SOLD
AMERICAN

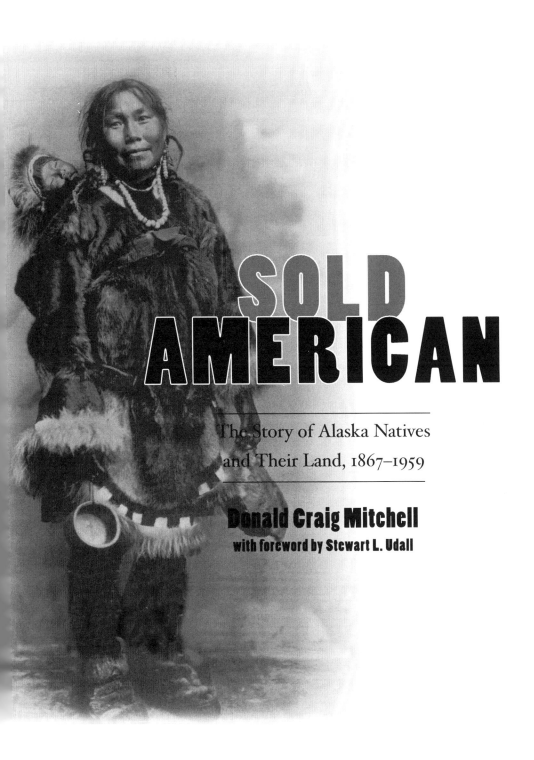

SOLD AMERICAN

The Story of Alaska Natives and Their Land, 1867–1959

Donald Craig Mitchell
with foreword by Stewart L. Udall

University of Alaska Press
Fairbanks

International Standard Book Number: cloth, 1-889963-37-2
                                     paper, 1-889963-36-4

Library of Congress Cataloging-in-Publication Data

Mitchell, Donald, 1947 Jan. 23–
    Sold American : The story of Alaska natives and their land, 1867–1959 :
the army to statehood / Donald Craig Mitchell.
    p. cm. — (Arctic Visions)
    Includes bibliographical references and index.
    ISBN 0-87451-800-8 (cl : alk. paper). — ISBN 0-87451-748-6 (pa : alk
paper)
    1. Indians of North America—Land tenure—Alaska. 2. Indians of
North America—Alaska—Claims. 3. Indians of North America—Alaska—
Government relations. 4. Indian title—Alaska—History. 5. Alaska Native
Brotherhood—History. 6. United States. Alaska Native Claims Settlement
Act—History. 7. Alaska—Ethnic relations. 8. Alaska—Politics and
government. I. Title. II. Series.

E78.A3M57 1997   1
333.2—dc20   96-4187

Printing in the United States of America by Data Reproductions

This publication was printed on acid-free paper that meets the minimum requirements for the American National Standard for Information Science—Permanence
of Paper for Printed Library Materials ANSI Z39.48-1984.

Publication coordination by Pamela Odom, University of Alaska Press.
Cover design by Dixon Jones, UAF Rasmuson Library Graphics
Text design by Deirdre Helfferich, University of Alaska Press, and Dixon Jones.

The Kinky Friedman lyric on page 1, quoted from the song "Sold American,"
copyright 1970, 1972 by Ensign Music Corporation. Reprinted with permission of
the Famous Music Publishing Companies.
Cover: Photograph of Inupiaq Eskimo Woman, 1903, by B.B. Dobbs. Courtesy
Alaska State Library.
The inset photograph of the 1929 Alaska Native Brotherhood Grand Camp, cour-
tesy of Tlingit and Haida Central Council Archives, and Sealaska Heritage
Foundation.

For James Lawrence McDonald,
one of the first to believe that what they told him was true

Contents

Foreword

Stewart L. Udall

TODAY, AT LONG LAST, CONGRESS celebrates the contributions that Native Americans have made to our national life. Indeed, in 1989 it authorized the Smithsonian Institution to construct a Museum of the American Indian in Washington, D.C., in order to "give all Americans the opportunity to learn of the cultural legacy, historic grandeur, and contemporary culture of Native Americans."

But for the first hundred years of the nation's existence the principal objective of Congress's inchoate Native American policy was not the celebration of indigenous cultures, but the removal of Native Americans from the land they used and occupied.

In 1783 the Treaty of Peace that ended the Revolutionary War extended the western boundary of the United States to the Mississippi River. During the war, the Continental Congress had pledged to grant war veterans land in "the distant and extensive territories, which appertain to the United States." And after the war, revenue that land sales west of the thirteen states generated was needed to pay the national debt.

But six months after the Treaty of Peace was ratified a congressional committee reported that Native Americans who occupied land west of the middle and northern states "are not in a temper to relinquish their territorial claims" and that the U.S. Army did not have the military capability to remove them. And even if the army had the capability, "numerous garrisons and an expensive peace establishment" would be required to hold the ground. For those reasons, the committee advised that it would be prudent for Congress to pay Native Americans "some compensation for their [land] claims," rather "than to hazard a war, which will be much more expensive."

From that realpolitik analysis of the respective military strengths of the parties in 1783 evolved Congress's policy that Native Americans should be persuaded to relinquish voluntarily the land they occupied and should be paid at least a token compensation for the relinquishments. In 1787 the Continental Congress codified that policy by including a provision in the Northwest Ordinance that directed

> [t]he utmost good faith shall always be observed towards the Indians, their lands and property shall never bet taken from them without their consent; and in their property, rights and liberty, they never shall be disturbed.

For a hundred years that admonition was honored in the breach. Government agents frequently negotiated in bad faith to persuade Native Americans to sign treaties they did not understand that extinguished their land occupancy rights on unfair terms. Congress also routinely refused to prevent whites from settling on land that treaties guaranteed that Native Americans could continue to occupy. Instead, when trespasses occurred, Congress sent new negotiators to persuade the dispossessed Native Americans "voluntarily" to relinquish more land.

In 1803 President Thomas Jefferson decided that Native Americans who occupied land east of the Mississippi River should be removed to land west of the river he recently had purchased from France. After the War of 1812, a number of removals were effectuated. At the urging of President Andrew Jackson, the most anti-Indian chief executive in our nation's history, in 1830 Congress passed a law that established removal as the preferred solution to the "Indian problem."

The most infamous "voluntary" removal occurred in 1838 when General Winfield Scott and the 7,000 troops under his command force-marched the Cherokees down the Trail of Tears from Georgia to Oklahoma. As a private who served under Scott described the scene:

> [T]he helpless Cherokees [were] arrested and dragged from their homes, and driven by bayonet into the stockades. And in the chill of the morning...loaded like cattle or sheep into wagons and started toward the west.

Over the ensuing decades, the demands by white settlers for land west of the Mississippi were insatiable. Since there was no additional territory to which Native Americans could be removed, Congress's solution to the problem was to persuade, and, when persuasion failed, to compel by force of arms, Native Americans who occupied land west of the river to relocate onto reservations whose boundaries in many cases were only vaguely defined. According to the historian Robert Utley,

> Virtually every major war of the two decades after Appomattox was fought to force Indians on to newly created reservations or to make them go back to reservations from which they had fled.

By the 1880s Congress's initial policy objective had been achieved. It then developed a new policy whose objective was to prepare Native Americans who resided on reservations for citizenship by instructing them how to assimilate into America's mainstream society. The individual who was most associated with Congress's assimilation policy was Senator Henry Dawes, who from 1881 to 1892 was chairman of the Senate Committee on Indian Affairs.

Given the situation as they saw it, Senator Dawes and the protestant clergymen and Bureau of Indian Affairs (BIA) officials who advised him had good intentions. But for most Native Americans the BIA's implementation of Congress's assimilation policy was a disaster, since by the end of President Herbert Hoover's administration in 1932 implementation of the policy had resulted in ninety million acres of reservation land having been transferred into white ownership, often by corrupt means.

In 1933 when President Franklin Roosevelt took office, Secretary of the Interior Harold Ickes, Commissioner of Indian Affairs John Collier, and Felix Cohen, the Department of the Interior's expert on Indian law, set about trying to repair the damage. In 1934 they persuaded Congress to enact the Indian Reorganization Act (IRA). Ickes, Collier, and Cohen intended the IRA to end the assimilation era. However, Senator Burton Wheeler and Representative Edgar Howard, the chairmen of the Senate and House Committees on Indian Affairs, and the other members of their committees who wrote the IRA believed, as Senator Wheeler would lecture Commissioner Collier, that Congress's Native American policy should continue to encourage Native Americans to as "nearly as possible adopt the white man's ways and laws."

In 1953 when Dwight Eisenhower became president, Congress reaffirmed its commitment to assimilation by passing House Concurrent Resolution No. 108, which made the termination of the federal government's relationship with tribes the official objective of Congress's Native American policy.

That was the situation in 1961 when I assumed office as Secretary of the Interior. Having been raised in an Arizona farm village near the Navajo,

Zuni, and Fort Apache reservations, I was familiar with the economic and social realities of reservation life. And during the three terms I served in the U.S. House of Representatives prior to my appointment as secretary I learned a lot about the plight of Native Americans because I had more Native American constituents in my congressional district than any other member of Congress.

Having a longstanding interest in Native American policy, I arrived at the Department of the Interior committed to doing what I could to try and right old wrongs by implementing Native American programs in a manner that would afford Native Americans an opportunity to make their own decisions, and by encouraging Congress to mobilize the resources of the federal government to improve economic and social conditions on reservations.

During the eight years I served as secretary of the interior, Senator Henry Jackson, the chairman of the Senate Committee on Interior and Insular Affairs, and many other members of congress from western states in which reservations are located still were committed to a "termination policy" as the means to hasten Native American assimilation.

Operating within that constraint, I and members of my staff such as Associate Commissioner of Indian Affairs James Officer and Robert Bennett, a member of the Oneida tribe of Wisconsin whom I appointed as the first Native American to serve as commissioner of Indian affairs since 1871, made a number of policy changes that we hoped would improve the situation.

The most important of those changes was our establishment of the principle that Native Americans themselves, rather than the BIA or the Indian Health Service, should administer education, health care, and other programs that the federal government provided for their benefit. In 1974, Congress ratified our self-determination policy by enacting the Indian Self-Determination and Education Assistance Act.

Despite the improvements that implementation of the self-determina-tion policy has made, at the beginning of the twenty-first century life on the reservations on which a majority of Native Americans continue to reside remains difficult. On too many reservations, inadequate housing, unemployment, underfunded schools, family dysfunction, high rates of infant mortality, and alcohol and substance abuse are prevalent. And little has been done, or at this point can be done, to return land that Congress acquired from Native Americans during the eighteenth and nine-teenth centuries through means that most Americans now consider dishonorable.

As Donald Mitchell describes in *Sold American*, his brilliant history of the federal government's dealings with Alaska's Indian, Eskimo, and Aleut peoples between Congress's purchase of Alaska in 1867 and Alaska statehood in 1959, Alaska Natives had a different historical experience from that of other Native Americans.

Because Alaska's winters are long and its rugged topography is not well suited for farming or ranching, few whites immigrated to Alaska during the nineteenth century, and few of those who did stayed. Because of the lack of white in-migration, there was no need for the federal government to remove Alaska Natives either from the land on which their villages were located or from the vast expanse of land on which they hunted, trapped, and gathered. Because their labor was needed, Alaska Natives also were afforded opportunities to participate in Alaska's non-Native natural resource development economy that Native Americans in the lower forty-eight states were denied. As *Sold American* describes, Alaska Natives enthusiastically made the most of those opportunities.

Contemporaneously, Congress authorized the Department of the Interior to operate schools in Native villages that afforded Alaska Natives an opportunity to acquire the English-language and other skills they needed to defend their own interests. In 1912 in southeast Alaska a group of educated Tlingit, Haida, and Tsimphsean Indians organized the Alaska Native Brotherhood (ANB). And in 1924 the ANB was instrumental in electing the Tlingit Indian leader William Paul to the Alaska Territorial legislature.

The ANB's participation in territorial elections began a tradition of Native involvement in Alaska politics that was unprecedented. In my home state of Arizona, for example, Native Americans were denied the right to vote until 1948 when my father, who was a justice of the Arizona Supreme Court, wrote a judicial decision that finally settled the question. But that same year, five Alaska Natives were elected to the Alaska Territorial Legislature from election districts that stretched from the coast of the Arctic Ocean to the southeast Alaska rain forest.

Their unique tradition of political involvement well served Alaska Natives in 1967 when they organized the Alaska Federation of Natives to lobby Congress to settle Native land claims on terms that included allowing Alaska Natives to obtain legal title to forty million acres of land. In 1971, Congress responded by enacting the Alaska Native Claims Settlement Act (ANCSA), which was then, and today remains, the most generous Native American land claims settlement in U.S. history.

The story of Congress's enactment of ANCSA is the subject of *Take My Land, Take My Life*, Donald Mitchell's second volume on the history of the U.S. government's dealings with Alaska Natives.

As that volume describes, many people—both Native and non-Native—participated between 1960 and 1971 in the effort to persuade Congress to settle Native land claims on fair terms. I am proud that as secretary of the interior I was able to contribute to that effort by imposing a "land freeze" in 1966 that prohibited the state of Alaska, the oil industry, and other third parties from acquiring rights to federal land in Alaska until Congress decisively settled Native land claims.

But those efforts would not have been as successful as they were if the political skills and intellectual imaginations of the leaders of the Alaska Federation of Natives had not reflected the Alaska Natives' unique political experience between Congress's purchase of Alaska in 1867 and Alaska statehood in 1959. *Sold American* tells the story of that experience. It is a remarkable never-before-told story that should be required reading both for general readers and for scholars who are interested in Alaska history or in the story of Congress's erratic Native American policies.

Acknowledgments

SO MANY PEOPLE SO gladly gave so much of their time, knowledge, and support to this project for so many years that a list acknowledging their individual contributions would be hopelessly under-inclusive. This book could not have been written without them and I owe them all an immense debt of gratitude. However, I particularly thank the archivists who with unfailing patience guided a rookie to and through the records on which so much of the *Sold American* story is based, particularly Renee Jaussaud, formerly of the Textual Reference Division of the National Archives, whose introduction to the records of the Department of the Interior was invaluable. In Washington, D.C., my great friends Jim Souby and Betty Barton and John and Scooter Cotton provided room and board and red wine at all times they were needed. Julie Petro came through in the crunch. John White helped with the title. Wanda Seamster prepared the maps. John Shively and William Van Ness (who took on the drudgery of reading the manuscript when it was 1,400-plus pages of boring-as-chalk facts) kept me going with the steadfastness of their belief that the project was worth the years the research entailed. I also thank Anne DeVries, Lynn Chase, Nancy Shute, Jane Angvik and Vic Fischer, Norman Cohen, Nancy Groszek, Larry Smith and Pam Brodie, and everyone else who helped keep my spirits up when they lagged during the long course of this project. And finally, I thank Gail Osherenko of the Institute of Arctic Studies at Dartmouth College, whose good offices were instrumental in persuading the University Press of New England to publish the first edition of *Sold American*, as well as Claus-M. Naske and Pamela Odom, the director and acquisitions editor at the University of Alaska Press, whose infectious enthusiasm and appreciation of the importance of the subject matter were equally instrumental in bringing the second edition home to Alaska.

Alaska

Introduction

Everything's being sold American.
No place to go—and brother no place to stay

Kinky Friedman

On the evening of July 15, 1741, Aleksei Chirikov, the captain of the eighty-foot Russian ship *St. Paul,* sighted the mountainous, heavily wooded coastline of a large island on the southern end of a group of islands off the northern coast of North America. The island later would be named Prince of Wales; the group of islands of which it is a part, the Alexander Archipelago; and the coast of North America, the Alaska Panhandle. However, all Chirikov knew at the time of his "discovery" was that he had accomplished the first goal the Russian admiralty had set for the expedition of exploration of which his ship was a part: he had crossed the expanse of ocean east of Siberia's Kamchatka Peninsula and reached the coast of North America.

Chirikov's was not the first attempt to do so. At the direction of Peter the Great, czar of Russia, Vitus Bering, a Dane sailing in the service of the Russian crown, embarked on the first Russian expedition to North America in 1728.[1] At the time, the Chukchi Peninsula, which protrudes into the Arctic Ocean from the extreme northeastern corner of Asia, and North America were thought to be joined by an isthmus. To test the theory, Peter ordered Bering to sail north from Kamchatka until he reached the isthmus and then east along the shore until he reached a city under the control of another European nation or encountered a European vessel.

Pursuant to those instructions, on July 13, 1728, Bering and a forty-four-man crew set sail in the sixty-foot wooden ship *St. Gabriel,* north from the mouth of the Kamchatka River across the Gulf of Anadyr to the southern coast of the Chukchi Peninsula. While anchored in a small bay a short distance west of the location at which the coast of the peninsula turns north, the *St. Gabriel* was approached by Chukchi Natives, whose curiosity had induced them to paddle their skin boats close to the ship. Speaking through Koriak interpreters, Bering asked the paddlers for information about the isthmus. The Chukchi informed Bering that "our land very near here turns to the left and goes far from there" and "no promontory of any kind extends from our land into the sea." The Chukchi also told Bering that there was a populated island to the east that could be seen from shore when the fog lifted.

Continuing along the coast, first east, then north, on August 11 the *St. Gabriel* passed west of the island mentioned by the Chukchi, which Bering named Saint Lawrence. Five days later the *St. Gabriel* reached sixty-seven degrees, eighteen minutes north latitude, a location far enough north for Bering to confirm that the coastline had turned west. As the Chukchi had foretold, the isthmus connecting Asia and North America did not exist.

Bering had no way to know that he had sailed over the isthmus for which he was searching, which, in his honor, would be named the Bering Land Bridge. For millions of years the land bridge had connected the Chukchi Peninsula and Alaska via Saint Lawrence Island until it was submerged by tectonic movements of the earth ten to twelve million years ago. During ensuing millennia the bridge reappeared when increased glaciation lowered the depth of the ocean. When the glaciers melted, the bridge submerged—a game of hide-and-seek that repeated itself on several occasions until 13,000 to 11,000 years ago, when the ice cap melted a final time and submerged the bridge 150 feet beneath the *St. Gabriel's* keel.[2]

Although Bering was convinced that the isthmus did not exist, his certainty that he could reach North America remained unshaken; and after returning to Kamchatka he reasoned that, rather than north, he should have sailed east. To test the theory, on June 5, 1729, Bering again embarked from the mouth of the Kamchatka River, this time sailing the *St. Gabriel* east until fog and wind forced him back to the mainland.

Temporarily abandoning the quest, the next year Bering made the arduous overland trek to St. Petersburg to report the results of his expedition to the Russian admiralty and lobby for a second expedition. If his theory that North America was east of Kamchatka was correct, Bering argued, then it was not far east, and if so, "it will be possible to establish trade with the lands discovered there to the advantage of the Russian Empire." The admiralty agreed, and the Empress Anna ordered Bering to organize a new expedition.

In December 1732 the Russian senate issued an ukase that detailed the expedition's objectives. With respect to the entanglement of Alaska

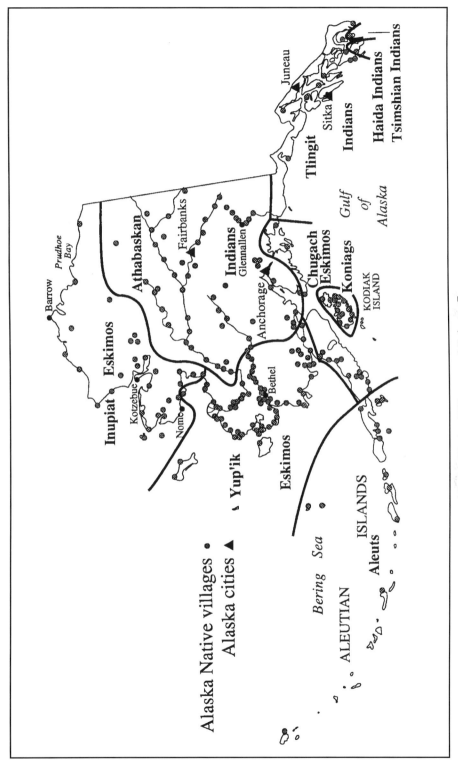

Alaska Native Villages and Ethnic Groups

Natives*—first with Russians and then with the multifarious agents of nineteenth-century American capitalism—the senate's instructions were prescient. Although they were to be treated kindly and given small gifts, any Natives that Bering encountered during his new exploration were to be interrogated to obtain information about the natural resources of the surrounding vicinity, particularly about whether fur-bearing animals were abundant. Bering also was instructed to explore any new land he discovered "to see if any valuable minerals and other metals are there." If minerals were found in quantities sufficient to give "evidence of profit," he was to notify the Russian commandant at Okhotsok "without letting it be known afar," and the commandant would send for the men and equipment necessary "to produce in every way a profit for the benefit and interest of Your Imperial Majesty."

On June 4, 1741, the *St. Peter,* commanded by Bering, and the *St. Paul,* commanded by Chirikov, who had served as a junior officer on the *St. Gabriel,* sailed from Kamchatka southeast across the North Pacific Ocean toward a peninsula labeled "de Gama land" on a map that had been prepared by the Russian Academy of Sciences. On June 13 the ships reached forty-six degrees, five minutes north latitude, a point from which, if Bering and Chirikov had sailed east, they would have reached the coast of North America south of the mouth of the Columbia River, which today divides the states of Oregon and Washington. However, having found no evidence of the nonexistent de Gama land, Bering turned the expedition north.

On June 20 the *St. Peter* and *St. Paul* were separated during a high wind, and after an unsuccessful attempt to reunite, each vessel sailed on toward North America alone. On July 15, Chirikov sighted Prince of Wales Island. Turning north, the *St. Paul* followed the coast of the Alexander Archipelago until July 17, when Chirikov ordered the ship's anchor dropped at the mouth of a bay on the western shore of Kruzof Island, a small island west of the present-day city of Sitka.

When the *St. Paul* was safely moored, Chirikov ordered Abram Dementief, the ship's mate, and ten other members of the crew to row one of the *St. Paul's* two longboats to shore to carry out the senate's instructions: to find Natives to interrogate to obtain information about the resources of the surrounding countryside and "to look for any distinctive rocks and earth in which one might expect rich ores." To assist the landing

---

* "Alaska Native" and "Native" refer collectively to all of Alaska's Indian, Eskimo, and Aleut peoples.

party in the latter regard, Chirikov gave Dementief a piece of silver ore to use as a template during his reconnaissance.

After loading the longboat with provisions and their muskets with powder and shot, Dementief and his men embarked, and the longboat soon disappeared behind a point of land that protruded into the bay. Moments later musket shots were heard, the signal that Dementief had reached the beach.

The landing party could not be seen from the ship, but over the next several days more shots were heard from shore, which Chirikov interpreted as a sign that all was well. However, when, after six days, Dementief had not returned, Chirikov ordered a second landing party ashore. When the longboat reached the beach, the crew dispersed into the forest, and shortly thereafter a plume of smoke rose from the point behind which Dementief's longboat had disappeared.

The next morning two canoes manned by Tlingit Indians rounded the point. Mistaking the canoes for longboats, Chirikov ordered all hands on deck to prepare the *St. Paul* to sail. When the canoes approached closer, the Russian captain realized his error. But by then it was too late. Upon observing the frenzied movements of the crew, the Tlingits turned their canoes and paddled back in the direction from which they had come.

Having lost both longboats, Chirikov was unable to send another landing party ashore or to refill his water casks. So he ordered the *St. Paul* to sail for Kamchatka, leaving Dementief and the members of his crew to an unknown (except to the Tlingits) fate.[3]

Whether the Indians had intended to attack the *St. Paul* but changed their minds after observing the Russians on deck or had approached the ship to satisfy a less malefic curiosity but were scared away by the crew's animation is not known. What can be said with certainty is that, if asked, Chirikov and the Tlingits would have agreed that, since they kept the longboat crews, the latter had gotten the better of the exchange. Over the succeeding two centuries, Alaska Natives would make similar statements with considerably less frequency.

Within a generation of Chirikov's "discovery" of Alaska, the Aleuts, the Alaska Natives who occupy the chain of volcanic islands that arc west from the Alaska Peninsula toward Kamchatka, were reduced in population to near extinction by disease and Russian atrocity.

In 1867, when the United States purchased Alaska from Czar Alexander II, the Russian employees of the Russian-American Company (the economic concession that the Russian government chartered in 1799 to administer the area) left southeast Alaska for home as terrified of Tlingit

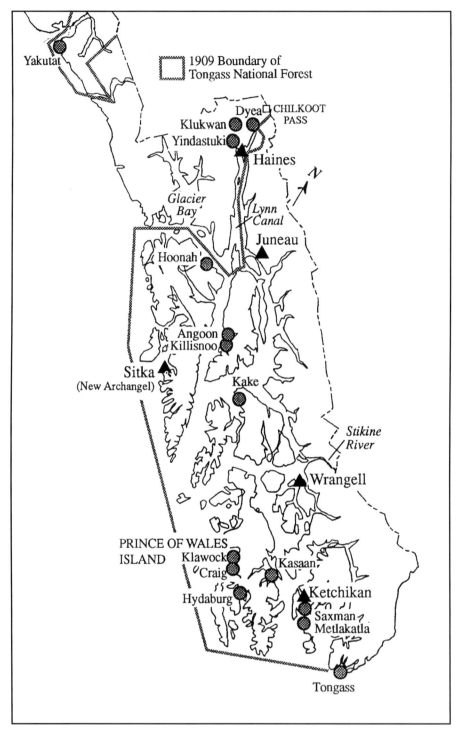

Southeast Alaska

Indians as the crew of the *St. Paul* must have been 126 years earlier when they realized that the vessels moving toward their ship were canoes rather than longboats. But within fifteen years of the October 1867 afternoon when the U.S. Army raised the Stars and Stripes over the Russian-American Company headquarters at Sitka, southeastern Alaska had been overrun by vagabonds, adventurers, and not a few criminals, who swept first up the Stikine River to a gold strike in the Cassiar Mountains, then north to the strike at Gold Creek (at what is now the site of the city of Juneau), and finally, at the close of the nineteenth century, over Chilkoot Pass to the Klondike goldfield.

In their wake, other whites confiscated islands that Tlingit and Haida Indians had occupied for a millennium. Seattle and San Francisco venture capitalists built salmon canneries that operated fish traps that made their absentee owners millions of dollars by overharvesting the Indians' most important subsistence resource. And Congress and the federal executive asserted the U.S. government's jurisdiction over the area and made decisions regarding the use of land and the exploitation of natural resources on which the Indians of Southeast Alaska depended for their sustenance, with slight regard for the impact of their decisionmaking on the indigenous population.

North of southeast Alaska, the Chugach, Yup'ik, and Inupiaq Eskimos, who lived along the coastline, and the Athabascan Indians, who roamed the interior river valleys, fared no better.

Only a few Russian-American Company trading posts operated north of Kodiak Island. But in 1848 first one, and within a year hundreds, of American whaling ships first sailed and then steamed through Bering Strait and into the Arctic Ocean to hunt bowhead whales and walrus—subsistence resources whose destruction, exacerbated by the whiskey the whalers traded when they put into shore, had a malevolent effect on the northern Eskimos.

In 1886 gold was discovered in the tributary creeks of the Fortymile River, which flows through interior Alaska and then into the Yukon River a few miles east of the Canadian border. Claims were staked, and road-houses, saloons, and stores were built on land that previously had been roamed by small bands of Athabascan hunters.

In 1899 thousands of whites, who had stampeded over Chilkoot Pass to the Klondike in 1897 and 1898, walked, mushed dogs, and (when the ice left the river) floated down the Yukon on their way to new gold-bearing ground at Cape Nome on the Seward Peninsula, spreading disease the indigenous population had no immunity to resist, ransacking cabins, and buying, bartering, and in many cases stealing sled dogs, boats, and food from the Indians and Eskimos who lived along the river.

By 1920 the stampedes were over, the price of gold had plummeted, and whites had left Alaska in droves, their number declining between 1909 and 1920 by 28 percent.[4] However, throughout rural Alaska the stampeders were replaced in influence by Bureau of Fisheries agents and the Alaska Game Commission and, at the outset of the Second World War, by the army. In 1940 five hundred servicemen were stationed in Alaska. By 1943 there were more than 154,000, most of whom were young men with little to do for recreation but hunt caribou and other large game on which Natives depended for food.[5]

When the war ended, thousands of servicemen returned to Alaska as civilians to take advantage of opportunities they believed would result from the availability of "unoccupied" free land. During the 1970s and 1980s they were followed by 200,000 more immigrants, who moved north for a job and easy access to Alaska's fortuitous oil wealth.

Each new wave of in-migration increased the pressure on fish and game and other natural resources that, prior to their usurpation by whites, supported the Native subsistence economy and the traditional cultures that have evolved from Indian, Eskimo, and Aleut participation in hunting, fishing, and gathering. As a consequence, with each succeeding wave, the Native subsistence economy and the cultures to which it gave life buckled—sometimes imperceptibly, sometimes to their knees.

None of this is new. White America's usurpation of Alaska's natural resources and its attendant adverse effect on the indigenous population is a matter of public record that Alaska Natives, particularly young Natives, today increasingly—and increasingly vocally—recite.

But while it has its uses, the rhetoric of victimization has consequential limitations. The rote invocation of the accusation that Alaska Natives are another of the nation's indigenous peoples who have grievances for which, no matter how many apologies are made, white America can never atone has succeeded in keeping Congress annually appropriating money to Native programs without pausing to ask itself why, which—given the new resolve on Capitol Hill to significantly reduce federal spending—is no small accomplishment. But nothing, including other people's tax money, is free. And the price Alaska Natives have paid for Congress's largess is to be trapped by the tens of thousands in a cycle of poverty and dependence on white institutions over which they have little control and from which there is no realistic expectation of escape.

Jean-Jacques Rousseau has been dead more than 200 years. If Rousseau's belief that the preindustrial society that existed in Alaska when Aleksei

Chirikov sighted Prince of Wales Island is "the best for man" and "the veritable prime of the world" ever were true, in Native villages throughout Alaska it is no longer relevant.

From Kaktovik on the wind-swept coast of the Arctic Ocean to Hydaburg on the southern end of the southeast Alaska rain forest, there is not a village whose Native residents are not more dependent today for their material well-being on economic systems and political institutions controlled by non-Natives who live outside the village than they are on hunting, fishing, and gathering. Of equal importance, Native participation in those systems and institutions has had as profound an effect on the evolution of traditional Native cultures as has the intrusion of the systems and institutions themselves into the fabric of village life.

As a consequence, if Alaska Natives are to acquire more control over the forces of change in their own communities than the little they have at present, their view of their situation must be informed by an understanding of how they have been and will continue to be changed by participation in the economic systems and political institutions they aspire to control, as well as energized by outrage over the bad acts perpetrated generations ago by the agents of the same systems and institutions.

Armed with such self-knowledge, Alaska Natives can make their own choices about their own future. If they have the collective strength of character to move in their chosen direction, then their survival as culturally distinct peoples may be a realistic possibility. If they do not, then Alaska Natives are destined, like the rest of us, to be consumed by a mass culture of which they are already—and in the eyes of many Natives too much—a part.

Whether Alaska Natives survive as culturally distinct peoples is no one's business but their own.

From 1969 through 1971 former U.S. attorney general Ramsey Clark served as Washington, D.C., counsel to the Alaska Federation of Natives, the statewide organization Alaska Natives organized in 1967 to lobby Congress to settle Native land claims. At the federation's 1983 convention Clark noted in his keynote address that "No mechanism, no organizational structure, no constitution [has] ever really preserved any important rights to a people where the people themselves by character and spirit were not passionately committed to its preservation."[6]

Assuming so, one hopes that if Alaska Natives are committed and careful in their fight for it they can obtain the social and economic justice that is their due as U.S. citizens without, as the cost of victory, having to relinquish still more control over the conduct of day-to-day life in their own communities. But for such a fight to stand a chance, Alaska Natives and

non-Natives who support the Native cause must have a clear understanding of Native involvement in events that, after passage of the requisite
amount of time, are arbitrarily labeled "history."

In that regard, two notes of caution. The first is that I am not a Native,
and this story of Alaska Natives and their land is not a history of the
Alaska Native people. Alaska Natives are perfectly capable of writing their
own history; some have, and more will do so. Rather, this volume describes
Alaska Native participation, between the Alaska purchase in 1867 and Alaska
statehood in 1959, in white Alaska's effort to transform Alaska's bountiful
natural resources into dollars and details how Natives, whites, and the
society they jointly developed have been changed because of it.

In particular, the narrative tells the story of how and why Congress was
persuaded that Alaska Natives should be compensated for the extinguishment of their legally cognizable possessory right—which the judiciary has
named "aboriginal title"—to use and occupy the land on which they and
their ancestors had hunted and gathered. And it tells the story of how and
why the decision was made that the Alaska Statehood Act, which Congress
enacted in 1958, would not extinguish that right.

When Alaska entered the union in 1959, the decision that statehood
would not compromise Native land rights set a series of unintended events
into motion that culminated in 1971 in Congress's enactment of the Alaska
Native Claims Settlement Act (ANCSA), a statute that paid Alaska Natives an unprecedented compensation for the extinguishment of their
aboriginal title.

The second note of caution is that this volume traces the history of
Native-white contact between the years 1867 and 1959 with a cursor guided
by the observation that, like all human beings, Alaska Natives tend to
assimilate the values embodied in the forms of economic and social organization in which they participate.

That is hardly an original insight. Social critics of such disparate views as
Karl Marx, on the left, and the late conservative legal scholar Alexander
Bickel, on the right, each have made the same point, albeit in different
contexts.

In 1971, ANCSA authorized Alaska Natives to be paid $962.5 million
and to select and be conveyed fee title to forty-four million acres of land as
compensation for the extinguishment of their aboriginal title. To manage
the money and hold title to the land, ANCSA required Natives living in
each of more than two hundred villages to organize a state of Alaska-
chartered business corporation in which each Native alive on December
18, 1971, and enrolled to the village received one hundred shares of stock.

ANCSA also divided Alaska into twelve geographic regions and required Natives living in each region to organize a regional state of Alaska-chartered business corporation in which each Native alive on December 18, 1971, and enrolled to the region received one hundred shares of stock.

The $962.5 million then was paid, and title to the forty-four million acres of land was conveyed, to the village and regional corporations. The regional corporations were required to distribute a percentage of the money they received to their shareholders, and village corporations were required to reconvey title to some of the land they received to individuals as well as to village municipal governments.

Although ANCSA corporation stock could not be sold or otherwise alienated (except by a court as part of a divorce settlement or to pay child support), the Act originally stated that the restrictions on alienation would terminate on December 18, 1991, and each corporation would be required to issue its shareholders new stock that could be sold or taken involuntarily to pay a shareholder's bad debts.

More than a quarter of a century after its enactment, ANCSA remains the most generous aboriginal claims settlement in U.S. history. However, Congress did not extinguish Native aboriginal title on fair terms simply to right an old wrong. Rather, the story of the Alaska Native land claims settlement is a story of America hoisted on the petard of its own rule of law and a story of how lucky breaks can happen to people who have the perseverance to deserve them.

The political struggle that preceded the enactment of ANCSA began decades earlier than most people realize and was considerably more bitter than many like to remember. But from 1929, when James Wickersham and William Paul persuaded the Alaska Native Brotherhood that Congress had an obligation to compensate the Indians of southeast Alaska for the extinguishment of their aboriginal title to land inside the Tongass National Forest, to the enactment of ANCSA in 1971, the preoccupying question was how much money Alaska Natives should be paid and how much land they should be allowed to own in fee title. The questions of to whom that title should be conveyed and who should manage the money were given considerably less attention.

Speaking through the text of ANCSA, Congress answered both questions by requiring Alaska Natives to organize business corporations. That decision had the practical consequence of mandating Native participation in a form of economic organization that embodies social values that are antithetical to those embodied in traditional cultures that have evolved from Native participation in hunting, fishing, and gathering.

When that fact became apparent, revisionist critics within and without the Native community began to argue from a brief written with the seeming wisdom of hindsight that a cynical Congress intended ANCSA to hasten the economic assimilation of Native people and the destruction of their traditional cultures.

Since the for-profit business corporation is the form of economic organization that fuels a national economy that enables citizens of the United States, including Alaska Natives, to consume a share of the world's wealth that far exceeds the share to which their presence as a percentage of the world population entitles them, Congress is guilty as charged of encouraging economic assimilation. Requiring Alaska Natives to organize business corporations is indeed the uncontradicted evidence ANCSA critics say it is that Congress intended Native economic assimilation to be a principal objective of the ANCSA settlement.

But that not particularly startling conclusion raises a more serious question. The fact that ANCSA critics rarely mention is that the idea of using state of Alaska-chartered business corporations to implement the settlement was recommended to Congress in 1968 by the Alaska Federation of Natives, rather than forced on Alaska Natives by Congress. Of even more importance, the federation's recommendation was not an anomaly. It was a logical consequence of the Alaska Native historical experience.

In the American West, most Indians who survived the military campaigns that the U.S. Army waged throughout the latter half of the nineteenth century to force them off what, when they had been removed at bayonet point, became known as the "public domain," were physically confined and economically marginalized on reservations. But in Alaska most Natives were allowed to remain in their villages; and when whites needed their labor, they recruited Natives to participate (albeit on unfairly rigged terms) in the commercial exploitation of the territory's natural resources for private economic gain. And beginning in the second decade of the twentieth century, whites (to achieve their own political objectives and again on rigged terms) encouraged Natives to vote in territorial elections.

Throughout the nineteenth and early twentieth centuries, Alaska Natives took advantage of both opportunities with a consistent enthusiasm. So it is small wonder that, when the political necessity to settle Native land claims afforded them a procedural opportunity to renegotiate the terms of Native participation in the Alaska economy, Native leaders recommended the business corporation to Congress as the form of social organization that they believed would facilitate Alaska Native exploitation of natural resources located on and under the land to which ANCSA authorized the corporations to be conveyed title. Nor is it a surprise that Native leaders did not fear allowing the state of Alaska, acting through a legislature whose membership included several of the same Native leaders, to regulate the internal operation of ANCSA corporations and the development of ANCSA corporation land.

For those reasons, the question ANCSA critics should be asking is not whether Congress intended Alaska Native participation as managers and shareholders of ANCSA corporations to encourage Native economic assimilation. Of course it did. Nor is the question whether, on the cusp of the twenty-first century, Native economic assimilation is a good thing. Alaska Natives answered that question in the affirmative generations ago. Rather, the question of most topical contemporary consequence is whether the ANCSA corporation has produced benefits for Alaska Natives that exceed the cost of the cultural disruption that the corporation's intrusion into the midst of village life has exacerbated.

"Iatrogenic" is a medical term that describes a pathology caused by treatment. When doctors vaccinate children against polio, for example, they know when they do so that one of every 2.4 million of the children who take the oral vaccine will be stricken with the disease as a consequence. But preventing 2,399,999 children from being crippled by polio is worth the cost of making one healthy but terribly unlucky child sick.

But at what point does the damage an iatrogenic pathology inflicts exceed the benefits derived from the treatment that causes it? A difficult question for the medical profession, it is an equally difficult question for anyone thinking about the costs and benefits of ANCSA corporations.

The social values embodied in the corporate form of organization are well known: the transformation of human beings into "shareholders," the transformation of land into an "asset" valued by its worth in the cash economy, the duty that a board of directors owes to a fictitious entity—the corporation—rather than to the human beings who own the corporation's stock, the expression of shareholder will through a majority vote of shares, and the equation of success with profitability.

The conflict between those values and the values embodied in traditional cultures that have evolved from Native participation in hunting, fishing, and gathering is immense. To mention but two, in traditional Native cultures conflict was resolved by consensus rather than majority vote, and an individual's social status was measured by the acquisition and distribution rather than the acquisition and retention of wealth.

For those reasons, the participation of Alaska Natives as managers and shareholders of ANCSA corporations, particularly ANCSA village corporations, has helped turn the world in Native villages on its head. For the corporations to succeed, Eskimo seal hunters on Saint Lawrence Island and Athabascan Indian salmon fishermen who live in villages along the Yukon River must participate more vigorously in corporate life than the average shareholder of General Motors.

But if they do, will they still be Eskimo and Indian? Is cultural assimilation a nonnegotiable by-product of economic assimilation? And if so, to what extent? And if so, at what point does their participation as managers and shareholders of ANCSA corporations so alter the way Alaska Natives look at themselves and their physical world that further participation is not worth the benefits the ANCSA settlement bestowed? And if the benefits are not worth the cost, why are they not? And if the question is close, who should decide? And besides, weren't Alaska Natives striving to assimilate themselves into the white economy and the mass culture it underpins prior to the enactment of ANCSA? If so, then what harm have ANCSA corporations done by hurrying Natives along in their previously chosen direction?

This story of Alaska Natives and their land from the Alaska purchase in 1867 to Alaska statehood in 1959 is told with those questions in mind. But before it is, there is an obligation that the introduction of every book must discharge.

Every work that purports to be nonfiction is the product of the inspiration, insights, and scholarship of many persons other than whoever is publicly saddled with responsibility for its content. Of the many people other than myself who are responsible for this book, the three most responsible are Ted Stevens, Sam Deloria, and George Washington.

Ted Stevens is Alaska's senior U.S. senator. In April 1983, Janie Leask, the president of the Alaska Federation of Natives, and I paid a courtesy call on Senator Stevens, who at the time was assistant majority leader of the U.S. Senate. When not attending to the nation's business on the Senate floor, Stevens was in the habit of spending his afternoons in the inner sanctum of the assistant majority leader's office, a comfortable, windowless cave down the hall from the Senate chamber, and that is where we found him when we came to visit.

When we seated ourselves and exchanged the ritual pleasantries, the senator asked our business, and Janie explained that she and I had flown to Washington to ask Stevens and the other members of Alaska's congressional delegation to try to persuade Congress to amend ANCSA to ensure that Alaska Natives would not lose control of their village and regional corporations after December 18, 1991, when corporation stock could be freely sold.

After listening to our pitch, the senator promised to do what he could and then gratuitously offered some advice. According to Stevens, the most serious problem the Alaska Federation of Natives would encounter on Capitol Hill was ignorance, since few members of Congress who voted for ANCSA in 1971 still were serving, and most members elected after 1971 knew little and cared less about Alaska Natives.

Subsequent events proved the situation less bleak than his prediction portended. But Ted Stevens's head count was accurate. Of the hundred senators who served in the 92d Congress in 1971, only ten were members of the 104th Congress. Of the 435 House members who served in the 92d Congress, only twenty-one were members of the 104th Congress. And no member of the professional staffs of the Senate and House Committees on Interior and Insular Affairs that exercised legislative jurisdiction over ANCSA during the 92d Congress still are employed on Capitol Hill.

So in addition to its value to Natives and non-Natives who are interested in Alaska history, in federal Indian policy, or just in reading a good story, the story of Alaska Natives and their land that follows, as well as *Take My Land, Take My Life*, the companion volume that tells the story of the enactment of ANCSA, is intended to be a contribution to the regeneration of Congress's lost institutional memory.

Philip "Sam" Deloria, a Standing Rock Sioux, is director of the American Indian Law Center. In August 1983, Deloria was a principal speaker at a conference commemorating the fiftieth anniversary of the Indian Reorganization Act of 1934, sponsored by the now defunct Institute of the American West at Sun Valley, Idaho.

Conferences of any kind are usually numbingly useless experiences, and Sun Valley, which is internationally famed for its fun, was an elegantly illogical site to assess the past fifty years of life in Indian country. But Ketchum, the town down the road, is one of my favorite places, and the Indian Reorganization Act recently had become a topic of renewed interest in Alaska, so I decided to attend. On the plane flight from Anchorage, I alternated my time between thinking about whether, if Ted Stevens was right about Congress's lost institutional memory, telling the story of Alaska Natives and their land would be worth the trouble I undoubtedly would get into for doing so, and finishing a recently published book about contemporary life in Indian country.

The book was a dreary cornucopia that documented the ups and downs of recent battles in which Native Americans in the lower forty-eight states had been involved to protect their land and economic rights. From the Taos Indians' struggle to persuade Congress to allow them to obtain title to Blue Lake, a religious site that Teddy Roosevelt, with a scribble of his pen in 1906, withdrew as a national forest, to the Pacific Northwest tribes' fight to enforce their treaty rights to harvest commercially valuable salmon runs, the events the book chronicled were depressing and predictable.

Depressing because there is nothing pleasant about white America's usurpation of natural resources at Indian expense. And predictable because every Indian I met on my read either was nobly fighting for his people or was a victim who had been put upon—a Manichean view of contemporary Native American life for which, after my years of involvement with Alaska Natives, I had long since lost patience.

Terrible things are happening in Indian country, and Native Americans need to know about their heroes and their victories if they are to maintain the strength to keep fighting to correct those things. But the fights are doomed from the outset if they are not waged with a realistic assessment of the strengths and weaknesses of the combatants. Native Americans fighting for their lives with the overly popularized myth of the victimized noble red man as their principal weapon is stupidity, not heroism. And perpetuating stereotypes such as those depicted in the book I read on my flight to Sun Valley is at best pandering and at worst racism.

But articulating that observation is one thing, and acting on it is quite another.

For thousands of years humankind has confused the messenger with the message, and Native Americans are no exception to that rule. As a consequence, it is difficult for academics, attorneys, and other white mercenaries who have been drawn to the Native American cause to speak their minds with candor without being accused of betrayal, a problem compounded by the fact that even mercenaries like to be liked.

These are hard thoughts about difficult choices, and they were on my mind when I arrived in Sun Valley. But as it turned out, they also were on Sam Deloria's mind.

On the third day of the conference, Deloria spoke to a mostly white audience on the era of Indian self-determination. The speech was an analysis of how the Economic Opportunity Act of 1964 helped transform Indian tribes from step-and-fetch-it vassals of the Bureau of Indian Affairs into local governments capable of administering federal programs without bureau supervision. But Deloria rambled across considerably more ground than the War on Poverty. Having been provided a podium from which to lecture white liberals on their sins, he proceeded to do so but with a touch so lightly sardonic that most members of the audience undoubtedly left for lunch thinking that Sam's remarks couldn't possibly have been directed at their work.

Whether they were or not is a matter between each of them and Sam. But Deloria's thoughts on the responsibility of the white mercenary significantly influenced my decision to research and write this story of Alaska Natives and their land. Warming to the subject, Deloria lectured his audience:

> Many scholars have been blinded by the romantic tradition. This approach to Indian history denies us our political life and our old people their humanity. Why do all old Indians have to be wise? Not all of your old people are wise. The romantic tradition imposes on us cultural notions that make you happy. It does not help us deal with complex problems.... We do not owe to the scholarly community any obligation to preserve or not to preserve Indian culture. But you can help us ... by writing realistically about what is happening, and by not ignoring what Indians are trying to do or say. There were a lot of missed opportunities in the era between 1960 and 1976. For a while we had a lot of things going our way and quite frankly we blew it. Unless there is scholarship by Indians and non-Indians that helps analyze why we blew it, the next time the cycle comes back we are not going to do it any better than we did the last time.[7]

George Washington is the well-known Father of His Country. If Ted Stevens is responsible for the idea for this book and Sam Deloria for the courage to write it, George Washington is responsible for the theme.

When Washington was inaugurated as president in 1789, the government over which he took charge had been in existence less than a year. Prior to that time the United States operated under Articles of Confederation.

The articles were written in 1777, but Maryland's foot-dragging delayed ratification until 1781, when Virginia agreed to abandon her claim to vast tracts of land on the western frontier. The capitulation was not a minor matter: for more than thirty years Virginians, as well as residents of other colonies, had speculated in the western lands.

George Washington, for example, was a member of the Ohio Company. In 1749, George III granted the Ohio Company two hundred thousand acres of land in the Ohio River Valley that also were claimed by France. After several years of conflict, in 1754 a French force overran the position occupied by Virginia troops south of the fork of the Ohio River, thus beginning the French and Indian War.

Benjamin Franklin was a member of the Indiana Company. In 1768 the Treaty of Fort Stanwix ceded the Indiana Company a large tract of land between the Ohio River and the Allegheny Mountains that previously had been claimed by the Ohio Company. Virginia's representative, Thomas Walker, signed the treaty and thereby acknowledged the Indiana Company's claim. However, doing so was not the act of disloyalty it seemed. Walker was an agent of the Loyal Company, which had been organized by a group of Virginia speculators that included Thomas Jefferson's father, Peter. In 1750 members of the Ohio Company took out caveats when Walker attempted to survey an eight-hundred-thousand-acre tract the Loyal Company had been awarded, disrupting the work and initiating a bitter rivalry that Walker must have been happy to further when, years later, he found himself in a position to compromise the Ohio Company's claim.[8]

A fascinating subject, the history of colonial land speculation will stop here, the point having been made that many of the nation's most revered patriots[9] were up to their elbows in the tomfoolery of land speculation.

But independent of their individual intrigues, both before and after the Revolution, land speculators shared a common problem: even if their title to a tract of western land was valid, the title was economically worthless as long as the Indians who occupied the tract resisted white settlement. For that reason and as George Washington noted in 1783, peace with the Indian tribes and the settlement of the western lands "are so analogous that there can be no definition of the one without involving considerations of the other."[10] But for both Indian and white, during the years the United States was governed by the Articles of Confederation, life along the frontier was lethiferous.

In 1783 the Treaty of Peace, which officially ended the Revolutionary War, marked the Mississippi River as the western boundary of the new United States. Not surprisingly, since no one asked their opinion before the boundary line was drawn, the Indians who occupied the land between the Mississippi and the strip of ground along the Atlantic seaboard that actually had been settled by whites paid the treaty no mind. And Congress was ill-equipped to deal with the recalcitrance.

Although the Articles of Confederation delegated to Congress the "sole and exclusive right and power" to manage affairs with and declare war against the Indians, the first power was tempered by the caveat that each state retained the same authority "within its own limits"; the second, by a loophole that authorized a state to take military action against an Indian tribe any time it "received certain advice of a resolution being formed by some nation of Indians to invade such state, and the danger is so imminent as not to admit of a delay." To make matters worse, the citizenry of the new nation opposed the federal government's maintaining a standing army, even to fight Indians. As a consequence, each time it wanted to take military action against a tribe or against whites trespassing on Indian land, Congress had to ask the states for the money and the men.

Despite that impediment, three weeks after the signing of the Treaty of Peace, Congress attempted to implement an Indian policy by prohibiting whites from settling, purchasing, or otherwise acquiring Indian land without its approval.[11] It then began negotiating with the tribes to obtain voluntary land cessions.

Each of the six treaties negotiated between 1784 and 1786 drew a line down the map of the frontier. One side of the line, usually to the west, was Indian country, in which any white caught trespassing could be punished by the tribe. The other side of the line, usually to the east, was open to white settlement.[12]

Negotiating Indian country boundary lines was a rational policy in theory. But in practice, Congress had no ability to prevent white trespasses west of the lines. As a consequence, by 1788 the situation was so out of control on the North Carolina frontier that Secretary of War Henry Knox reported to Congress that "an actual although informal war of said white inhabitants against the said Cherokees" was raging, which he blamed squarely on the "avaricious desire" of the whites.[13] And the situation was the same northwest of the Ohio River.

To separate the combatants, in 1789, when he assumed the presidency, George Washington urged Congress to use its new constitutional authority "to regulate commerce with the Indian tribes" to implement a new Indian policy.

The policy Washington recommended had three parts. Part one was a new effort to protect Indians from exploitation and their land from trespass. To that end, the Indian Trade and Intercourse Act that Congress enacted in 1790 prohibited trade with Indians except by persons licensed by the federal government, and voided all Indian land sales except sales "made and duly executed at some public treaty, held under the authority of the United States."[14]

Part two was an intensified effort to persuade Indian tribes to voluntarily cede more land. To that end, between 1789 and the end of Washington's second term in 1796 the federal government negotiated ten new treaties.[15]

Part three was the co-optation of individual Indians, particularly tribal leaders, into learning to think and act white. Although he had not read Marx or Bickel, Washington intuitively believed that Indian attitudes about the world and their place in it would evolve toward his own through Indian participation in the economic system in which he participated. And the way to encourage Indian participation was to teach Indians to covet the same material goods that whites coveted. Once Indians began wearing cotton shirts and drinking coffee out of china cups, so the theory went, they would be predisposed to abandon hunting for the plow. And when they were so disposed, they would reason on their own to the conclusion that they no longer needed vast tracts of undeveloped land.

The way to encourage Indian addiction to the goods to which whites were addicted, Washington reasoned, was to make the goods available. As he noted in a memorandum that listed subjects he needed to remind himself to mention to Congress: "would not a trade on public ground, with all the bordering tribes of Indians (if they can once be made sensible of their folly by the superiority of our arms) be an effectual mean of attaching them to us by the strongest of all ties, interest."[16]

But there was a problem. Whiskey peddling and rapacious skullduggery disqualified most frontier traders from employment as agents of the American dream. For that reason, as introduced, the bill that Congress enacted as the Indian Trade and Intercourse Act of 1790 contained a provision that authorized the federal government to purchase trade goods for its Indian agents. But the Senate objected and the authorization was omitted from the version of the bill enacted into law.

Five years later the Senate relented, and Congress appropriated money to open two government trading posts, called factories, one at Colerain in eastern Georgia and the other at Tellico in what is now east central Tennessee.[17] A year later Congress authorized the president to open factories "at such posts and places on the western and southern frontiers, or in the Indian country, as he shall judge most convenient."[18] And between 1795 and 1821, thirty-two factories were established west and south of the thirteen original states, although not all operated simultaneously.[19]

The factories' inventory included wool blankets, more than 150 different kinds of cloth, cotton shirts, earrings, rings, headbands, brooches, plumes, ostrich feathers, rouge, vermilion, iron pots, knives, brass and copper kettles, tin pans and cups, jugs, crockery, glasses, mugs, forks, spoons, candle and bullet molds, bellows, salt, sugar, flour, raisins, currants, tea, coffee, spices useful as otter and beaver bait, cinnamon, nutmeg, cloves, ginger, allspice, mace, various medicinal drugs, eye glasses, tobacco, muskrat and beaver traps, guns, rifles, gun powder, powder horns, flints, hoes, spades, scythes, plows, harnesses, cotton gins, spinning wheels, blacksmith and carpenter tools, building materials, compasses, violins, and seeds for growing wheat, corn, cotton, onions, radishes, turnips, beets, cabbage, lettuce, peas, beans, melons, and cantaloupe. The only important accoutrements of white civilization not stocked on factory trading shelves were whiskey and playing cards.

Indians paid for the items they purchased with furs, as well as deer tallow, bear oil, beeswax, snakeroot, maple sugar, cattle, deer and buffalo horns, cotton, and feathers. The federal government used the revenue it earned selling Indian furs to purchase more inventory, although the system usually operated at a loss. In that fashion the factories set about trying to turn Indians into consumers eager to keep the new necessities of life coming by participating in white postcolonial America's economic exploitation of the western wilderness.[20]

Although an interesting idea, unfortunately for sociologists, Washington's experiment was not afforded a fair test. Between 1795, when the first factory opened, and 1822, when the last factory closed, Indians whom Washington hoped his factories would transform into consumers with a psychological stake in the society that produced the objects of their consumption were subjected to a constant and deadly physical assault. As Washington advised Congress in 1795 about a situation that had worsened throughout his presidency:

> [I]t is necessary that we should not lose sight of an important truth, which continually receives new confirmations, namely, that the provisions heretofore made with a view to the protection of the Indians, from the violences of the lawless part of our frontier inhabitants are insufficient. It is demonstrated that these violences can now be perpetrated with impunity. And it can need no argument to prove, that unless the murdering of Indians can be restrained, by bringing the murders to condign punishment, all the exertions of the government to prevent destructive retaliations, by the Indians, will prove fruitless.... To enforce upon the Indians the observance of Justice, it is indispensable that there shall be competent means of rendering justice to them.[21]

Despite the president's urging, Congress had no stomach for disciplining whites in order to protect the physical safety and property rights of Indians. As a consequence and contrary to the civics lesson the factories had been opened to teach, white avarice and atrocity taught that if Indians voluntarily opened their land to the postcolonial economy, the white settlers who daily were forcing their way into Indian country at gunpoint would not allow Indians to receive a fair share of the material wealth that development of the land would produce.

It is no wonder, then, that no matter how much, thanks to Washington's factories, they learned to enjoy wearing cotton rather than buckskin, cooking with skillets, and drinking coffee and tea, Indians continued to resist the confiscation of their lands.

The death knell for the factory system was rung by John Jacob Astor, the proprietor of the American Fur Company, who, unlike the land speculators with whom he undoubtedly lunched, cared less about acquiring title to Indian land than he did about acquiring Indian furs. For the American Fur Company, the government factories were business competitors whose market share by 1818 had grown to the point that Astor's managers advised him that unless the factories soon closed it would be "imprudent" for him "to continue interested in the trade."[22] To eliminate the threat to his company's balance sheet, Astor ordered his agents to sabotage the factories' operations in the field and then to present the problems they created to Congress as proof that Washington's experiment was a mismanaged disgrace.

With Astor's "evidence" in hand, Missouri senator Thomas Hart Benton captained the effort to persuade Congress to abolish the factory system.[23] When he did so, Benton was not a disinterested public servant who by coincidence shared Astor's policy objections to factories. In 1820, St. Louis fur traders had arranged Benton's election to the Senate, and when he arrived in Washington, the senator boarded at the same hotel as Ramsey Crook, Astor's lobbyist. As a Benton biographer would note of the arrangement, Crook "already knew Benton" and was "not there by accident."[24] And indeed he wasn't. In fact, the senator was so involved in Astor's affairs that in 1822 (the year he persuaded Congress to enact the statute that ordered the factories closed), Benton, a lawyer among other vocations, won a $5,000 judgment in a lawsuit he had filed on behalf of the American Fur Company against a factory employee who had refused to allow Astor's traders to operate on the Des Moines River.[25]

At the White House, Astor's lobby emitted a similarly corruptive scent: when he signed the bill that Benton pushed through Congress, President James Monroe owed Astor $5,000 (a substantial sum in 1822) that Monroe had borrowed during the War of 1812 and did not repay until 1828, when he sold a group of slaves.[26]

Thanks to Benton and Monroe, the American Fur Company trading monopoly again was secure. But once the factories closed, the two most efficient means remaining to quiet Indian objections to the opening of their land to white settlement were removal and homicide, strategies the U.S. government employed throughout the remainder of the nineteenth century with inconsistent enthusiasm but to an ultimate, if bloody, success.

Avarice and racism denied Washington's experiment a fair chance to work its magic. For that reason and as will be explored both in the pages ahead and in *Take My Land, Take My Life*, the opportunities that, beginning in 1867, whites afforded Alaska Natives to participate in the economic exploitation of Alaska's natural resources may be the first fair test of Washington's theory that economic assimilation will alter Native American attitudes to non-Native American advantage. If so and assuming that Alaska Native involvement in designing the terms of and implementing the ANCSA settlement is a reliable standard of measure, it is a test that, to date, Washington's theory of human psychology arguably has passed with flying colors.

1

Soldiers

In regard to the tribal and uncivilized Indians on Baranof Island, and the adjacent islands and coast, you will exercise the most careful vigilance, as these Natives are known to be both warlike and treacherous.... It is suggested that they be prohibited from entering or remaining within your garrison during the night, and it may be well to have guns charged with grape and canister always bearing on their village, ready at an instant's warning to destroy them.... if any member of a tribe maltreat a citizen of the United States the whole tribe and especially its chief will be held responsible for the offense or crime committed by one of its members, unless they expel such criminal or deliver him to us for punishment.

Maj. Gen. Henry Halleck, San Francisco, California, September 6, 1867[1]

Misrule has been the fate of this Territory ever since the hoisting of the stars and stripes over it.... An effort is being made to have the military return to Alaska, and in the name of humanity and common sense I ask, what for?

Isaac Dennis, Deputy Collector of Customs, Fort Wrangell, Alaska, October 31, 1877[2]

In 1925, Calvin Coolidge observed that "the chief business of the American people is business" and today is still vilified for his candor. But the president's only sin was describing national purpose in language average citizens could understand. For eighty years prior to Silent Cal's spilling the beans, the same concept applied to foreign policy had been known as Manifest Destiny. This was the lofty-sounding public rhetoric invented to justify the United States grabbing land from its neighbors to enable "our yearly multiplying millions"—as John Sullivan, the newspaper editor who coined the phrase in 1845, euphemistically called the legions of European immigrants who were off-loading in New York harbor—to exploit North America's natural resources for profit—a little for themselves and a lot for the railroad magnates, mine owners, and cattlemen who controlled the economy of the American West with rapacious eyes on their balance sheets.

Manifest Destiny has an archaic, jingoistic ring to the modern ear, but during its years of good service the slogan summarized a broad consensus. After all, nineteenth-century America would have answered if asked, if money can't be made in the West, why would anyone bother moving there?

But money could be made, and in the name of Manifest Destiny President James Polk sent America to war with Mexico in 1846, to win California and what today are the states of Arizona and New Mexico, and rattled sabers to acquire the Oregon Territory from the British. Most important to the story of Alaska Natives and their land, in 1867, Secretary of State William Henry Seward purchased Russian America from Czar Alexander II.

The idea that the United States should do so had been kicking around for years. Not wanting to spend the money necessary to assert real sovereignty over a distant and unsettled (by Russians) geography, since 1799 the czar's government had managed Aleksei Chirikov's "discovery" as a commercial concession chartered to the Russian-American Company. It was a simple arrangement: the czar gave the Siberian entrepreneurs who pioneered the sea otter trade an exclusive franchise to exploit all of Russian America's natural resources, and they gave the czar and his friends equity positions in the business.[3]

As part of the deal—in addition to making money for the Russian government and the men who ran the Russian-American Company—the company agreed to perform the government's work. As the Russian minister of finance explained the arrangement: "Aside from a trading and hunting monopoly, the government has granted to the company a portion of its power to govern a distant and extensive country, where it now has the full responsibility for all local administration. In this respect the company is not only a commercial society, but, to a certain extent, a governmental power."[4]

Most governments have armies, but because of the expense the Russian-American Company did without, a deficiency of which both Britain and the United States were well aware. While a fortuitous diplomacy avoided the indignity of Russian America being seized by the British during the Crimean War, by 1857 the untenable nature of the situation was obvious to the czar's brother, Grand Duke Konstantin, who urged his sibling to cut his losses before the United States inflicted them.

> I think we would do well to take advantage of the excess of money at the present time in the Treasury of the United States of America and to sell them our North American colonies [Konstantin privately advised the Russian minister of foreign affairs]. This transaction would be very timely, as we must not deceive ourselves and must foresee that the United States constantly aim to round out their possessions and desiring to dominate undividedly the whole of North America, will take the aforementioned colonies from us and we shall not be able to regain them.[5]

The grand duke's advice was grounded on precedent, not prescience. In 1841 the Russian-American Company had abandoned Fort Ross, its outpost in northern California, in no small part because the influx of American settlers had prevented the company from expanding its land holdings. In 1849, American whaling ships began cruising through Bering Strait and then northeast along the Alaska coastline, hunting bowhead whales, whose baleen and oil created great fortunes in Boston and New Bedford.

Other American businessmen also began looking north. In 1852, San Francisco venture capitalists began exporting ice from Sitka and Kodiak Island and in 1855 obtained a twenty-year franchise from the Russian-American Company to export coal, timber, and salmon.[6] By the 1860s there was growing agitation in the Pacific Northwest to open the waters of the Alexander Archipelago to fishing and the archipelago's ports to trade by American fishermen and businessmen who already were surreptitiously engaged in both.

When Eduard Stoeckl, the Russian ambassador, complained to the State Department about American encroachments, his protests were routinely disparaged by a government sympathetic to the interlopers. As Stoeckl subsequently explained to his employer: "To the complaints which the Imperial mission at Washington has more than once had occasion to make on this subject, the federal government has invariably replied to us that it is for ourselves to take the necessary precautions against these marauders and that the United States cannot assume the guard of our coasts."[7] By December 1866, Alexander II had had enough and, as his brother had urged nine years earlier, instructed Stoeckl to negotiate a sale.

Secretary of State William Henry Seward was eager to deal. A holdover from Abraham Lincoln's war cabinet, Seward, a former governor of and senator from New York, manifestly believed in Manifest Destiny, and for years he had believed that acquiring Russian America was part of it. As early as 1852, Sen. Seward persuaded his colleagues to support the American whaling industry by sending the navy to chart Bering Strait.[8] And he had long been unimpressed with the Russian-American Company's efforts to colonize a geography within which it obviously did not belong. As Seward explained to a crowd in Minnesota that had turned out to hear him stump for Abraham Lincoln during the 1860 election: "Standing here and looking far off into the Northwest, I see the Russian as he busily occupies himself in establishing seaports and towns and fortifications on the verge of this continent. [And I can say to him,] 'Go on, and build up your outposts all along the coast, even up to the Arctic Ocean—they will yet become the outposts of my own country.'"[9] Seven years later Secretary Seward made good on Sen. Seward's boast.

In March 1867, Seward and Eduard Stoeckl shook hands, and for $7.2 million ($200,000 of which Stoeckl used to hire newspaper editors to write editorials supporting the appropriation and to bribe members of Congress who controlled it),[10] Alexander II sold his claim to Russian America. The Senate ratified the Treaty of Cession in April, and the deal was done.

But now that it owned Walrussia, as newspapers that opposed the acquisition called "Seward's Folly," how was the United States to know that the jurisdiction it had purchased the privilege of asserting over an area one-fifth the size of the continental United States would be respected? To ensure that it would be, Secretary of War Edwin Stanton ordered Gen. Henry Halleck, the commander of the army's Division of the Pacific, to send a detachment of soldiers to Alaska (as Manifest Destiny's newest neighborhood now was known) to raise the Stars and Stripes over New Archangel, the Russian-American Company headquarters on Baranof Island in the Alexander Archipelago. The Americans renamed the site Sitka.

For Halleck, the assignment was more dangerous work for troops already spread thin. An austere military theoretician who was known in the lower ranks as "Old Brains," Halleck had ended the Civil War as chief of staff of the Union army. But after Appomattox most of his troops mustered out, and Halleck was ordered to San Francisco to command the Division of the Pacific. The division's military jurisdiction encompassed three states (California, Oregon, and Nevada) and three territories (Arizona, Idaho, and Washington), and the division had one principal military objective: fighting Indians.

In 1867 the assignment was serious business. Since 1865, Paiutes had been waging a guerrilla war in Oregon and Idaho. In Arizona, between 1866 and 1870, Halleck's regulars fought 137 engagements against Indians, losing twenty-six of their own men, and claiming to have killed more than six hundred red men.[11] To the east of the territory the Division of the Pacific patrolled, Kiowas and Comanches were raiding along the Texas border; and Gen. Winfield Hancock and his subordinate, Lt. Col. George Armstrong Custer, had 1,400 men in the field in the summer of 1867, fighting Cheyenne and Sioux who were mauling white settlements in Kansas and Nebraska.

When Secretary Stanton ordered Gen. Halleck to dispatch troops to Alaska to police an inhospitable terrain populated by a few whites and tens of thousands of Indians, Eskimos, and Aleuts who had not been consulted either when Aleksei Chirikov claimed their land or when Seward purchased it, Halleck anticipated that there might be trouble. To find out how much, he sent Lt. Col. Robert Scott to reconnoiter the situation.

> It is probable that our people will attempt settlements here [Sitka], and farther north toward Cooks Inlet [Halleck explained to his scout]. Should such settlement of the ceded country be resisted by the Indians in our own territory, or in British Columbia, a serious Indian war, with numerous complications may ensue. It is therefore desirable for all parties that every proper measure should be taken to anticipate and prevent such results.[12]

When he returned from his reconnaissance, Scott confirmed Halleck's premonition. Predicting that "difficulties" would "in all probability arise" between whites and Indians, Scott recommended that "a show of military power be made at the earliest practicable moment to the Kakes, Hunnos [Hoonah], Chilcat [Chilkat] and Hoods na hoos [Angoon]" Indians who lived in villages scattered throughout the Alexander Archipelago.[13]

To put on the show, Halleck could spare only 250 actors: 10 officers and 240 enlisted men. Having so few troops available to undertake a job that, improperly performed, could get a lot of people killed required a commanding officer who was experienced under fire. Happily (for the army), there was just such a man available: Bvt. Maj. Gen. Jefferson Columbus Davis.

A slight, dark-haired man with a thick chin beard and haunted blue eyes that war had wearied beyond their years, Jefferson Davis was a professional soldier and as hard a man as they come. Raised in southern Indiana, Davis, the eighteen-year-old grandson of Kentucky Indian fighters, escaped his father's farm by enlisting in 1846 as a private in the Third Indiana Infantry, a volunteer company that the Hoosier colonel James Lane organized to fight Mr. Polk's war with Mexico. South of the border, forced marches, brain-frying heat, dust, and pointless death made the boy a man. And the man had a large talent for life in that world. In 1885, James Fry, a fellow soldier who had known Davis for more than thirty years, described him as "brave, quiet, obliging, humorous in disposition, and full of ambition, daring, endurance, and self-confidence."[14]

The description was not hyperbole. In 1848, when the Mexican War ended, Davis's superiors commissioned the twenty-year-old volunteer, who had risen through the ranks to sergeant, as a second lieutenant in the regular army as a reward for bravery exhibited the previous year during the Battle of Buena Vista. From that day forward, Davis's life was the army, in which his reputation would be made fighting Johnny Reb and a black opprobrium justly earned for the murder of a fellow officer.

On the predawn morning of April 12, 1861, Davis was officer of the guard at Fort Sumter, the federal redoubt at the mouth of Charleston Harbor, when the mortar rounds that began the Civil War began raining on his battlement. Rewarded for bravery during the bombardment, Davis was promoted to captain in May and, being a Hoosier, was ordered to Indianapolis to assist Oliver Morton, the governor of Indiana, to recruit volunteers. But where Capt. Davis wanted to be was on the killing field, and on August 1, Morton made it possible by commissioning Davis as colonel of the Twenty-second Indiana Volunteers.

James Fry later would recall that Davis "felt that he was a born military chieftain."[15] And by every account he was.

On August 10, Col. Davis fought well under Gen. Nathaniel Lyon when Lyon's Federals were routed by Confederate troops at Wilson Creek, Missouri. Unfazed by the defeat, during the succeeding months, Davis and the men he commanded killed and captured rebels with such consistent success that, in December, Henry Halleck, who recently had succeeded John Frémont as commander of Union forces in Missouri, awarded Davis a brevet promotion to brigadier general. Three months later the soundness of Halleck's judgment was demonstrated when the division Davis commanded held its line against a ferocious gray-coat fuselage at Pea Ridge, saving the field for an important Union victory.

But when a war hero misdirects his easy propensity for homicide, the consequence is cold-blooded murder, not valor. And in September, Jefferson Davis dipped his arms elbow-deep in blood that would leave an indelible stain.

As Davis subsequently set the mordant stage: "About the middle of August [1862], my health becoming very much impaired by hard work and exposure; I asked for and obtained a leave of absence, and after turning over my command to Brig. Gen. Robert Mitchell, left for Indiana."[16] When he returned to duty, Confederates were threatening the Union force at Louisville, Kentucky. A few days after he joined the defense of the city, Davis by happenstance tangled in an exchange of insults with Gen. William Nelson, the Union commander, who brusquely ordered his insubordinate subordinate to remove himself to Cincinnati. Several days later, when Gen. Don Carlos Buell assumed Nelson's command, Davis was ordered back to Louisville, where, on the morning of September 29, he reported to Buell's headquarters at a local hotel.

When Davis entered the lobby, he found Nelson leaning against the front desk. He approached Nelson and confronted him about the earlier insult. When Nelson haughtily dismissed Davis as a "dammed puppy," the former Indiana farm boy who had held hard ground from Buena Vista to Pea Ridge snapped a wad of paper into Nelson's face with the stroke of thumb and forefinger that boys use to shoot marbles. In response, the six-foot two-inch, 300-pound Nelson gave Davis, who was five inches shorter and 175 pounds lighter, the back of his hand across the smaller man's face and then strode out of the room.

Humiliated by the blow, Davis, who was unarmed, borrowed a revolver from a friend and set out after Nelson, whom he found at the bottom of the stairs to Buell's quarters. Leveling the gun at the larger man's heart, he fired a single shot point-blank. Nelson, undoubtedly in shock, climbed the stairs to the second floor, where he dropped and died.[17] James Fry, one of the first officers on the scene, later recalled that "Davis, though greatly agitated, showed no signs of rage."[18] And indeed, in 1866, Davis would shrug off the incident as simply "a personal difficulty with General Nelson."[19]

Placed under military arrest, Davis, whom Nelson's friends wanted hanged, did not stay arrested long. Although he regarded Nelson's murder as a "high crime,"[20] General Buell had no officers to spare for a court-martial and within days left Louisville to do killing of his own. When no charges were filed, Davis was returned to command, albeit with a new reputation as a good man to have with you in a fight but whom it was dangerous to cross.

On a battlefield where great armies daily were committing the same crime under official license, craven murder was a misdemeanor for which more killing could atone. In December, Davis commanded his division during the awful butchery that Blue and Gray inflicted on each other at Stones River. And the next fall, Davis lost "nearly fifty percent killed and wounded" in "the bloodiest field I ever saw" at Chickamauga.[21]

But his division fought well, and Davis was rewarded by being assigned the command of a division of the Fourteenth Corps of the army Gen. William Tecumseh Sherman set against Atlanta. Davis quickly won Sherman's respect. As Sherman recalled the performance, "General Davis handled his division with artistic skill."[22] In August 1864, when the commander of the Fourteenth Corps, Gen. John McAuley Palmer, resigned, Sherman gave Davis both Palmer's command and his final brevet promotion, to major general.

But if Davis's hard-driving professionalism allowed Sherman to ignore Nelson's murder, it did nothing to lessen Davis's facinorous reputation.

When Sherman's army departed Atlanta and began cutting a swath through Georgia to the sea, a ragtag band of freed slaves trailed behind. Sherman considered the trekkers a nuisance and tried to discourage them from delaying his troops, but he had little success. Davis, whose Fourteenth Corps was at the rear of one of Sherman's columns, had considerably more.

Since the bridges had been destroyed, Davis's troops forded streams on pontoons. When a crossing was completed, the pontoons were moved ahead to the next stream.

Pursuant to that procedure, when the Fourteenth Corps reached Ebenezer Creek, the pontoons were put down and the troops crossed, leaving the straggling band of refugees to do the same at first light. However, during the night, Davis ordered the pontoons moved to the front of his column.

As a consequence, at dawn his unwelcome camp followers, many of whom couldn't swim, had the Hobson's choice of trying to swim the creek anyway or being shot by rebel cavalry. Since he heard Davis's side of the story firsthand, Sherman's post-hoc justification of his subordinate's action is worth quoting:

> The truth was that, as we approached the seaboard, the freedmen in droves, old and young, followed the several columns to reach a place of safety. It so happened that General Davis's route into Savannah followed what was known as the "river-road," and he had to make constant use of his pontoon-train—the head of his column reaching some deep, impassable creek before the rear was fairly over another. He had occasionally to use the pontoons both day and night. On the occasion referred to, the bridge was taken up from Ebenezer Creek while some of the camp-followers remained asleep on the farther side, and these were picked up by Wheeler's cavalry. Some of them, in their fright, were drowned in trying to swim over, and others may have been cruelly killed by Wheeler's men, but this was a mere supposition. At all events, the same thing might have resulted to General Howard, or to any other of the many most humane commanders who filled the army. General Jeff C. Davis was strictly a soldier, and doubtless hated to have his wagons and columns encumbered by these poor negroes, for whom we all felt sympathy. . . .[23]

While Sherman dismissed the incident as simply more of war's regrettable bad fortune, Davis was vilified by the abolitionist press. However, Sherman's explanation may have been accurate.

When the war ended in 1865, Davis, who at the time was military commander of the Department of Kentucky at Louisville, was appointed Kentucky commissioner of the Freedmen's Bureau, the agency Congress created to supervise reconstruction. Aware that Davis "had been previously reported as hostile to negroes," Gen. O. O. Howard, the head of the

Freedmen's Bureau, who, having ridden with Davis on Sherman's march, thought he knew the man of whom he spoke, was "fearful" of putting Davis in charge of reconstruction in a state in which "regulators" were terrorizing blacks and law and order was being ripped ragged. "But I was greatly mistaken [Howard later apologized in his memoirs]. [Davis] settled difficulties between the negroes and white men with satisfaction to both, and punished the lawless with such promptitude that even the bloody and much-feared 'regulators' were obliged, where he could reach their haunts, to suspend their base work of terrorism which they had undertaken among the freedmen and their teachers."[24]

So Jefferson Davis may have been what Sherman said he was: a professional solider who had seen and survived the unspeakable cruelty behind humankind's veneer and who, when he deemed doing so necessary, could remorselessly inflict it himself. In any case, if, as Col. Scott warned, the Indians in southeastern Alaska intended to resist the U.S. purchase of their territory, Jefferson Davis was a man on whom Henry Halleck knew he could depend to set the situation straight.

On the afternoon of September 18, 1867, the two companies of troops assigned to the Alaska command—one infantry, the other artillery— marched through San Francisco from their barracks to the wharf, where, joined by Davis and his wife Mariette, they boarded the *John L. Stevens* for the steamship voyage to Sitka. The parade was not Manifest Destiny's most patriotic celebration. As Edward Ludecke, one of the infantrymen who made the march, would remember in his dotage: "As the soldiers, equipped in heavy marching order, tramped along the streets no maidens waited on the corners with roses for their buttonholes; and no enthusiastic crowds gathered to cheer them on their way. The public disfavor of the purchase of Alaska was made manifest by an absolute disregard of the troops marching to take possession of it."[25]

A month to the day later, the activation of Davis's Alaska command attracted little more local attention. Mariette Davis described the pageantry as follows:

> The ladies (there are five here besides myself) went over in the town to witness the proceedings, which were not very imposing. Our troops joined the Russian soldiers who were assembled in the grounds surrounding the Governor's house, where were the flag-staff and the Russian flag. After the soldiers had gone through their exercises, the Russian commissioner made a speech to which General [Lovell H.] Rousseau [the U.S. commissioner] responded, then amid the firing of guns and beating of drums the Russian flag was hauled down; at least the attempt was made to lower it, but as it caught and was torn in two

it required the aid of some three or four Russian soldiers before it came down. General Rousseau's son then ran up our flag, three loud cheers were given, the soldiers dispersed, officers and ladies went into the Governor's house and drank some wine; the stars and strip [sic] floated over Sitka and Russian America was ours.[26]

But what was "ours?" All that could be said for certain was that Sitka was firmly under the control of Mariette Davis's husband's war-tested iron hand.

In 1867, Sitka, which had been built in 1804 by Alexander Baranof, the Russian-American Company's first manager, was a pleasant name for a dilapidated log fort on Crescent Bay, a stunningly beautiful cove on the west side of Baranof Island, a large island in the Alexander Archipelago located a few miles east of Kruzof Island, where Aleksei Chirikov lost his longboats in 1741.

Surrounded to the north and east by a jagged topography of glaciated mountains and to the west by a dormant volcano, the mouth of Crescent Bay, which opens into Sitka Sound, is ringed by small, rugged islands. As a harbor, however, the bay is far from ideal because it is exposed to the weather and bottomed by rocks of such irregularity that, rather than dropping anchors, the Russian-American Company tethered its ships to chain cables.

At the west end of the bay, a rocky promontory commands the view, and on the mountainsides a near impregnable forest of spruce, hemlock, and cedar descends the steep terrain to tidewater. Overcast skies and misting drizzle predominate over the sun, and October, when Jefferson and Mariette Davis arrived, is the wettest month of the year.

The town, such as it was, was a log-hewn testament to decades of discordant relations between the Russian-American Company and the local Tlingit Indians. Its most important architectural characteristic was a palisade, a high log fence that started on the beach north of the promontory and then ran upward and eastward along the knoll above the beach before making a ninety-degree turn back to the bay.

Inside the palisade, Sitka was a one-street town of mostly log buildings, many of which were rotting in the drizzle. As Del Norte, a newspaperman who accompanied the army to Sitka on the *John L. Stephens,* reported to his readers in San Francisco, "there is a less use of boards here than any other civilized town I have visited." The only structure Del Norte thought had any "architectural beauty" was the Russian Orthodox church, a spacious plank-built structure with a spire and chiming bells.[27]

Bvt. Maj. Gen. Jefferson Columbus Davis.
NATIONAL ARCHIVES, WASHINGTON, D.C.

In addition to Mariette Davis, sixty-five civilians witnessed the raising of the Stars and Stripes.[28] The thousand Tlingit Indians who lived in the village on the other side of the palisade were not invited to the festivities. But if Jefferson Davis viewed the Indians with disdain, the Indians thought the same of the army. As Davis reported to his superiors two years after he assumed his command, by that date the Indians of Southeast Alaska had become more "reconciled to the change of government over them," but many still "frequently take occasion to express their dislike at not having been consulted about the transfer of the territory. They do not like the idea of the whites settling in their midst without being subjected to their jurisdiction, in some instances they have expressed a determination to exact tribute for the privilege of trading among them."[29]

For Davis, having hundreds of surly and, when trifled with, dangerous Indians—whom the Russians called "Kolosh"—living in close proximity was an unnerving predicament that he inherited from the Russian-American Company.

The company originally had been headquartered on Kodiak Island, six hundred miles across the Gulf of Alaska to the northwest, a location that

Sitka after the purchase of Alaska by the United States.
WILLOUGHBY COLLECTION ACC. NO. 72-116-506, ALASKA AND POLAR
REGIONS DEPARTMENT, UNIVERSITY OF ALASKA FAIRBANKS.

allowed the *promyshlenniki,* as the roughneck Russian peasants who labored in the company's employ were known, to keep the Native Aleuts and Koniags,* who did most of the sea otter hunting, on the job, whether they wanted to be or not. But overhunting soon decimated the islands' otter colonies.

There were other otter colonies in the Alexander Archipelago, but two impediments obstructed the Russian-American Company's effort to exploit them: the Tlingit Indians and the English and American traders who bartered for Tlingit furs in impudent violation of the czar's right of discovery. As early as 1787, English traders had made such inroads in southeastern Alaska that Gregory Shelikhof, the Siberian trader whose company dominated the Russian-American sea otter trade prior to the organization of the Russian-American Company, complained to his government that "the great profits which belong to the Russian citizens are being usurped by people of other nations who do not own the adjoining land and have no rights to this sea."[30]

Of the seventy-two recorded American trading voyages to Southeast Alaska between 1787 and 1806, sixty-one began in Boston,[31] which is why the Tlingits called all American traders "Bostons." The Bostons traveled in ships whose holds were filled—like floating Wal-Marts—with merchandise

---

* Koniags are the Alaska Natives indigenous to Kodiak Island.

whose quality of manufacture was markedly superior to that of Russian goods. As a consequence, the Americans had a competitive advantage over Russian-American Company traders, which they compounded by shrewd and aggressive salesmanship.

According to Vassilii Berkh, a crewman on the Russian frigate *Neva* who observed the trade in 1804: "Knowing that the aborigines of these coasts spend the winters in hunger because of their lack of foresight, [the Bostons] loaded their ships with wheat, hardtack, flour and molasses. Cruising in summer among the islands they were able to spot which tribes were short of food supplies and coming there in winter they bought all their furs at very advantageous prices."[32]

Transience also afforded the Americans a second advantage. As Russian-American Company directors Michael Buldakov and Benedict Kramer explained in 1808:

> ...beginning in 1792 from ten to fifteen seagoing vessels of citizens of the North American United States have been coming there [to southeast Alaska] each year to bypass the company and trade with the American savages living in various places on the islands and the mainland, exchanging goods that they bring—especially weapons, such as cannons, falconettes, rifles, pistols, sabers, and other destructive things and gunpowder, which they even teach the savages to use.[33]

Since he wanted to establish a permanent presence in the Alexander Archipelago, Alexander Baranof prohibited Russian-American Company employees from selling the hangman the noose.[34] But when Baranof asked the Bostons to exercise similar restraint, according to Kyrill Khlebnikov, who knew Baranof well, the American captains "answered him with laughter."[35] As Baranof described their attitude, "I more than once told them that such goods (guns and powder) ought not to be bartered to such barbarous people because they often caused bloodshed amongst themselves and sometimes, as has happened, they even over-power vessels. . . . But they paid little heed to this, saying, "We're traders, we're after profits [and] there's no law against it."[36]

Since he could not compete with the Bostons for Tlingit pelts, Baranof decided to circumvent the Tlingits as a source of supply by sending Russian-American Company hunters into their territory. To that end, in 1798 Aleuts in the company's employ ventured into Chatham Strait, the channel that divides Baranof and Admiralty Islands, and located otter colonies throughout the area. In response to the discovery, Baranof sailed south from Kodiak in 1799 to supervise construction of a trading post and permanent base of operations on Baranof Island, which he sited a few miles north of Crescent Bay and named Saint Archangel Michael.[37] The compound included a warehouse, a two-story barracks, and a log palisade. Inexplicably, the palisade was the last structure built and consequently was unfinished when the compound was overrun.

Like any competent group of businessmen who have a monopoly, the Tlingits resented Baranof's attempt to break theirs. Ivan Kuskov, who supervised one of the Aleut hunting teams, described the Indians' grievances to Baranof, after meeting angry Tlingits from southeast Alaska villages in May 1802, as follows:

> The toions [headmen] of the above-mentioned settlements came into the tent and complained against our hunters, using many rude and insolent expressions, accusing them of always causing outrages, robbing the chattels placed with the dead, etc. They mentioned that our Sitka partovshchiki [Aleut hunters] had also robbed the dead at the Kuiuvsk settlement [southeast of Saint Archangel Michael], that they had been caught and that the beaver [sea otter] pelts had been taken from them. In addition they said that we hunted furs in their waters causing them to suffer great shortages in clothing and other necessities for which they barter with the Europeans.[38]

Actually, by the time Kuskov passed along their complaints, the Tlingits had settled on a plan to drive the Russian-American Company out of southeast Alaska. The previous winter, Indians from villages as far south as Prince of Wales Island had gathered at Angoon, the Tlingit village on Admiralty Island, to discuss attacking Saint Archangel Michael. According to two Yakutat Indians who attended the meeting, the plan was abetted by Bostons whose ship was wintering in the harbor at Angoon and who—according to Kuskov, who heard the story from the Yakutats—told the Indians that their vessel "would not call there again because they did not have enough beaver [sea otter] pelts for exchange and told them straight out that unless they liquidated our Novo-Arkhangel'sk fort [Saint Archangel Michael] below Sitka together with our party, they themselves, the Kolosh, would be the losers.[39]

So the decision was made, and in June—with muskets and shot supplied by Tlingits who had been supplied by American and English traders—Indians from villages throughout the Alexander Archipelago attacked Saint Archangel Michael. Most Russians and Aleuts were caught outside the compound, and all were overwhelmed. Twenty Russians and 130 Aleuts died, most beheaded, and the women were taken as slaves.[40]

Baranof was outraged by the effrontery and, after two years of planning, in the spring of 1804 set sail from Kodiak with 120 Russians and 800

Aleuts to settle the score. Luckily for Baranof, the Russian frigate *Neva,* under the command of Urey Lisiansky, arrived at Kodiak shortly after his departure. When he learned of Baranof's mission, Lisiansky weighed anchor for Sitka Sound.

When they arrived at Crescent Bay, Baranof and Lisiansky discovered that the Indians—who had anticipated their coming—had constructed a fort, complete with cannon and a six-foot-high, two-log-thick palisade, inland from the mouth of Indian River, which flows into Sitka Sound east of the bay. When negotiations with the Indians failed to produce an agreement to allow the Russian-American Company to build a new trading post on the promontory overlooking Crescent Bay, Baranof and Pavel Arbusof, one of the *Neva's* junior officers, each leading a group of Russians and Aleuts armed with field cannon, attacked the Indian River fort.

The assault was a fiasco. Struggling through thick underbrush, Baranof and Arbusof did not reach the Tlingit redoubt until late in the day. When they arrived, as Baranof tells the story, "the very thickness of the wood of the fort made it hard to do it any significant damage, while we were exposed from all sides, and, in addition, dusk was falling."[41] Quickly routed by disciplined musket fire, the Russians and Aleuts broke for the beach with the Tlingits in pursuit; if the *Neva's* guns had not covered the retreat, they would have been annihilated. As it was, ten Russians and Aleuts died, and twenty-six were wounded, including Baranof, whose arm was punctured by a musket ball. His injury required Baranof to relinquish command to Lisiansky.

The next day, rather than attacking again on foot, the Russian captain began firing the *Neva's* cannon at the Tlingit compound. Although the fort was out of range, the bombardment induced a new round of negotiations, which proceeded inconclusively until Lisiansky learned that the Indians had sent a message to Angoon requesting reinforcements. In response, Lisiansky issued an ultimatum: if the Tlingits did not surrender the Indian River fort, the *Neva's* guns would be rafted close enough to shore to obliterate it.

The next morning an eerie silence emanated from the Tlingit compound, broken only by the beating wings of ravens circling the encampment. Upon investigation, the Russians discovered that the fort had been abandoned except for two old women, a small boy, and the corpses of the dead, which included the bodies of children and several dogs who had been killed to prevent the Russians from hearing the retreat[42]—haunting evidence of the fate the Indians believed awaited them all if Lisiansky had discovered the evacuation.

Reinforcements from Angoon would not have saved the Sitka Tlingits from the *Neva's* guns. But even if they would have, they never came, which explains why the Indians of southeast Alaska, who, had they acted collectively, easily could have rid themselves of Baranof and Lisiansky in 1804 and of Jefferson Davis in 1867, did not do so.

In 1804 as many as ten thousand Indians lived in fourteen villages scattered throughout the Alexander Archipelago and the surrounding mainland.[43] Each village was divided into clans and the clans into houses. Each clan owned names, songs, animal crests, and most important, the right to use particular beaches, hunting areas and fishing grounds, and trade routes.[44] Violations of those property arrangements began blood feuds, both within villages and between them. Feuds that ended in violence also erupted over affairs of honor; Tlingit society was a rigidly class-conscious world in which some clans, houses, and families were more equal than others, and all were better than the slaves who occupied the bottom rung of the hierarchy.

For reasons not known to non-Tlingit history, when Baranof arrived at Crescent Bay in 1804, the Sitka and Angoon Indians were blood-feuding. When Indians from villages throughout the Alexander Archipelago met at Angoon in 1802 to plan the attack on Saint Archangel Michael, no Sitka Tlingits attended. As a consequence, according to Ivan Kuskov, the group agreed that "should the Sitka Kolosh refuse to take part in the attack, they also were to be massacred."[45]

Although the Sitka Tlingits did participate in the attack, two years later their relations with the Angoon Tlingits were, if anything, worse. Several days after the Sitkans abandoned the Indian River fort, an emissary from Angoon arrived at Crescent Bay and asked to speak with Lisiansky. The purpose of the visit was not to talk peace or trade. Rather, as the Russian captain explained in his journal, the Angoonian had come to ask permission for his people "to make war against and subjugate the Sitcans [*sic*]," whom he described as a "mad race" that should be destroyed because its members "did not deserve to be considered as an independent people." Startled, Lisiansky declined the offer, professing astonishment that "a people, who, allied to their neighbors by the tie of frequent marriages, ought at least, to be on terms of good fellowship, if unwilling to acknowledge them as brethren of the same cast."[46]

Upsetting to Lisiansky, in the Tlingit world such bad attitude was de rigueur, and the Sitkans were hardly above reproach. In 1852, for example, when forty Stikine Tlingits from Wrangell Island journeyed to New Archangel to trade, the Sitkans, with whom they had been engaged in a blood feud for more than twenty years, butchered every one.[47]

In any case, Baranof burned the Indian River fort and built his own, New Archangel, on the promontory overlooking Crescent Bay. Profiting from past experience, this time the company's Aleut conscripts expeditiously constructed a sturdy log palisade, a sensible precaution since Lisiansky's victory did not extend beyond the beach.

In 1812 Baranof moved the Russian-American Company's headquarters to New Archangel but was so terrified of Tlingits that he refused to allow any to live near his settlement. And for good reason: Russians and Aleuts were attacked whenever they ventured outside it.

As a consequence, company gunboats chaperoned the Aleuts on their hunts. In 1805 when a gunboat accompanied Aleut hunters paddling three hundred *baidarkas* (as Aleut kayaks were called) on a hunting expedition, they were attacked by Tlingits throughout the trip. In 1807 a large Aleut hunting party was attacked east of Baranof Island. In 1809, Aleut hunters who spent the summer on Sitka Sound were constantly harassed by hostile Tlingits. In 1810, an Aleut hunting party guarded by two company vessels ventured as far south as the Queen Charlotte Islands. On the return trip the expedition was attacked at every landfall.[48]

The situation was sufficiently dismal that when he succeeded Baranof as company manager in 1818, Leontii Hagemeister demanded hostages as a guarantee for good behavior. However, the Indians refused to provide any unless the Russian-American Company did the same. So Hagemeister delivered up two creole (mixed-blood) boys whose loss he undoubtedly could have endured had the experiment gone awry.[49]

Whatever benefit New Archangel may have gained from the exchange, outside the palisade the attacks continued. That summer, in an ambush near Prince of Wales Island, twenty-five Aleuts died, and Camille de Roquefeuil, the captain of the French vessel *Bordelais* with whom Hagemeister had contracted to protect his hunters, had to swim for his life from the beach through ice water to the safety of his ship.[50]

Several months later, Hagemeister was replaced by S. I. Ianovskii, whose sensible response to the de facto guerrilla war his employees were fighting was to ask the Russian-American Company board of directors for permission to move his headquarters back to Kodiak Island.[51] But the permission was denied, and in 1819 and again in 1820 every Aleut hunting party that ventured into Sitka Sound was attacked.[52]

In December 1820, Ianovskii was replaced by Matvei Muraviev, a naval officer whom Russian-American Company historian Hector Chevigny has described as "one of the navy's best men," "able, popular, scholarly and strongly liberal in view."[53] As fearful of Tlingits as Baranof had been, Muraviev reasoned to a contrary result regarding how to deal with them.

> Baranof would not let [Indians] live in the fort or even on the nearby
> islands, but he did allow them to come to trade, in daytime only, and
> sent them off at night [Kyrill Khlebnikov, who knew both men, ex-
> plained in 1833]. Chief manager Muraviev permitted them to live near
> the fort. He believed that if their goods and women and children lived
> under the cannon this would be good leverage for security and that
> under this situation they would not be able to carry out their secret
> plots.[54]

Attracted to the bright lights of the big city, five hundred Tlingits accepted
Muraviev's offer.

Of necessity, the Indians' proximity transformed New Archangel into a
military garrison within which the cannon mounted on the parapets and
on board the ships anchored in Crescent Bay were kept loaded twenty-four
hours a day. The ships maintained two watches, twelve men walked a constant guard, and throughout the night each guard fired a musket shot each
hour to confirm that his position had not been overrun. If the Tlingits
attacked during the night, drums and bells were ready to sound the alarm.
If they attacked during the day, a red flag was ready to be unfurled at the
top of the promontory at the west end of Crescent Bay to signal anyone
unlucky enough to have been caught outside the palisade.

According to Khlebnikov, writing in 1833, the precautions were justified
since "every year [the Kolosh] chiefs make plans for attacking the fort" for
the same reasons they had destroyed Saint Archangel Michael in 1802. As
Khlebnikov described the grievance more than three decades after Ivan
Kuskov first heard it, "[The Indians] contend that we have taken the areas
where their ancestors lived, and that we have deprived them of all the
advantages of hunting, and use of the best fishing places."[55]

About that, Matvei Muraviev could do nothing. But like George Washington, Muraviev believed that—over time—Tlingit participation in Russian
commerce could transform hostile Indians into complacent consumers
whose interest in acquiring Russian trade goods would lessen hard feelings
about the Russian-American Company's usurpation of their territory. As
Muraviev insightfully advised in 1825, "Trade should be directed not only
for company profit, but also so that we may establish friendship with the
Kolosh and so that they will have a friendly attitude toward the Russians."[56]
Unfortunately, like George Washington's, Muraviev's plan was denied a fair
test, since a black market trade made the Tlingits' already bad attitude
substantially worse.

The Russian-American Company maintained two price lists, one for
Indians and another, considerably more generous, for its employees.

Taking advantage of their discount, the employees regularly purchased trade goods at the company warehouse that they bartered to the Indians for halibut, whale and seal oil, ducks, geese, eggs, herbs, berries, crabs, shellfish, and other fresh food that otherwise was not available on the Russian table.

The Tlingits quickly learned to obtain the better of the exchange. As Kyrill Khlebnikov despaired, a Russian would "often exchange an item that cost two rubles for a bowl of berries," a bargain so bad that Khlebnikov thought "the well-being of the company and of society demand that this be eliminated as much as possible immediately."[57] And if that was not bad enough, the Indians also operated a brokering business—bartering furs to the Bostons for American trade goods that they then bartered to Russian-American Company employees at exorbitant rates of exchange.

Finally, Tlingit entrepreneurs made money pimping. As Khlebnikov, who lived at New Archangel from 1817 to 1832, described the cottage industry, "Many of them bring their slaves and young girls and invite the Russians to use them. The owner takes everything that the girl receives. And this new branch of their industry also brings them every possession the promyshlenniks have. Officials of the company are involved in these relations, as well as many visitors who have come to the colonies aboard ships from Europe."[58]

Willing to pay usurious prices for food and American trade goods and falling over themselves to buy women that Tlingit men enjoyed for free, in the Indian mind the Russians neither commanded respect nor engendered fear. As a consequence, Russian-American Company employees lived in a constant and well-founded terror of their own making.

As late as 1855, Tlingits attacked New Archangel straight on, firing through the palisade from the church the Russians had built for Tlingit use on the Indian side of the wall. Two Russians died, and nineteen were wounded.[59] In 1862, Capt. Pavel Golovin, who visited New Archangel in 1860, informed the Russian government that "until recently no Russian dared go fifty paces out from the New Archangel fortress unarmed. At present this hostility does not exist, but trade relations are carried on only with the Sitka Kolosh who live only ten sazhens [seventy feet] from New Arkhangel. The Kolosh who live in the straits are not hostile to us, but neither are they friendly. They themselves say that they 'tolerate the Russians.'"[60]

With respect to Muraviev's decision to allow the Indians to build a village next to New Archangel, Golovin thought the idea good but the execution bad.

There is no doubt that this measure would have been quite advantageous [he reported] if at the same time [Muraviev] had gradually tried to bring the Kolosh and the Russians together, and to introduce [the Kolosh] to luxury items, and thus to install in them the desire for new goods so that they would try to find a way to acquire them. This they could have done by working in the harbor, and by doing such work, without realizing it, they would have become accustomed to our way of life, to obedience, and they would have replaced company laborers who are at the present time procured at great expense and with great difficulty.[61]

But as dismal as the situation was, Golovin concluded that there was cause for hope because Johan Furuhjelm, a Finnish mining engineer who had been appointed company manager in 1859, finally was putting trade to proper use.

At present the Kolosh work willingly [Golovin optimistically reported to St. Petersburg], and their needs increase more and more. Prior to this they used to receive 100 puds of flour from the company per year, but now they receive more than 100 puds per month, and it has not yet been a whole year since they started working for us. Think of the result if this system had been adopted twenty years ago! There is no reason to doubt that it will be just barely possible to bring the Kolosh into complete submission over time by peaceful means.[62]

But if Golovin's official assessment was upbeat, his private opinion of the situation was more realistic. The Indians living on the other side of the palisade are "intelligent, warlike and savage," Golovin wrote his mother in December 1860. They are "always armed with knives" and "often have revolvers and guns which they get from the English and Americans. They are all good shots and they are brave but they fear canister shot and balls.... The result is that New Archangel is constantly in a state of siege."

The Kolosh are not allowed to enter the settlement [Golovin reported home], so trade takes place in the market in the following manner. A building has been constructed below the battery in which they put all the goods which the Kolosh generally need. Behind the building in the Kolosh settlement there is a small empty bit of land enclosed by a high palisade—this is the market. The Kolosh enter through a draw-wicket gate, which, if necessary, can be instantly let down. There is a window in the wall of the building or warehouse which is closed from inside with a heavy shutter. When the Kolosh come into the market in the morning and bring their goods, consisting of wild goats, game, fish and potatoes, the window in this little shop is opened, and the Company prikashchik receives the goods from each Indian at a set price and gives him either marks or goods in return, also at a set rate. The Kolosh are not allowed to sell their goods to any foreigner living in New Archangel. When the trade with the Kolosh is ended, the inhabitants of New Archangel come to the shop and buy however much they need of goat, potatoes and fish at a set rate, also paying in marks. Because the Kolosh are so dangerous the company has for some time been thinking of banishing them from the settlement altogether, but they are afraid that in that case there would be no fresh provisions in New Archangel, because Russians do not go out to hunt in the forest, have very few gardens, and have no livestock except pigs.[63]

That was the extent of the authority the Russian-American Company wielded outside the New Archangel palisade when Jefferson Davis arrived at Sitka. Since the Treaty of Cession ceded "the territory and dominion *now possessed* by his said Majesty [the czar] on the continent of America and in the adjacent islands," the revisionist argument that Alexander II did not "possess" Alaska when the United States purchased it is supported, at least insofar as southeast Alaska is concerned, by historical truth. And the situation was similar elsewhere.

In 1796 Baranof built a permanent settlement at Yatukat Bay on the northern end of the southeast Alaska Panhandle, which he named Novorossiisk (New Russia). In 1805 Novorossiisk was overrun, twenty-seven colonists were killed, and when an Aleut hunting party reached the site after the attack, nothing remained but ashes.[64]

The authority the Russian-American Company exercised over most of the rest of Alaska was similarly illusory. Between 1818 and 1841 the company constructed three palisade-encircled forts and five defenseless trading stations, called *odinochkas*, north of Kodiak Island. Several of the *odinochkas* were overrun, and Athabascan Indians burned the *odinochka* on the Yukon River at Nulato three times before torching it a fourth and massacring the proprietors in 1851.[65]

Even at the locations at which the Russian-American Company protected its employees with palisades, what the company "possessed" was the ground the logs enclosed. St. Michael Redoubt, built in 1833 on a tundra island at the mouth of the Yukon River, was protected by an eleven-foot-high palisade, two watchtowers and six three-pound cannon.[66] In 1836, Eskimos from Sledge Island, twenty-five miles west of the present-day city of Nome, paddled their kayaks across Norton Sound to St. Michael, where they ambushed a group of Russians gathering wood on the beach, killing one and wounding seven.

The motivation was money (of sorts), since prior to the Russian-American Company's arrival their central location had allowed the Sledge Islanders to tithe the trade between the Chukchi in Siberia, the Eskimos who lived along the Alaska coastline, and the Athabascan Indians who lived inland. According to the Russian lieutenant Lavrentiy Zagoskin, who visited St. Michael in 1842, "seeing their influence weakened year by year after the arrival of the Russians at Norton Sound, an area in which from time immemorial they had themselves collected a heavy tribute in furs, [the Sledge Islanders] determined to destroy the fort."[67]

However, the plan was aborted when several wood gatherers escaped the ambush and sounded the alarm. Eskimos armed with bows and arrows could not scale an eleven-foot barricade defended by flintlocks and cannon.[68] But controlling an acre or two of ground inside a log fence is hardly tantamount to the Russian-American Company "possessing" northwestern Alaska.

The one area the company did possess was the Aleutian, Pribilof, and Kodiak Islands. Actually five separate groups of islands, the Aleutians arc 1,100 miles west from the Fox Islands, located west of the Alaska Peninsula, to the Near Islands east of Kamchatka. Fifty-seven volcanos dominate the horizon, a geologic peculiarity that makes the Aleutians one of the most seismically unstable areas in the world. The islands are windswept and usually shrouded in dense, damp weather. However, the volcanic topography is rich in wildlife, including, when the Russians arrived, sea otters.

Aleksei Chirikov's discovery of Prince of Wales Island has been described. On July 20, 1741, Vitus Bering, whose ship, the *St. Peter,* had separated from Chirikov's in the North Pacific, discovered Alaska on his own when the *St. Peter* dropped anchor off Kayak Island in the northeastern corner of the Gulf of Alaska, five hundred miles north of Chirikov's landfall. But after all the hardship he endured to get there, Bering stayed a day and then sailed for home.

Four months later, after passing the last of the Aleutian Islands and less than two hundred miles from Kamchatka, disaster struck when the *St. Peter* ran aground on a small island where, to let the historian Hubert Howe Bancroft tell the story, on December 8 "in a miserable hut half covered by the sand which came trickling down upon him through the boards that had been placed to bar its progress," Bering died.[69]

The members of the *St. Peter's* crew who survived the winter subsisted on seal, whale, and sea otter meat. There were so many otters that the following summer when the survivors reached Kamchatka, their homemade boat contained nine hundred pelts, each worth eighty to a hundred rubles.[70] Bering's 546-man expedition had cost 360,000 rubles,[71] which demonstrates the fortune that 72,000 to 90,000 rubles worth of otter pelts represented and explains why Russian hunters soon set sail, first for the island on which Bering had died and then for the Aleutians.

In 1745 Mikhail Nevodchikof, who had crewed on the *St. Peter,* guided the *Evodokiia* on the first Aleutian foray. In September, when the *Evodokiia* anchored off Agattu, the second of the Near Islands, the indigenous population—called Aleuts—had lived on the Aleutian Islands for ten thousand years. Most Aleut villages—congregations of communal dwellings dug into the earth and covered with driftwood, grass, and dirt—were located on the north shores, protected in the lee from the gale winds that blow from the North Pacific. But good location is no defense against atrocity.

When crew from the *Evodokiia* went ashore at Agattu to refill their water casks, the landing party encountered a group of curious Aleuts. When one asked to inspect a Russian musket, he was refused, and when a second grabbed the rope that tethered the crew's longboat, he was shot. Later, on Attu, a neighboring island, the *Evodokiia's* hunters took a lascivious shine to several Aleut women. When their men tried to protect them from sexual attack, fifteen more Aleuts were shot.[72]

And so it began.

In 1753 when the Russian ship *Ieremia* wrecked off Umnak, one of the Fox Islands on the eastern end of the Aleutian chain, the survivors were attacked with throwing boards and darts.[73] In 1758 when the *Kapiton* wrecked on a reef off a small island east of Agattu, the survivors were met by Aleut arrows. In 1762 when Russian hunters raped Aleut women on one of the Shumagin Islands south of the Alaska Peninsula, their men retaliated by attacking the Russian camp, killing six and wounding seven.[74] The same year, Aleuts armed with clubs and bone knives attacked Russian hunters on Unalaska Island. Twenty Russians were killed, and their corpses were strewn along the beach.

But Aleut resistance soon ended. Two years after the Aleut attack on Unalaska Island, the Siberian merchant-navigator Ivan Maksimovich Solov'ev trapped three hundred Aleuts in an earth fort on the same island, which he exploded with gun powder. When the survivors staggered from the rubble, they were shot or stabbed to death with sabers. According to Vassilii Berkh, the first historian of the Russian occupation, Solov'ev's take-no-prisoners solution to the Russian "Indian problem" broke the Aleuts' will, and they never mounted another organized defense of their territory.[75]

Within a decade, Aleut conscripts were hunting sea otters under the supervision of *promyshlennik* overseers. And like the Crow and Pawnee who signed on with the U.S. Army to fight Sioux and Cheyenne on the western plains, in 1784, Aleuts helped Gregory Shelikhof conquer the Koniags who lived on Kodiak Island east of the Aleutians.

But the Aleutian and Kodiak Islands and the initially unpopulated (except by fur seals) Pribilof Islands to the north were the only geographies within which, in 1867, the Russian-American Company's authority was unchallenged. For that reason and no matter how time-worn the misconception, the Treaty of Cession did not convey to the United States fee title to Alaska's 375 million acres of land. Rather, what the treaty conveyed was Alexander II's acquiescence to Manifest Destiny asserting the U.S. government's jurisdiction over Alaska's vast geography and the indigenous peoples who lived in it.

Today the distinction is important to Alaska Natives who are increasingly preoccupied with the ideology of indigenous self-determination. But it is of no other contemporary consequence because, when Jefferson Davis arrived at Sitka, he immediately set about mooting the difference.

As mentioned, when Davis assumed his Alaska command, Indian wars were raging across the western frontier. The fiercest fighting occurred during the years 1867-1869, and between 1866 and 1891 hostile Indians killed 932 blue-coat regulars, including Gen. George Armstrong Custer and the other members of the Seventh Cavalry who died at the Little Big Horn River in 1876.[76]

In the war zone, troopers in the regular army considered their adversaries—combatants and civilians alike—to be a subhuman form of life that, like grizzly bears and buffalo, could be removed from its natural habitat with a clear conscience.

Jefferson Davis's patron, William Tecumseh Sherman, who, when Davis arrived at Sitka, was directing the army's war against the Sioux from his headquarters at St. Louis, had the conventional army wisdom's view of the situation. In December 1866 when a Sioux war party killed Capt. William Fetterman and seventy-nine troopers who were in the field trying to kill them, for example, Sherman advised Ulysses S. Grant, the commanding general of the U.S. Army, that the correct response to the insult was to "act with vindictive earnestness against the Sioux, even to their extermination, men, women and children."[77]

In San Francisco, Henry Halleck was of a similar hard-nosed mind. Prior to Jefferson Davis's departure for Sitka, Halleck counseled his new field commander that "past history has shown that most of the difficulties which have occurred in [Alaska] between the Natives and foreign settlers have arisen from a violation of tribal laws or rules in regard to the rights and duties of their females" and that preventing "abuses which too frequently result from the unrestricted intercourse of avaricious traders and ignorant but vindictive Natives" was the key to keeping the peace. Then, ignoring the incongruity with his previous sensibility, Halleck ordered that "if any member of a tribe maltreat a citizen of the United States the whole tribe and especially its chief will be held responsible for the offense."[78] The possibility that Davis carrying out that order might be as egregious an "abuse" as the abuses Halleck wanted Davis to prevent was beyond the general's comprehension.

But if a racist, Halleck was no fool. As a soldier busy fighting Indians himself, he had a modicum of self-awareness of the past failures of his own policy. Misreading history, he also thought that the Russian-American Company had somehow managed to occupy Alaska without the "continual hostilities" that were raging across the frontier. So as an afterthought he urged Davis to give the whole problem "your careful and serious consideration in assuming the command of a military district in which there are some 50,000 Natives and a population of only a few thousand whites and creoles"[79]—sensible advice that Davis, as much a man of his time and profession as Henry Halleck and William Tecumseh Sherman, ignored.

When she met Jefferson Davis at Sitka in 1870, Sophia Cracroft, the niece of the lost English explorer, Sir John Franklin, thought he was "stamped with earnestness."[80] And from the beginning Davis was eager to put on the "show of military power" that Col. Robert Scott had recommended be made "at the earliest moment."

Less than a month after he assumed his Alaska command, Davis reported to the Division of the Pacific headquarters in San Francisco that

> the Indians at present are at peace with the whites, but many of the tribes are at war with each other. I am convinced, however, that they generally look upon the transfer of their country to the "Yankees" with distrust, and might in a very short time be induced to give up their old quarrels among themselves and unite in a common cause against us. To be fully prepared for such an emergency we should leave nothing undone.[81]

Expanding on the suggestion, a week later he advised that

> the Indians inhabiting the little village just outside the palisades protecting the town number, from what I can learn, about twelve hundred in all. They are at present at peace, but have the reputation of being very hostile and insolent. They fear the Americans and look with considerable mistrust upon us. I have been compelled to arrest some of

> them for thieving, etc. etc. Notwithstanding they evidently fear us,
> they frequently boast that they can and will whip us someday.[82]

Read between the lines, his reconnaisance indicates that, like the Russian-American Company managers before him, Davis considered himself something of a prisoner inside the Sitka palisade.

Assuming so, the palisade, which Frank Louthan, a local sutler, described as "a rude defense line of upright logs,"[83] was an inadequate barricade. To beef it up, Davis continued the security measures Matvei Muraviev had pioneered. Cannon were aimed at the Indian village around the clock, and the gate in the wall between the village and the town was closed at 6:00 P.M., after which, as Sophia Cracroft noted in her diary, "no Indian may be seen."[84] To ensure that none were, at dusk soldiers rousted loitering Tlingits out the gate.

If the Indians were as potentially "hostile and insolent" as Jefferson Davis said they were, it should have been in the interest of the outnumbered whites to stay on good terms with them. But that is a twenty-first-century assessment of self-interest to which the residents of nineteenth-century Sitka were incapable of reasoning. Racism denied Indians their humanity; and if Indians were not human, their lives had no value.

In March 1869 a Tlingit from Chilkat River broke the glass of a showcase in Frank Louthan's store. When the glass broke, the Chilkat ran into the street and quickly outdistanced Louthan's clerk, James Parker, who returned to the store, grabbed his rifle, and resumed the chase. Not knowing that Parker had gone for his weapon and thinking that the race was over, the winner sat down behind the Russian Orthodox church to catch his breath. When Parker suddenly rounded the corner, the Chilkat leaped to his feet and sprinted for the palisade gate. But before he reached it, Parker aimed at the fleeing Tlingit's back and fired, and the Indian died face-down.

After deciding that the showcase glass likely had been broken during an attempted petty theft, the board of inquiry Davis appointed to investigate the homicide concluded "that if there were no more reasons for shooting than those brought out in evidence, ... the act was not justifiable."[85] But since the dead man was an Indian, not only was no sentence imposed, Parker shortly thereafter was appointed U.S. customs inspector at Alaska's port of entry at Tongass, an old Tlingit village site on an island on the southern tip of the Alaska Panhandle south of the present-day city of Ketchikan.[86]

By November, however, Parker was back in Sitka after having been hired by the city council as town marshall. In December, Marshall Parker fatally shot his second Indian in the back, this time a Sitkan whom he accused of breaking into a building. Capt. George Brady, the officer who investigated the incident, found the explanation incredible. "From Parker's own statement to me," he reported, "I believe the shooting was unjustifiable and cowardly in the extreme."[87]

At that point, Parker's maleficent trigger-finger became an embarrassment even to Jefferson Davis, who ordered the body attached to it locked in the guardhouse "until such time as a competent court might demand him for trial, or his release be ordered by proper authority."[88] But like Davis when he was jailed for the same offense, Parker was only briefly detained. The Sitka city council, knowing when it saw a good man unjustly accused, petitioned for its constable's release. By April, Parker was free, "based on the fact of his impaired health consequent to his confinement."[89]

Not surprisingly, when the situation, like an old sock turned inside out, was the reverse and an Indian killed a white, Jefferson Davis had a decidedly different sense of justice.

In an incredibly stupid act of feigned camaraderie, on January 1, 1869, Davis invited three prominent Tlingits to his quarters and gave each man a bottle of whiskey to celebrate the New Year. Instead of returning to the village to drink it, the Indians sat down in front of the customs house and proceeded to get rousingly drunk. When dusk came and soldiers began sweeping Tlingits out the palisade gate, a fracas ensued between the soldiers and the inebriates. One of the Indians, known to whites as Sitka Jack, was arrested; but the two others escaped through the gate, one—a Chilkat River Tlingit named Cholckeka—with a rifle he wrestled from a sentry.

Rather than allowing the Chilkat to sleep off a drunk for which he was responsible, when the incident was reported to Jefferson Davis, he ordered soldiers to arrest Cholckeka and recover the gun. However, when the troopers ventured into the village, a second fracas erupted—this time on Tlingit ground—during which the detachment was fired on and a soldier shot.

The next morning, on Davis's order, four armed vessels that were anchored in Crescent Bay moved in front of the village and readied their combined twenty guns to fire whenever Davis, who positioned himself on the palisade parapet, gave the signal by dropping a white handkerchief.

Nine hundred twenty-one Indians lived in the Sitka village, 556 of whom were women and children.[90] And at the moment of decision the demographics were determinative.

According to a soldier who was there, when Cholckeka, surrounded by armed Indians, stood his ground below the parapet and refused to surrender, Davis several times started to give the signal, each time stopped, and then, folding his handkerchief, said that he couldn't bring himself to "destroy so many innocent people for one man."[91]

Instead, he descended the parapet and strode alone out through the palisade gate and into the crowd of Indians to make the arrest himself. Luckily for Davis, the time he took to make the walk apparently afforded Cholckeka an opportunity to look again at the ships whose cannon were aimed at the village because he allowed Davis to escort him to the guardhouse, where he spent the next thirty days subsisting on bread and water.

Earlier that morning, Davis had instructed his troops to shoot any Indian who tried to leave the village. But with Cholckeka in custody, Davis lifted the order. Unfortunately, according to William Dodge, the mayor of Sitka, "the post commandant, who was drunk, either did not promulgate the [new] order or afterward reissued the first order on his own responsibility." In either event, the next day when a canoe full of Indians pushed off from the beach, a sentry opened fire, killing two. One was a Chilkat, the other a Kake, as the Indians who lived on Kuiu Island east of Sitka were known.

When he was informed of the homicides, Davis refused to acknowledge the sentry's mistake. After all, no one had been killed but two Indians. Not surprisingly, the Kakes who were members of the trading party of which the decedent had been part had a different opinion. As Frank Louthan, who dealt with them daily, subsequently explained, Tlingits were

> tractable and kind when kindly treated, but vindictive and exacting full compensation for wrongs inflicted, come from what quarter they may. All difficulties, even that of killing one of their number, is measured by an estimated value, "so many blankets," or the equivalent in money, or what they may elect. The failure to promptly pay for a real or supposed injury is at once the signal for retaliation.[92]

In other words, in the Tlingit world the penalty for homicide was money damages. And if damages were not paid, the penalty was death. And if the perpetrator was not available, the penalty could be imposed on relatives, members of the offender's clan, or residents of his village.

Demanding justice, the Kakes asked Davis to pay compensation. When Davis refused, according to Frank Louthan, the Indians adopted "their extreme remedy 'an eye for an eye, a tooth for a tooth.'"[93] On their way home to Kuiu Island they imposed sentence on two white prospectors who, unlucky enough to have met the Kakes' canoe in Chatham Strait, were killed to settle a debt that could have settled with a few trade goods.[94]

Jefferson Davis saw the situation differently. The fact that there was no difference between the Kakes' holding every white accountable for the bad behavior of his sentry and Henry Halleck ordering Davis to apply the same standard to discipline Tlingit transgressions was a lost irony. So when the prospectors' deaths were reported, Davis decided to use the mess his bad judgment and the post commandant's dereliction had made of things as an excuse to finally put on Col. Scott's "show of military power."

Commandeering the *Saginaw,* a side-paddle shallow-draft steamship that the navy had stationed at Sitka, Davis set out for Kuiu Island to, as he subsequently explained, "demand the surrender of the murderers" and if the Indians refused to produce them, "to seize a few of their chiefs as hostages, until they were given up."[95] By the time he arrived, however, the Kakes, who saw the *Saginaw* coming miles out, had prudently removed themselves. As a consequence, as Davis subsequently reported to his superiors, "nothing was left to be done except to burn their villages which I ordered done. These villages containing in all twenty-nine houses were destroyed," as well as "quite a number of canoes."[96]

The extent to which the arson convinced Indians throughout the Alexander Archipelago that Davis's employer, the U.S. government, was powerful and ruthless enough to crush further resistance to its rule is not known. What is known is that, for the next five months, Indians with furs to trade avoided Sitka, a de facto economic boycott that damaged what there was of the town's private-sector economy. Of equal importance, although the Kakes' grievance against Davis's sentry had been settled, the Chilkat's death remained unatoned.

That debt was not settled until May, when the ubiquitous Frank Louthan sailed from Sitka in a small schooner to trade at Chilkat River. According to Louthan, who lived to tell the tale, several days after he dropped anchor, Indians swarmed over his gunwale "bent on satisfaction, either in property or life, for the man killed at Sitka nearly five months previous."[97] Negotiating through the locked door of his cabin, Louthan assured the Chilkats that Jefferson Davis would compensate them for his sentry's mistake. And if for some reason Davis refused to do so, Louthan promised to pay the debt.

The trader then wrote Davis a letter that explained the situation and asked him to pay up, which a Chilkat named Kieshie, a brother of the decedent, carried to Sitka. When Davis read it, he refused. Luckily, when Kieshie returned empty-handed, Louthan convinced the Chilkats that his word was better than Davis's judgment, and they allowed him to return to Sitka to make good on it—which he did with thirteen blankets and a coat.

While he was out $50 worth of trade goods, Louthan profited from the experience. As he subsequently described what he learned: "I feel quite sure that in this simple settlement I arrested serious trouble to myself and probably to the government. I made afterwards a similar settlement with the Chilkats in Sitka, for one of their men killed by a young man [James Parker] in my employ. I can safely say that dealt with in this way, there need never be any serious complication of Indian affairs in this territory."[98]

Even Jefferson Davis learned something. In December, when James Parker murdered his second Indian, Davis kept the peace by paying the Sitka Tlingits fifty army blankets as compensation for the wrongful death.

So ended the "Kake war." William Dodge blamed the carnage on the drunk post commandant who neglected to inform the wharf sentry that the order to shoot Indians leaving the village had been rescinded. According to Dodge, "the officer through whose culpable action two white men met their death was never punished. He boasts 'that there is not power enough to dismiss him from the army, let him do what he likes.' This is all wrong, and such conduct is not calculated to ennoble any one, whether white or Indian."[99]

Had Jefferson Davis reasoned to the same result, he might have concluded that racism and bellicose overreaction were as poor a basis for an Indian policy in Alaska as they were on the western frontier. But he didn't. As a consequence, the stupidity that precipitated the Kake war was not an isolated occurrence.

In the spring of 1868 the Alaska command was reinforced with four companies of artillery, slightly less than four hundred men, which Davis deployed to Cook Inlet, Tongass, and Wrangell. Wrangell was a trading post, originally named Redoubt Saint Dionysius, that the Russian-American Company built in 1834 on an island at the mouth of the Stikine River, which drains the west side of the spine of mountains that demarks the boundary between the Alaska mainland and British Columbia 120 miles southeast of Sitka.[100] In 1839 the Russian-American Company leased Redoubt Saint Dionysius and the right to trade in its vicinity to the Hudson's Bay Company, which renamed the post Fort Stikine.

Before the Russian-American Company settled in their neighborhood, the local Tlingits—known as Stikines—had built a thriving business brokering furs to the Bostons. They obtained the furs from Athabascan Indians—called Sticks—who lived up the Stikine River. The Stikines tolerated Redoubt Saint Dionysius because the Russian-American Company did not try to disrupt their commercial relations with the Sticks, but they took violent umbrage when the Hudson's Bay Company attempted to do so. According to Hubert Howe Bancroft, "In 1840 an attempt was made [by the Stikines] to scale the [Fort Stikine] stockade; in 1841 the Indians destroyed the aqueduct which supplied the fort with fresh water, and the beleaguered garrison only saved themselves by seizing one of their chiefs, whom they held as hostage."[101]

In 1842 the fort was surrounded by two thousand Indians who had assembled to rid themselves of it, but they were scared off when George Simpson, the governor of the Hudson's Bay Company's North American operations, fortuitously arrived with two Russian-American Company gunboats.[102]

Because of the Stikines' truculent reputation, when Jefferson Davis's troops occupied Fort Stikine (which the army renamed Fort Wrangell), the post, like Sitka, was encircled by a log palisade that Gen. O. O. Howard, who inspected the premises in 1875, described as "trees fifteen feet high," with "heavy double gates made of logs fastened together" and cornered by blockhouses.[103] And, again like Sitka, a large Tlingit village was located outside the south wall.[104]

The trouble occurred the December after the Kake war. Seventy years apart, the soldiers and the Indians told different stories of how it began, the most plausible of which is that of the Indians. According to the Tlingit version, on Christmas Eve 1869 soldiers stationed at Fort Wrangell invited several Tlingits, including an Indian named Si-wau and his wife, Kchok-een, to a Christmas party in a building outside the palisade. In the midst of the festivities, Si-wau, drunk, threw Kchok-een, who had been dancing with one of the soldiers, down the inside staircase of the building in which the party was being held. The door to the room occupied by Jacob Mueller, the post quartermaster, and his wife, who was "one of the [fort's] laundresses," opened onto the vestibule at the bottom of the stairs. Responding to the commotion, Mrs. Mueller opened her door and, seeing Kchok-een sprawled on the floor, pulled her into the Muellers' room to shield her from further assault. Si-wau, who had descended the staircase to retrieve his wife just as the Muellers' door was closing, angrily bit off the end of

Mrs. Mueller's third finger, which, since the door was not quite shut, was protruding between the door and the jam.[105]

When the mayhem was reported, Lt. William Borrowe, the duty officer, ordered twenty soldiers, commanded by Lt. M. R. Loucks, into the village to arrest the sozzled perpetrator. He also sensibly ordered the detachment "only to use their arms in case of resistance or in self-defense." Pursuant to that instruction, when he arrived at Si-wau's longhouse, Loucks stationed eight men outside and ordered the other twelve to follow him in and form a line along the wall "with instructions to fire whenever I should give the signal."

When the soldiers entered and deployed, Si-wau was sitting near the fire with nothing on but pants. When Loucks announced that he was under arrest, the Indian rose and began putting on his vest at such a slow pace that the lieutenant decided that Si-wau "wished to trifle with me." Loucks' account of what happened next must be read in its entirety:

> Si-wau appeared less and less inclined to come away, and in this, the latter part of the parley, he became impudent and menacing in raising his hands as if to strike me. I admonished him against such actions, and tried my utmost to avoid extreme measures in arresting him. About this time, Esteen, probably apprehending danger to his brother Si-wau, rushed forward in front of the detachment, extending his arms theatrically and exclaiming, as I supposed under the circumstances, "Shoot me; I am not afraid." Si-wau seeing this, also rushed upon the detachment, endeavoring to snatch a musket away from one of the men on the right of the detachment. Still wishing to avoid loss of life if possible, I tried to give him two or three saber cuts over the head to stun without killing him. In doing this I had given the preconcerted signal (by raising my hand) to fire. I should judge about six or eight shots were fired during the melee, and only ceasing by the Indian Si-wau falling at the feet of the detachment dead. Esteen and the others running to their holes [i.e., the sleeping planks located around the perimeter of the single large room], everything became quiet. I then directed the detachment not to renew the firing until further orders. I had Esteen pulled out, and discovered he was bleeding profusely from a wound in his right arm near the shoulder. Two handkerchiefs were tied around his arm above the wound to check the bleeding. My first thought was to arrest him also, for interference, but afterward considering that he was intoxicated, and that his interference was to protect his brother Si-wau, who, in my opinion, was in the same condition of intoxication, I concluded that he had been sufficiently punished, and directed that he be carried over to the hospital for treatment, and that the dead Indian should be carried over to the guard-house.[106]

If the slapstick is not lost on the contemporary reader, it also was not lost on the Indians who witnessed it. In the Tlingit world, the army had committed another wrongful death for which compensation was due.

The debt was paid hours later when Si-wau and Esteen's father, a Tlingit named Scutdoo, encountered Leon Smith, a trader who lived in a cabin on the beach outside the palisade. Shots were heard, and Smith's body was found riddled with bullet holes. Smith died that night, and the next morning Lt. Borrowe sent Lt. Loucks into the village to deliver an ultimatum: if Scutdoo did not surrender by noon, the fort's six-pound cannon would begin shelling the village. When the Indians answered that the wanted man would not turn himself in, Loucks "told them all again that their village would be destroyed like the Kake village last winter."

The fact that the Kake village was uninhabited when it was put to the torch, while the Wrangell village was full of women and children and the old and infirm—none of whom had had anything to do with Smith's death—was a distinction without consequence. When Scutdoo failed to appear at the designated hour, the six-pound gun began firing.

> I opened with solid shot in the house in which I knew the murderer, Scutdoo, resided [Borrowe subsequently explained]. Several shots struck the house, but the Indians maintained their position and returned the fire from the ranch [i.e., village], several of their shots striking in close proximity to the men.... Firing was kept up on their part all of the afternoon, and a slow fire from the six-pounder gun on the village was maintained until dark.

The next morning the Stikines resumed their counterattack, and Borrowe resumed "the fire from th[e six-pound] gun with shot and from the mountain howitzer with shell." The exchange ended when "after four shells had been fired, two bursting immediately in front of the houses, and two solid shots just through the house of the principal chief, Shakes, a flag of truce was seen approaching the post."

Outgunned, the Stikines laid down their weapons, Scutdoo surrendered, and the next day Borrowe appointed a jury composed of himself, Lt. Loucks, the post surgeon, and a trader named William Lear, the decedent's business partner. Since Scutdoo admitted the homicide, the jury's job was to impose a sentence, which of course was death.

Two days later the prisoner was hanged and his body left swinging until nightfall as an example to other misbehaving Indians. However, Scutdoo's last word on the subject is evidence that the Tlingits considered Leon Smith's death to be justice, not miscreancy. According to Borrowe, when the jury pronounced sentence, Scutdoo responded that "he would see Mr. Smith in the other world, and, as it were, explain to him how it all happened; that he did not intend to kill Mr. Leon Smith, particularly; had it been anyone else it would have been all the same."

It is interesting to speculate whether Lt. Borrowe would have cared what mayhem Si-wau had committed if "Mrs. Mueller" had not been white, or if she was an Indian, the woman of a white man. And it is useful to compare Scutdoo's punishment to the penalty Jefferson Davis imposed on James Parker for the murder of two Tlingits.

Davis was not so introspective. As he explained to his superiors in San Francisco, "After a very thorough investigation of the whole affair, I am satisfied Lt. Borrowe acted with promptness and good judgment; a less decided course would probably not have settled it with as little bloodshed as the one pursued. I anticipate no further trouble with this tribe for some time to come." If avoiding "further trouble" was the objective, the way for the army to have best achieved it would have been by withdrawing. Although Jefferson Davis would not have agreed with that reasoning, by mistake Congress did.

From the nation's inception, the citizenry was uncomfortable with the idea of maintaining a standing army in peacetime, so much so that in 1860 the U.S. Army numbered fewer than 20,000 men. While troop strength rose during the Civil War to over a million (most of whom were volunteers), when the war ended almost all mustered out, and in 1866, Congress reduced the authorized strength to 54,302. When the South remained well behaved, Congress slashed further. In 1869 it reduced the number of infantry regiments from forty-five to twenty-five, and in July 1870, seven months after the shelling of the Wrangell Indian village, it reduced the authorized strength of the enlisted army to 30,000.[107]

When it did, Congress could have cared less about how the troop reduction might affect Jefferson Davis's ability to assert its authority over Alaska—about which, in 1870, Congress also could have cared less. But the effect was significant. The Alaska command was disbanded as an administrative unit, four of its six companies were withdrawn, and by September every post but Sitka (including Fort Wrangell) had been abandoned.[108]

Impaired by jaundice and with little to do, in 1871, Davis was rotated out of Alaska to New York City, where he supervised recruiting at that station. In April 1873 when Kintpuash (the Modoc Indian leader known to whites as Captain Jack) murdered Gen. Edward Canby, the commander of the Division of the Pacific's Department of the Columbia, at a peace parley at Tule Lake, California, Davis inherited Canby's command. Under his supervision, Kintpuash was hunted down and hanged. The next spring, Davis was given command of the Omaha, Nebraska, barracks and, still in the army, died in 1879 in Chicago of pneumonia that may have been exacerbated by liver failure brought about by jaundice. He was fifty-one years old.[109]

With Davis gone, the Sitka garrison stayed within its walls until 1875. In 1872 gold was discovered in British Columbia in the Cassiar Mountains near the headwaters of the Stikine River. By the summer of 1874 the rush was on, and by the end of the year stampeders who flooded into the area had dug nuggets and panned dust worth almost $1 million.[110]

The quickest and easiest way to the diggings was to travel up the Stikine River by steamboat. The happenstance transformed Wrangell from a quiet (since the army's departure) Indian village in which William Lear, the deceased Leon Smith's business partner, operated a small trading post into a whiskey-besotted mining camp.

When it was abandoned in 1870, Maj. John Tidball, a senior officer at Sitka, sarcastically touted the army's nonaccomplishments at Fort Wrangell as follows: "it established no settlement; it attracted no [white] population; it opened no industry; it developed no resources of the country; it guarded nothing, observed nothing, commanded nothing."[111]

Thanks to the influx of stampeders, the need to maintain order finally gave the army a mission. However, like the Cassiar strike, the army's return to Wrangell was short-lived.

Unlike the opening of the American West, the Alaska purchase did not unleash a torrent of white settlement. Ten years after becoming U.S. territory, Walrussia still was populated almost exclusively by Indians, Eskimos, and Aleuts. And experience by that date had shown that when unruly Natives needed disciplining, unless their village was conveniently located next to a fort, they could not be reached by foot or on horseback, the army's customary modes of transportation.

Jefferson Davis recognized the problem early on. Less than three weeks after he arrived at Sitka, he advised his superiors in San Francisco that "the cooperation of a navy vessel with the military forces on this coast is very necessary to secure a continuation of the present peaceful states of affairs.... I think this matter of considerable importance and would respectfully ask the early attention of the General commanding the Department to the subject."[112] And two years later, the ride Davis hitched on the *Saginaw* when he burned out the Kakes proved the point.

The untenable nature of the army's situation finally came to a head in February 1877, when the Sitka officers' quarters were destroyed by fire.

In 1868, when Congress—for a fleeting moment—turned its uninterested attention to Alaska, it had extended the laws of the United States "relating to customs, commerce and navigation" to the territory,[113] all of which were enforced by the U.S. Revenue Marine (the precursor of the Coast Guard). Consequently, instead of rebuilding the officers' quarters, Secretary of War George McCrary and John Sherman, the secretary of the treasury (the department in which the Revenue Marine was located), decided that the Revenue Marine should assume responsibility for policing the territory.

To that end, in April McCrary ordered Secretary Sherman's brother, William Tecumseh Sherman (who by that date was commanding general of the U.S. Army) to abandon Sitka and Fort Wrangell "upon the arrival of the revenue cutter now fitting out under the control of the Treasury Department,"[114] and in June the troops departed on the steamer *California*. Left behind at Sitka to work out their new relationship with the Indians who lived next door were twelve to fifteen white men "of various nationalities," five Russians, and 270 creole men, women, and children.[115]

After more than seventy years of repeated Russian and American insults, there was some working out to do.

When he visited Sitka in 1875, Gen. O. O. Howard, the commanding officer of the Department of the Columbia (of which the Alaska command was then part), met with Anahootz, the leader of the Kokwantons, one of the Sitka Tlingits' two major clans. Anahootz began the meeting by reminding the general that he had been doing his best to live peacefully even though "nine of my people have been killed or wounded by white men." While the Kokwantons had no complaint against Maj. J. B. Campbell, the commander of the Sitka garrison, whom they considered a fair man, they had "hard feelings against some of the store-keepers here, who treat them like dogs." "[The Indians] are paid for labor with a little hard-tack or flour," the Tlingit headman explained, "and if they complain are kicked from the stores."[116]

Two years later, when the army departed, the storekeepers' accounts receivable came due. According to Charles Thorne, the captain of the *California,* when the steamer tied up at Sitka on its first trip back after transporting the army out, Indians "thronged his vessel while at the dock, and were generally haughty, insolent, and overbearing in their manner." More ominously, Sitka Jack, the leader of the Kiksatis, the Sitka Tlingits' other major clan, who had been jailed in 1869 when he and Cholckeka had gotten drunk on Jefferson Davis's whiskey, threatened Thorne that when the thousand Tlingits who were at their summer fish camps returned to the village "they intended to seize all the government buildings and other valuable property at Sitka."[117]

When the *California* reached Port Townsend, Washington, and Thorne reported Jack's threat to William Gouverneur Morris, the Treasury Department agent at that locale, Morris urged his superiors to permanently station a revenue cutter at Sitka.

> The inhabitants of Sitka are slumbering upon a volcano [he advised], and some day it will belch forth and engulf them ... many of these Indians have wrongs to redress and injuries to be made good, inflicted upon them while the country was in the hands of the military.[118]

Three months later, Sitka Jack proved Morris's prediction correct when the revenue cutter *Corwin,* which had been docked at Crescent Bay, weighed anchor. When the vessel and its guns were gone, Jack and a group of friends tore down a section of the log palisade behind which Sitka's white population had huddled since 1804.[119] The vandalism had the practical consequence of turning all of Sitka into an Indian village in which whites henceforth lived at Tlingit sufferance.

Any doubt to the contrary was resolved the following spring, when the *California* docked at Sitka with a cargo that included equipment and men that a San Francisco firm, Cutting & Company, had shipped north to build a salmon cannery. Among the inventory were eighteen Chinese who had been hired to manufacture tin cans. When the Indians saw the Chinese, according to William Gouverneur Morris, who witnessed the scene, "a general howl arose and the wildest excitement was manifested." With the help of a translator, Morris and the Cutting & Company manager tried to explain the limited involvement of the Chinese in the enterprise. But the explanation fell on deaf ears. According to Morris, "had the Chinamen landed before a proper understanding was had every man of them would have been ruthlessly murdered, and God only knows, when the sharks tasted blood, where it would have ended."

The concern that generated the roused ferocity was local hire. "The point of the controversy was that [the Indians thought] the Chinamen had been imported to catch the fish," Morris subsequently explained. In the Tlingit view, "It was their country and John Chinaman should not come. A very strong argument, it must be admitted."

The impasse finally was broken without violence when Cutting & Company's manager agreed to buy his fish from Indian fishermen and to ship the Chinese south when they had manufactured an agreed upon number of cans. The bargain struck, the Tlingits allowed the Chinese ashore and, according to Morris, "in a very short time as many Indians as could be set profitably to work were hired by Mr. Hunter [the Cutting & Company manager] to discharge his material." "Thus ended what might have proved a very serious affair. But it only goes to show how utterly helpless are the white population when the anger of the Natives is aroused."[120]

The next year Tlingit anger would be roused badly enough for a gunboat finally to be ordered to Sitka on permanent station. The circumstances were not dissimilar to those that precipitated the Kake war.

In 1878 six members of the Kiksatis clan who had hired on as crewmen on the sealing schooner *San Diego* drowned in a boating accident. As Tlingit law demanded, Katlean, a rising Kiksatis leader, asked Mottram Ball, the Sitka customs collector, who, after the army's departure, was the U.S. government's ranking representative, to pay one thousand blankets per man as compensation for the deaths. To avert trouble, Ball wrote to the *San Diego's* owner in San Francisco, urging payment. But the owner refused. In the meantime, in January 1879, two Kiksatises named Kotkowat and Okhkhonot murdered a white man at a hot springs outside Sitka. A reward was posted, and Annahootz, the leader of the Kokwanton clan, captured the two, who were summarily locked in the old army guardhouse.

Angered by the disparity of treatment, Katlean, drunk, shortly thereafter warned a trader that if Sitka's whites did not pay compensation for the six dead Kiksatises with blankets, they would pay with lives. The threat was not idle talk. On the evening of February 6, 1879, the whites and creoles in their houses behind what was left of the palisade heard raucous noise on the other side, during which an Indian named Mary, who was the woman of a former soldier, came in from the village to report that Katlean and the Kiksatises were coming to settle accounts.[121] Terrified, the townsmen gathered their women and children and, arming themselves, prepared for a fight they could not have won.

Luckily for all concerned, when Katlean and his men reached the palisade, they were met by Annahootz, the rival clan leader, who (perhaps having decided that if the whites were killed the guns on the next revenue cutter that docked at Crescent Bay would obliterate the village) blocked the way. A scuffle ensued, one of the Indians with Annahootz was stabbed, and Katlean retreated.

The next morning the survivors of the almost-massacre organized a public safety committee, distributed arms, and appointed a night guard. Then, as luck again would have it, in the midst of the preparations the *California* unexpectedly steamed into the harbor. Several days later, when it cast off and headed south, the two Kiksatises—Kotkowat and Okhkhonot (who were transported to Portland and hanged)—and as many women and children as could afford the passage were on board, as was a petition to the British on Vancouver Island to send help.

They did, and on March 1 the H.M.S. *Osprey*, with 141 men and six guns anchored at Crescent Bay, followed the next day by the revenue cutter *Wolcott* and, after a flurry of publicity that swirled around the incident, in June by the navy warship U.S.S. *Jamestown*, commanded by Capt. L. A. Beardslee.[122]

Gen. Rousseau's son had run the Stars and Stripes up the flagpole at the Russian-American Company headquarters twelve years earlier to mark the United States' symbolic assertion of jurisdiction over Alaska. The arrival of Beardslee's floating fort on permanent station sent the message that the United States was in Alaska to stay.

If the Tlingits needed a last lesson to clear away any lingering doubt, they got it three years later.

In October 1882 a harpoon gun bomb exploded and killed Tith-klane, a Tlingit from the village of Angoon, during a whale hunt in Kootznahoo Inlet on the west side of Admiralty Island. As compensation for the death, Tith-klane's relatives demanded two hundred blankets from his employer, the Northwest Trading Company. To secure the debt they seized the boat in which the accident occurred and took several whites hostage.

When the incident was reported at Sitka, E. C. Merriman, the captain of the U.S.S. *Adams*, the navy warship that had relieved the *Jamestown*, commandeered the revenue service cutter *Corwin*, which he needed to navigate the shallow water in front of the village, as well as a smaller vessel—the *Favorite*—on which he loaded a howitzer and a Gatling gun, and set out for Angoon. When the ships loaded with sailors and marines appeared, the Indians quickly freed their hostages. In 1951 Tith-klane's nephew, a Tlingit elder named Billy Jones, who was thirteen years old when the events occurred, described what happened next.

The *Corwin* and the *Favorite* steamed first to Favorite Bay south of the village, where "boats and food being packed for winter [at the Indians' summer fish camps] was machine gunned." Then "sailors was brought ashore with axes to finish what the guns could not destroy."

> After they have destroyed the foods at our camps they moved into Angoon and started to open fire on the village. After the firing, sailors and marines were brought ashore bringing with them oakum and kerosene. Busting into houses the sailors and marines set fire[s].... Having no power or means to prevent this disaster my Native people fled to the north side of Angoon. I taking my younger brother with

me. Natives from Killisnoo [two miles south of Angoon] and other camps came to witness this happen. The next day my mother told me that six children have suffocated from the fire.[123]

William Gouverneur Morris, who had relocated from Port Townsend to Sitka to be collector of customs and who watched the flames from the *Corwin's* deck, subsequently lauded Merriman's burning of the village to Secretary of the Treasury Charles Folger, calling it a "most severe, but eminently salutary" punishment that was "the very thing that was needed." A believer in Manifest Destiny's grand design, Morris understood that arson and infanticide were costs of doing business, since whites could not commercially exploit Alaska's untapped natural resources safely until the Natives, starting with the Tlingit Indians, acknowledged the U.S. government's jurisdiction over what previously had been their ground. As he explained the concept to Folger, "Once let it be understood by the Siwashes [i.e., Indians] that the life of a white man is sacred, and that they will be severely handled if they harm him, there will be no danger or difficulty in small parties traversing the country in search of mineral and other wealth."[124]

E. C. Merriman ordered the matches struck. But the command that he do so was issued fifteen years earlier by Gen. Henry Halleck when he instructed Jefferson Davis that if an Alaska Native mistreated a United States citizen "the whole tribe and especially its chief" were to be held responsible. The edict made arson, homicide, and every other -cide morally permissible. That is why it was unusual for a man as hardened to nineteenth-century necessity as Jefferson Davis to have refused to drop his handkerchief to spare innocents in the Sitka Indian village the collective fate Henry Halleck had ordered as punishment for misbehavior (refusing to surrender Cholckeka, the Chilkat who had absconded with a soldier's rifle) of which, from Halleck's perspective, all were equally guilty.

But infrequently accidents did happen, even in the post-Civil War army, whose job, both literally and metaphorically, was clearing the country of Indians. And during the army's decade in Alaska there were two. The first— Jefferson Davis being struck by conscience in 1869—has been described. The second, committed by a common soldier at Fort Wrangell in 1877, would, two months after the *California* transported the army south, bring a man north, who, over the next thirty years, would shape the Alaska Native fate into a configuration dramatically different from that which awaited Native Americans elsewhere.

2

Missionaries

It will be much cheaper to spend a few thousand dollars in now educating [Alaska Natives] to citizenship, than a few years hence millions to fight them, when the encroachments of the whites shall drive them to desperation.

Sheldon Jackson, February 1880[1]

On the afternoon of August 10, 1877, the steamship *California* docked at Wrangell harbor. Among the passengers on deck straining to catch sight of the log fort and the Indian village and the raucous mining camp that by that date was roaring next door to the village were a very large woman and a tiny, barely five-foot-tall man. On the voyage north their shipmates must have been struck by the incongruity of the couple's appearance. But upon examination, the straitlaced countenance that joined the two in a commonality of important interest would have been apparent. These were serious people bent on serious work—or to be precise, Presbyterian missionaries who had come to Wrangell to bring the Tlingit Indians news of the Protestant God and information about how best to get along with the civilization that served him.

The woman was Amanda McFarland, a widow later described by a co-worker as "two hundred pounds of good nature."[2] In 1867 McFarland and her husband, the Rev. D. E. McFarland, established the first Presbyterian mission in the New Mexico Territory. In 1875 the McFarlands were assigned to work among the Nez Percé on the border between Oregon and Idaho, but the Rev. McFarland, who had been in ill-health, died before the couple arrived at their station. Amanda, overcome by the loneliness that is the frequent lot of the relict, moved to Portland, Oregon, where she was recruited by the Rev. Aaron Lindsley of the First Presbyterian Church of that city to teach at the Indian school that recently had opened at Wrangell.

The man was Sheldon Jackson. Forty-three years old in 1877, Jackson had been born in Minaville, New York, northwest of Albany, into a family that was locally prominent.[3] When he was an infant, Jackson's parents relocated ten miles south to Esperance, where they joined the local Presbyterian church and shortly thereafter experienced a recommitment to the faith. "From this time onward," according to Jackson biographer Robert Laird Stewart, "the word of the Lord was the law of the household and all its affairs were ordered in cheerful obedience to its requirements."

Growing up, Jackson was smaller than other children and had terrible eyesight. Between his slight physical stature and the pervasive religiosity of his household, the boy evolved a temperament, again in the words of Robert Laird Stewart, "adverse to all that was rough and demoralizing, whether in sport or in sober earnest." He also was afflicted with dyspepsia, a disorder of the stomach and digestive tract.

In 1855, Jackson graduated from Union College in Schenectady, New York, and, having been pushed from boyhood to enter the ministry, enrolled at Princeton Theological Seminary. At Princeton several of the students who attended the weekly prayer meeting in which Jackson participated were enthusiasts of the world missionary movement, and the young novitiate fell under their influence.

At the time, the Presbyterian Church divided its missionary work between the Board of Home Missions and the Board of Foreign Missions. According to a church historian, "the basic aim of the Presbyterian home mission movement was to retain the allegiance of Presbyterians as they moved westward, by organizing them as quickly as possible into self-supporting churches."[4] The Board of Foreign Missions, by contrast, operated missions throughout the third world and in the Indian Territory in what today is the state of Oklahoma.

Captivated by the romance of service in exotic venues, during his last year at Princeton, Jackson applied to the Board of Foreign Missions for a missionary appointment. The application was accepted, but because of his frail health the board declined to send Jackson abroad. Instead, he was sent to the Indian Territory to teach school at Spencer Academy, an Indian boarding school on the Choctaw reservation. Jackson and his bride, the former Mary Voorhees, whom he married shortly after he graduated and was ordained into the ministry, reached Spencer in October 1858.

Jackson's short career as a teacher was a disaster. He had little natural aptitude for the work. And to compound the problem, the theory then in vogue was that the most effective way to teach Indian students the gospel and the values of the culture that prized it was to beat it into them. As Jackson explained in a letter to his parents written a month after he arrived at Spencer:

My boys are mostly large, and give me a good deal of trouble. The missionaries here say it was just what they had to pass through. They like to try a new teacher, and they do it in every conceivable way. Our surest mode of discipline is whipping. This I dislike very much. If you should deprive a boy of his meal it would make a good deal of noise in the tribe, but if you should whip him until the blood runs there would be nothing said about it. So I have to whip them. It is strange how you can calm them down. One of them doubled up his fist to intimidate me, but the only effect was to secure him a severer whipping. They are very impudent and stubborn, if allowed to have their own way, and sometimes won't answer a word; sometimes refuse to go to class. One day, I found under the seat of one of the boys a large hunting knife whetted to a keen edge. I took it in keeping for him. Recently one of the larger boys wrote me that if I attempted to whip another boy, he would whip me. By the advice of the other teachers I took the suit of clothes which belonged to him when he came, and calling him to my room was about to turn him out, when he broke down completely and said he did not mean it, and promised good behavior in the future, if I allowed him to stay. He afterwards said the same thing before the whole school. When we get a superintendent, the bad cases are to be turned over to him. I wish we could have one soon.

Jackson soon thereafter contracted malaria, which provided the rookie pedagogue an excuse to resign before one of his students made good on the threat to extract retribution for his reliance on the lash.

After transferring to the Board of Home Missions in 1859, Jackson was sent to organize a Presbyterian church at La Crescent, a farming town in southeastern Minnesota, a task for which he quickly proved well suited. Except for a brief several-month sojourn as a Union army chaplain during the Civil War, Jackson spent the next decade in southeastern Minnesota organizing small-town churches.[5] Had this vocation been pursued to its conclusion, it would have ended in a deservedly obscure retirement for its practitioner. However, Jackson was saved from the humdrum by a presumptuous ambition that was driven by a prescient understanding of how the transcontinental railroad would transform the American West.

The idea of building a railroad to link the Pacific Coast to the maze of track that crisscrossed the country east of the Mississippi River had been discussed since the 1840s. But there had been no political consensus between North and South on the choice of a route. When the South left the union in 1860, the need for consensus disappeared, and a northern route was chosen. By 1865 a largely Irish work crew was busy laying track for the Union Pacific Railroad west from Omaha, Nebraska, and a largely Chinese work crew was busy doing the same for the Central Pacific Railroad east from San Francisco.

Although no one in the hierarchy of the Presbyterian Church had the insight, Jackson, by 1868 an obscure thirty-one-year-old pastor of the Presbyterian church in Rochester, Minnesota, west of La Crescent, reasoned on his own that when the trains began running, economic development along the new road would accelerate, and population growth was the handmaiden of development. New people meant new towns. And every new town needed a church that Jackson aspired to organize.

In August, Jackson informed the Board of Home Missions by letter that "for four years and more the brethren have been urging me to enter the general work, but, in the providence of God, the way never seemed to be open until now." He then modestly reported that "men of prominence in the West" have proposed that the Synod of Iowa divide its jurisdiction and "give me the northern part."

Making good on the prediction and undoubtedly as a consequence of Jackson's having urged the membership to do so, two months later the synod sent the Board of Home Missions a resolution noting that "in view of the rapidly increasing population of our state, now numbering about one million souls, and of the several lines of railroads being constructed through the state, with the numerous villages and cities springing up along them and over our vast prairies, we believe that in order to render the plan of district missionaries effective, more than one is required in Iowa."

The resolution then urged the board to hire Jackson "as soon as [its] funds permit" to organize new congregations throughout a jurisdiction that would encompass "the North Western Railroad and the territory lying between it and the Minnesota line." But whatever its members may have thought of the idea, the Board of Home Missions' budget did not permit hiring another missionary, and the Iowa synod's request was denied.

The board's decision should have ended the matter. But Jackson, whom Richard Henry Pratt, the headmaster of the nineteenth century's most famous Indian school, later characterized as having a "bull dog tenacity,"[6] was undaunted. Having earlier wrangled an invitation to meet with the Board of Home Missions executive committee to brief the committee on the work that needed to be done on the frontier, Jackson proceeded east to do so.

The executive committee withstood his proselytizing, but Jackson refused to take a repeated no for an answer. When he returned to Minnesota, Jackson jury-rigged an alternative plan that was seared with the tinge of genius: if the Board of Home Missions would not hire him to organize churches along the railroad line, he would obtain the job piece-meal.

In January 1869, Jackson resigned as pastor of the Rochester Presbyterian Church and that spring traveled to Iowa to attend the annual meetings of the local presbyteries. At each stop he asked each presbytery to appoint him as its superintendent of missions within the territory encompassed by its jurisdiction. Since he was willing to work free, every presbytery agreed to do so. In April the Presbytery of Des Moines appointed Jackson as its missionary for central and western Iowa, and the Presbytery of Fort Dodge, whose jurisdiction began immediately to the north, did the same. The same month, the Presbytery of the Missouri River, whose jurisdiction stretched from the river of that name west to California, appointed Jackson as "superintendent of missions for Western Iowa, Nebraska, Dakota, Idaho, Montana, Wyoming and Utah or as far as our jurisdiction extends."

Ten days later, May 10, 1869, the golden spike was driven into the rail bed at Promontory Point, Utah, officially joining the Union and Central Pacific tracks; and Sheldon Jackson, his jurisdiction complete, controlled all Presbyterian missionary activity between the Missouri River and the western slope of the Sierra Nevada mountains.

But building the empire of small-town churches that Jackson had positioned himself to assemble required more than a paper jurisdiction. It required money—a commodity his new employers had none of but which Jackson already had been busy raising.

The key to Sheldon Jackson's extraordinary success as a frontier missionary was his talent for generating his own cash flow. During one of his years at Princeton, Jackson had worked as a fund-raiser for the American Systematic Beneficence Society, a summer job that had taken him as far west as Leavenworth, Kansas, to solicit money from fifty-three different congregations.[7] The experience taught the young would-be pastor that he had a knack for the hustle and that, if properly asked, Presbyterians—particularly Presbyterian women married to men wealthy enough to allow them to do so—were willing to donate substantial sums of money for church work other than through the offering plate.

Putting those insights to practical work, Jackson spent the summer of 1864 in New York soliciting Presbyterian congregations for donations to construct his Rochester church and returned to Minnesota with $5,000.[8] Building on that success, in 1869, Jackson began a direct-mail campaign that solicited wealthy Presbyterians to support his new work on the frontier that for its day would have been the envy of Richard Viguerie. Over the succeeding twenty months, the recipients of his appeals contributed

$10,000. The money allowed Jackson not only to pay himself a salary but to hire ten missionaries, whom he assigned to stations in Iowa, Nebraska, Wyoming, Colorado, and Utah.

In May, Jackson moved his wife and children from Rochester to Council Bluffs, Iowa, a small town near the Union Pacific railhead at Omaha, and then departed for Wyoming to organize a Presbyterian church at Cheyenne. Continuing on, between July 15 and August 17, Jackson traveled 2,300 miles by train and 1,200 miles by stagecoach to organize eight new churches in Nebraska, Wyoming, and Montana.

The political dust he raised inside the Presbyterian Church by hitting the ground running so hard forced the Board of Home Missions to hastily reconsider its decision not to hire Jackson for work he no longer needed its approval to perform. After doing so, the board appointed Jackson as its missionary for Nebraska, Wyoming, and Colorado, a jurisdiction narrower than the jurisdiction he had acquired piecemeal.

In August 1870, Jackson moved his headquarters to Denver and shortly thereafter expanded his missionary activities to include Indians.

As mentioned, the Board of Foreign Missions, rather than the Board of Home Missions for which Jackson worked, was responsible for converting the Indians who lived in the Indian Territory to Presbyterianism. But thousands of Indians lived within Jackson's new jurisdiction outside the Indian Territory. And after traveling through it, Jackson became convinced that, until they were educated, children who were members of those tribes could never be converted, nor could their parents. As he reminisced in 1904,

> I was sent to the frontier as a young missionary to do missionary work among the Indians, but as I looked over the field I could do little without the aid of a missionary teacher. I wrote Dr. [Henry] Kendall, then secretary of the Board [of Home Missions], that we must have a teacher to go into the homes of the Indians to gather the children, and to open the way for the minister. Later I came into contact with the Mexicans, with the same result. To my appeal, Dr. Kendall replied that the Board did not have a cent to devote to employing missionary teachers. "We can send you a preacher though." To which I wrote back: "They won't come to hear preachers: send us a teacher."

As usual, the board's problem was money, which Jackson, with characteristic ingenuity, set about raising.

Years prior to Jackson's becoming interested in Indian education, wealthy Christian women on the East Coast had organized women's auxiliaries through which they funneled financial support to Indian schools. The most prominent of the auxiliaries was the New Mexico, Arizona, and Colorado Missionary Association, whose members' donations supported Indian schools at Santa Fe and Las Vegas. Tapping into the same source, in 1870, Jackson mailed fund-raising appeals to Presbyterian women, addressed, in the words of Robert Laird Stewart, "in behalf of the many thousands of benighted women and ignorant children, within the limits of our territorial possessions and of our presbyteries and synods, who were living without the knowledge of God, and were as utterly neglected as the perishing multitudes in far-away heathen lands."

To institutionalize the practice, Jackson started the *Rocky Mountain Presbyterian* in 1872. Ostensibly published to keep his western congregations informed of each others' activities, the paper, which was widely distributed in the East, contained articles that described the work of women's auxiliaries among the Indians as a regular feature.

Predictably, Jackson's new endeavor angered the Presbyterian establishment. The Board of Foreign Missions rightly feared that, since tithing Presbyterian women was a zero-sum game, Jackson's fund-raising would reduce its ability to solicit money from the same women. And since he again had circumvented its authority, the Board of Home Missions also objected to Jackson's scheme.

But atrophied church patriarchs were no match for their younger opponent's talent for bureaucratic infighting and self-promotion.

Jackson first shrewdly recruited the Rev. Henry Kendall, the secretary of the Board of Home Missions, as a co-conspirator. He and Kendall then invented a front organization, the Woman's Home Missionary Society, whose membership initially consisted of Jackson and Kendall, to lure women delegates attending the annual Presbyterian General Assembly into Indian work. As Jackson told the story in 1904, "While at the General Assembly we would announce that there would be a Woman's Home Mission rally, and it was not hard to fill the largest hall or church with women who would come in response to such an invitation."

The simple, if deceitful, tactic worked to excellent effect. In 1872 and again in 1873 the General Assembly passed resolutions that urged Presbyterian women to support Jackson's work with the Indians. The premeditation with which Jackson and Kendall pursued their goals is revealed in a letter Kendall wrote in 1875, in which he urged Jackson to visit as many East Coast synods as possible because "other things being equal... here is the money." Jackson made the trip and had considerable success drumming up support for his program, an effort that culminated in 1876, when the General Assembly urged every Presbyterian synod to organize a women's group to help Jackson educate Indians.

In no small part, Jackson's success as a fund-raiser was a product of the force of personality he brought to bear on the task as he crisscrossed the country on his lecture tours. However, his success on the stump did nothing to quell protests from the Board of Foreign Missions. But by 1878, Jackson felt confident enough to force a confrontation by demanding that the Board of Home Missions call a national convention of Presbyterian women to organize a Woman's Board of Home Missions to parallel the Woman's Board of Foreign Missions, which provided financial support to the Board of Foreign Missions.

When the Board of Home Missions refused to do so, Jackson called his own convention, an ad hoc group that met in Pittsburgh in May and whose work culminated seven months later in the organization of the Woman's Executive Committee of Home Missions. Frances Haines of Elizabeth, New Jersey, Jackson's principal female ally, was elected secretary, and the committee designated the *Rocky Mountain Presbyterian* as its official newspaper.

Contemporaneously with his effort to establish an independent source of funding for Indian schools on the frontier, Jackson turned his attention to Alaska.

Insofar as Alaska Natives were concerned, Jackson's recognition that schoolteachers were Christianity's shock troops was not an original insight.

In 1793, Gregory Shelikhof (the Siberian fur trader whose business was merged, after his death, with several other trading companies to form the Russian-American Company) petitioned Catherine II to send Russian Orthodox priests to minister to the Natives on the Aleutian and Kodiak Islands. At the empress's direction, the following year the Archimandrite Ioasaf and seven other priests arrived at Kodiak equipped with a gold-plated communion set.[9]

In 1796, Ioasaf consecrated the first Russian Orthodox church in Alaska at St. Paul's harbor on Kodiak Island. The church suffered its first martyr the same year, when the Hieromonk Juvenal, who had accompanied Ioasaf to Russian America, was beaten to death by Eskimos at Lake Iliamna. One theory regarding the homicide is that it was a consequence of Juvenal voicing the view to Eskimo parents that the best way for their children to learn about the Russian Orthodox God was for him to remove them to the Shelikhof trading company settlement on Kodiak Island, where they could be raised in an environment in which they would not be corrupted by their parents' animist beliefs.[10]

If that was his view, then Juvenal was a hieromonk ahead of his time because acculturation was not the standard the Russian Orthodox Church used to measure success in the field. Rather, the priests gauged their usefulness to God by the number of baptisms they performed. In 1796, for example, the Hieromonk Makarii, the priest stationed on Unalaska Island, proudly reported that he had baptized 2,442 Natives and performed 536 marriages.[11]

Of course, the idea that Aleuts or any other Natives knew what a baptism was was utter nonsense. Few understood Russian, and fewer still understood the story of Jesus of Nazareth. For that reason, Gregory Shelikhof's son-in-law, Nikolai Rezanov, who assumed the principal management of his father-in-law's company after the older man's death and in 1799 arranged its merger into the Russian-American Company, considered the priests to be officious meddlers and disparaged their baptisms as "bathing."[12]

The facts support Rezanov's bad attitude.

After visiting Russian America in 1818, the Russian sea captain Vasilii Golovin complained that, although many Natives on Kodiak Island spoke some Russian, they had no understanding of the teachings of the church. When asked why they had agreed to be baptized, the Natives to whom Golovin posed the question answered that the priests had paid for the privilege, as indeed they usually did. After the obligatory dunking, the priest would place a white cloth (usually a blouse) on the baptized as a symbol that the neophyte had been clothed with the robe of righteousness. Allowing oneself to be briefly submerged while a man in a strange costume, chanting a strange language, hung a cross around your neck was a small inconvenience to endure to acquire a shirt imported from Europe and perhaps a leaf of tobacco.[13]

Forty-three years later, the situation was the same.

In 1861, Pavel Golovin reported that most of the Chugach Eskimos who lived near the Konstantin Redoubt on Hinchinbrook Island in Prince William Sound were members of the Russian Orthodox Church. However, the Chugaches had adopted the faith "partly because of the zeal of the missionaries and partly, as is true with all savages, because they find some personal benefit in it."[14]

In southeast Alaska the Tlingit Indians' lack of interest was worse. Although the Russian-American Company had constructed a church for Indian use outside the New Archangel palisade, in December 1860, Golovin wrote his family that services are rarely held there because the Kolosh simply do not attend. Many of them have been baptized, thanks to gifts and entertainment, but they do not like to go to church without being rewarded in some way. If someone were to announce that they would receive a cup of vodka after each service they attended, then of course the church would always be full to overflowing; but without this they do not go to pray.[15]

Golovin's view of the matter clearly was influenced by Johan Furuhjelm, the manager of the Russian-American Company. In April 1861, Golovin wrote to his mother that his traveling companion, a Russian named Sergi Kostlivtsov, had agreed to assist in the baptism of an important Tlingit chief. "[Company manager] Furuhjelm says that he could baptize all of them at once in the Kolosh River," Golovin reported home, "if he could declare that every baptized man would be given a blanket and two cups of vodka and a dinner."[16]

Golovin's description of the baptism in which Kostlivtsov participated does little to belie Furuhjelm's sarcasm:

At 8:00 A.M. Kostlivtsov christened one of the Kolosh toions [chiefs]. This great lout was forcefully shoved into a large tub, and when he emerged from it, they put a cross on him. For a few moments he stood as if he were dazed, and not because of the cold water, because these people bathe in the sea in ten degrees of frost; he himself said he did not know what had happened, but he felt just as if he were drunk.

As a reward for participating in the ritual the new Christian received a frock coat trimmed with silver lace, a pair of trousers with a stripe down the side, and a free dinner.[17]

Dunking grown men in tubs of water on the theory that the immersion will compel belief in a God about whom they know little and could care less about is a procedure that is unlikely to induce authentic religious conversion. However, with the exception of the baptisms that the priest Veniaminov, who spoke fluent Aleut, performed between 1824 and 1834 on the Aleutian Islands, where his ministry reportedly met with better than average success, the baptism Golovin witnessed six years prior to the transfer of Alaska to the United States depicted the rule rather than the exception.

In Golovin's view, after sixty-seven years of trying, the Russian Orthodox Church had failed in its mission—not because of its message but because of its tactics. "It is no wonder," he reported in 1861, "that [the Natives] are not convinced of the superiority of the Christian faith, for not one of the missionaries in the colonies has the slightest knowledge of their language, and, consequently, cannot converse with them."[18]

Golovin's solution to the problem was the same as Sheldon Jackson's. Before Alaska Natives could be converted, they had to be educated.

> If missionaries are only appointed in order to somehow christen a certain number of Natives per year, and to show in their reports that the number of converts has increased, and once a year to go to visit a few settlements located close to our redoubts and odinochkas, then the colonial missionaries more or less fulfill their obligations faithfully [Golovin advised]. But if the appointment of missionaries is meant to spread Christian teachings among the savages, and to set a fine example—by word and deed to modify their customs, and to help them in need, to heal them of bodily and spiritual ills, and systematically to teach them to adjust to settled and industrious lives, and primarily to influence the upbringing of their children, and finally to bring about a condition wherein the savages themselves will desire to be converted— then in that case, not one of our past or present missionaries has fulfilled his task.

"[A]s long as the Kolosh remain illiterate and religious beliefs are not implanted in them and they do not feel a genuine need to accept Holy Baptism, it is not wise to entice them into Orthodoxy with the help of various lures."[19]

Golovin's recognition that "influenc[ing] the upbringing of [Native] children" was the key to persuading the next generation of Alaska Natives to accept the Russian Orthodox catechesis places his view of the matter in the mainstream of contemporary educational theory. As John Dewey, America's preeminent theoretician of the philosophy of education, long ago observed, children are the "future sole representatives" of the social group of which their parents are members. For that reason, if the older members do not communicate—or are prevented from communicating— their "ideals, hopes, expectations, standards, [and] opinions" to their children, the cultural life of the group will die with the older members. For Dewey, "education, and education alone, spans the gap" between every society's young and old.[20] Or as Ivan Illich, a decidedly more radical theoretician than John Dewey, has described the same concept: the schoolhouse is "the repository of society's myth."[21]

Assuming so, if the Russian-American Company and the Russian Orthodox Church had been seriously interested in communicating the religious and other myths of Russian society to Alaska Natives, they would have opened schools for their children. But while the company and the church operated schools at Kodiak, New Archangel, and several other locations, most students were creoles, the offspring of Native mothers and Russian fathers. For example, of the twenty-seven boys who attended the boys' school jointly operated by the Russian-American Company and the Russian Orthodox Church at New Archangel in 1860, six were sons of lower-ranking company managers, twenty were "children of scribes, master craftsmen and laborers," and only one was a full-blood Tlingit.[22]

Initially, the U.S. government had less interest in educating Natives than the next to none the Russian-American Company had had. But by happenstance the purchase of Alaska coincided with the development of a new federal Indian policy that, as it evolved over the subsequent decade, emphasized education.

By 1867 the United States had negotiated numerous treaties with the western tribes. In exchange for their relinquishment of vast tracts of land, the treaties guaranteed the members of the tribes whose leaders had signed them that they would not be disturbed on the land their tribe retained. However, white demand for Indian land being insatiable, the United States soon violated its treaty commitments, and the breach of contract led to war that by the mid-1860s was raging across the western plains.

Both sides committed atrocities. In August 1862, for example, the Santee Sioux, who had been driven to the brink of literal starvation by their confinement on small reservations on the Minnesota River, murdered between 400 and 800 whites during an uprising in southwestern Minnesota. In turn, in November 1864, the First Colorado Cavalry under the command of John Chivington, a Methodist minister known as the "Fighting Parson," butchered between 200 and 450 Cheyenne and Arapaho, a majority of whom were women and children, at Sand Creek, Colorado. As retribution for Sand Creek, in January 1865 and again in February 1,000 Cheyenne and Sioux attacked Julesburg, a white settlement in northeastern Colorado, and raided homesteads and stagecoach stations along the Platte River.

And so it went.

Appalled by the Sand Creek massacre and increasingly skeptical of the army's ability to win the guerrilla wars Indians were waging from the Dakota prairie south to Texas, in March 1865, Congress established a commission chaired by Sen. James Doolittle of Wisconsin, the chairman of the Senate Committee on Indian Affairs, to investigate the situation. Submitted in January 1867, the Doolittle Commission's report blamed most of the mess on the frontier on "the aggressions of lawless white men" and the attendant "destruction of that game upon which the Indian subsists," particularly the purposeful extermination of the buffalo herds.[23] Responding in July, Congress authorized Commissioner of Indian Affairs Nathaniel Taylor to try to negotiate an end to the fighting.

Encouraged by the new interest in nonmilitary solutions to the "Indian problem," clergymen interested in reforming the federal government's Indian policies lobbied Congress; and in 1869, Congress responded by creating a Board of Indian Commissioners composed of men "eminent for their intelligence and philanthropy" to advise the secretary of the interior in his administration of Indian affairs. Although the statute that established the board made no mention of religious affiliation, it was privately understood that board appointments would be divided among the Protestant denominations.

The subsequent work of the Board of Indian Commissioners was so inextricably associated with the administration of President Ulysses S. Grant, who ascended to the presidency the year the board was established, that the Indian policy the board advocated became known as the Grant Peace Policy. In 1873 Secretary of the Interior Columbus Delano outlined the elements of the policy as follows.

First and foremost, Indians were to be moved "as rapidly as possible" onto reservations, where they would be physically distant "from such contiguity to our frontier settlements as otherwise will lead, necessarily, to frequent outrages, wrongs, and disturbances of the peace." Once confined, Indians would be transformed into farmers and taught "pursuits as are incident to civilization, through the aid of the Christian organizations of the country now engaged in this work." If a tribe refused to move onto its assigned reservation and trouble resulted, its members would be punished for their misbehavior "with all needed severity," a result that would teach "that it is better to follow the advice of the government, live upon reservations and become civilized, than to continue their native habits and practices." As long as reservation Indians were well behaved, the Department of the Interior would ensure that food, clothing, and other consumer goods were purchased for their use at "fair and reasonable prices." Indian agents appointed on the recommendation of the religious denominations involved in Indian work were to oversee the reservations in a manner intended to bring Indian "intellectual, moral and religious culture" into closer alignment with white society.

Finally, the linchpin of the Grant Peace Policy was education. Church schools, such as Spencer Academy, where Sheldon Jackson had taught, were to be opened on the reservations to teach Indian children "a better way of life than they have heretofore pursued" so that they would "understand and appreciate the comforts and benefits of a Christian civilization, and thus be prepared ultimately to assume the duties and privileges of citizenship."[24]

The Peace Policy's emphasis on reservations had something for every white. For those who wanted to homestead or prospect Indian land, forcing more tribes onto reservations was a way to open more Indian land to white settlement. To that end, in the same report in which he described the Grant Peace Policy, Secretary Delano informed Congress that implementation of the new policy already had resulted in the acquisition of more Indian land.

> Satisfactory progress has been made within the year [he proudly announced], in the reduction of the area of existing reservations, in the exchange of reservations lying within the range of advancing settlements and railroad construction for other locations equally desirable for all purposes of Indian occupancy, as well as in bringing tribes upon reservations for the first time, and in the removal of other tribes to the Indian Territory.[25]

For the Board of Indian Commissioners and other whites interested in the Indians' welfare, reservations were places of refuge within which people such as themselves could protect an uncomprehending and uncivilized people until they learned to make their way in the white world.

However, while they were the centerpiece of the Grant Peace Policy, no reservations were established in Alaska for the simple reason that, unlike the situation on the western frontier, there were not enough whites who aspired to expropriate enough Native land to make forcing Natives onto reservations at gun and bayonet point worth the trouble.

That is not to say that the idea was not considered.

In the summer of 1869, Vincent Colyer, secretary of the newly appointed Board of Indian Commissioners, visited Alaska on an inspection tour. Traveling on the steamer *Newbern,* Colyer stopped at Tongass, Wrangell, Sitka, and the Kodiak, Aleutian, and Pribilof Islands.

At each stop in southeast Alaska, Colyer invited the principal Tlingit chiefs to dinner and was impressed with their table manners.

> The chiefs ate with their forks [he subsequently reported, and] when it came to the pudding they used their spoons, and on having the almonds and raisins placed before them they used their fingers, the same as those around them. In all they behaved with perfect propriety, and the most fastidious could see nothing in their demeanor to find fault with. I mention these trifles to show their wish and ability to imitate white men.[26]

At St. Paul, one of the Pribilof Islands, the Aleuts Colyer met asked if it was true that in the United States all men were created equal and, if so, whether they ever would be allowed to vote for president. "I said yes, I hoped so," Colyer reported; then "they shook my hand warmly, and when we left the shore gave us three slow but very loud cheers, which our officers and men returned with a will."[27] Colyer also was happily surprised to find that several Aleut children played the accordion.

But if delighted that the Natives he met were so busy learning to act white, Colyer was not blind to the problems for which he held whites responsible: the use of alcohol as a trade good and physical abuse by the army being the two most serious. When the *Newbern* docked at Tongass and Wrangell, Colyer was appalled by the amount of beer and whiskey that was off-loaded to the local traders. Of the physical abuse Colyer witnessed, two incidents merit mention.

At Kodiak, Colyer watched the army detachment that Jefferson Davis had stationed at that location spend their pay.

> It was the same here as down in the Cherokee country, at Fort Wingate, and at Sitka [Colyer reported]. The day after the men were paid many of them were beastly drunk, and while in that condition the Natives had a hard time of it. The officers tried in vain to restrain them. I passed by one creole cabin at Kodiak, from the interior of which issued the shouts of drunken soldiers, while at the porch stood a little Indian girl the very picture of despair and distress.[28]

And when the *Newbern* docked at Wrangell on the voyage south, Colyer met an Indian, "his face badly cut and bleeding," who had been beaten by two "half drunken discharged soldiers" who were members of "a party of over one hundred discharged soldiers who had come down on our steamer from Sitka, and were on their way to San Francisco. Some of them had been drummed out of the service for robbing the Greek church at Sitka, and for other crimes."[29]

When he returned home, Colyer sent Felix Brunot, the chairman of the Board of Indian Commissioners, a trip report. In addition to urging that Indian agents be stationed at various locations and that schools to educate Native children be opened throughout the territory, Colyer recommended that the "wild tribes" (the Eskimos and Athabascan Indians about whom Colyer had heard but had not traveled far enough north to meet) "be placed upon reservation[s]" and "amply provided for and protected when there,"[30] although he saw no need to confine the "nonwild tribes" (i.e., the Tlingits, Aleuts, and Koniags).

Since no whites wanted their land, there was no reason to establish reservations even for the "wild tribes." However, Colyer's recommendation regarding Native education was accepted. The Board of Indian Commissioners and Secretary Delano both urged Congress to appropriate money for that purpose; and after considering the matter, the Senate Appropriations Committee added $50,000 to the Office of Indian Affairs Appropriations Act, enacted in July 1870 "for the support of industrial and other schools among the Indian tribes not otherwise provided for."[31]

While the text of the act did not mention Alaska, the members of the Appropriations Committee privately understood that Alaska was where $45,000 of the $50,000 would be spent. However, Francis Walker, a statistician by trade who became commissioner of Indian affairs in November 1871, refused to spend so much as a dime in Alaska because, in his judgment, Alaska Natives were not members of "Indian tribes" as the term was used in the Appropriations Act. If so, then no matter what the senators who served on the Appropriations Committee may have intended, the Office of Indian Affairs had no legal authority to spend money to educate Native children.[32]

There the matter stood until 1872, when the Board of Indian Commissioners urged Secretary Delano to urge the president "to place the Indians of Alaska under the care of the Department of the Interior, with a view to the early commencement of measures for their education and advancement in civilization" and that the money previously appropriated "be devoted to that purpose."[33] In response, Commissioner Walker advised Delano that "I have never believed that the Natives of Alaska were Indians within the meaning of the Constitution, any more than are Esquimaux or Kanakas, and I am disposed to avoid entirely the use of the word Indians as applied to them."[34] However, Walker also had a self-serving reason for objecting to the board's request: he recently had asked Congress to reappropriate the $45,000 that had been unofficially earmarked for Native education into his discretionary account. If Congress did so, Walker explained, "I am entirely satisfied that the balance of the appropriation remaining could be applied with much larger results of good to tribes nearer at hand, and with which the Government has long sustained relations."[35]

Caught between the Board of Indian Commissioners and his commissioner of Indian affairs, Secretary Delano washed his hands of the matter. On the one hand he explained in a letter to the Speaker of the House of Representatives, "it is the duty of the Government to bring this semi-barbarous and uncivilized people under the influence of the beneficial provisions made for the Indian tribes now under the jurisdiction of the Indian Office." But on the other, it was "exceedingly doubtful" whether Alaska Natives "belong to the same race or family of men as the Indians of North America," and "I cannot, as an executive officer, undertake in the course of administration to expend the funds of the nation in its discharge without clear warrant of law."[36]

When Felix Brunot learned of Delano's letter, he sent Rep. J. P. C. Shanks, the chairman of the House Committee on Indian Affairs, a draft bill that, had it been enacted, would have placed Alaska Natives "under the management and control of the Department of the Interior" and authorized the commissioner of education, the official who supervised the Bureau of Education (an agency independent of the Office of Indian Affairs that through bureaucratic anomaly was housed inside the Department of the Interior) to establish schools "under competent Christian teachers . . . for the instruction of said Native inhabitants in the English language, the common branches of English education, the principles of republican government, and such industrial pursuits as may seem best adapted to their circumstances."[37]

But Congress, famed then as now for its inability to resolve arcane policy disputes, declined Brunot's invitation to settle the legal status of Alaska Natives and quietly added Walker's reappropriation to the 1873 Office of Indian Affairs Appropriation Act.[38]

Since Congress and the Department of the Interior did not consider Alaska Natives to be members of congressionally recognized "Indian tribes," throughout the army's ten-year tenure in Alaska neither the Office of Indian Affairs nor any other federal agency exhibited any interest in their welfare. The dereliction created a policy vacuum that allowed Sheldon Jackson a free hand to customize the federal government's Alaska Native policy to his personal specifications.

How and when Jackson became interested in Alaska is a matter of dispute. In *Alaska,* his book on the subject published in 1880, Jackson describes how "on my long stage trips, while establishing churches through the Rocky Mountain Territories, I had often thought of that distant section of our country, and the vague hope would sometimes cross my mind that I myself might yet be permitted to go there."[39] *Alaska* also relates that as early as 1876, Jackson had urged the Board of Home Missions to send missionaries to Alaska.[40]

There also is another version of the story.

Jackson's brazen self-promotion so enraged members of the Presbytery of Oregon, who considered the Rev. Aaron Lindsley, the pastor of the First Presbyterian Church of Portland, the true founder of the Alaska church, that the presbytery commissioned the writing of a history of the Wrangell mission that paints Jackson as an eleventh-hour interloper.

What seems clear is that the Rev. Lindsley became interested in Alaska in 1869 after talking with former secretary of state William Henry Seward about the subject when Seward passed through Vancouver, British Columbia, on his way east after visiting Sitka. As a consequence of the conversation, Lindsley lobbied both the army and his church "to secure the establishing of evangelical missions among this neglected people." But nothing came of Lindsley's advocacy until 1877.

As previously described, by 1876 the gold strike in the Cassiar Mountains had transformed Wrangell into a hell's roaring mining camp. Although the Stikine Tlingits traditionally had controlled the mouth of the Stikine River, the new bustle was irresistible to Indians from elsewhere, who, prior to the flood of white prospectors into the area and the army's reoccupation of Fort Wrangell, had been rightly afraid to venture into Stikine Tlingit territory uninvited. In May 1876 four Tsimshian Indians from Fort Simpson, British Columbia, the Hudson's Bay Company trading post 160 miles to the south, set out in their canoe for the Stikine River to look for work in the Cassiar mines. However, when they stopped at Wrangell they found employment cutting firewood for the army.

Having been converted to Christianity at Fort Simpson, where the Rev. Thomas Crosby operated a Methodist mission, on Sundays the Tsimshians began holding prayer meetings, which a number of Stikine Tlingits began attending. The meetings were such a success that, at the Rev. Crosby's urging, one of the Tsimshians, known as Clah, wintered at Wrangell to continue the prayer meetings and open a school. As many as ninety Indians soon attended, many of whom were adults.

Unable to interest his superiors in sending Clah any help, Crosby wrote Gen. O. O. Howard, the commanding officer of the Department of the Columbia, who supervised the Alaska detachment from his headquarters in Portland, to inform Howard of "what God is doing for Alaska" and ask him to arrange for one of the other denominations to send a missionary to Wrangell. Howard passed Crosby's letter on to Aaron Lindsley,[41] who lived across the street from Howard in Portland and with whom, as Howard years later reminisced, he had "talked with ... twenty times in 1875 about opening missions in Alaska."[42]

Lindsley arranged for Howard to send John Mallory, a Presbyterian missionary who happened to be in Portland, to relieve Clah. But shortly after he arrived at Wrangell in May, Mallory's lungs began to hemorrhage, and he returned south. Lindsley then persuaded Amanda McFarland to take the job. Then, according to the Presbytery of Oregon's account of events, "on the eve of Mrs. McFarland's departure for Alaska, Dr. Sheldon Jackson, having arrived at Portland on a visit, and being desirous of seeing the regions beyond, acted as an escort, going up and returning by the same trip of the mail-steamer."[43]

But Jackson was not the total Johnny-come-lately the presbytery's version of history makes him out to be. The previous winter, J. S. Brown, a soldier stationed at Fort Wrangell who had been touched by the sincerity of Clah's effort to teach Tlingits the gospel, also had written Howard to urge the general to arrange for a missionary to be sent to Wrangell. "I am not a church-member," Brown wrote, "but am making this appeal for these poor people from the dictates of a heart that I trust may never be deaf to the cry for help from the heathen."[44]

As with the Rev. Crosby's letter, Howard passed Brown's letter on to Aaron Lindsley. In May, Lindsley passed the letter on to the Rev. Howard Stratton, who was on his way to Chicago to attend that year's Presbyterian General Assembly. There Stratton passed the letter on to Sheldon Jackson. Jackson, the master propagandist, immediately recognized the public relations value of Brown's melodramatic plea and arranged for the letter to be published in the *Chicago Daily Tribune*. He also distributed a copy to the Board of Home Missions with a recommendation that the board send a missionary to Wrangell. The board agreed and in June offered the job to the Rev. Francis Robinson. But Robinson declined the invitation in order to take a similar post in California.

Contemporaneously, Jackson, who by then had returned to Denver, set out on another of his trips through the West, stopping first at Boise and then continuing on to Walla Walla on the Washington and Oregon border in a stagecoach that he shared with "a scrofulous Chinaman and a gambler far gone in consumption."[45] When he arrived at Walla Walla, he found the region in an uproar over the Nez Percé who, having ignored an ultimatum from Gen. Howard to move onto a reservation, had been killing settlers along the Snake River and on June 17 had killed thirty-four of Howard's troopers during a skirmish. Since whites in the surrounding towns were too preoccupied with the Indian uprising to talk about organizing churches, Jackson detoured west to Portland to visit Lindsley. There he learned of

Amanda McFarland's impending departure for Wrangell and decided to accompany her.

After settling in at her new station, McFarland, armed with "four bibles, four hymn books, three primers, thirteen first readers and one wall chart,"[46] began teaching school in the Wrangell dance hall, with Clah and Sarah Dickinson, a Tlingit woman who was married to a white trader, assisting in the work. Several days later, Sheldon Jackson returned to Portland on the *California.*

Aaron Lindsley clearly is entitled to the credit for arranging to send the first Presbyterian missionary, John Mallory, and the second, Amanda McFarland, to Alaska. But Lindsley's involvement in the field soon was lost in the swirl of activity that Sheldon Jackson generated in annexing Alaska to his missionary empire.

While McFarland spent the winter in Wrangell teaching Tlingits the alphabet, Jackson spent his in New York and elsewhere in the Northeast touting her work to Presbyterian congregations. According to Florence Hayes, who later wrote a history of the Presbyterian mission in Alaska, at each stop on his tour Jackson concluded his stump speech with the plea: "I left Mrs. McFarland without books, schoolhouse, helpers, money, friends, only a few converted but morally uninstructed Indians, with a great many heathen about her. What will you do for her?"[47]

The hyperbole produced immediate results. Aaron Lindsley raised $600 to send McFarland to Wrangell. Between October 1877 and December 1879, Sheldon Jackson raised more than $12,000 to keep her there.[48]

In addition to fund-raising, Jackson also arranged for the Board of Home Missions to hire two missionaries, John Brady and S. Hall Young, who were assigned to Sitka and Wrangell, respectively.

Brady arrived at Sitka in March 1878, where he was joined by Aaron Lindsley's niece, Fannie Kellogg. In April, Brady opened a school in the abandoned Sitka army barracks and within a month reported to Jackson that thirteen Tlingit students were reading from the primer, and another twenty-five had learned the alphabet. But eight months later, Brady abruptly resigned, and his school closed; and Fannie Kellogg, who had married Hall Young, joined her husband at his station at Wrangell. However, the next year Alonzo Austin, a friend of Brady's from New York, reopened the Sitka school.

In 1881, Capt. Henry Glass, who had succeeded L. A. Beardslee as commander of the *Jamestown,* the warship the navy had assigned to permanent station at Sitka three years earlier, ordered the Tlingits living in the Sitka

Indian village to send their children to the Presbyterian school. Sheldon Jackson's description of Glass's enforcement of his edict is worth quoting:

> He first caused the Indian village to be cleaned up, ditches dug around each house for drainage, and the houses whitewashed. These sanitary regulations greatly lessened the sickness and death-rate among them. He then caused the houses to be numbered, and an accurate census taken of the inmates—adults and children. He then caused a label to be made of tin for each child, which was tied around the neck of the child, with his or her number and the number of the house on it, so that if a child was found on the street during school hours the Indian policeman was under orders to take the numbers on the labels and report them, or the teacher each day would report that such numbers from such houses were absent that day. The following morning the head Indian of the house to which the absentee belonged was summoned to appear and answer for the absence of the child. If the child was willfully absent, the head man was fined or imprisoned. A few cases of fine were sufficient. As soon as they found the captain in earnest, the children were all in school.[49]

Indian education at Wrangell proceeded differently. Four months after she opened for business, between seventy and eighty "scholars," as McFarland called her students, regularly attended class.[50] But being a missionary, McFarland was not content to teach the alphabet, and by February she had concocted a "plan of opening a Home for young girls."[51] She decided to do so, she subsequently wrote Jackson, after a white trader named Forman

> went to the parents of my favorite sc[h]olar, a bright little girl of thirteen, and actually bought her for twenty blankets. I determined to rescue her if possible, as I heard that she was taken to his house by force. She begging and crying not to go. I succeeded in getting her away, and her mother has promised to keep her at home. But her father is a hard wicked man, and I tremble every day lest Forman offers him a little more, and again gets possession of the child.[52]

Forman was not the only white who considered Tlingit teenagers a recreation within his budget. For McFarland the problem was doubly vexing because the more successful she was at teaching her female scholars the social graces, the more valuable they became in the marketplace. As she complained to Sheldon Jackson, being "pretty and smart," they are "just the ones the white men will try to get possession of."[53]

McFarland's solution to the problem was to move girls whose virtue she considered in jeopardy out of the longhouses in the Indian village in which their parents lived and into her home.

> Mrs. Dickinson [McFarland's classroom assistant] has brought a woman to me, who is the mother of one of my school girls (a pretty little girl of thirteen) [McFarland wrote Jackson in September 1878]. [She] was about to start up the river with the child [to the Cassiar mines] to (as she expressed it) make money to buy muck a muck for winter. The woman is determined to go herself but after long persuasion she consented to leave the child with me. So you see the "Home" is already started.[54]

The next month she acquired two more borders, a fourteen-year-old who McFarland had heard "was about to be taken up the river by her heathen mother to be sold" and a "bright little girl of twelve years" who had told McFarland that "her mother wanted to let a white man have her."[55]

When Jackson read her letters, he immediately began raising money to build McFarland a proper boardinghouse. To that end, Jackson and a Mrs. Julia McNair Wright wrote a series of articles, which Jackson published in the *Rocky Mountain Presbyterian,* that alerted the paper's subscribers to the plight of Tlingit Indian girls who would be sold by their parents into a lascivious slavery unless the readers sent Jackson money to prevent it. As Mrs. Wright shamelessly concluded one of her articles: "O mothers of our church, every one of you who holds a baby girl on your knee, see in her face the pleading of that babe cast out in cold woods to die! In the name of Him who blessed the little children, give something, even if the veriest mite, to this Home."[56] As Jackson knew they would (as he later described it), "contributions flowed in from the St. Lawrence to the Gulf."[57]

In July 1879, Jackson, whose experience in Alaska to that date had been limited to escorting Amanda McFarland north two years earlier, returned to Wrangell accompanied by the Rev. Aaron Lindsley and the Rev. Henry Kendall and their wives.

During the trip, Jackson left his group to do some exploring on his own. He hitched a canoe ride with a passing Chilkat trading party south to the Anglican mission at Metlakatla, British Columbia.[58] As the canoe cut through the water, Jackson, who had a comfortable seat in the middle of the dugout rather than a paddle, had a leisurely opportunity to ponder the future, during which he conceived his two-part plan for Alaska that he immediately set about implementing when he returned to Denver.

From Tongass north to Point Barrow the number of Native children who needed educating exceeded even Jackson's ability to raise the money that would enable the Board of Home Missions to open schools for them. There was, however, an obvious deep pocket. As Jackson described part one of his plan to the Board of Home Missions after his return from Alaska, "We need government aid to establish boarding-schools in Sitka and at Fort Wrangell."[59]

But the financial commitment Jackson actually wanted from the federal government was considerably larger.

When Jackson returned from his first trip to Alaska in 1877, Henry Kendall had written Secretary of the Interior Carl Schurz (undoubtedly at Jackson's instigation) describing the Presbyterian Church's efforts to open a school at Wrangell. The letter concluded:

> [W]e are willing to do this and co-operate with your department in building up at the several central points of population industrial schools, where, in addition to the rudiments of an English education, the men shall be taught the carpenter and other industrial pursuits, and the women sewing, cooking, housekeeping, nursing, etc. To give efficiency to this wise and humane policy of the government it would be wise to ask an appropriation of $_____, to be disbursed under the direction of the Hon. Commissioner of the Bureau of Education, Department of the Interior.[60]

But nothing had come of Kendall's request.

Two years later, when Jackson returned from his second trip to Alaska, he and Kendall wrote to Schurz again, requesting that he "take such action as in your judgment will secure congressional aid in the school work among the Native races of Alaska."[61] In response, Schurz advised the clergymen to eliminate the middleman and directly petition Congress for an appropriation.[62]

Alaska historian Ted Hinckley has described Sheldon Jackson as "a born lobbyist."[63] And by every account he was. Taking Schurz's suggestion to heart, Jackson convened a meeting of "the friends of education in Alaska" in New York City to organize a campaign to lobby Congress. To that end, the group drafted a petition urging Congress to appropriate $50,000 to establish "schools for the instruction of the Native population and creoles of Alaska," which Jackson and the Rev. John Lanahan, the pastor of the Foundry Methodist Church in Washington, D.C., signed.[64]

In January 1880, Jackson and Henry Kendall journeyed to Washington to meet with Secretary Schurz, who, although sympathetic to the idea that the Department of the Interior should open schools for Natives, counseled that "the status of Alaska [Natives] was [so] entirely different from that of any of the races on this continent; that there would have to be special legislation for Alaska."[65]

To generate congressional support for the idea, Jackson booked himself into several Washington, D.C., churches to lecture the congregations on the "extent, resources, climate, people, their conditions and needs" of Alaska, prior to which he sent members of Congress a letter advertising his appearances. "Affairs in Alaska are claiming public attention [he wrote], and as Congress is asked to legislate with reference to that country and believing that you will be interested in any facts bearing on that question, permit me (having twice visited there in the interest of schools) to invite your attendance."[66]

Undoubtedly at Jackson's urging, on January 29, Sen. Henry Blair of New Hampshire introduced a resolution in the Senate that requested the Committee on Education and Labor "to inquire what, if any, provisions have been made for the education of youth in Alaska."[67] Four days later, Sen. Henry Dawes of Massachusetts introduced the petition that Jackson and Lanahan had signed in New York City, which was referred to the Appropriations Committee.[68] However, since every appropriation must be preceded by an authorization and no statute authorizing an appropriation for Native education had been enacted, the Appropriations Committee referred the petition to the Committee on Education and Labor.[69]

In March, Jackson delivered a letter to Sen. James Bailey, the chairman of the Education and Labor Committee, that explained why, in Jackson's judgment, Congress needed to appropriate money for Native education. The letter also explains why the Department of the Interior would administer Alaska Native programs through its Bureau of Education rather than the Bureau of Indian Affairs for almost half a century (as Felix Brunot first recommended in 1872).

> The appropriations for schools among the Dakota, Montana and other Indians are administered through the Indian Bureau [Jackson reminded Bailey. But] in the case of the Alaska Natives it is proposed to administer through the Educational Bureau of the Department of the Interior, for the following reasons: 1st. Among the Dakota, Montana and other Indians ... [the responsibility of the Indian Bureau] is a mixed one. It not only educates, but to some extent feeds, clothes, and issues annuities. But with the Alaskans there are no treaties or annuities needed. It is purely and solely an educational work, and as such more properly comes under that branch of the government.[70]

Jackson also prepared a fact sheet that listed the reasons Congress should appropriate money for Native education. The reason listed third reaches to the quick of Jackson's Native policy. According to the fact sheet, not spending money to open Native schools would be pound-foolish because "it will be much cheaper to spend a few thousand dollars in now educating those people to citizenship, than a few years hence millions to fight them, when the encroachments of the whites shall drive them to desperation."[71]

The spin was astutely calibrated to take advantage of the budding recognition on Capitol Hill that killing Indians had been inordinately expensive. The total cost of the wars the U.S. government waged against Indians has never been calculated. But in 1870 the federal government estimated that, to that date, the U.S. Treasury had spent $1 million per dead Indian.[72] And Secretary of War Robert Lincoln subsequently estimated the cost of the military campaigns waged against Indians between 1872 and 1882 as $223,891,264.[73]

Assuming so, then co-optation clearly was the most fiscally responsible policy. Among others, Rutherford Hayes, who succeeded Ulysses S. Grant to the presidency in 1877 and for whom Secretary Schurz worked, was of that view.

In 1878, Hayes reported to Congress that the preceding year the Bannocks and northern Cheyennes had caused disturbances. To prevent future uprisings, the president recommended that a mounted "Indian auxiliary" be organized "for the purpose of keeping the Indians on their reservations." But hiring Indians to guard Indians was a short term solution.

> [W]hile the employment of force for the prevention or repression of Indian troubles is of occasional necessity, and wise preparation should be made to that end [Hayes acknowledged], greater reliance must be placed on humane and civilizing agencies for the ultimate solution of what is called the Indian problem.... We owe it to them as a moral duty to help them in attaining at least that degree of civilization which they may be able to reach. It is not only our duty—it is also our interest to do so. Indians who have become agriculturists or herdsmen, and feel an interest in property, will henceforth cease to be a warlike and disturbing element. It is also a well authenticated fact that Indians are apt to be peaceable and quiet when their children are at school, and I am gratified to know, from the expressions of the Indians themselves, and from many recurring reports, that there is a steadily increasing desire, even among Indians belonging to comparatively wild tribes, to have their children educated.[74]

But if, by 1880, the Native education policy that Sheldon Jackson urged on Congress was mainstream, there was a minor glitch: unlike the Bannocks and northern Cheyennes, Alaska Natives had not killed enough whites to necessitate Congress' spending money to teach their children not to do so. As a consequence, the 46th Congress adjourned without action by the Education and Labor Committee on the Jackson-Lanahan petition.

When the lack of interest became apparent, Jackson, working with Commissioner of Education John Eaton, a close friend and fellow Presbyterian minister, reorganized his lobby. In April 1881, Eaton wrote to Jackson to ask for information about the education situation in Alaska, and in December, Jackson sent Eaton a detailed report.[75]

When the 47th Congress convened the same month, the Senate adopted a resolution, introduced by Sen. Blair, that requested a copy of Jackson's report,[76] and in January 1882, Blair arranged for the Senate to print two thousand copies at Senate expense.[77] While Blair's involvement was orchestrated by Eaton, it was choreographed by Jackson.[78]

Henry Teller was appointed secretary of the interior by President Chester Arthur when Arthur assumed the presidency after James Garfield (who had succeeded Hayes) died in office in September 1881, after having been shot by a disgruntled office seeker. In February 1882, John Eaton urged Teller to support a congressional appropriation of money for Native education. Teller passed Eaton's recommendation on to Arthur, who passed the recommendation on to Congress.[79]

In response to the president's urging, Rep. Jonathan Updegraff, chairman of the House Committee on Education and Labor, introduced a bill that authorized the commissioner of education to establish schools in Alaska.[80]

For Sheldon Jackson, the Updegraff bill was significant progress. But most probably because, when compared to other demands on its members' time, the need to open schools for well-behaved Natives in a venue as distant as Alaska was a small-ticket item, the Education and Labor Committee failed to report the bill—which is not to say that Jackson did not attempt to persuade it to do so.

People who have not spent time on Capitol Hill do not appreciate the value that, to the present day, members of Congress place on constituent mail. Jackson did, and, at his instigation, mail supporting the Updegraff bill poured in. Updegraff received petitions from such disparate locations as Covington, Kentucky; Homer, Illinois; Mount Pleasant, Iowa; and West Liberty, Gallipolis, Cincinnati, and Jefferson County in his home state of Ohio, each urging an appropriation for Native education.

The Senate received similar mail. During the spring of 1882, Sen. Preston Plumb, chairman of the Public Lands Committee, who would play a pivotal role in deciding the scope of Congress's commitment to Native education, received six petitions from constituents in Kansas. Similarly, Sen. Blair, who represented New Hampshire, received petitions from two New Hampshire churches, as well as from the Nashua, New Hampshire, Board of Education.

To generate the memorials, Jackson printed petitions with the name of the sponsoring organization and the signature lines blank, which he mailed to groups throughout the country.[81] He also sent selected members of Congress copies of *Alaska*, his recently published book, as well as Native handicrafts and at least one bear rug.[82]

But despite the full court press, the Updegraff bill remained stalled in committee. In desperation, on July 7, Rep. John Hill of New Jersey rose on the House floor during debate on a sundry appropriations bill and offered an amendment to appropriate $50,000 "to be expended by the Commissioner of Education, under the direction of the Secretary of the Interior, for the use of schools at such points in Alaska as may be designated by the Commissioner of Education."[83]

Hill was not a member of the Education and Labor Committee, which had jurisdiction over the Updegraff bill, or of the Appropriations Committee, which had reported the sundry appropriations bill. Nor had Hill cleared his amendment with Rep. Frank Hiscock, the chairman of Appropriations Committee. As a consequence, Hiscock raised a point of order that the amendment was new legislation that "properly belongs to the Committee on Territories or the Committee on Indian Affairs."[84] And as it should have been, the point of order was sustained.

So whether Sheldon Jackson liked it or not, there would be no appropriation for Native education until Congress enacted legislation that authorized it. That being the case, Jackson either had to persuade the Education and Labor Committee to report the Updegraff bill or to arrange to add an authorization for an appropriation for Native education to a bill that Congress might pass. However, aware of the procedural situation, Jackson already had hedged his bet.

By 1882 the handful of whites who resided in southeast Alaska had spent fourteen years lobbying Congress for a civil government. Three days after the October 1867 afternoon on which Jefferson Davis assumed command at Sitka, Thomas Murphy, a local tailor, organized a meeting "to consider the propriety of organizing a civil government for the Territory."[85] The meeting resulted in the writing of a municipal charter and, in November, in

Sitka's first municipal election, even though there was no legal authority to hold one.[86]

Acknowledging the defect, in September 1868 the first issue of the *Alaska Times,* Sitka's first newspaper, editorialized that "we are strongly in favor of a civil government and directly opposed to military rule."[87] The following spring the Sitka Chamber of Commerce adopted a resolution at its first meeting that urged Congress "to establish at an early day, a territorial government."[88]

In response to white Sitka's urging, in 1869, Rep. James Ashley, chairman of the House Committee on Territories, introduced a bill to provide Alaska with a civil government. But Congress adjourned, and the bill died. In 1871 a scaled-down proposal that designated Alaska as a county of the Territory of Washington and gave the county three seats in the Washington Territorial Legislature passed the House but died in the Senate.[89] Congressional interest in the subject then waned until 1880, when the Senate Committee on Territories organized a subcommittee, chaired by Sen. Manning Butler of South Carolina, to hold hearings on Alaska civil government.

After expressing his support for the idea, Sheldon Jackson, the Butler Subcommittee's first witness, used his time at the witness table to educate Butler and the other members of the subcommittee to his view of the factual assumptions on which Congress and the Department of the Interior would base their Alaska Native policy for more than a century.

> The people of Southeastern Alaska, the Indians, live in comfortable plank houses, from forty feet by sixty feet ordinary size [*sic*] [Jackson lectured]. They have comfortable clothing; many of them dress in European clothing. The ready-made clothing-store of the United States has reached Southern Alaska. They have plenty of comfortable food. It is not necessary that the United States should feed or clothe them, or make treaties with them. This enables us in our Indian policy to take a new departure; and treat them as American citizens. All that is necessary to be done is to afford them government and teachers, which they cannot procure for themselves.[90]

As a consequence of the hearings, Sen. Butler introduced a bill to establish a civil government in Alaska (albeit without a provision that authorized an appropriation for Native education),[91] to which Congress responded with the same yawn of indifference that the Updegraff education bill later met. Having felt the mood, on March 29, Jackson contacted Butler to express his concern, but the senator was optimistic, writing Jackson on April 1 that "there must be some misapprehension about the Alaska bill—

I shall call it up in about ten days if I possibly can and press it to a vote ... my purpose is to pass it this session if I can."[92]

But Jackson's political judgment was better than Butler's sense of timing, since the bill was not brought to the Senate floor prior to the adjournment of the 46th Congress.

When the 47th Congress convened in January 1882, Rep. Melvin George and Sen. La Fayette Grover, both of Oregon, each introduced an identical Alaska civil government bill[93] that most likely was written by Jackson, Commissioner of Education Eaton, and Mottram Ball, the customs collector at Sitka. In an unofficial election that whites living in southeastern Alaska had held the previous September, Ball had been elected "to represent this district of the territory in the 47th Congress of the United States."[94] Jackson, Eaton, and Ball also consulted Sen. John Miller of California.

In 1868, Miller, who at the time was the San Francisco customs collector, was one of a group of businessmen that organized the Alaska Commercial Company to purchase the assets of Hutchinson, Kohl and Company, which, the previous year, had purchased the Russian-American Company's buildings and inventory. Miller became president of the Alaska Commercial Company in 1869 and in that capacity arranged a lease with the federal government that gave the company a twenty-year franchise to kill fur seals for their pelts on the Pribilof Islands rookeries, where hundreds of thousands of seals annually congregate to breed.[95] In 1881, when the California legislature elected Miller to the Senate, the senator resigned his position as president of the company that had made him rich but retained his interest in the business, which in addition to the fur seal monopoly and a series of trading posts would, by 1890, include canneries in the vicinity of Kodiak that collectively annually packed several hundred thousand cases of salmon.[96]

Since citizen Miller had major money at stake, Sen. Miller was a lukewarm supporter of civil government. As one of Alaska's most successful absentee businessmen, the senator understood that commerce requires an environment in which contracts can be enforced and that Alaska was not such a place. In 1868, for example, Vincent Baronovitch, the owner of the schooner *Pioneer*, hired John Cashoaroff to make a trading voyage between Sitka and Kodiak Island. The *Pioneer* left Sitka with $4,000 in trade goods that Cashoaroff bartered with the Natives for furs worth $12,000. When he reached Kodiak, Cashoaroff sold the furs and the remaining trade goods and then, to add insult to injury, sold the *Pioneer*. Since Alaska was a military district, Baronovitch's only avenue of redress was to appeal to Jefferson Davis: "In the absence of a proper civil tribunal within the territory or, in fact, any civil authority whatever which is able to reinstate me in my rights and repossess me of my property, I respectfully apply to you as commanding this Department and request that you may take such steps as may be within your authority."[97] That was not a way to conduct business.

But while a civil government would improve the Alaska Commercial Company's ability to locally enforce its contracts, Sen. Miller was disinclined to require his company to comply with the new laws and pay the new taxes that would be applicable inside an Alaska civil government's jurisdiction. So to placate Miller, the George-Grover civil government bills stopped the northern boundary of Alaska's civil and judicial district at the north end of the Alaska Panhandle.[98]

But the bills did not accede to the senator's view on Native education.

In January 1882, Commissioner of Education Eaton wrote Jackson, who was living in New York City, that "[Mottram] Ball called this morning and informed me that Sen. Miller thought there had better be no educational clause in the territorial bill, that is, the bill organizing the Territory; but that it better be offered separately."[99] But when introduced, the George-Grover bills included a section that authorized the Bureau of Education "to organize one or more schools for the education in industry and letters of the children of the district."

In the Senate, the Grover bill was referred to the Committee on Territories, where the measure again was sent to Manning Butler's subcommittee. Since Sen. Miller was not a member, when the committee reported the subcommittee's substitute for the Grover bill as introduced, the new text expanded the Alaska civil government's jurisdiction to encompass the entire territory. But if Miller lost that round, so did Sheldon Jackson, because the subcommittee simply replaced the text of the Grover bill with the text of the civil government bill that Sen. Butler had introduced in the previous Congress and that did not contain an authorization for an appropriation for Native education.[100]

Jackson had better luck in the House. In April the House Committee on Territories reported a substitute for the George civil government bill that retained the education provision thanks in no small part to Jackson's persuasive performance as a witness during the committee's hearings on the measure.[101]

But while the authorization for an appropriation for Native education now was safely buried in the George civil government bill, by summer it was apparent that the House of Representatives was no more interested in passing the Committee on Territories' version of the George bill than the House Education and Labor Committee was in reporting the Updegraff education bill. And it was at that point that, undoubtedly at Sheldon

Jackson's urging, Rep. Hill tried to add the Alaska education appropriation to the sundry appropriations bill.

With Congress rushing to adjournment, in January 1883, Mottram Ball urged House members who supported the Committee on Territories' rewrite of the George bill to try to bring the bill to the floor by moving to suspend the House rules, a parliamentary tactic that requires a two-thirds affirmative vote. On February 1, Ball wrote Jackson that "the chance for passage of the House bill looks very fair. An effort will be made to call it up next Monday and we want to press all our force to secure the requisite two-third vote for its consideration. If you can help any, I know you will."[102] But four days later, a motion to suspend the rules was offered on the floor, and it passed but by less than two-thirds of the votes cast.[103] So the motion failed, the 47th Congress adjourned in March, and the George civil government bill died.

To resurrect it, Jackson moved to Washington, D.C., in October to assume day-to-day command of the Alaska lobby.[104] He began by mailing circulars to schoolteachers throughout the nation, urging them to "flood their congressmen with petitions asking special attention to the claims of Alaska." And petitions from teachers and other interested citizens in more than twenty-five states began flooding into congressional offices.[105]

In November, Mottram Ball, who remained on the job although his unofficial commission as Alaska's representative to the 47th Congress had expired, visited the White House to lobby President Arthur to include a statement supporting a civil government for Alaska in his annual message to Congress. When Arthur did so, Ball pridefully bragged to Jackson that "I do not know whether any others saw [the president] about it, but unless they did, or even *if* they did, the almost identical reference in his message with the language of my brief written statement to him makes me flatter myself that he did use and rely on it."[106]

When the 48th Congress convened in December, Sen. Benjamin Harrison of Indiana introduced a new Alaska civil government bill that was referred to the Committee on Territories.[107] Three days later, Rep. William Phelps of New Jersey wrote Jackson that three different civil government bills had been introduced in the Senate and that "unless anticipated by others I shall prepare a bill made up of what seem to be the best features of the three and introduce it early next week. A provision for education will be in the draft."[108] As good as his word, on December 11, Phelps introduced an Alaska civil government bill in the House.[109]

Sheldon Jackson's involvement in writing the Harrison and Phelps bills was apparent to Mottram Ball, who on January 25 wrote Jackson: "Early this month I went to Washington and think I recognize your work in the bills of Senator Harrison and Mr. Phelps and the numerous petitions in the Senate."[110]

To the untutored eye, Jackson's influence seemingly was not all-pervasive since the Harrison civil government bill did not include an authorization for an appropriation for Native education. However, at Jackson's request, the same day Sen. Harrison introduced the civil government bill, Sen. Orville Platt of Connecticut, a member of the Committee on Territories, introduced a bill that authorized an appropriation to finance the opening of schools in Alaska.[111] Sen. Harrison quietly arranged for the Senate to refer it to the Committee on Territories, rather than to the Education and Labor Committee to which the bill should have been referred.[112]

Two weeks after it was introduced, the Committee on Territories reported the Harrison civil government bill to the Senate. The speed with which the measure moved through the committee had a simple cause.

At the end of the 47th Congress, Sen. Alvin Saunders of Nebraska, chairman of the Committee on Territories, retired, and at the beginning of the 48th Congress was succeeded by Harrison. Civil War general and future president of the United States, Benjamin Harrison was a devout Presbyterian who for more than forty years served as an elder of the First Presbyterian Church of Indianapolis. As such, he was a committed Jackson ally. And Jackson, who undoubtedly had asked Harrison to introduce the bill, wanted the measure enacted.

During the Committee on Territories' consideration of the Harrison civil government bill, Jackson persuaded the senators who served on the panel to agree to add the Platt bill's authorization for an appropriation for education to the civil government bill when the latter measure reached the floor of the Senate. As Sen. Augustus Garland, a committee member from Arkansas, subsequently explained, the education amendment was not a "necessity," but "it was suggested to the committee and discussed by the committee in view of the anomalous condition of that country, and, in fact, the somewhat anomalous form of government we are compelled in the first instance to provide for it; and it was thought best to put some provision in reference to education in that Territory."[113]

On January 21, 1884, the Harrison civil government bill was called to the floor of the Senate. And on the second day of the debate, Harrison moved the Senate to amend the bill by adding the text of the Platt education bill.[114]

Rather than being accepted by the Senate pro forma, the amendment was vigorously opposed by Sen. Preston Plumb of Kansas, who was adamant that the federal government not spend taxpayer money to educate the children of Alaska Commercial Company employees and other whites who, in Plumb's view, were in Alaska only long enough to get rich. "I have no objection," Plumb informed Harrison, if the amendment was modified to limit the federal government's pedagogical responsibilities "to the Indians who are there and who are the proper subjects of national charity."[115]

Harrison rejected the suggestion because he thought it would be difficult for the few whites in Alaska to organize their own schools, and the recalcitrance stiffened Plumb's resolve because it proved his point.

If whites were as scattered throughout the expanse of the territory as Harrison said they were, Plumb retorted, then "if this section is carried out there will be a great many schools in a great many places in Alaska where they would not be considered necessary in any other portion of the habitable globe."

Having his back up, the senator from Kansas then shifted his ground. Why, he inquired, should the federal government assume responsibility even for educating Native children when "we have not done that with any other tribe of Indians under our jurisdiction. If we are to carry out the principle which is here established, what are we to do with the fifty thousand Indian children on this side of the Rocky Mountains, and who have been heretofore very imperfectly provided for if this is to be the scale the government is to adopt with reference to their children?"[116]

While he did not object to a reasonable appropriation for Native schools, Plumb orated, the Committee on Territories' amendment was "too wide, it is too ample, too expensive, too loose, and will lead to nothing but expense and trouble and annoyance."[117]

Given Preston Plumb's stature in the Senate, the Committee on Territories' amendment about a subject few other senators cared about was in trouble.

One of the senators who did care was Henry Dawes of Massachusetts, chairman of the Committee on Indian Affairs and the Senate's acknowledged expert on Indian policy. When Dawes was given the floor, he counseled his colleagues that educating Native children was worth the cost because it was past time for Congress to begin learning from its mistakes.

By 1884 the white rush for Indian land on the frontier had destroyed the Indian hunting economy. But few Indians had been assimilated into the white economy. As a consequence, after spending millions of dollars fighting Indians, Congress now was spending millions more to support them. Unless Congress pursued a new policy in Alaska, it would face the same problem there. "There are multiplying year by year in that section of country [Dawes lectured], a body of uncivilized people upon our border coming upon us in some time to come, how near we could not tell, as an ignorant, uneducated mass of people whom we should perhaps be obliged to support as we are obliged to support those of a kindred class here in our midst." For Dawes the solution was simple. The federal government had an obligation to educate Natives "enough to understand the institutions under which they live and the laws they are called upon to obey." "[E]very single one of them who can be brought up in intellectual capacity to understand the value of the institutions under which we live [he argued] is an actual donation of so much wealth to the nation itself.... we should make haste to avail ourselves, if I may use the expression, of this raw material out of which it is possible for us to make valuable citizens of the United States."[118] When Dawes concluded his remarks, the Senate recessed for the day.

Sheldon Jackson undoubtedly witnessed the debate from the visitors' gallery, for two days later, Sen. George Vest, a member of the Committee on Territories from Missouri, remarked on the floor that "I see upon my desk this morning, and I presume it is upon the desk of every other Senator, a statement of the Native tribes of Alaska. This paper, coming from the superintendent of the Presbyterian missions in Alaska."[119]

If he was present, Jackson would have understood that, despite Sen. Dawes's wise counsel, Sen. Plumb had left the floor unpersuaded. Assuming so, Jackson apparently went to work, since by morning Senators Harrison and Plumb had negotiated a compromise.

At the beginning of the day's debate, Harrison congenially remarked to Plumb

> that the committee are [*sic*] not at all wedded to the phraseology of this bill, that if the section now under discussion seems to him to be too broad, to involve too much the idea of a school system, the committee have [*sic*] no possible objection that it shall be simplified and limited in its terms. They only desire that there shall be here a suitable appropriation for education, and that its expenditure and use shall be committed to the Commissioner of Education under the supervision of the Secretary of the Interior.[120]

Harrison having announced the bottom line (and the fix being in), Plumb now was happy to stay within it. "If the Senator will indulge me a moment," he requested, "I will say that I have drawn an amendment, which I shall read now in order to ascertain whether it covers the point according to the opinion of the Senator from Indiana"—which, of course, it did. The

Plumb amendment authorized the secretary of the interior to make "equal and proper provision for the education of the children of school age in the Territory of Alaska, without reference to race" and appropriated $25,000 to enable him to do so.[121]

Harrison's only objection was that since the amendment did not reference the commissioner of education, the secretary of the interior was free to delegate responsibility for Native education to the commissioner of Indian affairs. That would be a mistake he argued because

> these Indians in Alaska have never yet become public charges. We have not been asked to make any appropriations in the way of annuities for them. If the question is wisely dealt with we shall never be asked to do so. Now as the management of Indian schools under the Indian Department has connected itself with the system of annuities, treaty annuities or annuities by special grants of Congress, I believe that it would be wiser to put the subject of education in Alaska in the hands of the Commissioner of Education, under the direction of the Secretary of the Interior.

But Plumb, who opposed Congress's micro-managing executive branch departments, objected, and when Harrison tried to amend the Plumb amendment to add a reference to the commissioner of education, the amendment to the amendment failed on a voice vote.[122] The Senate then adopted the Plumb amendment and two days later sent the Harrison civil government bill to the House of Representatives. The House passed the bill without amendment, and on May 17, 1884, President Arthur signed the measure into law. Alaska's whites finally had a civil government. And Sheldon Jackson finally had his appropriation for Native education.

Now that the money was in hand, Jackson began lobbying for the job of spending it.

In June the Rev. Henry Kendall wrote Sen. Shelby Cullom of Illinois to ask that he urge Secretary of the Interior Henry Teller to appoint Jackson general agent of education in Alaska. Cullom replied that "as soon as I can find an opportunity I will see the Secretary and urge Dr. Jackson's appointment."[123] Kendall sent similar letters to other influential members of Congress,[124] and the secretaries of the American Missionary Association and the Board of Domestic Missions of the Episcopal Church also endorsed Jackson.[125]

Contemporaneously, Jackson arranged to have himself appointed pastor of the Sitka Presbyterian Church and superintendent of the Sitka Presbyterian School. At the end of the summer, he then chaperoned T. W. Bicknell, the president of the National Education Association, on a tour of southeast Alaska.[126] In October, when he returned from the excursion, Bicknell wrote Jackson that "our Alaska trip was the crowning success ... and all were enthusiastic over the scenes and experience which your zeal and generalship brought within our observation.... I will write today to Secretary Teller [that] you are the man for that business [i.e., appointment as general agent of education] and no other knows anything about it."[127]

As he repeatedly had been urged to do, on March 2, 1885, Teller delegated responsibility for Alaska education to the commissioner of education, rather than the commissioner of Indian affairs.[128] On April 9, Commissioner of Education Eaton recommended to Teller that a general agent be appointed to administer the Alaska education program and that although Jackson's old rival, the Rev. Aaron Lindsley, had nominated his son-in-law, Hall Young, for the position, "in looking for the proper person to become such an agent, I find no one either so well qualified or so strongly recommended as Mr. Sheldon Jackson."[129]

With Teller's approval, four days later, Eaton appointed Jackson general agent of education at a salary of $1,200 per year, a modest sum that—ignoring the line between church and state—the Board of Home Missions supplemented by keeping Jackson on its payroll.[130]

On May 1, Rep. F. A. Johnson of New York, a member of the subcommittee that had reported the Harrison civil government bill to the House of Representatives, wrote Jackson to congratulate him "on the reward you are now receiving for your long, unwearied, and very efficient labors on behalf of that distant portion of our country." "I say without any hesitation," he concluded, "that in my humble judgment to you more than to any other one man or agency is due the success thus far attained in the direction of the establishing of a form of government and the improvement in the condition of the inhabitants of Alaska."[131]

Even discounting hyperbole, the kudos was merited. Henceforth, the federal government's Alaska Native policy would part company with the policy that governed its dealings with Indian tribes whose members had been confined on reservations. And more than Commissioner Eaton or Secretary Teller or Senators Harrison, Dawes, or Plumb, Sheldon Jackson was the Alaska policy's principal architect.

If there was any doubt, Jackson's first report as general agent of education reaffirmed the objectives of the policy he had lobbied.

> [T]he government has never treated [Alaska Natives] as Indians [the report reminds], and it would be a national calamity at this late day to

subject them to the restrictions and disabilities of our Indian system. Among those best known [i.e., the Tlingits] their highest ambition is to build American homes, possess American furniture, dress in American clothes, adopt the American standard of living, and be American citizens. They ask no favors from the American government, no annuities or help, but simply to be treated as other citizens, protected by the laws and courts, and in common with all others furnished with schools for their children.[132]

To that end, on June 1, 1885, the Bureau of Education opened its first classroom at Juneau, the beginning of a school system that during Jackson's tenure as general agent would expand to fifty-two schools.[133]

But mocking its superintendent's lofty talk about treating Natives "as other citizens" by educating their children "in common with all others," from its inception the school system the Bureau of Education operated in Alaska was as racially segregated as any Jim Crow school system in the Deep South.

As mentioned, the text of the education section of the Alaska Organic Act (as the Harrison civil government bill was known subsequent to its enactment) required the secretary of the interior to "make needful and proper provision for the education of children of school age in the Territory of Alaska, without reference to race." But in every town that had an appreciable white population, the Bureau of Education operated two schools—one Native, one white. Of the forty-seven schools the bureau operated in 1904, for example, thirty-five were Native, and twelve were white.[134]

The Bureau of Education's segregated classrooms had a simple cause. Despite his assimilationist rhetoric, Sheldon Jackson was a man who was as much a product of his time as Jefferson Davis and Henry Halleck were. And in that time racial segregation was as American a tradition as bunting on the Fourth of July.

Segregated schools had been upheld by the courts as early as 1849.[135] And eleven years after Jackson's appointment as general agent the U.S. Supreme Court decided *Plessy v Ferguson*,[136] a decision that upheld a Louisiana statute requiring Negroes to travel in segregated railroad cars.

Race relations in Alaska reflected the national mood. In 1888, for example, Native and white children at Douglas, a small southeastern Alaska mining town near Juneau, briefly attended the same school. White parents were so angry that Jackson instructed the teacher to "dismiss her Native pupils at 12 o'clock and in the afternoon teach the white children." But the white parents objected to their offspring having to sit on seats that previously had been occupied by Native children, and the conflict was not resolved until Jackson sent a second teacher to Douglas to open a white school.[137]

The white protests at Douglas were not an isolated incident. As Sarah Haynes, the teacher at the Native school at Juneau, reported to the Bureau of Education in 1910: "The prejudice of the whites against the Indians was clearly shown a year ago on Memorial Day when a number of the pupils of the white school refused to march in line because the Indian band led the parade."[138] And during Jackson's era the Presbyterians operated two churches at Sitka: one Native, one white.[139]

In 1900, Congress gave the Bureau of Education's segregated school system de jure recognition when it authorized whites living in towns with populations of three hundred or more to organize municipal governments and operate their own schools.[140] Whites living outside the incorporated towns soon demanded the same arrangement; and in 1905, Congress enacted the Nelson Act,[141] which authorized whites living in any "camp, village, or settlement" in Alaska to petition for their own school district. Enrollment in Nelson Act schools was statutorily limited to "white children and children of the mixed blood who lead a civilized life." Native children would continue to be educated by the Bureau of Education.

Sheldon Jackson wholeheartedly supported the arrangement. As he explained to the House Committee on Territories in 1904,

> As a rule [white and Native children] are separate. In some of the Native towns where there are only three or four white children, and for the sake of getting any schooling at all, the white children are glad to go into the Native school; but where there is a sufficient number, as for instance at Juneau before it became an incorporated town, the Bureau of Education maintained separate schools for the white and Native children as it does now at Sitka. Where there are enough white children the Bureau of Education organizes a white school, and if there are a number of Native children at the same place it also has a Native school.[142]

When asked whether he objected to the bifurcation, Jackson replied, "No; we have no objection. It is working well for the schools already established."[143]

As was usually the case, Jackson's view of the matter was determinative. The same day he testified before the House Committee on Territories, the Nelson Act was debated in the Senate. Sen. Henry Teller of Colorado, former secretary of the interior, expressed concern that the Act might prevent Native children from attending school if there were not enough Native children living in a white town for the Bureau of Education to justify the expense of operating a Native school, to which Sen. Nelson, the bill's sponsor, retorted that "the bill meets with the approval of Dr. Jackson of the Bureau of Education who is interested in the schools in Alaska. I submitted the bill to him, and he concurs in its provisions."[144]

Jackson's casuistic enthusiasm for segregated classrooms symbolizes the contradiction inherent in the Native policy Congress and the Department of the Interior pursued at his direction. The policy's professed goal was to use the schoolhouse to transform Native children into "citizens" who possessed white values, attitudes, and work habits. Among its other estrangements from reality, the social theory the policy was intended to implement ignored the fact that the new citizens would be sent out the schoolhouse door to make their way in a patently racist world.

That is not to say, given the inevitabilities that Alaska Natives faced, that Sheldon Jackson's commitment to assimilation—as opposed to his support for segregated classrooms—was wrong. To the contrary: by 1884 (the year Jackson persuaded Congress that opening schools was the key to solving the "Native problem"), the continued intrusion of whites into areas of Alaska that Natives previously had exclusively used and occupied and the intrusion of an endless array of manufactured paraphernalia into the fabric of the traditional Native subsistence-based material culture were foregone conclusions.

Assuming so, and regardless of the fetid aroma that Sheldon Jackson's confidence in his own cultural superiority emits into the contemporary atmosphere and of the repugnance of his easy embrace of segregated schools, the assimilationist Native policy that Congress and the Department of the Interior pursued at his direction was conceptually correct. As we shall see, William Paul and other Tlingit Indian leaders, who in the 1920s began organizing their people's defense against political and racial discrimination and economic exploitation, could not have done so if they first had not acquired the English language and other skills that Jackson's teachers taught as part of the assimilationist curriculum.

But to return to the story. In 1885, the year Jackson opened the first Bureau of Education school at Juneau, the Presbyterian Church transferred the schools it was operating in southeast Alaska at Wrangell, Hoonah, Haines, and Howkan to the bureau. The same fall, Salomon Ripinsky, whom Jackson described as "a Russian Hebrew, who had received a liberal European education,"[145] opened a bureau school on Unalaska Island. But while progress was being made, more schools were needed than Congress ever would appropriate enough money to enable the Bureau of Education to open.

Jackson understood the problem, and doing something about it was the second part of the plan he concocted during the canoe ride he hitched to Metlakatla in 1879 with the passing Chilkat trading party. Not only were there more schools needed than Congress would fund, there were more heathens in Alaska than the Presbyterian Board of Home Missions ever would have enough missionaries to convert. So there was no reason to be greedy.

To spread the wealth, in 1880, Jackson organized a meeting of representatives of Protestant denominations.[146] As he explained to the Board of Indian Commissioners in 1895,

> [W]e tried to improve on what the churches had done in other lands. We did not want Presbyterians and Congregationalists and Methodists and Baptists and Friends all huddled together in one corner of Alaska. We did not want half a dozen missionary societies working in one corner with 6,000 people, and leaving thousands of barbarians outside without any chance to hear the gospel. So we called a convention in New York City of the great missionary bodies; and, with a large map of Alaska before them, they decided on their separate missions.[147]

Each denomination was given a monopoly on the saving of Native souls. The Yukon River was given to the Episcopalians, Kodiak Island and Cook Inlet to the Baptists, the Aleutian Islands to the Methodists, the Kuskokwim and Nushagak Rivers in southwestern Alaska to the Moravians, and the northwest coast to the Congregationalists. The Presbyterians retained southeast Alaska and assumed responsibility for Point Barrow.[148]

While it had no force of law, Jackson's division of the evangelical pie was taken seriously. In 1887, for example, the Quakers, who were not party to the agreement, established a mission at Douglas and in 1891 did the same at Kake. Both locations were within the Presbyterian jurisdiction. Negotiations ensued, and in 1912 the Quakers transferred the Douglas and Kake missions to the Presbyterians; in exchange, the Presbyterians transferred a mission in Jamaica to the Quakers. Like the buildings, the Indian friends were chattel in the transaction. Each Tlingit who had been a Quaker was issued a certificate that instantaneously transformed the bearer into a Presbyterian.[149]

But a denomination agreeing to accept a paper jurisdiction was one thing. Committing the money and missionaries required to enter the field was quite another. To encourage the Moravian Church to do so, Jackson visited the church headquarters at Bethlehem, Pennsylvania, in 1884 to urge its leaders to send missionaries to minister to the Yup'ik Eskimos in southwestern Alaska.[150] The church leaders agreed, and in the summer of 1884 sent the Rev. Adolphus Hartmann and the Rev. William Weinland to explore the Kuskokwim River drainage. The following summer the Rev. and Mrs. Weinland and a second couple, the Rev. and Mrs. John Henry Kilbuck, returned to the Kuskokwim and selected a site for a mission, which they named Bethel, near a trading post operated by Edward Lind, an Alaska Commercial Company trader.

In September 1886 the Bethel mission opened a day school with six students, and Jackson hired Weinland as a Bureau of Education teacher so that the school could be supported in part by the bureau.[151] In theory, Jackson was Weinland's supervisor, but as a practical matter, Weinland was on his own. As Jackson subsequently explained, "If I wish to visit the school at Bethel, I take the mail steamer from Sitka [where Jackson was living at the time] to San Francisco, 1,600 miles, then wait until some trading vessel sails for Unalaska, 2,418 miles, then wait again until some trading vessel has occasion to visit the mouth of the Kuskokwim River, 461 miles, and go from thence in a bidarka (sea-lion skin canoe) 150 miles up the river."[152]

Other denominations followed the Moravians, including the Catholic Church, a denomination Jackson pointedly had not invited; in 1888 the priests established a mission and boarding school on the lower Yukon River at a location they called Holy Cross.[153]

By 1890 various denominations operated schools at such disparate locations as Yakutat, Unalakleet, Nulato, Anvik, Tununak, Bethel, Woody Island, and Cape Prince of Wales. The Alaska Commercial Company operated schools on the two Pribilof islands, and the Bureau of Education operated sixteen schools, principally in southeast Alaska and on Kodiak and the Aleutian Islands.[154] Still fund-raising on the side, in 1890, Jackson opened a school for the Eskimos at Point Barrow with money donated by Margaret Louise Shepard, a wealthy Presbyterian dowager from New York City whose maiden name was Vanderbilt.[155]

While they disagreed on questions of religious dogma, the missionary teachers all agreed that the reason they were in the field was to steal the minds of children. They also agreed with the unfortunate Hieromonk Juvenal, whose advocacy of the idea may have provoked his murder, that the most efficient way to do so was to remove Native children from their households.

That was the reason Amanda McFarland opened her home for girls at Wrangell, the reason Catholics opened their boarding school at Holy Cross, and the reason Presbyterians would open theirs at Sitka. As Jackson explained to the Board of Indian Commissioners in 1887, "The Sitka school, which is the only real effort to reach the children (for although there are several other schools in existence, yet they are day schools only), is a boarding school, where the children are taken from the parents, who sign away a girl until she is eighteen and a boy until he is twenty-one. The influence is therefore continuous."[156]

Two years later, the Jesuit Paschal Tosi, who supervised the Catholic school at Holy Cross, explained the assimilationist rationale for boarding schools as follows:

> In my opinion the only plan by which these people can be raised to some degree of civilization is through the establishment of good boarding schools, where the children can be taught, besides English speaking, reading, and writing, some kind of work calculated to promote their welfare and home comfort. The children should be removed as far as possible from contact and association with the elder ones of their race, and at a proper age legally married, and helped to make a comfortable home for themselves. Then we may expect them to continue to improve and bring their children up to a still higher degree of usefulness. Those who imagine that a few years of preaching and teaching in day schools will suffice to civilize and christianize wild native tribes are, in my opinion, greatly mistaken. Of course the day school is perhaps better than none at all as a means of making them christians, but how will it do much in the way of advancing them toward a true civilization I can not see. Too much has been said and written in favor of day schools, upon which a great deal of money has been wasted. For my part, I have seen too much of the workings of day schools during my many years of experience among the Indians to permit me to say much in their favor as a means to the accomplishment of any permanent good to the people they are ostensibly intended to benefit.[157]

But whether they attended a village day school or a mission boarding school, for every Native "scholar" the core curriculum was English.

Words are the symbols of the society that invents them. Taken together, a particular society's words form a pattern that reflects the members of that society's social and economic relationships—both between each other and with the physical world. As Aldous Huxley described the concept, "Words are magical in the way they affect the minds of those who use them.... Conduct and character are largely determined by the nature of the words we currently use to discuss ourselves and the world around us."[158]

For that reason, so the theory went, if Native children could be persuaded—and if not persuaded, then forced—to speak English words to describe their social and physical reality, the process of their doing so would imbue them with the values, attitudes, and aspirations of white European culture; and over time they would abandon the values, attitudes, and aspirations of their Tlingit-, Athabascan-, Yup'ik-, or Inupiaq-speaking parents.

To hasten that day, Bureau of Education and mission school teachers prohibited Native children from speaking their parents' tongues. L. F. Jones, a teacher at the Sitka boarding school in 1908 explained why:

> [E]very thing should be done to encourage and help the Natives to acquire the English. This would give them a tongue to communicate with the English speaking peoples who are bound to populate their country and with whom they must, in the future, altogether deal.... [B]y dropping their dialect and acquiring the English, they would the more rapidly get away from the heathen customs and advance in civilization. Those who know no English are great sticklers for old customs. Those, on the other hand, who speak English are the ones that are getting away from the old customs.[159]

The English-only edict was sternly enforced. To cite one of hundreds of illustrative examples, when Charles Replogle, a Quaker missionary who, beginning in 1893, spent a decade teaching at the Bureau of Education Native school at Douglas, heard an Indian student speaking Tlingit, he would soak a sponge with hot peppers and a bitter-tasting resin and then rinse the verboten vocabulary from the offender's mouth.[160]

For reasons to which any parent can relate, Tlingit parents objected to the degradation of their language. But during the hours their children were inside the schoolhouse there was little, other than refusing to allow them to be there, that they could do about it. So they voiced their opposition through a stoic silence that whites misinterpreted as acquiescence, as they not infrequently do today when confronted by the same tactic.

In 1887, for example, the Sitka newspaper the *Alaskan* happily reported that

> The Indian people are accepting with good grace the determination of the mission authorities to allow no language to be spoken by them but the English. Formerly there was much objection on the part of the parents to their children being prevented from conversing in their native tongue but now the feeling has entirely changed and the Indians, both young and old, who have been brought under the influence of the mission, seem anxious to adopt the new language and to follow in the footsteps of civilization.[161]

Given the number of Tlingits who attended school at Sitka during the last decades of the nineteenth and the first decades of the twentieth centuries and who spoke Tlingit, the reporter who filed the story got it wrong. But the error was not an isolated mistake. Rather, it reflected certainty of their cultural superiority on the part of Sheldon Jackson and his teachers. According to that line of thinking, Natives acted differently from whites because no one had taught them how they should act. Assuming so, once Bureau of Education and mission school teachers obviated their ignorance by communicating information about the benefits, material and otherwise, they could derive from the new way of living, the Natives to whom the teachers communicated the information would voluntarily conform their behavior and their attitudes to the norms of white society.

While there is more validity to the theory than many who live in today's brave new world of mandatory multiculturalism care to admit, during Sheldon Jackson's tenure as general agent of education not enough Natives attended school, particularly boarding school, to enable his teachers to work their magic on more than a few.

The 1900 census records 29,536 Natives living in Alaska.[162] But as late as 1907, only 2,500 children were enrolled in Bureau of Education schools that operated in only a quarter of the more than two hundred Native villages. And attendance was sporadic. Territory-wide, in 1907 the average daily attendance was 1,100.[163] And in southeast Alaska in 1912, the average daily attendance was 350 out of an enrollment of 1,039.[164] For that reason, as late as 1945, Roy Peratrovich, a Tlingit leader about whom more will be said, "recommend[ed] to our [Alaska Native Brotherhood] local camps [in each southeast Alaska village] the practice of teaching our older men and women how to write their names."[165]

In ill health, Sheldon Jackson resigned as general agent of education in 1908 and the next year died in Asheville, North Carolina, where he had traveled to deliver yet another lecture on Alaska.[166] He was seventy-five years old.

What, if anything, did Jackson accomplish during twenty-three years as general agent? The wisdom of his policies may be debated, but his stature as the dominant theoretician of the federal government's Alaska Native policy cannot be questioned. Because of Jackson, the Bureau of Education, rather than the Bureau of Indian Affairs, administered federal Native policy and programs. Because of Jackson no reservations were established on his watch. And to the present day, Jackson's shade dominates the debate over the proper federal-Native relationship.

Before returning Sheldon Jackson to his place on the shelf of Alaska history, mention should be made of the second flaw in his intellectual construct (the first being his blithe embrace of segregated schools).

As described, George Washington believed that encouraging Indians to become psychologically addicted to trade goods that only the white economy could provide was the long-term solution to the "Indian problem." Sheldon Jackson shared that view and intended the Bureau of Education's curriculum to transform Native students into consumers who, when they graduated, would possess vocational skills adequate to enable them to participate in the economy that produced the goods that their teachers had taught them to covet. As Jackson explained the process in 1886,

> As instruction creates new wants, and is so intended by the Government, it is but proper that instruction should go farther and so train the hand that the newly created wants can be supplied. Or, in other words, the work of the Alaska school system is not only to teach reading, writing, and arithmetic, but also how to live better, how to make more money to live better, and how to utilize the resources of the country in order to make more money.[167]

But the theory assumed that the same whites who refused to allow their children to attend school with Native children would allow Native children who learned English and a trade a fair opportunity, when they reached adulthood, "to utilize the resources of the country in order to make money."

For Jackson, who was not a stupid man, the estrangement of that assumption from reality should have been apparent. The Equal Employment Opportunity Commission did not exist. Nor could the Bureau of Education nor the Presbyterian nor any other church guarantee Natives jobs at fair wages, nor prevent whites from expropriating the economic benefit derived from land and natural resources to which Natives had a legitimate claim.

Since they couldn't, what was accomplished by a policy whose goal was to transform Alaska Natives into Economic Man without providing the new Alaska Native Economic Man a fair opportunity to participate in white Alaska's development of the Alaskan economy?

First, as Jackson intended, his teachers encouraged their Native students to consider an ever expanding array of manufactured goods that only money could buy to be necessities of life. The students' enthusiastic embrace of a new material culture accelerated the diminishment of their reliance on the traditional hunting and fishing economy that for generations had allowed Alaska Natives to be self-reliant.

Second, at locations at which whites had use for their labor, Natives who had attended Jackson's schools competed for low-paying wage work. Unaware of the Faustian bargain into which they entered, self-sufficient hunter-gatherers hired on as bottom-rung members of a new social order.

However, it would be unfair to lay responsibility for that dark side of the nineteenth-century part of the story of Alaska Natives and their land solely at Sheldon Jackson's door because the sixty-five teachers the Bureau of Education employed during Jackson's final year as general agent, while important, were not the exclusive agents of social change in Native villages. As mentioned, in a vast geography that contained more than two hundred villages and thousands of children, relatively few Native children attended school. And even if more had, the majority of Natives were adults.

As a consequence and as we shall see, for most Natives making their way in Alaska during the last decades of the nineteenth and the first decades of the twentieth centuries, their participation as unskilled labor in the white economy, rather than their attendance at school, was the principal assimilative experience. Which is not to say that Alaska Natives were at all times merely pawns in an economic game in which they were allowed to make no moves. As they had since the days of Baranof and the Bostons, Natives who attended school and Natives who didn't had a clear, if intuitive, understanding of such basic economic concepts as the advantage monopoly confers and the opportunities for profit that can be found in the spread between supply and demand.

Because of this understanding and in spite of the fact that they had no control over the initiation of economic activity in their neighborhoods, Natives, when afforded the chance, exploited whites in the same way that whites, on more numerous occasions, exploited them.

3

Capitalists

When the Native has thus become useful to the white man by supplying the markets with fish and fresh meat, and when he has become herdsman and teamster with reindeer he has not only assisted the white man in solving the problem of turning to use of civilization the vast territory of Alaska, but he has also solved his own problem. If useful to the white man as a self-respecting and industrious citizen he has become a permanent stay and prop to the civilization and his future is provided for.

SHELDON JACKSON, March 10, 1904[1]

WITH THE EXCEPTION OF missionaries and schoolteachers, most whites who came to Alaska during the first forty years subsequent to the Alaska purchase did so for a single good reason: to make money. Of the many schemes, almost all involved catching or extracting one of the territory's abundant natural resources. But killing fur seals, canning salmon, mining gold, and the like involved backbreaking work that, happily for the whites who needed it done, Natives who attended one of Sheldon Jackson's schools and Natives who didn't all were eager to perform.

So few Natives attended school that Jackson and his teachers are entitled to minor credit for the enthusiasm with which Alaska Natives competed for wage work. Rather, the credit is due the desire for modernity that lurks in every human's nature. As George Washington theorized they would if allowed the chance, once they accepted that the whites who began appearing in their neighborhoods were in Alaska to stay, Alaska Natives, like moths attracted to the light, were eager to labor at whatever work whites wanted done in order to acquire manufactured goods that, prior to the arrival of whites, Natives didn't know they needed.

In southeast Alaska, in the days of Baranof and the Bostons, the Tlingit and Haida Indians worked when they felt like working to obtain sea otter and other fur-bearing animal pelts and fresh food that the Russians and the Bostons wanted, which they bartered for goods of American, European, and Russian manufacture that they wanted. As a consequence, after half a century spent learning the art of commercial negotiation, the Indians with whom traders at Sitka and Wrangell did business during the first years subsequent to the Alaska purchase had a perspicacious understanding of the value of monopoly. As William Dodge, who arrived at Sitka in 1867, described the situation in 1869:

> One peculiar characteristic of the Alaska tribes, such as the Haidas, Stikines, Sticks, Kakes, Kootznoos, and Sitkas is their individual intelligent independence.... For half a century educated into traders by the Russian American and Hudson's Bay Companies, as well as by small traders, who trade contraband, they have become keen, sharp-witted, and drive as hard and close a bargain as their white brothers, and since the federal occupation of the country this fact is more apparent.... [A]s a rule they stand as the immediate agents between the white traders and the interior Indians, and in this exhibit a jealousy worthy the Jews. Many purchase from the whites hard bread, rice, shoes, blankets, and etc., and take these together with salmon, which they cure themselves up the various rivers to the interior tribes, with whom they in turn trade for mink, martin, lynx, fox, bear, and other skins. Returning to the whites, these Indians again exchange for articles of traffic. They never allow the upper country Indians to come to the white settlements to trade with the Chilkats and Tarkens [sic]; death would follow the attempt. Hence is evinced a monopoly powerful and extensive in character. Nor will the Coast Indians permit any white man to pass to the upper country to trade[. T]he penalty they threaten is the same. All trade must be made with and through them.[2]

But the Tlingit trading monopolies were too sweet an arrangement to last. The Stikine Tlingits' control, both of their trade route up the Stikine River and of economic activity at Wrangell, their village near the mouth of the river, was the first to go.

As mentioned, by 1875 the gold strike in the Cassiar Mountains had transformed Wrangell into a mining camp so raucous that the army sent troops to reoccupy Fort Wrangell and maintain order. Since the new work to be had chopping firewood, stevedoring supplies, and lightering freight by canoe upriver to the mines was located in their village, the Stikines assumed that they were entitled to the jobs. But Indians from villages throughout the Alexander Archipelago and as far south as Metlakatla, British Columbia, poured into Wrangell to compete for the work. According to the Presbyterian missionary Hall Young, who arrived at Wrangell in 1878, "opportunities for work at wages, which were small but seemed large to the Natives, as well as the gathering of a number of merchants to Fort Wrangell with supplies of new, strange and attractive goods, drew the attention and presence of the Indians from eighteen to twenty different tribes and from distances ranging from sixty to four hundred miles."[3]

When the Stikines refused to allow the interlopers to settle in their village on the south side of the Fort Wrangell palisade, their uninvited guests built their own village on the north side. In 1879 the *Alaska Appeal* described the increasingly chaotic scene as follows:

> The town of Wrangell, Alaska, has caused quite a revolution in the fur trade of the southeastern part of the Territory. Ten or eleven well-stocked stores and the presence during seven months of the year of a large number of miners more or less provided with "dust" have attracted the Indians from all parts of the neighborhood, who formerly took their peltries to Sitka or Port Simpson [British Columbia]. The gratifying result of this change is the concentration of a larger number of Indians than any other trading center of this region can boast of. Some 2,000 Natives can at times be seen swarming about the place, especially in the spring of the year, before the annual exodus to the mines. Another means of attracting the Natives and their trade is the employment of hundreds of their young men in freighting by canoe, wood-chopping, and various kinds of labor. The fur trade, which, in spite of competition, is quite remunerative, enables the business men of Wrangell to invest considerable means in fitting out prospecting and exploring parties, and in this way even the Indians pay indirectly for the development of their country's resources.[4]

The arrival of more and more Indians exacerbated an increasingly tense situation.

> When you were here you know that canoes were carrying freight up the river pretty fast [Isaac Dennis, the deputy collector of customs at Wrangell, privately reported in June 1878 to William Gouverneur Morris, the customs collector at Port Townsend, Washington]. Well, the news spread over the country like wild-fire, and a few days after your departure the Indians were coming in from all quarters by hundreds. Everything passed off peaceably until the 21st May, at which time the canoes became so plentiful, and all wanting to carry freight up the river, that the Stikine Indians became alarmed and jealous because of the competition. They made threats, and this created trouble and excitement among the outside Indians. All came to me with their complaints, and bothered me to death almost, but I lived through it. On the 22d and 23d we loaded forty canoes with freight. These forty canoes carried in all about two hundred and fifty Indians as crews.[5]

In less than a decade their inability to protect their position inside the new economy at Wrangell reduced the Stikines to psychological indigence.

You Boston people know different things and are different from us [Shakes, the Stikines' chief of chiefs, lamented to Sheldon Jackson when Jackson met with the Stikine clan leaders when he visited Wrangell in September 1881]. Up the river was our place, but not our place now and when we go up there they say you belong to Boston and because we want to obey you, we don't speak strong words to them. And when [indecipherable] comes up river or at Wrangell we don't say anything about it because we want you to help us.

We can't get any money now [Shakes continued]. If we were like white people and had plenty of money, we would use it for our children but we are poor. Long time ago they were the middle men selling up the river and had plenty of money, but now because we are Boston people we have no money....

Having heard a rumor that Jackson had been trying to get them money from far away, Shakes and the other headmen thanked him for his efforts. But what the Stikines wanted was access to a technology that, until recently, they hadn't known that they'd needed: "If you get us a sawmill we will obey you, no matter what, [promised Joseph Davies (the English name of another Stikine)]. Everybody want a sawmill but don't like to tell you, so I speak for them. Everyday I hear people say they want a sawmill. If he give us this thing, then we will do what they tell us. If you give it we will never make you sorry."

Davies then reminded Jackson how much more cooperative the Stikines had been than other Tlingits, particularly the Chilkats. "I guess the Chilkat chief will laugh at us," Davies lamented, "if [he] hear[s] that we bring fish to the [McFarland] Home [for Girls]."[6]

The Chilkats, who lived in three villages along Chilkat River, which flows into Lynn Canal 110 miles north of Sitka, and a fourth on Chilkoot River, which flows into the canal a few miles north of the mouth of Chilkat River, could be contemptuous because, in 1881, only a few whites had intruded into their territory.

During the years immediately subsequent to the Alaska purchase, the Chilkats regularly traded at Sitka. But unlike the Stikines, they refused to allow whites to prospect the river drainages that empty into Lynn Canal. As a consequence, Jefferson Davis considered the Chilkats to be "the most formidable and hostile Indians" in Alaska.

They carry on trade with the tribes living on the upper Yukon [River] and are reported to be very wealthy Indians [Davis reported in 1868 to his superiors in San Francisco]. They have thus far persistently resisted all attempts of the whites to locate among them. I can learn of no expeditions having been made up the Chilcot [*sic*] River by the whites—yet it is the most direct, and I think the most practicable, route to the Yukon.[7]

The Chilkats did, however, make exceptions to their rule: two whites, William Henderson and James Strichan, spent the summer of 1879 prospecting in Chilkat country, where Henderson reportedly lived several months the previous year.[8] But the Chilkats maintained control over the Lynn Canal watersheds throughout 1870s, until Klotz-Kutch, the principal chief, self-servingly cracked open the door.

In September 1879, Klotz-Kutch hosted a potlatch at which a barrel of distilled molasses was consumed by his guests, after which a brawl erupted; several Chilkats were killed, and Klotz-Kutch was shot. When he learned that Chilkats were shooting Chilkats, L. A. Beardslee, the captain of the *Jamestown,* the navy warship that recently had been stationed at Sitka, saw his chance.

He encouraged a group of Chilkats who had been living at Sitka to return to Chilkat River to help Klotz-Kutch. Beardslee instructed his emissaries to tell Klotz-Kutch that they had been sent "to help him keep his people in order" and that, in return for the favor, Beardslee "expected him to always use his influence to secure good treatment to any white men who should come to his country to trade." In addition, Beardslee "would be pleased" if Klotz-Kutch "would let white miners go into the interior to prospect the country for precious metals, which, if found, would enrich the Indians also."[9]

The extra men apparently proved decisive, since Klotz-Kutch accepted the quid pro quo by sending Beardslee word that whites no longer would be prevented from prospecting Chilkat territory.

In May 1880 nineteen prospectors departed Sitka for Chilkat River, chaperoned by seventeen sailors from the *Jamestown,* whose launch prudently was armed with a Gatling gun.

One of Klotz-Kutch's conditions for safe passage was that prospectors not trade with the Athabascan Indians who lived on the far side of Chilkoot Pass, the trail to the headwaters of the Yukon River that began at the head of Lynn Canal. Predictably, a prospector named Steele and a companion immediately violated the agreement, and Klotz-Kutch sent word to Beardslee that if the offenders were not removed from his jurisdiction, both men would be killed. In the meantime, a new round of fighting broke out when the Chilkats got drunk on another barrel of distilled molasses and one of Klotz-Kutch's nephews killed the Indian who had wounded his uncle the previous September.[10]

To deal with both matters, Beardslee chartered the Northwest Trading Company steamer *Favorite* (since the *Jamestown* would have been difficult to maneuver in Lynn Canal) and embarked for Chilkat River, where he negotiated the release of Steele and his associate and, after summoning Klotz-Kutch and the other Chilkat headmen, ordered them to order their people to stop killing each other.

The meeting concluded with a demonstration. "After the interview [Beardslee subsequently reported] we exhibited to them the howitzer and gatling, firing a number of rounds from both; the action of the gatling, which was mounted on a pivot block aft, so that we could sweep two-thirds of the horizon, was particularly interesting to them, as it taught them what one man could do to a fleet of canoes coming from all directions."[11]

In November 1881, Beardslee's successor, Capt. Henry Glass, returned to Lynn Canal to deliver the same message. According to Carrie Willard, the Presbyterian missionary Sheldon Jackson sent with her husband to open a mission at the mouth of Chilkoot River, when the principal chiefs assembled, Glass reiterated that "if they harmed the whites who came among them, he would storm their village and blockade their river. He then showed them what the big guns [mounted on his vessel] were made of by firing quite a number of balls and bombshells, which shook our house, although sent in an opposite direction."[12]

Allowing the Willards to settle in their midst more subtly debased Chilkat authority. In October 1879, Hall Young and the naturalist John Muir explored the Alexander Archipelago by canoe. During the trip, Muir "discovered" Glacier Bay, the inlet west of Lynn Canal that President Calvin Coolidge would designate in 1925 as a national monument, after the Tlingits he and Young hired to paddle their canoe guided him to it.[13] Young and Muir then continued on to Yindestukki, the Chilkat village at the mouth of Chilkat River, where Young preached the gospel through an interpreter and prior to departing met with the Chilkat headmen to offer to send a missionary to build "a new Christian town where they could speedily learn the white man's ways and Christian habits and where their children could be educated as Boston men and women."[14]

Apparently deciding that it would be more convenient to do their trading close to home rather than to continue transporting their furs to Sitka, the Chilkat chiefs accepted the offer and selected Portage Cove on the north side of the finger of land that protrudes between the mouths of Chilkat and Chilkoot Rivers as the site for Young's new town. The next summer, George Dickinson, a white trader who had been living at Wrangell, and his Indian wife, Sarah, who had been helping Amanda McFarland teach school, opened a trading post at Portage Cove for the Northwest Trading Company.

In July 1881 the Dickinsons were followed by Sheldon Jackson, who arrived with lumber for a mission house, a church bell, and Carrie Willard and her husband, Eugene. Jackson named the new mission Haines in honor of Frances Haines of Elizabeth, New Jersey, who three years earlier had helped Jackson organize the Woman's Executive Committee of Home Missions.

To protect the monopoly that had made them rich, the Chilkats forbade the Athabascan Indians who lived at the headwaters of the Yukon River (who, like the Athabascans who lived at the headwaters of the Stikine, were known as Sticks) to trade with whites, just as they forbade whites to trade with the Athabascans. The consequence, according to Aurel Krause, a German geographer who boarded with George and Sarah Dickinson the winter of 1881-1882, was that the Sticks "all had to leave their wares with the Chilkat for comparatively low prices."[15]

Within months of their arrival, the Willards disrupted that generations-old arrangement when, in February 1882, Mr. Willard bartered for a squirrel parka from a visiting Stick with the same amount of flour, shot, and powder he would have paid a Chilkat for the item. According to Carrie Willard,

> Early next morning, before we could get our breakfast, we were set upon by some head-men, of whom Cla-not was spokesman.... He charged us with having robbed them; for, said he, "the Sticks are our money; we and our fathers before us have gotten rich from them. They are only wild: they are not men; and now you have told them these things and taken away our riches." Mr. Willard told him that he spoke the truth to all men, nor would he lie for any: he told him that a certain advance on prices here was just and right when they carried their goods into the interior, but that it was wrong to hinder the Sticks from coming here, and that when they brought their skins here it was only right that they should buy and sell at the same prices which the Chilkats did.[16]

As Carrie Willard condescendingly lectured in a letter to friends on the East Coast, "The Chilkats have lied to the Sticks and cheated them, and to prevent their coming to the coast to trade have told them horrid stories of the whites, and that they would be killed if they came. The few who have ventured here have been dogged about by the Chilkats, and look like hunted things. We have, however, gotten hold of every one and told them of Christ."[17]

But while the Willards were meddlesome, the Chilkat barter economy was under pressure from a considerably more serious source: the money to be made working for whites for wages.

By the early 1880s the Northwest Trading Company, headquartered at Portland, Oregon, operated trading posts throughout southeast Alaska, such as the post George Dickinson opened at Haines and a reduction plant at Killisnoo on Admiralty Island that rendered whale oil, which the company sold to tanneries in Oregon and California.[18] The businesses all ran on Indian labor. Indians trapped the animals whose pelts were bartered at company trading posts; they hunted the whales whose oil was rendered at Killisnoo; and at the entrance to Lynn Canal, they corded the wood that fueled the *Favorite's* boilers.[19]

But of the new economic activity that whites brought to southeast Alaska during the first years subsequent to the Alaska purchase, the salmon cannery had the most profound effect on Indian life.

Within three years of the purchase, three commercial salmon fisheries were operating in the Alexander Archipelago, one near Sitka and one each at the villages of Kasaan and Klawock on Prince of Wales Island.[20] They all relied on Indian labor. As O. B. Carlton, superintendent of the Sitka saltery explained in 1869,

> Last season I employed American [i.e., white] labor, but found it to be expensive both in transportation and wages to make it pay. This year I employed Russians mostly, and find the expense about one-half of last season, but find them too indolent to employ to advantage. Next season I shall employ Indians altogether, except coopering, and I have no doubt but they can also be taught that trade. I found them willing and industrious, and kind when properly treated.

And most important, Carlton concluded, "They will work for less pay than Americans or Russians."[21]

In 1879, Sheldon Jackson toured the Cutting & Company cannery that had opened near Sitka the previous summer and liked what he saw.

> We found all the operations, from the catching of the salmon to the boxing of the cans ready for market, were carried on by the Indians under the supervision of white men [he happily reported]. It was a new sight to see over a hundred Indian men working as steadily and intelligently as the workmen in an Eastern factory. It is an opening up

of new avenues of support—a partial solution of the problem, how to elevate and civilize the Indians.[22]

The technology for canning salmon had been perfected in the 1860s. The first cannery on the Pacific Coast began operating in California in 1864, and four years later the North Pacific and Trading Company, a California corporation, began canning salmon at Klawock, a Tlingit village on the west coast of Prince of Wales Island.[23]

In the marketplace, salmon canned in Alaska competed against salmon canned on the Columbia River on the Washington-Oregon border. According to Hubert Howe Bancroft, writing in 1886, the reason Alaska canneries made their absentee owners millions, notwithstanding the extra freight charges they paid to ship their product to market, was that "salmon can be bought from the Natives in Alaska at less than one fifteenth of the price paid on the Columbia."[24] Indeed, in 1879 white fishermen on the Columbia River earned fifty cents a salmon, while Indian fishermen in southeast Alaska were paid one to five cents.[25]

To take advantage of the differential, in 1883 the Northwest Trading Company and Kinney Brothers of Astoria, Oregon, both built canneries at the mouth of Chilkat River that offered work to every Chilkat who wanted it.

And they all did.

Initially, the Chilkats naïvely assumed that inside their territory what they said still went. And in June, when the first run of salmon arrived at Chilkat River, they made the point by going on strike. "The people are almost crazy to make money [Carrie Willard reported in a letter to friends]. Both canneries have stores, and prices have been brought down to fairness. At the same time, the prices of fish have run up till the Indians can make fifteen dollars a day fishing. What they are striking for now I do not know."[26]

But we do.

As it had been five years earlier when the Indians at Sitka had almost massacred the Chinese imported by Cutting & Company to manufacture cans, the issue was local hire. According to Eliza Ruhamah Scidmore who visited Chilkat River in 1883, "In the rivalry and competition of the first year between the Pyramid Harbor [Northwest Trading Company] and Chilkat [Kinney Brothers] canneries, the price of salmon rose from two to fifteen cents for a single fish, and the Indians, once demoralized by opposition prices, refused to listen to reason when the canneries had to, and Chinese cheap labor was imported."[27]

Unbeknownst to the Chilkats, Chinese canning of Tlingit-caught fish actually was already a standard industry practice. According to William

Gouverneur Morris, when he visited the North Pacific and Trading Company cannery at Klawock in May 1878, "they had 350,000 tin cans made. This labor is all done by Chinamen."[28] The same year, Cutting & Company imported Chinese to manufacture cans for the cannery it opened near Sitka. And in 1883 when Eliza Scidmore visited the Kinney Brothers cannery at Cape Fox on the southern tip of the southeast Alaska mainland, she observed that "most of the work is done by the Indians, but a few Chinamen perform the work which requires a certain amount of training and mechanical skill."[29]

The Chilkats' enthusiasm for the cannery payday wreaked havoc on the traditional barter economy. The salmon that migrated up the Chilkat River were so abundant and of such a superior quality that, in addition to fishing for themselves, the Chilkats routinely caught extra fish that they bartered to Indians from villages as far south as Wrangell. But salmon that previously had been bartered now were being delivered to the canneries. As a consequence, in September, Carrie Willard reported:

> Canoes are coming daily from below Juneau, Sitka, Hoonah and Fort Wrangell to get salmon at [Klukwan,] the upper [Chilkat River] village. These people say they have been standing all summer waiting for the fish to come, but in all they had gotten but forty dried. Winter is coming on, and [the Chilkats] have made no provision for it; usually they have by this season great store-houses full of dried salmon and salmon oil—not only enough for themselves, but for trade with the lower tribes—and they will, I fear, have nothing left of their summer earnings with which to buy flour or any other food.[30]

The ease with which the Chilkats made the transition from fishing for themselves and for barter to fishing for whites for wages occurred throughout the Alexander Archipelago. However, labor unrest continued over the issue of local hire.

In addition to the Chinese they imported to operate the canning machines, at Chilkat River the Northwest Trading Company and Kinney Brothers managers hired whites to fish alongside Chilkat fishermen. The consequence? "The Chilkats resented the presence of white fishermen," Eliza Scidmore, who conducted the 1890 census in southeast Alaska, reported that year. "[And] the presence of the governor [of Alaska] and a man-of-war were [sic] required to settle the troubles."[31]

Sending the navy and its Gatling gun to intimidate Indians into working for whatever wages absentee cannery owners decided to pay was a regular occurrence. In 1890, when John Muir made his second visit to Chilkat

River, the Northwest Trading Company and Kinney Brothers canneries were paying Chilkat fishermen ten cents per salmon.[32] But prior to the 1891 season the cannery managers decided to increase their profit margins by lowering the price to five cents. When the Chilkats were told that their wages had been cut fifty cents on the dollar they refused to fish. The managers again summoned the navy, and in July the *Pinta,* the navy gunboat on station at Sitka, steamed to Chilkat River.

Despite the urging of the *Pinta's* captain, O. W. Farenholt, that they do so, the Indians continued to refuse to fish for five cents a salmon. Farenholt warned that, presumably through the use of the *Pinta's* Gatling gun, he intended to preserve order. He then weighed anchor and returned to Sitka. When the *Pinta* docked, the *Alaskan,* the Sitka newspaper, reported to its readers that "it was not known whether or not the [Chilkat] Indians [who were 'cross and somewhat sullen'] would accept the terms insisted upon by the canneries, and it is possible that another visit there [by the *Pinta*] may be necessary."[33]

As it did at Chilkat River, the salmon cannery transformed Tlingit life throughout the Alexander Archipelago. As Eliza Scidmore described the scene in 1890 after inventorying the archipelago for the census, "a large number of Native men, women, and children find work both in the cannery and in catching fish" at Loring on Revillagigedo Island north of the present-day city of Ketchikan. And many Indian fishermen were "bringing fish to the cannery in their canoes" from as far away as "a distance of forty or fifty miles."[34] Indians also were fishing for or working in canneries at Yes and Burroughs Bays on the Behm Canal, at Turk's Salmon Saltery southeast of Tongass, and at canneries at Salmon and Lake Bays on Prince of Wales Island and at Point Ellis on Kuiu Island.

By 1897 nine canneries were operating in southeastern Alaska, and twenty more were operating at locations as far north as Cook Inlet and as far west as Bristol Bay in southwestern Alaska and Chignik on the southern coast of the Alaska Peninsula. The annual pack, which had been 8,159 cases in 1878, increased to 909,078 cases,[35] and the need for Native labor, both then and years hence, increased accordingly. In July 1911, for example, the *Thlinget,* the newspaper published at the Indian boarding school the Presbyterian Church operated at Sitka, reported that that season's "salmon pack promises to be the largest known since the beginning of the fishing industry in Alaska.... Every Native person in Alaska that is able to work (and there are very few that are not) are busy. Even the little folks are earning money wrapping the cans. Everyone is so busy that the steamers have difficulty in getting men enough to unload the ships as they come in."[36]

Southeast Alaska Indian salmon cannery workers.
WICKERSHAM COLLECTION PCA 277-2-134, ALASKA STATE LIBRARY.

And in September the *Thlinget* reported that the canneries still were operating, "which will keep many of the children out of school this month. They would come in in time but are not paid until all the work is finished."[37]

By 1914 four thousand Indians, Eskimos, and Aleuts, a work force that the federal Bureau of Fisheries estimated to be one-third of the Natives who lived along the coast, were employed in the Alaska salmon canning industry.[38]

Interestingly, like the Chilkats, Indians throughout the Alexander Archipelago initially considered the new commercial fisheries to be an Indian monopoly. In 1879, when a white named Haley attempted to fish for cod in Chatham Strait east of Baranof Island, Indians who lived in the vicinity forced Haley to purchase his cod from them, rather than catch it himself.[39] And in 1880, Ivan Petroff, who conducted that year's census, reported that "the few small sloops engaged in the business in this region depend altogether upon the inclination of these Natives to exert themselves in obtaining their cargos." Because the Indians fished with bark lines and wood hooks, they were less efficient than white fishermen, a fact of southeast Alaska economic life, Petroff reported, that "frequently detained [white fishermen] for many weeks awaiting a cargo that could easily have been secured within five or six days by white men."[40]

Ten years later, in July 1890, word reached Sitka that Tlingit Indians were preventing the Baranof Packing Company schooner *Active* from fishing at Sitkoh Bay on the southern tip of Chichagof Island, and Lt. R. E. Cootz and a squad of marines were ordered to the scene. When the marines arrived, they discovered that two rival groups of Tlingits, each asserting the exclusive right to the salmon that spawned in the streams that emptied into the bay, had joined forces to prevent William Murphy, the captain of the *Active*, and his crew from fishing.

Lt. Cootz tried to persuade the white and Indian fishermen to negotiate an arrangement, but the talks terminated when Murphy rejected the Indians' demand that each member of his crew pay a royalty of twenty-five cents per day. At Cootz's suggestion, the Tlingits then returned with him to Sitka to have the controversy settled by the civil authorities.[41]

How the dispute was resolved is not known. What is known is that, to keep the peace, the civil authorities began issuing certificates decorated with a large red seal that purported to guarantee Indian fishermen the exclusive right to fish in particular waters.

The practice outraged the white residents of Sitka. "Improbable as it may seem," the *Alaskan* railed in November,

certificates guaranteeing fishing rights in the streams of S.E. Alaska
are as yet issued to the Natives by civil representatives of the government [presumably Lyman Knapp, an attorney from Vermont whom
President Benjamin Harrison appointed governor of Alaska in 1889],
despite the admonition received by them last summer in the Sitkoh
Bay trouble, which, if it had not been promptly checked ... would
undoubtedly have resulted in bloodshed. There is not the slightest
foundation of law for such action on the part of our civil officers ... it
is most urgent not only to stop the issue of such worthless documents
but to call in and cancel them all as they can only be inducive in
creating serious trouble between the Natives and the whites and to
undermine the little authority which our civil government can at present
exercise ... that the whites will not respect such an unlawful exercise of
power on the part of the authorities and will be driven to an armed
conflict with the Natives is beyond question.[42]

The *Alaskan's* protest accomplished its objective since the practice of
issuing certificates stopped, with predictable result. As Jefferson Moser,
the captain of the U.S. Fish Commission steamer *Albatross,* described the
situation after surveying the Alaska salmon fishery in 1897,

A Native, whose ancestors have lived on a certain stream for many
generations, and whose rights are respected by other Natives, supplies
a certain cannery with his catch, as possibly he has been doing for
years. A rival cannery tells the Native he must sell his catch to it, and
that otherwise their men will fish the Native's stream. The result is
overfishing, complaints, bad feeling, blows, and threats of bloodshed.
So far as can be learned, there are now no legal rights or title to any
fishing grounds in Alaska except what force or strategy furnish.[43]

In addition to salmon, there was a second part of the traditional Tlingit
and Haida material culture that Indians were as eager to sell as whites were
to buy.

In 1774, Juan Herandez, the senior naval officer at San Blas on the western coast of Mexico, who had been sent north in the *Santiago* to reconnoiter
the extent of Russian and English encroachment on territory claimed by
the Spanish crown, arrived at Dall Island, an island north of Dixon Entrance that today marks the border between southeast Alaska and British
Columbia. After dropping anchor off the Queen Charlotte Islands a few
miles to the south, the *Santiago* was approached by three canoes manned
by Haida Indians, the Indians who occupied the Queen Charlottes as well
as the southern half of Prince of Wales Island to the north in what a
century later would be known as Alaska. When the Haidas came alongside,

one of the *Santiago's* officers tossed a cracker wrapped in a handkerchief into one of the canoes; the precursor of a trade that the next day began in earnest. To entice the Spaniards to part with trade beads, iron, and European clothing, the Haidas bartered their own clothing, as well as blankets, cedar bark mats, hats, dishes, boxes, and spoons of their own manufacture. "Thus," according to Douglas Coe, the historian of the northwest coast curio trade, "on the occasion of the first contact of Europeans with the northcoast Indians, the trade in artifacts had begun."[44]

By the Alaska purchase in 1867, the sale to whites of clothing, hats, masks, blankets, baskets, boxes, bowls, utensils, carvings, and similar items was an established Indian business.

When Sophia Cracroft visited Sitka in 1870, she went "into a shop where Indian curiosities are sold, and bought some."[45] Escorted by one of Jefferson Davis's officers, she also went on a shopping tour through the Indian village.

> We went into several [Tlingit longhouses, Sophia confided to her diary] not merely to inspect, but in search of baskets and other queer things.... We saw a quantity of boxes (and have bought a small one) made of one piece of wood.... A very few women were making baskets, and for those brought out to us they asked absurd prices, so there was plenty of bargaining until the right highest price was accepted.[46]

For most whites who traveled in southeast Alaska during the first years subsequent to the purchase, items of Tlingit and Haida Indian manufacture had an exotic allure, and many acquired large collections. During his reconnaissance of the territory in 1869, Vincent Colyer, the secretary of the Board of Indian Commissioners, purchased a number of items for the Smithsonian Institution.[47] Sheldon Jackson also was a collector. But he was hardly alone. In 1878, when Jackson wrote John Brady, the new Presbyterian missionary at Sitka, to send him some items, Brady responded that "they are scarce here now" because "someone down below sends up nearly every steamer for $50 worth."[48]

The willingness of collectors like Colyer and Jackson to pay money for household items taught the Indians of southeast Alaska that their material culture had economic value in the white marketplace. The tourist trade transformed the avocation of selling items that originally had been made for Indian use into the business of manufacturing curios. Sheldon Jackson and John Muir helped found the industry by promoting Alaska through the books and newspaper articles both men published about their travels through Manifest Destiny's newest neighborhood. But the business took off when the transcontinental railroads and the Pacific Coast Steamship Company began jointly marketing a summer trip through the Alexander Archipelago.

The steamship *Dakota* inaugurated what become known as the Inland Passage Tour in 1882. The next summer the *Idaho* transported the first boatload of tourists into Glacier Bay.[49] And the summer after that, the Pacific Coast Steamship Company began making regular runs to Glacier Bay from ports in the Pacific Northwest; in the maiden season it transported 1,650 passengers.[50] The Inland Passage Tour proved so popular that the company soon had four vessels on the route and still couldn't handle the business.

In the summer of 1890, 5,007 tourists made the trip.[51] The following June the *Alaskan* celebrated the arrival of the first tour boat of the season by happily announcing that all space on the ships that worked the trade had been booked through the middle of August.[52]

At Wrangell the curio trade early on became an important segment of the local economy.

> With all its rickety appearance there was no small amount of business doing in Wrangell [Lt. Frederick Schwatka reported when he arrived at that location in 1883]. No less than four or five fair sized backwoods stores being there, all apparently in thrifty circumstances. Indian curiosities of all kinds were to be had, from carved spoons of the mountain goat at "two bits" apiece to the most elaborate idols or totemic carvings. A fair market is found for these articles among the few visitors who travel in this out-of-the-way corner of the earth, and when the supply is exhausted in any line the Natives will immediately set to work to satisfy the demand.[53]

At Sitka the situation was the same. "The curio craze had seized them all," the *Alaskan* reported of the tourists who visited Sitka in 1889: "The old and curious handiwork of the Indians of ages ago filled them with delight. The work of the Natives of the present day was highly spoken of and marveled at especially. The engravings on silver bracelets was [*sic*] also most admired. Curios of great age, old stone implements, bones a hundred years old, ancient skulls, in fact, the contents of grave yards have been carried away by the tourists."[54]

The next year the *Alaskan* described the Tlingit side of the transaction:

> Steamer day is salesday in Sitka for the Native women. Along the pavements, on the veranda of the Custom House, at the roadside, and

on the wharf are clusters of women and children crouched on the floor
or ground displaying their wares consisting of baskets, mats, silver
bracelets, silver spoons, goat horn and wooden spoons, moccasins, small
boats, paddles, totems, grotesque figures, and a great variety of mytho-
logical curiosities which are eagerly purchased by tourists as souvenirs
of their visit to Alaska.[55]

At the core, the curio trade was a cross-cultural admiration society:
white tourists gave Indians money in order to acquire items of Indian
manufacture, and the Indians then paid the money to white traders in
order to acquire items of American and European manufacture. The most
detailed description of the trade was recorded by the travel writer Eliza
Ruhamah Scidmore, who toured the Inside Passage in 1883 on the *Ancon*
and repeated the trip the following summer on the *Idaho*.

When the *Ancon* stopped at Cape Fox, Scidmore found that the prices
the Indians working at the Kinney Brothers cannery charged were so high
that "even the most insatiate and abandoned curio-buyers made no pur-
chases."[56]

Indian women selling baskets and curios at Sitka.
CASE & DRAPER COLLECTION PCA 39-777, ALASKA STATE LIBRARY.

The *Ancon's* stop at Kasaan, a village on the eastern shore of Prince of Wales Island, was more productive. By the time the passengers debarked and walked to the village, the salesmen had their wares on display. "An old blind man, with a battered hat on his head and a dirty white blanket wrapped around him, sat before one bark hut, with a large wooden bowl filled with carved spoons made from the horns of the mountain goat." "These spoons," Ms. Scidmore informed her readers, "once in common use among all these people, are now disappearing, as the rage for the tin and pewter utensils in the traders' stores increases."[57]

Most of the *Ancon's* passengers were amateur collectors who

> found themselves worsted and outgeneralled on every side in this rich market of Kasaan by a Juneau trader, who gathered up the things whole-sale, and, carrying them on board, disposed of them at a stupendous advance. "No more spoon," said the old blind chief as he jingled the thirteen dollars that he had received from this trader for his twenty beautifully carved spoons, and the tourists who had to pay two dollars a piece for these ancestral ladles echoed his refrain and began to see how profits might mount up in trading in the Indian country.[58]

"In the stores the curio departments are well stocked," Scidmore reported from Wrangell, "with elaborately carved spoons made of the black horns of the mountain goat; with curiously-fashioned halibut hooks and halibut clubs; with carved wooden trays and bowls, ... [and] with stone pipes and implements handed down from that early age."

Outside the stores, Indians marketed their wares directly to tourists who wandered through the Indian village searching for bargains. "In all the houses the Indians went right on with their breakfasts and domestic duties regardless of our presence," Scidmore reported somewhat wonderingly. "The white visitors made themselves at home, scrutinized and turned over everything they saw with an effrontery that would be resented, if indulged in in kind by the Indians."[59]

At Juneau, the site of a recent gold strike and the *Ancon's* next port of call, the hustle was the same. As Scidmore subsequently described the scene,

> Indian women crouched on the wharf with their wares spread before them, or wandered like shadows about the ship's deck, offering baskets and mats woven of the fine threads of the inner bark and roots of the cedar, and extending arms covered with silver bracelets to the envious gaze of their white sisters. There was no savage modesty or simplicity about the prices asked, and their first demands were

Indian women selling baskets and curios at Douglas, a mining town across Gastineau Channel from Juneau. ANCHORAGE MUSEUM OF HISTORY AND ART.

generally twice what the articles were worth. They are keen traders and sharp at bargaining, and no white man outwits these Natives.[60]

Continuing north, the Inland Passage Tour included an obligatory stop at Chilkat River. Again according to Scidmore, when the *Idaho* dropped anchor at the Northwest Trading Company cannery and the passengers were lightered to shore, "they made a hasty rush for the Indian tents that were scattered in groups along the narrow clearing between tide-water and mountain wall." The Chilkats stocked miniature totem poles and canoes, pipes, masks, wooden forks and spoons, bone sticks topped with totemic carvings, fish and small toys carved from soapstone, copper bracelets, knives and arrow-tips, granite mortars and axes, and blankets. The blankets, which sold for $20 to $40 depending on "the fineness of the work, the beauty of the design, and the anxiety of the purchaser," were woven from dyed mountain goat fleece. Black dye was made from coal, yellow from a local moss, and blue by boiling seaweed and copper.[61]

When Scidmore returned to southeast Alaska in 1890 to conduct the census, she was startled by the acculturation that the salmon cannery and the curio trade had wrought during the six years since her last visit.

> While living in permanent villages and enjoying trade with the whites ever since the beginning of this century the most astonishing changes have come over these people within ten years [Scidmore reported in her census]. Closer trade relations, resulting from the establishment

of so many canneries, have brought them more in contact with the whites, and they have been almost too quick to lay aside their old ways and adopt others. Wars and uprisings are wholly a thing of the past; witchcraft and slavery have about disappeared; cremation has given way to earth burial; the one lodge with the central fireplace where several branches of one family lived under patriarchal rule, has given way to log cabins or clapboarded and bay-windowed cottages; the blanket is cut and sewed into a fitted garment, and ready-made clothing is the men's usual garb. Government schools and mission schools have taught the young generation, and the mines, canneries, and sawmills have been so many industrial schools for the elders.... It is the Tlingit's aim to dress and live as the white man, and he fills his home with beds, tables, chairs, clocks, lamps, stoves, and kitchen utensils, and even buys silk gowns for his wife. He is no longer picturesque, distinctive, or aboriginal. Even his canoe has cotton sails instead of the old bark mats, and the oar works simultaneously with the paddle. The blanket and the beaver skin are not currency nor units of value.... They have been keener than the whites in seeing the possibilities of the tourist trade and sell their heirlooms and the crudest copies of their heirlooms for fabulous sums. Each year the cedar-bark baskets are more coarsely woven, and the trader's dyes have long replaced their own soft and harmonious colorings. They weave Chilkat blankets of coarse German yarn instead of the silky fleece of the mountain goat, and they manufacture antiques, even stone-age relics, with the shrewdness of Europeans.... The winters are given up to rest, and recreation of milder kinds than of old, card playing, dancing, and other travesties of the white man's ways, delight them. Soon there will be only the color of the skin to distinguish these fishermen, miners, and day laborers from any others around them....[62]

But if, during the 1880s, the salmon cannery and the tour boat, rather than the schoolhouse, were the white institutions most responsible for altering Tlingit and Haida attitude, during the 1890s their influence was overshadowed, both in southeastern Alaska and in Native villages elsewhere in the territory, by the rush for gold.

The gold strike in the Cassiar Mountains actually was located in British Columbia. But in 1870 a modest quantity of gold was discovered on the Shuck River ninety miles north of Wrangell.[63] And two years later gold-bearing quartz was discovered at Silver Bay five miles east of Sitka.

In 1879 a mining engineer named George Pilz built a stamp mill to process ore at Silver Bay. As Pilz reminisced in 1922, just as they refused to allow Chinese to work at the Cutting & Company cannery, "the Sitka Indians would not let me employ any other tribe of Indians to work on the quartz properties near Sitka, though there were hundreds of them ready and willing to work for me at one dollar a day."[64]

However, Pilz found work for the Indians idled by the Sitkans' local hire edict: he taught them how to identify gold-bearing ore and then issued a standing offer to pay for ore samples that proved valuable. "Nearly every tribe brought me some," Pilz recalled years later, "the Chilkats, the Hoonup from Chichagoff and Cross Sound and Icy Straits, the Hoochinoos from Admiralty Island, the Auks from Auk River and present Juneau, the Takoos from Takou and Windham Bay, Schucks from Sumdrum, and different others."[65]

When promising ore samples arrived, Pilz grubstaked sourdoughs (as veteran prospectors later would be called) to investigate the areas from which the samples had been obtained. Pursuant to that arrangement, in the summer of 1880, Pilz sent two down-on-their-luck veterans of the Cassiar gold rush, Joe Juneau and Richard Harris, to prospect the eastern shore of Gastineau Channel, the narrow tendril of sea water northeast of Sitka that separates the east side of Douglas Island from the southeastern Alaska mainland. In August, Juneau and Harris discovered pay dirt on a stream that flowed into the channel from the mainland. They named it Gold Creek, and in October they struck a mother lode in a valley at the headwaters of the creek, which Harris named Silver Bow Basin.

Forty years after the fact, Pilz recalled that he had sent Juneau and Harris to Gastineau Channel because Cowee, the Tlingit chief whose people, known as Auks, lived along the waterway, had sent him promising ore samples. However, in a more contemporaneous account, Eliza Scidmore, who visited Juneau—as the mining camp that sprang up around a small cove south of the mouth of Gold Creek was named—in 1883 reported that "in 1879 the Indians gave fine quartz specimens to the officers of the U.S.S. *Jamestown*, claiming to have found them on the shores of Gastineau Channel"[66] and that L. A. Beardslee passed the ore samples along to Pilz.

Either way, the Auks were responsible for both the discovery on Gold Creek and the Silver Bow Basin strike. And according to Walter Pierce, a prospector who lived in Juneau at the time, an Indian, undoubtedly an Auk, discovered gold on the eastern shore of Douglas Island a short distance back from the beach and subsequently showed his find to a white prospector named Pierre "French Pete" Erussard. Erussard, who staked the location, later sold his claim to John Treadwell, who combined it with other claims to form the world-famous Treadwell Mine.[67]

In 1880 when Joe Juneau and Richard Harris discovered gold at Gold Creek, the Auks lived in three villages in the vicinity of Gastineau Channel, one at Stephens Passage at the southern entrance, another on the east side of Douglas Island, and a third on the east side of Admiralty Island to the north. A second group of Tlingits, known as Takus, lived in four villages along the Taku River, which flows into Stephens Passage below the channel.[68]

Auks had a summer fish camp at the mouth of Gold Creek, but there was no village either on the creek or around the cove about which Juneau soon was bustling. However, when the German geographer Aurel Krause arrived in December 1881, he found more Indians than whites. As Krause contemporaneously described the scene: "Many Auks have settled near the new prospector's town of Juneau where they can work for the whites as diggers, carriers, or woodcutters for fairly high wages of one to two dollars a day.... The Taku have, just like the Auks, [also] settled in large numbers near the prospector's town."[69]

When the Auks moved to Juneau, they pitched tents on the beach between the mining camp and the cove, a proximity that Henry Glass, the captain of the *Jamestown,* considered close enough for trouble. To prevent it from happening, Glass persuaded the Auks to relocate north to the mouth of Gold Creek. When they abandoned the Taku River for Juneau, rather than moving next to the Auks, the Takus built their own village on the south side of the cove.[70] As a consequence, when Eliza Scidmore visited in 1884, she described Juneau as fifty houses "with a village of Taku Indians on one side of the town, and Auk Indians on the other."[71]

When the ownership of the claims staked at Douglas and along Gold Creek was sorted out and the mines opened, stamp mills were built to process the ore, and whites who had been "prospectors" became "miners" and "stamp mill workers" who worked regular hours for regular pay—a sociological phenomenon that quickly transformed Juneau from a rough-and-tumble mining camp into a mill town.

Just as they had congregated during the 1870s at Wrangell, Indians from villages throughout southeast Alaska came to Juneau looking for work that, since not enough whites wanted it, they quickly found. When John Healy, a frontiersman from Montana, arrived in Juneau in November 1885, he reported that most of the miners employed at the Treadwell mine were "Indians and Chinamen" because whites would only work "long enough to get a prospecting stake."[72] The next summer there were new openings at the mine after nativist white vigilantes at gunpoint forced the eighty Chinese who worked alongside the Indians to board a steamship for Wrangell, never to return.[73]

Tlingits filled the vacancies; in 1908, T. A. Rickard reported after visiting the Treadwell Mine that in the big open-cut or pit only Indians are employed, because they can keep steady while perched on narrow benches overlooking the cavernous hole. They work by day only. All the young Indians speak English well. They get instruction at the Silkoh [Sitka Presbyterian] mission [boarding school] and the schools for Natives established by the American government twenty years ago. In the Treadwell mine from sixty to eighty of them are employed. They are mostly machine-men, that is, operating air drills; they work steadily all the year round, and receive the regular wages, $3.50 per shift.[74]

Throughout the nineteenth-century American West, legions of itinerant white prospectors—more attracted to camp town life than to wage work—stampeded from gold strike to gold strike and kept moving west. When they reached Alaska, they kept moving north, first from Wrangell and Sitka to Juneau and then from Juneau over Chilkoot Pass to the Yukon River.

For generations prior to the arrival of L. A. Beardslee and his Gatling gun, the Chilkat Indians had controlled the trade route over the pass, which begins at the mouth of the Taiya River at the head of Lynn Canal. Following the river uphill thirteen miles through rugged coniferous terrain, at the tree line the trail continues two miles up a talus of loose rock to the base of the pass. The last half mile from the base to the summit is so steep that at times the trail appears to ascend straight into the sky up a ladder of boulders so large and a course so vertical that a hiker must drop to all fours to reach the top where, on the eastern side, the trail gently descends across an alpine plateau to a series of lakes that empty into the upper tributaries of the Yukon River.

The first white to cross Chilkoot Pass was a Hudson's Bay Company trader whom the Chilkats apprehended in 1864 or 1865.[75] In 1875 a prospector named George Holt, guided by a Chilkat, hiked the pass to prospect the headwaters of the Lewis River, a tributary of the Yukon, and then returned to Sitka for the winter.[76] Stories about the trip circulated through town, and in 1878 a group of Sitka prospectors attempted to retrace Holt's route. But when they reached Lynn Canal, the Chilkats refused to allow them to do so.[77] And since the army had departed and the *Jamestown* was not yet on station, nothing could be done about the affront.

As mentioned, the following summer the Chilkats' resolve to keep white prospectors from intruding into their territory weakened when they allowed William Henderson and James Strichan to investigate the Lynn Canal drainages. And that fall it cracked when the Chilkat headmen agreed to allow Hall Young to construct "a new Christian town" at the mouth of

Indian packer at Klukwan, the principal Chilkat Indian
village. PHOTOGRAPH BY G. T. EMMONS, NEG. NO. 11216, COURTESY
DEPARTMENT OF LIBRARY SERVICES, AMERICAN MUSEUM OF
NATURAL HISTORY.

Chilkoot River. Several months later, L. A. Beardslee's perspicacious diplomacy persuaded Klotz-Kutch to allow every white prospector who wished
to do so to cross Chilkoot Pass.

But while they now allowed whites to make the hike, since Chilkoot
Pass was their trade route, the Chilkats charged a toll. It was "not very
flattering to one's feelings to be obliged to pay a dirty, greasy, disgusting
looking savage one dollar, demanded in a half threatening manner, for the
privilege of passing through Uncle Sam's domain," Walter Pierce, who paid
to cross Chilkoot Pass in 1884, subsequently complained. "Yet this tribe is
very powerful, and to quarrel with them would make the trip impossible."[78]

Although a useful means to compel whites to acknowledge Chilkat authority, the toll produced little revenue. Transporting supplies over the
pass was considerably more lucrative since their monopoly allowed Chilkat
packers to set their own wages. In 1884 when Walter Pierce crossed the
pass, his packers charged $12.50 per hundredweight. "They had an under-

standing with each other not to pack for less," he complained, but "we had to pay it or do our own packing."[79]

A wonderful arrangement for the Chilkats, by 1886 so many whites wanted their supplies packed that the Indians' monopoly could no longer be tolerated. As John Healy described the situation that March, "The Indians pack from tide water to the head of the lakes, a distance of thirty-five miles, for which they have heretofore charged ten cents per pound, but now I understand that they are charging twenty cents per pound. This may cause trouble, as there will be several hundred men on the trail in the next sixty days."[80]

As Healy predicted, the conflict came to a head the next month when fifty prospectors camped at Haines sent word to Sitka that the Chilkats were demanding "exorbitant sums of money for their services in packing," and by "threats of immediate violence" had prevented the prospectors from hiring other Indians (presumably from Hoonah, the village southwest of the entrance to Lynn Canal) to pack for lower wages. The message concluded by urging H. E. Nichols, the captain of the *Pinta,* "to protect said prospectors and miners from harm, as well as hardships now imposed upon them by said Chilkat Indians."[81]

In response to the request for assistance, Nichols immediately steamed to Lynn Canal on the *Pinta* and anchored off Haines. The Gatling gun solved the problem without needing to be unsheathed by visually reminding the Chilkats of the downside consequences of behavior of which the navy disapproved.

But while Nichols had a clear conscience, one member of the *Pinta's* crew was troubled by the heavy-handedness. A graduate of Annapolis, Lt. George Thorton Emmons was the eldest son of Rear Adm. George Foster Emmons, who in 1867 had captained the *Ossipee,* the navy vessel that transported Gen. Lovell Rousseau to Sitka to oversee the flag raising that transferred Alaska to the United States. In 1882 the younger Emmons began his own tour of duty in the Alexander Archipelago, where he soon developed a lifelong interest in ethnology.[82]

Emmons also liked and genuinely respected Indians. For that reason, while the *Pinta* still was on station at Lynn Canal, Emmons wrote a letter that was published in the *Alaskan,* in which he argued the Indians' case. Emmons began by reporting that when Nichols ordered the Chilkats to stop charging their toll, they had responded that "we make our trail for our own use, if others wish to use it should they not compensate us for our labor? The white man builds a wharf and all who land goods over it must pay." Emmons agreed with the argument but admitted that, because they were Indians, the Chilkats' logic was unavailing. "No one can well deny that in point of justice their claim is well-founded," Emmons conceded, "but law and justice are not synonymous in dealings with the Native."

Emmons also expressed the left-of-liberal view that, since Chilkoot Pass was "their country," "the privilege of packing should be accorded to them" and that, as to the fee Chilkat packers charged for their labor, the prospectors at Haines "had a very indefinite idea of the exact meaning of the term 'exorbitant'" because "$12 to $13 was a miserable equivalent for the packing of a hundred pounds" up a nearly vertical rock face. "If endurance and strength ever earn their wages they do in this case most assuredly," Emmons concluded, and then he predicted that "as soon as these people learn the true relation existing between labor and money their demand will be still more exorbitant."[83]

If they did not appreciate the value of their labor in the white marketplace, Chilkat packers understood the concept of supply and demand.

In June, when the prospectors who summoned the navy had safely crossed over the pass, the *Pinta* returned to Sitka. A month later a prospector named Jack Wade and two of Wade's friends arrived at Haines, where they negotiated an arrangement with the Chilkats to pack their supplies over the summit for $10 per pack. But when the packers and their clients arrived at Dyea, the trailhead at the head of Lynn Canal, the Indians raised the price to $13. When Charles John Seghers, one of three Jesuit priests Wade and his friends had met at Haines and with whom they had agreed to hike the pass, attempted to intervene, an argument was set off that ended when Klamat, the head Chilkat packer, hit Seghers in the face.[84]

Outnumbered—11 whites to 108 Indians—the prospectors and priests retreated inside the two-room trading post that John Healy and his brother-in-law, Edgar Wilson, had opened at Dyea several months earlier. After letting Wade and the Jesuits ponder their predicament for a few hours, the Chilkats announced that they would work for $12 per pack, and the offer sensibly was accepted.[85]

Over the next decade the scenario repeated itself on numerous occasions. In 1896, for example, Harry de Windt contracted with Chilkats to pack his supplies for $9 per hundredweight. But when his freight was moved to the tree line, the Indians raised the price to $12. "[T]he scoundrels knew, as we did," de Windt raged, "how helpless we were up here." Having no alternative practical choice, de Windt paid.[86]

When the *Pinta* was on station at Lynn Canal, however, the Chilkats lost their negotiating edge. After rightly concluding that "there will be no trouble with [the Indians], unless the gunboat now in Alaska waters is hauled off,"[87] in the spring of 1886, John Healy opened his trading post at Dyea for the express purpose of breaking the Chilkat's trading monopoly with the Stick Indians. The shove-aside proceeded with speed, and the following summer Klanot, the head Chilkat packer, complained to J. S. Newell, the new captain of the *Pinta*, that Healy was improving the trail up the pass so that he could charge his own toll. Klanot argued to Newell that "we used to get all the furs from the Stick Indians, but they now trade with Mr. [Healy], which ought to satisfy him without taking our trail."[88]

But Healy wasn't satisfied. When the *Pinta* transported a Canadian survey party to Dyea, Healy hired Sticks to carry the Canadians' supplies from the summit to the lakes that empty into the Yukon. The gunboat's presence allowed the encroachment on the Chilkat packing monopoly to proceed without incident. Healy assumed that what he said now went; and the next spring, when he contracted with a group of prospectors to transport their supplies, he hired Indians from Sitka to do the packing.

But when Healy's new employees arrived for work, the Chilkat packers were waiting, and a fight erupted during which Klanot, the head Chilkat packer, shot the head Sitkan, a Tlingit known to whites as Big Tom. Big Tom, wounded, wrestled away the revolver, which he proceeded to use as a bludgeon to cave in Klanot's skull while a second Sitkan stabbed the Chilkat in the back with a knife. But the victory, fleetingly Pyrrhic, had its own fatal consequence when a Chilkat avenged Klanot's murder by murdering Tom.[89]

The bloodletting reaffirmed that, no matter what John Healy thought of the matter, if prospectors wanted Indians to pack their supplies, the Indians they hired would be Chilkats. But just as the Chilkats tried to leverage their monopoly over the supply of packers to raise their wages, prospectors who needed their supplies packed used their control over the demand for packers to try to lower them.

> According to the ethics of the trail the price for packing should not be bid up [William Laskell, who crossed Chilkoot Pass in 1896, subsequently explained about the ground rules that the prospectors imposed on each other to hold down costs]. If one party put up the price in order to secure quick service, every other Indian on the trail would know it in an inconceivably short space of time, and all would throw down their packs at once, contracts or no contracts. They would refuse to carry for less than the man in a hurry was willing to pay. One man who had plenty of money, it was said, bid up the price, and as a result received a very cold ducking in the creek.[90]

If prospectors thought the Chilkat packers' rates were high, as George Emmons argued in 1886, the service was worth the cost since each packer carried a hundred-pound load for $10 to $13.[91] And many carried more than a hundred pounds. Omer Maris, who crossed Chilkoot Pass in 1896, reported that the loads his packers carried averaged 120 pounds "but thirty or forty pounds more is not uncommon."[92] Maris also reported that one Indian packed a 220-pound organ.

Hauling a hundred-plus pounds for three days up a trail that ends with a half-mile climb up a nearly vertical rock face was exhausting work. And on reflection, even Harry de Windt, whose packers extorted an extra $3 per pack, was awed by the accomplishment.

> I must admit [he reported when he'd finished complaining] that when I saw the crushing weights carried by the Indians and the perilous trail over which they were borne, I ceased to wonder that the Dyea men had struck for higher wages. A Tlingit Indian will pack one hundred and twenty pounds with ease up places where an unencumbered white man would be toiling on his hands and knees.[93]

The situation soon would change. In 1885 four sourdoughs washed gravel bars on the Stewart River, a tributary of the upper Yukon, for $35,000 in gold. The next summer a hundred men were panning gravel throughout the area,[94] and in September gold was discovered on the Fortymile River, which flows into the Yukon forty miles below the Stewart.[95]

Each summer thereafter the money being made on the Fortymile drew more prospectors over Chilkoot Pass. And by May 1895, Arthur Lewin, who was camped at Lake Bennett on the far side of the pass, reported that "about five hundred people are ahead of us and there are four hundred all along the lakes and the mountains behind us."[96]

The increase in traffic frayed the Chilkat monopoly to the point that, by 1895, John Healy and Edgar Wilson were skimming the cream off the business by hiring out a string of horses to pack supplies from Dyea to Sheep Camp, the way station at the tree line. However, since the trail from Sheep Camp to the summit was too steep for horses, the Chilkats maintained their monopoly on the upper portion of the route.[97]

But more and more prospectors packed their own supplies, and in 1897 the hundreds who did became tens of thousands.

In August 1896 a Stick Indian whose white name was Skookum Jim was camped with a Stick named Tagish Charley and a white named George Carmack at the mouth of the Klondike River, which empties into the Yukon above the Fortymile. When Jim stooped to drink from a stream that flowed into the Klondike (subsequently rightly named Bonanza Creek), he noticed specks of gold. After working the gravel several days confirmed that the metal was plentiful, Carmack staked the area and, leaving Jim to guard the site, floated with Tagish Charley down the Yukon on a log raft to the Fortymile to record the claim.[98]

The news that a large quantity of gold had been discovered on the Klondike quickly filtered south, and by May 1897 a thousand whites were camped at Dyea on their way over Chilkoot Pass.[99]

In July the rush became a stampede when the *Excelsior* docked at San Francisco with the first load of miners from the Bonanza Creek diggings, who collectively carried $587,000 worth of gold,[100] a figure that the two major San Francisco newspapers, each of which maintained a telegraph link with newspapers in New York City,[101] inflated to $2.5 million.

Incited by the misreporting, sixty thousand people from cities and towns across the nation, the majority of whom were single men who had been living on the margin in an America that in 1897 was recovering from a national economic depression, set out for Dawson, the new mining camp at the mouth of the Klondike River. Of that number, forty thousand reached southeast Alaska. And of that number, twenty-eight thousand hiked Chilkoot Pass or the longer but easier nearby White Pass.

The Royal Northwest Mounted Police, whose jurisdiction over the Klondike goldfield (which was located in Canada) began at the summit, required each stampeder to bring a year's supply of food and other items necessary to survive the winter, a grubstake that amounted to roughly 1,150 pounds per person. As a consequence, by August 1897 the trailhead at Dyea was gridlocked with freight.

While the Chilkat packers were flotsam lost in the sea of argonauts, the stampede provided enterprising Indians a new profit center. Since the water at the head of Lynn Canal was too shallow for steamships to anchor close to shore, the first problem a *cheechako* (as greenhorn stampeders were called) encountered at Dyea was off-loading his supplies to the beach—a task that, for a price, Chilkats who owned canoes and Chilkats who didn't were happy to perform. According to Peggy Sand, when the steamship on which she and her stampeding husband, Davy, had booked passage dropped anchor at Dyea, at low tide "Indians waded waist deep in the ice-cold water, carrying the passengers and the outfits on their shoulders to the beach."[102]

But like the Stikines when there was money to be made at Wrangell, the Chilkat stevedores, some of whom were pocketing $40 to $60 a day, quickly faced competition from other Indians. When the news of the money that Chilkats were earning reached Sitka, according to the *Alaskan,* it "went through the ranch [i.e., the Indian village] like a whirlwind and in a short time it seemed as if all the Natives in the village were getting ready to start for this new Eldorado, where fortunes were to be made in short order." Within hours seven large canoes with fifteen- to twenty-man crews set out on the 200-mile paddle to Dyea, as did a second fleet the following day.[103]

By fall, thousands of stampeders were packing their own supplies over Chilkoot Pass. But other than how to put one foot in front of the other, *cheechakos* knew next to nothing about climbing mountains, particularly during a winter as snowbound as that of 1897-1898.

During February and March, storms of incessant ferocity made movement up the pass next to impossible. The morning of April 2, when the sky finally cleared, six feet of wet snow were hanging from the cornices above the summit. Yet at first light hundreds of stampeders returned to the trail— until the first cornice broke loose and the snow that crashed down buried three men. When it did, the rapacity that had triumphed over common sense gave way to fear: *cheechakos* turned tail and scrambled down the mountain. But before they reached safety, a second wall of snow broke loose and buried more than sixty men.

Not one of the dead was an Indian. According to Peggy Sand, who was at Sheep Camp that morning, "The Indian packers had warned the people of this danger, telling them that it was especially bad at this time of the year. The heavy snow from the night before obliterated the trail, causing exceptionally hard going toward the summit ... the Indians refused to travel, warning everyone against a possible snowslide."[104] A legendary event in the story of the Klondike stampede, the avalanche did nothing to stem the tide. The dead that could be were dug free, and the living returned to the trail.

All told, the Klondike diggings produced more than $150 million worth of gold. But by the summer of 1898 every foot of ground in the vicinity of Bonanza Creek had been staked. When they reached Dawson, *cheechakos* had three options: they could work a claim for $15 a day in wages, they could lease a claim and pay an absentee owner 20 to 50 percent of the profit their labor produced, or they could move on.

The first year eight thousand departed, most by floating 1,850 miles down the Yukon River to St. Michael, the former Russian-American Company trading post located on an island a few miles northeast of the mouth. There passage could be booked on one of the steamships that made the run to Seattle. According to Albert Brooks, head of the U.S. Geological Survey in Alaska, who witnessed the scene: "In the fall of 1898 there were many small boats at St. Michael which had been laboriously built on the upper lakes and whose crews had traced the whole course of the river without even attempting to prospect."[105]

The next summer the flotilla would expand into an armada. But gold fever had begun disrupting life in Native villages along the Yukon River years prior to the Klondike strike.

In 1887, Jack McQuestern, an Alaska Commercial Company fur trader who first arrived on the Yukon in 1873, opened a store at the mouth of the Fortymile River to supply the new diggings at that location. Within months cabins were built around the store, as well as a blacksmith shop, a sawmill, and a dozen saloons.[106] And just as the Cassiar and Silver Bow Basin strikes attracted Tlingit Indians to Wrangell and Juneau, the Fortymile diggings attracted Athabascan Indians who heretofore had roamed the river valleys of the upper Yukon in small family bands. According to William Greenfield, who toured the mining camp in 1890,

> Around the trading posts at Forty Mile creek there are a number of log cabins built and inhabited by [Indians] the year round, and they fully appreciate the advantages of stoves and clothing from the states. The younger men are more fastidious in their dress than the average white man. They are industrious and fairly enterprising, many of them working successfully at mining for wages paid by the whites, and some are mining on their own account. They make excellent boatmen, poling a boat with skill, boats built of sawed lumber being preferred for river navigation to their own birch canoes. Docile and peaceable, both among themselves and with the miners, they are strongly imbued with the teachings of the English missionaries with whom they had more or less intercourse for many years previous to occupation of the country by the United States. Formerly their chief subsistence was caribou and moose meat, and fish they only used during the summer and fall, but since the arrival of the miners they depend each year more and more on white men's provisions. Obtaining pay for work, they also avoid the necessity of hunting for furs to buy provisions with, as used to be the case in former years; hence the falling off of the supply of furs from that section.[107]

In 1894 a mining camp named Circle City was staked to supply a gold strike that Sergi Cherosky and Pitka Pavaloff, two Athabascan creoles (their fathers were Russians who had traded at the Russian-American Company post at Nulato), had made two years earlier on Birch Creek, which empties into the Yukon below Fort Yukon, the former Hudson's Bay Company trading post at the mouth of the Porcupine River. Although Birch Creek was a major strike, neither Indian benefited. As Pavaloff's sister subsequently explained, "My Brother, Pitka, and Cherosky staked claims but not knowing anything about mining and how to stake claims, they lost all their claims to the white men."[108]

The likely reason Pavaloff and Cherosky "lost" their claims was that they were Indians. In addition to establishing a civil government and authorizing the secretary of the interior to open schools, the Alaska Organic Act that Sheldon Jackson lobbied through Congress in 1884 extended the 1872 Mining Act to Alaska. The 1872 Act authorized "citizens of the United States" to organize mining districts and stake claims. But in 1892 most Indians, including half-breeds like Cherosky and Pavaloff, were not citizens. So if he found gold, an Indian had no right that the law of the United States recognized to protect his discovery.

There were, however, other ways for Natives along the river to earn a dollar. Chilkoot and White Passes were the quickest routes to the Klondike. But until July 1900, when the White Pass and Yukon River Railroad began running over White Pass from Skagway, the White Pass trailhead mining camp on Lynn Canal, the most convenient freight route was up the Yukon.

The Alaska Commercial Company, whose steamboat *Yukon* began traveling the river in 1869 to supply the company's upriver trading posts, dominated the trade until 1892, when John Healy persuaded a group of Chicago investors to organize the North American Transportation and Trading Company. For the next six years the Alaska Commercial Company and the North American Transportation and Trading Company divided the freight business—until Skookum Jim discovered gold on Bonanza Creek. By July 1898 thousands of stampeders were camped at St. Michael waiting to book passage upriver,[109] and by the end of the summer sixty steamboats, eight tugs, and twenty barges, operated by more than thirty companies, were making the run to Dawson.[110]

Except for three or four Alaska Commercial Company traders, between the Alaska purchase in 1867 and the gold strike on the Fortymile in 1886, St. Michael was populated almost exclusively by Yup'ik Eskimos who had relocated to the trading post from one of the surrounding villages. And even after the need to supply the miners who were prospecting upriver transformed St. Michael into a bustling transportation center, in 1890 only 30 of the community's 101 residents were white. According to John Sidney Webb, who landed at St. Michael in June 1897, Eskimos did "all the labor in unloading the vessels, moving cargos, and getting the goods in and out of the huge warehouses," since they were physically present on the job site and willing to work. However, the Eskimos were not a model proletariat. "Whenever a Native has got the particular thing he came for, be it a tin can or a rifle," Webb complained, "he quits work. Even under the stress of his extreme desire for tobacco or tea, nothing can induce him to work more than every other day."[111]

To navigate the river, the transportation companies hired Athabascan Indians, who lived upriver from the Eskimos, to pilot their steamboats as well as to stevedore and fire the boilers. According to Alice Palmer Henderson who traveled from St. Michael to Dawson the summer of 1897 on the *Healy,* "Indians who work on the boats are the village aristocrats, rich, blasé, and traveled,"[112] particularly the pilots, whose skills were in demand. A fact of economic life the Indians understood and were quick to exploit. "[T]he Indian pilots have become the servant-girl problem of the Yukon," Henderson captiously reported, "demanding tremendous pay and increasing privileges."[113]

But Henderson had no need to worry, since whites soon took the jobs. Lt. John Cantwell, captain of the *Nunivak,* the U.S. Revenue Marine steamboat that patrolled the river between 1899 and 1901, explained in 1902:

> In the early days of traffic on the Yukon the crews of the steamers, with the exception of the officers, were almost exclusively made up of Natives, but with the beginning of the new commercial era on the river the more exacting duties and harder work required of the crews of the competing steamers soon caused the indolent and pleasure-loving Natives to be driven out of this field of employment and their places were filled by white men. At the present time no Natives are employed on the river steamers except in the capacity of pilots, and even as such they are not satisfactory, and their services are being dispensed with as soon as white men can be found with a sufficient knowledge of the river channels to take their place.[114]

The river traffic also started a lively curio trade. At St. Michael the Eskimos sold carved walrus ivory for what Alice Henderson described as "big prices."[115] But Anvik, the Athabascan village 457 miles up the Yukon, was "the best place on the river for curios." However, after browsing the inventory, Henderson was incensed that the prices had increased since her visit the previous year, a change for which she blamed a San Francisco florist who purportedly had purchased one thousand birch baskets.[116]

The river traffic also created other opportunities for Native employment. Most steamboats fired their boilers with wood, on average $15,000 worth on the round trip between St. Michael and Dawson at $8 per cord.[117] To satisfy the demand on the lower river, Eskimos corded driftwood that the ice that floated downriver each spring left littered along the shore. And according to Cantwell, the Yup'iks understood the concept of supply and demand as well as Chilkat packers and Anvik basket makers.

> During the summer of 1901 [Cantwell reported to his superiors] a number of steamers were unexpectedly delayed at the mouth of the [Andreafski] river [120 miles above the mouth of the Yukon] by the presence of ice in the harbor of St. Michael where they were bound. Fuel became somewhat scarce before the opening of navigation, and the thrifty Eskimos met the increased demand for wood by steadily increasing the price for what they had on hand. The original price per cord had been fixed at $8, but when they learned that some of the vessels were short it gradually rose until it reached $45 per cord![118]

As late as 1900, Indians sold wood at Nulato, the former Russian-American Company trading post on the middle portion of the river.[119] However, since there was money to be made, Indian woodcutters, like the Indian steamboat crews, were pushed out of the business. As Cantwell reported in 1902, "Very little wood is now cut by the Natives of the interior for sale. The more energetic white man has almost entirely driven the indolent and easy-going Native from the field."[120]

But if anyone could cut wood, only Natives possessed the skill to provide food. According to Alice Henderson, when the *Healy* entered the Yukon and began moving upriver, the vessel was approached by two Eskimos who, paddling their kayaks alongside, "brought strings of duck, wild goose, and other game from the flats about us to sell to the boat."[121]

The following summer, on the *Leah's* run to Dawson, the passengers dined on king salmon that the cook purchased from Native fishermen for twenty-five cents per fish. And in October 1900, Lt. Cantwell reported that his crew was "almost entirely dependent upon the Native men for our supply of moose meat"[122] and that the Indians sold the *Nunivak* whitefish for twenty-five cents per pound.[123] Cantwell also reported that "caribou, deer, and bear meat is brought into the [mining] settlements [along the Yukon] by the Indians for sale to the whites regularly throughout the winter" and that "grouse of several varieties and ptarmigan are also shot and trapped in large numbers by the Natives and sold at very reasonable prices."[124]

The fur trade that had been conducted since Russian-American Company traders first pushed up the river had been conducted by barter, but the Bureau of Education and mission schools and the steamboat traffic taught Natives who lived along the Yukon about money. According to Alice Henderson, "Almost everybody I met in Alaska opposed the missions to the Indians. Miners said that they lost all their virtue and gained all the white vices the minute they could read. But I think the main objection was ... that they now understood the value of money, and had raised their prices for work and sales. Only a year ago, they cared nothing for money, it was only barter with them."[125]

Cantwell independently vouched for the change of attitude: "[The Natives] understand the use of money, and in disposing of their wares they usually demand a part at least of the purchase price in cash. Apparently this desire to handle money is not for the purpose of hoarding it, for as a general thing they end in spending the last cent they have obtained from the trader before leaving the store."[126]

In addition to reconfiguring the local economy, the river traffic had a calamitous social consequence. Prior to the stampede to the Klondike, cabins, boats, and supply caches routinely were left untended. While it is dangerous to generalize about the behavior of any group of people, the safety of private property along the river can be attributed to the honesty of an indigenous people uncorrupted by dealings with whites. As Alice Henderson explained in 1897,

> The Indians of the Yukon, though all Tinnehs, are divided into many classes, speaking entirely different languages. But in their astonishing honesty they are as one. You might leave valuables with them for years, articles, I mean, considered valuable by them, even a rifle, beloved of their barbarian hearts, and you would find them intact to a pin upon your return, unless they might have learned to steal from some "civilized" man. This absolute honesty is very strange among a people without laws either of God or man. A man who has hired large numbers of Yukon Indians for years told me that he had never had but one case of theft, although nothing was watched. One of his crew stole a ham. He said nothing to the offender, but simply sent ahead a runner to the Indian's village, where he informed the tribe of the theft. When the boat reached the hamlet, the thief was put off. That was his sole punishment. When the boat returned the poor fellow rushed aboard and begged piteously to be allowed to earn the ham a dozen times. He was completely ostracized by the village, his own wife wouldn't speak to him. He was taken back, and upon ample restitution, word was sent to his village that the Indian had atoned. When a new boat was being built at St. Michael, the Natives, Eskimo these, carefully picked up the nails dropped by the carpenters and returned them, though they were highly pleased if given some.[127]

But Eden never lasts. When word reached Dawson at the beginning of the winter of 1899-1900 that gold had been discovered at Cape Nome on the southern coast of the Seward Peninsula, northwest across Norton Sound from St. Michael, Lt. Cantwell watched the "advance guard of the army of travelers bound for the new gold fields of Nome" trudge downriver past the *Nunivak's* winter moorage at the mouth of Dall River above Rampart City, a mining camp on the middle Yukon.[128] The main force quickly followed.

In January 1900, C. A. Booth, the commander of the army post at Fort Gibbon below Tanana,* reported that, "a few whitemen have passed here on the ice in route to Cape Nome."[129] Two months later he amended his report to note: "There appears to be a stampede from the upriver country to Cape Nome as parties of men varying from two to twenty per day pass downriver on the ice."[130]

In the spring, when the ice went out, the stampeders built boats. Again according to Cantwell,

> Hundreds of small boats, scows, and rafts were now daily seen on their way down stream, filled with men and women of all classes and nationalities bound for Nome or other places from which reports of new gold discoveries had spread to tempt them into making the long, wearisome journey. As we made our way slowly down the river these adventurous parties were constantly being overhauled, and hardly a day passed that we were not called upon to render assistance to some wrecked or stranded party, or to settle some question of disputed ownership of property between discontented and quarreling travelers. It was not unusual to see, floating down the river side by side, the two ends of a boat which had been cut into equal parts and patched up so as to afford transportation to both portions of some disputed party which had taken this novel and heroic means of settling its differences. Most of the boats were constructed in the crudest manner and loaded to the guards with everything likely to be of value or profit in a mining camp. Boats and rafts, piled high with shovels, picks, stoves,

---

* While it periodically sent expeditions north to reconnoiter the terrain, between 1877 and 1897 the army did not station troops in Alaska until February of the latter year, when soldiers were sent to Dyea and Wrangell to maintain order after large numbers of prospectors who had heard the word-of-mouth news that gold had been discovered on the Klondike began arriving at those locations. In September 1897, Lt. Col., later Gen., George Randall and a small detachment of troops established Fort St. Michael on the island of the same name above the mouth of the Yukon River. In 1899 forts were built and garrisoned upriver at Rampart, below the mouth of the Tanana; Circle, the mining camp that supported the Birch Creek diggings; and Eagle on the Canadian border. The same year, troops also were sent to Nome.

clothing, food supplies, etc., in the midst of which, perhaps, an assort-
ment of restless and hungry dogs gave vent to their discontent in
lugubrious howls; scow loads of horses gazing wistfully at the green
shores, with now and then a lonely cow or beef cattle, worried and
stung night and day by clouds of vicious mosquitos, floated by us on
the placid surface of the mighty river, all bound for that distant land of
promise and prospective wealth, Nome.[131]

As they descended the Yukon, the stampeders vandalized caches and
cabins and stole dogs. "In the majority of cases the animals are enticed
away from their owners by travelers who pass by the Indian settlements on
their way up or down the river," Cantwell reported, "and before any action
by the authorities is possible all trace of the theft has disappeared."[132] The
theft of boats was the same: "When the river opens in the spring many of
the travelers by sled are left without means of continuing their journey, and
much complaint is heard of the loss of small boats."[133]

The rush to Nome also had a pestilential consequence. In June 1900
smallpox broke out at St. Michael,[134] and on July 3 every steamship that
docked was quarantined. But while no new smallpox cases were reported,
measles and influenza swept through the Eskimo village.

In July when R. G. Obert, the army surgeon stationed at St. Michael,
visited an Eskimo fish camp seven miles northeast of the port, he found a
family, six of whom were children, debilitated by disease. According to
Obert, "A wife and one son were lying dead and unburied in a separate
tepee, a short distance removed, surrounded by a litter of young puppies
and the older dogs of the family." Only one person in the camp could care
for herself. "The father was in a precarious condition, unable to be moved
to the launch, and will in all probabilities succumb," he reported. "The
older son 'Dan' was breathing at a rate of about thirty per minute, the lungs
being completely congested; the girl was in a state not much better, while
the younger children, including a nursing babe, were afflicted with an incessant cough."[135]

By early August thirty Eskimos in the vicinity of St. Michael were dead,
and according to James White, the doctor on board the *Nunivak,* "Many
bodies were found out on the tundra and along the beaches unburied."[136]

In July, Gen. George Randall, who commanded the Military District of
North Alaska from his headquarters at St. Michael, had been informed that
the Eskimos who lived at the mouth of the Yukon River were sick and that
those who survived would starve during the winter because they were too
weak to fish for salmon during the summer. In response to the emergency,
Randall ordered his quartermaster to purchase food and clothing from the
local trading companies for Lt. Cantwell to distribute along the river.

When Cantwell and the *Nunivak* arrived at the first village at the river mouth, the eleven Eskimos alive were out of food, and six others were dead. Moving on, "night and day we pushed on up the river," Cantwell reported, "visiting every Native camp where signs of life could be observed, and everywhere the same condition of suffering and distress was found to exist.... In many cases the corpses of those who had died were left entirely unburied in the tents because there was no one strong enough to perform the work of burial."[137]

At Pitkas Point, a hundred miles upriver, of the sixty-five Eskimos alive in the village all were sick, and twelve others were dead. At Dogfish village, twenty of twenty-seven residents were dead, several of whom had been unearthed from shallow graves by dogs that fed on the corpses. At Holy Cross mission, fifty-seven Natives were dead and every Native alive was sick. According to one of the priests, 62 of the 130 Natives who lived in the vicinity and 12 of the 80 children who boarded at the mission school had died.[138]

At the next village 150 were ill, and 37 dead.[139] Cantwell recorded a similar count at every fish camp and village for a thousand miles upriver to the *Nunivak's* winter moorage at Dall River.

But death did not stop with the *Nunivak*. On August 20, G. B. Twinehart, who reconnoitered the situation from the deck of the *St. Sarah* as far upriver as Circle, wrote Gen. Randall that: "On my way up the river I have inquired somewhat closely into the conditions of the Indians and find that the reports to the effect that they are dying in great numbers have not been exaggerated, and I find further that owing largely to the sickness practically no provision has been made to lay in their usual winter food."[140]

South of the Yukon River, the villages along the Kuskokwim River had the same body counts. "Where last summer I had about eight hundred people under my control," the Russian Orthodox priest at Chauthbaluk upriver wrote Gen. Randall in December 1900, "there are not over four hundred or five hundred left at the present time."[141] And downriver at the Moravian mission at Bethel, where fifty-seven had died, Joseph Herman Romig, the first doctor on the Kuskokwim River, described the scene as follows:

> The story is about the same for every village. There were not enough well ones to care for the sick, and in many cases the sick were in serious need of care. The rain was almost incessant and of the kind peculiar to the regions of the Bering Sea—cold and misty. The people could not keep dry; their houses and tents leaked, and the ground was like a wet sponge, for such is the nature of this mossland during the

rainy season. Consequently colds were contracted, increasing the misery due to the influenza and preparing the way for pneumonia. Pneumonia was the real cause of death in a large percentage of the cases. The misery of the people seemed to be complete. They were cold, they were hungry and thirsty and sick, with no one to wait on them. The dead remained for days in the same tent with the living, and in many cases they were never removed. Those that recovered left the tent to fall on the dead as the only covering for the remains of relatives and friends. Children cried for food, and no one was able to give it to them. At one place some passing strangers heard the crying of children, and upon examination found only some children left with both parents dead in the tent. Thus the story continues from the source to the mouth of the river.[142]

North of the Yukon River, the Eskimos who lived on the Seward Peninsula fared no better. As it is today, in 1900 the Seward Peninsula, a 200-mile-long, 100-mile-wide finger of tundra-covered permafrost that juts west from the body of the Alaska mainland toward Siberia, was occupied by Inupiaq Eskimos. While the winters are long and the environment harsh, the Inupiat provided for their sustenance by hunting, fishing, and gathering. But by 1898 when gold was discovered at Cape Nome, almost half a century of bad behavior by white whalers had dislocated the subsistence economy and disrupted the traditional culture that had evolved from Inupiat hunting, fishing, and gathering.

In 1845, Thomas Welcome Roys, captain of the American whaling bark *Josephine,* who was recuperating from an injury at Petropavlovsk, a Russian military post on the Kamchatka Peninsula, was told by a Russian officer about the whales he had observed north of Bering Strait. His curiosity piqued, when he returned to Sag Harbor, New York, his home port, Roys began reading accounts of arctic exploration and soon was convinced that the waters north of Bering Strait were an untapped whaling ground. However, since venturing into an uncharted sea littered with pack ice was risky business for the New England investors who financed whaling voyages and terrifying for the crews that manned them, Roys made no mention of his theory prior to departing Sag Harbor in command of the whaling bark *Superior* in 1847. But when whaling in the South Atlantic and western Pacific produced no great success, in 1848, Roys turned the *Superior* toward Bering Strait.

Roys's first attempt to navigate the strait ended in failure when his crew, terrified of the pack ice, forced its captain to turn back south of St. Matthew Island. Roys's second try was successful, but barely. As the *Superior* rode the current of a windless sea north between East Cape, Siberia, and

Cape Prince of Wales, Alaska, seven walrus-skin boats called umiaks, each manned by forty Inupiat, were sighted cutting through the water toward the ship. With the exception of a revolver that, according to Roys, "would not go unless you threw it," Roys and his crew were unarmed. However, the wind picked up, and the *Superior* disappeared into the weather before the Eskimos paddled close enough to make their intentions known.[143]

Rejecting renewed objections from his crew, Roys kept the *Superior* on course through the strait and into the Chukchi Sea, where the vessel soon was surrounded by large, docile whales. The chase boats were lowered, and the destruction of the bowhead whale population of the Arctic Ocean began. In October the *Superior,* its hold brimmed with whale oil, sailed into the harbor at Honolulu, where an article describing Roys's success subsequently was published in the local newspaper. The word now out, by 1850 more than two hundred whaleships were whaling north of Bering Strait.

Between 1848 and the demise of the commercial whaling industry in 1915, American whalers killed more than 21,000 bowheads.[144] They also killed more than 148,000 walrus[145] for both their ivory and their blubber (blubber from an average walrus rendered twenty pounds of oil). Over 134,000 of that number were shot between 1867 and 1880. The consequence? Henry Woolfe, a veteran whaler, reported in 1890:

> To write at this date upon the killing of walrus would be absurd. The huge, obese beast is now almost extinct in Arctic Alaska, and where in former years herds of these animals might be seen covering the floating ice pack today it is a rarity to see one. To the whaleman belongs the obloquy of having slaughtered the walrus by thousands for their tusks. Now the Natives along the coast from Point Hope to Point Barrow consider it a very lucky catch to shoot ten walrus during the season, where formerly five hundred to six hundred were obtained. The King Island and Diomede people still secure from fifty to sixty walrus yearly, but the supply becomes smaller every season.[146]

Eskimos on the west coast of the Seward Peninsula, in the vicinity of Bering Strait, and on Saint Lawrence, King, and the Diomede Islands in the middle of the strait, depended on walrus meat for food, used walrus skin to make clothing and tent and boat covers, and carved walrus ivory into utensils and ornaments. But just as the Tlingits hunted sea otters and caught salmon for the Bostons and the canneries, the Inupiat enthusiastically participated in the whaleship fleet's destruction of the walrus herds and bowhead whales on which their traditional way of life depended. John Bockstoce, the authoritative historian of the Alaska commercial whale fishery, has described their involvement:

During the heyday of walrus hunting in the 1870s a number of Natives
were signed aboard [the whaleships], often with their skin boats, to
help in butchering the animals. In the 1880s many of the ships began
taking several Natives for the season to serve as ordinary seamen and
occasionally as boatsteers. During the 1890s, with many ships wintering at Herschel Island [in the Canadian Arctic east of Point Barrow],
whole families were signed aboard for two years or more, the women
to serve as seamstresses, the men as hunters and dog drivers in the
winter and as seamen in the summer....[147] In a sense, traditional Eskimo whalers became commercial whalers the moment they discovered
that their baleen* was a valuable trade item. Before, whalebone had
been a by-product of the [subsistence] hunt for meat and blubber.
When the Eskimos realized they could trade what had been surplus
for manufactured goods, the whale hunt for Eskimos became a commercial enterprise. In the 1890s, with the industry's pressing need for
manpower, most Eskimos chose to work directly for the [whaling
shore] stations [that had been established at Point Barrow and Point
Hope and several other locations along the coast] or the ships. From
1890 to 1898 whaleships made sixty winterings east of Point Barrow,
and most of the ships carried several Native families to act as hunters
and seamstresses. At the same time the Brooks Range, the great mountain range that traverses northern Alaska, had been largely abandoned
by the interior Eskimos who had moved to Point Barrow and Hershel
Island to seek employment.[148]

Inupiaq employees of the shore whaling stations and the whaleships
annually earned $100 to $250 in trade goods. Eskimos who hunted on their
own bartered baleen, walrus ivory, and furs for what the traffic would bear.
But of the items in the whaleship and trading schooner inventories, the
Inupiat most valued alcohol and breech-loading rifles.

In 1873, Congress prohibited selling Natives either commodity. But
whaleships and trading schooners routinely stocked both. In 1879, for example, George Bailey, captain of the Revenue Marine cutter *Richard Rush,*
reported that that summer eleven ships had stopped at Kotzebue Sound
north of Bering Strait to trade "large quantities of liquor, breech-loading
arms and ammunition."[149] And when the *Timandra* ran aground on Nunivak

---

* Also known as whalebone, baleen is the ten- to twelve-foot-long keratinous
plates that hang from the upper jaw of whalebone whales such as the bowhead,
which the whales use to filter the plankton on which they feed from sea water. A
large bowhead may contain several thousand pounds of baleen. A naturally elastic
material, throughout the nineteenth century whalebone was used to manufacture
corset ribs, whips, fishing rods, and similar items. In 1892 at the whaleship fleet's
home ports in New England, baleen sold for more than $5 a pound.

Island on her way to Bering Strait the same year, her hold was loaded with breech-loading rifles, ammunition, and barrels of rum.[150] So much alcohol was being traded for baleen that George Bailey believed that

> one of the principal causes of the improvidence of the north coast Indians, and their neglect to provide food for winter, is the demoralizing effects of rum sold by the arctic traders. It is reported that it is sold in such large quantities as to keep whole villages drunk and quarreling the best part of the season.... This is undoubtedly killing them off, or causing them to be careless in providing food for the winter, whereby many of them die of starvation.[151]

Bailey's concern about the genocidal consequences of the trade was not rhetoric.

In 1871 thirty-two whaleships were caught in the ice and abandoned at Point Belcher, twelve miles northeast of Wainwright on the northwestern coast of Alaska north of Bering Strait. In 1905 the whaleman John Kelly, a longtime resident of the northern Arctic, reported that when the crews left,

> the Natives boarded the ships, removed the bread, liquor and medicines—not knowing what flour was, they threw it away. Natives gathered from all along the Arctic coast and one grand debauch took place—drinking, howling and killing each other till, like the Kilkenny cats, there were none left. The village was shunned for years by passing natives, who, hearing dogs and wild animals wrangle at night, thought the place inhabited by demons. Twenty years afterward, frozen bodies were still stark and stiff in some of the huts. When the liquor gave out, they took to drinking tinctures and extracts, and when the food supply was exhausted they were unable to reach other villages.[152]

Kelly is not a reliable informant because, although he may have viewed the corpses, it is doubtful that he witnessed the "drinking, howling and killing" he says were responsible for creating them. However, Kelly's conclusion that the Inupiat at Point Belcher starved to death because they were drunk when they should have been hunting is supported by corroborative evidence.

In September 1879 when the trading schooner *Pauline Collins* stopped at Saint Lawrence Island, J. J. Nye, the ship's captain, found the three villages on the north side of the island littered with bodies. The Eskimos at Gambell, the village on the northwestern end of the island, told Nye that the dead had starved the previous spring when the wind had pushed so much pack ice so close to shore that village hunters had not been able to reach open water to hunt the whales, walrus, and seals they needed to feed their families.[153]

The following June, when the Revenue Marine cutter *Corwin* anchored off the northern shore of Saint Lawrence Island, its captain, C. L. Hooper, "found the [first] village entirely deserted, with sleds, boat-frames, paddles, spears, bows and arrows, etc., strewn in every direction." At the second and third villages, both deserted, Hooper discovered sixty-six bodies and many fresh graves. And at Gambell, two hundred of the village's five hundred residents were dead.[154]

The Eskimos at Gambell told Hooper the same story they had told Nye—that the deaths were a consequence of starvation that had occurred in the spring of 1879 when ice conditions prevented villagers from hunting. But even assuming so, Hooper theorized, the dead could have avoided their fate.

> [The Eskimos on St. Lawrence Island] live directly in the track of vessels bound into the Arctic Ocean for the purpose of whaling or trading [the Revenue Marine captain subsequently reported]. [T]hey subsist upon whales, walrus, and seals, taking, as already stated, only so much as is actually needed for their immediate wants, never providing for the future. They make houses, boats, clothing, etc., of the skins of walrus and seals, and sell the bone and ivory to traders for rum and breech-loading arms. So long as the rum lasts they do nothing but drink and fight. They had a few furs, some of which we tried to buy to make Arctic clothing, but, notwithstanding their terrible experience in the past, they refused to sell for anything but whiskey, breech-loading rifles, or cartridges.[155]

The next spring the naturalist John Muir's experience at Gambell paralleled Hooper's:

> On the morning of the twenty-eighth [of May 1881] we came to anchor near an Eskimo village at the northwest end of St. Lawrence Island. It was blowing and snowing at the time, and the poor storm-beaten row of huts seemed inexpressibly dreary through the drift. Nevertheless, out of them came a crowd of jolly, well-fed people, dragging their skin canoes, which they shoved over the rim of standard ice that extended along the shore, and soon they were alongside the steamer, offering ivory, furs, sealskin boats, etc., for tobacco and ammunition. There was much inquiry for beads, molasses, and most of all for rum and rifles, though they willingly parted with anything they had for tobacco and calico. After they had procured a certain quantity of

these articles, however, nothing but rifles, cartridges, and rum would induce them to trade. But according to American law, these are not permitted to be sold.[156]

Whether or not alcohol caused the tragedy on Saint Lawrence Island is a question that has no definitive answer. Whaling historian John Bockstoce discounts the possibility.[157] "Even if an extraordinarily large amount of alcohol had been traded to the Natives," Bockstoce has argued, "it is difficult to believe that the quantity would have been sufficient for them to remain crippled from the effects of drink all winter."[158]

But the Eskimos on the northern coast of Saint Lawrence Island did not have to stay drunk all winter. If whale and walrus hunting had been good the previous fall and, as a consequence, Eskimos on the northern coast of Saint Lawrence Island had large amounts of baleen and ivory to barter when a whaleship or trading schooner stopped to trade, an entire ship's hold of alcohol might have been exchanged for the Eskimos' inventory. If that is what occurred, and if, as a consequence, hunters in villages on the northern coast of Saint Lawrence Island stayed drunk long enough for the villages' food supplies to have been consumed; and if then, when they sobered, the wind jammed the pack ice onto the beach, famine would have been the consequence.

The supposition is consistent with a contemporaneous description of the havoc alcohol wrought at Gambell. In 1894, Vene Gambell, who had been recruited by Sheldon Jackson to open a Bureau of Education school, arrived in the village that would be named in his honor after he and his wife and daughter drowned in a shipwreck.

> During the second and third winters my wife and I often spoke of what a peaceable village it was, and how few quarrels and altercations occurred [Gambell wrote]. [T]he tribe was like one large, harmonious family. Uniform kindness and good humor seemed to be the rule of life. The supply of food was sufficient in these years, and everybody seemed quite content. Wherein, do you suppose, lay the secret of such marked good-fellowship and peace, and why was this hamlet of semi-savage Mahlemuits, wholly unprovided with police courts, lawyers, or laws of any sort, more peaceful than any civilized village in our own country? It was because no intoxicants could be procured. There were none on the island.

In the fall of 1897, Gambell's peace was shattered when a whaleship put ashore an Inupiaq woman from Point Hope, a village on the mainland north of Bering Strait. The woman's name was Hoonakia.

Three weeks later two children knocked on the schoolteachers' door. Both were crying, and one had a bruise on her face. To determine what had happened, Gambell and his wife donned their parkas and set out for the sod house in which the children lived. Upon entering, they found the children's parents and five or six other Eskimos slumbering in a stupor on the floor. And sitting in the glow of the oil lamp next to a huge basket filled with furs, parkas, mittens, and other items that had been bartered for her ware was Hoonakia.

As Gambell described the scene,

> Suspended over the lamp was a large, sheet-iron can, the contents of which were boiling and simmering with a singing noise. To the nose of the can was affixed a rude kind of gooseneck, contrived from a large, hollow bone; and from this the barrel of a gun projected to one side, passing through a kind of pan which Hoonakia was heaping up with bits of ice. At the far end of the gun barrel, on the other side of the pan of ice, was set a little copper kettle, into which dripped a tiny stream of liquor.

According to Gambell, Hoonakia's knowledge of the alchemy for distilling molasses engendered anarchy and violence: "During the next three weeks the village was in an uproar night and day. One woman was beaten nearly to death in a brawl. A man had been stabbed and a girl, named Taskekia, had disappeared; no one knew where she had gone.... Many of the men had altogether ceased to hunt, and had even exchanged their walrus lances and guns for liquor."

Hoonakia soon was the wealthiest Eskimo in the village. And most important, the men did not hunt until the village's uninvited guest had exhausted her supply of molasses.[159]

Whatever the cause of the deaths that occurred on Saint Lawrence Island, the presence of the Revenue Marine cutter that began patrolling the whaling grounds the summer of 1879 reduced, but hardly ended, the alcohol and firearms trade in U.S. waters. In 1884, M. A. Healy, who succeeded C. L. Hooper as captain of the *Corwin,* reported:

> Owing to the continued and determined efforts of the *Corwin,* and notwithstanding the lax enforcement of the law regarding liquor permits to vessels clearing for this Territory, I am happy to state that the whiskey traffic in northern Alaska has almost entirely ceased. The beneficial effects of our annual cruises are apparent in the changed condition of the Eskimos. Sickness has decreased; the people are better clothed; more attention is paid to their boats; food is plentiful; fur,

bone, and ivory for trade are abundant, and the large number of healthy young children in every village dissipates former fears that the race might become extinct.[160]

But Healy's optimism was misplaced, since the whaleship captains adjusted to the Revenue Marine cutter's presence on the grounds by moving the alcohol trade to Siberia. As Healy less exuberantly reported in 1885, "At Cape Tchaplin (Indian Point) [Siberia] Indians visited the vessel in an intoxicated condition and Omalik (chief) informed us that about fifty barrels of rum were concealed on shore, which had been traded for by his people with American whaling vessels.... All the liquor had been disposed of by the whalers before they enter the United States domain."[161]

Contrary to Healy's initial assessment, the Revenue Marine cutter's presence merely created a new class of Chukchi middlemen who brokered the whalemen's rum to Inupiat from the American side of Bering Strait for baleen and walrus ivory that they then traded to the whalemen for more rum.

The new distribution system had the same disruptive consequences as the old.

Since, as he later bragged, all "the ships used to do it when the coast guard [i.e., the Revenue Marine cutter] wasn't around," in 1877, George Gilley, captain of the schooner *William H. Allen,* traded whiskey to fourteen Eskimos at Wales, the village on the western tip of the Seward Peninsula. The next morning the still-drunk Inupiat paddled back to the *Allen* to demand another drink. When the ship's mate struck one of the Eskimos, a melee erupted during which the mate was stabbed to death.

> I'm telling you those Kanakas [i.e., the *Allen's* Hawaiian crew] went crazy [Gilley told Charles Brower in 1886]. They grabbed axes and spades and lit into the dammed Eskimos, driving 'em forward under the fo'castle-head in no time. And that was just the beginning. Soon's they had 'em cooped up there, they'd yank 'em out with boat-hooks, one by one, and knock 'em on the head and toss 'em down into the oomiak alongside.

Every Eskimo, but one, was murdered.[162]

In 1890, Harrison Thorton, the Bureau of Education teacher at Wales, reported that whaleships still were trading alcohol, their captains having learned nothing from the incident on board the *Allen*.[163] And despite the prohibition on trading breech-loading rifles, Thorton's inventory showed that of 152 guns in the village, 67 were breech-loading.[164]

For Thorton, the combination of guns and alcohol proved fatal in 1893 when three villagers shot the schoolteacher through the door of his house with a whale gun to avenge the homicides that George Gilley's crew had perpetrated sixteen years earlier.

Several months after Thorton and his wife, Neda, arrived in the village, an Eskimo named Elignok, three of whose sons had been murdered during the fracas with Gilley, broke into the Thortons' house, drunk. As a consequence, the two teachers "ate and worked and slept with loaded arms at hand."[165] According to Neda Thorton, "We did not fear the people when they were sober, but feared from the whiskey, for when they were drunk they shot at us, and Mr. Thorton felt the peril."[166]

Thorton was murdered at midnight of the day two barrels of alcohol arrived in the village from Siberia.

But neither Thorton's death nor the Revenue Marine cutter's seasonal presence ended the alcohol trade along the Siberian and Alaska coastlines. In 1902 a Chukchi from East Cape was arrested after an Inupiaq from Wales, to whom he had sold alcohol, stabbed a relative while drunk. At his trial in Nome the Chukchi testified that he had acquired his inventory from a white named Newton (probably E. W. Newth), captain of the whaleship *Jeanette,* in exchange for ivory, furs, and baleen.[167]

And when Inupiat such as the enterprising Hoonakia learned to distill alcohol, the whalers began bartering the raw materials needed to do so. In the winter of 1900 a sourdough named Scotty Allan mushed his dog team across Bering Strait from Wales to East Cape. On the return trip, Allan stopped at Big Diomede Island, where he found the entire village drunk on alcohol that had been distilled from flour, prunes, and oatmeal bartered from a whaleship.[168] When John Kelly visited Wales the same year to conduct the federal census, stills were operating in thirty-seven of the village's sixty-three sod houses.[169] And as late as 1905, E. J. Knapp, the schoolteacher at Point Hope, Hoonakia's home village, urged the U.S. government to stop the alcohol trade:

> Knowing full well the appetite which the Natives have for intoxicants and the value of the pelts and the [whale] bone which they accumulate from year to year to trade with, the whalers come supplied with cheap whiskey, which they peddle out in exchange for the Native commodities they so much covet. The Natives of the Diomedes have from time to time obtained so much whiskey from whalers that they sometimes travel along the north coast of the Seward Peninsula as far eastward as Kotzebue Sound and the surrounding country trading it to others.

> The whaling fleet always arrives in the Arctic before the revenue
> cutter does, and in cruising northward succeeds in keeping the cutter
> a little outdistanced. The whaling fleet usually arrives off Point Hope
> anywhere from two to three weeks before the cutter appears there.
> When the whaling fleet is at Point Hope, the cutter is at Nome or in
> that neighborhood, and when the cutter reaches Point Hope the whal-
> ing fleet is at Point Barrow, and by the time the cutter reaches Point
> Barrow ... the whaling fleet will have gone to the eastward.[170]

The reason American whalers and traders in the northwestern Arctic so
disdainfully ignored the prohibition on bartering alcohol is that the profit
they earned doing so was astronomical.

After being shanghaied in San Francisco, William McIntosh did a con-
scripted tenure in 1905 as a member of the crew of the whaler *Charles
Hanson*. As was routine, prior to entering the Arctic Ocean, the *Hanson*
stopped at the Chukchi villages on the Siberian side of Bering Strait to
barter the thousand gallons of alcohol it had on board, which had been
diluted with water in a ratio of two to one. McIntosh, who witnessed the
scene, described the mechanics of the exchange as follows:

> When his [whale]bone and skins had been brought on board the
> Native was invited into the cabin where a bottle and glass were set
> before him, and in a short time his two hundred pounds of bone was
> bartered for twenty gallons of alcohol, say $10, a box of hard biscuits,
> $1, and a sack of low grade flour at fifty cents, in all $11.50, while the
> two hundred pounds of bone will realize in the eastern market $6 per
> pound, or in other words the captain got $1,200 worth for $11.50.[171]

The trade also had a concupiscent benefit. Again according to McIntosh:

> During the seven weeks referred to the ship was more or less crowded
> with Natives night and day, (at this time we had the midnight sun), and
> a large proportion of them were often girls, ranging from 12 to 20 years
> of age. These young girls were enticed into the officers' quarters and
> into the quarters of the seamen and there debauched, the unfortunate
> creatures receiving for their favors a handful of hardtack or an old
> shirt. These are not mere statements but actual facts of which the
> writer was often an eyewitness.... Some of the sailors who visited us
> from the other whaling vessels informed the writer that their captains
> were never without one to three Natives in their cabins at all times,
> and when they made any attempt to get away they were locked in....
> From information which I obtained from officers of the *Charles Hanson*,
> who had been whaling in the Arctic ocean for several years past, the

same conditions exist on the American side from Cape Prince of Wales up to Herschel Island.[172]

From the Seward Peninsula, where the fleet regularly put in at Port Clarence, a harbor northwest of Nome, north through Bering Strait and then north and east around the Alaska coastline to Herschel Island in the Canadian Arctic, whaleships disrupted the Inupiaq subsistence economy and culture in three important respects.

First, as mentioned, the Eskimos enthusiastically participated in the destruction of the bowhead whales and walrus herds that, prior to the arrival of white whalers and traders with alcohol, breech-loading rifles, and other accoutrements of white civilization, had supported an age-old sustenance. Henry Woolfe described the scene along the coastline north of the Seward Peninsula in 1890:

> The coast Natives abandon their winter houses as soon as the first sign of thaw is visible, erecting tents at convenient spots along the coast where seals can be shot amid the shore and ground ice, and there await the arrival of vessels whose masters are known to be inveterate traders. Off Point Lay, at Icy cape, Wainwright inlet, and Point Belcher are the points of rendezvous for both the Natives and the ships.... Everything in their possession, from large bundles of whalebone to the smallest ivory or bone carving, is brought for trade by these people.[173]

Second, alcohol, and then access to the knowledge and raw materials required to distill it, disrupted family and village relations, provoked constant violence, and too frequently resulted in the death of inebriates.

And third, the sexual contact between Eskimo women and white whalers left a staggering number of Inupiat syphilitic. According to Henry Woolfe, when he spent the winter of 1889-1890 at the shore station at Point Barrow,

> my time was taken up in large measure in treating cases of syphilitic origin, and had it not been for the supply of medicines belonging to a corporation, which effected partial cures in the patients, the number of Natives to prosecute the spring whaling catch would have been materially reduced. The keeper of the United States relief station at Point Barrow was unable to contribute the least aid to the unfortunate of both sexes who came to the station to ask for medical assistance.... The blight bids fair to depopulate the coast, nearly every infant bearing marked indications of the curse, and unless it be for the presence of some white man in their midst, who will administer to their sufferings

as far as he is able, the afflicted wretches drag out a miserable existence until death claims them.[174]

And consistent with Woolfe's assessment of the pervasiveness of the
epidemic, the doctor on board the *Bear* during the Revenue Marine cutter's
patrol of the whaling grounds the following summer reported that 85 percent of the several hundred Eskimos he examined during the cruise were
syphilitic.[175]

Other than at Port Clarence and the shore stations at Point Barrow and
one or two other isolated locations, the whalemen did not establish a permanent physical presence, either on the Seward Peninsula or farther north.
However, within months of the discovery of gold in 1898 at Cape Nome on
the southern coast of the Seward Peninsula, the stampeders who rushed to
the diggings did so in a huge way.

According to Josephine Earp, when she and her husband, Wyatt, arrived
in the summer of 1899, the beach at Nome, where "every conceivable type
of supply was stacked," was a "bedlam," and the town, such as it was, was "a
messy sprinkling of tents and a half dozen very rough lumber shacks."[176]
But by September, when Arthur Wines reconnoitered the site, more than
two hundred frame buildings had been erected or were under construction.[177] And according to Alfred Brooks, who arrived a month after Wines,
except for a few stores and warehouses, "all the large buildings were saloons, dance halls, or gambling houses."[178] By June 1900 the population of
Nome was 12,488, and by the end of the summer 20,000 people were
camped along the beach.[179]

The sudden presence of a bustling new city had predictably baleful
effects on the local Inupiat. The first was the outbreak of disease. On July
2, 1900, Gen. Randall reported to the adjutant general in Washington,
D.C.: "Health conditions at Nome serious: measles, typhoid fever and
smallpox in camp. Eighteen cases latter disease reported yesterday, and
disease spreading."[180]

Just as it had traveled up the Yukon from St. Michael, the epidemic
quickly escaped Nome to ravage villages as far west and north as Wales. As
Frances Kittredge, writing from Nome on July 23, described the situation
to a friend: "there is a dreadful epidemic of measles and pneumonia among
the Eskimos all along the coast. Dr. Kittilsen said the last he heard twenty-
four Eskimos had died at Cape Prince of Wales, and that the percentage of
deaths there was much smaller than anywhere else. It would seem from the
stories as if the Eskimo race was nearly being wiped out."[181]

Toleef Brevig, the Bureau of Education teacher at Teller on the north shore of the harbor at Port Clarence, theorized that whalers who had been infected with measles when they went ashore at Nome were the source of the misery.[182] But whatever the cause, the consequences were devastating. Brevig recorded them in his diary:

> JULY 13—two dead.

> JULY 17—Sekeoglwok brought in his two-year-old daughter and asked if we would care for her. Her mother had died during the night at their place by the reindeer herd.... The little daughter died during the night, but according to her father's wish I administered Christian baptism to her.

> JULY 19—Tautook's wife was reported as having died out at the reindeer herd; and two families came into the station to seek help.

> JULY 20—Three additional families, all sick, arrived at the station. They brought with them a young boy whom they had found alone on the strand. We received him, to be cared for among the many other homeless ones.

> JULY 21—At three o'clock in the morning a woman came with a child in her arms and two little girls walking at her side. She had left her husband in a tent two miles to the east, believing him to be very near dead.

> JULY 22—Tautook came into the mission station with his sick child. He also brought three small boys and two girls, his brothers and sisters. Four of them were also sick. Wocksock's wife whose husband has died, came in with her only living son, Ablikak. Her other son and daughter had died out by the herd.... Two more died in the tents the same day. Three others were reported found dead upon the strand.

And so it went, until

> AUGUST 23—Getaugu's wife died this forenoon. The epidemic seems by this time to have passed its high mark. There are fewer deaths, and those who yet remain, though very weak and convalescing slowly, are able to walk about. During this epidemic, for several weeks we had as many as seventy-two to care for.[183]

The outbreak of disease accelerated the reloaction of local Inupiat to Nome.

> The sick and destitute Natives living within a few miles of Nome and who have been reported as being in great need of food and of medical

attention will be collected ... and placed on the beach at a safe and
convenient distance east of Cape Nome [Gen. Randall's aide-de-camp
informed the commander at Fort Davis, as the post that a detachment
of Randall's troops constructed at Nome had been named]. The Department Commander directs that you furnish them with subsistence
and medical attention until such time as their physical condition will
enable them to provide for themselves.[184]

As a consequence, in less than a month 159 Eskimos were camped on the
beach.

When the Natives arrived a few of them were without food, money or
property of any value. Perhaps half of them had a small amount of
money or food. Several had rolls of bills, the amount unknown to me
[the camp doctor reported in August]. Now it is a common sight to
see Natives playing poker with silver dollars. The army ration provides
them food, and it is their habit to buy luxuries, and to gamble with the
money earned by fishing and trading.[185]

Word of the new fun to be had spread, and each summer from that year
forward, Inupiat from Wales, Teller, Sinuk, Mary's Igloo, Sledge, King and
Diomede Islands, and other Seward Peninsula and Bering Strait villages
sailed their umiaks to Nome to trade furs and ivory and work for wages
longshoring freight or on one of the mining crews.[186] The residents of each
village lived at a separate location—the King Islanders, for example, camped
on the beach east of town, while Inupiat from the Diomede Islands camped
on the sand spit to the west.[187]

Each year more villagers made the trip. In August 1904 the *Nome Nugget*
reported that "a larger number of Eskimo than usual at this season of the
year have congregated in Nome, the majority being camped on the sandspit"
and that many were sick and "in want" because the prices being paid for
their ivory, furs, and curios had declined.[188] The next summer, according to
the *Nugget,* four to five hundred Inupiat were camped incommodiously on
the beach.[189]

As the number of Eskimos who visited Nome each summer increased,
so did the number who stayed. And too many of those who did needed
public charity.

The condition of the Eskimo in and around Nome is too well known
by the people of Nome to need much comment here [a writer to the
Nugget lectured in December 1904]. They have, on more than one
occasion, gone down "in their jeans" so that the Eskimo would not

Eskimo man walking the beach at Nome (c. 1900).
ANCHORAGE MUSEUM OF HISTORY AND ART.

starve in the golden streets of Nome. Even this fall the Rev. Dr. Ryberg
[the pastor of the First Congregational Church of Nome], with the
aid of the people, had to erect cabins and supply them with food for
the winter.[190]

Nome's white citizenry considered the Eskimos a parasitic nuisance. In
August 1901 the *Nugget* interviewed an Inupiaq from Wales who was camped
on the sandspit. When asked why he and his friends had made the journey,
the Eskimo responded that "the people have come to trade because they
have heard so much of Nome from the Natives who have been here and
gone back to their homes." However, when an inspection of the campsite
revealed only a few pieces of ivory and a several pairs of seal-soled fur
boots, called mukluks, the *Nugget* theorized that the real purpose for the
visit was to have a good time. "Day and night frenzied men and women
stagger about the sandspit, making both day and night hideous by their
cries, moans and lamentations," the *Nugget* reported disapprovingly. "These
Natives will stay in Nome as long as they can get whiskey. In the meantime
the fishing season is passing and next winter they will die of disease and
starvation."[191]

The following week the *Nugget* reported that many of the 150 Inupiat camped at one site on the beach had been seen staggering about or lying in a stupor in their tents. And every Eskimo who had been capable of responding when asked the question told the *Nugget's* reporter that they had obtained their whiskey by bartering furs and ivory to whites. "The time for the Natives to catch their winter supply of fish is fast going by," lamented F. H. Gamble, who supervised a Bureau of Education program that Sheldon Jackson had concocted in 1890 to try to transform Inupiaq hunters into reindeer herders. "They have traded all their ivory and skins away and have not enough provisions in hand to keep them two months of the long arctic winter. The proper authorities should see that these Natives are compelled to leave for their different homes for some have stated that they expect to stay all winter."[192]

And initially, that was the how the problem was handled. In 1901 and 1902, Eskimos camped on the beach in the fall were loaded on board the Revenue Marine cutter *Bear* and transported back to their villages.[193] In 1903 the *Bear* was not available, and alternative means were employed to persuade the Inupiat to break camp. Hugh Lee, the Bureau of Education teacher at Wales, for example, traveled to Nome to hurry Inupiat from the village for which he was responsible home to go hunting.[194]

Eskimos who refused to leave were ordered off the beach.

> When Capt. D. H. Jarvis was still in the revenue service [the *Nugget* reminisced in September 1905] along about this time of year, while in Nome, he would visit the Natives' camp, and quietly tell them that by midnight of the next day he did not want to see a Native boat on the sandspit or elsewhere. The Natives know Capt. Jarvis and the *Bear* and the hint was always sufficient. By midnight the last boat filled with Eskimos could be seen moving to the westward.[195]

But each summer more Inupiat returned.

> The shiftless, good-natured Native is getting all of the worst and almost nothing of the best of civilization [the *Nugget* lamented]. Eskimo men, women and children are on the streets of Nome at all hours of the day and night, hanging about the stores and saloons, learning plenty of vice and little good. Under present conditions they are a nuisance to the community and of little good to themselves.... They are tolerated simply because they are good natured and never hostile.[196]

Eskimo women at Nome (c. 1900).
DOBBS COLLECTION PCA 12-29, ALASKA STATE LIBRARY.

The unwelcome visitors were a drain on the municipal treasury. In December 1902 two Eskimo men and one woman died (one of the men was from Port Clarence and the other from one of the Diomede Islands), and two children were burned when an oil lamp set the cabin in which they were living on fire. At its next meeting the Nome City Council was informed that the Bureau of Education refused to pay the children's hospital bill because they lived in Nome and therefore their health care was a municipal responsibility. At the same meeting, the local undertaker submitted a $150 bill for the burial of the three adults, which the council indignantly refused to pay. As the *Nugget* later editorialized, "The City of Nome cannot be expected to take care of every sick or disabled Native who is dumped within the city's boundaries."[197]

Shortly thereafter, C. E. Ryberg, pastor of the First Congregational Church, who previously had been involved in organizing public charity for Nome's Inupiat, struck upon a solution to the city's problem that was a recycled version of the Grant Peace Policy that the Board of Indian Commissioners had invented thirty years earlier to rationalize forcing Indians onto reservations and out of white hair throughout the American West. If

Eskimo children in a walrus skin umiak on the beach at Nome (c. 1900).
ANCHORAGE MUSEUM OF HISTORY AND ART.

the Inupiat in Nome were a nuisance and an expense, Ryberg reasoned, they should be relocated to a place where Christians like himself could protect them from the rapacity of whiskey-peddling whites and train them for future citizenship.

To that end, in August 1903, Ryberg purchased twenty acres of land and a building at the mouth of Quartz Creek, which empties into Norton Sound nineteen miles west of Nome, with money donated by a wealthy mine owner.

> [The Quartz Creek colony] will be a social settlement [the *Nugget* explained] having in mind the moral and mental welfare of the people. It will be an attempt to keep the Eskimo off the streets and to teach the children at least enough to prepare them for citizenship. It is an experiment that will require time, and, of course, money, but one that will doubtless relieve the citizens of Nome, and will help toward a final solution to the problem.... The reservation plan is not always a good one, but it seems the only feasible one with the Indian at a certain stage of his development.[198]

Ryberg explained his own thinking on the subject as follows:

> A fact to be remembered by all who interest themselves in the Eskimo
> problem is that the tribal and village life of the Eskimo has been to a
> very large extent destroyed by the advent of the white man. The miner
> uses all their driftwood, fills the salmon rivers with a muddy silt, wrongs
> the wives and daughters of happy Native homes, and, most of all, gives
> them all the "hootch" [i.e., liquor] they want.... This destruction of
> the old settlements between St. Michael and Kotzebue Sound has cre-
> ated a homeless, improvident, roaming class of Natives that naturally
> drift to Nome and the other camps along the coast. They spend their
> summers making and selling curios and trinkets, and consequently the
> long winter finds them without food, clothing and proper shelter. Many
> live in a small tent all winter. Often they would come to the parsonage
> at midnight and ask for a blanket because they were too cold to sleep.
> This roaming, homeless class is constantly increasing and is becoming
> a serious menace to the rest of the Natives, because of crime and
> disease. When the poor Natives come to us at Nome, sick, starving,
> dying, we find it hard to take care of them. The city authorities will do
> nothing, because they say it is the duty of the government. The hospi-
> tal will not take them because they have no money. One poor Native
> boy watched over the corpse of his dead mother two days and two
> nights to keep the dogs from eating her, until finally the city authori-
> ties decided to bury her as a city charge. The military authorities have
> strict orders to do as little as possible for the Natives. The federal
> authorities can do nothing. Therefore the needy Natives are forced
> upon individual charity. The struggling pioneers of Northwestern Alaska
> should not be required to take up the heavy burden of the helpless
> Eskimo in addition to the burden of the many unfortunate ones of
> their own race. This the government should see to at once and send
> proper relief. Seeing how serious the problem of this roaming criminal
> class of Natives was becoming, I conceived the idea of colonizing them
> at some convenient place.[199]

Nome's white citizenry thought the Quartz Creek colony an excellent
solution to the city's problem. But there was a dissident, a woman who
signed her letters to the editor of the *Nugget* "An Early Settler." She pre-
sciently argued that relocating Nome's Eskimos to Quartz Creek would
decrease, rather than increase, their self-sufficiency.

Originally, the "Early Settler" reminded *Nugget* readers, the Nome Inupiat
had lived in villages scattered along the coastline. Because the communities were widely distributed through the natural environment, the Eskimos
had been able to hunt enough animals and catch enough fish for food and
gather enough driftwood for fuel to be self-supporting. But the two hundred Inupiat that Ryberg wanted to congregate at Quartz Creek would

exceed the ability of the natural resources of the surrounding vicinity to support them. Assuming so, then the Eskimos who relocated would have to be supported by public charity. "Help them through this winter," "Early Settler" counseled, "but let them return to their old homes, where they can make a living and have houses. At Quartz Creek they have very little prospects of supporting themselves, either now or in the future."[200]

The "Early Settler's" advice was ignored, and by November eighty-five Eskimos who had been living in Nome had been persuaded to relocate to Quartz Creek, where William McKnight, who had been hired as the colony's "superintendent," was busy teaching the children English. However, according to the *Nugget*, "All they have to eat is tomcod and a few seals,"[201] a shortfall that McKnight predicted would be temporary. "The Natives are anxious to help themselves," he reported on one of his trips into town, and the Quartz Creek Inupiat soon would be self-supporting. "Just now, however, their trading goods are all gone, having been exchanged for a little grub and forty-rod whiskey."[202]

As a consequence and as the "Early Settler" predicted would be necessary, the hat was passed, and $400 in money and supplies was collected and sent to Quartz Creek; the army contributed 1,600 pounds of food.[203] A month later, McKnight quit and was replaced by Peter Bayne, a veteran whaler of facinorous reputation.

But staff turnover was not the only problem. As the *Nugget* reported in January 1904, when Ryberg returned from inspecting his tundra utopia, "The Natives got the idea that the provisions recently secured for them were to be at once distributed, but they were quickly disabused of the notion. Each is compelled to do something for what he gets, and they are thus taught that they cannot receive provisions and sit down and eat them, and await another supply. They now understand the situation and take it kindly."[204]

Bayne's solution to the problem, Nome's assistant district attorney explained after touring Quartz Creek, was to require the Eskimos to "pile wood, [or] catch tomcod or seal before they can have anything from the mission. The Natives thus get the result of their own work and also provisions if they work. If they do not work, they get nothing."[205] Bayne also put the Quartz Creek Eskimos to work cording driftwood to sell in Nome.[206]

Two years after it began, the Quartz Creek experiment ended when Bayne resigned and Ryberg left town. Nome's white citizenry soon thereafter lost interest in the project, although several Eskimo families continued to live at the site.[207] In 1906 the Methodist Church began a similar experiment in social engineering when it opened a mission and boarding school at an abandoned village at the mouth of the Sinuk River, which flows into Norton Sound seven miles west of Quartz Creek.

By 1909 the Sinuk mission had a population of more than a hundred Inupiat, most of whom had lived in one of the surrounding villages, including Quartz Creek.[208] While several Eskimo families relocated to the mission, most Nome Inupiat stayed where they were, and by 1908 so many Eskimos were underfoot that local Bureau of Education employees flirted with the idea of adopting the Ryberg removal plan as official government policy.

"The authorities have now under consideration the question of removing the Eskimos from the neighborhood of this city in order to save them from the contamination which almost invariably results with the lower class of whites," the *Nugget* reported, as if the Quartz Creek colony and Sinuk mission experiments had never been conducted. "Not only will the Natives who are now here be sent away, if the plans fructify, but all the Natives who live away from the city will be prevented from approaching."[209] But that patently unlawful scheme proceeded no further than talk, since 250 of the 2,600 persons living in Nome in 1910 were Inupiat.*[210]

However, by that date there were not enough whites left in Nome to care. The bowhead whale population had been hunted to near extinction and, with several unimportant exceptions, the gold rushes were over. As a consequence, whaleships had all but disappeared, and the thousands of stampeders who had camped along the beach had long since packed up and moved on. And more would do so throughout the territory over the next ten years.

The out-migration afforded Alaska Natives a respite from the social disruption that forty years of whites settling their neighborhoods without asking had engendered. But the downturn was temporary; by 1910, Alaska's there-for-the-digging-up natural resources had caught the eye of eastern venture capitalists. However, before it could gain momentum, the new wave of white in-migration that their investments would have set off fortuitously was slowed by a nascent national political movement. But if the new political force to be reckoned with unintendedly did Alaska Natives an important service, it was a service for which Alaska Natives would pay a heavy price.

---

* Ironically, over the decades during which Nome has languished in the post-gold rush doldrums, the community has evolved into an Eskimo town—so much so, that in 1971, Congress designated Nome as a "Native village" for the purpose of settling the land claims of the local Inupiat. Of the 3,505 persons who resided in Nome in 2000, 1,789 were Eskimo.

4

Conservationists

In the early part of the century when consevation of our natural resources very properly became a lively national issue, Alaska appeared to be the one area left under the flag where the people's property could be saved from despoliation. Mindful of all the mistakes which have been made here—and for which I for one will readily admit we are just beginning to pay—a great padlock was placed on Alaska. One grievous error was made. No formula was established to unlock that padlock on proper occasions. In their anxiety to save something for future generations the conservationists forgot that a wise policy allows proper use by the present generation.

ALASKA DELEGATE E. L. "BOB" BARTLETT, January 7, 1948[1]

IN 1924 THE HISTORIAN Jeannette Nichols described the previous half-century of muddled confusion over land ownership as "a persistent annoyance throughout Alaska's history."[2] And indeed it had been. On October 18, 1867, when the son of Gen. Lovell Rousseau, ran the Stars and Stripes up the flagpole at Sitka, fee title to all but a few hundred of Alaska's 375 million acres of land instantaneously vested in the United States. While the vesting was a legal fiction, for whites who moved to Alaska during the first years after the purchase it was a lawyer's way of thinking that had real-world consequences since they could not "own" the ground under their houses and salmon canneries and mining claims until Congress enacted laws that authorized the United States to convey its title. But since most members of Congress could have cared less about what went on in Alaska, for seventeen years no such laws were enacted.

The inattention denied whites legal certainty that other whites would not claim the land on which they made improvements or the gold under the ground on which they staked mining claims. And insofar as "fee title ownership" of their village sites and other land they physically occupied was concerned, the situation was the same for Alaska Natives.

From 1865 until the Alaska purchase in 1867 a Russian named Ivan Petroff operated a trading post that the Russian-American Company maintained on Cook Inlet. After the purchase, rather than returning to Russia with the company's other Russian employees, Petroff, an expatriate from St. Petersburg who had earned U.S. citizenship by serving in the Union army during the Civil War, relocated to Washington Territory, where, for reasons known only to himself, he reenlisted in the U.S. Army. In 1868 the army ordered Private Petroff to Alaska, where he was stationed as the company clerk at Fort Kenay, an outpost Jefferson Davis garrisoned on the Kenai Peninsula, close by trader Petroff's former place of business. When his enlistment expired in 1870, Petroff moved to California, reenlisted, deserted, was jailed, and deserted again. While living in San Francisco as a fugitive whom the army didn't care to try to find, Petroff, who had a gift for languages, was hired by the historian Hubert Howe Bancroft to locate and translate documents for a history of Alaska that Bancroft intended to produce.[3]

In 1880, Bancroft sent Petroff on a document-acquisition trip to Washington, D.C., where he made Sheldon Jackson's acquaintance and shortly thereafter joined Jackson and Mottram Ball in their effort to persuade Congress to enact legislation granting Alaska a civil government.

That February, when the Senate subcommittee that had been organized to investigate the subject held hearings on Alaska civil government, Petroff, who followed Jackson to the witness table, urged the senators to include a provision in their bill that would authorize the United States to convey fee title to all individuals—white and Native—who currently occupied particular tracts of land. "If the land laws of the United States are to be extended over the territory," Petroff counseled, "I think it not only just but necessary that some provision should be made to protect those persons who are holding land now in their possession, as far as practicable, if they do not hold too much."

But how much land was "too much?"

"If those in possession of land now were secured in their right to prove up and acquire title to 160 acres," queried Sen. James Slater of Oregon, "that, as a general thing, would cover the acreage of their residences?" To which Petroff responded: "Yes sir, it would."[4]

When the hearings concluded, Sen. Manning Butler, chairman of the subcommittee, introduced the panel's Alaska civil government bill in the Senate.[5] To resolve the land ownership problem, section 7 of the bill extended "all laws now in force for the survey, sale, and other disposal of the public lands" to Alaska and gave "bona fide [white] residents and citizens" a preemptive right to obtain fee title to the land they occupied or on which they had made improvements. Section 7 also provided that "at each settlement in said territory" the "Indians shall not be disturbed in the possession of lands actually in their use and occupation." But in codifying Sen. Slater and Ivan Petroff's meeting of minds, the Native right of occupancy was limited to not more than "160 acres each."

Two years later, when Rep. Melvin George and Sen. La Fayette Grover of Oregon introduced their Alaska civil government bill, section 8 of the bill tracked section 7 of the Butler bill by extending the public land laws to Alaska, with the proviso that "the Indians in said district shall not be disturbed in the possession of any lands actually in their use or possession." However, unlike section 7 of the Butler bill, section 8 of the George-Grover bill did not limit the protection for Native possessory rights to 160 or any other specified number of acres.

Congress's enactment of the George-Grover bill would have allowed whites the same opportunity to acquire fee title to land in Alaska that the public land laws afforded in states and territories west of the Mississippi River. But the same year that the George-Grover bill was introduced, Noah McFarland, commissioner of the General Land Office, the Department of the Interior agency responsible for administering the public land laws, advised Congress that "investigations made during the past year have developed the existence of much fraud under the shield of the pre-emption, homestead, and timber culture laws."[6] If anything, McFarland understated the problem.

For that reason, the senators who served on the Committee on Territories had no interest in allowing laws that were being used to steal public land throughout the American West to be used to steal public land in Alaska. But by 1883 prospectors were panning for gold throughout southeast Alaska, and Joe Juneau and Richard Harris had discovered the Silver Bow Basin mother lode. So S. 153, the civil government bill the Committee on Territories reported to the Senate in December 1883 in lieu of the Grover bill, extended the Mining Law of 1872 to Alaska but not the homestead or any of the other public land laws.

Whether Sheldon Jackson lobbied the committee not to allow whites other than miners to obtain title to the Alaska public domain is not known. But he well may have since, in addition to the disinclination to risk new scandal, the senators justified their decision not to extend any of the other public land laws to Alaska on the ground that doing so would compromise "the rights of the Indians to the land, or some necessary part of it." The report on S. 153 that the committee sent to the Senate expresses the concern:

> It would be obviously unjust to throw the whole district open to settle-
> ment under our land laws until we are advised what just claim the
> Indians may have upon the land, or, if such a claim is not allowed,
> upon the beneficence of the government. These objections did not
> seem to the committee to apply to the proposition to extend the min-
> ing laws over Alaska. We have, therefore, subject to such limitations as
> were necessary to protect actual occupants, provided for putting the
> mining laws in force.[7]

To prevent prospectors from staking mining claims on land that "actual occupants" actually occupied, S. 153 included a proviso that prohibited "Indians or other persons in said district" of Alaska from being disturbed "in the possession of any lands actually in their use or occupation."

When the bill was debated on the floor, the Senate enlarged the protection the proviso afforded, at the urging of Sen. Preston Plumb of Kansas, chairman of the Committee on Public Lands and the same senator who later objected to the Committee on Territories' Native education amendment.

A militant abolitionist who had been born and raised in Ohio, in 1856, when he was nineteen years-old, Plumb had been the leader of the Grisslies, a band of abolitionists that ran guns to Topeka, Kansas, when the free-state town was threatened by proslavery border ruffians. The next year Plumb settled in Emporia, a new town southwest of Topeka, where he published a newspaper until returning to Ohio to attend law school. Admitted to the bar in 1861, the future senator returned to Emporia, opened a law office, and made his first foray into politics by winning election to the Kansas legislature.

Serving as a solon only briefly, in 1862, Plumb resigned to join the Eleventh Kansas Infantry, which saw considerable front-line action during the Civil War. When the war ended, Plumb reopened his law office and reentered the Kansas legislature. He served until 1877, when his colleagues elected him to the U.S. Senate. When he arrived on Capitol Hill, the freshman Jayhawker was appointed to the Committee on Public Lands; he ascended to the chairmanship in 1881.[8]

In 1865 the company of Kansas volunteers that Plumb commanded spent the final months of the war patrolling the Overland Trail mail route that ran from St. Joseph, Missouri, to Salt Lake City, an assignment that required Plumb and his men to fight a number of military engagements in Wyoming and Nebraska against marauding Indians.

His attitude influenced both by that experience and by having lived for more than twenty years on the frontier, according to his biographer, Sen.

Plumb "entertained all the prejudices of the pioneers against [Indians] as a people." But notwithstanding his belief that they were "incapable of any high degree of development and unsuited for higher occupations," as chairman of the Committee on Public Lands, the senator "was always careful to see that the Indians were accorded their legal rights under treaties."[9]

Consistent with that characterization of motive, when the debate on S. 153 began on the Senate floor, Plumb offered an amendment to the proviso that prohibited mining claims from being staked on land actually used or occupied by Indians, to also prohibit claims from being staked on land "now claimed by them." "I do not want to make the condition of things up there worse than they are now," Plumb explained, but "I propose that the Indian shall at least have as many rights after passage of this bill as he had before."[10]

Sen. Benjamin Harrison, who as chairman of the Committee on Territories was the floor manager of the bill, thought the Plumb amendment unnecessary. But since he also thought it harmless, he accepted it.

> It was the intention of the committee to protect to the fullest extent all the rights of the Indians in Alaska and of any residents who had settled there, but at the same time to allow the development of the mineral resources of that territory, if there are such resources, as seems to be believed [Harrison explained]. As the amount of territory that could be taken up under the mining law would be very small, and as the prospectors or claimants under the law could not invade, under this bill, the actual territory occupied by anyone, we supposed the provisions of the bill were sufficient; but I do not care to antagonize seriously the proposition of the Senator from Kansas.[11]

Harrison was as aware as anyone that as the frontier moved west, homesteaders and prospectors and cattlemen had continually "invaded the actual territory occupied by Indians." Thus his assertion that, because the Alaska Organic Act (as the Alaska civil government bill was known subsequent to its enactment) would forbid such trespasses, prospectors would not therefore trespass on land physically occupied by Alaska Natives was perfidiously cynical, hopelessly naive, or some confused combination of both.

One of the most egregious incidents proving Harrison wrong occurred in January 1900 at Erakutserk, a small Inupiaq village on Daniel's Creek, fifty-one miles east of Nome, where four miners who had staked claims near the village were run off at gunpoint by a rival group of prospectors.[12] In their frenzied search for pay dirt, the interlopers then began digging through the permafrost under the village. According to an Eskimo named Katuganah, whose sod house was above one of the tunnels,

> [W]hen the white men first started to dig under my house I was not notified. I warned them not to proceed with the work. They continued, and I was powerless to stop them. I went to Nome for supplies. When I returned I went into all the tunnels to try and stop the work. The white men would not listen when I told them that the house would cave in, but showed me timbers and logs and told me that they could brace the house up with them. After a few days, while we were occupying the house, fires were built in the tunnels and we were smoked out of our house. At that time we were all sick. My brother Orock ... tried to put the fires out by pouring water on them. The white men promised they would put the fires out by and by. This they did, but began firing in the tunnels again after a few days. All the members of the families were in bed at the time. I woke up suffocating and roused the others.... We escaped through the window. When the white men built fires for a third time, we had to quit our house and go into camp on the tundra. As soon as we left our house we all became very sick. One morning I tried to wake my brother Neulano, but he was dead. Some white men had dug a hole just along side of my brother Neulano's tent and thrown the wet dirt against it making the tent floor wet. My brother was then too sick to be moved. I also warned the men who were sinking shafts to stop work, but they told me that they had as much right to sink shafts as the other men had to tunnel under my house.[13]

By the time a detachment of soldiers from Fort Davis, the army post at Nome, arrived to investigate the claim jumping, a second brother had died from pneumonia. According to Lt. H. Erickson, one of the army officers at the scene, both deaths were a consequence of "the exposure attendant to the [dead Eskimos'] flight from their home."[14]

Assuming so, how did the army deal with a trespass so violative of the Alaska Organic Act's prohibition on whites staking mining claims on land Alaska Natives actually occupied? Capt. E. S. Walker, who commanded the detachment, first ordered the trespassers to board up their tunnels. But as Walker subsequently reported to his superiors at Fort Davis, when the miners refused to do so, instead of arresting the trespassers, he merely "advised Lieutenant Erickson to try and collect enough to reimburse the Natives."[15]

To their credit and unlike the army, the clerks at the General Land Office tried to enforce the letter of the law.

Because Congress had refused to extend the public land laws (other than the Mining Law of 1872) to Alaska, the small but steadily increasing number of whites who were settling in southeast Alaska could not obtain ownership of the land under their houses and salmon canneries. As John Healy, the trader who tried to end the Chilkat monopoly on packing supplies over Chilkoot Pass, complained in 1886: "If Congress would only extend the land laws to Alaska, thousands of people would soon establish good homes along the islands and the mainland ... were it so that men could acquire title to lands other than mineral the country would soon settle up."[16]

In response to continued white protests, in 1891, Congress finally extended the townsite laws and authorized corporations and U.S. citizens to obtain fee title to trade and manufacturing sites of up to 160 acres.[17] However, consistent with the concern that he had expressed seven years earlier during the debate on the Alaska Organic Act, Sen. Plumb included a proviso in the 1891 Act that prohibited town and trade and manufacturing sites from being staked on land "to which the Natives of Alaska have prior rights by virtue of actual occupation."

To ensure that the prohibition would be observed, the General Land Office required each trade and manufacturing site applicant to file an affidavit in which he certified "that no portion of the land [described in his application] ... is occupied or claimed by any Natives of Alaska."[18] And when the area described in an application was surveyed, if the survey revealed that land inside the boundaries was used or occupied by Natives, the survey was rejected.

In 1896, for example, the Fort Alexander Fishing Station filed an application to obtain title to 132 acres surrounding the company's cannery on the Nushagak River near Bristol Bay. But when the survey revealed that the acreage included a creek on which residents of a nearby Eskimo village depended for drinking water, the General Land Office rejected the survey.[19]

But no matter how competently the clerks in the General Land Office handled their paperwork, whites continued to stake mining claims and build canneries on and otherwise expropriate Native-occupied land. The usurpations not infrequently provoked violence.

In 1898, R. T. Yeatman, the commander of the army detachment that had been sent to maintain order on the American side of Chilkoot Pass, urged the General Land Office to reject a trade and manufacturing site application that Jack Dalton had filed because Dalton had run a Chilkat

Indian off the land,[20] most probably at gunpoint because the Chilkat tried to regain the property by attempting to shoot Dalton but missed.

According to Yeatman's superior, Gen. H. C. Merriam, commander of the Department of the Columbia, the Chilkat's escalation of the conflict "made it necessary to send a detachment of troops from Dyea to maintain the peace." But Merriam expected more trouble. As he subsequently advised the commissioner of the General Land Office: "The Indians of Alaska, like all the rest of humanity, will certainly resent outrage and robbery, if they are not protected under the laws."[21]

But the Chilkats were not "protected under the laws," and by 1900 the situation had deteriorated to the point that Henry Hovey, Yeatman's successor as commanding officer of the troops stationed at the head of Lynn Canal, urged Gen. George Randall, to whom Hovey reported, to urge the Revenue Marine to send a cutter to patrol the waterway.

> The establishment of canneries along the inland waters has brought acutely before the authorities the question of the rights of the Indians and white men with reference to each other [Hovey wrote Randall]. The Indians claiming that certain inlets and arms of the sea are so exclusively their property that the white men have no right to fish, hunt or prospect in the same.... [I]t is claimed that men who have gone into these inlets, after being warned by the Indians, have never returned. Evidence on this point is conflicting, but the Chilkat Indians, in view of the Horton murder which occurred last fall, and which was concealed until spring, and the fact that others have disappeared, are showing a spirit, when punishment was properly meted out by the court, which indicates an intention on their part to ultimately bring the matter to a focus in the shape of actual trouble.... [T]here is likely, during the next year, to be trouble with these Indians ... Since the active entrance of the white people into this section, the question of supremacy is becoming more and more acute, and must ultimately come to one trial, unless an ounce of prevention, in the form which I suggest, is provided as soon as possible.[22]

But if, when the *Pinta* and its Gatling gun disappeared, the Chilkats tried to reestablish control over their territory, by 1900, Indians elsewhere in southeast Alaska were resigned to whites settling where they wished and exploiting what natural resources they wished to their advantage and at Indian expense.

But they understood the injustice. In 1898 the leaders of clans from a number of villages met in Juneau with John Brady, the former Presbyterian missionary whom President McKinley recently had appointed governor of

Alaska, and Frank Grygla, the Juneau General Land Office agent. For generations, Kah-du-shan, a clan leader from Wrangell, reminded Brady, Indians had hunted fur-bearing animals and fished for salmon. But then the army arrived.

> [T]he business men followed the soldiers [Kah-du-shan explained]. They commenced to trade with our people. Our people did not object, did not say anything to them. By and by they began to build canneries and take creeks away from us, where they make salmon and when we told them these creeks belonged to us, they would not pay any attention to us and said all this country belonged to the President, the big chief at Washington. We have places where we used to trap furs; now the white man get up on these grounds. They tell us that they are hunting for gold.... We know that the white people get lots of gold money out of these places as well as out of the Yukon River. Here at this place as well as other places they take our property, take away ground, and when we complain to them about it, they employ a lawyer and go to court and win the case. There are animals and fish at places where they make homes. We are not fish. We like to live like other people live. We make this complaint because we are very poor now. The time will come when we will not have anything left. The money and everything else in this country will be the property of the white man, and our people will have nothing. We meet here tonight for the purpose for you to write to the chief at Washington and to let them know our complaint. We also ask him to return our creeks and the hunting grounds that white people have taken away from us.

Each Indian made a similar speech. And the longer they talked, the angrier Brady became. "[T]here is trouble ahead for them if they entertain such notions as they expressed here," the governor sputtered when the last Indian finished. And Frank Grygla was of a similar mind.

> Now if it is your intention to class yourselves with the western states Indian it is all right, but I think it is a dishonor to you and against your own interests [Grygla tongue-lashed]. We think the Tlingit almost equal to the white men, but if you do not want to be educated, we cannot help you.... You must decide for yourselves whether you are to be classed as aborigines like the wild men of the west, but do not ask us afterwards what we should do.[23]

The idea that—rather than being sequestered on reservations like "western states Indians"—all Kah-du-shan and his people wanted was a fair opportunity to hunt fur-bearing animals and catch salmon so they would have furs and fish to sell to whites for money to spend to build saw-lumber houses with glass window panes and purchase store-bought clothes from mail-order catalogs was a concept beyond Brady's and Grygla's ethnocentric comprehension.

But the governor and the General Land Office agent were not alone in their ignorance. The idea that Natives should have the same right as whites to exploit natural resources for personal economic gain was a concept beyond the comprehension of most whites. For that reason, whites who came to southeast Alaska to pan for gold, can salmon, and turn a dollar any other way that proved profitable continued to subjugate Native land and economic rights to white advantage—until 1902, when the Tlingit and Haida Indians received unintended help from an unexpected quarter.

In 1868, Oliver Kelly, a visionary Minnesota farmer, organized the Order of the Patrons of Husbandry, a farmers' organization, modeled on the Masons, that also was known as the Grange. Kelly's timing was perfect. During the first decades after the Civil War, homesteaders farming public land in the West and established farmers in the eastern and southern sections of the country had a common interest in organizing to fight the usurious tariffs and other predatory actions of the railroads that monopolized the transport of their crops to market. As a consequence, by 1875 every farm town in America had a local Grange, and the national organization had 761,000 members.[24]

In the West and the South, the Grange's influence waned by 1880 and would elsewhere by 1900. But the Grange left a lasting mark. The idea its members championed—that the public should be protected from the maleficence of private monopoly—captured the national imagination. And a complementary idea of equal moral suasion emerged that by the turn of the century was known as "conservation."[25]

When natural resources located on land owned by the public were developed, conservationists argued, the development should benefit the public, rather than simply line private pockets. As Gifford Pinchot, the second most influential spokesman for the new way of thinking about natural resource development, explained in 1909: "Conservation is the most democratic movement this country has known for a generation. It holds that the people have not only the right but the duty to control the use of natural resources, which are the great sources of prosperity. And it regards the absorption of these resources by the special interests, unless their operations are under effective public control, as a moral wrong."[26]

Pinchot, a Yale-educated rich kid who helped to invent the vocation of forest management and ended his career as governor of Pennsylvania, was the conservation movement's principal theoretician. But President

Theodore Roosevelt became the titular leader of the movement in December 1901, when he included several paragraphs (written by Pinchot and a group of friends) in his first message to Congress that argued the conservationist case to the nation.

The president's precursory involvement with conservationism began in 1883, when he made a hunting trip to Dakota Territory. When his wife Alice died the following year, the twenty-five-year-old widower purchased a ranch in the badlands and embarked on a financially disastrous career as a gentleman cattleman.

In 1885, Roosevelt wrote a book about his adventures in Dakota Territory that George Bird Grinnell, the editor of *Field and Stream* magazine, who had spent considerably more time on the frontier than the author had, disparaged in a review that Grinnell published in his magazine. When Roosevelt presented himself at Grinnell's New York City office to complain, the ersatz cowboy and the editor hit it off and subsequently became friends. The relationship allowed Grinnell, who at his death in 1938 was eulogized as "the Father of American Conservation," to talk up his views on the subject to the future president.

Alarmed that big game was being hunted to extinction, Grinnell, as early as 1884, had advocated the organization of an "association of men bound together by their interest in game and fish, to take active charge of all matters pertaining to the enactment and carrying out of the laws on the subject."[27] Putting the idea into practice to protect birds, the year after he met Roosevelt, Grinnell organized the Audubon Society, which within a few years exploded into a fifty-thousand-member mass movement.

During his periodic sojourns to Dakota Territory, Roosevelt, his thinking about the subject influenced by Grinnell, watched overgrazing by cattle transform the badlands into a high plain desert and watched sport and market hunters denude the range of large game. Increasingly troubled by the ecological destruction, when he returned to New York City from yet another badlands hunting trip, in December 1887 Roosevelt invited Grinnell—together with his brother, Elliott Roosevelt; his cousin, Jay West Roosevelt; and six friends, each of whom was a socially prominent sportsman—to dinner at his Madison Avenue town house.

That evening, between courses, Roosevelt proposed to his guests that they organize a club whose membership would be limited to one hundred gentlemen who were devoted to "manly sport with the rifle" and who would "work for the preservation of the large game" throughout the nation and the enactment of "legislation for that purpose."[28] The idea was enthusiastically received, and the next month the Boone and Crockett

Club—named in honor of its founder's boyhood heroes, Daniel Boone and Davy Crockett—was organized. Roosevelt, whose club after all it was, was elected president.[29]

For the next thirty-five years the Boone and Crockett Club's socially prominent and politically connected cadre of sportsmen exercised a pervasive influence over implementation of the nascent conservation agenda.

One of the first conservation techniques club members helped to pioneer was the land withdrawal.

The idea that private individuals should not be allowed to obtain ownership of public land that contained natural resources of national importance was not new. As early as 1817, Congress authorized the president to withdraw oak and cedar forests from the public domain "for the sole purpose of supplying timber for the navy of the United States."[30] But that delegation of authority was an exception to the usual rule that Congress reserved to itself decisions regarding which tracts of land to close to private entry. In 1832, for example, Congress segregated a township surrounding a salt springs at what is now Hot Springs, Arkansas.[31] In 1864, Congress transferred ownership of the Yosemite Valley to the state of California.[32] And in 1872, Congress established Yellowstone National Park in Wyoming.

But four years after the organization of the Boone and Crockett Club, Congress gave the president unprecedented authority to make land withdrawal decisions in its stead.

By 1877, when President Rutherford Hayes appointed Missouri senator Carl Schurz to the position of secretary of the interior, the brazen theft of timber from the public domain was a fact of every day western life. As Schurz later described his failed effort to end the looting: when he discovered that "enterprising timber thieves [were] not merely stealing trees, but stealing whole forests" and tried "to stop at least the commercial depredations upon the property of the people," he was chastised by western state congressmen "all solemnly protesting against my disturbing their constituents in this peculiar pursuit of happiness."[33]

As a consequence no action was taken, and by 1884 the thieving had become such a scandal that Noah McFarland, commissioner of the General Land Office, urged Congress to protect "all distinctly timber lands of the United States" by establishing "permanent timber reserves."[34] McFarland's successor as commissioner urged the same action; and in 1888, William Steele Holman, chairman of the House Committee on Public Lands, who was as outraged as Schurz was by the looting, broached the idea to his colleagues. But with an important change.

In 1873, John Aston Warder, an Ohio horticulturist, had been exposed during a trip to Europe to the idea that forests should be protected and professionally managed. In 1875 he sponsored the first national conference on forestry, during which the thirty-odd participants organized the American Forestry Association.[35] In 1882 the association helped organize the American Forestry Congress, an umbrella organization that lobbied Congress and state legislatures to enact legislation to protect forest lands. To that end, in January 1888 the Forestry Congress petitioned Congress to withdraw forest lands from the public domain and submitted a bill whose enactment would accomplish that objective. In the House the bill was referred to the Committee on Public Lands.[36]

Groups as disparate as the Fruit Growers Convention of California, the Maine State Grange, and the Pennsylvania Forestry Association also submitted petitions. And in February, when William Steele Holman introduced H.R. 7901—an omnibus bill that consolidated all of the public land law reform bills that had been referred to his committee—section 8 of the bill contained a provision that, as Holman explained on the floor, "protects [forest] lands from speculators."[37]

Section 8 accomplished that objective by adopting a concept the American Forestry Congress had included in its bill: rather than Congress's enacting statutes that established forest reserves statute by statute, section 8 delegated the president authority to "set apart" federal timber land "as public reservations."

While the Forestry Congress conceived the idea, Boone and Crockett Club member William Hallett Phillips, a Washington, D.C., attorney who served as the club's unofficial lobbyist, is credited with persuading Holman to include section 8 in his bill.[38]

H.R. 7901 passed the House but died in the Senate when the Senate Committee on Public Lands refused to report the bill prior to adjournment. But in November, Benjamin Harrison was elected president, as was a new Congress.

Responding to the national anger that organizations such as the Grange had spent twenty years provoking against the abuses of monopoly, in 1890 the new Congress enacted the Sherman Anti-Trust Act. And the next year it enacted a bill that repealed the preemption and timber-culture laws, which, unbeknownst to most members (since it had not been included in the versions of the bill that had initially passed the House and Senate), included a rewritten version of section 8 of H.R. 7901, which, subsequent to its enactment, became known as the Forest Reserve Act.

Who persuaded the six members of the House-Senate Conference Committee to include the Forest Reserve Act in the final version of a bill that the House and Senate voted into law before the text was printed (so most members had no idea what they had voted for) is a matter of dispute. Secretary of the Interior John Noble, a close friend of William Hallett Phillips (who subsequently became a member of the Boone and Crockett Club and who is said to have told the conferees that President Harrison would veto the bill unless the Forest Reserve Act was included)[39] is generally credited with the achievement.

In any case, at Noble's urging, Benjamin Harrison exercised his new authority in September 1891 by signing a proclamation that established a 1.2-million-acre forest reserve on the south side of Yellowstone National Park, and a month later he signed a proclamation that established a 1.19-million-acre reserve in Colorado. While the size of the withdrawals provoked howls of protest in the West, Noble was undeterred. In December, at the American Forestry Association's annual meeting, he pledged "to cooperate in all ways to protect the forestry resources of the country."[40] On Noble's recommendation, Harrison signed a proclamation that established an 811,000-acre reserve in New Mexico; and prior to leaving office in March 1893, he signed twelve other proclamations.

One of the twelve, signed in December 1892, designated Afognak Island, a heavily timbered island northeast of Kodiak, as the first forest reserve in Alaska.[41] The president signed the Afognak proclamation without consulting the more than three hundred Natives who lived on the island. But Harrison's disregard for Native land rights pales when compared to that of Theodore Roosevelt. Among the many conservationist actions Roosevelt took during his presidency were three Forest Reserve Act proclamations that withdrew almost all of southeast Alaska as the nation's largest national forest.

The first proclamation, signed in 1902, designated Prince of Wales, Kuiu, Kupreanof, and Chichagof islands as the Alexander Archipelago Reserve. The idea of creating the reserve was neither Roosevelt's nor Gifford Pinchot's. (By that date, Pinchot was chief of the Department of Agriculture's Division of Forestry; in 1897 he had been sponsored by his friend Roosevelt for membership in the Boone and Crockett Club.)[42] Rather, the reserve was urged on the president by George Emmons, the navy officer who sixteen years earlier had publicly defended the Chilkat Indians' effort to maintain control of their trade route over Chilkoot Pass.

Emmons, after fourteen years on station in southeast Alaska, had been reassigned in 1896 to shore duty in New York. He retired from active duty in 1899 because of ill health. Thereafter, he spent his winters in Princeton, New Jersey, and his summers in southeast Alaska collecting Tlingit and Haida artifacts. With time on his hands, in 1901, Emmons conceived the idea of a southeast Alaska forest reserve, and that summer, during his annual artifact collecting trip, began writing a report entitled "The Woodlands of Alaska," that argued the case for doing so.

Fortuitously, when he returned to Princeton in the fall, the navy ordered Emmons to Washington, D.C., to help the State Department prepare its negotiating position regarding a dispute that had arisen with Canada over the location of the boundary between southeast Alaska and the Yukon Territory. The assignment required Emmons to mcct occasionally with the president, whose acquaintance he previously had made in 1897 when Roosevelt had served a brief tenure as assistant secretary of the navy.

Roosevelt quickly came to respect the retired officer's judgment and subsequently told Secretary of the Interior Ethan Hitchcock that Emmons "has given me more aid in reference to Alaska than any other man."

Taking advantage of the relationship, Emmons met with Roosevelt in April 1902 to talk about his idea for a forest reserve. After hearing his Alaska expert out, the president not only was receptive but read "The Woodlands of Alaska" and enthusiastically passed the report along to Hitchcock, with the recommendation that Emmons's "forest reservation scheme strikes me favorably," so "if it is proper have it done." When Hitchcock let the matter languish in his in-basket, Roosevelt ordered the secretary to direct his staff to draft a proclamation, which the president signed two weeks later.[43]

When he hatched his plan, Emmons had been politically astute enough to know that the General Land Office would oppose the establishment of a forest reserve in southeast Alaska if the boundaries too obviously impeded white settlement. For that reason, the boundaries he proposed excluded the mainland on which Dyea and Skagway, the towns at the Chilkoot and White Pass trailheads, and Juneau were located, as well as Baranof Island, on which Sitka, the oldest white town in southeast Alaska, was located. But they encircled the major islands on which Tlingit and Haida Indian villages were located because, as far as the General Land Office was concerned, the islands were uninhabited, although eight hundred Indians lived on Prince of Wales Island, a hundred lived on Kuiu Island, five hundred lived on Kupreanof Island, and five hundred more lived on Chichagof Island.

The boundaries of the Alexander Archipelago Reserve excluded the land surrounding Juneau and Sitka, but when the white residents of those com-

munities learned that the president had closed seven thousand square miles
of southeast Alaska to private entry and unregulated commercial logging,
they were outspokenly outraged. By contrast, the Indians whose villages
now were inholdings inside a national forest were silent. There was, however, a protest, of sorts, voiced on their behalf. "We are trying to induce
them to give up their old communal houses," the Rev. Harry Corser, the
Presbyterian missionary at Wrangell, complained to Secretary Hitchcock,
"but if these islands are made into a reservation, it will be impossible for
them to go and get the logs to make the lumber to build homes."

Not only that, but if local sawmills could not cut timber inside the
Alexander Archipelago Reserve, the prohibition would end Corser's effort
to turn the members of his Tlingit congregation into wage laborers, since
there would be no wage-paying jobs for them to labor at.

> The Indians, the more advanced ones, receive by far the larger part of
> their support from the timber industry [Corser lectured]. They make
> good loggers, and it has been hoped that by encouraging them in this
> industry they would take a long step toward civilization. But this pro-
> posed reservation puts a stop to this ... from a moral standpoint is it
> right to prohibit Indians from logging on property which they have
> inherited from their ancestors, and which has been considered by them
> and respected by them as property, as much as any white man's prop-
> erty is considered as property by the law?[44]

Hitchcock undoubtedly did not forward Corser's letter to the president.
But if he had, it would have made no difference because Roosevelt had no
empathy for talk about Indian land rights. As he once railed when asked
his opinion of the idea: "To recognize the Indian ownership of the limitless
forest and prairies of this continent ... necessarily implies a similar recognition of every white hunter, squatter, horse thief, or wandering cattleman."[45]

In 1907, Roosevelt signed a second proclamation, which designated
Baranof Island and part of the southeast Alaska mainland as the Tongass
National Forest, into which the Alexander Archipelago Reserve subsequently was merged. And in 1909 he signed a third proclamation, a month
prior to leaving office, which expanded the boundaries to encircle the entire southeast Alaska Panhandle and archipelago.

The Tongass National Forest ended at Yakutat, but the Roosevelt conservation agenda extended farther north. "I acted on the theory that the
President could at any time in his discretion withdraw from entry any of
the public lands of the United States and reserve the same for forestry, for
water-power sites, for irrigation, and other public purposes," Roosevelt

later explained. "Without such action it would have been impossible to stop the activity of the land-thieves."[46]

Consistent with that view of the matter and at Gifford Pinchot's urging, in 1907, Roosevelt signed a proclamation that withdrew 4.9 million acres of coastline surrounding Prince William Sound as the Chugach National Forest.[47] And six days prior to leaving office he signed executive orders that established five bird and game refuges in Alaska.

In addition to persuading the club's founder to carve forests and wildlife refuges out of the Alaska public domain, Boone and Crockett Club members also persuaded Congress and the president to carve out parks. At the instigation of Charles Sheldon, chairman of the club's game committee, Congress established Mount McKinley National Park in 1917. And in 1925, at the instigation of George Bird Grinnell, President Calvin Coolidge signed a proclamation that designated Glacier Bay, which John Muir "discovered" in 1879 and which since 1883 had been the northern terminus of the Inland Passage steamship tour, as a national monument.

For Alaska Natives, the land inside the boundaries of Mount McKinley National Park and Glacier Bay National Monument would be forever lost. But the proclamations and executive orders that closed land inside the boundaries of the Tongass and Chugach forests and, in the years ahead, closed millions of other acres of Alaska to private entry unintentionally protected Native land rights. The withdrawals hindered first whites and then (in 1959 when it entered the union) the state of Alaska from obtaining title to land inside the boundaries. And at one important location a withdrawal order stopped a natural resource development project that, had it proceeded, would have attracted thousands—and potentially tens of thousands—more whites to Alaska than the few who moved to the territory between the end of the turn-of-the-century gold rushes and the beginning of the Second World War.

By 1900 it was common knowledge that the Ahtna, the Indians who live along the Copper River, which empties into the Gulf of Alaska at the southeastern entrance to Prince William Sound, mined copper. After exploring the area in 1885, for example, Lt. Henry Allen reported that "the minerals of the Copper River have long been a source of speculation, owing to pieces of pure copper, knives and bullets of the same metal, having been brought down to the coast by the Natives."[48]

The first copper discovery, the Billum claim, was staked in 1899 after an Ahtna showed the location to a pair of bedraggled miners. The second, the Nicolai claim, was staked the same year, when an Ahtna chief of that name traded the location for store-bought food that enterprising prospectors brokered for the information. The third, the Bonanza claim, was discovered the following summer on the side of a cliff in the Wrangell Mountains, twenty miles northwest of the Nicolai claim.[49]

The Bonanza claim contained the richest copper ore in the world, assaying at 75 percent pure copper at a time when copper mines in Utah and Nevada were earning a profit smelting ore that contained 2 percent.[50] Of course, unlike the situation in Utah and Nevada, the cost of building a world-class mine on the side of a mountain in an Alaska wilderness two hundred miles from tidewater and then transporting the ore to steamships that would float the rock to a smelter would be exorbitant. But if the investment was made, the profit would be exorbitant. And for that reason the money was available.

Stephen Birch, a New York City mining engineer, was in Valdez, a small town on Prince William Sound, a mountain range west of the discovery, when the prospectors who staked the Bonanza claim recorded their find. Appreciating the quality of the ore, Birch, who was in Alaska scouting investment opportunities for Henry O. Havemeyer, the president of the national sugar refiners' trust, organized the Alaska Copper Company, a paper shell that purchased the Bonanza claim from the discoverers for 25,000 of Havemeyer's dollars per man.[51]

But now that he owned the Bonanza claim, the cost of developing it was too much for Havemeyer. So in 1906 when the U.S. Supreme Court refused to hear the appeal of a lawsuit that had settled a dispute over the Alaska Copper Company's ownership of the Bonanza claim in their favor,[52] Havemeyer and Birch took the project to Dan Guggenheim, the scion of Guggenheim Brothers, the family holding company that controlled the American Smelting and Refining Company, the trust that controlled the nation's metal smelting industry. But the cost of developing the Bonanza claim also was too much for Guggenheim Brothers. So Dan Guggenheim took the project to John Pierpont Morgan, one of the richest men in America, whose New York City investment bank was large enough to assemble the necessary capital.

Morgan signed on and organized a joint venture with Guggenheim Brothers and a group of investors (that included Havemeyer) that became known as the Alaska Syndicate. The venture, which Stephen Birch, who managed the project, described as a "gentlemen's agreement,"[53] was simple: Guggenheim Brothers contributed the Bonanza claim and the know-how needed to build and operate a world-class mine, and the Morgan bank advanced Guggenheim Brothers the money it needed to bring the project on line.

At the time Dan Guggenheim took the Bonanza claim to Morgan, the Morgan bank was financing the Northwestern Commercial Company, a holding company that owned the Northwestern Steamship Company, whose ships dominated the run between Seattle and Nome; the Pacific Packing and Navigation Company, which operated a group of salmon canneries; and a railroad right-of-way from Valdez to the Yukon River.[54]

Since it needed a railroad to move ore from the Bonanza claim to tidewater and steamships to transport the rock from Alaska to the Guggenheim Brothers' smelter in Tacoma, Washington, the syndicate purchased a controlling interest in the Northwestern Commercial Company.

The steamship fleet became a profit center. But in 1911 the canneries were sold, and the Valdez railroad right-of-way went unused after the syndicate selected Cordova, a tidewater townsite southeast of Valdez, as the southern terminus of its Copper River and Northwestern Railway.

A monumental feat of engineering that required six thousand men, $28.5 million, and four years to lay, the Copper River and Northwestern track ran two hundred miles from Cordova to Kennecott, the mining complex the syndicate constructed on the Bonanza claim. Between 1911, when the first ore train steamed into Cordova, and 1938, when the road shut down, Copper River and Northwestern Railway trains hauled millions of tons of copper that, smelted and sold, earned the syndicate's investors tens of millions of early-twentieth-century dollars.

But for Theodore Roosevelt and his fellow conservationists, they would have earned tens of millions more.

From the outset of his involvement with the Bonanza claim, Dan Guggenheim had no intention of simply mining copper. As he explained to the *New York Times* in 1906, "We want to go into the territory and build railroads and smelters and mining towns and bring men there and populate the country where it is habitable and do for [Alaska] what the earlier figures in American railroad building did for sections of the great West."[55]

But extending the Copper River and Northwestern Railway from Kennecott north to the Yukon River and operating the smelters Dan Guggenheim wanted to build in Alaska could not occur until the syndicate secured a reliable local source of cheap energy to run its trains and fire its smelting furnaces. In 1906 "energy" meant "coal." And to Dan Guggenheim's seeming good luck, in 1902 a half-billion-ton field of it had been discovered on Bering River, which flows into Prince William Sound south of the mouth of the Copper River and only fifty-seven miles southeast of Cordova. As a consequence, at the time he decided to participate in the development of the Bonanza claim, Guggenheim assumed that his railroad would run on and his smelters would be fueled by Bering River coal. And but for the conservation movement flexing its muscle, they would have.

At the turn of the century, most coal burned in Alaska was imported from British Columbia, as was three-quarters of the coal consumed in California.[56] To encourage coal production in its northernmost possession, Congress extended the federal coal-land law to Alaska in 1900.[57] But in a wonderful catch-22, the law required coal claims to be staked on surveyed land, and neither the Bering River coal field nor the Matanuska coalfield, which had been discovered at the north end of Cook Inlet, had been. So the 1900 Act prohibited what Congress had intended it to authorize. In 1904 Congress tried to remedy the problem by enacting an Alaska coal-land law that authorized an entryman to stake a single 160-acre coal claim on unsurveyed land.[58] Significantly, the Act also prohibited entrymen from pooling claims prior to staking them.

In the summer of 1904, Clarence Cunningham, a speculator from Idaho who arrived in Alaska with a pocketful of powers of attorney, staked thirty-three 160-acre coal claims in the Bering River field for himself and thirty-two Washington state businessmen.

Knowing the syndicate needed coal, in 1907 the Cunningham group offered Dan Guggenheim a one-half interest in the corporation the members of the group organized to develop their 5,280-acre holding, which was estimated to contain 50 million tons of coal. The arrangement also granted Guggenheim the right to purchase coal mined on the claims for $2.25 a ton and granted the Copper River and Northwestern Railway the right to purchase coal for $1.75 a ton.[59] Since British Columbian coal later sold at Cordova for as much as $14 a ton,[60] Guggenheim quickly accepted the offer.

But the deal was never consummated.

In 1903, Theodore Roosevelt had put capitalists like Dan Guggenheim and John Pierpont Morgan on notice that he was serious about the commitment to the conservation ethic he had expressed in his 1901 message to Congress. He unexpectedly vetoed a bill that authorized private investors to construct a hydroelectric dam on the Tennessee River on the ground that, since the water that produced the hydroelectric power was owned by the public, the public was entitled to a fair share of the profit to be made selling it.[61]

In accordance with that philosophy, Roosevelt wanted Congress to amend the federal coal-land law to require coal land to be leased, rather than for fee title to continue to be given away to speculators. As he explained in December 1906, "It is not wise that the nation should alienate its remaining coal lands. The withdrawal of these coal lands [until Congress has an opportunity to enact a statute that authorized leasing] would constitute a policy analogous to that which as been followed in withdrawing the forest lands from ordinary settlement."[62]

Consistent with that view of the matter, a month earlier Roosevelt signed an order that withdrew all coal land in Alaska from entry under the 1904 Alaska coal-land law. But while the order closed the Bering River coal field to new entries, it could not invalidate claims that previously had been staked. So if the Cunningham group's claims (in which Dan Guggenheim held a one-half interest) were valid, the syndicate could acquire the coal it needed notwithstanding Roosevelt's effort to prevent it from doing so. But the syndicate never did because, as Richard Ballinger, the commissioner of the General Land Office, later admitted to Congress, the claims were "technically" invalid since the men who had given Clarence Cunningham their powers of attorney had agreed to pool their claims before their agent, Cunningham, staked them.

In December 1907, Louis Glavis, the twenty-three-year-old head of the General Land Office in Portland, informed Ballinger of the illegality. When he did, Ballinger, who prior to his appointment as commissioner had been the mayor of Seattle, confided to his politically naïve subordinate that "he was a friend of many of the [Cunningham] claimants,"[63] and then, several weeks later, ordered his staff to approve the claims; although the order was rescinded when Glavis protested.

At Ballinger's urging, that spring congressmen sympathetic to the syndicate attempted to amend the 1904 Alaska coal-land law to validate all pending claims and authorize members of the Cunningham group and other entrymen to consolidate their holdings into 2,560-acre tracts. But their timing was horrible; as Secretary of the Interior James Garfield subsequently noted, seven years of Roosevelt preaching from his bully pulpit had "awakened" the nation to the need to prevent the "misuse" of the public domain, "whether by way of waste or monopolistic and speculative control."[64]

As a consequence, Rep. Herbert Parsons, a Roosevelt Republican from New York who served on the House Committee on Public Lands, had little difficulty in adding a section to the bill that required coal claims validated by the legislation to be forfeited if they subsequently were acquired by an "unlawful trust," or were managed "in restraint of trade in the mining or selling of coal," or if a corporation that acquired them from the entrymen gained control of more than the allowed 2,560 acres. Parsons's conservationist conditions were so onerous that in May, when Roosevelt signed the bill, the *New York Times* reported that "in the opinion of many persons" the 1908 Act was "the most radical measure of legislation enacted during his administration."[65]

So the effort to validate the Cunningham group's claims post hoc had failed, and the claims would have to be approved pursuant to the requirements of the 1904 Act, with which the Cunningham group could not comply. The subsequent and ultimately failed effort to have the General Land Office approve the claims anyway engendered what Charles Bonaporte, Roosevelt's attorney general, later would describe as "the most notable unbroken succession of colossal blunders known in American politics."[66]

In March 1909, when Roosevelt's handpicked successor, William Howard Taft, succeeded Roosevelt as president, he appointed Ballinger, who had resigned as commissioner of the General Land Office the year before, as secretary of the interior. When Secretary Ballinger resumed what Louis Glavis considered to be behind-the-scenes maneuvering to arrange for the claims to be approved, Glavis appealed for help to Gifford Pinchot, the chief of the Department of Agriculture's recently renamed Bureau of Forestry.

Aware of the situation, in February 1909, Pinchot had persuaded Roosevelt to sign a Forest Reserve Act proclamation that extended the southeastern boundary of the Chugach National Forest to encircle most of the Bering River coal field so that the Bureau of Forestry could have a say in the approval of the Cunningham group and other Alaska coal-land law entries.[67] Pinchot also disliked Ballinger, "a stocky, square-headed little man"[68] with whom he had warred during the secretary's year as commissioner of the General Land Office. So Pinchot arranged for Glavis to argue his case against Ballinger to President Taft.

For Taft, allowing the earnest young General Land Office employee to do so was a career-altering mistake.

After hearing Glavis out, rather than disciplining Ballinger, Taft (whose brother Henry, a prominent New York City attorney, represented the Morgan bank)[69] fired Glavis for insubordination. Glavis astutely responded to the censure by writing a long article entitled "The Whitewashing of Ballinger," which *Collier's Weekly*, one of the nation's most influential magazines, published in November 1909.[70]

The publicity set off a political firestorm that roared white hot when Taft fired Gifford Pinchot two months later for committing the guilty-as-charged offense of helping Glavis—whom Pinchot lauded to Congress as a "vigorous defender of the people's interests"—take his case against Ballinger (and in which Taft now was implicated) to the press and then to Capitol Hill.[71]

The hearings Congress held on the Glavis-Ballinger-Pinchot-Taft donnybrook kept the controversy before the public for months. More important, after hearing Pinchot's spin on the story, Theodore Roosevelt decided that "on many important points" Taft had "twisted around the [conservation] policies I advocated."[72] Their disagreement over the Ballinger-Pinchot affair contributed to a political estrangement between the former and present chief executives that in 1912 provoked Roosevelt to challenge Taft for the Republican nomination for president. And when Taft won that contest, Roosevelt fractured an already deeply divided Republican Party by running in the general election as a third-party candidate, an act of political hubris that cost Taft a second term by electing Woodrow Wilson.

That was the national consequence.

In Alaska, the white populace's attitude was mixed. Individuals, most of whom lived in Cordova, who thought they would benefit economically if Dan Guggenheim was allowed the coal he needed—to build his smelters, extend the Copper River and Northwestern Railway to the Yukon River, and open the country in between—were outraged that Glavis (who had argued in *Collier's Weekly* that allowing "monopoly" to gain control of the Bering River coalfield would be a "national menace") and his friends had locked up Alaska. "[I]t is urged by the lock-and-key conservationists that we must fix things so that the next generation cannot undo what we have done," the *Alaska-Yukon Magazine*, a pro-Guggenheim publication, editorialized in the same issue in which it disparaged conservationist attacks on Ballinger as "unjust and villainous." "[E]very year's delay in the opening of the territory is a year wasted to every man or woman who could live more prosperously or happier if the opportunity were offered."[73]

However, at Nome, where its monopoly allowed the Northwestern Steamship Company to charge as much as the traffic could bear to transport freight from Seattle, the *Gold Digger* newspaper demonized the syndicate as the "Guggenheim vampire which has already started its blood-sucking operations, and is laying its plans for the complete subjugation of the country to its will."[74] And since their town had been bypassed as the southern terminus of the syndicate's railroad, most Valdez residents felt the same.

But if the blood-sucking vampire was denied the coal it needed to extend the Copper River and Northwestern Railway to the Yukon River, how was Alaska to realize its economic destiny in a political environment in which conservationism had monopoly capital on the run?

Bloodied by his public fight with Pinchot, in March 1911, Richard Ballinger resigned as secretary of the interior. Making use of the opportunity, Taft tried to repair the damage the fracas had inflicted on his standing with the Roosevelt wing of the Republican Party by appointing Walter Fisher, a past president of the Conservation League of America whose credentials as a conservationist were impeccable, to fill the vacancy.

Secretary Fisher agreed with the conventional wisdom that a railroad from Prince William Sound to the Yukon River was the key to "opening" Alaska and that opening Alaska was in the national interest. In October, in a speech to the American Mining Congress, he announced a new Alaska development policy.

Fisher began by telling the roomful of mining executives that he agreed with Louis Glavis and Gifford Pinchot that the syndicate should not be allowed to acquire an ownership interest in the Bering River coal field. "We have already seen in this country the injurious effects of the joint or common ownership of coal fields and railroads," he lectured. "We should not repeat in Alaska or elsewhere the mistakes that have been made."

But that said, if they were denied a dependable source of low-cost coal, neither the syndicate nor any other source of private capital would be willing to spend the millions of dollars it would cost to build a railroad to the Yukon River. For that reason, "if private interests do not care to undertake the task [of laying track]," Fisher informed the Mining Congress, "the government itself should do so."[75]

The suggestion was a logical extension of mainstream conservationist doctrine. When it subsidized the construction of the transcontinental railroad, Congress had not demanded an equity interest in the Union Pacific and Central Pacific Railroads. And monopoly had been the result. So if Congress financed an Alaska railroad, Fisher argued, "I see no reason why the government should not own the road outright, whether it operates it or leases to an operating company."[76]

Theodore Roosevelt, although retired from public office, still was America's most prominent conservationist, and he agreed with Fisher's view of the matter. And President Taft, despite his support for Richard Ballinger, continued to think of himself as a Roosevelt conservationist. In February, acting on his secretary of the interior's recommendation, Taft urged Congress to finance and then to authorize the federal government to operate an Alaska railroad.

In August, Congress created a commission to study the matter, and in February 1913 the commission recommended that Congress finance an extension of the Copper River and Northwestern Railway to the Yukon River.

In 1902, John Ballaine, a Seattle promoter financed by Chicago investors, had organized the Alaska Central (later renamed the Alaska Northern) Railroad to run track from Seward, a townsite Ballaine had purchased at Resurrection Bay on the west side of Prince William Sound, north along the east side of Cook Inlet to the Matanuska coalfield and then into the interior. By 1906, when Theodore Roosevelt closed Alaska coal land to entry, Ballaine had laid seventy-one miles of track. But with the Matanuska field off limits, the incentive for investors to continue financing the Alaska Northern disappeared. Therefore, the commission recommended that, in addition to extending the Copper River and Northwestern Railway, Congress also should extend the Alaska Northern.

When he assumed office a month after the commission submitted its report, President Woodrow Wilson—who, although he was a Democrat, was as progressive a conservationist as Roosevelt—was supportive of the idea of a government road.

> A duty faces us with regard to Alaska which seems to me very pressing [Wilson informed Congress in his first State of the Union address]. Alaska, as a storehouse should be unlocked. One key to it is a system of railways. These the government should itself build and administer, and the ports and terminals it should itself control in the interest of all who wish to use them for the service and development of the country and its people.[77]

At Wilson's urging, in 1914, Congress authorized the president to build an Alaska railroad along whatever route he decided was appropriate, and in April 1915, Wilson announced that the federal government would purchase the Alaska Northern and extend its track from Turnagain Arm to the Matanuska coal field and then north to Fairbanks, a mining town on the Chena River, an inland tributary of the Yukon.

Within a week, two thousand whites, each looking for a government construction job, were camped in tents at the mouth of Ship Creek on the east side of Cook Inlet on the site that the Alaskan Engineering Commission, the agency the Department of the Interior created to construct the road, selected as its principal supply depot. When the Postal Service opened an office on the site, it named the tent city Anchorage.[78]

Budgeted at $35 million, when President Warren Harding opened the Alaska Railroad in 1923 by driving a gold spike into the rail bed, more than $56 million ($450 million in 1996 dollars) had been spent to lay 470 miles of track and construct support facilities.[79]

As the railroad's balance sheet soon would prove, however, every dollar spent was a dollar wasted by fabulists whose mystical faith in "development" had allowed their dislike of Dan Guggenheim and John Pierpont Morgan to overcome their common sense.

Once the trains began running, so the sophistry went, their presence would spur the mining and export of coal and other minerals and bring thousands of homesteaders to settle along the right-of-way. "[W]e should think of Alaska as a land not only of mines and fisheries, but of towns, farms, mills, and factories, supporting millions of people of the hardiest and most wholesome of the race," Wilson's secretary of the interior, Franklin Lane, explained to the Senate Committee on Territories in 1913. "[I]t seems to me there is less of a hazard as to Alaska's future if the government of the United States owns the railroads which will make its fertile interior valleys accessible from the coast and bring its coal, iron, copper, and other mineral resources within the reach of the world."[80] And when he drove the last spike, President Warren Harding perorated before swinging the sledge that "it is not possible to liken a railway to a magician's wand, but the effect to me is the same."[81]

Lane and Harding were deacons of the faith. But no member of the congregation was as true a believer as James Wickersham. Born in 1857 and raised in a southern Illinois farm town, Wickersham moved to Springfield, the state capital, when he was nineteen. He read law in the Springfield law office of John McAuley Palmer, the former Union army general from whom, the world being a small place, Jefferson Davis had inherited command of the Fourteenth Corps during the Civil War. In 1880, Wickersham was admitted to the bar, married, and, to make ends meet, went to work for the federal Census Bureau, where he lasted three years before relocating with his wife and infant son to Tacoma in Washington Territory.

After opening a law office, in 1884 the twenty-seven-year-old newcomer ran as a Republican for probate judge. He was elected, and in 1886 was reelected to another two-year term; but in 1888 he was defeated for a third. While he remained active in the local Republican Party, for the next ten years Wickersham practiced law. In 1898 he reentered public life by winning election to the Washington House of Representatives. Shortly thereafter, he was instrumental in arranging for the legislature to elect Addison Foster, a fellow Tacoma attorney, to the U.S. Senate. In 1900, Foster returned the favor by recommending Wickersham to President McKinley for a patronage appointment as either consul general to Japan or district court judge in Alaska. Wickersham wanted to be an ambassador,

Alaska District Court Judge James Wickersham.
WICKERSHAM COLLECTION PCA 277-7-107, ALASKA STATE LIBRARY.

but in June 1900 he was appointed judge of the third division of the Alaska district court.

The seat of Wickersham's court was at Eagle, population four hundred, a Yukon River mining camp a few miles downriver from the Canadian border.[82] Traveling by riverboat, steamship, and dog team, for the next seven years Wickersham presided at trials and other judicial proceedings along the Yukon, as far north as Cape Prince of Wales on the tip of the Seward Peninsula, as far west as Dutch Harbor in the Aleutian Islands, and as far south as Juneau.

In 1904, President Roosevelt appointed the traveling judge to a second four-year term. But the Senate refused to confirm the appointment principally because of the opposition of Sen. Knute Nelson, a member of the Senate Judiciary Committee who had met the nominee the previous summer when a subcommittee of the Senate Committee on Territories (on which Nelson also served) visited Alaska. As a consequence, Wickersham remained on the bench only because Roosevelt reappointed him each time Congress recessed.

By September 1907, however, Wickersham had had enough and resigned. He was fifty years old, there was no possibility he would be confirmed to a second term, his wife was in ill health, and as he explained in his resignation letter, he was a "poor" man.

In 1903, Wickersham had relocated his court from Eagle to Fairbanks. Elbridge Barnette, a Klondike stampeder who had a large, if insouciant, talent for the con, had founded Fairbanks two years earlier on the Chena River, which flows into the Tanana River, a major tributary of the Yukon. After having lived there almost five years, when Wickersham left the bench, he opened a law office in Fairbanks, and in less than a month hustled retainers that exceeded the $5,000 annual salary he had been earning as a judge.

But what Wickersham wanted more than good money was big money. To obtain it, he needed a big client, which is exactly who he thought he had on the hook.

In 1903, Wickersham had presided at the trial in Valdez in which the ownership of the Bonanza copper claim had been challenged by the men who had grubstaked the prospectors who had sold the claim to the Alaska Copper Company, the corporation Stephen Birch had organized with Henry O. Havemeyer's money.[83] During the trial, Wickersham and Birch not only became acquainted but socialized after hours, an impropriety that today would be a violation of the code of judicial conduct.

In 1906 when Wickersham traveled to Washington, D.C., to try to persuade the Senate to confirm his appointment to a second term, he visited Birch in New York City. Among other men of monied consequence, Birch introduced him to Dan Guggenheim, with whom Birch was busy organizing the Alaska Syndicate. Birch also urged Wickersham to quit the bench and hire on as the syndicate's Alaska counsel, to which Wickersham responded that he "would be willing to make some arrangement on that line."[84]

Remembering the conversation, Wickersham wrote Birch in April 1908 suggesting that, now that he was in private practice, the syndicate should retain him as its counsel for $15,000 a year. However, Birch already had hired a Seattle law firm to handle the syndicate's legal work and suggested that Wickersham consider joining it. Instead, Wickersham announced his candidacy as an Independent Republican in the August election for Alaska's nonvoting delegate in the U.S. House of Representatives, an office that Congress had created two years earlier.

After years of traveling the territory at government expense, Wickersham was one of the best-known men in Alaska. But in addition to the advantages of name recognition, he decided to run for delegate because the half-term incumbent, a Tanana Valley miner named Tom Cale with whom Wickersham had been aligned the previous fall during an intra-Republican fight with Territorial Governor Wilford Hoggatt, was rumored to have decided that he would not stand for reelection. If Cale retired, Wickersham reasoned, his supporters would support Wickersham rather than "Seattle John" Corson, the candidate the Hoggatt wing of the Alaska Republican Party had nominated. And in the end, that is how the election turned out.

In 1906, Theodore Roosevelt had appointed Hoggatt, a southeastern Alaska mine owner, as territorial governor on the recommendation of David Jarvis, a former Revenue Marine officer with whom Roosevelt was acquainted and whom Stephen Birch later hired to manage the syndicate's businesses. So Governor Hoggatt, with whom Wickersham by 1908 had fallen out, and his candidate, Corson, were syndicate men.

But so was Wickersham, who was a friend of Jarvis's and an acquaintance of Birch's and, prior to declaring his candidacy, had tried to work for the syndicate. Not only that, but Wickersham assumed that Jarvis would support his candidacy and that the syndicate, through Birch, would help finance the campaign.

However, in July, Jarvis wrote to say that he was committed to Corson and, as Wickersham recorded in his diary, "strongly advised me to keep out of the race." As a consequence, Wickersham immediately, and with no sense of the hypocrisy attendant in doing so, "revised my address [i.e., stump speech]" to "put in a strong plank against Guggenheim domination in mining and transportation matters in Alaska."[85]

In doing so, the man who had hoped to make his fortune helping the syndicate maximize its profits transformed himself into a tribune of the common man, publicly promising that, if elected to Congress, he would "oppose in every way possible the control of transportation or mining business within Alaska by the Guggenheims or any other dangerous combinations."[86]

If cynical, the strategy worked; the shedding of one political skin for another allowed Wickersham not only to easily win the 1908 election but, less easily, to win the next five elections as well.

Prior to deciding to run against the syndicate, Wickersham had campaigned on a populist platform that included an eight-hour workday in the mines, a territorial legislature (which prior to declaring his candidacy he had privately opposed Congress's creating), and a railroad to connect Fairbanks to ice-free tidewater. "It costs more to bring a sack of flour from St. Michael up [the Yukon River to the Tanana River and up the Tanana to the Chena River to] here than it does to get it around the world," Wickersham argued during his first campaign appearance in Fairbanks. Assuming so, the way to lower freight rates was to foster competition by "getting a railroad from the coast to the City of Fairbanks." For that reason, the candidate promised that if he had "the honor to represent you in Washington" he would do "everything I can to get a railroad from the coast into the interior of Alaska."[87]

Once elected, Del. Wickersham made good on candidate Wickersham's pledge by becoming Capitol Hill's most vocal proponent of the idea that, since the syndicate had been prevented from doing so, Congress had a responsibility to build and operate a railroad connecting Fairbanks to Prince William Sound. In arguing that case, Wickersham repeatedly promised that if Congress would pay the cost of construction, the Alaska Railroad would pay its own way. Even if the Cassandras were right, he argued in 1914 on the floor of the House, that the railroad would not immediately spur new development, inbound freight, passengers, and the coal that would be mined and exported when the trains began running would annually generate $2 million, more than enough to cover the road's operation and maintenance costs.[88]

Wickersham's accounting was patently fatuous. But in March, Congress passed and President Wilson signed the Alaska Railroad Act.

During the years of debate that preceded the enactment of the Act, not a public word was said by Wickersham or any other member of Congress about the impact a railroad would have on Alaska Natives whose villages and hunting areas would be located along the right-of-way. However, in 1915 when Congress recessed and Wickersham returned home for the summer, he gave the matter some thought.

Wickersham, who was fifty-seven years old and serving his fourth term as delegate, had been looking forward to the break from the hurried pace of life on Capitol Hill. But after two days in Fairbanks, its most prominent citizen confided to his diary that the backwater mining town was "oh so dull." So to break the monotony, he hitched a steamboat ride down the Chena River to the Tanana and then down the Tanana River to the Tolovana.

After setting up his camp at the mouth of the Tolovana, Wickersham hiked up a hill to take in the view, which he thought looked like an "Indian paradise, ducks, geese, swans, and all kinds of game—large and small." But it was a paradise whose time he was sure was ending. "The Indians protest against the entrance of the white men into their hunting grounds," Wickersham noted to himself, "but in vain."[89]

While camped, Wickersham paid a courtesy call on Sit-tsu-dau-tuna (known to whites as Alexander), who was chief of the Athabascan Indian village at the mouth of the river. The next day Alexander, dressed in "feathers, beadwork, and a mooseskin jacket," paid his own courtesy call, during which the two men wiled away the afternoon talking about "game laws, reservations, schools, etc."

For Alexander the visit was unnerving. The future that Wickersham assured him was coming was so apocalyptic that when he told the headmen of the surrounding villages about the conversation they refused to believe that Wickersham could have said what Alexander said he had. But upon reflection, they were troubled enough to ask for a meeting.

In July the chiefs of seven Tanana Valley villages met in Fairbanks with Wickersham, Thomas Riggs, a member of the Alaskan Engineering Commission, and C. W. Richie and H. J. Atwell, the local General Land Office agents. In addition to Alexander, the Indian delegation included Chief Joe from Salchaket, Chief John from Chena, Chief Thomas from Nenana, Chief Charley from Minto, Chief Ivan from Coskaket, and Chief Starr from Tanana.

"What you told Alexander the Natives did not believe and came here to find out," Chief Starr opened the meeting by telling Wickersham. Wickersham responded that "Alexander told you the truth."

> I told Alexander that the white people were building railroads in this country now [Wickersham, warming to his theme, continued]. White men are coming out and taking up the land; they are staking homesteads, cultivating the land raising potatoes and all kinds of crops ...there are many, many white men in the United States, as many as there are trees on the hills here, and in a few years many of them are coming to Alaska ... the white men coming from the United States are going to keep taking up this land until all the good land is gone, and the Indian people are going to have to move over ... and when all the good land is gone, the white men are going to keep on taking more land. After a while the Indian will have no land at all.

As a sponsor of the Alaska Railroad Act, Wickersham was as responsible for the calamity he prophesied as anyone. But he was not unsympathetic to the Indians' plight, although his solution was hardly innovative: before the trains began running, he advised, the Indians should accept title to a small amount of land so that whites could settle on the rest.

Alaska Delegate James Wickersham (middle row, fifth from left) and the chiefs of seven Tanana Valley Athabascan Indian villages meeting at Fairbanks in July 1915.
ALBERT J. JOHNSON COLLECTION ACC. NO. 89-166-372, ALASKA AND POLAR REGIONS DEPARTMENT, UNIVERSITY OF ALASKA FAIRBANKS.

If they agreed to that arrangement, Wickersham told the chiefs, there were two ways their people could do so: 160-acre allotments (the Indian equivalent of homesteads) and reservations. If they wanted allotments, "you can pick out that land and stake on it and live there forever with your children," Wickersham explained. If they wanted reservations, "you and your people could build an Indian town there. You could have a church there, a school, and an Indian agent, an official agent of the President, who would show you how to plow land and raise potatoes and other crops."

When Wickersham concluded his sales pitch, the chiefs discussed the matter among themselves, and when the meeting reconvened, Chief Ivan announced the verdict. "We don't want to go on a reservation," he told Wickersham. And Chief Alexander was of a similar mind. "We want to be left alone. As the whole continent was made for you, God made Alaska for the Indian people, and all we hope is to be able to live here all the time."

Since Wickersham had decided prior to the meeting that reservations were the solution to a problem that—other than in his own mind—had not yet arisen, he refused to take the collective no as the answer. "A reservation is not a prison," he argued, "a reservation is more for the purpose of helping the Indians ... [I]t would be a good thing to make a reservation five miles square [around a village] and keep the white men off." But the chiefs were adamant that there would be no reservations.[90] And the issue soon was moot.

Except at Nenana, south of Fairbanks—where Chief Thomas had the poor luck of having the Alaska Railroad run its track through his village, which the Alaskan Engineering Commission commandeered as a supply depot—the land rush Wickersham predicted did not occur. Not only did thousands of whites not settle along the right-of-way, during its first six years of operation the railroad ran an $8.1 million operating deficit.

Alarmed by the torrent of red ink, in 1930 the U.S. Senate sent three members to Alaska to investigate the situation. After holding twenty-two hearings along the right-of-way, the senators gloomily concluded that the development and export of coal and other natural resources that the trains had to haul in order to earn enough money to enable the railroad to pay its operating expenses was uneconomical and would remain so indefinitely.

> There is little or no merchantable timber for export [the senators lamented in their report]. While there is an abundance of coal [in the Matanuska field], it is of a character that has failed to develop an export demand. There can be no exportation of agricultural products as the region cannot produce in competition with the states. The fisheries are along the coast and contribute little to the outgoing volume of freight.... As a matter of fact, furs and the precious metals are the chief exports of the region, and, of course, contribute little to the outgoing traffic on the road.[91]

And if that was not bad enough, the railroad was ruining the private economy that did exist. In 1920, there had been 220 truck farms along the right-of-way but, in 1930, there were only 168. The reason was that locally grown produce could not compete with produce the railroad's freight rates made economical to import from Seattle. But if the freight rates were raised high enough to make locally grown produce competitive, the railroad would lose more money than it already had because, as the senators accurately concluded, "if a farming industry should develop, it must do so at the expense of farm products now being shipped in, and naturally would cause a reduction in freight income."[92]

So despite the Alaska Railroad's having "opened" the country, until tens of thousands of army troops were ordered to Alaska at the beginning of the Second World War, white population growth along the railroad right-of-way was next to none. Between 1929 and 1939, the population of Seward, where the track began, increased by only 114, the population of Anchorage by only 1,218, and the population of Fairbanks, where the track ended, by only 1,354.

It is interesting to speculate what the white population growth in southcentral and interior Alaska would have been if Alaska coal land had not been closed to entry and the conservationist hue and cry that Louis Glavis provoked had not prevented the Alaska Syndicate from acquiring the Cunningham group's coal claims.

As late as 1910, Alfred Brooks, the head of the Alaska Division of the U.S. Geological Survey, complained that there were "millions of acres of low-grade placer ground and thousands of quartz deposits [in Alaska that are] now unable to operate on account of the high cost of British Columbia coal," which "could be worked at a profit" if low-cost Alaska coal was available.[93] For that reason, it also is interesting to speculate about how much of the future that James Wickersham prophesied to Alexander and the other Tanana chiefs would have come to pass if the syndicate had acquired the Cunningham group's coal claims and extended the Copper River and Northwestern Railway to the Yukon River and then used its supply of low-cost energy and its line of credit at the Morgan bank to develop marginal mineral deposits.

But if Theodore Roosevelt and his fellow conservationists unintentionally prevented whites from settling on land on which Alaska Natives hunted and gathered, they charged a fee for the service.

The same decade in which Roosevelt created the Tongass and Chugach National Forests and conservationists denied the syndicate access to the Bering River coalfield, the Boone and Crockett Club successfully lobbied Congress to enact a statute regulating hunting in Alaska.

When Europeans arrived in North America in the sixteenth century, the continent teemed with wildlife. But by the closing decades of the nineteenth century, Manifest Destiny's pertinacious march westward had taken its toll on game animals. "In 1875, while traveling through Montana," George Bird Grinnell subsequently reported, "I frequently saw parties of skin hunters engaged in killing elk, deer and antelope for their hides, and their wagon-loads of flat dried skins stacked up as high as loads of hay, on the way to Fort Benton to be shipped down [the Missouri] river."[94]

To the east, when Theodore Roosevelt made his first trip to Dakota Territory in 1883, antelope, elk, grouse, ducks, and grizzly bears occupied the range. But over the next five years Roosevelt watched "swinish game-butchers" denude the badlands of large game.[95]

In 1887 when Roosevelt organized the Boone and Crockett Club, he and Grinnell had neither the inclination nor the power to halt the westward migration that was destroying wildlife and their habitats. Instead, club members lobbied for forest reserves and wildlife refuges and parks, as well as legislation to prohibit market hunting and unsportsmanlike hunting practices.

To the latter end, in 1900, Boone and Crockett Club member John Lacey, a Republican member of Congress from Iowa, sponsored the Lacey Act, the first federal wildlife protection statute, which prohibited game animals and game birds that had been taken in violation of state law from being shipped in interstate commerce. And in 1902, Rep. Lacey introduced the Alaska Game Act.[96]

Throughout the Russian-American Company occupation, Natives bartered game and fish to company employees as food and supplied sea otter and other fur-bearing animal skins. When the United States purchased Alaska in 1867, they continued to provide the same services. In doing so, however, Natives hunting for the white marketplace had the same ability to cause the same damage to game populations in Alaska that George Bird Grinnell and Theodore Roosevelt had watched white hunters, hunting for the white marketplace, inflict on game populations in Montana and Dakota Territory.

By 1900 the concern was not theoretical. Indians killing deer in order to sell their skins to whites was egregious enough in southeast Alaska that Howard Kutchin, the special agent to whom the Treasury Department had assigned the daunting task of preventing the Alaska commercial salmon fishery from being overfished, persuaded Sen. George Perkins of California to introduce a bill to prohibit the killing of game animals in Alaska exclusively for their hides.[97] After investigating the situation in 1901, a Juneau grand jury petitioned Congress to take the same action.

> It is an acknowledged fact [the jury reported] that thousands of deer are killed annually for their hide, which sells for the paltry sum of forty cents, while their carcasses are left to decompose or be devoured by wild beasts. Congress has sadly neglected to make any provision for the protection of our game, the natural meat supply of the Natives and of the miners and prospectors who are hundreds of miles from the

markets of the district, prospecting and developing our great mineral resources.[98]

And Alaska governor John Brady made a similar plea to Secretary of the Interior Ethan Hitchcock:

> Congress should enact a game law for this district [Brady advised]. The wanton slaughter of deer has been carried on to a great extent in southeast Alaska by the Natives. In the winter and spring, when the snow is heavy upon the mountains and even to the beach, these animals seek the shores of the island. They become weak, and when run into a snowdrift can be killed with a club. A single Native has been known to bring in as many as 150 skins of animals which he has killed in this fashion. He makes no attempt to use the meat. All he wants is the skin to sell at the store.... This can all be corrected by prohibiting the exportation of deer hides from Alaska."[99]

In response to those and other admonitions, in February 1902, Rep. Lacey and Madison Grant, a fellow member of the Boone and Crockett Club, wrote the bill Lacey introduced in the House of Representatives,[100] which Congress quickly passed and Theodore Roosevelt, who was personally outraged "about [the] game slaughter in Alaska,"[101] quickly signed.[102]

The Alaska Game Act, as the measure was known, established bag limits and open and closed hunting seasons and imposed restrictions on the methods and means of hunting. The Act also prohibited the sale of "hides, skins, or heads of any game animals or game birds." And it prohibited the sale of game meat "during the time when the killing of said animals or birds is prohibited."

The territory-wide prohibition on the sale of hides (including those of both animals other than deer and deer that had been killed for their meat) and the prohibition on the sale of game meat during the eight- to ten-month closed seasons significantly disrupted the Native economy. With a stroke of his pen and no prior notice, Roosevelt had instantaneously eliminated two of the few ways Natives could earn money to purchase coffee, flour, store-bought clothing, and other trade goods that Sheldon Jackson and his teachers and the whites for whom they performed wage work had spent a generation encouraging them to covet.

To acquire firsthand information about the nation's northernmost possession, in the summer of 1903 the Senate Committee on Territories sent a four-member subcommittee to Alaska, which was chaired by William Dillingham of Vermont, and included Sen. Knute Nelson, whose animus for James Wickersham later forced the jurist off the bench and, albeit indirectly, into Congress.

By the time the senators began their tour, the hardship that enforcement of the Alaska Game Act was inflicting on Alaska Natives was apparent. When the subcommittee held a hearing at St. Michael, P. C. Rickmers, the master of the Northern Commercial Company steamship *Sadie*, which traded with Inupiat as far north of Bering Strait as Kotzebue Sound, recommended that "The game law should not apply to the Eskimos."

"During the [September 1-October 31] open season, when the law allows the walrus to be taken, they are not present [in the waters surrounding the northern villages]," the captain explained, because the animals "follow the ice where they can't be reached at that time." And at Kotzebue Sound, as a consequence of the prohibition on the sale of skins, the Inupiat "have nothing whatever now except salmon ... [as their] means of living ... because there are no stores." "The last time I was up there," Rickmers reported, "the Natives came along the sides of the ship with hundreds of black bear skins, but we were unable to give them flour and provisions for them because there is a penalty of $200 under the game law."[103]

But if it hurt Natives, enforcement of the Alaska Game Act inconvenienced whites.

"Up to this last winter the Eskimo brought in many ptarmigan for sale," John Strong, editor of the *Nome Nugget*, complained when the senators reached the Seward Peninsula. "They used to sell them in large quantities, but under the law they have not been able to do so."[104] And at Sitka the Chamber of Commerce urged the senators to urge Congress to amend the Alaska Game Act to extend the deer season because "there is no fresh meat in this town of Sitka now."[105]

After hearing complaints at every stop, John McLain, who traveled with the subcommittee, summed up the situation as follows:

> For [Alaska Natives] the government of the United States has done practically nothing, while legislation conceived in the interest of white men has pretty nearly destroyed their most productive source of revenue. The game laws have operated disastrously to their declining trade in furs by making it unlawful to kill some of the most important fur-bearing animals when their pelts are at their best, and prohibiting the white traders to deal in them or send them to market. It is charged also that these game laws are taken advantage of by some unscrupulous dealers to beat down the prices paid the Indians for such as are bought, on the ground that the traffic is dangerous and that therefore the dealer cannot afford to take the risk unless he gets his goods at

very low figures. From both standpoints the operation of the law bears
hardest upon the Native. This is a sample of legislation enacted at
Washington by a body of men few of whom have ever taken the pains
to visit the country personally and see enough of it and its needs to
make laws intelligently for its government.[106]

And when they returned to Washington, the subcommittee reasoned to
the same conclusion. "The first measure for the relief of the Natives," the
senators recommended in their trip report, "should be the absolute repeal
of the game laws in as far as their provisions prohibit hunting and trapping
by aborigines and Natives and the sale of skins so taken."[107]

To that end and at Sen. Dillingham's request, in February 1904, Sen.
Redfield Proctor, Dillingham's fellow senator from Vermont, introduced a
bill to amend the Alaska Game Act that, according to George Bird Grinnell,
ignited an "earnest struggle" with the Boone and Crockett Club, which the
club easily won. "After much discussion and the production of not a little
testimony by both sides," Grinnell later reported, "Sen. Dillingham withdrew the bill."[108]

The following summer, Theodore Roosevelt asked George Emmons, his
Alaska expert, to investigate the condition of Alaska Natives. Emmons did
so and subsequently advised Roosevelt to urge Congress to amend the
Alaska Game Act to permit Native hunters to sell meat to whites during
closed seasons because preventing Natives from market hunting "deprives
the Native of his self-support, and limits the white in his fresh food supply."[109]

Since Emmons's recommendation was not the one Grinnell and other
Boone and Crockett Club members had wanted, it was ignored. And in
1908 when Congress rewrote the Alaska Game Act, the prohibition on the
sale of game meat during closed seasons was reenacted, and the secretary
of agriculture (the federal official responsible for administering
the Act) was authorized to adopt regulations that imposed even greater
restrictions.

In 1912, Secretary of Agriculture James Wilson did just that when he
adopted a regulation that prohibited the sale of deer meat in southeast
Alaska, even during the open season.[110] He did so because, with money to
be made, whites were selling southeast Alaska deer meat throughout the
territory. In 1908, for example, A. G. Shoup, the deputy U.S. marshal at
Sitka, reported that

> since the season opened there has been an average monthly shipment
> of over two hundred deer from this place alone ... and I think that

other places where the mail steamer Georgia calls on Baranof and Chichagof Islands have furnished a proportionate number. The captain of this steamer told me not long ago that he had himself bought and sold over sixty deer in one week. One of the Sitka dealers has a standing contract to furnish a dealer in Cordova with a half a ton of venison per week, and a revenue cutter officer told me that he was able to buy Sitka venison this summer as far west as Dutch Harbor, and that's over twelve hundred miles away.[111]

The year after work on the Alaska Railroad began, Secretary of Agriculture David Houston adopted a regulation that prohibited the sale of moose and sheep meat in the construction camps because, as the superintendent of the Chugach National Forest explained to his superiors in Washington, D.C., the "government railroad has stimulated pot hunters as never before."[112]

Given the number of workers the Alaskan Engineering Commission was feeding in its camps, prohibiting market hunting along the railroad right-of-way was a reasonable conservation measure. But the regulation that imposed the prohibition, capriciously and with no consideration of the effect on Native hunters, also prohibited the sale of moose and sheep meat throughout all of southcentral Alaska, including the Copper River valley hundreds of miles and a mountain range east of the right-of-way.

In 1917, Frank Foster, a white who lived in McCarthy, a mining camp in the Wrangell Mountains east of the Copper River, wrote Charles Sulzer on behalf of an Ahtna named John Good-la-tah. Sulzer was serving as Alaska's delegate in the U.S. House of Representatives while James Wickersham's ultimately successful challenge to Sulzer's certification as the winner of the 1916 election was being decided.

> [Good-la-tah] cannot compete with the Swedes and Bohunks in the mines, the only labor market, nor will the white man hire him [Foster explained]. He says this country belongs to him and his ancestors and now the government which stops him from getting the where withal to buy sugar, flour and tea under the plea of game protection has permitted and is permitting the cannery people to take practically all of the salmon from the Copper River as they come up to spawn, making it impossible to catch enough for dog feed or food for himself and his family. The only source of revenue left to him after the salmon supply was cut off, was the sale of sheep meat to miners and prospectors too busy to hunt for themselves. He would like to have the departmental ruling [prohibiting the sale of moose and sheep meat] relaxed as to Indians. There are only a few of them, and they are fast disappearing.[113]

Sulzer forwarded the letter to Edward W. Nelson, chief of the Bureau of Biological Survey (the agency inside the Department of Agriculture that administered the Alaska Game Law), who summarily denied Good-la-tah's request. "While regretting the hardship to which the Indians are subjected owing to changed conditions in their region," Nelson wrote Sulzer, "it does not appear feasible to make an exemption in their favor as to the sale of game, since to do so would nullify the very object of the prohibitory regulation."[114]

If market hunting was an important part of the cash economy of Native villages located near white towns and mining camps, in most villages the fur trade was the most important. But the Bureau of Biological Survey's regulation of that activity also wreaked havoc.

To complement the authority that the 1908 Alaska Game Act delegated to the secretary of agriculture to regulate the taking of game animals, in 1920, Congress enacted a statute that delegated the secretary authority to regulate the taking of fur-bearing animals. In turn, the secretary assigned responsibility for exercising that combined authority to Edward W. Nelson and the Bureau of Biological Survey. In 1921, Nelson sent Ernest Walker to Juneau to organize an Alaska Division of the bureau, which initially consisted of Walker as chief fur and game warden and a half dozen deputies.

Since he controlled the information on which bureau officials in Washington, D.C., relied to pass judgment on his recommendations for regulations, Chief Warden Walker had a free hand to impose whatever restrictions on Native hunting of fur-bearing animals he pleased.

Soon after he arrived on the job and with no prior notice to affected Native hunters, Walker decided to prohibit the use of firearms to take fox, mink, marten, ermine, land otter, muskrat and beaver. And on his recommendation, in September 1921, Secretary of Agriculture Henry Wallace adopted a regulation that imposed criminal penalties for violation of that restriction.[115]

In December, Frank Cassel, the deputy warden on Akutan, one of the Aleutian Islands, radioed Walker that enforcement of the regulation was inflicting significant hardship on Aleuts who customarily hunted foxes with rifles and had few, if any, traps.[116] The same month, Frank Williams, a trader at St. Michael, wrote Edward W. Nelson to urge that the regulation be repealed because "it will work a very serious hardship on the Natives who depend on hunting for [a] living as it is next to impossible for them to catch enough [fox] in traps to afford them a living." And to add to the unfairness, "many of the outlying districts will not learn of this new rule until next spring or summer and to enforce this rule against skins killed in ignorance of the rule will be decidedly unjust."[117]

In January when he returned from a trip to the Yukon River during which none of the Eskimos in the hunting camps he visited along the way had heard of the new regulation, Frank Waskey, a trader at Bethel, the Moravian mission on the Kuskokwim River, wrote Nelson to make a similar request. "[T]his provision, if enforced," he warned, "will be the cause of serious hardship to many Native families in the Yukon and Kuskokwim deltas.... With food conditions as they are now, the tundra being alive with large red mouse, shrews and other small mammals, trapping is out of the question as far as Mr. Fox is concerned."[118]

The following month, Esmalka, the chief of Nulato, an Athabascan village on the Yukon River, telegraphed Dan Sutherland, who had been elected delegate to the U.S. House of Representatives the previous November, when James Wickersham retired after serving six terms. "We the people of Nulato beg you to intercede for us to let us hunt with twenty-two gauge rifles muskrats and beaver," Esmalka pleaded. "With traps only we cannot make a living."[119] Sutherland passed the telegram on to Nelson, and on February 16 the firearms regulation was repealed. But by the time it was, the fox season closed in two weeks, the beaver season closed in six weeks, and in any case there was no way to notify Natives in remote villages and hunting camps who had heard of the regulation that it no longer was in effect.

The firearm prohibition fiasco was not an isolated incident. Rather, it is representative of Ernest Walker and other Bureau of Biological Survey employees' self-certain lack of caring for the consequences of the enforcement of their policies on the day-to-day lives of Alaska Natives.

In November 1922, for example, Frederic Goodman, the Episcopal missionary at Point Hope, an Inupiaq village north of Kotzebue Sound in the northwestern corner of Alaska, wrote Dan Sutherland to ask the delegate to persuade the Bureau of Biological Survey to amend its regulation which opened the fox season in the northwestern Arctic in December.

> The present law entails a cruel hardship and loss to our people [the missionary wrote]. By December 1st the surface of the Arctic Ocean has been frozen over for a month and the foxes have been steadily migrating to the ice to follow the polar bears and clean up their leavings. Last week I had to supply eleven almost destitute families with provisions to tide them over until they can start fox-hunting on December 1st, whereas if the season had opened the first week in

November, when there were plenty of foxes around, our people would
not have been reduced to this pitiable condition.[120]

Sutherland forwarded Goodman's letter to Edward W. Nelson, who, after reviewing the matter, wrote Sutherland that "you can rest assured that
we look on every suggestion of this kind with sympathetic interest and
where the changes recommended can reasonably be made we try to conform to local desires."[121] But the regulation was not amended.

The hardship the Inupiat at Point Hope suffered was typical of the
hardship Natives throughout the territory endured trying to comply with
the endless schemes the Bureau of Biological Survey concocted in the name
of conservation.

In the spring of 1923, Frank Dufresne, the deputy warden at Nome,
recommended that beaver hunting, which the previous year had earned
hunters (most of whom were Native) more than $250,000, be prohibited
throughout the territory. Neither Dufresne in Nome nor Ernest Walker in
Juneau nor Edward W. Nelson in Washington, D.C., had any way to know
the condition of beaver populations throughout the length and breadth of
Alaska. In fact, beaver were scarce at some locations and abundant at others. After surveying the upper Kuskokwim River in February 1924, for
example, J. W. Warwick, one of Dufresne's fellow deputy wardens, reported
that beaver at that location were plentiful.[122]

Nevertheless, as was routine, Dufresne's recommendation was accepted;
and in August, Secretary of Agriculture Henry Wallace adopted a regulation that closed Alaska to the taking of beaver. But by that date many
hunters had moved to their winter camps. As George Parks, head of the
General Land Office in Alaska, wrote Edward W. Nelson in September,

> As you know, most of the trappers in the Yukon and Kuskokwim drain-
> age basins must take their outfits to the scene of their operations
> during the high water in July and August. A great many of these men
> purchased their winter outfits and had gone into the hills before the
> order [announcing the closed beaver season] reached them. They will
> not return until some time after the breakup next spring; consequently
> they will all come in with a winter's catch of beaver.[123]

The bureaucracy took Parks's expression of concern to heart, and three
weeks later the member of the Washington, D.C., staff who supervised
regulation of the taking of fur-bearing animals wrote Chief Warden Walker
a letter marked "confidential." After conceding that Parks's letter contained "lots of truth," the writer cautioned Walker that "here is a situation

which will require great care in handling properly in order that the Bureau may not be open to what might be termed just criticism…. We shall have to handle this matter with 'gloves,' because we never would secure a conviction against a party who honestly trapped beaver and never received notice of the close season."[124]

Protecting the bureau's reputation was paramount. The lack of data justifying a territory-wide closure and the hardship and anxiety such a closure would inflict on Native hunters and their families were considerations of no moment.

Bureau of Biological Survey employees intentionally engendered exactly that kind of anxiety to enforce their edicts, no matter how arbitrary the edict or unfair its enforcement. In 1922, for example, Frank Dufresne heard that Eskimo hunters at Mary's Igloo, an Inupiaq village north of Nome, were using steel traps, a practice the bureau recently had prohibited. Entering the village incognito, Dufresne instructed the Bureau of Education teacher to gather the villagers at the school.

> Appearing before my surprised audience with the steel traps I revealed my identity, and with all the force within me went after the violators [Dufresne proudly informed his superiors]. Secured eleven confessions, took their names and told them the penalty for their actions. They were much terrified and pleaded ignorance of the regulations. I took this under consideration—looked the matter up and found that no copy of the 1922 laws had ever reached the village. After sweating them what I thought a proper time, I then switched to an explanation of the fur, fish and game laws; how they came to be; the absolute need for them, and how these laws were made for their own protection. In the simplest language and aided by interpreter I think they were made to see a new light. The older head men of the village in answering talks concurred exactly in what I had said and promised me they would restrain any of the other men from breaking the laws again. Ordered every trap pulled up and brought into the village. Strange as it may seem this was done early the following day.[125]

The files of the Bureau of Biological Survey contain myriad other examples of the racist caprice with which bureau employees exercised the power of the government for whom they worked to regulate Native hunting and trapping. But the situation could have been worse, since the 1902 and 1908 Alaska Game Acts at least allowed Natives to hunt during closed seasons to feed their families.

However, in 1925, Congress enacted a new Alaska Game Act that delegated the secretary of agriculture (i.e., the Bureau of Biological Survey) authority to regulate Native subsistence hunting, a power that bureau employees long had coveted and wasted little time abusing.

The bill John Lacey and Madison Grant wrote and Lacey introduced in the U.S. House of Representatives in 1902 allowed "native Indians" and "Eskimos" who killed game animals and game birds "for food or clothing" to do so during closed seasons.[126] To afford similarly situated whites the same privilege, when the bill was reported to the floor, the House Committee on Territories expanded the subsistence hunting exemption to allow "miners, explorers, and travelers on a journey" to hunt during closed seasons—but only when "in need of food."[127]

When Congress rewrote the Alaska Game Act in 1908, it decided to require "travelers on a journey" to make do but continued the subsistence hunting exemption for "miners" and "explorers," although, unlike the subsistence hunting opportunity the Act granted to Natives, miners and explorers could hunt during a closed season only "when in need of food."[128]

From the beginning, whites in Juneau and other southeastern Alaska towns who were not miners or explorers or travelers on a journey resented the fact that Indians could hunt during closed seasons and they could not. To rectify the "injustice," in 1915, Alaska governor John Strong urged Congress to amend the 1908 Act to prohibit Natives from hunting during closed seasons except when necessary "to prevent starvation." In 1916 the Department of Agriculture drafted a bill that contained that and several of Strong's other suggestions, but Alaska delegate James Wickersham objected to its introduction.[129]

So the next year the governor tried again. "Under the present law these Natives claim the right to kill game at any time," Strong advised Secretary of the Interior Franklin Lane. "In interior Alaska it is perhaps desirable that some differentiation be made in the case of Indians, but on the Pacific coast of Alaska, there does not seem to be any valid reason for the Indians to kill game at their pleasure during the close season."[130] But Strong's advice again was disregarded, and complaints from whites continued.

In 1921 the Juneau district attorney informed Thomas Riggs, the Alaskan Engineering Commission official who in 1915 had attended James Wickersham's meeting with the Tanana chiefs and whom President Woodrow Wilson in 1918 had appointed to succeed John Strong as governor, that the Native subsistence hunting exemption in the 1908 Act meant what it said. Riggs asked Edward W. Nelson for a second opinion, and Nelson, in turn, referred the matter to R. W. Williams, the solicitor of the Department of Agriculture. After rereading the Act, Williams told Nelson to tell Riggs that the Juneau district attorney was correct. "[N]atives may kill game animals and birds at any time for food or clothing," Williams reiterated, "whether necessity for food or clothing exists or not."[131]

But their attorney's pronouncement of the law did nothing to lessen the hostility of the men who enforced it. The same year that Governor Riggs telegraphed his query, Alfred Bailey, the deputy warden at Juneau, informed his superiors that

> [t]he Natives feel they have a right to the game at any time, and in any quantity, and as they use absolutely no judgment in their killing, shooting does and fawns, and as long as an animal remains on its feet, it is no wonder that the game is decreasing in southeastern Alaska. It is time that the Indian was considered as being amendable to the law as well as a white, for their condition along the southern coast is far in advance of the Natives of the interior, and most of them are well to do. Many Natives, living in Juneau, take their big fishing boats to some favorable locality, and salt down enough deer to last them all winter, and these same Indians have probably made more money in the past season than many whites.[132]

Bailey's description of the situation was nonsense, since there were very few—most likely no—fishermen in the Juneau Indian village who earned more money than whites. By white standards, most Indians in southeast Alaska were third-world poor. And they all depended on deer meat to feed their families.

But Alfred Bailey's was not the only bad attitude that belied the real facts of the matter. Although he repeatedly had been told that the Bureau of Biological Survey had no authority to regulate Native subsistence hunting, Chief Warden Walker repeatedly attempted to do so.

In 1924, for the first time in Alaska history (as will be discussed in the following chapter), Indians in southeastern Alaska, voting as a block, elected one of their number to the territorial legislature. When they did, Walker wrote Edward W. Nelson to ask: "Is it possible that by such voting they have sacrificed their rights as Natives under the [Alaska Game Act subsistence hunting] exemption and thereby come under the same status as those who are not Natives?"

When Nelson said no, Walker ignored the answer and instructed his deputy wardens to require Indians to prove they were in need of food before hunting in southeast Alaska during closed seasons: "It is not anticipated nor desirable that the wardens should undertake such rigid application [of his new interpretation of the exemption] as will work hardships on parties in isolated locations where domestic supplies of fresh meat are not available. But they should exercise care to overcome the laxity and excessive abuse of this privilege which has developed in the past."[133]

The chief warden's interpretation contravened both the plain meaning of the text of the Act and the legal opinion R. W. Williams, solicitor of the Department of Agriculture, had issued three years earlier and which, when queried, he reaffirmed. "It is quite clear that Congress intended to permit Natives to kill the game animals and birds protected under the Act at any time for the purpose of securing food or clothing," Williams advised Edward W. Nelson after being asked to review the legality of Walker's new interpretation. "I find no authority in the Act which would authorize the Secretary of Agriculture to limit the privilege conferred upon these Natives by Congress."[134]

While Walker's interpretation of the 1908 Act was knowingly unlawful, in 1925, Congress enacted a new Alaska Game Act that gave the Bureau of Biological Survey almost all of the authority the chief warden wanted. And the authority Congress withheld, Walker took.

The 1925 Act was the culmination of five years of work by Edward W. Nelson. Born in New Hampshire in 1855, raised in Chicago, and interested in the natural sciences from an early age, Nelson briefly studied biology at Johns Hopkins University before applying for a job at the Smithsonian Institution, where he met Spencer Baird, the director of the U.S. National Museum. Through Baird's good offices, the twenty-two-year-old would-be scientist secured an appointment as a meteorologist at the station the U.S. Signal Service maintained at St. Michael, the Alaska Commercial Company trading post at the mouth of the Yukon River.

Arriving at St. Michael in 1877, for four years Nelson traveled through western and northern Alaska by dog team, kayak, and Revenue Marine cutter, first south through the Yukon-Kuskokwim River delta and then north along the coast to Point Barrow. Along the way he recorded his observations of the Eskimos he encountered. They were published in 1899 as a monograph that is still a standard text.[135]

Like many members of his generation, Nelson was a conservationist. However, his Hobbesian view that, unless restrained by government, whites and Natives would hunt game to extinction was honed by a guilty conscience. When he left Alaska in 1881, Nelson moved to Arizona to help his brother work a ranch. As he reminisced about his life as a cowboy to Frank Dufresne in 1926:

> [F]or the next six years, we killed game at all seasons of the year, without a thought to its future, just as did everyone else, and we would

have resented any curtailment of these privileges at the time. This, you must remember, is the natural attitude of mind of men in a more or less wild country who feel that the country and all in it should be at their service. The trouble is now with the modern developments such an attitude if given full swing becomes absolutely destructive to wildlife, and consequently it is necessary to make rather stringent laws and attempt to enforce them as far as possible.[136]

In 1890, Nelson gave up his career as a ranch hand and joined the Bureau of Biological Survey, in whose employ he spent fourteen years conducting zoological and botanical studies in Mexico before coming in from the field in 1907 as the bureau's chief naturalist. By the time he was appointed chief of the bureau in 1916, he also was a member of the Boone and Crockett Club.

The new chief, having had an adventure there in his youth, had a personal interest in Alaska. He soon decided that the 1908 Alaska Game Act was outmoded and after visiting the territory in 1920 began writing a new one, completed in 1921.

Elimination of the Native subsistence hunting exemption was a prominent feature of Nelson's bill. Except when they were "in urgent need of food," the bill prohibited Natives from hunting during closed seasons. And in southeast Alaska the bill prohibited Tlingit and Haida Indians from hunting at all during closed seasons.

But to Nelson's undoubted surprise, when he read the text Governor Riggs objected to prohibiting Indians "in urgent need of food" from hunting in southeast Alaska during closed seasons, a position that, when pressed, even Ernest Walker grudgingly conceded made sense. "I believe that Riggs' idea is right in regard to this," the chief warden advised Nelson, "if the provision is made strong that there must be real and actual need for the meat."[137]

So Nelson made the change, and the version of his bill that Del. Dan Sutherland introduced in the U.S. House of Representatives in 1922[138] and that was enacted into law in 1925 required Native hunters throughout the territory to observe the same closed seasons as white hunters except when "in absolute need of food and other food is not available."[139] However, soon after the Sutherland bill became law, the Indians of southeast Alaska were quietly written out of the emergency subsistence hunting provision.

The new Act established a five-member Alaska Game Commission composed of one representative appointed from each of Alaska's four judicial districts, plus Ernest Walker, the senior Bureau of Biological Survey employee in Alaska. The commission's principal task was to write regulations for the bureau to recommend to the secretary of agriculture. Not surprisingly, although the majority of the hunters who would be expected to comply with the regulations were Native, no Natives were appointed to the commission.

President Calvin Coolidge signed the 1925 Alaska Game Act in January. In May, Secretary of Agriculture Howard Gore adopted the first regulations developed by the Alaska Game Commission and approved by the Bureau of Biological Survey. Regulation 8 identified the Natives who would be allowed to hunt during closed seasons when "in absolute need of food." While the Act granted the privilege to "any Indian or Eskimo," regulation 8 restricted the privilege to Indians and Eskimos who had not severed their tribal relations by "adopting a civilized mode of living" or "exercising the right of franchise."[140]

At the time Ernest Walker and the other members of the Alaska Game Commission wrote regulation 8, they knew that a significant number of Indians in southeast Alaska had "exercised their right of franchise" in the 1924 territorial election. And they knew that a majority had adopted "a civilized mode of living" by wearing store-bought clothes and aspiring to wage employment. As a consequence, no matter what the text of the 1925 Act stated (and as Edward W. Nelson initially had intended), Tlingit and Haida Indians henceforth would be required to hunt on the same terms as whites. So even if he had hungry children, an Indian caught hunting deer in southeast Alaska during the eight-month closed season could be fined $500, jailed six months, or both.

During its thirteen years of regulatory life,[141] regulation 8 unlawfully inflicted incalculable hardship. In 1932, for example, the crash of fur prices that the depression brought on, together with a poor commercial salmon harvest, reduced Indians in southeast Alaska to a destitution that in some cases bordered on literal starvation. In response to the emergency, George Parks, the former head of the General Land Office's Alaska office whom President Calvin Coolidge had appointed governor of Alaska in 1925, asked H. E. Terhune (who by that date had succeeded Ernest Walker as chief warden) to ask the Bureau of Biological Survey to modify regulation 8 to allow Indians in southeast Alaska who were in absolute need of food to hunt deer during the closed season. Terhune agreed to do so and wired his superiors in Washington, D.C., as follows:

> Upon considering provision of law permitting taking by prospectors, travelers and certain Natives as controlled by regulation eight, we find that Natives of southeastern section do not come under provisions as these Natives have all severed tribal relations or exercised right of franchise. Governor believes and am inclined to concur with him that

it would be good policy if possible to have Secretary either formally or informally waive the inconsistent wording of regulation eight immediately and authorize commission to issue special permission to individual Natives to take limited number deer for food. We are not now checking over Natives very closely for deer killed during closed season and have unofficially indicated we would not prosecute if no sale involved, but they are afraid and will not take chance without specific authorization and we would prefer to have it so if legally possible that we may keep check on them.[142]

But the request was denied. Instead, Terhune was instructed to issue permits that authorized their holders to each take one deer. To obtain a permit, an Indian hunter was required to file an application in which he certified "that I am without the necessary food supplies to sustain the lives of myself and my family, and that I do not have the finances or credit to procure such food nor can I secure work to obtain the finances to purchase such food."

During the winter and spring of 1932, Terhune issued eighty-seven permits. But given the Hobson's choice of violating the law or going hungry, most Indians, particularly those in villages distant from Juneau and the other white towns, risked arrest—at least in their own mind—to feed their families. "[F]rom all the information we are able to obtain this special privilege relieved a great deal of the distress among the Natives," Terhune informed Paul G. Redington, who in 1927 had succeeded Edward W. Nelson as chief of the Bureau of Biological Survey. However, "it goes without saying that many Natives, as well as whites, living in outlying places away from towns and villages, kill such animals as are needed for food regardless of permits."[143]

In August, Secretary of Agriculture Arthur Mastick Hyde adopted a regulation that authorized the Alaska Game Commission to issue permits to Indians who had voted or adopted a civilized mode of living, which authorized the holder to take one deer during the closed season.[144] But to prevent unfavorable publicity, at Terhune's suggestion the regulation was not printed in the regulation book the commission annually distributed.

The purposeful and patently unlawful enforcement of the 1925 Alaska Game Act completed the conservation movement's intrusion into Alaska Native life. As had the soldiers, missionaries, and capitalists who preceded them, both in Washington, D.C., and in Juneau, conservationists routinely decided on their statutory and regulatory edicts without consulting the Natives, who they expected to immediately and with no complaint conform their behavior to the latest policy pronouncement.

But while the importance of his contribution to the story of Alaska Natives and their land is to the present day not fully appreciated, in 1920 a Tlingit Indian who believed that Alaska Natives were entitled to the same political and economic rights as whites and who possessed both a perspicacious understanding of realpolitik and a large and egocentric personal ambition, returned home to southeast Alaska. And by 1925, when President Calvin Coolidge signed the Alaska Game Act, his organization of the Tlingit and Haida Indians into the United States' first Native American polity had set the relationship of, first, the Indians of southeastern Alaska, and then all Alaska Natives, with the U.S. and Alaska territorial governments and the men who ran them on a portentous new course.

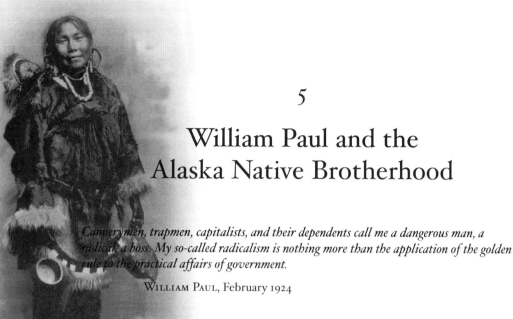

5

William Paul and the
Alaska Native Brotherhood

Cannerymen, trapmen, capitalists, and their dependents call me a dangerous man, a radical, a boss. My so-called radicalism is nothing more than the application of the golden rule to the practical affairs of government.

WILLIAM PAUL, February 1924

It is just too bad that [William Paul] cannot restrain his greed for he is an intelligent and immensely bright half-breed Indian and has a wide and influential power among his own people. He could do much good if he would only follow honest paths.

JAMES WICKERSHAM, October 1935[2]

ON OCTOBER 28, 1912, twelve Indian men assembled at Juneau to attend a conference on Indian education that William Beattie, the superintendent of Bureau of Education schools in southeastern Alaska, had organized.[3] But for their black hair and brown skin, the men could have been mistaken for white: each wore a suit coat and tie and leather shoes and spoke English. Although only four of the twelve were from Sitka, the majority had attended the Sitka Industrial Training School, a boarding school the Presbyterian Church had operated at that location since 1887 and that recently had been renamed the Sheldon Jackson School in memory of its founder.[4]

Indeed, the men were testaments to the success of the Native education program Jackson had begun thirty-five years earlier when he escorted Amanda McFarland to Wrangell: they were Indians who, after being educated by Jackson's teachers and worshiping in his church, had repudiated the culture and language of their birth.

The conference had been convened to allow "civilized" Indians and Bureau of Education teachers to exchange ideas as to how they could work together to hasten the assimilation of the "uncivilized." But before returning home, the civilized Indians held their own meeting.

Whether "civilized" or "uncivilized," Indians were not citizens. As a consequence, since the Mining Law of 1872 limited the right to stake mining claims to "citizens of the United States and those [immigrants from other countries] who have declared their intention to become such," no Indian who discovered gold could keep it. As Jefferson Moser, captain of the U.S. Fish Commission steamer *Albatross,* described the problem after listening to southeast Alaska Indians voice it in 1897, "The Natives urge that the law prohibiting them from owning mining claims is very hard to endure; that they wear the same clothes, eat the same food, obey the same laws as the white man, and are far more orderly than the white communities, and that they should have the same rights."[5]

Of equal importance was the fact that, because they were not citizens, Indians who lived in Juneau and Sitka and the other white towns could not vote in municipal elections or, since 1906, in the territorial election for delegate to the U.S. House of Representatives.

In 1910, Peter Simpson and Ralph Young (two Indians from Sitka who later attended the education conference) complained about the unfairness of it all to Joseph McAfee, the secretary of the Presbyterian Board of Home Missions, when McAfee visited the Sitka Industrial Training School. The clergyman suggested that the Indians of southeast Alaska organize themselves for their own self-improvement.[6]

Three weeks prior to the education conference the sensibility of McAfee's suggestion was demonstrated when the citizens of Alaska went to the polls to elect the members of the new territorial legislature that Congress had recently authorized them to organize. As a consequence, as William Beattie subsequently explained:

> After the [education] conference had closed the English speaking Indians [held a meeting at which they] formed a temporary organization of the Alaska Native Brotherhood, an organization which purposes to work for the uniting and general uplift of the Native people in every way possible. It is the hope of the members of the temporary organization to effect a permanent organization in the fall of 1913 at a convention of delegates from every village in this district.[7]

In 1896, Russian Orthodox priests who had been dispatched from Russia to reinvigorate their church in southeast Alaska organized the Society of Temperance and Mutual Aid of St. Michael the Archangel, a temperance society in which Indian members of the Sitka Russian Orthodox Church participated. By 1905 the priests had organized similar organizations at Juneau, Hoonah, Angoon, and Killisnoo.[8] Not to be outdone, during the same years two members of the Sitka Industrial Training School staff organized a weekly prayer meeting in the Sitka Indian village that evolved into a Presbyterian temperance society called the New Covenant Legion.[9] Simpson and Young had been members of the legion,[10] so they were aware of precedents for organizing groups dedicated to Indian self-improvement. But the Alaska Native Brotherhood (known as the ANB) was openly imitative of a third organization, the Arctic Brotherhood, the largest white men's club in territory, whose Sitka chapter maintained "a fine lodge and ante-rooms."[11]

Founded in 1899 by drunken stampeders in the bar of a steamship making the run to Skagway, the hell's-roaring trailhead town at the head of Lynn Canal and by that date the gateway to the Klondike goldfield, the Arctic Brotherhood was organized into local chapters called camps. By 1909 there were twenty-five camps into which ten thousand men had been inducted, and each year members of the local camps held a convention called a Grand Camp.[12]

The civil government Congress gave Alaska in 1884 had a governor and a judiciary but no legislature or representation in Congress. As part of the Arctic Brotherhood's effort to persuade Congress to grant Alaska a delegate to the U.S. House of Representatives, the 1903 Grand Camp inducted President Theodore Roosevelt into the brotherhood at a ceremony held in the Seattle Opera House. And in 1906, when Congress granted Alaska a delegate, the first three men elected to the office (the third was James Wickersham) were members of the brotherhood.

Building on that success, the 1909 Grand Camp inducted President William Howard Taft.[13] In August 1912 when Taft signed the Act that authorized the citizens of the territory to elect a legislature, the event, which was widely heralded in Alaska, demonstrated what a social club with a political agenda could accomplish. The ANB was organized three months later.

When they returned to Sitka, Peter Simpson and Alfred Young organized ANB Camp No. 1. Camp No. 2 was organized at Juneau and Camp No. 3 at Douglas. Imitating the Arctic Brotherhood, in 1913 members of the three camps convened a Grand Camp at Sitka at which Peter Simpson was elected grand president.

The forty-two-year-old Simpson[14] was not an Alaska Native; he was a Tsimshian Indian who had been raised in Metlakatla, a town for "civilized" Indians in northern British Columbia that William Duncan, an Anglican missionary, had founded in 1862.[15]

After a court in Victoria, British Columbia, ruled that the government of British Columbia and the Anglican Church, rather than Duncan and the Tsimshians, owned the Metlakatla townsite, Duncan and eight hundred

Tsimshian followers emigrated to Alaska in 1887. They built a new town, which Duncan again named Metlakatla,[16] on Annette Island a few miles north of the Alaska-British Columbia border. When he toured Metlakatla the spring after the Tsimshians arrived, Sheldon Jackson met a number of boys and young men who told him that they wanted more education than the few years they had received at the grade school Duncan operated. Always on the lookout for new "scholars," Jackson offered to enroll as many Tsimshians as wanted to attend in the Sitka Industrial Training School. More than two dozen accepted the offer, one of whom was Peter Simpson.[17]

When he completed his class work at the Sitka Industrial Training School, Simpson married an Indian woman whom he had met on campus and then moved with his wife into a cottage on the training school grounds.[18] In 1892 the Simpsons relocated to Gravina, a small island across the Tongass Narrows from Ketchikan, the bustling white fishing town that was growing up around a salmon saltery that had been established several years earlier. There Peter and a friend who also had attended the Sitka Industrial Training School constructed a sawmill and opened a store, which they operated until 1904, when a fire destroyed the mill and most of the village in which the employees resided.[19]

After the fire, Simpson moved first to Juneau and then to Sitka, where, by 1912, he had established a reputation as a master boat builder[20] and "very religious man"[21] who served as an elder of the Sitka Presbyterian Church.

"Civilized" Indian founders of the Alaska Native Brotherhood; Peter Simpson (fifth from left). ALASKA NATIVE ORGANIZATION MEMBERS COLLECTION PCA 33-1, ALASKA STATE LIBRARY.

Sheldon Jackson (foreground) at Metlakatla, Alaska, in 1888 with William Duncan (far right) and the Tsimshian Indian boys Jackson enrolled at the Sitka Industrial Training School. Peter Simpson and Edward Marsden are in this group.
PHOTOGRAPH NO. 400 SIR HENRY S. WELLCOME COLLECTION, NATIONAL ARCHIVES—ALASKA REGION.

But in at least two Presbyterian eyes he remained a heathen. After meeting him in 1914, W. B. Adams, a Board of Home Missions official, reported to his superiors that Simpson had been so "spoiled by the attention he received at the [Presbyterian] General Assembly," to which he had been invited several years earlier, that he had "gone back so far that it was necessary to depose him from the eldership." Adams also passed along the slander that Simpson "hunted and fished on Sunday" and "played at the Native dances."[22]

But even Adams conceded that the lamb he accused of having strayed from Calvin's fold was "by far the cleverest Native and smoothest talker I met in Alaska."[23] And whatever Adams's displeasure with his behavior, had he been asked, the clergyman would have approved of Simpson's thinking, since the Tsimshian was adamant that it was past high time for Indians to stop living like Indians. "Education, good character, truth and honesty is the style to-day," Simpson lectured the training school student body in 1911. But too many young Indians wanted to speak English, wear store-bought clothes, and work for wages while they continued to maintain their parents' connections to the old ways of living. "[N]o man can serve two masters," he warned, and until Indians abandoned "the old life," and began living the "new, noble Christian life," the "doors of opportunity" would remain "barred against us."[24]

For Peter Simpson and other "civilized" Indians, the way to unbar the doors of opportunity was to become citizens. A resolution the Indians who attended the Juneau education conference adopted argued the case as follows:

> It is the paradoxical position of the Alaskan Indian that he is not a citizen nor an alien, nor, like the plains Indian, a ward of the government.... We believe that there is absolutely no reasonable doubt that there are many Indians who by reason of their ability to read and write English, their adoption of civilized customs and manner of life, their knowledge of and conformity to the government laws, and their manifest loyalty to the flag of the United States, are qualified for American citizenship, and we believe that it is a gross injustice to withhold it from them or to leave them in an indefinite position.[25]

But while its members wanted citizenship, the ANB initially had no political strategy to assist them to attain it. Rather than trying to figure one out, when the second ANB Grand Camp convened at Sitka in November 1914, the twenty-three delegates spent their time discussing how to persuade other Indians "to forswear all old customs and tribal ties that may, in any manner or degree whatsoever, hinder or detract from [their] fitness for worthily bearing the responsibilities and honors of American citizenship."[26] But if that was true in 1914, in 1919 the Grand Camp set a new course that, for decades hence, would be dominated by a remarkable force of personality.

William Lewis Paul was born in 1885 at Fort Simpson, British Columbia, the Hudson's Bay Company trading post twenty miles south of the Alaska–British Columbia border.

His mother, Matilda (whose Tlingit name was Kah-tli-yudt and who was called Tillie by whites), was the second daughter of James Kinnon, a Scot who traded furs for the Hudson's Bay Company, and Kut-xoox, a Stikine Tlingit.[27] When Tillie was an infant, Kut-xoox learned that Kinnon, with whom she was living at his employer's headquarters at Victoria, British Columbia, was arranging to send his daughters to Scotland. To prevent him from doing so, Kut-xoox gathered her children and, with the help of a nephew of her sister's husband who happened to be in Victoria trading furs, set out by canoe for Wrangell, her home village seven hundred miles to the north.

Traveling at night to avoid capture by unfriendly Indians, Kut-xoox months later reached her destination. She and her daughters were taken in by her sister's husband, Yuk-ah-yus-snook (known as Snook), the leader of one of the principal clans whose members lived in the Wrangell Indian village.

Kut-xoox soon thereafter died of tuberculosis, and Snook adopted Tillie into a life of privilege. After interviewing Matilda in 1931, the writer Mary Lee Davis described her childhood as "the characteristic rearing of the high caste Tlingit child, in the old manner."[28] But if she grew up attended by Snook's slaves, Jefferson Davis's troops gave the toddler an unintended lesson about the world in which she would live as an adult when the army shelled the Wrangell Indian village in December 1869 to force Snook and the other clan leaders to deliver Scutdoo, the Indian who shot Leon Smith, to the hangman.[29]

When his adopted daughter was thirteen, Snook negotiated her marriage to Gahl-shak, an important Tsimshian (known to whites as Abraham Lincoln) from the Indian village at Fort Simpson. Tillie would have none of it, so the two adults struck a reasonable bargain: Snook allowed Gahl-shak to take his child bride to Fort Simpson, and Gahl-shak agreed that the two would not marry until Tillie agreed.

When the wedding party reached the Tsimshian village at Fort Simpson, three weeks spent traveling in close quarters with Gahl-shak on the canoe trip south had hardened Tillie's resolve never to agree to the union. Her adamancy set off a test of wills that was not resolved until Gahl-shak tired of the contest and allowed the Rev. Thomas Crosby to move Tillie out of the village and into the Home for Girls that he and his wife operated at the nearby Methodist mission. Crosby later recalled how it happened: "[A] girl, who came from the mouth of the Stikine, had been sold to a man old enough to be her grandfather. We had to take her to the Home and protect her, as she said she would never live with him. She was a modest child, about fourteen years of age. We kept her for a time in the Home, against much opposition from the head tribe of the village."[30]

According to a daughter-in-law, under the Rev. and Mrs. Crosby's supervision, Tillie

> learned to sleep in a bed and to make it up neatly. She learned to use a fork instead of her fingers. She saw plates, cups and saucers and used them instead of spoons made of mountain sheep horn. She swept and dusted and even carried flat stones from the beach to make paths in the mission gard[en]. She learned to sit in a chair at a table for her meals ... [and] she learned about God and his son, Jesus the Christ.[31]

When Snook learned that his adopted daughter was performing slave work for missionaries, he demanded that Crosby send her back to Wrangell. But Crosby refused until Snook agreed to allow Tillie, who under Crosby and his wife's tutelage had become an enthusiastic Christian, to board at the Home for Girls that Amanda McFarland recently had opened.

When she returned to Wrangell and began attending school, Matilda Kinnon quickly became McFarland's star pupil,[32] so much so that she was privately tutored by S. Hall Young, the local Presbyterian missionary, for whom she translated sermons and Bible lessons. According to her daughter-in-law, Tillie "was ever grateful to Dr. Young for the excellent training she received in this way. I never knew her to make a mistake in English grammar."[33]

In 1882 seventeen-year-old Tillie, who by that date was missionary-mannered and had matured into a strikingly beautiful woman, left the McFarland Home to marry Louis Paul Pyreau, the son of a French-Canadian fur trader and an Indian woman from Tongass, a small Tlingit village on a small island of the same name located at the extreme southern tip of the Alexander Archipelago.

Shortly after their marriage, the Board of Home Missions certified the Pauls (as the couple was known after Louis dropped "Pyreau" because the French word was too difficult for many Indians to pronounce) as lay missionaries, and Sheldon Jackson assigned them to minister to the Chilkat Indians at Klukwan, the principal Chilkat village on the river of the same name.[34] In June, Caroline Willard, the missionary at Haines mission, wrote Jackson that "we were enabled to send Louis and Tillie to the upper village on Saturday. They will fix themselves up as comfortably as possible in the large house until I can get some way to send them more comfortable things."[35]

But sending two young Indians to preach the gospel and teach the alphabet to Indians as proud of their high status in the traditional culture as the Chilkats was a doomed project. After only a month on the job, Caroline Willard reported to Jackson that "Louis and Tillie came down today, very blue and homesick."[36]

Quitting Klukwan the next summer, in July 1883, Louis and Tillie canoed down the Chilkat River to Haines, where they boarded a steamship for Wrangell to await the birth of their first child, a son Tillie named Samuel Kendall Paul after S. Hall Young (whose first name was Samuel) and Henry Kendall, the secretary of the Presbyterian Board of Home Missions.

In 1885, Sheldon Jackson reassigned Louis and Tillie to Tongass, where Tillie taught school and Louis operated a trading post. On May 7, 1885, Tillie's second son, William Lewis Paul, was born at Fort Simpson, where the Pauls had gone to await the birth. Then, nineteen months later, Louis Paul disappeared.

At Hall Young's urging, Tlingits at Tongass, Cape Fox, and Kasaan had agreed to abandon their villages and relocate to nearby Annette Island, where the Presbyterian Church would assist them in building a town for "civilized" Indians—like Metlakatla, the town William Duncan had built south of Fort Simpson for civilized Tsimshians.[37] To that end, in December 1886, Louis Paul, a white teacher named Samuel Saxman, and an Indian named Wah-koo-se-at set out from Tongass to stake the new townsite.

Navigating a canoe through open water in winter is treacherous work, but according to W. H. Bond, the collector of customs at Tongass (which was Alaska's first port-of-call): "Louis was considered one of the best canoemen that we had."[38] However, even for an expert, conditions can be dangerous, particularly when a bone-chilling wind kicks up and the temperature falls below freezing, as it did after the staking party departed.

When the New Year arrived and the three men had not returned, Louis's brother George and a Captain On organized a search party that several days later found the canoe "driven upon a rock and bound under a fallen tree."[39] A paddle and supplies were found with the wreckage, but the bodies were never recovered.

Three days after George Paul and Captain On returned to Tongass, Tillie gave birth to a third son, whom she named Louis in memory of her husband.

Grief-stricken, the young widow was easy prey. Louis's white partner carried off the trading post inventory, and a shipment of furs Louis sent south prior to his death disappeared. But Tillie struggled on as best she could until Sheldon Jackson, who rightly felt an obligation, brought her to Sitka, where she went to work at the Sitka Industrial Training School as a laundress.

For her sons, the relocation was a life-altering event. Rather than growing up in an Indian village, the Paul brothers were raised in a missionary culture in which they were taught to speak, dress, and think white; their mother, the pride of the McFarland Home for Girls, wholeheartedly supported such a repudiation of their parents' traditional culture. As William Paul's son Fred years later would recall the story he had been told as a boy, "Gramma forbade all of the three sons from speaking Tlingit and spanked them if they did."[40]

The discipline had its intended effect, and Tillie's three boys soon had more in common with white children than with Indian children. By Christmas Eve 1896, eleven year-old Master William Lewis Paul (as he signed his correspondence) had learned enough about Christian ritual to petition as follows: "I am very glad that Christmas time came around now for I want to ask you a favorit," he wrote to Saint Nick. "I am trying to mind mama very much, if you will bring a few things to put in my stockings such as a top, ball, nuts and candy." And to avoid the possibility of confusion during the delivery, he pinned the following note to the sock he hung on Tillie's fireplace: "Please, Santa Claus, don't make a mistake, the stocking on the lower damper is Louie and the one on the highest is William."[41]

William Paul lived at the Sitka Industrial Training School eleven years, during which time he forged friendships that would last a lifetime. "We had for playmates and schoolmates a wonderful set of boys who were to become the leaders of the next generation," he later reminisced. "They were my pals then and later."[42]

But in an important respect, William Paul's education was different from that of Peter Simpson and other Indians who enrolled at the Sitka Industrial Training School when they were teenagers or young adults. Surrounded from toddlerhood by missionaries who emitted a pervasive confidence in their intellectual and cultural superiority, Paul evolved an opinion-about-every-subject intellect. His mind, once made up, could be as unwavering as the trajectory of an anvil dropped from the roof of a building. As Fred Paul would describe his parent decades later, with the restraint of understatement: "Sometimes my father unnecessarily made enemies, whether intended or not. He was strong willed and nobody could influence him. He never lost an argument in his own mind."[43]

But if the missionaries at the Sitka Industrial Training School influenced the development of his know-it-all personality, Lt. Col. (later Brig. Gen.) Richard Henry Pratt taught William Paul his politics. In 1875, Pratt, a Civil War veteran who after the war re-enlisted to spend the next decade fighting Indians, escorted a group of Kiowa, Comanche, and Cheyenne prisoners to an army prison at St. Augustine, Florida. He then spent three years as their jailer.[44]

After dealing with them day to day on the frontier, Pratt decided as early as 1867 that Indians were as intelligent as whites, but "the reservation and other systems we have adopted for and forced upon them" have "walled [them] off from participating in our civilization."[45]

Acting on that startling (for its time and place) insight, Pratt cut the hair of his Indian prisoners and issued them army uniforms whose buttons and trousers they were expected to keep polished and pressed. He then gave them guns, for which he had to "pledge my army commission" to his commanding officer,[46] and ordered them to guard themselves. When that

Indian students at the Sitka Industrial Training School.

experiment worked, he sent them into the community to pick oranges for a local grower, to beachcomb for "sea beans" that were polished and sold to tourists, and in the case of at least one Indian, to work as a porter at the railroad station.

Warden Pratt also arranged for women volunteers from St. Augustine to teach his prisoners English. And according to Pratt, "Most of the young men learned to write fairly intelligent letters during the three years of their imprisonment."[47]

The success of the experiment convinced Pratt that "neither the Indians of the United States nor the Native people of Alaska would ever find rest and their true place except through quitting being Natives and Indians and participating as citizens in all the affairs of what is their government as well as ours."[48]

For that reason, Pratt opposed sequestering Indians on reservations. As he lectured in 1904, "Both experience and common sense prove that segregating on race lines is an enemy of the nation and of the race so segregated, and that wide opportunity and wide contact are absolutely necessary to secure the best development."[49] "To civilize the Indian, get him into civilization," Pratt repeatedly advised. "To keep him civilized, let him stay."

In 1879, Pratt persuaded Secretary of the Interior Carl Schurz and Secretary of War George McCrary to allow him to open a boarding school in an abandoned cavalry barracks at Carlisle, Pennsylvania, to field test his theory that, as he later explained to Sen. Henry Dawes, "Education and industrial training for Indian youth" would "in a very short period, end Indian wars and, in a not very long period, end [the necessity for] appropriations to feed and clothe them."[50]

"The [sixty Sioux, Cheyenne, Kiowa, and Pawnee] boys [who had been brought to Carlisle from the reservations on which their parents lived] have been organized into companies as soldiers," Pratt reported in 1880. "They have been uniformed and drilled.... [and t]his has taught them obedience and cleanliness."[51] Washed, scrubbed, and neatly dressed, when they weren't marching on the parade ground, the boys spent half their day in the classroom and the other half learning a trade. When they finished their schoolwork, the girls Pratt brought to Carlisle were taught to sew and do housework.[52] And boys and girls both were sent on summer "outings"—as Pratt called the work assignments during which his students boarded with white families in the surrounding communities.

The Carlisle Indian School quickly attracted a cult following among the Protestant clergymen, Bureau of Indian Affairs officials, and congressmen who were active in the late-nineteenth-century Indian policy reform movement.

> In a little more than a year these children have been brought from a very low point of natural ignorance and barbarism to the possession of many of the benefits of civilization [an inspection committee enthusiastically reported to Commissioner of Indian Affairs Hiram Price after visiting Carlisle in 1881]. We cannot forbear the decided expression of our judgment that this method of dealing with this unhappy people is, by the results attained in this and kindred schools commended as eminently wise, and deserving of much wider adoption. In fact, we cannot hesitate to express our conviction that it ought to be made a fundamental feature of national policy in our future dealing with the Indian tribes.[53]

Sheldon Jackson, who was living in Denver, was a Carlisle enthusiast who, as Pratt reported in 1880, "brought to us one Apache and ten Pueblo children from New Mexico."[54] In 1884, when Jackson, who by that date had shifted his attention to Alaska, decided to open a boarding school at Sitka modeled on Carlisle, he wrote to Pratt for advice.[55] And when the Sitka Industrial Training School was up and running, in 1894, Jackson began sending Pratt his most promising students, one of the first of whom was Samuel Kendall Paul, age eleven. On his fourteenth birthday, William Paul followed his brother to Carlisle.

Richard Henry Pratt. NEGATIVE NO. 12-I-I,
CUMBERLAND COUNTY HISTORICAL SOCIETY AND THE
HAMILTON LIBRARY ASSOCIATION, CARLISLE, PENNSYLVANIA.

At the Sitka Industrial Training School, Sheldon Jackson's missionaries taught their students how to speak English and to dress and act white. At Carlisle, Richard Henry Pratt taught his students to demand the political rights and economic opportunities that he was adamant were their due. And during the two and a half years he spent at Carlisle, William Paul was profoundly influenced by Pratt's militancy. "At best, Carlisle was a tenth grade institution," he reminisced decades later. "But with General Pratt there to inspire us, it was truly a university wherein Indians of leadership

Tillie and William Paul in 1902.
EARLY PRINTS COLLECTION PCA 01-3907,
ALASKA STATE LIBRARY.

quality got acquainted and blazed the way to a political solution of their troubles."[56]

In February 1902, William Paul graduated from Carlisle at a commencement ceremony that Sheldon Jackson was in the audience to witness.[57] Rather than returning to Alaska, when he left Carlisle, Paul moved to Philadelphia, where he went to work in a print shop at the trade for which he had trained.[58] But the ambitious teenager soon decided that he wanted more from life than to spend it wearing a blue collar and hired on as a night watchman in a chocolate factory so that he could attend afternoon classes at a local business college, from which he graduated in 1903. Paul then returned to Carlisle, where he enrolled in the preparatory school at Dickinson College, whose campus was a few miles from Pratt's.[59]

Although he wanted to stay in Pennsylvania, in 1904 his mother, who had resigned her job at the Sitka Industrial Training School and moved to Wrangell, asked Paul to come home. Since Tillie was in poor health and Paul's brother Samuel was living in the East and his brother Louis was attending Carlisle, he reluctantly agreed.

After living five years in Pennsylvania, he soon found Wrangell, where there was too much rain and too little to do, claustrophobic, and by the fall of 1905 the ambitious twenty-year-old was looking for an excuse to leave. He found it in Tillie's attic: a torn copy of a catalog for Whitworth, a small (176 students)[60] Presbyterian college in Tacoma, Washington.

When he wrote to Whitworth for a new catalog, the president wrote back to say that, although classes had begun two months earlier, he still could enroll for the fall semester.[61] Within days, Paul raised $125 and booked steamship passage to Tacoma.

At Whitworth, the young Indian found that his several years at Carlisle and his year at Dickinson prep had been poor preparation for college. So, rather than Whitworth College, he enrolled in Whitworth College Academy, a preparatory school. "I went to my classes and sat by myself, digging away to catch up," he later recalled. But he mastered the work and, in 1906 transferred into the college; when he felt academically secure, he turned his attention to extracurricular activities. "I promptly got on the football team [on which he was the starting quarterback], then the basketball team, then the baseball team," he years later reminisced. "[I] helped edit the *Whitworthian* [the school magazine], helped start the literary society, and later made the debating team with George Rossman (later a Supreme Court Judge of Oregon), [and] became the leading man in the senior class play."[62]

He also kept the school's books (one of the jobs at which he labored to work his way through) and fell in love with Frances Lackey, a classmate who was the daughter of missionary parents.

Undoubtedly influenced by Frances, when he graduated in 1909, Paul enrolled in a California seminary, at which he studied for the Presbyterian ministry until he ran out of money. As the Alaska Presbytery's education committee explained in April 1911, "Mr. W. L. Paul was at Anselmo Seminary for two years but became too poor to attend further until he could strengthen his finances. He is now at Aberdeen, Washington [Frances Lackey's hometown], clerking in a store."[63] By that date he also was a husband, having married Frances the month before.

From Aberdeen, the Pauls moved to Portland, where William found work as a bank clerk, and in November he became a father when a son, William Lewis Paul, Jr., was born. The next year the Pauls relocated to California, where William worked in San Francisco as an assistant cashier for the Fidelity and Deposit Company of Maryland, and where a second son, Frederick Paul, was born in 1914.

Several years later, when the Fidelity and Deposit Company of Maryland opened a branch office in Portland, Paul moved his family north and settled into life with a steady paycheck as the branch office field agent. But he remained intellectually restless. As Fred Paul later recalled, "Even riding a streetcar [my father] always had a book, usually not fiction."[64] When he wasn't reading nonfiction, William began studying law through the La Salle University correspondence program.

He also had a dream. In 1902, Paul had been a member of a quartet that sang at his Carlisle graduation.[65] In years hence he continued singing and according to Frances,

> began taking voice lessons after we returned to Portland. It was a proud day when his teacher, Taglieri, began including in his newspaper ad, "teacher of William Paul." He joined the Apollo Club, the foremost singing organization in Portland.... He became tenor soloist of the First Methodist Church. He joined the [Knights Templar of the York Rite] Masonic Lodge [where Will was impressed into singing and it was proposed that he take the degrees in exchange for permanent singing].... The organist of the Apollo Club impressed Will into filling in the quartet in a big downtown lodge in an emergency and Will sight-read the whole evening's program. He became a regular member of the quartet. We [also] joined the First Presbyterian Church.... The First Presbyterian Church choir loft was not large enough for a chorus choir, so they substituted three persons on each voice. Will became one of the three tenors.[66]

But singing was more than a recreation. When William and Frances visited New York City on a trip made during the years they lived in California, Paul conceived the ambition of singing in the opera. Of course, world-class voice training cost considerably more money than an insurance agent with a wife and two children to support could save from his wages. But there was a place where big money could be made and made quick.

In 1905, Tillie had married a Tlingit from Wrangell named William Tamaree. When Tamaree visited his stepson and his family in Portland in 1920, according to Frances, he brought "stories of the money to be made in Alaska in fish traps" that were being used to catch salmon (and about which more will be said). "Our ambitions were stirred," Frances recalled in her memoirs, "[and we decided to go] to Alaska to build a fish trap and get rich, [and] then go to New York where Will would continue his voice development and probably become famous."[67]

The move was intended as temporary. "My wife and I planned that we would earn enough money to return to New York where I would study for the grand opera as a robusto tenor," Paul subsequently related. But like all of his big money schemes, his noncareer as a fish trap magnate ended in financial ruin. Rather than building a trap (since he likely did not have the money needed to purchase the materials required to do so), Paul fished, most likely with William Tamaree, at Salmon Bay west of Wrangell.[68] But "the fish didn't run," and he "didn't make enough money to get back to Seattle."[69]

But if the poor fishing season destroyed the dream of singing at the Met, it changed the course of Alaska Native history when, in November, Louis Paul asked his brother to accompany him to the 1920 ANB Grand Camp, which, by happenstance, was being held at Wrangell.

Like his brothers, Louis had been raised at the Sitka Industrial Training School and attended Carlisle. He later followed William to Whitworth, although he didn't graduate. He also attended Chemawa, a Bureau of Indian Affairs boarding school in Oregon, and a business school in Portland, after which he joined the army. Stationed at Haines during the First World War, Louis mustered out in 1918 and moved to Wrangell.[70]

At the time, Edward Marsden, a Tsimshian from New Metlakatla, was the most prominent Indian in southeast Alaska. Fred Paul, who knew Marsden during the 1920s, remembered him as "a brilliant man." And when Marsden arrived at the Sitka Industrial Training School with the group of Tsimshians that included Peter Simpson, Sheldon Jackson recognized the boy's talent and subsequently arranged for him to enroll at Marietta College in Ohio, from which Marsden graduated in 1895. He then enrolled at and in 1898 graduated from a Presbyterian seminary.

When Marsden returned to Alaska, Jackson stationed the rookie pastor at Saxman, a new village the Tongass and Cape Fox Indians had built near Ketchikan (since William Duncan by then had built Metlakatla at the village site on Annette Island), which had been named in honor of Samuel Saxman, the teacher who had disappeared with Louis Paul in 1886.[71]

The Rev. Edward Marsden was not a political militant. Although he occasionally had visited Richard Henry Pratt during the years he lived in Ohio, Marsden's politics were as conservative as his table manners. No matter how unfair the economic and social discrimination to which they were subjected, Marsden objected to Indians doing anything to end it other than to keep trying to look and act and think white. According to his biographer,

> While Edward Marsden was a warm supporter of the Alaska Native Brotherhood in its early years, he became critical of some of its policies as time passed.... From hearsay it would seem that he believed the organization was pushing into questions and making demands, especially in the political-economic field, about which only a small number of its members were able to speak intelligently. Though his white opponents in those days rated him as a radical in some respects, a number of his Indian brethren thought him too conservative. He

seemed to think that they were more concerned with attempts to force the government to eliminate fish traps, increase certain appropriations, build hospitals and to pass a general citizenship law than they were with their own preparation and qualifications for individual and moral progress.[72]

As far as Louis Paul was concerned, Marsden's suspicion was on the mark. At the 1914 ANB Grand Camp and apparently at several Grand camps thereafter, Marsden had been elected grand secretary. However, at the 1919 Grand Camp, held at Juneau, Louis Paul was elected to the office.

Like his brother William's, the youngest Paul's thinking about his and other Indians' place in the world had been molded by Richard Henry Pratt. And putting Pratt's theory of Indian equality into action, Louis took the 1919 Grand Camp by storm. The Rev. R. A. Buchanan, a Presbyterian minister Louis tried to have fired because Buchanan refused to allow Indians to join the Sitka Red Cross, reported to the Board of Home Missions:

> Last year at their convention in Juneau [Louis Paul] made a flaming "red" speech in which he said that if he had his way he would burn every government Native school in Alaska. He is against the Board [of Home Missions], against the government, Native Bolshevik, against anything and everything that draws any line of distinction, no matter how faint, between white and Native. And anything which does this is to him like the red rag to the angry bull.[73]

In 1924, Louis wrote his own account of the 1919 Grand Camp:

> Six years ago the writer, secretary of the Grand Camp of the Alaska Native Brotherhood, joined that organization and then began to urge the principles obtained from that greatest of Indian educators, General Pratt. The convention of Juneau six years ago brought forth a platform which urged the prevention of the reservation system in Alaska; the establishing of the legal status of Alaskan Indians as citizens; one territorial school system, without segregation and equal opportunity to assimilate education; [and] development of competent Christian citizenship.[74]

But although Louis Paul reordered the ANB agenda, he lacked the skills to implement it. The next year that task fell to William. As William Paul later told the story, "The last thing my wife said to me as I went to attend the first session of the [1920] ANB [Grand Camp] was 'Don't you let them elect you to any office for we are not going to stay in Alaska.' I gave the usual reply, but when I returned to our home, I had to tell her that

Peter Simpson (left), the Reverends Sheldon Jackson (middle), and
Edward Marsden (right). ALASKA NATIVE ORGANIZATION MEMBERS
COLLECTION PCA 33-25, ALASKA STATE LIBRARY.

[Louis had been elected Grand President and] I was the new Grand
Secretary."[75]

Prior to William Paul assuming the office, the grand secretary had no
responsibility other than to answer the occasional mail. But William decided that the grand secretary had an obligation to implement the Grand
Camp's resolutions. Although that should have been the grand president's
responsibility, according to Fred Paul, "my father, being my father, with the
kind of personality [he had], he was going to see to it that he used whatever imprimatur the Indians gave him."[76]

But before setting about the work in December 1920, Paul, who by then
had completed his La Salle University correspondence course, took the

Alaska bar exam. As Frances Paul, who heard it from "a traveling salesman before Will got home," later told the story,

> [I]n 1920 a committee of three lawyers was appointed to prepare a set of written questions and later there was an oral examination by the district judge.... It seems the committee was all set to prevent Will's passing the test. It would never do to have an Indian a member of the bar. For three whole days Will had answered questions on the type-writer and was beginning to suspect some prejudice was at work. The salesman reported that a man in the smoking room of the Revilla Hotel [in Ketchikan] had called out to one of the committee, "How are you coming with failing that Indian?" The committeeman answered, "No go. The damn son of a bitch knows more law than the judge does."[77]

When he was admitted to the bar, Paul proudly wrote to Richard Henry Pratt: "I am the first man of Indian blood to be admitted in Alaska. There was a very strong prejudice among some of the attorneys but I was too well prepared to be denied. Out of 231 questions, I missed only 21."[78]

Ironically (since he had returned to Alaska to get rich operating one), the first fight attorney Paul picked was over fish traps.

As has been described, in the 1880s Indians throughout southeast Alaska had eagerly gone to work catching salmon that they sold to canneries for a fraction of the money white fishermen were paid on the Columbia River. But at least they were paid something. However, in 1907, James Heckman, the superintendent of the cannery at Loring, north of Ketchikan, invented the fish trap—a configuration of iron pipes and nets hung from floating logs.[79]

When they encountered the nets, migrating salmon would swim into the trap and eventually into a "pot" from which they could be scooped into a scow and transported to a cannery. After his invention caught 400,000 salmon during the 1907 fishing season, Heckman began marketing the de-vice for $500 per trap.

During the 1908 season, Heckman's traps threw so many Indian fisher-men out of work that Tlingits living in the Sitka Indian village organized a protest meeting in January 1909.

"By using this new invention of making easy money and making quick money it not only ruin our fishermen, but it going to ruin the great Alaska fishing industry," an Indian named Kathlean told the group, after which the fishermen sent the secretary of commerce and labor, the federal offi-cial who regulated the Alaska commercial salmon fishery, a petition that demanded that fish traps be outlawed: "We are not permitted to own land outside of our own crowded villages [the petition reminded]. Now the government has allowed fish traps to be used near the mouth of salmon streams to take our salmon. In doing this it is taking away our means of making our own living. Not only this, but in a few years the traps will destroy the fishing business entirely."[80]

The plea was ignored, and during the summer of 1909 eighty traps operated in Alaska waters.[81] And by the summer of 1920, the season William Paul moved to Wrangell, 484 traps, most of which were owned by the canneries to which the salmon the traps caught were delivered, were fishing in southeast Alaska.[82]

That November the Indians who attended the 1920 ANB Grand Camp spent considerable time rhetorically shaking their fists at the technology that had destroyed their ability to earn a fair wage, after which they voted to send their new grand secretary "to represent the Native fishermen" before Congress.[83] To enable him to do so, when the delegates from Camp No. 1 returned to Sitka, they passed the hat and hosted a dance that raised $500 to pay for Paul's steamship and railroad tickets and other expenses.[84]

As a consequence, in January, Louis Paul reported to Richard Henry Pratt that William was in Washington, D.C., where George Emmons, the retired navy officer who in 1886 had defended the Chilkats' defense of their Chilkoot Pass trade route and who in 1902 had persuaded Theodore Roosevelt to create the Alexander Archipelago Reserve, had written "a letter of introduction [for William] to Sen. Dillingham with a request that influence be brought to bear for right and justice for the Indians of Alaska."[85]

The reason traps fished with impunity was that the secretary of commerce had no authority to prevent them from doing so.[86] So when Rep. Wallace White, the chairman of the House Committee on Merchant Marine and Fisheries Subcommittee on Fisheries and Fish Hatcheries, introduced a bill to allow the secretary to regulate commercial fishing in the waters in which traps operated, the 1921 Grand Camp sent Paul back to Washington to testify before White's subcommittee.

"In 1916 31,000,000 salmon were taken with 558 traps and seines," Paul explained when he seated himself at the witness table in January 1922. "[But] in 1921, but 14,000,000 salmon were [taken] by 550 traps and seines." The decline was so precipitous that the commercial fishery should be closed. However, because of the "terrible hardship" a closure would inflict on Indian fishermen, Paul urged the committee to abolish traps instead.

"In 1921 the Ship Island trap, situated about forty miles north of Ketchikan, caught over 900,000 salmon in twenty days," Paul explained.

And "The Sawyer-McKay trap has the reputation of catching over 1,000,000 salmon each year in thirty days." But a salmon caught in a trap is a salmon that cannot be caught by a fisherman. "I frequently saw from twelve to twenty-five seine boats at Eagle Creek [on the north side of Prince of Wales Island] and no depletion resulted," Paul testified. "[But] last year there was not a single seining crew that stayed there." And the Indians who still fished were destitute.

During the 1921 season an Indian from Wrangell named Charley Jones fished his boat with a six-man crew. "At the end of the fishing season [the crew] had coming to them $17.70 per share, on which those men must live from the end of the fishing season to the next fishing season," Paul told the committee. "Gentlemen," he concluded by lecturing, "we have a right to live in something better than poverty."[87]

Three weeks after Paul testified, Rep. White introduced a new bill[88] that the Committee on Merchant Marine and Fisheries reported to the House of Representatives in March. The text of the measure prohibited fish traps

> in any bay, inlet, or estuary in Alaska, the width of which at its entrance is three miles or less, or within any channel or passage connecting larger bodies of water, where the width of said channel or passage is three miles or less, or within one mile of the entrance to any bay, inlet, or estuary, which is two miles or less in width at its entrance, or within one mile of the mouth of any stream into which salmon are accustomed to run.[89]

While his mission had been accomplished, when Paul departed Capitol Hill, the cannery owners' lobbyists swung their weight, and the bill died when the House adjourned without passing it. And when the White Fisheries Act was enacted in 1924, the section that prohibited traps was gone.[90]

But if the cannery owners won the round, William Paul's visit to Sen. Dillingham in 1921 and his testimony before the Subcommittee on Fisheries and Fish Hatcheries in 1922 were the first times an Alaska Native lobbied Congress on its home ground.

Paul's next historic first was winning election to the territorial legislature.

In 1868 the Fourteenth Amendment to the U.S. Constitution conferred citizenship on all persons who had been born in the United States and were "subject to the jurisdiction thereof." Sixteen years later, in *Elk v Wilkins*,[91] the U.S. Supreme Court decided that the Fourteenth Amendment did not confer citizenship on Native Americans because Indians were subject to the jurisdiction of their tribes rather than to the jurisdiction of the United States.

In Alaska, since neither Congress nor the federal executive recognized the political existence of Native "tribes," Natives had been subject since 1867 to the criminal and civil jurisdiction of the United States. Nevertheless, the unanalyzed conventional wisdom assumed that *Wilkins* controlled and that Alaska Natives were not citizens.

Three years after *Elk v Wilkins* was decided, Congress partially reversed its holding by including a section in the Dawes Allotment Act that conferred citizenship on Indians who lived "separate and apart from any tribe" and had "adopted the habits of civilized life."[92]

Whether an Alaska Native satisfied those criteria was a question of fact. So to figure out what the facts were, in 1915, William Beattie, the superintendent of Bureau of Education schools in southeast Alaska, and his friend Edward Marsden[93] persuaded the territorial legislature to enact a statute that established a procedure for issuing Natives certificates that attested that they had satisfied the Dawes Act citizenship test.[94] But the Dawes Act did not precondition citizenship on obtaining a certificate, and the fact that it did not allowed James Wickersham to survive two razor-close elections.

In 1916, Democrat Charles Sulzer, a southeast Alaska mine operator who had served in the territorial senate, was certified as the winner of that year's delegate election by 19 votes out of 12,861 cast. Wickersham contested the certification, and the U.S. House of Representatives eventually declared him the winner by 31 votes.

Natives cast the deciding ballots. At Afognak and Seldovia, a village on Cook Inlet, Wickersham received 72 of the 100 votes cast.[95] At Koggiung, a village on Bristol Bay, Wickersham received 25 of 28 votes cast by Eskimos with Russian names who signed their ballots with a mark.[96] Wickersham also received the majority of the votes cast at Unalakleet, an Eskimo village north of St. Michael.[97]

When his election contest was debated on the floor of the House, Wickersham argued that the votes he received at Afognak, Seldovia, Koggiung, and Unalakleet had been cast by Natives who lived "separate and apart from any tribe of Indians" and had "adopted the habits of civilized life." But when his supporters prevented thirty Indians from Klawock, a Tlingit village on the west coast of Prince of Wales Island, from voting, Wickersham defended the exclusion of those Indians (who would have cast their ballots for Sulzer) by arguing that they were not citizens because (as will be discussed in the following chapter) President Woodrow Wilson had withdrawn the land around Klawock as a reservation. As a consequence, Wickersham sanctimoniously perorated: "They have no right to vote because they are classed as reservation Indians."[98]

When Sulzer and Wickersham faced off again in the 1918 election, the outcome was a repeat: Sulzer was certified the winner by thirty-three votes. After Wickersham contested the election, the U.S. House of Representatives declared him the winner by thirty-seven votes.[99] Although Indians at Klawock and Hydaburg, the two southeast Alaska villages located inside reservations, voted at polling places Sulzer supporters controlled, Wickersham supporters tried to prevent Indians who supported Sulzer from voting at other locations.

In both delegate elections, Indian voters in southeast Alaska were pawns whose positions on the political chessboard were manipulated by Wickersham and Sulzer, each to his own end. But when William Paul returned to Alaska in 1920, he immediately understood that Indian votes could be cast to Indian advantage. As he explained to the 1920 ANB Grand Camp: "[T]he way for the Natives to get what they want is for them to put their own men in the legislature."[100] Since a substantial percentage of the residents of southeast Alaska were Indians, if Indians voted as a bloc for an Indian candidate, they had the votes to elect him (southeast Alaska's four seats in the territorial house of representatives were elected at-large).

William Paul decided early on that the first Indian that Indian votes elected should be William Paul. But before he could stand as a candidate, Paul had to settle the question of whether the Indians of southeast Alaska were citizens who were entitled to vote.

To that end, in November 1922 he filed a lawsuit on behalf of George Mason, a Tlingit whom L. M. Churchill, one of the election judges at Wrangell, had refused to allow to vote in that year's April primary election.[101] "This move on our part (for which our enemies blame me entirely) is creating a great stir here," Paul wrote Richard Henry Pratt two days after he filed suit. "I hope we lose in the district court so that we can appeal it, but I am afraid we will win in which case the decision is merely local, although even at that it will insure our rights in many directions."[102]

But in March 1923, Paul dismissed Mason's suit when a Ketchikan grand jury indicted Charley Jones, the Indian fisherman Paul had mentioned in his testimony before the Subcommittee on Fisheries and Fish Hatcheries, and Tillie Paul Tamaree.

At the November 1922 general election Jones, who "could not read or write,"[103] had tried to vote, but L. M. Churchill refused to allow him to do so. Jones later in the day encountered Tillie Paul Tamaree on the street and told her the story. Tillie escorted the illiterate Tlingit back to the polling place, where, bending before Tillie's indignant insistence, Churchill allowed Jones to swear that he was a citizen and then gave him a ballot.[104]

Four months later a Ketchikan grand jury indicted Jones for illegal voting and perjury[105] and indicted Tillie for "the crime of inducing an Indian not entitled to vote to vote."[106] According to William Paul, the jury did so because the Wrangell city council had decided that Jones was the best defendant to prosecute to obtain a court ruling that illiterate Tlingits were not citizens.[107]

Initially, James Wickersham, who in 1920 had retired as delegate and was practicing law in Juneau and was in Ketchikan attending the term of court during which the indictments were returned, agreed to defend Jones for $500.[108] But in October, when the case came to trial, Jones was indigent, so William Paul represented the defendant for free.

The verdict turned on whether the all-white jury believed that Jones had "voluntarily taken up his residence separate and apart from any tribe of Indians" and had "adopted the habits of civilized life."[109] For Arthur Shoup, the U.S. attorney, the fact that Jones could not speak or read and write English was determinative evidence that he had not adopted the habits of civilized life. Louis Paul explained the prosecution's theory in a letter to Richard Henry Pratt: "The one fault they have with him is that he speaks but little English."[110]

When the trial began, L. M. Churchill and the other prosecution witnesses testified that Jones was an illiterate who took pride in being the successor of Shakes, the traditional chief of Wrangell. They also testified that the defendant lived in an unpainted house in the Indian village. William Paul countered by calling Jones to testify (presumably through an interpreter) that he sent his children to the Bureau of Education school, paid city taxes, regularly purchased Liberty Bonds, and routinely donated to the Red Cross.

After weighing the evidence, the jury decided that, notwithstanding his illiteracy or the fact that he resided in an Indian neighborhood, Jones lived "separate and apart from any tribe of Indians" and had "adopted the habits of civilized life." As a consequence, he was a citizen and had not perjured himself when he asserted that status.

For William Paul, who was ecstatic over his win, the verdict was precedent "that there is no 'tribe of Indians' in the legal sense in Wrangell, or anywhere else where the same form of tribal organization prevails."[111] It also was precedent for the legal principle that, regardless of whether they spoke English or had a certificate issued pursuant to the territorial legislature's Native Citizenship Act, the Indians of southeast Alaska were citizens who were entitled to vote.

When he passed the bar exam, Paul moved first to Juneau and then, in 1923, to Ketchikan, were he opened a law office. And in Ketchikan in January 1924, Paul announced his candidacy in the May primary election for one of the four Republican nominations for southeast Alaska's four at-large seats in the territorial house of representatives.[112]

As part of a plan that may have been hatched as early as 1920, in February 1923, Paul, who had been trained at Carlisle as a printer, had begun publishing the *Alaska Fisherman,* a monthly newspaper that provided its owner a means to disseminate his name and political views throughout southeast Alaska, and particularly to the increasing number of young Indians who could read.

Putting the paper to its intended use, Paul dedicated an entire page of the February 1924 edition to promoting his candidacy: "People who have known me from my earliest childhood know that I have not changed in character during all this time. On account of my present views, cannerymen, trapmen, capitalists, and their dependents call me a 'dangerous man,' a 'radical,' a 'boss.' My so-called radicalism is nothing more than the application of the 'golden rule' to the practical affairs of government."

The article then described Paul's progressive Republican platform, which included home rule, abolishing fish traps, "publicity for every letter or document filed with our public officers except in criminal prosecution," requiring public utilities to file financial statements, and increasing the mining tax.[113]

The same month that the *Alaska Fisherman* announced his candidacy, the candidate, who recently had purchased a small gasoline-powered boat, set out from Ketchikan to organize his vote.[114]

Today, candidates for the Alaska legislature routinely spend tens of thousands of dollars each election on polling, airplane travel, television and radio commercials, and computer-generated direct mail. William Paul's 1924 campaign was of a simpler era. When he docked at a village, he would call a community meeting. After talking up the ANB and organizing a local camp if one had not previously been formed, he then would explain why voting could make a difference. After that he would conduct a class to teach Indians who could not read a ballot how to cast one. After the primary, Arthur Frame, a candidate for Republican national committeeman whom the Indian vote William Paul turned out helped to defeat, honored Paul's effort by damning it.

The Indians were thoroughly organized by William L. Paul, a half-breed who was a candidate for the legislature on the Republican ticket [Frame complained]. Paul was also assisted by certain white politicians who were anxious to secure the Indian vote. The great majority of the Indians were unable to read or write, or speak the English language and schools were held by Paul and others under his direction, in which they were taught to mark their ballots and the names of the candidates for whom they should vote. The Indians also carried marked sample ballots into the booths from which they marked the official ballot.... It is estimated that at least six hundred illegal votes were cast in the First Division.... At the fall election it is thought that several hundred more votes of this kind will be cast, as the squaws will be broken in by that time.[115]

Stripped of its racism, Frame's description is accurate.

Instead of attacking his progressive positions on fish traps or the mining tax during the weeks prior to the primary election, Frame and Paul's other conservative Republican opponents played the race card.

A plan is on foot to extend to the Indians of Alaska all the privileges of whites, including the right to sit on juries, to vote irrespective of mental qualifications, and to send their children to the white schools to mingle, regardless of physical condition, with white children [a typical anti-Paul newspaper advertisement warned]. Unless those who are opposed to having Indians in the legislatures and white schools and on juries also organize, the Indians are certain to have the balance of power.[116]

Rather than responding, Paul continued teaching illiterate Indians how to mark their ballots. In May when the ballots were counted, the strategy was vindicated: he finished second out of thirteen Republican candidates.[117]

For the conservative white politicians and businessmen who controlled the government and economy of southeast Alaska, Paul's victory was horrifying evidence that Indian bloc voting was the clear and present danger to their hegemony that they had feared it might be.

When one considers that opposition to the fox farming industry, which is making such fine headway in southern Alaska, was among the things which brought 700 to 1,000 Indians to the polls at the recent primary to vote as one man and thus upset the expressed will of the majority of the self-determining votes [the *Daily Alaska Empire,* Juneau's leading newspaper, editorialized], the danger of permitting the Indians to vote until they have become qualified to do so through education and recognition of the responsibilities of citizenship is apparent.[118]

Between the May primary and the November general election the attacks on Paul intensified as the Democratic candidates campaigned on the promise to disenfranchise Indian voters.

> The establishment of a literacy test for voters of all races alike is the big issue in Tuesday's election [Frank Boyle, the Democrat who was challenging Dan Sutherland, who in 1920 had succeeded James Wickersham as delegate, announced]. Without it, the government of the territory of Alaska, its institutions, its schools, the government of some of its towns, their institutions and public schools, will inevitably pass into the hands of those controlling the votes of thousands of illiterates.

In the end, the campaign to get out the anti-Indian vote was effective but not effective enough to prevent Paul from defeating James J. Connors, a Democrat and member of the Juneau city council, for the fourth of southeast Alaska's four seats in the territorial house of representatives by thirty-four votes. Connors beat Paul in Juneau and Ketchikan by 607 votes, and Paul beat Connors in Sitka and Wrangell by 147 votes. But the election was decided in the villages—Chilkat, Hoonah, Yakutat, Kake, Craig, Metlakatla, Klawock, Killisnoo, Angoon, Kasaan, and Hydaburg—where Paul outpolled Connors 615 to 65.[119]

If, for the Indians of southeast Alaska, Paul's win was not victory enough, four months prior to the election, President Coolidge signed a bill into law that reversed *Elk v Wilkins* by granting Indians citizenship.[120] But if the living "separate and apart from any tribe of Indians" and adoption of "the habits of civilized life" citizenship test no longer could be invoked to deny Natives the vote, they still could be disenfranchised through the enforcement of a literacy test.

Anti-Native politicians first tried to force a voter literacy test bill through the territorial legislature during the 1923 legislative session.[121]

> While there are isolated instances among the Indians wherein individuals have gone to school and have fitted themselves for the obligations incident to the exercise of the elective franchise, an overwhelming percentage of these Indians are, to my knowledge, illiterate [Rep. Royal Shepard, a Juneau insurance agent whom Paul would defeat in the 1924 primary election, advised his colleagues when the bill was reported]. In numbers this class of voters [in southeastern Alaska] constitutes about one thousand, which in a total voting population of seven or eight thousand holds the balance of power. The

Indian having but a vague knowledge of our institutions and government, lend themselves readily to the machinations of political
charlatans.[122]

The "political charlatan" Shepard referred to without naming was William Paul, who, representing the ANB, had testified against the bill. Nine
days after the bill passed the territorial house of representatives, Ernest
Walker, the Bureau of Biological Survey's chief Alaska fur and game warden, reported to his superiors in Washington, D.C., that "Paul has political
aspirations and through the Alaska Native Brotherhood can control the
Native vote. For this reason he has been feared by politicians. Aiming at
such mass voting the House of the present Legislature has just passed a bill
prescribing qualifications for voters.... It was freely admitted that it was
aimed at the mass voting of Natives by the 'Master Mind' as Paul was
called."[123]

However, in the end, the effort to end William Paul's political career
before it began failed when the Senate rejected the voter literacy test bill
on a tie vote,[124] and the 1923 territorial legislature adjourned.

In 1925, when the new legislature convened,* a new voter literacy test
bill was the first measure introduced.[125] But this time William Paul was a
member of the body. And in a skillful, if cynical, display of realpolitik he
brokered a compromise: the bill was enacted, but illiterates who had voted
in the 1924 election were exempted from complying with it.[126] The arrangement allowed Paul and other southeast Alaska Republican legislators who
were members of the progressive wing of the party and who had been
elected with Indian votes to keep their political base, but it disenfranchised Natives elsewhere in the territory who had not voted in the 1924
election.

But the fight to prevent a voter literacy test was not over. Having been
outmaneuvered in Juneau, territorial senator Anthony J. Dimond, a Valdez
attorney who represented the Alaska Packers Association (the trust whose
shareholders owned a majority of the salmon canneries and fish traps that
operated in southeast Alaska) and who in 1923 had publicly characterized
Paul's testimony opposing that year's voter literacy test bill as "a shameful
thing,"[127] took the anti-Indian case to Rep. Wallace White, the sponsor of
the 1924 White Fisheries Act. Dimond apparently was acquainted with
White as a consequence of having lobbied the congressman on behalf of
the Alaska Packers Association.

---

* Unlike the Alaska State Legislature, the territorial legislature met biennially.

Alaska House of Representatives, 7th Alaska Territorial Legislature (1925);
William Paul (third from left). WINTER & POND COLLECTION PCA 87-2507,
ALASKA STATE LIBRARY.

At Dimond's urging, in February 1926, White introduced the voter literacy test bill that had passed the territorial legislature (but without the
provision that exempted illiterates who had voted in the 1924 election) in
the U.S. House of Representatives.[128] In March, the Committee on Territories reported the measure,[129] and less than three weeks later a motion was
made on the floor of the House to call the bill up for a vote.[130] But the
measure was passed over when Alaska delegate Dan Sutherland persuaded
several Republican colleagues to object. He did so because, as the leader of
the progressive wing of the Alaska Republican Party, Sutherland had as
much to lose as William Paul if the bill was enacted. In the southeast
Alaska villages in which he had campaigned with Paul, Sutherland had
defeated Frank Boyle, his Democratic opponent in the 1924 election, by a
vote of 640 to 69.

When the vote on the Alaska literacy test bill was delayed, William
Paul, who was an elder of the Ketchikan Presbyterian Church, resource-
fully acquired a steamship and railroad ticket to Washington, D.C., by
arranging to represent the Alaska Presbytery at the Presbyterian General
Assembly, which was held in May at Baltimore.[131] He then joined Sutherland
on Capitol Hill.[132]

On June 30, Sutherland inserted an eight-page statement in the *Congressional Record* that described the voting situation in Alaska, explained why illiterates who had voted in the 1924 election should be allowed to continue to vote, and listed the states whose voter literacy test statutes exempted illiterates who previously had voted.[133] The voluminous legal citations that litter the statement indicate that Paul, rather than Sutherland (who was a miner by trade, not an attorney) was the author.

In February 1927 when the Alaska voter literacy test bill finally was called up for debate in the U.S. House of Representatives, Sutherland arranged for James Strong, a Republican from Kansas, to offer an amendment to exempt illiterates who had voted. Since Maine, Wallace White's home state, had a similar exemption in its voter literacy test statute, White's objection was seen as disingenuous, and the amendment was accepted on a voice vote.[134] So amended, the bill passed Congress and into law.[135]

Before it did, in November 1926, William Paul was easily reelected to a second term in the territorial house of representatives.[136] It was the apex of a political career that two years later would be destroyed by a scandal of his own making.

William Paul (detail of previous photograph).
WINTER & POND COLLECTION PCA 87-2507,
ALASKA STATE LIBRARY.

At the core, Paul's sententious self-confidence masked a defect of character, a disorientation of moral compass, that would prevent him from realizing a potentially heroic destiny. Given the choice between spending his time building a law practice and spending his time organizing ANB camps, writing articles for the *Alaska Fisherman,* and teaching illiterate Indians how to cast ballots, Paul almost always chose the latter. But he also wanted and was in constant need of money. And each time he was tested, his ability to rationalize avarice consistently trumped his common sense.

Although ostensibly retired from politics, throughout the 1920s, James Wickersham was Alaska's most prominent Republican. And Dan Sutherland, Wickersham's protégé and successor as delegate, was the leader of the progressive wing of the Alaska Republican Party. But after twice delivering the southeastern Alaska Indian vote to the Wickersham-Sutherland faction, William Paul was a king maker. Wickersham noted in October 1927 in his diary: "Had dinner [in Ketchikan] with William L. Paul and his nice family—after which we went to his office and laid plans for candidates for the spring primary election."[137]

In addition to himself, the members of the slate of progressive Republican candidates Paul participated in organizing included Charles Benjamin, a member of the territorial house of representatives from Wrangell. Benjamin would run against Forest Hunt, the incumbent Republican territorial senator from Ketchikan, for the Republican nomination for Hunt's seat.[138]

The challenge to Hunt was a consequence of a schism between the progressive and conservative wings of the Republican Party. During the 1927 session the legislative priority of progressive Republican legislators was a home rule measure, which William Paul introduced, that became known as the Controller Bill. Had it been enacted, the bill would have transferred all of the responsibilities Congress had empowered the territorial legislature to bestow from the appointed governor to an elected board chaired by the territorial controller.

In April the bill passed the house but died in the senate when a tie vote failed to overturn a parliamentary ruling by senate president Bartley Howard, a conservative Republican from Anchorage, that the bill could not be considered.[139]

Forest Hunt voted to overturn Howard's ruling but nevertheless was blamed for the defeat. In March, when the senate organized, Hunt first promoted his own candidacy for senate president. When it became apparent that he could not be elected, instead of joining Will Steel, southeast Alaska's other senator, in the progressive Republicans' effort to elect Charles Brown (a progressive Independent from Nome) as president, Hunt cast the vote that elected Bartley Howard. As Wickersham noted in his diary when he failed to talk Hunt out of his own candidacy, "I do not think it will defeat our progressive legislation—but no one can ever be sure. If it does, the burden will be on Hunt's shoulders."[140]

Since the defeat that Wickersham feared Hunt's disloyalty would engender had occurred, Hunt would be disciplined by being removed from the Republican ticket. And with Paul's Indian votes, Charles Benjamin easily defeated Hunt in the April 1928 primary election by a vote of 1,740 to 560.[141]

"The returns from the Republican primary in the First Division show that William Paul still controls the organized Indian vote in many precincts almost or quite to a man," the *Daily Alaska Empire* raged. "The manner in which Indian precincts turned from Sen. Hunt because they were told to do so by their chief makes that plain."[142]

Forest Hunt had a similar view, and in a letter the *Empire* published a week prior to the November general election he publicly tongue-lashed Paul as "the most egotistical, bigoted, and malicious political aspirant known to me, whose veneer of Christian pretense is exposed by revengeful methods."[143]

But Hunt was not adverse to employing his own revengeful methods. Conspiring with John Frame, a prominent Ketchikan Republican who disliked Paul, and George Grigsby, a Ketchikan attorney who was Dan Sutherland's Democratic opponent in the delegate election, by the time the *Empire* published his letter, Hunt was well on his way to settling the score. Several days earlier the *Ketchikan Alaska Chronicle* had published a letter from Hunt in which he accused Paul of secretly taking money from the cannery owners whose fish traps Paul had made his political reputation campaigning to abolish.[144]

The accusation immediately became the talk of Ketchikan. Its subject responded by publishing an advertisement in the *Chronicle* announcing that at the Republican campaign rally on the Friday evening prior to the election "William L. Paul Will Answer the Hunt-Frame Questions."[145] To add to the drama, on the day of the rally the *Chronicle* published an advertisement in which the Ketchikan Democratic Club accused Paul of having received a $1,250 check the previous February from the Nakat Packing Corporation and $300 per month since that date from "similar sources."[146]

That evening William Paul's political career ended onstage at the Coliseum Theater when, before a packed house, he admitted that Hunt's and the Democratic Club's accusations were true. Paul confessed that he had been paid $6,000 by the Nakat Packing Corporation and several other cannery companies to lobby Dan Sutherland to introduce a bill whose enactment would allow trap owners to permanently lease their sites.[147]

The next day the *Chronicle* drove the knife home with the front-page headline: "Paul Confesses Accepting Cannery Funds."[148] Even more pointedly, the *Daily Alaska Empire's* headline informed Juneau that "Paul Betrays Indian Followers."[149] After reading the story, James Wickersham noted in his diary that "the *Empire* had an ugly attack against Paul—put out by Hunt of Ketchikan charging Paul with having sold out to the cannery interests on the trap site matter! Poor Hunt is bitter and a hard loser."[150] But hard loser or not, Hunt had his issue. "[I]t comes rather as a shock" the *Chronicle* piously editorialized, "for Mr. Paul, the gentleman who has and still declares that he favors abolition of traps, to say that he accepted a big fee to go to the national capitol to advocate that for which he always stood against.... On his own confession he is not entitled to re-election."[151]

On the eve of the election, Paul tried to control the damage by speaking in his own defense on a Ketchikan radio program.[152] But the effort fell short. When the votes were counted, of the eight candidates for southeast Alaska's four seats in the territorial house of representatives, Paul finished seventh, losing the fourth seat by 367 votes.[153]

To his credit, Paul accepted the defeat with marmoreal grace. "I believe in 'the voice of the people,'" he announced, "so I have no complaints to make at the result of the last election."[154] But to his discredit, he was blind to the nature of his error.

On stage at the Coliseum Theater, Paul had defiantly argued that he had done nothing wrong since "a lawyer having a general practice has the right to accept fees from any source he can get them," and my "work as a private attorney and my work as a legislator is a different thing."[155] But Paul repeatedly had publicly pledged during his campaigns that he was "against the fish trap in any form" and "would kill the system of fish traps at one blow if that were possible."[156] So the fact that a man as intelligent as Paul would profess not to understand why Indian and progressive white voters might feel that he had betrayed their trust is astounding.

Paul's undoing began the summer of 1927 when a Ketchikan fisherman named William Irvine put a trap in the water at a site at which the J. L. Smiley Company usually operated a trap. When the Smiley Company filed a lawsuit, district court judge Thomas Reed ruled that Irvine's trap was not trespassing because the Smiley Company had no property interest in its site. Since trap sites routinely were abandoned at the end of one fishing season and reoccupied the next, Reed's decision had the practical consequence of announcing that trap sites now belonged to the fishermen who, at the beginning of each fishing season, reached them first.[157]

The cannery owners who operated their traps as private monopolies immediately concocted a plan to nullify Reed's ruling. And in November, D. E. Skinner invited James Wickersham to Seattle to discuss it.

Skinner made his first fortune operating the largest lumber mill in the world. During the First World War he made his second fortune when the Skinner-Eddy Corporation, of which he was a principal stockholder, made millions of dollars building ships.[158] And to make millions more, the Skinner-Eddy Corporation purchased Alaska Consolidated Canneries,[159] which operated canneries and fish traps throughout southeast Alaska.[160]

When the two men met, Skinner asked Wickersham to write a bill to allow trap owners to lease their sites for a nominal rent and then to lobby Congress to enact it.[161] Wickersham agreed to draft the bill for $7,500 (plus a $7,500 bonus if the measure was enacted).[162] But he declined to lobby Congress and instead recommended William Paul for the work. As Wickersham recorded his reasoning in his diary, "Paul ought to be bound over to keep the peace and for that purpose ought to go to Washington—at least at first—to assure Dan [Sutherland] that the Indians and fishermen will be satisfied with the plan!!"[163]

If cynical, Wickersham's political judgment was astute since William Paul was both the leader of the southeast Alaska fishermen who wanted fish traps abolished and a friend and political confidant of Dan Sutherland. So if Paul asked Sutherland (who Wickersham knew also wanted fish traps abolished) to support the bill, his doing so would increase the odds that Sutherland might be willing to do so.

When Wickersham proposed the idea to Paul, Paul quickly agreed to sign on.

Over time, attorneys become their clients. Lawyers who represent rich people get rich, lawyers who represent poor people stay poor, lawyers who represent Mafia hit men get whacked, and so on. Unlike Wickersham, whose client list included a coal company and aspiring public utility monopolists, most of William Paul's clients were Indians. And since most Indians were poor, so was Paul. In fact, he was so short of cash that when Wickersham invited him to Juneau to discuss Skinner's project, he had to lend Paul $75 to purchase his steamship ticket.[164]

But that is not the entire story. In November 1927, William Paul was forty-two years old. His eldest son, William, Jr., was a sophomore at Ketchikan High School, and his second son, Fred, was thirteen. By that date he also had two younger children, five-year-old Robert and a three-year-old daughter, Frances, to support, plus his wife and his wife's mother, who had moved into the Paul household when she was widowed. But even though he wanted money and his family needed it, rather than working at his law practice, Paul spent his time working on the nonpaying projects that interested him, a preoccupation that left his family impecunious. As Fred Paul years later would recall,

> Dad's interest was in the Native movement. One of the family stories we have is that my mother kept book on him as to the amount of hours he was spending practicing law as compared to being the editor of *The Alaska Fisherman*.... From time to time he'd get some enthusiasm going to make [the newspaper] profitable and he'd have someone go out and solicit ads and stuff. But that wasn't his interest. His interest was in writing his political essays. When mother realized he was spending ninety percent of his time in political matters, she went back to teaching school.[165]

So when James Wickersham offered big easy money, Paul readily agreed to trade on his friendship with Dan Sutherland.

As part of the plan, in January 1928 the *Alaska Fisherman* published a copy of the Wickersham trap site lease bill and a letter from its author, which argued that the bill's enactment was necessary "to preserve order between warring trap men, to compel them to pay a license fee and to recognize the rights of the public."[166] Significantly, the letter made no mention of the fact that the publisher of the newspaper in which it appeared had been hired to lobby the bill.

In February, Paul met with Skinner and several other cannery owners in Seattle, negotiated his fee, and then continued east, where his nascent career as a cannery lobbyist quickly ended in disaster. As Wickersham subsequently raged in his diary, "Paul has made a fool of himself in Washington!"[167]

On February 24, Paul sent a telegram informing Haakon Friele, the Alaska superintendent of the Nakat Packing Corporation, that Dan Sutherland refused to introduce the trap site lease bill. But rather than leaving town, Paul—by then apparently worried that his involvement in the failed plan would be found out—tried to cover his tracks and in the process made a bad situation for his clients substantially worse. With the help of Sen. Charles Curtis of Kansas (whose acquaintance he likely made through James Wickersham's good offices), Paul obtained an appointment with President Calvin Coolidge, during which he lectured the president on the mismanagement of the Alaska commercial salmon fishery.[168]

When Wickersham read the press account of the meeting, he rightly concluded that Paul was "playing politics." As he noted in his diary, "This is a beautiful alibi in case of a political accusation!"[169]

When Henry O'Malley, the commissioner of the Bureau of Fisheries, the Department of Commerce agency that regulated the Alaska commercial salmon fishery, learned of the meeting, he was livid. Wickersham confided to his diary: "[I]nstead of cultivating a friendly O'Malley when he got there [Paul] went over his head with the aid of Sen. Curtis and presented his grievances to the President in such a way as to make O'Malley furious.... Friele and others who are putting up for Paul's expenses to Washington are sore and bitterly disappointed—for O'Malley's now abusing and threatening the canners!"[170]

James Heckman, the inventor of the fish trap, was a friend of Forest Hunt and had attended the meeting in Seattle at which Paul negotiated his fee. So Paul knew, or should have known, that Hunt and other political enemies would learn that he was being paid by the cannery owners.

In 1928 the owners' influence in the territorial legislature was as pervasive as the influence oil companies wield in the Alaska legislature today. As a consequence, Paul also knew, or should have known, that his Indian and progressive white constituents would consider trading for hire on his friendship with Dan Sutherland in order to advance the economic interests of the owners was a breach of political trust equivalent to a present-day Alaska lawyer-legislator elected on an environmental platform secretly representing an oil company.

But to the end, Paul's propensity for self-rationalization prevented him from acknowledging the public hypocrisy of his private behavior. Dan Sutherland, however, was more realistic. Sutherland wrote Louis Paul the month after the election: "William's friends in the [Alaska Native] Brotherhood may be right about wanting him not to run for office again.... It is to be regretted that William ever became involved in that trap business or that he took the money from the packers."[171]

What was William Paul's legacy as a legislator? When it was over, Wickersham privately lauded Alaska's first Native legislator as one of the "two outstanding strong men" in the 1927 legislature. And he was.

The first Paul bill enacted into law gave watchmen at fish traps and elsewhere a lien for their wages. Other Paul bills that passed the legislature increased the fish trap tax (vetoed), increased maintenance payments for school buildings, authorized divorced and widowed Native women who were unable to support their children to receive a small stipend unless the children were being cared for by the Bureau of Education, authorized a

school to be built at Yakutat and another to be repaired at Douglas, prohibited indigents from being incarcerated because they were too poor to
pay their fines (vetoed), authorized the construction of public libraries
(vetoed), and authorized first-class cities to tax property owners to construct roads and sewers (vetoed).

Before leaving his political career, there is a codicil that typifies Paul's
penchant for poor judgment. Prior to the 1928 election Paul wrote Edward
Marsden a letter in which he gratuitously savaged George Grigsby, the
Ketchikan attorney who was Dan Sutherland's Democratic opponent in
the delegate election, as a "crook, gambler" and "wife beater." Why he did
is curious. Marsden, who by that date was pastor of the Presbyterian Church
at Metlakatla, years earlier had persuaded the Tsimshians to quit the ANB
because he objected to Paul's having transformed the organization from a
self-improvement club into a William Paul campaign organization.[172] So
Marsden was no friend.

Indeed, the Sunday prior to the 1928 election, Marsden, who had been
in Ketchikan when Paul's acceptance of money from the cannery owners
had been the talk of the town, appeared with Grigsby at a political rally at
Metlakatla at which he urged his congregation to repudiate Paul's leadership. "It is true that Mr. Paul received fees from the canneries," Marsden
intoned. "I want to assure you that he met temptation, and that he fell."[173]

Several days after the election, Marsden passed the "wife beater" letter
along to Grigsby, who, after reading it, stormed with his wife into Paul's
Ketchikan law office (which shared a common wall with a pool hall) to
demand a retraction. Paul answered, "George, if that's why you came here,
turn around and go out." Frances Paul's description of what happened next
at the scene she witnessed is worth quoting.

> Grigsby answered by aiming a blow at Will's face, knocking off his
> glasses.... Will [then] rushed Grigsby bang up against the pool hall
> wall, which caused the habitues of the pool hall to erupt into our
> office. Another time he had Grigsby on the floor and Mrs. Grigsby
> flung herself on top of them and clawed Will's neck with her finger-
> nails.... We had a wood stove for heating and there was a wood box.
> Mrs. Grigsby picked up a two-by-four from the wood box and pre-
> pared to enter the fray but was disarmed by one of the pool hall men.
> She began hitting Will with her purse and it flew open spilling the
> contents all over the floor which diverted her interest. At the last, Will
> knocked Grigsby into the wood box where he sat doubled up until
> some of the pool hall men pulled him out and took him away.[174]

According to James Wickersham, who did not witness the brawl, "Paul succeeded in beating Grigsby at the assaulting game, blackens his eyes, cut his face with his fists, nearly broke a leg for him and otherwise, etc. Paul [then] went off to Sitka to attend the ANB Convention. Grigsby is confined to his home."[175]

Since George Grigsby was one of Forest Hunt's co-conspirators, blackening his eyes may have been a solace. But like it or not (and he did not), William Paul's political career was over. However, while he had been repudiated by the southeast Alaska electorate, inside the smaller world of the ANB he retained his influence.

According to the *Alaskan,* a newspaper Louis Paul began publishing in 1926 in Petersburg, a white fishing town that had grown around a cannery north of Wrangell, when the 1928 Grand Camp convened at Sitka, Paul cleared the air by "[taking] up the political situation and the charges made by the [Ketchikan] *Chronicle* and Juneau *Empire.*" And his rhetorical talent for self-congratulatory rationalization carried the meeting hall. As the *Alaskan* reported when the publisher's sibling concluded his defense, "The spirit of harmony and understanding extended William Paul proves that he has completely vindicated his character in every respect."[176] In fact, the delegates unanimously elected Paul to the first of two consecutive terms as ANB grand president.[177]

When they did, the delegates had no way to know that Paul's election would result the next year in the presence of a guest at the 1929 Grand Camp who would start the Indians of southeastern Alaska—and eventually all Alaska Natives—on a historic new journey.

Throughout the 126-year Russian "occupation" of Alaska, the Indians of southeast Alaska had asserted hunting, fishing, and trade rights over particular lands and waters and transportation corridors. Since few whites had any interest in moving north, when the United States purchased Alaska in 1867, the Indians were not dispossessed either of the land they used and occupied or of their fishing sites and trade routes. Rather, the usurpation began ad hoc and continued piecemeal when prospectors drifted into southeast Alaska searching for gold and whites began competing with Indian fishermen.

Between 1902 and 1909, Theodore Roosevelt's proclamations creating the Tongass National Forest closed most of southeastern Alaska to private entry, although at disparate locations whites continued to build towns, open mines, and operate canneries. Of equal importance and abetted by the National Forest Service and the Bureau of Biological Survey, whites also evicted Indians from more than a hundred islands throughout the archipelago.

Encircled by a seawater fence, small islands are natural pens in which to raise foxes. When that fact became apparent, in 1901 a white named Jim York released blue foxes on Sumdum Island south of Juneau.[178] And by 1923 the National Forest Service had leased 140 islands inside the Tongass National Forest to fox farmers.[179]

In 1921 the Forest Service and the Bureau of Biological Survey instructed their employees to prohibit fox farm lessees from disturbing "totem poles, Native burying grounds, and lands cultivated by Natives."[180] But they were not told to stop leasing islands that Indians used or occupied. As a consequence, conflicts between fox farmers and Indians continued to escalate.

By 1924 the situation was so egregious that, on behalf of the ANB, William Paul wrote a letter of complaint to Edward W. Nelson, chief of the Bureau of Biological Survey, stating that the Forest Service was conspiring with whites to steal Indian land.

> Our first cause of complaint against the fox farmer is that in nearly every instance the fox farmer has stolen the islands from the Indian occupant [Paul wrote]. He makes an affidavit to the effect that there are no Indian claims. The Forestry Department has confided to me that they have made in the past no adequate investigation of the affidavit of the applicant, but have granted a lease of the island with a view of facilitating the so-called "new business." Then Mr. Fox Farmer armed with a lease from the government approaches Mr. Indian and tells him that Uncle Sam has given him the island and "please get off." In nearly every case the Indian is a very peaceful person engaged in hunting his mink, land otter and other fur-bearing animals on the coveted islands. His shack stands there and has stood in some cases on the very same site held by his ancestors for generations.

"It does not improve matters any merely because the thief is now armed with a lease from the government," Paul concluded.[181]

In response, Nelson wrote William Greeley, chief of the Forest Service, that he "assume[d] that you do not desire to have the Natives treated harshly." If so, there was a solution to Paul's problem. "If Indians should be living on any island which is to be leased for fox farming purposes, the Forest Service might well require that the applicant have the lessor pay the Indian some reasonable sum for his house or other structures and his squatter's rights," Nelson counseled. "In that way the Indian might move to another locality without feeling that he is being ruthlessly crowded out of the home of his ancestors."[182]

But even that modest suggestion was ignored, and the evictions continued. In March 1925 the Indians at Hoonah, the Tlingit village on the
northeastern corner of Chichagof Island, petitioned Nelson as follows:

> A number of our people have cultivated gardens and have buildings
> erected on Pleasant Island. We have all used this island for protection
> when we have been driven ashore by storms as we travel from place to
> place in our small boats. Now we understand it is to be taken up by fox
> farmers and that we shall not be allowed to land upon it under any
> consideration. As nearly every other island in the whole of Icy Straits
> has been set aside in the same way, we do most earnestly ask relief.[183]

Eight months later, when the 1925 ANB Grand Camp convened at
Hydaburg, the Haida Indian village on the south side of Prince of Wales
Island, the delegates joined in Hoonah's condemnation: "[Fox farmers have]
driven the Indians of southeastern Alaska from their homes on many islands. The home of at least one Indian widow with six children has been
destroyed and her garden products actually used by the beneficiaries of the
Forest Department officials in Alaska. Another Indian, a very old man,
was forced out of his island and his home and smokehouse actually made
to serve as fox pens."[184]

Peter Simpson and William Paul attended the Grand Camp. As mentioned, Simpson had emigrated to Alaska after a court had decided that
the government of British Columbia and the Anglican Church, rather than
the Tsimshian Indians, owned the Metlakatla townsite. Thirty-eight years
later, Simpson still was so bitter about the decision that, according to William Paul, his anger "burned within him."[185]

Not being an Alaska Native, Simpson was hesitant to voice his feelings
during the discussion that preceded the vote to adopt the resolution that
condemned the fox farm leasing program. But at some point during the
Grand Camp, the Tsimshian pulled Paul aside. "This land is yours," he said.
"Why don't you fight for it?"[186]

Simpson's assertion that the Tlingit and Haida Indians "owned" southeast Alaska piqued Paul's interest. When he returned to Ketchikan, he
researched the question and discovered the legal theory of aboriginal title.

In 1823 in *Johnson v M'Intosh*[187] the U.S. Supreme Court held that the U.S.
government's title to those portions of the public domain being used or
occupied by Native Americans whose ancestors' use and occupancy pre-
dated the nation's existence was subject to an Indian right of occupancy—an
"aboriginal title"—that only Congress could extinguish. In the coterminous states, Congress had extinguished aboriginal title by Senate ratification

of treaties the federal executive negotiated with various tribes, in which the United States agreed to pay money and distribute sundries to tribal members as compensation for the land the treaties ceded.

In 1871, Congress directed the president to stop negotiating treaties, but in 1925 the concept of aboriginal title still was good law.

Assuming so, between 1902 and 1909, Congress had extinguished the Tlingit and Haida Indians' aboriginal title to the land inside the Tongass National Forest when Theodore Roosevelt (acting in Congress's stead by exercising the authority he had been delegated by the 1891 Forest Reserve Act) signed the proclamations that established the forest. But Congress had not compensated the Indians for the extinguishment, even though the U.S. government's past dealings with other groups of Native Americans was precedent that it should have.

To obtain compensation, the Tlingit and Haida Indians had to persuade Congress to either pay direct compensation or enact a statute that authorized them to file a lawsuit in the U.S. Court of Claims to obtain a money judgment for the value of their extinguished aboriginal title.

According to William Paul, the need to persuade Congress to authorize a Court of Claims lawsuit was obvious. But when he presented it at the 1926 ANB Grand Camp, the delegates thought the idea that the Indians of southeast Alaska had a right to be paid for the loss of their use and occupancy of the Tongass Forest was a fantasy. For that reason, "it took me four years," Paul recalled, "to persuade my people to endorse my idea to sue the government for compensation for the land taken from us."[188]

That is William Paul's often-told story of how he invented the Alaska Native land claims movement. But the telling is a self-promoting prevarication.

Between 1925, when Peter Simpson purportedly voiced his "why don't you fight for it" admonition, and 1932, when it ceased publication, the *Alaska Fisherman,* whose pages Paul used to promote his political candidacies and to talk up the projects in which he was interested, made no mention of its publisher's alleged "idea to sue the government for compensation for the land taken from us."

The reason is that the idea was James Wickersham's rather than William Paul's.

On eight occasions during the twelve years Wickersham served as delegate, Congress enacted legislation that authorized an Indian tribe to sue the United States in the Court of Claims to obtain a money judgment for the value of land taken from its members in violation of a treaty. And in 1925, Congress enacted a statute that authorized the Muckelshoot, San

Juan Islands, Nook-Sack, Suattle, Chinook, Upper Chehalis, Lower Chehalis, and Humptulip tribes and bands of Indians in Washington state to file suit.[189]

During several of the Congresses in which he served, Wickersham had been a member of the House Committee on Indian Affairs, so he was aware of the precedents. He particularly was aware that the statute that authorized the Washington state tribes to file suit authorized the Indians' attorneys to keep 10 percent of the judgment they won as a fee.

During the years subsequent to the 1925 Grand Camp, Wickersham heard the same complaints about white usurpations of Indian-occupied land that had been voiced at Hydaburg. And he undoubtedly also discussed the problem with William Paul. The Indians' complaints got Wickersham to thinking. Even though the United States had not negotiated a treaty with the Indians of southeast Alaska when it purchased the territory in 1867, the law recognized that the Indians possessed an aboriginal title to the land they used and occupied. Assuming so, Wickersham reasoned, then Congress had the same obligation to compensate the Indians of southeast Alaska for the extinguishment of their aboriginal title as it had to compensate the Indians whose land had been taken in violation of treaty guarantees.

But before he could lobby Congress to enact a statute that authorized him to file a lawsuit on behalf of the Tlingit and Haida Indians (which he intended to prosecute for 15 percent of the judgment as his fee), Wickersham needed a client. The way to obtain one, he reasoned, was to associate the ANB's grand president as his co-counsel. As Wickersham explained in his diary entry of March 12, 1929,

> I am incubating a scheme of organizing the Tlingit Indians and having them apply to Congress for compensation for their lands, fishing rights, etc. etc., in connection with Paul when I go down to Ketchikan next week. Many of them have complained to me about the United States taking their garden sites, fishery places, hunting grounds, etc., and I think they are entitled to compensation such as Washington state Indians are now seeing through Acts of Congress.[190]

The following week, as he left for Ketchikan on the evening steamer, Wickersham noted to himself that

> I hope to get a scheme established with Wm L. Paul's assistance to recover from the United States the tribal values for the Tlingit Indians of their lands and properties taken by the United States and its citizens without treaty or any other rights—but just by force! *If I can get*

Paul interested we will act as the attorneys for the Tlingits—as a tribe—through Congress, etc.[191] (emphasis added)

After meeting with Paul, Wickersham summarized their discussion as follows:

> I proposed to [William Paul] the project of attempting to secure the passage of an Act of Congress to permit the Tlingit and Haida Indians to bring suit in the Court of Claims to recover the value of the home lands, fishing sites, etc., taken by the United States without compensation. We agreed to join as attorneys and work together as attorneys for the Indians. I wrote out the agreement and he is considering it.[192]

Hands were shaken, and in April, Wickersham wrote a contract for "the Tlingit and Haida Indians" to sign, designating him and William Paul as their attorneys. Then he drafted a bill to introduce in Congress.[193]

On November 15, Wickersham noted in his diary that the next week he intended to "present the matter of organizing the suit" at the ANB Grand Camp at Haines and would ask the delegates "to appoint a committee to assist in the matter and sign a contract to pay myself and Paul as their attorneys a fee of fifteen percent upon what we can recover."[194]

On the evening of November 19 he did so, and after listening to Wickersham pitch his proposal, the delegates organized a committee to consider the matter. Wickersham subsequently summed up his meeting with the group: "They seem greatly interested and exhibit a shrewdness and careful attention to their own interests that is gratifying to me. I assume their report [favoring the project] will be adopted and if so myself and Wm. L. Paul will act as their attorneys."[195]

The Grand Camp adopted the committee's report. And that is how the Alaska Native land claims movement began.

In January 1930, Dan Sutherland introduced Wickersham's Court of Claims bill in the U.S. House of Representatives.[196] But the Committee on Claims, to which it was referred, took no action on the measure prior to adjournment.

The previous fall, Sutherland (who, during his five terms in Congress, had "scarcely [been able to] make both ends meet financially")[197] had announced that he would not seek reelection. When he did, many of his former supporters urged Wickersham to run for his old seat. Although he was seventy-three years old, he was in good health. So Wickersham decided to make the last hurrah, and in November 1930 he defeated George Grigsby, who again was the Democratic candidate, by 286 votes.

1929 Alaska Native Brotherhood Grand Camp, Haines, Alaska; Grand President
William Paul (front row, center), Louis Paul (front row, fourth from right).
PHOTOGRAPH COURTESY TLINGIT AND HAIDA CENTRAL COUNCIL ARCHIVES,
AND SEALASKA HERITAGE FOUNDATION.

When the new Congress convened, in December 1931, Del. Wickersham
persuaded Sen. Lynn Frazier to introduce attorney Wickersham's Court of
Claims bill in the Senate.[198] It was referred to the Committee on Indian
Affairs, which Frazier chaired. Wickersham also persuaded Frazier to urge
the Senate to pass the bill over the objection of Commissioner of Indian
Affairs Charles Rhoads (who opposed the measure principally because there
was no precedent for paying a group of Native Americans compensation
for the extinguishment of aboriginal title that had not been recognized by
a treaty). The Senate did so, but despite Wickersham's effort to steer the
measure through the House of Representatives, the bill died in the House
Committee on Indian Affairs.

When the 73d Congress convened in 1933, the bill was reintroduced.[199]
But not by James Wickersham. Instead, the bill was introduced by Alaska's
new delegate, Anthony Dimond, the territorial senator who in 1926 had
lobbied Congress to disenfranchise illiterate Native voters.

The previous November the fifty-one-year-old Dimond had easily defeated Wickersham, who had the bad luck to be a Republican candidate in an election held in the trough of the depression. Franklin Roosevelt's name at the top of their ticket carried almost every Alaska Democratic Party candidate into office.

At a campaign appearance two weeks prior to the election, Dimond told a standing-room-only white audience that he supported allowing the Tlingit and Haida Indians to file a lawsuit in the Court of Claims because "if they have been wronged, certainly they ought to have the right to sue for compensation."[200]

By that date, Dimond likely believed what he said, although prior to the 1932 election he had been no particular friend of the Indian. But even so, his public support for the idea also was part payment of a debt that he owed both to the ANB and to William Paul, who by then was working to turn out the Indian vote for Dimond and other Democratic candidates after he had tried and failed to extort money to do so from James Wickersham and other leaders of his own party.

By any standard of ethical measure, Paul's behavior during the 1932 election was shameful.

James Wickersham had as many faults as most men, but he understood the value of political loyalty. When he ran for delegate in 1930, Wickersham also understood that, despite the scandal that had resulted in his defeat in 1928, William Paul still could influence as many as two thousand Indian votes. For that reason, when Paul, who wanted to return to office, held on in the 1930 primary election to win one of the Republican nominations for southeast Alaska's four seats in the territorial house of representatives, Wickersham welcomed him onto the Republican ticket. Paul, in turn, turned out the Indian vote for Wickersham. And in southeast Alaska villages, Wickersham defeated George Grigsby by 373 votes, which—added to the Indian votes he received at Juneau, Sitka, Wrangell, and Ketchikan—were both the margin and the cushion of his narrow territory-wide 286-vote victory.

Although he received 2,094 of 5,117 votes cast, of the eight candidates for southeast Alaska's four seats in the territorial house of representatives, William Paul finished a distant sixth.[201] The new defeat brought Alaska's first Native ex-legislator hard aground on an increasingly desperate reality.

As has been discussed and as Fred Paul later would describe the situation during the years he came of age, his father "was never a money maker."[202] But that allegiant understatement does not do justice to Paul's financial desperation after losing the 1930 election. During his first years in

Ketchikan, his law practice apparently had had a modest positive cash flow. But the spring after the 1928 election, the flow stopped.

The previous year, President Coolidge had appointed Justin Harding, a politically connected Republican member of the Ohio legislature, as U.S. attorney for southeast Alaska. As a matter of policy, when a fisherman was cited for violating a commercial fishing regulation Harding routinely seized his boat. If the fisherman pleaded guilty and paid his fine, the boat was released. But if he pled not guilty, the boat remained impounded until the case came to trial after the fishing season.

In September 1928 an Indian named Maxfield Dalton was apprehended, under questionable circumstances, setting his net in the water off the coast of Prince of Wales Island minutes prior to the opening of a commercial fishing period. As was his policy, Harding seized Dalton's boat. When Robert Peratrovich, who owned the vessel, complained that Dalton was innocent, Harding offered Peratrovich what William Paul later described as the usual "sporting proposition": if Dalton pleaded guilty and paid a $400 fine, Peratrovich could have his boat back. But if Dalton pleaded not guilty, the boat would remain impounded until the case came to trial.[203] Given the Hobson's choice, Peratrovich told Dalton to plead guilty and then paid Dalton's fine.[204]

Two months later, at the 1928 ANB Grand Camp at which William Paul was elected grand president, the delegates adopted a resolution—undoubtedly written by Paul—that described Harding's enforcement policy as "official blackmail" and intemperately demanded that the attorney general of the United States fire Harding for abuse of office.[205] However, not only did his attorney general not do so, President Coolidge appointed Harding to fill the judicial vacancy that had been created the previous spring, when Thomas Reed, the U.S. district court judge for the First Division, died of a heart attack.

Since Harding would be the only judge who regularly heard cases in the region of Alaska in which William Paul practiced law, prudence counseled restraint. Instead, Paul mailed the Senate Judiciary Committee a copy of the ANB resolution that accused Harding of misconduct. After Harding was confirmed without controversy, Paul filed a petition for a writ of review that requested Judge Harding to set aside Maxfield Dalton's conviction on the ground that U.S. attorney Harding had coerced his guilty plea.

Why, other than allowing hubris to compromise his judgment, Paul did not file a motion to disqualify Harding is a mystery. And even though Paul did not request him to do so, since ruling on the merits of the petition required him to judge his own conduct, Harding should have voluntarily recused himself. But he did not. Instead, when Maxfield Dalton's case was called, Judge Harding opened the hearing by tongue-lashing Dalton's attorney, a public condemnation to which Paul the next morning responded by finally filing a motion that demanded that Harding disqualify himself. Harding responded by fining Paul $175 for contempt.[206]

Represented by James Wickersham, Paul appealed his contempt conviction to the circuit court, which vacated it. Not only had Paul behaved properly, the appellate court ruled that if he had behaved improperly, it was in not filing his motion before "the application for writ was called up before a judge who it appears from the record had been an attorney in the case."[207]

But the victory was Pyrrhic. He had called Harding to public account, but by doing so Paul now was disliked by the only judge in southeast Alaska. And no client wants to hire an attorney who is on bad terms with the judge who will decide his case.

The effect on Paul's law practice was ruinous. His few white clients and his few paying Indian clients drifted away, and his always marginal financial condition deteriorated to hand-to-mouth. "As a youngster of fifteen or sixteen I didn't realize the impact of Dad's conviction by Judge Harding on his law practice," Fred Paul wrote years later. "It was only when I read my mother's unpublished memoirs that I learned the real impact.... Those were tough days."[208]

They were so tough that when James Wickersham spoke with him the week after the 1930 election, "Paul said he was broke" and asked the delegate-elect to hire him as his staff assistant.[209] But Wickersham already had promised the job to someone else.

Even if he hadn't, Wickersham would not have offered the job to Paul because by then Wicksham knew Paul well enough to know that he "would insist on dictating my course of action in especially the fisheries, and if I exhibited any independence he would be disloyal at once."

Wickersham did, however, offer to use his influence with his and Paul's acquaintance Charles Curtis (the senator from Kansas who had been elected vice-president two years earlier) to try and get Paul a job in the Hoover administration.

But Wickersham's exercise of influence would take time, and by February, Paul had decided that he had no time left. Wickersham's account of his meeting with Paul, when the two men talked on the dock at Ketchikan as the steamship on which Wickersham was traveling put into port, is both a poignant description of William Paul's personal despair and an astute analysis by a professional politician of what Paul might have made of himself.

> Paul tells me he is considering moving to Seattle to practice law! [Wickersham recorded in his diary]. I tried to dissuade him—but when I discovered his trouble arises from the fact that his wife, a highly educated and good white woman is chagrined and humiliated over his constant defeats in the elections "because he is an Indian" I cannot blame him so much. Still I think it better for him to remain in Alaska—though he might really do better and be more happy in Seattle than in his own country. Paul is very ambitious and makes the political mistake of becoming a perennial and unsuccessful candidate for office instead of remaining a successful "political boss"—which he could do easily through his control over some 2,000 Indian votes in southeast Alaska. As a controlling influence with his mass of voters he would be in constant and powerful control, but as a candidate of less than a majority vote, he is in a weak position and constantly defeated. Better [to] be a successful and influential "boss" than [an] unsuccessful and defeated candidate—but he does not see it that way.[210]

In 1931, Paul moved his family to Seattle, where, after being admitted by reciprocity to the bar, he opened a law office that was as unsuccessful as his Ketchikan practice had been—so unsuccessful that in November he wrote to Wickersham to ask for a $600 loan.[211] Wickersham refused to make the loan because, as he recorded in his diary, by that date he had decided that Paul was "a natural grafter" who "always wants money."[212]

But Wickersham kept his word. In February 1932 he visited Vice President Curtis to ask Curtis to speak to Charles Dawes, the head of the Reconstruction Finance Corporation that Congress had created a month earlier as part of Hoover administration's effort to end the depression, about hiring Paul to work in his agency. Curtis told Wickersham to tell Dawes that Paul was "a good and competent man," who ought to be hired. But despite the recommendation, Dawes declined to do so.[213]

By the following May, Paul had given up on Seattle and, leaving his family there, had returned to Ketchikan. He telegraphed Wickersham to ask for a $500 loan, which Wickersham refused.[214] It was then that the "boss" of the southeast Alaska Indian vote decided to sell it. Having decided to run for reelection, in February, Wickersham contracted to pay Louis Paul (who, in addition to publishing his own newspaper, the *Alaskan,* when William moved to Seattle had become publisher of the *Alaska Fisherman*) $50 a month ... between March and November 1932 "for publicity in election matters."[215] But as thanks, in June, Wickersham, who was attending the Republican National Convention in Chicago, received a "mean letter" from Louis. As Wickersham recorded the content, "[Louis] and 'Billy' want money for their influence—sale of Indian vote."[216]

While he was disgusted by the shakedown, Wickersham needed what the Pauls were selling. So when he stopped in Seattle on his way home to Juneau Wickersham talked with Henry O'Malley, the commissioner of the Bureau of Fisheries, "about Wm. L. Paul and other things of political character." O'Malley agreed to "see if some of the cannery interests would not employ Paul." Wickersham also visited with Edward Allen, an attorney who represented the Nakat Packing Corporation, and "talked about Paul to him."[217]

To add bathos to the situation, three days later, Frances Paul presented herself at Wickersham's hotel because William had told her to do so. As Wickersham described in his diary, she "asked me to give her $200 ... for [steamship] tickets" and "to pay the household bills and go to Ketchikan." Wickersham angrily declined because her husband's "insulting and threatening letters justify my action."[218] Several days later he relented and made the loan.

However, rather than being thanked, when he arrived in Juneau, Wickersham was repaid in William Paul scrip.

First, William Grant, a former Republican legislator, passed along a letter he had received from Paul in which, according to Wickersham's diary entry, Paul said "he would not support me or the Rep[ublican] ticket." Wickersham then received a letter from Louis Paul that, again according to Wickersham's diary entry, announced that "the Indians will not support the Rep[ublican] ticket because the candidates will not give him $1,500, [agree to] appoint Billy to an office and put the *Petersburg Press* [against which the *Alaskan* competed for advertising] out of business."[219]

Three days later the shakedown intensified when William Paul met in Juneau with Wickersham and Albert White, the head of the First Division Republican Committee. Wickersham's diary describes the confrontation:

> Paul made demand to be appointed my [staff assistant], that I submit to a platform written by him, and put of [*sic*] larger contributions etc. I talked frankly and forcibly to him. Told him I would not appoint him my clerk; that his proposed attack on [Henry] O'Malley [in his platform] was a fool thing to do, but that I would submit to a plank against fish traps. We had a bitter talk and he left mad and declared he would fight me! and urge the Indians all to vote against me!! So that's that. It will probably defeat me!![220]

Albert White, however, was not about to allow William Paul to cost Wickersham or any other Republican candidate two thousand Indian votes. So that evening he capitulated. As Wickersham the next day described the bargain: "[White] made an arrangement with Paul to stay in and support the Republican Party—the [First Division Republican] Com[mittee] has agreed to pay him $250 per month for three mo[nths] to work among and organize his people and promised him that after the election they will—if we win—try to get him an appointment.... I approve the matters bringing peace and will aid in keeping it."[221]

Although Wickersham did his best, on July 23 he made a startling discovery. When he had talked with Edward Allen about William Paul in Seattle, Allen had told Wickersham that at Henry O'Malley's suggestion he had written to his client, the Nakat Packing Corporation, to urge the company to hire Paul as its Alaska representative.[222]

When Wickersham encountered Haakon Friele, the company's Alaska superintendent, on the evening of the day he learned that Albert White had agreed to pay Paul $250 a month, he told Friele "fully about the political situation" and suggested that, rather than the Nakat Packing Corporation paying Paul, the company should pay what it wanted to contribute to the cause to the First Division Republican Committee "and let it act."[223] Two days later, Friele reported back that, unbeknownst to him (and apparently unbeknownst to Edward Allen), the Nakat Packing Corporation had been quietly paying Paul since 1928. According to Wickersham's diary entry, "Wm L. Paul has been on the payroll of the Nakat Co[rporation] up to Jan[uary] 1st [19]32 when he was dropped—then it was Paul became too poor and began to bombard me for money!!" As Wickersham privately recorded his disgust: "He will not even stay bought."[224]

And he didn't. In 1920, John Rustgard, a prominent Republican and former mayor of Nome, had been elected territorial attorney general. In 1924 when Rustgard stood for reelection, Paul initially had supported Henry Roden, a Juneau attorney who was running as an independent. But concerned that his support for Roden would cost his own candidacy Republican votes, a month before the election he publicly repudiated Roden and urged his Indian supporters to vote the straight Republican ticket.[225]

However, Paul disliked Rustgard. And in 1929 when he passed a letter he had received from Dan Sutherland along to James Wickersham in which Sutherland had confided that he intended to retire prior to the 1930 election, Paul had urged Wickersham to run for his old seat because, as Wickersham recorded in his diary, "Paul ... will not support Rustgard."[226]

In 1932, when he returned to Ketchikan, Paul was aware that Rustgard, whose third term as attorney general was ending, would again be the Republican nominee. So he circulated a petition that 250 (undoubtedly Indian) voters signed, which, under the territorial election law, put Paul's name on the November ballot as an independent candidate for attorney general.

But the candidacy was a canard. Although his nominating petition was filed in April, pursuant to the election law, Paul was not officially a candidate until he accepted the nomination by signing the petition. Nine days after he promised—in exchange for $250 a month from the First Division Republican Committee—to turn out the southeast Alaska Indian vote for Republican candidates (including Rustgard), Paul signed the petition, and the next day announced his candidacy.[227]

William L. Paul
Independent Candidate for Attorney General
Solicits your vote on his record of progressive political activity through the past twelve years. If elected he will use this office to test the validity of the fish trap on the ground that they are operating as a special privilege, in violation of law. He will prosecute those traps which are used to violate Section V of the fishery laws of 1924--which laws provide that no one "shall fish for take or kill by any means" salmon for commercial purposes in Alaska. He will assist in securing all possible control of territorial powers and divorce of all bureau control.

William Paul campaign advertisement published in the September 1932 edition of the *Alaska Fisherman*.
PHOTOGRAPH COURTESY OF FRANCES PAUL DEGERMAIN.

But the announcement was just another scheme to turn a dollar, since Paul sent Henry Roden to tell Rustgard that he would quit the race if Rustgard would agree to hire him after the election as an assistant attorney general. While the evidence is conflicting,[228] the weight of it is that Rustgard agreed to do so. But after mulling over the bargain, he subsequently not only reneged but told Albert White to throw Paul off the First Division Republican Committee payroll—because Republican money should not be used to pay Paul to campaign against a Republican candidate.

When he learned that White had stopped his paycheck, Paul, with truly guileless temerity, publicly complained that he had been performing the work for which he had been hired "to the best of my ability."[229] He then declared himself a "free agent" and, financed by Cash Cole (a Juneau businessman who was the Republican nominee for territorial auditor and who had his own reasons for disliking Rustgard), in October set off on a campaign trip through southcentral and interior Alaska.[230]

No matter how William Paul behaved, James Wickersham would have been buried in the 1932 Democratic election landslide. But he also was a victim of Paul's mendacity.

Two weeks after Paul promised Albert White that he would get out the Indian vote for the Republican ticket, Wickersham recorded in his diary that "Henry Roden tells me that Paul is going to support me vigorously—that he—Paul—is anxious to be endorsed for District Judge and will ask me if I will support him if the [Republican] Organization—[Edward] Rasmuson [Alaska's Republican National Committeeman] and [Albert] White will do the same."[231] But in October, when he spoke during his campaign trip before audiences at Fairbanks and Anchorage, Paul announced that he intended to remain neutral in the delegate election.[232]

When he returned to Juneau, however, neutrality soon was replaced by behind-the-scenes support for Anthony Dimond.

Between Grand Camps, the business of the ANB was conducted by an executive committee composed of the grand officers and past grand presidents.

In July, Wickersham had noted to himself that he could "no longer trust" Paul because he "is threatening and trying to get money from both sides!"[233] Consistent with that premonition, late in October, Dimond, James J. Connors (whom Paul had defeated in the 1924 election and who recently had been elected Alaska's Democratic national committeeman), and John Troy, the yellow dog Democrat publisher of the *Daily Alaska Empire*, met with the ANB executive committee, of which Paul was a member as a past grand president.

Dimond, Connors, and Troy told the committee that if the brotherhood would abandon its usual support for the Republican ticket and get out the Indian vote for Democratic candidates and if Franklin Roosevelt won the presidential election, the Alaska Democratic Party would treat the ANB as if it were a Democratic organization—a status that would allow the executive committee a share of the political patronage (i.e., federal jobs) the party would have to distribute. The executive committee agreed. Troy also made a sidebar agreement with William Paul to get out the Indian vote in exchange for cash payments and the promise of a job after the election.

In November, Paul delivered on his side of the bargain. To cite the vote count in six southeast Alaska villages, in 1930, Wickersham outpolled George Grigsby in Hoonah, Kake, Klawock, Angoon, Hydaburg, and Yakutat, 447 votes to 92;[234] but in 1932, Dimond defeated Wickersham in the same villages by a vote of 477 to 117.[235]

But if Paul double-crossed Wickersham, James J. Connors double-crossed Paul by reneging on the promise to allow the ANB executive committee a say in the distribution of patronage. When that fact became apparent, in March 1933 the executive committee adopted a resolution, addressed to "the acknowledged Democratic Party leaders of Alaska," that reminded Dimond, Connors, and Troy of their agreement and demanded that the executive committee be allowed "to speak on all matters of patronage proposed to be given to Natives of the First Division."[236] The resolution also identified eight Indians the committee wanted to be given jobs, one of whom was William Paul, who had finished a distant third in the three-way race for attorney general.[237]

Simon Hellenthal, a Juneau attorney and well-connected First Division Democrat, discussed the executive committee's demands with Connors and Troy, whom President Roosevelt had appointed territorial governor. Afterward Hellenthal wrote Anthony Dimond that

> it seemed to be the consensus of opinion that it would be best to recognize the recommendations of the Alaska Native Brotherhood the same as we would recognize the recommendations of any civic organization such as the Order of the Elks or Order of Moose ... it would be very difficult for us to recognize them as a political organization, which they are—but should not be.... We do not feel that we want to antagonize the Natives and want to recognize them as far as possible, and wish to reward them for services rendered; but if we start in to buy their vote, this has to be done continually, and that is the thing we must avoid.[238]

William Paul was hardly in a position to complain about bad faith, but that did not prevent him from doing so. "The ANB has not been given any consideration whatever," he complained to Dimond in a letter written the week after Hellenthal wrote his, "but to this I am now reconciled for I can see that those leaders were playing me for a sucker."[239]

To add injury to the insult, Connors also reneged on the agreement to pay Paul to turn out the vote. "I was in hopes that Connors would pay me the balance of the money promised for my work on your behalf last fall," Paul complained to Dimond. "The best that I have gotten so far has been from Troy who says, 'We will see.' Perhaps if you wrote them that they should keep their promise, it might get results. The balance is $250."[240]

In that environment of distrust, in March, Anthony Dimond introduced Wickersham's bill to authorize the Tlingit and Haida Indians to file a lawsuit in the Court of Claims in the U.S. House of Representatives. The measure was referred to the Committee on Indian Affairs, which refused to consider the measure until Harold Ickes, the new secretary of the interior, communicated his position on the bill; Ickes did not do so prior to Congress's adjournment.

When the new Congress convened, Dimond reintroduced the bill,[241] and in March 1935, Ickes wrote the Committee on Indian Affairs that, while he supported the measure in concept, he wanted amendments. Ickes personally knew next to nothing about the content of the amendments he advocated. He simply passed on recommendations that had been sent to him by Commissioner of Indian Affairs John Collier, who received them from Paul Gordon, the Bureau of Indian Affairs' director of Alaska education. (For reasons that will be described in the following chapter, in 1931 the administration of Alaska Native programs had been transferred from the Bureau of Education to the Bureau of Indian Affairs.)

As far as Gordon was concerned, rather than compensation for the taking of a property right, any money the Court of Claims awarded would be a windfall that the bureaucracy for which he worked, rather than the Indians, should control.[242]

For that reason, the most important amendment Gordon urged Collier to press Ickes to recommend to Congress eliminated the per capita distribution of the judgment money that Wickersham had written into the bill. Instead, the Gordon amendment required the Bureau of Indian Affairs to hold the money in trust for the "economic security and stability" of the Indians of southeast Alaska in the aggregate[243] so that it could be spent— with Bureau approval—to purchase fish traps, canneries, logging camps, and mining claims whose operation could provide Indians employment that would "develop stability and self-sufficiency in a normal way."[244]

As a courtesy, in the previous Congress, John Collier had given Anthony Dimond a copy of the letter his staff had written for Ickes to send to the Committee on Indian Affairs, as well as a copy of the Gordon amendments. Dimond passed both documents along to James Wickersham and William Paul, as well as to Frank Booth and Judson Brown, the ANB grand president and grand secretary.

In May 1934, Judson Brown telegraphed Dimond that "William Paul has full authority of said matter" (i.e., deciding the Brotherhood's position on the Gordon amendments).[245] And in November, Paul wrote Dimond that eliminating the per capita distribution was acceptable. "In the long run, I think it will work out best for the future of the Indian and his descendants," he wrote, "especially when one sees what can be done with them with the aid of whiskey."[246]

Since the ANB had signed off on the one that was most important, when Secretary Ickes sent the Gordon amendments to the Committee on Indian Affairs, Dimond signed off as well. As amended, the bill passed Congress, and in June 1935, Franklin Roosevelt signed the measure into law.[247]

In addition to eliminating the per capita distribution, the bill the president signed differed from the original Wickersham bill in several other respects. One was that the Wickersham bill authorized the Indians (without identifying which Indians) to select their attorneys. But the bill enacted into law required a committee elected by all of the Indians in southeastern Alaska to select the attorneys and required the secretary of the interior and the commissioner of Indian affairs to approve the committee's choices.

In his letter to Dimond, William Paul had protested giving the secretary and the commissioner a veto. He also objected to electing a committee because

> [t]he only organization that we have that can act is the Alaska Native Brotherhood, and they are acting by convention and by appointed committees which contain educated men who are fully competent to draw up a fair contract.... We plan to submit to the committee of the ANB in each town a contract which is to be signed by each person so desiring upon which the fee of the attorneys is fixed at ten percent as full payment for their services. The Indians will agree to advance costs of the suit but these sums are to be returned in the event of success.[248]

Paul's objection was a valid criticism, but it was disingenuous. Since 1929 when James Wickersham sold him on the idea, Paul had assumed that the ANB would select the attorneys and that he and Wickersham would be the attorneys selected.

Sticking with that plan despite the fact that Congress had rewritten the bill to preclude it, at the November 1935 ANB Grand Camp, Paul had the delegates organize a five-member committee, which then selected him "to represent the [Tlingit and Haida] tribes, with authority to appoint co-counsel," a job he shortly thereafter offered to Wickersham.[249]

By that date Wickersham had had a crawful of William Paul. He still wanted the case but was wary. He also was put off by his co-counsel's avarice. As Wickersham recorded on December 10 in his diary:

> Before Paul left [on a trip to Washington, D.C., about which more will be said] he appointed his wife treasurer [of the Indian committee] and she is sending out notices and receipts asking the Indians to send in the money to her. It will of course be spent for Paul—as an attorney—instead of the preparation of the case! He is engaged on a commission of what judgment we get—not on what she can get the Indians to pay![250]

Two days later, Wickersham noted to himself that the project was "a mess already!"[251] And over the next two years things got worse.

Between the Bureau of Indian Affairs' indecisiveness and William Paul's machinations—first a demand to be paid an equal share of the attorney's fee, then a demand to be named "lead" attorney—months became years.

By November 1937 when the ANB Grand Camp convened at Kake, the eighty-year-old Wickersham had had enough. He refused to have William Paul involved with the lawsuit in any way. And he was disgusted that Congress had "betrayed" the Indians by eliminating the per capita distribution in order to allow "the most extravagant and selfish Bureau in the government service" to spend the judgment money. So he informed the Grand Camp by telegram that "I will not accept employment" as the attorney to file the Court of Claims lawsuit.[252]

But if his clever idea and eight years of work to take advantage of it for Wickersham had come to nothing, he had the comfort of knowing that his "co-counsel" also would not be handling the case—because in July his co-counsel had been disbarred.

Having kept his bargain with Anthony Dimond, James J. Connors, and John Troy, Paul had been confident after the 1932 election that he would be rewarded with a job whose status was commensurate with his inflated view of the value of his services. For that reason, he modestly offered himself for appointment to replace Henry O'Malley as commissioner of the Bureau of Fisheries. And as a backup he had the ANB executive committee recommend his appointment as U.S. attorney for southeast Alaska.

Anthony Dimond acknowledged that Paul was owed, but his view of how much was more tethered to the earth. In April 1933 he suggested to Connors that Paul might "profitably be appointed to the office of Assistant District Attorney or of United States Commissioner at Ketchikan."[253] Dimond also asked Frank Bell, whom President Roosevelt had appointed to replace Henry O'Malley as commissioner of the Bureau of Fisheries, to find Paul "a responsible position in connection with the Alaskan fisheries."[254]

But Connors, who privately had no use for the man to whom he had lost the 1924 election, wanted Paul out of southeast Alaska. "I do not think it would be good politics to have him appointed in the United States Attorney's office in this division," Connors responded when he rejected Dimond's suggestions. Nor did he want Frank Bell to hire Paul to help regulate the southeast Alaska commercial salmon fishery.[255]

As a consequence, Bell offered Paul the job of supervising the Pribilof Islands fur seal rookeries in the middle of the Bering Sea, a reward for services rendered that Paul, who accurately characterized the "offer of seal-herder" as "kind of a joke," rejected.[256]

But if he refused to herd seals, how would he get out of what he later described to Anthony Dimond as "my [financial] wilderness?"[257]

Wandering in his wilderness so muddled Paul's judgment that in January he had filed a lawsuit in Ketchikan against District Court Judge Justin Harding. The complaint sought $100,000 as compensation for income Paul alleged he had lost since 1929 when Harding wrongly cited him for contempt, and "persons, hearing of the said order adjudging contempt, and knowing that the plaintiff was prejudiced before the said district court, ha[d] ceased [hiring Paul as their attorney]."[258] Since he had been sued in his own court, Harding recused himself. However, before he did so, he transferred the lawsuit to Fairbanks. Had the case come to trial (which for technical legal reasons it would not have), Paul "planned to call at least twenty witnesses." Instead, in May when Fairbanks District Court Judge E. Coke Hill refused to move the lawsuit to Anchorage (which Paul argued would save him $4,000 in witness travel expenses), Paul dismissed the case.

After that truly desperate moneymaking scheme ended in ruin, Paul next tried to trade on his new political connections to acquire a fish trap. "[T]here is absolutely nothing left to do," he wrote Dimond. "[B]eing pressed by my own necessities (feeding seven mouths besides educating four of them), I am obliged to apply myself to anything that is legitimate."[259]

To that end, Dimond, who continued to acknowledge the debt, imposed on Frank Bell to have the Bureau of Fisheries adopt a regulation that opened a trap site for Paul. Bell then arranged for Nick Bez, who operated a number of traps, to set Paul up in business.

In December 1933, Bez invited Paul to lunch in Seattle, during which (after mentioning that Frank Bell had said that a friend, undoubtedly

Anthony Dimond, had asked him to do something for Paul) Bez proposed that the two men form a partnership to operate a trap—Paul contributing the site and Bell the money needed to construct and operate it. Paul agreed, and the lunch partners organized the Lewis Fish Company.

The fix in, on February 1 the Bureau of Fisheries adopted a regulation that opened a trap site at Tenakee Inlet, and a week later the Corps of Engineers issued the Lewis Fish Company a permit. But before Paul could put his trap in the water, Jim Davis and F. A. Berg (to whom the Corps of Engineers also had issued a permit) put their trap in the water at the Tenakee Inlet site.[260] Paul then filed a lawsuit to eject the interloping trap, which he subsequently dropped in exchange for a third of Davis and Berg's profits during the 1934 season (only).

Paul later said he relinquished the Tenakee Inlet site because Bez had agreed to relocate the Lewis Fish Company trap to a site near Admiralty Island. In 1935, Bez began operating a trap at that location but denied that he was doing so as part of the Lewis Fish Company partnership. Paul then sued Bez and lost,[261] another scheme gone awry.

By then, President Roosevelt had appointed an Oregon attorney named George Alexander to replace Justin Harding on the First Division bench. So Paul relocated to Juneau, where Frances found work teaching in the Bureau of Education school and William opened a law office.

But within months, Paul was crosswise with another judge. The episode began when the wife of an Indian named Jimmie Watson drowned. In keeping with Tlingit custom, the decedent's mother sent another of her daughters to Watson to take the dead daughter's place. When the second daughter was settled in, the mother asked Watson to "give her his gasboat in recompense for the death of her first daughter." When Watson refused, the mother sent her son to the U.S. attorney to complain that Watson was unlawfully cohabiting. When Watson and the second daughter were jailed, they hired William Paul, whose advice to his clients was to get married, which they did.[262]

The day after the new Mr. and Mrs. Watson exchanged vows, Paul encountered W. S. Pullen, a member of the grand jury that was considering whether to indict the couple, in the courthouse elevator. On the ride between floors, Paul stupidly lobbied the juror not to do so. Pullen reported the conversation to Judge Alexander, who convened a hearing at which Paul admitted the unlawful contact. Alexander cited Paul for contempt and suspended his license to practice law for ninety days.[263]

But that was the least of William Paul's problems. James Wickersham recorded the first hint of the trouble to come in his diary:

Wm. L. Paul is in trouble—charged with meddling with [Grand] Jurors, etc. The people of Petersburg sent witnesses to me and asked
that they be called before the Grand Jury in relation to other matters—this morning I learned that they are also to complain about Paul's
embezzlement of a large sum of money, which he collected and failed
to pay over in a cannery case arising at Petersburg. It is just too bad
that he cannot restrain his greed for he is an intelligent and immensely
bright half-breed Indian and has a wide and influential power among
his own people. He could do much good if he would only follow honest paths.[264]

Five days later Wickersham noted to himself that

[a] very interesting matter is pending before the Grand Jury—the indictment of Wm. L. Paul for obtaining money under fraudulent
pretenses!! I am informed by rumors that the Grand Jury has not
brought in the indictment and wishes to adjourn without doing so, but
the judge is said to have told the Pros[ecuting] Attorney he would not
discharge the Grand Jury until a full examination of the various charges
of bad practices against Paul had been examined and indictments returned! The town is full of such rumors, but whether they are true or
not I do not know!! Anyway Paul is scared![265]

If he was, Paul's apprehension calmed when the grand jury adjourned
without returning a true bill.

Several weeks later, when the 1935 ANB Grand Camp convened at
Wrangell, the delegates asked Paul to travel to Washington, D.C., to lobby
Congress to amend the Indian Reorganization Act of 1934 (about which
more will be said) to allow Alaska Natives to participate in the new economic development and other programs the Act authorized. Since Judge
Alexander had shut down his law practice, Paul agreed to do so (and likely
had lobbied for the work), although, since the brotherhood had no money,
the work paid next to nothing.

Paul spent the winter and spring of 1936 in Washington. He was there in
May, when George Folta, the assistant U.S. attorney in Juneau, filed a petition in the district court in Juneau that asked that Paul be disbarred.[266]

The dour son of an immigrant miner who had died of black lung disease
in the Pennsylvania coalfields when his son was a toddler, Folta had been
raised in rural Washington state, where his mother had relocated after her
husband's death. In 1912, at age nineteen, he graduated from a Tacoma
secretarial school and moved to Alaska. In 1915, John Strong, the former
publisher of the *Nome Nugget,* whom President Woodrow Wilson had

appointed governor in 1913, hired Folta, first as a clerk and then as the governor's secretary. Folta retained the position when Thomas Riggs, the member of the Alaska Engineering Commission who had met with James Wickersham and the Tanana chiefs in 1915, succeeded Strong as governor in 1918. In 1921, Warren Harding, the new Republican president, fired Folta and every other Democrat who held a patronage position in the Alaska territorial government, so Folta hired on as a court reporter for Thomas Reed, southeast Alaska's district court judge. He began reading the law, was admitted to the bar in 1927, and soon thereafter was appointed as an assistant U.S. attorney in Juneau.

During his thirteen years in the job, Folta acquired a deserved reputation as a hard-nosed prosecutor who won all but one of the twenty-six murder indictments he tried.[267] A father who would be remembered by his son as a man of "unwavering moral stamina" who neither smoked, drank, nor gambled in an era in which most men did all three, Assistant U.S. Attorney Folta also disliked William Paul "with a passion."[268] As Robert Peratrovich's brother, Roy, years later would remember when asked, "[Folta] said William Paul was such a damn crook he should be behind bars."[269]

But even discounting Folta's take on events as prejudice, the incidents described in the disbarment petition he filed were devastating.

The first count alleged that in 1930 Paul had hired George Collins to guard property that Paul had attached on behalf of the Union Oil Company. When Union Oil won its case, Collins sent the company a bill for his services. Paul first advised Union Oil that it was not responsible for the debt, then, representing Collins, filed a lawsuit against his former client to recover it. When Union Oil settled the case for $175, rather than passing the wages on to the man who had earned them, Paul pocketed the money.

The second and third counts alleged that Paul had unlawfully converted mining equipment to his own use. The fourth count alleged that he had sold Patrick (Paddy the Rat) Henry a building located on land Paul knew he did not own. The fifth count alleged that in 1930 Paul had obtained three thousand cases of canned salmon from the Wrangell Narrows Packing Company, a Petersburg cannery, as compensation for wages the company owed to Indian fishermen. Paul then sold the fish in Seattle and pocketed the proceeds, which were more than $3,000.

The sixth and seventh counts alleged that two clients had paid Paul to file divorce papers, but the papers had not been filed and Paul had refused to return his fees. And the eighth count alleged that when he had represented an Indian in a land dispute, Paul had introduced evidence that impeached his client's case.[270]

Desperate times can make awfully strange bedfellows. Proving the adage, Paul hired George Grigsby, the attorney who had conspired with Forest Hunt to orchestrate his defeat in the 1928 election and whose eyes Paul had blackened, to represent him in the disbarment proceeding.

Rather than Judge Alexander deciding the truth of the facts George Folta had alleged in his petition, Grigsby asked Alexander to appoint a bar committee, composed of R. E. Robertson, A. W. Fox, and James Wickersham, to hear testimony and render a proposed decision; Alexander agreed. But when he was offered the job, Wickersham minced no words in turning it down: "I have quite recently declined to associate with Mr. Paul in an important case because of my unwillingness on account of my fixed belief that he is not worthy of my confidence as an associate attorney," he wrote Alexander. "I ought to be excused for a fixed prejudice against him."[271]

In March 1937 the bar committee—composed of A. W. Fox; Howard Stabler, a former U.S. attorney (who replaced Wickersham); and G. W. Nostrand, the former secretary of the Juneau Bar Association (who replaced R. E. Robertson, who also refused to serve)—gaveled itself into existence to take testimony. Although he was notified, Paul did not attend the hearing.

After listening to the testimony of Folta's witnesses and then to Frances Paul, who, ever loyal, was the only witness who testified for the respondent, the committee found that Paul had committed the offenses described in the petition.

Judge Alexander accepted the committee's finding and, on July 31, 1937, signed the disbarment order. When he did so, he singled out pocketing the money from the sale of the Wrangell Narrows Packing Company salmon as the most egregious offense.

> [Paul's] conduct in this case [Alexander remarked], besides showing a wanton disregard for the interests of his clients and of his duties and obligations as a lawyer and an officer of this court, is rendered even more reprehensible by the fact that his victims, for the most part, were Indians, or Natives as we generally call them up here, and members of his own race, who looked to him with almost childish faith as one who could be implicitly trusted by them with their affairs, and their claims for the most part represented their entire season's (or year's) earnings.[272]

What was William Paul's response? He indignantly wrapped himself in the bunting of self-rationalized self-justification.

When George Folta filed his disbarment petition, Paul told an old friend that his new friends "the Demos are after me."[273] But after declining to testify in his own defense and then being found guilty as charged, Paul shifted his ground and began arguing—albeit without saying so explicitly—that he, rather than the Indian fishermen whose wages he had embezzled, was the victim because the ANB had not paid him for the years of work he had performed on its members' behalf. Paul field-tested that defense four months after his disbarment in a letter to the 1937 ANB Grand Camp (which, for reasons that will be described in the following chapter, Paul did not attend).

> We Native people of Alaska are a peculiar people [Paul wrote]. We are the most harsh people in condemning what we consider wrong in others. This is especially true in money matters. And yet everybody knows that you cannot get any work done without spending money. Up to the present time, you have solved that problem by electing men who were spending their own money largely. This era is passing. You should bear in mind that you can only act thru agents who are really your "tools." These tools do not select themselves. You do it. The value of the tool is of course determined by the work which it does for you.... I have been your tool since 1920. For most of my work, you have not paid, but have left me to carry the entire burden.

The letter itemized $5,350 of unpaid accounts receivable for work that began in 1923 (when Paul defended Charley Jones in the prosecution that established the principle that the Indians of southeast Alaska were citizens) and ended in 1936 (when Paul spent six months in Washington, D.C., lobbying Congress to amend the Indian Reorganization Act). Paul then demanded that the brotherhood "make a settlement with me so that nobody can say that you have not done your part."[274]

As a summary of the time he had expended over the years on the projects in which he had been involved to advance the political rights of and improve economic opportunities for the Indians of southeast Alaska, Paul's accounting was, if anything, conservative. It also is true that during his first years of prominence his work on behalf of the ANB was as courageous as it was important, since many whites considered Paul a dangerous and impudent Indian. As early as 1923, for example, Ernest Walker, the Bureau of Biological Survey's chief fur and game warden, reported to his superiors that "Paul is not well thought of by the white population of southeastern Alaska. They generally feel that he is 'bleeding' the Natives under the pretext that he is working for their interests. He has succeeded in arousing some hitherto undeveloped racial antagonism."[275]

But not all the men who had no use for William Paul were white. A group of younger members of the ANB, led by Cyril Zuboff, who had been elected grand president in 1934 and 1935, and Frank Johnson, who was elected grand president in 1936 (after having served an earlier term in the office in 1931), intensely disliked Paul. As Louis Paul passed along after his brother was disbarred, "I had a report direct from Juneau and from the marshall's office that Zuboff and Johnson were both very active in their effort to have charges brought against William."[276]

Cyril Zuboff and Frank Johnson both had legitimate grievances. But Johnson's was particularly justified since he was from Kake, the village of the fishermen from whom Paul had embezzled the year's wages they were owed by the Wrangell Narrows Packing Company.

So while the facts upon which he constructed it were true as far as they went, Paul's "whatever I did wrong I did because the Alaska Native Brotherhood didn't pay me for my work" defense of the peculations of which he was as guilty as George Folta charged is not exonerative. Because simply put, when he thought he could get away with doing so, William Paul kept his personal finances afloat by stealing from clients.

After the death of Arnold Tyonbee, H. R. Trevor-Roper described the renowned historian as "a good man ruined by the accidental operation of venial faults."[277] Adjusted for time, place, and context, the same can be said of William Paul, whose character was as riven by mendacity and avarice as it was graced by a lifelong commitment to the defense of Native political and economic rights. Half a lifetime later, James Hawkins, who between 1958 and 1962 served as Alaska area director of the Bureau of Indian Affairs, would remember Paul, who by then was a septuagenarian, as a "conniver" who would "wrap himself in the flag of Native rights."[278] So would Roy Peratrovich, one of the most respected of all Tlingit leaders, who in 1988 would recall that "William had an angle" on "everything he did."[279]

The tragedy is that Paul allowed an occasionally near-pathological predisposition for mendacious misjudgment to compromise his ability to perform the important work he loved and for which he was wonderfully suited. As Roy Peratrovich later aptly noted, "If he'd handled it right, we'd still be carrying him on a pedestal."[280]

But even a life of disgrace must be lived.

Ironically, at the time he was disbarred, Paul finally was employed by the Bureau of Indian Affairs at the job he had been promised prior to the 1932 election (and about which more will be said). And after he was disbarred, he was not fired. George Folta, whose dislike for the subject of his account was such that his story must be heavily discounted, subsequently described how Paul's termination three months after his disbarment came about as follows:

> Cyril Zuboff, then President of the ANB, forwarded certified copies of the complaint and judgment in the disbarment action to Washington, and demanded Paul's removal [from his Bureau of Indian Affairs job]; but, it did not appear that disbarment on such grave charges was sufficient. It was not until Paul, in his official capacity, solicited a bribe on the promise that he would procure the award of the contract for the operation of the Metlakatla cannery (subject to the supervision of the Secretary of the Interior) to the person solicited, that he accomplished his undoing. His offer necessarily involved the circumvention of the law with reference to competitive bidding. But Paul misjudged the character of the person whom he approached. The letter was turned over to W. A. Pries, who operated the cannery under the [Bureau of Indian Affairs Indian Reorganization Act] contract which was about to expire. Pries flew to Juneau, placed the letter upon the General Superintendent's desk and demanded the immediate dismissal of Paul. Confronted with this evidence of his crime, Paul resigned. But the whole affair was apparently kept a secret....[281]

However it happened, when her husband lost his paycheck, Frances supported the family teaching school. And the next summer Paul, who by then was fifty-three years old, labored as a commercial fisherman in Bristol Bay. But ever enterprising, when William Paul, Jr., returned to Juneau in 1939 after graduating from the University of Washington Law School, father and son used the ANB to organize Indian fishermen and cannery workers into an AFL-recognized bargaining unit that employed the elder Paul as secretary of the union.

Ten years after his disbarment Paul had a brief public rehabilitation. In the 1946 election, Republican candidates won enough seats to gain control of the territorial house of representatives. In January 1947 when the 18th Alaska Legislature convened its sixty-day biennial session, the members of the House, on a thirteen to eleven party-line vote,[282] hired the sixty-one-year-old Paul (who despite his defection to Anthony Dimond and the Democratic ticket during the 1932 election had remained a Republican) as their chief clerk (i.e., staff assistant).

If two years later Paul had any interest in serving as chief clerk during the 19th Alaska Legislature, his opportunity to do so was foreclosed when the Democrats regained control of the territorial house of representatives

Alaska House of Representatives, 18th Alaska Territorial Legislature (1947):
Chief Clerk William Paul (seated). THELMA ENGSTROM COLLECTION,
PHOTOGRAPH COURTESY OF CATHY ENGSTROM MUNOZ.

in the 1948 election. But by that date Paul was preoccupied with the Tlingit and Haida Indian land claim.

As has been described, Paul did not conceive the idea that Congress had a responsibility to compensate the Tlingit and Haida Indians for the extinguishment of their aboriginal title inside the Tongass National Forest. And he had only passing involvement in persuading Congress to enact the statute that authorized the Indians of southeast Alaska to file a lawsuit in the Court of Claims. But in the decades ahead, William Paul's participation in the effort, first to win compensation for the Tlingit and Haida Indians, and then to persuade Congress to compensate all Alaska Natives for the extinguishment of their aboriginal title, would be as important as Paul's continued presence in the story of Alaska Natives and their land would be ubiquitous.

6

Reservations

If a reservation that belongs to ten or two hundred Indians is a racial affair, then, it seems to me, a piece of property that belongs to ten or two hundred white persons is just as much a racial affair. But none of the opponents of the reservation policy have ever suggested, so far as I know, eliminating exclusive ownership of specific tracts of Alaskan land by white persons, even though it is on the land owned by white persons that racial discrimination most frequently occurs. The fact is, of course, that nobody has ever suggested the establishment of reservations for the "Indian race." All that has been suggested is that Indian property rights should be respected, and Indians should be permitted to acquire lands collectively rather than smply on an individual homesteader basis.

FELIX COHEN, August 28, 1944[1]

ON MARCH 6, 1929, the U.S. Senate confirmed Ray Lyman Wilbur, the president of Stanford University, as secretary of the interior. Prior to being recruited by President Herbert Hoover into his cabinet, Wilbur had been a member of the Indian Rights Association. Since its founding in 1882 by Herbert Welsh, a socially prominent Philadelphian whose uncle had been the first chairman of the Board of Indian Commissioners, the association had been one of the most influential of the white "friends of the Indian" organizations of the late nineteenth and early twentieth centuries. In 1923, Wilbur also had been a member of the Committee of One Hundred, a group of distinguished Americans that Secretary of the Interior Hubert Work organized to advise President Calvin Coolidge on Indian policy. So Wilbur arrived at his new workplace with a personal interest in Indians.

Like most Indian policymakers of his era, Wilbur was as ardent an assimilationist as Richard Henry Pratt. As he subsequently would describe his solution to the nation's "Indian problem," "The Indian must be prepared for a life in which he will no longer be a person apart, but a productive citizen working side by side with other productive citizens of many races. He must give up his role as a member of the one race that holds aloof, while all other races enter our American melting pot and emerge as units of a great new people."[2]

Putting that view into practice, the month after his confirmation, Wilbur announced that at the Department of the Interior "the Indian shall no longer be viewed as a ward of the nation, but shall be considered a potential citizen." "As rapidly as possible he is to have the full responsibility for himself," the new secretary explained. "In order to bring this about it will be necessary to revise our [Indian] educational program into one of a practical and vocational character and to mature plans for the absorption of the Indian into the industrial and agricultural life of the nation."[3]

To achieve those objectives, Wilbur and Charles Rhoads, a Philadelphia banker and past president of the Indian Rights Association whom Herbert Hoover had appointed commissioner of Indian affairs, reorganized the Bureau of Indian Affairs. As part of the reorganization, Wilbur asked Congress in 1930 to allow him to transfer responsibility for the administration of village schools and other Alaska Native programs from the Bureau of Education to the Bureau of Indian Affairs.[4]

He did so because in 1930 there were no employees still working at the Department of the Interior who remembered that, in 1885 and at Sheldon Jackson's urging, Secretary of the Interior Henry Teller had assigned the Bureau of Education responsibility for operating schools in Native villages in order to prevent the Bureau of Indian Affairs from treating Alaska Natives as dependent wards of the government. Equally important, Wilbur also was not aware of the adamancy with which the Alaska Native Brotherhood (ANB) objected to the idea that the legal status of the Indians of southeast Alaska was no different from that of reservation Indians.

Dan Sutherland, who in 1920 had succeeded James Wickersham as Alaska's delegate in the U.S. House of Representatives, was aware. And in December 1930 when the House Committee on Appropriations, on Wilbur's urging, sent the House of Representatives a bill that appropriated money to the Bureau of Indian Affairs to finance Alaska Native programs, Sutherland offered an amendment to appropriate the money back to the Bureau of Education. "[T]he aborigines [of Alaska], are not considered Indians," the delegate lectured his colleagues.

> They are not wards of the government of the United States; they are absolutely a free people and have never yet been classified with the plains Indians under the supervision of the Bureau of Indian Affairs ... the Native people of Alaska do not want to come under this bureau. They live in dread of it. They take the position that they are not in the same class with the Indians of the plains of the United States.[5]

While Sutherland's protestation accurately communicated the ANB's view of the matter, his amendment was defeated on a voice vote, the appropriations bill was enacted, and in March 1931, Wilbur signed a secretarial order that transferred responsibility for the administration of Alaska Native programs to the Bureau of Indian Affairs.[6]

But soon after he did, his attorneys apparently began having second thoughts.

Before a federal agency may spend money, the expenditure must be authorized by an act of Congress, after which the money must be appropriated. If Dan Sutherland was correct that, as a matter of law, Alaska Natives were not "Indians," then the Snyder Act, which Congress enacted in 1921 to authorize the Bureau of Indian Affairs to spend money for the care and assistance of "Indians," did not apply to Alaska Natives. And if it did not, then the Bureau of Indian Affairs was not authorized to spend money on many Native programs, even though the money had been appropriated.

To tie up the loose end, in February 1932, Edward Finney, the solicitor of the Department of the Interior, issued a legal opinion that, after a cursory review of the relevant statutes and court decisions and next to no analysis of their content, happily concluded that "no distinction has been or can be made between the Indians and other Natives of Alaska so far as the laws and relations of the United States are concerned ... their status is in material respects similar to that of the Indians of the United States."[7]

Had Sheldon Jackson been alive to see it happen, he would have been outraged by the adventitious sleight-of-hand Finney employed to justify post hoc an administrative action to which Jackson also would have objected.[8] But since Ray Lyman Wilbur and Commissioner of Indian Affairs Rhoads believed that the principal mission of the Bureau of Indian Affairs was to help hasten Native Americans' assimilation into the "American melting pot," Jackson would have approved of Wilbur's and Rhoads's policies, which included the eventual transfer of education and other Indian programs to state governments and the abolition of the Bureau of Indian Affairs. The same cannot be said, however, of Jackson's attitude toward the policies of Wilbur's and Rhoads's successors.

Ten months after Solicitor Finney issued his legal opinion, Franklin Roosevelt routed Herbert Hoover in the 1932 presidential election. And in March 1933 when he was sworn into office, the new president appointed Harold Ickes, a blunt-speaking fifty-nine-year-old Chicago attorney, to replace Wilbur as secretary of the interior. Although Roosevelt was a Democrat and Ickes was a Republican, Ickes had organized the Western Independent Republican Committee for Roosevelt during the presidential campaign.[9] More important, he also was a connected member of what remained of the progressive wing of the Republican Party, which Roosevelt wanted to mollify by bringing one of its leaders into his cabinet.

In the 1920s, Ickes's wife, Anna, began spending a portion of each year in New Mexico at a small adobe house that Ickes built near the Navajo reservation. Through Anna, her husband became interested in the fight the Pueblo Indians and a group of whites who supported the Pueblo cause began waging in 1921 to persuade Congress not to enact a bill that New Mexico senator Holm Bursum had introduced; its enactment would have allowed white settlers to obtain title to land that an 1848 treaty granted to the Pueblos. In fact, Ickes became so interested in Indians and their problems that, until he adjusted his ambition upward after the election, he initially hoped that Roosevelt would appoint him commissioner of Indian affairs.

Instead, when he was appointed secretary of the interior, Ickes arranged for the president to offer the commissionership to John Collier.

Unlike the blustery Ickes, Collier was an emotionally withdrawn, forty-eight-year-old native of Atlanta, Georgia, whose view of the world and of his place in it had been scarred by the "deep physical and spiritual depression" into which he had fallen when he was sixteen years old, after his mother's early death from drug addition and his father's subsequent suicide.[10]

After briefly attending Columbia University and drifting for a year through Europe, by 1907, Collier was a committed twenty-three-year-old critic of the capitalist values of the society he was certain had destroyed his parents. So he embarked on a career in social work that began in New York City with Collier trying to persuade as many European immigrants as would listen not to abandon their traditional folkways. Mabel Dodge, the bohemian doyenne with whom Collier became acquainted in Greenwich Village, subsequently and quite accurately described the pensive social worker as "a small blond Southerner, intense, [and] preoccupied," who "because he could not seem to love his own kind of people, and as he was full of a reformer's enthusiasm for humanity ... turned to other races and worked for them."[11]

In the winter of 1920, Dodge invited Collier, who had recently relocated to Los Angeles, to visit her at her home near Taos Pueblo, north of Santa Fe. Collier did so and, after attending a dance and several other events inside the pueblo, experienced an epiphany. The man who thirteen years later would administer the nation's Indian policy decided that Taos Pueblo was a utopia whose members' seemingly mystical connection to nature and communistic social organization were models that, extended to the mass

Commissioner of Indian Affairs John Collier.
NATIONAL ARCHIVES, WASHINGTON, D.C.

culture, could save humankind from the avarice and materialism Collier detested.

Although he returned to California to teach sociology at a local teachers college, Collier abandoned the academy in 1922 to throw himself into the fight against the Bursum bill. To that end, he was instrumental in organizing and then in arranging to be appointed executive secretary of the American Indian Defense Association, a new white "friends of the Indian" organization that provided Collier a full-time salary to lobby on behalf of Indian causes. After a decade of doing so, when Harold Ickes arrived at the Department of the Interior in 1933, John Collier was a prominent member of the small group of whites who were professionally engaged in attempting to influence Indian policy.[12]

At a personal level, the new secretary of the interior had little use for the man he recommended to Roosevelt. But as Ickes privately explained several days after the president announced Collier's appointment as commissioner,

[N]o one exceeds him in knowledge of Indian matters or his sympathy with the point of view of the Indians themselves. I want someone in that office who is the advocate of the Indians.... I want a man who will respect their customs and have a sympathetic point of view with respect to their culture.... John Collier, with whatever faults of temperament he may have, has to a higher degree than anyone available for that office, the point of view towards the Indians that I want in a Commissioner of Indian Affairs.[13]

With Ickes's blessing, when he arrived at the Bureau of Indian Affairs, Collier set about repudiating the tangle of policies that had evolved during the long consensus (both inside the Department of the Interior and on Capitol Hill among the members of the Senate and House Committees on Indian Affairs) that the solution to the "Indian problem" was to encourage reservation Indians—and if they refused to be encouraged, to compel them—to abandon their tribal relations and learn to think and act and live like whites. The capstone of Collier's effort to reverse course was a bill he delivered to Congress in February 1934.[14] Its enactment, as the commissioner subsequently would describe the measure's principal objective, would end "the long, painful, futile effort to speed up the normal rate of Indian assimilation."[15]

To help Collier write it, Nathan Margold, the new solicitor of the Department of the Interior, recruited a New York City attorney named Felix Cohen. Twenty-six years old when he hired on, Cohen possessed a compendious intellect that from adolescence had been honed around the dinner tables of the New York City intelligentsia, of which his father, Morris Raphael Cohen, a philosopher of distinguished reputation and member of the faculty of the City College of New York, was a prominent member. When he was only eighteen, in 1926, Cohen graduated magna cum laude from City College, then quickly earned a Ph.D. in philosophy at Harvard and in 1931 a law degree from the Columbia Law School.

When he earned his own Ph.D. at Harvard, Morris Cohen had roomed with Felix Frankfurter, after whom Cohen named his first son. In 1932 when Franklin Roosevelt ascended to the presidency, Frankfurter, who by then was a politically connected member of the Harvard Law School faculty, drew on his influence with the new administration to install his favorite former students in positions of high government service. One of them was Nathan Margold.[16] Prior to enrolling at Harvard Law School, Margold had been a student of Morris Cohen's at City College. And when Margold arrived at Harvard, Cohen vouched for his former pupil, telling Frankfurter that Margold was a "fine chap" whom his old friend should

Felix S. Cohen. YALE COLLECTION OF WESTERN AMERICANA,
BEINECKE RARE BOOK AND MANUSCRIPT LIBRARY.

"encourage."[17] Twelve years later, Margold returned the favor by recruiting Morris Cohen's son into the Department of the Interior.

A tall, thin man with wavy hair and wire glasses, Felix Cohen is remembered by colleagues as a "kind and warm" personality who, unlike the dour Collier, had an easy sense of humor. But notwithstanding their differences of temperament, Cohen and Collier shared a similar view of the world and of Native Americans' place in it. As Rita Singer Brandeis, whom Cohen recruited into the solicitor's office in 1944, would remember of her mentor, Felix Cohen was a "romantic" who had "a rose-colored picture of Indians." And like John Collier, he "didn't like the industrialized kind of society that we had"[18]—so much so that throughout his fourteen years at the Department of the Interior, Cohen refused to own an automobile.[19]

The bill John Collier conceived and Felix Cohen helped to write was enacted by Congress in a substantially modified form in June 1934 as the Indian Reorganization Act (IRA). The IRA codified policy objectives that— in a swirl of analytical confusion—cross-pollinated Collier's and Cohen's Rousseauistic preoccupation with protecting traditional Native American cultures with a new program intended to accelerate Indian assimilation.[20]

To achieve the first objective, the IRA abandoned compelled assimilation as the goal of Indian policy by repealing the Dawes Allotment Act (which since 1887 had mandated the dismemberment of reservations through the sectioning of reservation land into tracts whose titles were conveyed to individual Indians) and by authorizing reservation Indians to (re)organize tribal governments. To achieve the second objective, the IRA encouraged the same Indians to organize federally chartered business corporations (which Collier later described as "state-owned enterprises")[21] that would develop natural resources and commercially exploit other tribal assets in order to enable tribal members to earn money to spend purchasing goods and services that the white economy produced off the reservations.

When Congress debated the IRA, no mention was made on the floor of either house that strengthening the reservation system in order to protect traditional cultures that had evolved over generations of Native American participation in hunting, fishing, gathering, and indigenous agriculture might be incompatible with the objective of encouraging Indian participation in the white economy. To the extent that he gave the matter thought, John Collier believed the two were compatible. As he unrepentantly would lecture from retirement in 1963: "Assimilation, not into our culture but into modern life, and preservation and intensification of heritage are not hostile choices."[22]

Regardless of the policy contradictions inherent in its content, the text of the bill Collier sent to Congress made no mention of Alaska Natives, whom neither Congress nor the Department of the Interior recognized as members of "tribes" and who, with several exceptions that will be discussed, did not reside on reservations. In February, when Collier testified on his bill before the House Committee on Indian Affairs and Alaska delegate Anthony Dimond, who was a member of the committee, asked how the bill's enactment would affect his Native constituents, Collier ducked the question.

Piqued by the evasion, Dimond responded by lecturing the commissioner that Alaska Natives did not share his preoccupation with saving their traditional way of life. To the contrary, Dimond explained, "There is a desire on the part of the Indians of Alaska as rapidly as possible to become part of the general political organization of the country, and, in fact, a good many of them have so become and, except that their lands are not taxed, they enjoy pretty much the status of their white neighbors."[23]

Insofar as the ANB was concerned, Dimond's description of Native attitudes was accurate. Prior to the hearing, Dimond had mailed a copy of Collier's bill to William Paul, who, after reviewing the text, responded that "there is very little that can apply to Alaska, and that appears to be entirely beneficial—the matter of education principally. Some people without an understanding of the legal position of the Alaska Native would think that these Natives would come under the bill. Such questions could be solved when we got to them."[24]

Guided by that advice, when the House Committee on Indian Affairs rewrote the bill, Dimond arranged to insert references to Alaska Natives at appropriate locations in the text to enable Natives to obtain the education and other benefits the bill made available, including the right to organize the same business corporations that tribes whose members resided on reservations were authorized to organize.

Unfortunately, when the House and Senate passed different versions of the bill, Dimond was not appointed to the conference committee that cobbled together the final text. Since their sponsor was not there, no one kept a close eye on Dimond's Alaska Native provisions. Several section references were unintentionally misnumbered, and the version of the bill that was enacted into law inadvertently excluded Natives from the section of the bill that authorized Indian tribes to organize business corporations. And only corporations could borrow money from a loan fund the bill established.[25]

To fix the problem, at Anthony Dimond's urging, in 1935, Felix Cohen drafted a bill to amend the IRA to authorize Alaska Natives to organize business corporations. But the bill also went an important step further.

Neither Cohen nor John Collier had been to Alaska. But both men were aware that the National Forest Service and the Department of the Interior General Land Office were assisting whites to settle on land on which Alaska Natives hunted, trapped, and gathered. And they were aware that—with the encouragement of the Department of Commerce Bureau of Fisheries and the Department of Agriculture Bureau of Biological Survey—white commercial fishermen, trappers, and sport hunters were disrupting the

Native hunting, fishing, and trapping activities on which the subsistence and the small cash economies of Native villages depended.

So Cohen and Collier decided to use the bill Cohen was writing as a procedural occasion to urge Congress to grant the secretary of the interior new authority to protect Native land use and fish and game harvest opportunities.

There were a variety of ways the bill could have been written to empower the secretary to accomplish those objectives. But since Cohen and Collier were committed to protecting traditional Native American cultures in the coterminous states by strengthening the reservation system, they decided to extend the same policy to Alaska by inserting a section into the bill delegating to the secretary of the interior authority "to designate as an Indian reservation" any public land in Alaska that Alaska Natives "actually occupied."[26] The bill also authorized Native residents of Native villages to elect village councils whose internal operation and governmental authority would be chartered by village constitutions approved by the secretary of the interior.

While the objectives John Collier and Felix Cohen intended the establishment of reservations in Alaska to achieve were antithetical to the objectives of the assimilationist Native policy that Congress and the Bureau of Education had pursued during Sheldon Jackson's two decades as superintendent of education, the idea that reservations should be established in Alaska had prior precedents. The most important was Metlakatla.[27]

As mentioned, in 1857 the Anglican missionary William Duncan began ministering to the Tsimshian Indians at Fort Simpson, British Columbia, the Hudson's Bay Company trading post twenty miles south of the Alaska-British Columbia border. After several years, Duncan decided that a whiskey-besotted trading post was a poor venue for civilizing Indians and that a better strategy would be to put the members of his Tsimshian congregation to wage-paying work at a location removed from the maleficence of the society for which their labor would prepare them for membership.

To field-test the theory, in 1862, Duncan persuaded four hundred Tsimshians to abandon Fort Simpson and relocate twenty miles to the south, where, at Duncan's direction, they built Metlakatla, an imitation white town in which Indians dressed in wool and cotton clothing lived in rows of single-family homes of English design that were bordered front and back by flower and vegetable gardens.

In theory, the Indians governed themselves through an elected town council. But in practice Duncan made the rules. The rules included abandoning traditional customs, a prohibition on the consumption of alcohol, compulsory education, compulsory attendance at the church whose spire dominated the skyline, and paying taxes.

Duncan also created an economy. In 1863 he purchased a schooner in which Metlakatlans transported their furs to market at Victoria. He built a cooperage where Indians constructed casks that were used to store "grease" that other Indians rendered from herring. He purchased looms on which Indian women wove blankets and clothing. And he opened a sawmill and a blacksmith shop and in 1882 a salmon cannery.

But the private autarchy William Duncan created was not to last. In 1882, Duncan became embroiled in a dispute with the Anglican Church and the government of British Columbia that in 1886 resulted in a court decision denying Duncan and his Tsimshian surrogates ownership of several acres of land near their townsite. Embittered that the near-despotic control he had wielded over Metlakatla for more than two decades had been broken, the next summer Duncan expatriated to southeastern Alaska, settling on Annette Island south of the present-day city of Ketchikan. The 800 Tsimshians who came with him (a group that included Peter Simpson and Edward Marsden) began building New Metlakatla.

Houses were raised, another church was erected, gardens were planted, and a sawmill, store, and salmon cannery, all owned by Duncan, soon were providing jobs.

The sight of sober, churchgoing Indians pursuing workplace livelihoods in an orderly imitation white town asserted an efficacious influence on the clergymen and Bureau of Education employees who operated missions and schools in the surrounding villages, within which most Indians lived in shacks and public drunkenness was pandemic. As a consequence, by the turn of the century, William Duncan was as legendary a figure in southeast Alaska as Sheldon Jackson.

Duncan agreed with Jackson that Alaska Natives should be taught to abandon their "Nativeness." But unlike Jackson, Duncan, who in 1891 had persuaded Congress to set aside Annette Island for the exclusive use of the Tsimshian Indians, believed that establishing reservations was the way to create an environment in which that objective could be achieved.

Sending Native children to school for a few years and then leaving them "to work out their own destiny" by "tak[ing] the same chances as the whites" had a "semblance of fairness about it," Duncan advised Congress in 1901. But "[f]or a race to be a fair one the competitors should be equally matched." And in Duncan's view, whites and Natives were no more equally matched than grown men were to children. To even the odds, Duncan urged Congress to set aside a tract of land, located at least five miles from the nearest

Metlakatla, Alaska (c. 1900). PHOTOGRAPH NO. 191, SIR HENRY S. WELLCOME
COLLECTION, NATIONAL ARCHIVES — ALASKA REGION.

white town, for each Native community in Alaska so that "every Indian shall have secured to him a foothold on the land of his fathers for a home where saloons and other demoralizing institutions shall have no place."[28]

Whatever the theoretical merit of Duncan's logistically impractical suggestion, for Superintendent of Education Sheldon Jackson and John Brady (a former Presbyterian missionary whom President McKinley had appointed governor of Alaska in 1897), reservations were anathema. As Brady excoriated the concept, "[T]he reservation policy has not worked well [in the western coterminous states] and has wrought mischief. It would not be good policy to introduce it into Alaska, where the [Native] people are self-supporting and of keen commercial instincts."[29]

In 1906, Brady and, in 1908, Jackson retired; and when Jackson died in 1909, Peter Trimble Rowe, the Episcopal bishop of Alaska, inherited his mantle as the recognized expert on Alaska Natives and their problems.

Appointed bishop in 1895, Rowe toured his new jurisdiction in 1896 by hiking Chilkoot Pass and then floating the Yukon to inspect Episcopal missions along the river. In 1897 he hiked the pass again, this time accompanied by thousands of whites stampeding to the Klondike goldfield.[30]

And over subsequent years, what he saw of the gold rushes the bishop didn't like.

"The condition of the native Indians of Alaska is deplorable," Rowe lectured the Senate Committee on Territories at a hearing in which he participated in January 1912. "In the great interior, along the Yukon, where there is a large stretch of country, the people are diseased. They are dying off rapidly. The trouble comes largely from the liquor that they are able to obtain." The Aleuts on the Aleutian Islands and the Athabascan Indians along the Copper River were in a similar poor condition and "would be extinct in a short time unless something was done for them," as would the coastal Eskimos.

William Duncan at age 70 (1902). PHOTOGRAPH NO. 14,
SIR HENRY S. WELLCOME COLLECTION,
NATIONAL ARCHIVES—ALASKA REGION.

Peter Trimble Rowe, Episcopal Bishop of Alaska.
EPISCOPAL DIOCESE OF ALASKA.

But Rowe had a solution. "[I]t might be wise," he counseled, "at this particular time, before all the available sites and streams in Alaska were taken up by the white population, to reserve some that would be available for the Indians, segregate them on these reservations, where, by a little management, they can support themselves, and where, most of all, they can be treated so far as their health is concerned."[31]

Before he departed the capital, Rowe likely offered the same advice to Commissioner of Education Philander Claxton. A college professor from Tennessee whom President Taft had appointed commissioner the previous July, Claxton had no firsthand knowledge of Alaska. And since it had been four years since Sheldon Jackson had retired from the Bureau of Education, Claxton also likely had no understanding of why the bureau had pursued the policies in Alaska that it had during Jackson's tenure as superintendent of education.

In any case, five months after Rowe visited Washington, D.C., Claxton and William Beattie, the superintendent of Bureau of Education schools in southeast Alaska, began implementing the bishop's recommendation.[32]

The previous year, Haida Indians on Prince of Wales, the southernmost island in the Alexander Archipelago, had relocated from the three villages in which they had been living to a new site, where they built Hydaburg, a model Indian town imitative of Metlakatla. At the Bureau of Education's request, in June 1912, President Taft signed an executive order that withdrew twelve square miles of land around Hydaburg "for the use of the Hyda tribe of Indians and such Natives of Alaska as may settle within the limits of the reservation."[33]

When they learned that they now were "reservation Indians," the Haidas feared they would be denied the civil rights that they had been trying to acquire by living like whites. In response to the Haidas' protestations, W. T. Lopp, chief of the Alaska division of the Bureau of Education, attempted to allay the Indians' anxiety by assuring the town council that "Hydaburg is in no sense an Indian reservation as we know them in the States, neither are your people 'reservation' Indians."[34]

But the Haidas' fear was not unfounded. On the Bureau of Education's recommendation, in 1914, President Woodrow Wilson signed an executive order that established a small reservation at Klawock, a Tlingit village north of Hydaburg. Two years later, when Klawock Indians attempted to vote in the 1916 delegate election, they were refused ballots because they were "reservation Indians." And at Alaska delegate James Wickersham's urging, the U.S. House of Representatives ratified the disenfranchisement.

As a consequence, the Haidas continued to object to the establishment of their reservation. In 1926, President Calvin Coolidge finally signed an executive order that abolished it.[35]

In addition to the reservation at Klawock, in 1914, President Wilson signed executive orders that established reservations on the Kobuk River in the northwest Arctic, along the coast of Prince William Sound, and at Fort Yukon on the Yukon River,[36] actions that Commissioner Claxton justified in his annual report to Secretary of the Interior Franklin Lane by arguing Bishop Rowe's case.

> [W]ith the influx of white men the village sites, hunting grounds, and fishing waters frequented by the Natives from time immemorial have often been invaded [Claxton explained]. Native settlements exploited by unscrupulous traders, and the pristine health and vigor of the Natives sapped by the white man's diseases and by the white man's liquor. To protect the Natives the Bureau of Education has adopted the policy of requesting the reservation by Executive Order, now, before Alaska becomes more thickly settled by white immigrants, of carefully

selected tracts to which large numbers of Natives can be attracted, and within which, secure from the intrusions of unscrupulous white men, the Natives can obtain fish and game and conduct their own industrial and commercial enterprises. To the humanitarian reasons supporting this policy are added the practical considerations that within such reservations the Bureau of Education can concentrate its work and more effectively and economically influence a larger number of Natives than it can reach in the small and widely scattered villages.[37]

Claxton also advised Lane that more reservations would be established "as rapidly as their locations and boundaries can be determined."[38] And to implement that edict, the Bureau of Education sent Charles Robinson, one of its teachers, to Cook Inlet to reconnoiter a site for a reservation in that locale.

After inspecting Kenai, Seldovia, Homer, Ninilchik, Beshta, and Susitna, Robinson settled on Tyonek, a village on the west side of the inlet. "The Natives are quite fond of Tyonek and its neighborhood," Robinson reported. "I am assured that there is no better fishing ground for nets anywhere on the shores of the inlet." A reservation whose boundaries would extend to the low tide mark was needed because white fishermen already were crowding out Indian nets on the beach in front of the village.

"[N]o white man would stand for it," Robinson observed. "But Natives do not possess the knowledge or the pluck to defend themselves against being thus victimized. A reservation expressly including exclusive net, weir and trap fishing rights is necessary if these Natives are to be protected in their fishing industry."[39]

Robinson's recommendation was approved, and in 1915, President Wilson signed an executive order that set aside 26,918 acres of land surrounding Tyonek as a reservation. Wilson also signed orders that established reservations at Klukwan and Chilkat in southeast Alaska. In 1916 and 1917 five more reservations were established, including a 316,000-acre reserve at Elim, an Eskimo village east of Nome.

Other than the small reservation at Fort Yukon, which had been personally recommended by Bishop Rowe,[40] no reservations were established on the Yukon River. The omission was not inadvertent.

In 1912, A. N. Evans, the Bureau of Education superintendent at St. Michael, urged Commissioner Claxton to urge the president to establish eight five-square-mile reservations along the Yukon River.[41] But whatever Claxton thought of the idea, when Clay Tallman, the commissioner of the General Land Office, asked the opinion of J. W. Barker, the Land Office agent responsible for administering the public land laws that encouraged

Commissioner of Education Philander Claxton (left) and William Duncan at
Metlakatla in August 1913 during Claxton's first visit to Alaska.
PHOTOGRAPH NO. 19, SIR HENRY S. WELLCOME COLLECTION,
NATIONAL ARCHIVES—ALASKA REGION.

whites to settle along the river, Barker was unenthusiastic. "I do not believe, from my observations along the Yukon covering a period of practically
three years, that the scheme of Mr. Evans to place the Natives on reservations will ever be practicable," Barker advised.

> It must be borne in mind that these Natives are far from being pau-
> pers. It may be that, in a sense, they are wards of the government, but
> they are self-supporting and as independent as only a Native knows
> how to be. They have taken up many of the customs and most of the
> vices of white men and, particularly among the younger generation,
> there is a noted tendency to hang around the settlements, such as
> Nulato, and do odd jobs of longshoring for the steamboats at a wage of
> fifty cents to $1 an hour, than to do as the older Natives do in the way
> of following fishing and hunting exclusively for a livelihood.... [I]f the
> creation of eight reservations, of the area requested by the Bureau of
> Education, would aid in the protection of the Natives, then I should
> heartily endorse such a plan ... but, personally, I do not believe, be-
> cause of the wandering instinct of these Natives, that it will ever be
> possible to confine them to such reservations as these.... [T]he best
> solution in the way of a reservation would be one about one half mile

square near such places as Nulato, Fort Yukon and other settlements along the Tanana and Yukon Rivers. This would enable the Bureau of Education and the Natives themselves to keep out undesirables at any time, and particularly at night time, when most of the mischief complained of by Evans is done.[42]

After mulling over Barker's objection, Tallman recommended that "one reservation" should be established, rather than Evans's eight, "in the Upper Yukon District and one in the Lower Yukon valley" at sites "to which the Natives could be attracted and upon which industries similar to those at Hydaburg could be established."[43]

When the rumor that the Bureau of Education intended to gather Indians living along the river onto a reservation reached Nulato and Koyukuk on the middle Yukon, the Indians commissioned Peter Kokrine, the half-breed son of a local trader, to draft a petition, which the Indians signed with their marks:

> We are peaceful law-abiding Natives, self-supporting, and want no reservation. We earn our living by hunting and trapping and selling of furs, chopping wood, fishing, and working for wages. There are many of us that are abled bodies and earn our living in this way and many of us have adopted the life of a civilized life and are living up to it, that is the reason why we don't see why we should be put on reservations.[44]

While the petition professed confidence that "you will grant our request," two weeks after he received it, Claxton approved a proposal to establish a reservation upriver at Koskaket, a village at the confluence of the Tanana and Cosna Rivers.[45]

But no matter what the commissioner of education may have decided, the Indians who roamed the interior river valleys were adamant that they would not move onto a reservation.

As described in chapter 4, the following summer Alaska delegate James Wickersham met in Fairbanks with the headmen of seven villages to try to persuade them to gather their people onto a reservation before the arrival of the tens of thousands of white settlers whom Wickersham was sure would begin homesteading the interior when the Alaska Railroad began running its trains.

But after hearing Wickersham out, Chief Thomas of Nenana responded for the group that "we don't want to be put on a reservation."[46] And several months later, when W. T. Lopp visited Tanana to talk about establishing a reservation at Koskaket, the Indians objected to the idea so vehemently that Lopp felt compelled to promise that "the government would take absolutely no steps to make any reservations for their protection until they thoroughly understood the meaning of such an act and favored it."[47]

Of course, if W. T. Lopp had been willing to spill blood, if Philander Claxton had been willing to urge that recommendation on Woodrow Wilson, and if the president had been willing to order the army to do so, the Indians living along the Yukon could have been gathered onto the Koskaket reservation at gunpoint. But the nation's revulsion over the army's massacre of 146 Sioux at Wounded Knee Creek on the Pine Ridge Reservation in South Dakota in 1890 long since had ended force of arms as a politically acceptable means to implement Indian policy.

So the Bureau of Education was left with persuasion, and persuasion had failed.

But if Indians along the Yukon River refused to be gathered onto a reservation, the Senate Committee on Indian Affairs was equally unenthusiastic about having the president establish reservations. "We know exactly how those things come about," Sen. Albert Fall of New Mexico complained in 1918 on the floor of the Senate. "Some clerk in the Indian Bureau of the Interior Department draws up a proclamation of withdrawal. It goes through the routine, and is finally approved and sent to the President of the United States as a message from the Secretary of Interior with his recommendation."[48]

So to end usurpation of its authority by the Bureau of Indian Affairs, in 1919, Congress prohibited the establishment of Indian reservations by "executive order, proclamation or otherwise."[49]

Although Solicitor Edward Finney would not declare Alaska Natives "Indians" until 1932, once Congress enacted its edict, no additional executive order reservations were established in Alaska until 1925, when Congress delegated to the secretary of the interior authority to establish "a system of vocational training" for Alaska Natives.[50]

The vocational training statute said nothing about withdrawing land, but the Department of the Interior solicitor apparently and quite creatively decided that it did. On Secretary of the Interior Hubert Work's recommendation, in September 1925, President Calvin Coolidge signed an executive order that established a 1,200-acre reservation at White Mountain, an Eskimo village northeast of Nome, for the use of the "Bureau of Education and of Natives of Alaska." And over the next half decade Presidents Coolidge and Hoover signed orders that established six more reservations, including, in 1930, a 768,000-acre reserve at Tetlin, near the Canadian border, that Secretary of the Interior Ray Lyman Wilbur recommended. According to Wilbur's spokesman, the withdrawal would advance the assimilative goal of assisting Bureau of Education employees in teaching Indians how to raise foxes. Then the executive order would be revoked (which it never was) and the land leased to individual Indians.[51]

So in 1935 when Felix Cohen wrote a section into the bill that amended the IRA to authorize the secretary of the interior to establish reservations for Alaska Natives, executive order reservations of disparate acreages were scattered around the Alaska topography.

That March, Anthony Dimond mailed a copy of Cohen's bill to the ANB executive committee, which governed the brotherhood between the organization's annual Grand Camps. Its membership was composed of past grand presidents, one of whom was Frank Johnson, who in 1931 had served a term as grand president and who in 1937 would do what he could to ensure that William Paul was disbarred.

When he read the bill, the forty-year-old Johnson, who (after attending the Sitka Industrial Training School and Salem Indian School in Chemawa, Oregon) had graduated from the University of Oregon in 1927 and returned to Kake to teach school,[52] was so rankled by its content that he drafted a petition, which 108 Kake Indians signed. The petition protested the inclusion of Alaska Natives in the IRA at all because they were "self-supporting people" with "self-government in the village under the laws of the Territory" who wanted whatever "we get from the government ... [to] come to us as it comes to other citizens and not as wards of the government.[53]

Had he been asked when he returned to Alaska in 1920, William Paul—parroting the Richard Henry Pratt line—would have agreed with Frank Johnson. But by 1935, Paul had decided that reservations could be exclusive economic zones, rather than the cages Johnson considered them to be. Metlakatla was again the precedent.

In 1916 when the Alaska Pacific Fisheries Company installed a fish trap several hundred yards from Annette Island, the Bureau of Education responded to the intrusion by persuading President Woodrow Wilson to sign a proclamation that extended the boundaries of the Annette Island reservation three thousand feet seaward of the low tide mark. When Alaska Pacific Fisheries refused to remove its trap, James Smiser, the U.S. attorney in Juneau, filed a lawsuit to obtain a court order that ordered the trap evicted. U.S. district court judge Robert Jennings issued the order, and in 1918 the U.S. Supreme Court upheld Jennings's decision.[54] As a consequence, the 1916 proclamation provided the Tsimshian Indians an exclusive right to fish within a half mile of Annette Island. Taking advantage of the opportunity, by 1934 the Annette Island Canning Company, which operated the

Metlakatla cannery, was fishing eight traps. That season it employed 182 Indians and earned a $51,000 profit for the village.[55]

Watching Metlakatla thrive while cannery company fish traps destroyed the livelihoods of Indian commercial fishermen who resided in other southeastern Alaska villages convinced William Paul to rethink his prejudice against reservations.

"Those of us who are believers of the late Gen. R. H. Pratt theory are very much opposed to the creation of further reservations," Paul explained in an April 1935 letter to John Collier. But "we have a large group of [Indian] grammar school graduates, high school graduates, college graduates and experienced carpenters, boat builders, cannery operators and miners who are virtually bums eking out an existence by fishing about three weeks each year during the month of August." To provide employment, the Indians of southeast Alaska "must have capital." And the way for them to get it was by organizing business corporations that could borrow money from the IRA loan fund to finance the commercial exploitation of salmon and other natural resources inside reservations.[56]

Seven months later the 1935 ANB Grand Camp convened at Wrangell. After listening to Frank Johnson and William Paul argue their discordant views, the delegates sided with Paul by a vote of 55 to 15.[57] Anthony Dimond described his understanding of the consequence of the vote in a subsequent letter to Paul:

> The original objections by some of the members and officers of the Alaska Native Brotherhood to this measure were based, as I understand, upon the proposition that they did not want to be placed in the status of reservation Indians and thus become in any larger sense wards of the government. Later you were able to convince them that no evil or damage was contemplated or could be brought about by the passage of the measure. The enactment of this bill, which you have approved and which has now been approved by all but one of the executive committee of the Alaska Native Brotherhood [i.e., Frank Johnson], is based upon the theory of the status of the Natives of Alaska toward the national government which I have entertained from the beginning, namely, that the government owes to these Natives a special duty and is bound in honor and in good morals to enact suitable measures for their benefit and their economic welfare. You doubtless realized when you gave your assent to this proposed legislation that if it should pass and the Secretary should reserve public lands in Alaska for the benefit of the Natives inhabiting the lands in question these Natives would enjoy substantially the same benefits and occupy the same status now enjoyed by the inhabitants of the Annette

Island Reservation, those benefits being principally exclusive use of the lands and of the surrounding waters for fishing.[58]

After voting their confidence in his judgment, the delegates asked Paul to personally communicate to Congress their position on amending the IRA. Since his license to practice law had been suspended and Paul was unemployed, he agreed to do so. When he arrived in Washington, D.C., the brotherhood's lobbyist quickly earned his $250 per month wage (which, according to the letter he mailed to the 1937 Grand Camp subsequent to his disbarment, he was never paid).

When he had written John Collier in April, Paul had complained that Felix Cohen's bill to amend the IRA to authorize Natives to organize business corporations was "unsuitable to Alaska because it is based upon tribal entity built around a reservation," which meant that Natives who did not live on reservations would not be eligible to organize corporations.

To solve the problem, Paul urged Collier to instruct Felix Cohen to rewrite the bill to authorize Natives to organize business corporations "without respect to the residence of such [Natives] upon reservations."

When Paul floated it, members of the Bureau of Indian Affairs bureaucracy who were as committed as John Collier and Felix Cohen to establishing reservations were lukewarm to the idea of allowing Natives who lived in white towns to organize corporations.

> I believe that Paul's suggested amendment might be added to the bill [Walter Woehlke, an old friend Collier's whom the commissioner had recruited onto his staff,[59] advised]. But I thoroughly disagree with his reasons for this amendment. I believe that in certain cases a chartered corporation might be organized without the reservation residence requirement, that such a provision might facilitate the rehabilitation of certain groups, but on the whole I believe that there should be Indian communities on their own land.[60]

But if Woehlke was unenthusiastic, Anthony Dimond, who by 1935 had twice been elected to Congress with the help of William Paul's southeast Alaska Indian votes, was considerably more so. The version of Felix Cohen's bill that Dimond introduced in January 1936 contained a proviso that authorized "Indian-chartered corporations in Alaska" to be organized "without regard to residence on any Indian reservation."[61]

Having succeeded in persuading Dimond to include his concept in the bill, Paul next worked out an amendment with Felix Cohen that established the standard to govern the eligibility of Natives who did not reside on reservations to organize corporations. As Paul and Cohen explained their meeting of the minds to John Collier:

> Because of the fact that there are apparently no recognized Indian reservations, tribes or bands in Alaska (except for the Annette Islands Reservation), it would be undesirable to carry over to this bill the requirement of the Indian Reorganization Act that organization be restricted to the Indians of a single tribe, band or reservation.... At the same time we recognize certain dangers in opening the advantages of credit to any group regardless of the basis on which the group is selected.[62]

To solve the problem, the amendment Paul and Cohen crafted authorized "groups of Indians in Alaska not heretofore recognized as bands or tribes, but having a common bond of occupation, or association, or residence within a well-defined neighborhood, community or rural district" to organize corporations.

Hands were shaken, the House Committee on Indian Affairs added the Paul-Cohen amendment to Dimond's bill, and in May 1936, President Roosevelt signed the measure into law.[63]

As events soon would prove, however, persuading Congress to allow Natives who shared a "common bond of association" to organize an IRA business corporation was merely step one of an audacious scheme.

At some point, Paul reasoned that if each village in southeast Alaska organized its own corporation, the amount of money each corporation would be allowed to borrow would be modest. And even if the amount was immodest, few Indians had education or experience enough to run a business.

So in November when the 1936 ANB Grand Camp convened at Metlakatla, Paul unveiled a plan to reorganize the brotherhood into a regional IRA business corporation that would borrow and then administer all of the loan fund money that the Bureau of Indian Affairs allocated to southeast Alaska.

Whatever its merit (and in retrospect there was considerable merit, since in 1971, Congress would require the Indians of southeast Alaska to organize a regional business corporation to administer much of the money they received pursuant to the Alaska Native Claims Settlement Act), consideration of Paul's plan ended before it began when the delegates tabled discussion of the idea on a motion made by Frank Johnson.

To add injury to the insult, the delegates then elected Johnson as the brotherhood's next grand president and amended the ANB constitution to require the executive committee to be elected. When the election was held, William and Louis Paul, both of whom were past grand presidents, were stripped of their seats.[64] "Fear, not sense governed the convention," Louis subsequently complained in a letter to the Ketchikan *Alaska Fishing News*. "The leaders did not talk of logical and real objections, they talked of losing rights of citizenship and becoming wards of the government…. Hysteria not sense prevailed. None of the delegates opposing this movement had made a study of the [Indian Reorganization] Act in its entirety."[65]

But while Louis was correct that the delegates did not give fair consideration to his brother's reorganization plan, William Paul was the root cause of his own vitiation.

When he joined the brotherhood in 1920, Paul was the best educated and most politically astute Indian in southeast Alaska. But over the years, younger men who had acquired their own educations joined the organization, each of whom wanted to participate in decisionmaking. But throughout his long life, Paul considered his own opinion about every subject to be the one that mattered most. And the acerbity could be grating. As Philip Drucker, a white anthropologist who attended the 1952 Grand Camp, described Paul at that late date,

> [H]e has from time to time unintentionally offended numerous important people among his socially sensitive compatriots…. The difficulty is compounded by the fact that Paul habitually utilizes many of the typical aggressive mannerisms of the trial lawyer, which are by no means congenial to traditionalist Tlingit.[66]

To compound the atmosphere of grievance that permeated the 1936 Grand Camp, Paul was not hesitant to misuse his influence with Peter Simpson and the other elderly former grand presidents who served on the executive committee.

Since 1933, Paul had waited with increasing financial desperation for Anthony Dimond to find him the patronage job he had been promised as payment for getting out the southeast Alaska Indian vote for the Democratic ticket during the 1932 election. Although James J. Connors, Alaska's Democratic national committeeman, vetoed offering Paul the jobs for which Dimond thought he was qualified, in August 1936 the debt was paid when John Collier hired Paul as a Bureau of Indian Affairs field agent assigned to implement the new Alaska amendments to the IRA.[67]

In January when Collier decided to hire a new agent, Paul was in Washington, D.C., so he was able to lobby for the work. As he privately assessed his chances in a February letter home, "I really have no fear about the job—I have the absolute confidence of the men here who will make the appointment.... The new [Bureau of Indian Affairs] Director of Education, Willard W. Beatty, is for me—likewise, [Assistant Commissioner of Indian Affairs William] Zimmerman, Collier, and who isn't?"[68]

One of the individuals who wasn't was Frank Peratrovich, who also applied for the work.[69] A prominent Tlingit from Klawock, who in 1949 would serve a term as ANB grand president, Peratrovich, unlike Paul, was a real, rather than an ersatz, Democrat. In 1944 he was elected to the territorial house of representatives and in 1946 to the territorial senate. So Peratrovich not only might well have been hired, but two days after Paul confidently predicted in his letter home that the fix for his appointment was in, Charles Hawkesworth, the assistant superintendent of the Bureau of Indian Affairs office in Juneau, passed along to James Wickersham the behind-the-scene news, which Wickersham recorded in his diary: "Delegate Dimond had offered the work of representing the Wheeler-Howard [i.e., Indian Reorganization] Act work for the Indians in Alaska to Frank Peratrovich—and had passed Wm L. Paul by in doing so. That he [Hawkesworth] thought Paul *would not be employed* by the Indian Affairs Bureau to work in Alaska, etc."[70] (emphasis in original).

Paul, however, had heard the same rumor. Two days before Hawkesworth passed along his understanding of the situation to Wickersham (and the same day Paul mailed his letter home), the ANB executive committee telegraphed Dimond that the brotherhood opposed the hiring of Peratrovich because of his "political interest."[71]

The extent to which the telegram, which most likely had been written by Louis Paul, derailed Frank Peratrovich's candidacy is not known. But nine months later when the 1936 Grand Camp convened at Metlakatla, the blood between Paul and Peratrovich was as bad as the blood between Paul and Frank Johnson. And Louis Paul's subsequent accusation that "jealous men who were aspirants for [the] position as field agent"[72] turned a majority of the delegates against his brother undoubtedly had a basis in fact.

But that self-serving observation ignores the fact that in November 1936 a disbarment petition was pending in the district court in Juneau, accusing Paul of stealing from Indian clients. And it ignores the sixteen-year accumulation of slights that Paul's termagant style had inflicted on brotherhood members, young and old. Indeed, Frank Peratrovich years later would tell Philip Drucker that he became a leader of the anti-Paul delegates because "he resented Mr. Paul's rather brusque manner of cutting off elderly Indians who took the floor [at Grand Camps] to make lengthy speeches."[73]

When the 1936 Grand Camp adjourned, Judson Brown, the brotherhood's new twenty-four-year-old grand secretary, informed Anthony Dimond by telegram that

> William Paul, field agent [Indian Reorganization] Act, has no authority express views Alaska Native Brotherhood. Action of ANB convention Metlakatla, Alaska, November 1936, not opposing [Indian Reorganization] Act, but opposed Paul's reorganization plan attempting convert entire ANB into commercial corporation with special privileges shown to members who have been in accord with him in his political activities. Law good and each community will organize under own charter free from dictatorship and selfish influence.[74]

But if coup had been counted, the next year when Frank Johnson hosted the 1937 Grand Camp at Kake, Paul, along with the other past grand presidents who had been removed from the executive committee and the delegates who were loyal to them, boycotted the event.

"A decided break has come in the Native Brotherhood movement," Charles Hawkesworth privately reported to his superiors. "William Paul, and his brother, Louis, were the moving forces of the organization, and associated with them were Peter Simpson, Ralph Young and Frank Price of Sitka, also Gideon Duncan and George Haldene of Hydaburg. All of these men are recognized leaders of Native life in southeast Alaska and none were in attendance at the Kake convention."[75]

But the next fall, boycott begat a counterrevolution when Cyril Zuboff (who had been elected grand president at the 1937 Grand Camp) announced that the 1938 Grand Camp had been canceled due to lack of interest. Seizing the opportunity, Paul immediately mailed each local camp a letter in which he announced that "the Old Guard tells the world that there will be a convention as provided in our constitution—November 14th is the date—the place will be Sitka, Wrangell or Juneau—white man's style."[76]

As promised, when the 1938 Grand Camp convened at Sitka, the "Old Guard" were in their seats and Paul again controlled a majority of delegate votes, which were cast to elect him to a fifth term as grand secretary.

But if Paul's sinecure inside the ANB was again (albeit momentarily) secure, by that date he had been fired by the Bureau of Indian Affairs from his job as field agent. The termination ended Paul's participation in the Department of the Interior's implementation of the Alaska amendments to the IRA.

Over the decade subsequent to his departure, the department's implementation would provoke a bitter fight over the establishment of reservations.

In a 1938 memorandum, John Collier described his vision of what the establishment of IRA reservations in Alaska could accomplish. In southeast Alaska, the commissioner candidly conceded, many Indians opposed reservations. But that said, "it is becoming evident to these southeastern Indians that some form of reserved area would be a reliable guarantee of the minimum rights essential to economic self-support." In the interior, once the Bureau of Indian Affairs identified "the extent of fur-bearing areas needing protection," reservations would protect Indian trap lines from being jumped by whites. And in the Arctic, Collier wanted to create an administrative area for the Eskimos "similar to that established by the Danes in Greenland."[77]

But regardless of the region of the territory in which a village was located, before the land around it could be withdrawn as a reservation, Collier required each village to obtain an Indian Reorganization Act constitution that, when approved by the secretary of the interior, authorized the Native residents of the village to elect a village council that then could petition for a reservation.[78]

Since few Natives and few Bureau of Indian Affairs village schoolteachers had heard of the IRA, bureau field agents (one of whom, until his firing, was William Paul) were sent into the field to explain how to write a constitution and petition for a reservation.[79] The agents set about their work, and between 1938 and 1941, Secretary of the Interior Harold Ickes approved forty-four village constitutions.

Although the IRA required a majority of the adult residents of a village to ratify the secretary's approval, the ratification votes were a formality; the teachers talked the constitutions up, and no one talked them down. In 1940, for example, *Indians at Work,* the magazine the Bureau of Indian Affairs published during John Collier's tenure as commissioner, reported the following vote counts: "Elim, 28-0; Stebbins Community Association, 30-3; Unalakleet, 80-0; Ketchikan Indians, 123-3; Minto, 64-0; Stevens, 24-0; [Ft.] Yukon, 67-0."[80]

The principal benefit a constitution conferred was authority for the Native residents of a village to elect a village council. But the guidelines John Collier issued to his field agents and teachers instructed that a council had no governmental authority until a reservation had been established for its village. "If at the time the constitution is being drafted the designation and approval of an Indian reservation for the community organizing is anticipated," the guidelines directed, "such powers may be included in the constitution, but limited to take effect *only* upon the designation and approval of a reservation for such community"[81] (emphasis added).

Since Collier intended Secretary of the Interior Harold Ickes to establish a reservation around each village, conditioning a village council's authority to exercise governmental power on the establishment of a reservation was a seeming technicality. But that is not how implementation of the Alaska amendments to the IRA proceeded.

By 1938 three villages had petitioned for reservations, one of which was Chandalar, the winter village of a small band of Gwich'in Athabascan Indians located on the headwaters of the Chandalar River, which flows out of the Brooks Mountain Range and into the Yukon downriver from Fort Yukon.

The Chandalar petition had been submitted by John Fredson, the first Athabascan Indian to earn a college degree. He had been hired by the Bureau of Indian Affairs the previous year to teach school in the village.[82]

The Gwich'in were seminomadic caribou hunters.[83] But by 1937 rifles and steel traps, coffee and flour, and the like had become necessities that the Indians obtained by trading furs at the Northern Commercial Company store at Fort Yukon.[84] Whites flying into the Brooks Range from Fairbanks in small airplanes had begun jumping Gwich'in traplines, and unless the trespass was stopped, it had the potential to destroy the Indians' access to the trade goods on which the Gwich'in were dependent. So when he learned about IRA reservations, John Fredson saw the establishment of a reservation as a means to protect Gwich'in traplines. "[The Gwich'in] realize that the time has come when such action is necessary to protect their fur and game," Fredson explained by letter in January 1938 to Claude Hirst, the Bureau of Indian Affairs' Alaska superintendent in Juneau.[85]

Fredson's letter arrived as Hirst was preparing to leave for Washington, D.C., to meet with employees of the General Land Office to negotiate a procedure for processing reservation petitions. In February, during the meeting he traveled east to attend, Hirst pitched Fredson's reservation to the Land Office officials with whom he met. When they realized that Hirst was serious about wanting to close more than a million acres of land to mineral exploration and white settlement, they were appalled.

The General Land Office would never agree to such a thing, L. W. Brady, one of the Land Office officials, responded, unless the Bureau of Indian Affairs could demonstrate that closing the land to entry would not economically disadvantage whites.

"Would you want a report to show that the land would never be of any use to whites?" Hirst asked. Brady replied, no, the report merely should indicate that the land had no "immediate prospective value." "But suppose there was an equal value to these people who have lived there all this time and to persons who might come in from San Francisco?" Hirst queried. In that case, Brady answered, "I presume that you would give more consideration to Natives than to whites," and the General Land Office would do the opposite.[86]

So the conflict was joined, and as late as 1944, John Collier would be advised by his staff that "half a dozen [public land] orders establishing Alaska reservations are hung up in one or another of the Interior Department bureaus—principally the Land Office."[87]

While intradepartment guerrilla war would rage inside the Department of the Interior throughout the 1940s, the Bureau of Indian Affairs won the first skirmish in 1943 when Assistant Secretary of the Interior Oscar Chapman (who supervised the Bureau of Indian Affairs) signed proclamations that established four reservations, one of which was a 1.8-million-acre reservation for the Gwich'in Indians.[88] Two days later, Secretary of the Interior Harold Ickes signed a land order that established a reservation at Karluk, a small village on the north shore of Kodiak Island.[89]

The gridlock broke because Harold Ickes ordered it broken. As Dale Doty, Ickes's administrative assistant, reminded Oscar Chapman, two months before Chapman signed the first proclamations, "The Secretary has stated that it is a fundamental policy of the Department to establish reservations for Alaskan Indians."[90] The reason again was Metlakatla.

The summer of 1938 when Ickes made his first tour of Alaska, the vessel on which his party was cruising through the Alexander Archipelago stopped at Hoonah, a Tlingit village on the northeastern side of Chichagof Island. "It was ramshackle, squalid, dirty and apparently poverty stricken," Ickes confided to his famous diary.[91] And according to Ernest Gruening, director of the Department of the Interior's Division of Territories and Island Possessions, who was traveling with the secretary, "most of the adults [were] intoxicated."[92] The scene was so upsetting that, when his boat docked at Juneau, Ickes telegraphed John Collier, ordering him to send Assistant Commissioner of Indian Affairs William Zimmerman to Alaska to investigate "living conditions [which] in some villages are worse than deplorable."[93]

Two days later the steamship on which Ickes was traveling to Seattle stopped at Annette Island. "[O]ne of the most interesting episodes of our entire trip," the secretary gushed. Metlakatla was "the best built, cleanest and most prosperous Indian village I have seen in these parts," with modern houses of the "American style," wooden sidewalks, and no liquor stores. "[A]fter some of the other villages I had seen," Ickes subsequently would remark, the Tsimshians' situation was "quite heartening."[94]

The Annette Island reserve, whose offshore boundary had stopped Alaska Pacific Fisheries from operating a trap that would have caught salmon on which the Metlakatla cannery depended for product, was a key to the village's prosperity. Because of the reservation, Ickes would write in 1944, Metlakatla is "probably the most completely self-supporting Native community in Alaska." And the Tsimshians who lived in it "are a living refutation of the charge that reservations are a peculiar kind of concentration camp within which Indians are deprived of the rights of citizenship."[95]

Thanks to his stop at Metlakatla, Harold Ickes returned from his summer tour of Alaska committed to reservations as the means to afford Alaska Natives economic justice.

Since only a handful of white trappers and prospectors were inconvenienced by the closure of more than 1.9 million acres of land to entry, the initial reaction in Alaska to the four reservations Oscar Chapman established by proclamation was indifference. But in Seattle and San Francisco the men who managed salmon canneries in Alaska immediately understood the threat that the Karluk reservation, whose northern boundary extended three thousand feet from shore and encircled more than eight square miles of water at the mouth of the Karluk River, posed to their balance sheets. A. K. Tichenor, the president of the Alaska Packers Association, advised his attorneys: "If it gets by at Karluk [the idea of establishing reservations in order to allow Native fishermen to catch salmon that white fishermen and fish traps now were catching in the waters surrounding Native villages] would gradually spread to include other areas throughout Alaska."[96] For that reason, "Our first consideration is blocking the establishment of Indian reservations."[97]

Two hundred Aleuts lived at Karluk, fifty-seven of whom were adults. During the summer the few dozen men earned their year's income fishing with beach seines. But the Aleut fishermen were not alone.

Each summer when the red salmon that spawned up the Karluk River began migrating in from the ocean, as many as 650 whites fishing in boats put out nets at the mouth of the river. If that was not enough competition, the cannery companies imported Swedes from the fishermen's union hiring hall in San Francisco to fish beach seines. As Assistant Commissioner of Indian Affairs William Zimmerman explained in 1940 when he urged Harold Ickes to establish the Karluk reservation,

The native Aleuts of Karluk have been forced out of their fishing area by outsiders who are transported to their village each summer from the states. The mouth of the Karluk River and the two miles of beach immediately in front of the village is the area desired and has been used by the Natives of Karluk for many years. The Natives are crowded out of this locality and are now forced to leave the village to work in canneries or fish in a far corner of the lagoon or beach which is known as the "rock dump."[98]

Pursuant to the Alaska amendments to the IRA, a reservation proclamation or land order did not take legal effect until the Native residents of the village for which a withdrawal had been made approved the establishment of the reservation by a majority vote cast by secret ballot.

In May 1944 the Karluk Natives approved their reservation by a vote of 46-0, after which the village council put out buoys to mark the outer boundary of an area at the mouth of the river within which it prohibited white fishermen to set nets. But W. C. Arnold, chief counsel and managing director (i.e., chief lobbyist) of the Alaska Salmon Industry, Inc., the trade association the cannery companies organized in 1940, subsequently reported after visiting the grounds when the salmon began running: "The white purse-seiners are generally disregarding the reservation boundaries."[99]

To try to force them to do so, prior to the 1945 fishing season the Karluk village council adopted an ordinance that required white fishermen to obtain a license from the council to fish in reservation waters. But none did. Prior to the 1946 season, the Fish and Wildlife Service (the Department of the Interior agency responsible for regulating the Alaska commercial salmon fishery) adopted a regulation (at the urging of Felix Cohen and the Bureau of Indian Affairs) that prohibited white fishermen from fishing in reservation waters unless the Karluk village council had authorized them to do so.

In response, seven cannery companies asked U.S. district court judge Harry Pratt to invalidate the establishment of the Karluk reservation on the ground that the Alaska amendments to the IRA delegated to the secretary of the interior authority to withdraw "public lands" as reservations—and Congress did not intend the term "public lands" to include water. Assuming that was so, W. C. Arnold, who represented the plaintiff companies, argued to Pratt that Harold Ickes therefore had no authority to establish a reservation whose boundary extended beyond the beach.

Judge Pratt agreed with Arnold,[100] and in 1947 the circuit court affirmed Pratt's decision.[101] But when the lawsuit reached the U.S. Supreme Court in 1949, the Court disagreed.[102]

However, for the Karluk Natives, the victory was Pyrrhic. By a unanimous vote the Court decided that Congress intended the term "public lands" in the Alaska amendments to the IRA to include water. But by a vote of 5 to 4 a majority of the justices held that a proviso of the White Act (the 1924 statute that controlled regulation of the Alaska commercial salmon fishery), which prohibited the fishery from being regulated in a manner that created an "exclusive or several right of fishery," also prevented the Fish and Wildlife Service from adopting the regulation that prohibited white fishermen from fishing in reservation waters.

Although at a first cursory reading it may seem so, the Court's decision in *Hynes v Grimes Packing Company,* which was written by Justice Stanley Reed, turned not on a technical analysis of the intent of Congress embodied in the texts of the White Act and the Alaska amendments to the IRA but on Reed's personal opinion that the Karluk Natives should not be allowed what he privately had decided would be an economic windfall.

When Reed circulated a draft of his decision inside the Court, Justice William O. Douglas, who would be one of the four dissenting justices, chided Reed:

> From the beginning a reservation has been a monopoly. This is ancestral land which the Indians are occupying.... Indian reservations in Alaska had long had exclusive fishing rights [e.g., the Annette Island reservation]. I have found nothing to indicate that the "equality" proviso of the White Act was designed to effect a reversal in Indian policy. The administrative construction has been to the contrary.... The right to create Indian reservations should, I think, carry with it a right to grant to the Indians in question the exclusive right to fish therein. The problem in Alaska has been to protect the Indians and the public against the packing houses, not to protect the packing houses against the Indians.[103]

After thanking Douglas for his note, Reed responded:

> I think [the decision I have written] is best for the Indians. If the Indians were given a monopoly of a three million dollar a year fishery like Karluk and if this Court did not decide that the reservation was temporary, it would be too much to give the Indians. If we hold that [the reservation] was temporary, and the Indians were given a complete monopoly both to fish and to exploit, the pressure would soon compel Congress to open so great and natural a resource to the public under suitable regulations.[104]

Whether granting the Karluk Natives a monopoly to fish in reservation waters was "too much to give the Indians" was a policy question. And if the Court upheld the regulation that excluded white fishermen, "the pressure would soon compel Congress to open [reservation waters]" was a prophecy. And both the policy question and the prophecy were irrelevant to the task of discerning the intent of Congress embodied in the two statutes that deciding the case required Reed to construe.

But the law means what five justices say it does. And with Stanley Reed, a socially conservative Kentuckian (described by William O. Douglas as "one of the most reactionary judges to occupy the bench in my time")[105] in their corner, the cannery companies won the round. Although the Bureau of Indian Affairs would score several points between 1943 and 1949, in the end, the companies would win the bout with a second judicial knockout.

Eight years prior to the announcement of its decision in *Grimes Packing Company,* the U.S. Supreme Court in 1941 decided *United States v Santa Fe Pacific Railroad,*[106] a lawsuit the Department of Justice had filed at the Department of the Interior's request to stop the Santa Fe Pacific Railroad from interfering with the Walapai Indians' occupancy of land in northwestern Arizona. As part of that decision, which was written by Justice Douglas, the Court held that the Justice Department attorneys were not required to prove that the Walapais' right of occupancy had been recognized by a treaty or statute. Rather, if the contested land was the Indians' "ancestral home," within which the Walapais occupied a "definable territory" to the exclusion of other Indians, then the Walapais held an aboriginal title to the ground that, unless the title had been voluntarily relinquished, gave the Indians a right of exclusive occupancy.

Felix Cohen worked on *Santa Fe Pacific Railroad* while he represented the Bureau of Indian Affairs in the intradepartment disputes that were preventing the establishment of IRA reservations in Alaska. Equally important, as Cohen subsequently would recall, when President Roosevelt transferred the Bureau of Fisheries to the Department of the Interior in 1939 as part of an executive branch reorganization,[107] the move brought "the protests of local Alaskans, Native and white, against absentee monopolization of fish traps ... to my attention."[108]

When he read the *Santa Fe Pacific Railroad* decision, Cohen realized the utility of its precedent. If the Walapai Indians possessed aboriginal title to land they exclusively occupied as a definable territory (even though their aboriginal title had not been recognized by Congress in a treaty or statute), Cohen reasoned, why didn't Alaska Natives possess aboriginal title to the waters surrounding their villages that they exclusively occupied as a definable territory (even though their aboriginal title had not been recognized by Congress in a treaty or statute)? "This established a basis upon which resident Alaskan Indian fishermen could challenge the absentee control of fish traps," Cohen later would recall of his thinking, "just as the Walapai Indians had challenged the control of their land and water holes."[109]

The month after he read the *Santa Fe Pacific Railroad* decision, Cohen informed John Collier that "I have come to the opinion that the Alaskan Indians have such rights in those areas which they have occupied from time immemorial as entitle them to preference in the allowance of fish trap sites."[110] The month after that, Solicitor Nathan Margold issued a legal opinion to that effect. Although signed by Margold, the opinion had been written by Cohen.[111]

When he was told that the Fish and Wildlife Service (as the Bureau of Fisheries had been renamed after merging with the Bureau of Biological Survey after it also had been transferred to the Department of the Interior as part of the executive branch reorganization) would be required to order cannery companies to dismantle their traps to afford Alaska Natives the exclusive right to catch millions of dollars worth of salmon, Ira Gabrielson, the director of the Fish and Wildlife Service, was incredulous.

But that is what Harold Ickes ordered done.

Each spring the Fish and Wildlife Service wrote regulations that set out the rules for the conduct of that season's Alaska commercial salmon fishery, which the secretary of the interior routinely approved. But at Nathan Margold's (i.e., Felix Cohen's) urging and over Ira Gabrielson's protestation, in March 1942, Ickes ordered the Service to add a new regulation to the season's package. The regulation, undoubtedly written by Cohen, prohibited whites from installing fish traps in waters that were subject to a Native right of fishery acquired "by virtue of aboriginal occupancy" and authorized Natives who claimed a right of aboriginal occupancy to "petition the Secretary of the Interior for a hearing with respect to the validity of such claim."[112]

> He isn't in a happy frame of mind these days [Ickes noted to himself after meeting with Gabrielson]. He has been having more or less of a feud with Margold and the Solicitor's Office. Gabrielson has a sneaking notion that he is as good a lawyer as Margold, but I can't agree with that. Recently Margold sent me an opinion to the effect that the Indian communities in Alaska had certain fishing rights which cannot be ignored. This may mean that some of the traps of white fishermen will have to be taken out, or at least terms made with the Indians.[113]

But that is not the way things turned out.

While Ickes enjoyed thinking of himself as "pro-Indian," after nine years as secretary of the interior he had been politically bloodied in numerous fights more consequential than the new one Nathan Margold had persuaded him to pick with the cannery companies. The nation was at war, and if the companies were forced to remove their traps, their lobbyists could fairly complain to their friends in the Congress that Ickes was disrupting an important food supply at a time of national crisis. To quiet a criticism that hadn't been voiced, Ickes decided to delay the adjudications of aboriginal fishing rights that the new Fish and Wildlife Service regulation obligated him to conduct. As he confided to his diary, "We need salmon too badly this year to run any chances, and we have the Japs to think of in addition."[114]

Ickes may have explained the political facts of life to his diary, but he did not explain them to William Paul. When he read the Fish and Wildlife Service's aboriginal fishing rights regulation, Paul understood its import and immediately set about implementing its edict.

Through his mother, Paul was a member of the Tee-Hit-Tons, one of the Tlingit clans at Wrangell. For years the Pacific American Fisheries Company had operated a fish trap at Point Colpoys that caught salmon that spawned at Salmon Bay on the north side of Prince of Wales Island in waters in which Tee-Hit-Tons traditionally fished. The month after the new Fish and Wildlife Service regulation was published, Paul petitioned Harold Ickes to direct the Fish and Wildlife Service to order Pacific American Fisheries to remove the Point Colpoys trap.[115]

In June, Paul (represented by his sons Bill and Fred, who by then both had graduated from the University of Washington Law School and been admitted to the Alaska bar) filed a lawsuit against Pacific American Fisheries.[116] On behalf of the Tee-Hit-Ton clan, that winter Paul filed a second lawsuit against Pacific American, and the following May he filed suit against Clarence Olson, the local Fish and Wildlife Service official responsible for enforcing the aboriginal fishing rights regulation.[117]

The Pauls also engaged in civil disobedience.

Because the Point Colpoys trap annually caught all of the fish that could be taken from the salmon run that spawned at Salmon Bay, the Fish and Wildlife Service had adopted a regulation that closed the bay to commercial fishing. To challenge the legality of the closure, in July 1942, Louis Paul and his son and three other Tee-Hit-Tons announced that they intended to set their nets in Salmon Bay, which they did. As they intended, they were arrested for fishing in closed waters.[118]

When John Collier and Felix Cohen learned of the arrests, they agreed with the misdemeanants that the regulation closing Salmon Bay to Tee-Hit-Ton fishermen was unlawful. But Louis Paul's timing was unlucky. Nathan Margold recently had been appointed to the bench and had been replaced as solicitor of the Department of the Interior by Warner Gardner, a New York attorney with whom Felix Cohen did not have the influence he had had with Margold. When the legal question reached his desk, Gardner sided with Ira Gabrielson.

> Dr. Gabrielson feels quite strongly that the Indians, whether or not they have aboriginal rights, are subject to the fisheries regulations to the same extent as white persons [Gardner advised Harold Ickes]. Commissioner Collier feels that aboriginal rights of the Natives are, while subject to reasonable regulation, sufficient to prevent a complete closing of the ancient fishing grounds. I am inclined to agree with Dr. Gabrielson.[119]

When he learned of the result to which Gardner had reasoned, Felix Cohen was livid.

> This is the first case during my nine years' connection with this Department in which we have upheld a deprivation of Indian property without compensation [Cohen complained to his new boss]. What is upheld by this decision is not a considered judgment of the Interior Department, based on hearings or investigations, reaching the considered conclusion that Indian aboriginal rights must yield to the needs of conservation. Rather this is a decision which is fictitiously imputed to a regulation issued by the Department of Commerce years ago, without investigation or hearing as to Indian rights, at a time when nobody thought these Indians had any aboriginal rights.[120]

Unmoved by Cohen's dehortation, in November, Gardner forwarded his advice to Harold Ickes, who accepted it and authorized Ira Gabrielson to amend the aboriginal fishing rights regulation to clarify that "this section shall not be construed as permitting any exercise of such rights contrary to any of the provisions of [the Fish and Wildlife Service's other fishing] regulations."[121]

Five months later, Judge George Alexander dismissed William Paul's lawsuits. Although Bill and Fred Paul appealed the dismissal of the suit against Clarence Olson, in 1946 the circuit court affirmed Alexander's decision. The brothers also had intended to appeal their uncle's misdemeanor criminal conviction, which is why Louis had arranged to be arrested. But as

Fred Paul years later explained, "We ran out of energy and money and that was the end of that."[122]

The cannery companies, however, had plenty of both.

When the Fish and Wildlife Service published its aboriginal fishing rights regulation, the Association of Pacific Fisheries and the Northwest Salmon Canners Association sent Harold Ickes a radiogram in which they demanded its repeal.[123] But once Ickes made his mind up, arguing with him was unproductive. "The only satisfactory way to handle the matter," Leland Groezinger, an Alaska Packers Association attorney in San Francisco, subsequently concluded, "is to secure congressional legislation."[124]

Three months earlier, Sen. Monrad Wallgren of Washington, an always reliable friend of the Alaska salmon canning industry, had introduced a bill at the cannery companies' request to prohibit fish traps from being closed except by future act of Congress.[125]

Congress adjourned without the Senate Commerce Committee, on which Wallgren served, having taken action on his bill. In March 1943 Wallgren reintroduced the measure.[126] But as reintroduced, the text contained a new clause mandating that the Alaska commercial salmon fishery be open to all citizens "free of all exclusive or several rights under any claim of occupancy, aboriginal or otherwise."[127]

The point did not escape John Collier. "This print sets up monopoly naked and unashamed," he railed to Assistant Secretary of the Interior Oscar Chapman, "and in other of its language effectively would destroy Indian fishing rights."[128]

At Collier's behest, Chapman informed the Commerce Committee that the Roosevelt administration objected to Wallgren's new language. But Wallgren gave only cosmetic ground by arranging for the Commerce Committee to delete the reference to aboriginal fishing rights from the version of the bill it reported to the Senate but retain the "no exclusive right of fishery" prohibition to which aboriginal fishing rights would remain subject.[129]

Although, for unrelated reasons, the Wallgren bill was not enacted, Harold Ickes continued to delay adjudications of aboriginal fishing rights. "I think it unfortunate that the war has interfered so seriously in securing a speedy administrative adjudication of these claims," Ickes wrote Louis Paul in May 1943. "At this point I can only renew my assurance that as soon as possible, after the present wartime conditions no longer interfere, every opportunity will be given for the presentation of facts in support of claims."[130]

But if his policy was delay, the secretary's interest in protecting Native fishing rights was sincere. As he lectured the Association of Pacific Fisheries and the Northwest Salmon Canners Association the following spring,

> It does not follow that a recognition of the rights of the Natives of Alaska will destroy the Alaska fishing industry. In the continental United States, Indians under the jurisdiction of this Department have many resources which are being fully utilized. Where there are mineral deposits on Indian reservations, those deposits are being mined. Where there are Indian forests, their lumber is going directly into war production. There is no reason to believe that the recognition of the rights of Alaskan Natives will result in a waste of the fishing resources of the Territory.[131]

What Ickes left unsaid, of course, was that, if the cannery companies were required to close their traps, they would have to purchase salmon. And if, as the Department of the Interior was trying to have happen at Karluk, white fishermen were prohibited from fishing in waters in which Natives traditionally fished, Native fishermen would have a monopoly on supply that, properly managed, could put many of the companies out of a multimillion-dollar business.

That certainly was William Paul's objective. During his brief career as a Bureau of Indian Affairs field agent, Paul had urged Claude Hirst, the bureau's Alaska superintendent, to approve an IRA business corporation for the Indians at Sitka and then to recommend that the bureau lend the corporation enough money to purchase the local cannery and the fish traps that supplied it. To ensure that the cannery would be profitable, Paul wanted the coastline and waters south of Sitka withdrawn as a reservation.[132] While it is easy to disparage the plan as yet another William Paul scheme, there was merit to the proposal.

In 1938 the Indians at Hydaburg organized the Hydaburg Cooperative Association, which in 1939 obtained a $115,000 loan from the Bureau of Indian Affairs that it used to build and begin operating a cannery.[133] In 1944 when the association applied for a new $280,000 loan, Assistant Secretary Oscar Chapman cautioned John Collier that "it is apparent that unless this group can be assured of the right to operate one or more fish traps, prospects of financial success are not very bright."

But there was a way to improve the odds: withdraw the waters around Hydaburg as an IRA reservation.

In response to the Haidas' demand that he do so, in 1926, President Calvin Coolidge had revoked the 1912 executive order that established the

Bureau of Education reservation at Hydaburg. But a decade of watching fish traps make their white absentee owners rich had caused the Haidas to reconsider their antipathy to becoming "reservation Indians." In 1938 when they organized the Hydaburg Cooperative Association, the Haidas petitioned the Bureau of Indian Affairs to replicate the situation at Annette Island by establishing a new reservation for Hydaburg, whose boundaries would enclose the waters surrounding the village within which cannery companies operated nineteen traps.[134]

When he read the petition, Donald Hagerty, the Bureau of Indian Affairs field agent in Juneau, decided on his own to redraw the boundaries to encircle only six traps.[135] And when they learned of the change, the Haidas were outraged.

> We did not ask for civilization, it was thrust on us and it taught us how to live without provision for the means with which to do it [Albert Brown, the secretary of the Hydaburg Cooperative Association, complained to Assistant Commissioner of Indian Affairs William Zimmerman]. The canning concerns already operating here have had it in their power to help us economically. We were however considered fair game and have been beat down to the last penny. So it is justice that we shall be given the privilege to earn an adequate living even if it inconveniences a little the people who have exploited us and our lands.[136]

But justice or not, intradepartment squabbles and America's entry into war prevented the Hydaburg reservation proposal from being forwarded to Harold Ickes for approval. And so it went until April 1944 when Felix Cohen, as he subsequently explained, "knowing that the Fish and Wildlife Service, as well as the chief operators in the [Alaska salmon canning] industry, had consistently and very vigorously, since February 1941, if not before, opposed any steps looking to the recognition of Native rights in Alaskan fisheries ... urged that the arguments for and against a prompt hearing of Indian claims be presented to the Secretary."[137]

So the matter was brought to Harold Ickes for a new decision, and in May, Ickes approved "proceed[ing] with hearings at the close of the current [fishing] season."[138]

To prepare the way, the next month Cohen made his first trip to southeast Alaska to interview potential witnesses. Throughout the tour his movements were shadowed, and Kenneth Simmons, the Department of the Interior attorney who accompanied him, was privately lobbied by H. L. Faulkner, the Alaska Packers Association's local counsel in Juneau. Faulkner subsequently reported to his client that Simmons had privately confided that he thought "Cohen's schemes for the Indians are crazy." Faulkner also passed along the gossip that Ernest Gruening, the former director of the Department of the Interior's Division of Territories and Island Possessions (whom President Roosevelt had appointed governor of Alaska in 1939), and Don Foster, the Bureau of Indian Affairs Alaska area director in Juneau, "have been very critical of the Paul family and their connection with these cases, and they made representations to Cohen that the Pauls were not trustworthy. Cohen made the statement that in such cases as this it required a 'crooked' attorney to get the Indians their rights restored to them."[139]

But crooked or not, by 1944, Bill Paul had filed petitions on behalf of Klawock, Tongass, Hydaburg, Chilkat, Douglas, Juneau, Sitka, and Wrangell. Each requested the secretary of the interior to hold a hearing to adjudicate the village's aboriginal fishing rights.[140] However, there was a legal question raised as to whether Paul had authority to do so.

A provision of the IRA required an "Indian tribe or tribal council" to obtain the secretary of the interior's approval to hire an attorney, and an 1871 statute required the secretary to approve contracts between attorneys and Indian tribes and attorneys and noncitizen Indians.

Although Alaska Natives had been citizens since 1924, and neither Congress nor the Department of the Interior recognized Native residents of Native villages as being members of "tribes," George Folta (who in 1940 had transferred from the U.S. attorney's office to the Department of the Interior to work for Nathan Margold as an assistant solicitor based in Juneau) was adamant that Bill Paul, whom he disliked as much as he did the younger Paul's father, not be allowed to represent the Indians who had retained his services. When Folta's protestation reached his desk, Felix Cohen was of a more equivocal mind.

> My own feeling is that unless Mr. William L. Paul, Jr., is disbarred (as was his father), or otherwise duly adjudged incompetent to practice, we ought to recognize the right of any Indians who wish to employ him to do so under proper safeguards as to all financial arrangements [Cohen advised John Collier]. This, however, is simply my personal view on a difficult question as to which I am perhaps inadequately informed.[141]

But Folta's antipathy prevailed, and the petitions Bill Paul filed were rejected on the ground that the secretary of the interior had not approved his attorney contracts. However, when Cohen visited Hydaburg, Kake, and Klawock during his trip to southeast Alaska, the members of the village councils with whom he met agreed to have Department of the Interior attorneys represent their communities. Cohen and Kenneth Simmons drafted new petitions for the three villages. Three weeks after Cohen returned to Washington, D.C., on July 26, Assistant Secretary Oscar Chapman announced that in September an administrative law judge would hold a hearing in each village to obtain evidence regarding aboriginal fishing rights.[142]

In 1942 when the aboriginal fishing rights regulation was published, Nathan Margold had urged Harold Ickes to appoint George Folta to do the judging.[143] But the following summer, when he defended Clarence Olson in the lawsuit that William Paul filed to force Olson to order Pacific American Fisheries to close its Point Colpoys trap, Folta had gratuitously argued in court that the Indians of southeast Alaska had no aboriginal fishing rights, even though his client, the Fish and Wildlife Service, had adopted a regulation that said they did. Fowler Harper (who was serving as solicitor while Warner Gardner was in Europe fighting the German army) subsequently censured Folta for the unprofessionalism: "I am troubled by the charge that in your cross-examination of witnesses you attempted to cast doubt upon the claim of the Tee-Hit-Ton tribe to any aboriginal fishing rights. I must say, judging from a transcript of some of the testimony that has been transmitted to me with the letters, that there appears to be some justification of this charge."[144]

With Folta disqualified for bias and time to find an administrative law judge growing short, Harper recommended Richard Hanna.

Hanna was a prominent New Mexico Democrat and former justice of the New Mexico supreme court. In 1918 he had represented the Pueblo Indians at the outset of the fight to prevent white settlers from acquiring title to Pueblo land.[145] When he served a brief tenure as a special assistant to the U.S. attorney general in 1936, Hanna had worked with Felix Cohen on the *Santa Fe Pacific Railroad* lawsuit, so the New Mexico attorney's impartiality was suspect. As Charles Jackson, the assistant director of the Fish and Wildlife Service, complained when the appointment was announced, "We hardly feel that Judge Hanna can be regarded as impartial, but we were not given an opportunity to pass on the question at all."[146]

Whatever the extent of Richard Hanna's pro-Indian bias, the mismatch over which he presided soon neutralized it.

The Indians at Hydaburg, Kake, and Klawock were represented by three Department of the Interior attorneys: George Folta, whose prejudice had disqualified him from judging the evidence he now was presenting; Kenneth Simmons, who purportedly privately believed that Felix Cohen's theory that the Indians of southeast Alaska had aboriginal fishing rights was "crazy"; and Ted Haas, a forty-one-year-old attorney from the Solicitor's Office in Washington, D.C., who recently had been appointed as the Bureau of Indian Affairs' chief counsel.

The cannery companies that collectively operated seventy-five traps in the waters surrounding Hydaburg, Kake, and Klawock sent five attorneys, including W. C. Arnold, who served as lead counsel. In September, when Richard Hanna gaveled the Hydaburg hearing to order, Arnold immediately moved that the session be adjourned because the Haidas' claim had "no basis in history or in law" and "the entire proceeding is unfair to the white people of Alaska and the whole United States."[147]

The motion was denied, and the first witness, Sam Davis, a Haida who had been born in 1865 and who testified through an interpreter, began telling Hanna how, prior to the turn of the century, whites paid the Indians for the privilege of fishing in traditional areas. Four other elderly Indians gave similar testimony, after which the hearing adjourned. The coterie of attorneys, newspaper reporters, government officials, and cannery superintendents in attendance moved to Klawock for the second hearing and then on to Kake for the third.

At each stop the routine was the same. Ted Haas would call elderly Indians who, speaking through interpreters, would testify to the locations at which residents of their village traditionally fished and would then describe the harm that fish traps and the Fish and Wildlife Service's regulation of Indian commercial fishermen had inflicted on the village economy. W. C. Arnold then would move to strike the testimony, and Hanna would deny the motion.[148]

When the Kake hearing concluded, Hanna held a fourth hearing at Ketchikan to allow representatives of such groups as the Ketchikan and Wrangell Chambers of Commerce and the Alaska Miner's Association to enter their outrage into the record.[149] Then Hanna moved south, where the hearing he held in November in Seattle lasted a week and had to be moved three times to accommodate the hostile overflow crowd.[150]

Through it all, the presentation of the Indians' case was woefully inadequate. To be fair to Ted Haas, even if his co-counsel had believed in their clients' case, the team he captained was no match for the cannery companies' top-dollar talent. Still, Haas, who in 1942 had assisted Felix Cohen research a treatise on Indian law that today remains a standard text, seems not to have understood the legal theory of the claims he bore the burden of proving. Edward Allen, the Seattle attorney with whom James Wickersham had spoken in 1932 about finding William Paul work and who in 1944 represented Libby, McNeill & Libby, a cannery company whose six canneries operated forty-eight traps, reported:

> The witnesses presented by the Indian Bureau were almost exclusively elderly men and were very few in number.... Practically all conceded that they do not wish to give up the white man's way of living and return to their former ways of living. Practically all of them admitted that their desire was to secure the commercial benefits obtainable by exclusive use and occupancy even though such commercial benefits were wholly the creation of the whiteman's development.[151]

But the crippling damage the Indian witnesses inflicted on their case was their testimony that residents of their villages had first allowed Indians from other villages and then whites to fish in their traditional areas.

Felix Cohen understood the consequence of those admissions early on, even if Haas did not. As he explained to John Collier when he returned from his trip to southeastern Alaska, the most important factual question Hanna would have to decide was "to what extent have Indians sold traps or trapsites to non-Indians or otherwise acted in a manner which may be held to constitute abandonment of particular areas formerly subject to Indian occupancy?"[152] And throughout his cross-examinations of the Indian witnesses, W. C. Arnold pressed the point.

Had the residents of Hydaburg, Kake, and Klawock tried to prevent whites from fishing in their traditional areas? The answer was no, which had a determinative influence on Richard Hanna's thinking. According to Edward Allen, Hanna "commenced the proceedings wholly in favor of the Indians and against us and wound up, I believe, with a complete change of heart."[153] And unbeknownst to Allen, his assessment was confirmed by J. Steele Culbertson, a Fish and Wildlife Service biologist who traveled with Hanna. "In discussing the hearings unofficially aboard the [Service vessel M.V.] *Brant*," Culbertson reported to his superiors, "Judge Hanna stated that according to the testimony thus far received, he was unable to see where the Indians had been injured through the development of the commercial fisheries."[154]

After reviewing the testimony presented in the 2,700-page transcript and the exhibits and briefs, in April 1945, Hanna sent Secretary of the Interior Harold Ickes his recommended decision. With respect to claims of aboriginal title to offshore waters, W. C. Arnold won another round. "So far as the fishing in ocean waters is concerned by these claimants," Hanna advised Ickes, "there is no substantial evidence in the record that [the Indians] engaged in such fishing prior to the development of commercial fishing, and the use of modern gear and power boats, or exercised any exclusive rights therein."

To the contrary, the Indian witnesses had testified that Indian fishermen fished close to shore at the mouths of spawning streams, and the extent of white encroachment on those areas was "not clear from the evidence presented." But of most portentous consequence, Hanna concluded that since the Indians had not prevented white fishermen from fishing at locations at which Indian fishermen traditionally fished, "this, together with the change in Indian economic conditions, has resulted in a substantial abandonment of aboriginal rights."[155]

When he read the decision, Ickes was surprised that it was "much less favorable to the Indians than I had expected,"[156] so he asked Felix Cohen to review Hanna's assessment of the evidence. But after doing so, Cohen reported that the opinion was "sound."[157] In July Ickes signed a decision document that accepted most of Richard Hanna's findings of fact and conclusions of law.[158]

The decision document announced that the Indians initially had possessed aboriginal title to 3.3 million acres of land and water. But since 1884 when Congress enacted the Alaska Organic Act,

> the Natives of Hydaburg, Klawock and Kake have ceased to maintain exclusive occupancy of approximately ninety-two percent of the foregoing described areas, either by reason of voluntary abandonment of lands once claimed or by acquiescence in the superior power and authority of the Federal Government in patenting or otherwise disposing of or controlling certain lands which effectively interfered with Indian use not only of the lands so disposed of but of other lands thereby separated from convenient access.

When that acreage was deducted, rather than 3.3 million acres, the Haidas held aboriginal title to 101,000 acres; the Tlingits at Klawock, to 95,000 acres; and the Tlingits at Kake, to 77,000 acres.

Ted Haas and W. C. Arnold, each for different reasons, thought the decision was a disaster, and both petitioned Harold Ickes to reconsider it.

For the cannery companies, Richard Hanna's (and Felix Cohen's) easy acceptance of the legal principle that to protect their aboriginal titles the Indians at Hydaburg, Kake, and Klawock should have resorted to violence to prevent whites from fishing at traditional locations and the U.S. government from "patenting or otherwise disposing of or controlling" land that they previously had exclusively used and occupied seemingly was a slam-dunk win. But the devil is in the details, and the decision extended the boundaries of the areas that remained subject to aboriginal title three thousand feet from shore.

"The press release that Ickes gave out was in my opinion exceedingly deceptive," Edward Allen complained to A. R. Brueger, who operated a cannery at Wrangell.

> It sounds as if he had turned down the Indians and given Alaska all the best of it [Allen cautioned, but] when we received the decision itself yesterday and had a chance to check it over, we find that he gives the Indians all the best of it. He not only upholds Indian aboriginal and possessory rights but makes definite awards of specific areas to the Indians and when we come to check these up on the map, we find they embrace long stretches of coastline. In other words, he picks out the most valuable acreage and turns it over to the Indians.... Also although he pretends to say that the Indians have no exclusive ocean fishing rights, he in effect holds that the ocean stops 3,000 feet off shore. Altogether, the decision is very bad.[159]

Ted Haas and W. C. Arnold's requests for reconsideration were granted. But in January 1946, Ickes issued a second decision that, except in minor detail, reaffirmed the findings of fact and conclusions of law that had been announced in the first decision.

While the experiment had not produced the result that he had assumed it would when he invented the idea of allowing Alaska Natives to petition for adjudications of aboriginal fishing rights, Felix Cohen intended the Hydaburg, Kake, and Klawock adjudications to "serve as a precedent for the rest of Alaska."[160] But by the time Harold Ickes issued his second decision, subsequent events had negated the value of the exercise as a template.

The previous April when Franklin Roosevelt died of a cerebral hemorrhage, Harry Truman inherited the presidency. Unlike Roosevelt, who over the years had grown fond of his secretary of the interior's legend-in-his-own-mind braggadocio, Truman disliked Ickes, whom he described off the record as a "shitass."[161]

However, Harold Ickes had no higher opinion of Truman and immediately began making plans to leave office before he was fired. Three weeks after he signed the second Hydaburg, Kake, and Klawock aboriginal fishing rights decision, the secretary found his excuse and resigned to protest Truman's appointment of Edwin Pauley, a man Ickes considered morally suspect, as under secretary of the navy.

When his resignation was announced, the *Pacific Fisherman,* the West Coast fishing industry's in-house newsletter, jubilantly editorialized that "no voice of lament has been heard in the Pacific fisheries at the passing of Harold L. Ickes as Secretary of the Interior." But if the *Pacific Fisherman* was delighted to be rid of the man who had "accepted the sophistries of the Margold Opinion [which had invented the concept of aboriginal fishing rights],"[162] Felix Cohen may have been of a more mixed mind.

On the one hand, Cohen may have reasoned, Ickes had been a reasonably dependable ally in the intradepartment fights in which Cohen and John Collier had been involved over the years to defend Indian interests. On the other hand, Ickes had pulled an important punch fourteen months earlier by scuttling Cohen and Collier's plan to establish additional reservations in Alaska.

Secretary Ickes did so at the urging of Under Secretary of the Interior Abe Fortas. Three years Felix Cohen's junior, Fortas possessed a natural intellectual talent that was the equal of Cohen's, although a contemporary would recall that people continually underestimated Fortas because he "look[ed] like a boy."[163] Unlike Cohen, Fortas also possessed an ultimately maledict ambition that, with the help of several life-altering scholarships, fueled a rocket-swift rise from Memphis, Tennessee—where his Orthodox Jewish parents had settled after emigrating from England—to New Haven, Connecticut. In 1933 at the age of twenty-three, Fortas was appointed to the faculty of the Yale Law School.[164]

When he attended Yale Law School, Fortas had been the "prize student"[165] of Professor William O. Douglas. When Douglas and other faculty members with whom Fortas was acquainted moved to Washington, D.C., to staff Franklin Roosevelt's New Deal, they brought Douglas's protégé into government service, first part-time in the Agricultural Adjustment Administration and then, in 1937, full-time working with Douglas at the Securities and Exchange Commission.

In 1939, Roosevelt appointed Douglas, then serving as chairman of the Securities and Exchange Commission, to a seat on the U.S. Supreme Court. Before departing for the bench, Douglas arranged for Harold Ickes to hire Fortas as counsel to the Department of the Interior Coal Commission. Two years later, Ickes named Fortas director of the Division of Power. And the year after that, Ickes arranged for Franklin Roosevelt to appoint the thirty-two year-old former Yale law professor, whom Ickes considered "one of the most brilliant lawyers in Washington,"[166] under secretary of the interior, the second ranking position in the department.

Insofar as Fortas's involvement can be determined, Harold Ickes did not consult his under secretary in 1943 when he approved Karluk and the four other reservations that he and Oscar Chapman established that year. But in December 1944, Fortas intruded into the implementation of the Department of the Interior's Alaska reservation policy at the request of Rep. Henry "Scoop" Jackson.

Unlike Abe Fortas and Felix Cohen, from his boyhood in Everett, Washington, a small town north of Seattle, through his graduation from the University of Washington Law School, the thirty-two-year-old congressman had been an undistinguished student. But the first-generation son of Norwegian immigrants had both an affinity for the grind (during his career as a newsboy, Jackson delivered 74,880 papers without receiving a complaint for tardiness)[167] and an audacious political ambition.

In 1938, only two years out of law school, Jackson organized a cadre of college-age volunteers whose door-to-door campaigning catapulted the twenty-six-year-old homeboy from obscurity to election as Everett's youngest county district attorney. Two years after that, Jackson's doorbell-ringing volunteers leveraged their candidate's short career prosecuting bootleggers and whorehouse madams into a seat in the U.S. House of Representatives.[168]

In 1940 when Jackson was elected to Congress, the Alaska salmon canning industry annually infused "a veritable blood transfusion into the arteries of [Pacific] Northwest commerce,"[169] as it had since the 1880s. Many cannery owners, many officials of the unions that provided much of their labor, and many of the businessmen who sold sundries to the owners and their workers lived either in Seattle or in Jackson's congressional district, which encompassed the entire northwestern corner of the state of Washington. To provide his constituents service, Jackson arranged to be appointed to the House Committee on Merchant Marine and Fisheries.

Three years later, in July 1944, Assistant Secretary of the Interior Oscar Chapman announced that an administrative law judge would hold hearings at Hydaburg, Kake, and Klawock to obtain evidence on aboriginal fishing rights. Representatives of the cannery companies and unions whose balance sheets and membership dues were at risk asked their friends on the Merchant Marine and Fisheries Committee to intervene.

Schuyler Bland, the chairman of the committee, responded by deputizing Jackson and Rep. Joseph O'Brien of New York as a two-member subcommittee to attend the hearings and report their view of the situation. As Jackson contemporaneously described the mission,

We have been requested by both the industry and its employees to investigate the fisheries situation in southeastern Alaska. We want to determine exactly what the Interior Department's policy will be in these matters. We are concerned because the industry, which has an annual output of $60,000,000 in Alaska salmon and employs 12,000 workers, is of tremendous economic importance to Alaska and the Pacific Northwest, particularly the State of Washington.[170]

But that seemingly candid explanation was subreptitious since it made no mention of Jackson's political stake in the matter. For a career politician like Scoop Jackson, the prospect of defeat in the next election is an omnipresent concern. And 1944 was an election year.

If the men who made their money canning salmon decided that members of the Washington state congressional delegation, such as Jackson and Warren Magnuson, whose congressional district included the city of Seattle, could not keep Harold Ickes's love affair with Indian fishing rights under control (so the worst case scenario thinking went), they might give their campaign contributions and their votes to competing candidates.

To try to preempt the possibility, the day after Oscar Chapman announced the Hydaburg, Kake, and Klawock hearings, Rep. Hardin Peterson, chairman of the House Committee on Public Lands and someone that Jackson knew Chapman paid attention to, telephoned the assistant secretary on the back channel. He asked Chapman to urge Harold Ickes to order Richard Hanna to postpone his hearings until after the election because "Congressmen Jackson and Magnuson were very much concerned, as these hearings would adversely affect them in November" and "Sen. Wallgren also feels deeply about these hearings being held in November."[171]

Chapman passed along the message. But Ickes refused to countenance delay, and in September, Jackson and Joseph O'Brien flew to southeast Alaska to attend the Hanna hearings.

Two months later the House of Representatives returned to the capital after the election (in which Jackson was elected to his third term). Schuyler Bland convened a closed session of the Merchant Marine and Fisheries Committee to allow the Alaska Indian fishing rights subcommittee to brief the members on the report Jackson and O'Brien had written about the situation and whose cover was marked "Confidential."

The concept of aboriginal rights to fishing grounds according to the information received by your subcommittee is a novel one [Jackson and O'Brien, speaking through their report, informed their colleagues]. Briefs submitted to your subcommittee by various interested parties show that this concept is legally debatable, and that there are serious legal questions as to whether the views of the Solicitor of the Department of the Interior would be sustained by the courts.

For that reason, no "exclusive fishing rights should be maintained." If the unexpected happened and the courts decided that the Indians had such rights, "legislative action would be advisable to insure the preservation of the fishing industry in Alaskan waters and to maintain the required output of fish." In the meantime, the report concluded, "no action should be taken by the Department of the Interior which will restrict these valuable fishing areas in such manner as will reduce the total salmon pack, pending the courts' decision regarding aboriginal rights."[172]

Acting on his own recommendation, on December 3, Jackson sent Abe Fortas a telegram from Everett asking for a meeting "in connection with the Alaska Indian matter" when he returned to the capital.[173]

When Hardin Peterson's phone call to Oscar Chapman produced no useful result and Richard Hanna subsequently announced that he intended to hold a fifth hearing in Seattle in October, Fortas had set the situation straight when Jackson demanded that the Seattle hearing be postponed because it was too close to home too close to the election. "This is an absolute contradiction to assurances you gave me in [our] telephone conversation a few days ago," Jackson complained to Fortas by telegram when Hanna mistakenly disavowed the rescheduling to which Fortas had agreed. "I'm sure you realize this places me in an intolerable position at a most critical time."[174]

When he received Jackson's first telegram, Fortas clarified Richard Hanna's confusion about the date of the Seattle hearing. When he received the second, Fortas calendared the meeting Jackson requested, and the two men met on December 7.

Six days later Fortas sent Harold Ickes a memorandum. After counseling that "I think it is necessary for us to spend the time needed to arrive at a resolution of the policy problems raised by the proposed creation of additional Native reservations in Alaska," the memorandum urged Ickes to appoint a committee, which Fortas volunteered to chair, to review the matter.[175]

When Ickes approved the recommendation the following day, his doing so instantaneously transferred control over implementation of the Alaska reservation policy from Assistant Secretary Oscar Chapman (who had line authority over the Bureau of Indian Affairs) to Fortas. And to make the situation for Felix Cohen worse, John Collier resigned the following month[176]—Collier's personal relations with members of Congress who controlled the enactment and funding of Indian programs having deteriorated during his twelve years as commissioner from not so good to beyond repair.

Through the winter and into the spring the Fortas review committee (to which Felix Cohen was appointed) patched together a new Alaska reservation policy whose announced goal was to limit reservation withdrawals to no more than 5 percent of Alaska's 375 million acres, regardless of the number of acres that were subject to Native claims of aboriginal title. But that was merely the beginning of the constriction.

Inside reservations, Natives would be conveyed legal title only to the land under their villages and then simply allowed to hunt and fish on the remainder of the acreage.

The policy also announced that reservations in southeastern Alaska, where "a quantity of land much smaller than the indicated average for the entire Territory is adequate for a decent livelihood on the American standard of living," would be considerably smaller than reservations that might be established for the Eskimos and the Athabascan Indians who lived north of the Alaska Panhandle. But even in the interior and the Arctic, "bona fide homestead entries on suitable tracts classified as agricultural land" and "sound mineral and other commercial developments which will not unduly interfere with the Native food and fur supply" would be allowed inside reservation boundaries.[177]

In July a copy of the Fortas review committee's Alaska reservation policy began circulating inside the Department of the Interior. Assistant Commissioner of Indian Affairs William Zimmerman was the senior Bureau of Indian Affairs official who had been on the job when the original Alaska reservation policy had been conceived. When the new policy reached his desk, Zimmerman protested that the review committee's handiwork was a "reversal of the policy to which the Department has been publicly committed since 1936."[178]

The previous summer Felix Cohen had returned from his trip to southeast Alaska with his enthusiasm for establishing reservations reinvigorated. As usual, the reason was Metlakatla.

As Cohen explained when he returned to Washington:

> We [i.e., Cohen and Kenneth Simmons] think of all the Indian communities we visited the only one in which this Department can take any real pride is Metlakatla. In 1887 this Department reserved for the Metlakatlans (refugees from Canada) an area of land and water

adequate for their needs. Except for schooling, which has been furnished by the federal government (and we have some doubt as to the necessity for continuing this arrangement), everything else essential in the building up of a civilized community has been done by the Indians and their white friends and employees, within the secure economic framework of the original reservation. We think the Department ought to try to give the same measure of justice and economic protection to other Indian communities in southeastern Alaska as it has given to Metlakatla.[179]

But since Cohen had been a principal draftsman of the Fortas review committee reservation policy, he was stung (by a guilty conscience?) by William Zimmerman's criticism. So stung that, while he conceded that the new policy "represent[s] a moderate retreat from the largest hopes of the Indian Office on the reservation program," Cohen nevertheless subsequently rationalized its content to Abe Fortas—as if the under secretary needed convincing—as "a fair and practical compromise of all the conflicting interests."[180]

If it did nothing to lessen Felix Cohen's pusillanimity, Zimmerman's protestation accomplished its purpose.

Abe Fortas had wanted Harold Ickes to announce the new Alaska reservation policy to the public the day after he signed the decision document that accepted Richard Hanna's Hydaburg, Kake, and Klawock aboriginal fishing rights decision, since doing so "would provide a fairly comprehensive indication of policy concerning the major land problems in Alaska."[181]

But when the decision document was published in the *Federal Register* on August 1, no mention was made of a new Alaska reservation policy. Several weeks later the review committee tried to mollify Zimmerman by modifying its work product in several unimportant respects, but by then the momentum to adopt a new policy had slowed. In December it died, when Abe Fortas resigned as under secretary and in January left the Department of the Interior to practice law.

A month later, Harold Ickes tendered his own resignation, after which Harry Truman, delighted to be rid of the "Old Curmudgeon" (as the seventy-one-year-old Ickes liked to call himself), nominated Julius "Cap" Krug to replace Ickes as secretary of the interior.

A thirty-eight-year-old engineer who had been raised in Wisconsin and then had worked for the Tennessee Valley Authority, Krug came to Harry Truman's attention during the war, when he served as chairman of the War Production Board. Krug candidly admitted during his confirmation hearing that he knew nothing about Native Americans or Indian policy.[182] He also knew nothing about Alaska. However, with Abe Fortas gone, the new secretary's ignorance was a clean slate on which the proponents of establishing reservations in Alaska immediately etched their mark.

For more than a year the paperwork to establish a reservation on Little Diomede Island, a barren chunk of rock in the middle of Bering Strait on which a small Eskimo village was located, had been languishing in a file drawer.

The U.S. Senate confirmed Krug's nomination to the Truman cabinet in March 1946. Several weeks later, Krug was sent the paperwork, and in April he signed a proclamation that designated Little Diomede Island as a "Native reservation."[183]

Because there were no trees (much less marketable timber) or gold on the island and no commercial salmon fishery in the surrounding waters, the reservation engendered no ruckus. But that would not be the case with reservations that might be established elsewhere. As a consequence, when Krug toured the territory in August, he was lobbied during his obligatory stops at Fairbanks, Anchorage, and Juneau by the territorial attorney general and other influential whites to put an end to the nonsense about reservations and aboriginal fishing rights that Harold Ickes had begun.[184]

In the meantime, after pondering the less than successful (in their view) adjudications of aboriginal occupancy at Hydaburg, Kake, and Klawock, Felix Cohen and Ted Haas had decided that what Haas had lacked was an expert witness. So they arranged for Walter Goldschmidt, a Department of Agriculture anthropologist, to spend the summer of 1946 traveling with Haas through southeast Alaska interviewing witnesses and preparing maps that depicted aboriginal use areas. Goldschmidt then organized the information into a lengthy report that documented Indian use and occupancy of the land and waters surrounding each village (other than Hydaburg, Kake, and Klawock).[185]

Cohen and Haas recruited Goldschmidt because they assumed that Julius Krug intended to continue to hold hearings to adjudicate Indian claims based on aboriginal occupancy. Krug announced during his August 1946 visit to Juneau that a hearing would be held at Klukwan in September,[186] but neither the Klukwan nor any other hearings were held. Instead, Abe Fortas's departure reenergized the effort inside the Department of the Interior to establish reservations.

In April 1946, Don Foster, the Bureau of Indian Affairs Alaska area director in Juneau, advised E. L. "Bob" Bartlett, who in 1944 had succeeded Anthony Dimond as Alaska's delegate in the U.S. House of Representatives, that he had recommended that 640-acre reservations be established at village sites "from Barrow clear down to the Kotzebue and Deering area," and that he intended to submit similar proposals for the remaining arctic and interior villages as soon as possible because "now that the war is over and the Territory is going to be flooded by all kinds and types of people, there is urgent need that these areas be established in order to protect the homes of people and to keep out through federal regulation undesirable traders, fly-by-night chiselers and, in many instances, to be able to control the missionary activities."[187]

But if Foster's goals were modest, William Zimmerman's were considerably more ambitious. Throughout 1947, Zimmerman served as acting commissioner of Indian Affairs while William Brophy, who had succeeded John Collier, recovered from an illness. For Zimmerman, protecting land around Native villages from trespass, and inexperienced Natives from exploitation, were laudable goals. But like Collier and Felix Cohen, Zimmerman considered the protection of the Native hunting, fishing, and trapping economy to be the principal reason reservations should be established.[188] To that end, by July 1947 the acting commissioner had forwarded proposals for three large reservations to Julius Krug: a 151-square-mile reservation at Hydaburg whose boundaries encircled the land and waters that Richard Hanna had determined still were subject to aboriginal title, an 800-square-mile reservation at Barrow, and a 2,300-square-mile reservation for Shungnak and Kobuk, two Eskimo villages on the Kobuk River in the northwestern Arctic.[189]

By October the Hydaburg reservation proposal had percolated far enough up through the bureaucracy that the Department of the Interior public affairs office issued a press release mistakenly announcing that Julius Krug had signed the Hydaburg reservation proclamation.[190]

When he learned through the public affairs office error that the establishment of a reservation at Hydaburg was imminent, Bob Bartlett was outraged. "To say I was astounded that the reservation proposal had reached such a stage without consultation with interested individuals or groups in Alaska or with the Alaska delegate in Congress is a gross understatement," Bartlett complained in a personal letter to Krug. "I earnestly hope your signature will not be attached to this or to any like proclamation until Alaskans have been heard on the subject."[191]

Embarrassed by the bungling, Krug instructed Oscar Chapman (who had been promoted from assistant secretary to under secretary when Abe Fortas resigned) to "confer with me" before "any contemplated action concerning establishment or expansion of any Indian reservation is taken."[192]

But the damage was done.

After the Republican Party won control of both houses of Congress in the 1946 election, in January 1947, Sen. Hugh Butler of Nebraska, a senior member of the reactionary Republican "Old Guard," became chairman of the Senate Committee on Public Lands, which, since the Committee on Indian Affairs had been disbanded, exercised legislative jurisdiction over Indian affairs. A Ray Lyman Wilbur assimilationist, the sixty-nine-year-old Butler believed that "the solution of the Indian problem in Alaska is not to set them apart from the other people or from modern life, but to give them the tools with which to compete on an equal footing with other people."[193]

As will be described in the following chapter, in the spring and summer of 1947, Butler learned firsthand the extent to which legal confusion over the validity of aboriginal land rights inside the Tongass National Forest was inconveniencing white southeast Alaska businessmen, with whom Butler, having been a businessman himself prior to entering the Senate, was empathetic. So when the Juneau and Ketchikan Chambers of Commerce asked him to do so, that December, Butler introduced Joint Resolution 162 in the U.S. Senate to repeal the section of the Alaska amendments to the IRA that delegated the secretary of the interior authority to establish reservations.[194]

Hugh Butler controlled an important committee, to which the secretary of the interior was accountable. And when Julius Krug had been sworn into office, he had promised to be "guided scrupulously by the will of the people as expressed through Congress."[195] As a consequence, when Butler introduced Joint Resolution 162, Krug decided not to sign the Hydaburg, Barrow, and Shungnak-Kobuk reservation proclamations until Congress decided whether it would repeal his authority to do so (although he allowed the Department of the Interior's lobbyists to publicly oppose Resolution 162). Felix Cohen summed up the situation in a private letter to Harold Ickes:

> I shall be surprised, albeit pleasantly so, if Secretary Krug actually sets up any new Native reservations in Alaska, although Secretaries [William] Warne and [Oscar] Chapman and the Indian Bureau have been pushing in this direction. Present Department policy seems to be to do nothing to protect its exposed Alaska flanks until Sen. Butler has further opportunity to throw legislative monkey wrenches.[196]

Butler gave the wrenches a hard throw, but in June 1948 a procedural objection raised on the floor of the U.S. House of Representatives during the closing moments of a last all-night session killed Joint Resolution 162 after its sponsor had shepherded its passage through the Senate.[197] Four months later, Oscar Chapman urged Krug to sign the three reservation proclamations, which had been gathering dust in his in-basket.[198] "[T]hese are the reservations that Assistant Secretary Warne discussed with you last spring," Chapman reminded him. "At that time you indicated that if the Congress did not repeal your authority to create Indian reservations in Alaska you would approve the establishment of these reservations."[199]

Krug, still skittish, decided to take no action until he discussed the matter with Alaska delegate Bob Bartlett and Alaska territorial governor Ernest Gruening.[200] He did so in December at a meeting during which Gruening, a stalwart assimilationist who in 1944 had publicly condemned the establishment of reservations in Alaska as "a form of inverted Jim Crowism,"[201] reasserted that objection, and Bartlett, who had a more restrained personal style, counseled Krug that "the reservation approach is not the best one."[202]

So Krug continued to do nothing, which is not to say that he was not being lobbied to act.

After fourteen years as a government attorney, Felix Cohen had resigned from the Department of the Interior the previous January to return to private practice. But the Alaska reservation policy still had a champion high inside the Department of the Interior bureaucracy.

In May 1947, Warner Gardner, who the previous year had been promoted from solicitor to assistant secretary, resigned. Julius Krug arranged for President Truman to appoint William Warne, the assistant commissioner of the Bureau of Reclamation with whom Krug had worked when both men served on the War Production Board, as Gardner's replacement.[203] At the Bureau of Reclamation, Warne, who, prior to entering government service, had been a California newspaperman, had no involvement with Alaska matters. But now that he supervised the Bureau of Indian Affairs and other department agencies that administered Alaska programs, the new assistant secretary spent August touring the territory.[204]

Doing so convinced Warne that Native land claims based on aboriginal occupancy had "to be settled before there can be any major development of Alaska"[205] and that establishing reservations was the means of settlement that would best afford Alaska Natives economic justice. As it had been for Harold Ickes in 1938 and Felix Cohen in 1944, visiting Metlakatla was the event that most influenced Warne's view of the situation. He subsequently explained the connection:

> I have never hidden my support of the idea of establishment of land reserves for Indian use in Alaska. I have testified before committees of the House and Senate and have made many talks ... telling the story of the difference between the villages of Metlakatla, which has a reserve that was established by law more than fifty years ago, and Kasaan [a small Tlingit Indian village on the east coast of Prince of Wales Island sixty miles northwest of Metlakatla] which has no reserve. Metlakatla is as fine a small town as I have known and I am from a background of small towns. Kasaan has almost disappeared and its people are a defeated people. Both are about the same distance from Ketchikan and, if anything, normally the greater outside pressures would have been on Metlakatla. There can be no other explanation than the reserve for Metlakatla and the lack of one for Kasaan for the differences between these two villages.[206]

During the fall of 1948 and throughout 1949, Warne repeatedly urged Julius Krug to sign the Hydaburg, Barrow, and Shungnak-Kobuk reservation proclamations. But as late as October, Warne had "told the people [of Hydaburg] in a meeting there that I doubted whether their petition [for a reservation] would be approved."[207] However, to Warne's delight, six weeks later it was.

When it was over and he could be gracious, Harry Truman would recall Julius Krug as "a kindly man" who "made a great Secretary [of the Interior] for a while."[208] But according to a reliable contemporaneous account of the conventional wisdom, Krug was "hopelessly naïve in political matters,"[209] so naïve that when he decided that Harry Truman could not win the 1948 presidential election he concocted a series of excuses not to campaign. When Truman astounded the pundits by triumphing, Krug's disloyalty soured his relationship with the man to whom he owed his presence in the cabinet, as well as with the powers behind the throne, including, among other Truman confidants, Clark Clifford, the president's unofficial chief of staff.

As a consequence, as early as May 1949, Ruth Bronson, the executive secretary of the National Congress of American Indians (whose involvement in the story of Alaska Natives and their land will be described in the following chapter), would pass along the back-channel news from her sources inside the Department of the Interior "that Krug is to go soon and that Oscar Chapman will take his place."[210]

But Krug held on until October, when he allowed the Bureau of Reclamation to become publicly embroiled in a politically embarrassing dispute with the Bureau of the Budget over the financing of dams in the Pacific Northwest.[211] Truman responded by finally sending his secretary of the interior a "Dear Cap" letter that curtly conveyed the message that it was time for Krug to quit.[212]

When Krug refused to depart, Truman dispatched Clark Clifford to tell him to begin packing. As Clifford later told the story,

> On November 3, 1949, I called on Krug in his office at the Interior Department to suggest that perhaps it would be better for everyone if he offered the President his resignation. Krug could not believe his ears. He asked me on whose authority I was speaking. When I assured him I was speaking on behalf of the President, something unexpected happened; he began to cry. This, I must admit, unnerved me more than almost anything else that I had experienced in dealing with high-level members of the government. Over the next few days, Krug tried without success, to get the decision reversed. Finally, the President asked me to tell Krug that if he did not announce his resignation, the White House would.[213]

On November 10, Krug resigned, effective December 1, and on November 30, as the soon-to-be ex-secretary was clearing off his desk, William Warne, who during his recent visit to Hydaburg had "resolved in my own mind to renew my recommendation if an appropriate moment should later arise," again urged Krug to sign the Hydaburg, Barrow, and Shungnak-Kobuk reservation proclamations. Twenty minutes later Krug did so.[214]

However, the Barrow and Shungnak-Kobuk reservations soon met an ignoble end, as would the Hydaburg reservation three years later.

As Ruth Bronson's sources had predicted, the day he accepted Krug's resignation, Truman nominated Oscar Chapman to succeed Krug as secretary of the interior.

Prior to his appointment as assistant secretary of the interior, Chapman had been active in Democratic Party politics in Colorado, his adopted home state, and in 1930 had managed the successful election campaign of Colorado senator Edward Costigan, with whom he was practicing law in Denver. So Chapman arrived at the Department of the Interior in 1933 with his political antennae fully extended. To keep them so, as soon as he settled in, the new assistant secretary began cultivating what by 1949 were excellent personal relations with the members of the congressional committees that asserted legislative and budgetary jurisdiction over his department.

Chapman was so personally popular with the senators who served on the Senate Committee on Interior and Insular Affairs (as the Committee on Public Lands recently had been renamed) that their recommendation to the Senate of his nomination as secretary of the interior was a foregone conclusion. That said, and even though Sen. Joseph O'Mahoney of Wyoming had replaced Hugh Butler as chairman of the committee when Harry Truman's "Give 'em Hell" presidential campaign had helped to elect enough Democrats in the 1948 congressional election to allow the president's party to regain control of the Senate, when Chapman testified at his confirmation hearing in January, he knew that senators sitting on the dais were livid over Julius Krug's eleventh-hour signing of the Hydaburg, Barrow, and Shungnak-Kobuk reservation proclamations.

Assistant Secretary Chapman had been involved elbow-deep in the implementation of the Department of the Interior's Alaska reservation policy. And Under Secretary Chapman had not objected to the establishment of the Hydaburg, Barrow, and Shungnak-Kobuk reservations. But to avoid being splattered with the political tar into which the committee members wanted to dunk Julius Krug, when asked by Sen. Guy Cordon of Oregon to comment on the subject, Secretary-designate Chapman responded, "I have felt for some time, and I feel more strongly about it every day, that we should take an entirely new look ... at the matter of reservations for the Indians of Alaska." And he promised Cordon that he would not establish additional reservations without holding public hearings to afford "people who are interested in Alaska ... an opportunity to be heard."[215]

When the Chapman confirmation hearing adjourned, Bob Bartlett and Ernest Gruening, who were in the audience, walked across Capitol Hill to Bartlett's office, where they composed a letter to Chapman that commended the secretary-designate's willingness to take a "new look" at the Alaska reservation policy and urged him to appoint a committee of white residents of the territory (because "it would be difficult for anyone of Native blood to view this question objectively") to advise him on the matter.[216]

Although Chapman did not do so, any cause that Bartlett and Gruening may have had for further worry abated in March when the White House announced that President Truman had appointed Dillon Seymour Myer as commissioner of Indian affairs.

The fifty-eight-year-old Myer, a former middle-rung bureaucrat at the Department of Agriculture, had made his reputation with the president during the four years he served as the hard-nosed administrator of the War Relocation Authority, the agency that operated the concentration camps in which 120,000 U.S. citizens of Japanese descent had been confined during the Second World War.

Myer had had no involvement with Native Americans or Indian policy prior to his appointment as commissioner. But he arrived at the Bureau of

Indian Affairs convinced that John Collier's preoccupation with strengthening the reservation system and protecting traditional Native American cultures had achieved nothing since 1933 other than to delay the assimilation of Native Americans into Ray Lyman Wilbur's "American melting pot."

Putting that view into practice, Myer set about dismantling as many Collier-era policies and programs as he had time, during the three years he served as commissioner, to repudiate.[217]

Since Myer considered reservations "prisons" from which it was past high time to set free the Indians who lived on them,[218] he had no intention of recommending the establishment of more reservations in Alaska. And even if Oscar Chapman had wanted to establish additional reservations over the objection of his commissioner of Indian affairs (and there is no evidence that he did), Chapman understood the clamor his doing so would set off on Capitol Hill.

Scoop Jackson provided an early preview. The U.S. Senate confirmed Oscar Chapman's nomination as secretary of the interior in January 1950. Two months later, Jackson (who, after rising through the back-bench ranks of the U.S. House of Representatives, had been appointed in 1947 to a seat on the House Committee on Appropriations) persuaded the members of the Appropriations Committee who were writing the Department of the Interior 1951 appropriations bill to add a paragraph to their report on the bill that ordered the Bureau of Indian Affairs not to spend so much as a dollar on the administration of reservations.

"A policy of placing Alaska Indians, Eskimos and Aleuts on reservations appears to be devoid of merit, retrogressive, unnecessary and indefensible from the standpoint of settling Native land claims" the report announced. "Therefore, none of the funds appropriated for the Bureau of Indian Affairs should be used in connection with pending reservation orders or reservation orders which might hereafter be signed."[219]

While it did not have the force of law, the Appropriations Committee's admonition, followed less than a week later by Dillon Myer's appointment as commissioner of Indian affairs, were two turns of the roll that, for Jackson and the reservation policy's other blood enemies, began in January, when Oscar Chapman volunteered to take a "new look" at the Alaska reservation policy. It continued into February, when the Eskimos at Barrow rejected their reservation by the lopsided vote of 231 to 29, and then into April, when the Eskimos at Shungnak and Kobuk did the same.[220]

Eben Hopson, a respected Inupiaq leader, years later recalled that the Barrow Eskimos rejected their reservation because the acreage was "too small," and if the federal government had required the Barrow Eskimos "to keep our activities limited to within that reservation" we "would not have been able to freely travel to our fish camps, caribou hunting grounds and all over the North Slope."[221] Since the Barrow Eskimos had voiced that complaint as early as 1946,[222] Hopson's recollection was accurate. But that was not the way Don Foster, the Bureau of Indian Affairs Alaska area director, saw the situation at the time.

"Actually what happened was that a lot of propaganda was poured into [Barrow] that confused the issue," Foster complained after the vote in a private letter to Felix Cohen. "For instance, William Paul, Sr., wrote the people and told them they should share in the oil that the navy had found and indicated in his letter that a reservation might jeopardize their claims" to the 35,000 square miles of North Slope tundra that President Warren Harding had withdrawn from the public domain in 1923 as a naval petroleum reserve.

And according to Foster,

> At Shungnak the people were subject to one of the dirtiest most underhanded campaigns that I have ever been connected with. The people were told that they would lose their freedom, their voting privileges, that they would be confined to the reservation, that the old people would lose their pensions, that there would be no aid to dependent children, that the wives would be stolen and that they would be slaves of the Alaska Native Service.[223]

But whatever their motivation for doing so, the Eskimos at Barrow and Shungnak and Kobuk had voted no; for Don Foster and Felix Cohen, Hydaburg was the only respite.

After a vigorous lobbying campaign waged by Foster and other Bureau of Indian Affairs employees who supported the establishment of the reservation and by whites who opposed it (including Bob Bartlett, who broadcast an election eve plea to vote no that a Ketchikan radio station beamed into the village), in April 1950 the Haidas accepted their reservation by a vote of 95 to 29.

As previously mentioned, in 1938 the Haidas had organized the Hydaburg Cooperative Association that in 1939 began operating a cannery. To be profitable, the cannery needed a dependable supply of salmon. But the three best trap sites in the surrounding waters were occupied: one by a trap owned by Robert Carlson, a white absentee owner from Seattle, and the other two by traps owned by the Nakat Packing Corporation and Libby, McNeill & Libby cannery companies.

Prior to the 1946 fishing season the Hydaburg cannery was able to acquire a trap (after struggling seven years without one) when Harold Ickes's decision that Haida aboriginal fishing rights extended three thousand feet from shore created enough legal confusion to enable the Hydaburg Cooperative Association to negotiate an agreement with Nakat Packing (which in addition to its own also operated the Carlson trap) and Libby, McNeill & Libby. In exchange for the Haidas agreeing to "withdraw their pending requests that the Secretary close down the [companies'] traps," the P. E. Harris cannery company agreed to install a trap south of the village and deliver "the entire production" to the Hydaburg cannery.[224]

When the agreement expired at the end of the 1947 season, Libby, McNeill & Libby refused to extend it. But Nakat Packing agreed to deliver fish to the Hydaburg cannery for the next five seasons in exchange for being allowed to operate its traps.[225]

That agreement held until 1950 when the Haidas voted to accept their reservation, and James Curry, the Washington, D.C., attorney who represented the village (and about whom considerably more will be said in the following chapter), notified Nakat Packing and Libby, McNeill & Libby that they henceforth would be charged rent to operate their traps in what were now reservation waters. Nakat Packing responded to the ultimatum by informing Curry that its agreement with the Hydaburg Cooperative Association allowed its traps to continue to operate through the 1952 fishing season. "If Nakat is successful in its view," Bill Paul, who was associated with Curry as Hydaburg's local counsel, complained to Don Foster, the Alaska area director of the Bureau of Indian Affairs, "Hydaburg Indians will be effectually deprived of the use of the three fish traps on their reservation until 1953, amounting to a loss to the reservation people of approximately $300,000."[226]

In 1947 when he had served the year as acting commissioner of Indian affairs, William Zimmerman, who had no ax to grind with either man, had approved Curry and Paul's attorney contract with the village of Hydaburg. But Dillon Myer, who particularly disliked Curry, refused to allow Curry and Paul to represent the Haidas in the fish trap dispute. Myer also refused to ask Mastin White, the Department of the Interior solicitor, to instruct his attorneys to do so.

To pressure Myer, in November, Curry flew to Hydaburg. At his instigation the town council and the IRA council that had been organized to govern the reservation jointly passed a resolution demanding that the Bureau of Indian Affairs remove the Nakat Packing and Libby, McNeill & Libby traps.[227]

When he returned to Washington, D.C., Curry mailed a letter to individuals on a list of white "friends of the Indian" that he had compiled over the years. He urged his correspondents to write their congressmen and demand that Dillon Myer protect Haida fishing rights. Many did so, and queries from Capitol Hill began appearing in Myer's mail. Working the problem from a different angle, Curry also wrote a letter that John Collier, who was teaching at the City College of New York, signed,[228] and the *New York Times* published. After labeling the situation at Hydaburg a "scandal" that "deserves citizen attention" the letter advised that "protests should go to the Secretary of the Interior."[229]

Curry's one-man public relations campaign had its intended effect. But to be fair to Dillon Myer, the previous December—the month after the Bureau of Indian Affairs received the Hydaburg councils' resolution—the Department of the Interior (without notifying Curry) asked the Department of Justice to file a lawsuit on behalf of the United States, the legal owner of the Hydaburg reservation, against Libby, McNeill & Libby to obtain a court order directing the company to remove its trap.[230]

The request was approved and in May 1951, Patrick Gilmore, the local U.S. attorney, filed the government's complaint in the U.S. district court in Juneau.[231]

In light of the subsequent charge that Gilmore and his client wanted to lose the case, it is interesting to note that the judge they allowed to decide it was George Folta, whom President Truman had appointed to the bench in 1947.

At the time, a statute required a U.S. district court judge to recuse himself from a case with which he had a prior connection to the subject matter.[232] Since Folta had served as Ted Haas's co-counsel in the adjudication that resulted in Harold Ickes's decision that the Hydaburg aboriginal use area included the waters that the reservation boundary now enclosed, the prior connection was disqualifying. But Folta did not withdraw.

Another statute required a U.S. district court judge to recuse himself from a case when a party filed an affidavit that alleged that the judge was prejudiced.[233] But despite Folta's past public and private statements in small-town Juneau that the Indians of southeast Alaska had no aboriginal fishing rights and despite his well-known animus toward reservations, no affidavit was filed—although Patrick Gilmore asked to do so.

> Judge Folta has said he will be fair [Assistant Attorney General Devitt Vanech instructed Gilmore after discussing the matter with Mastin White], and we do not believe an affidavit should be filed. While he

was opposed to the policy of establishing Indian reservations, there is no question as to the validity of such reservations since *Hynes v Grimes Packing Company* [the 1949 U.S. Supreme Court decision that upheld the establishment of the Karluk reservation]. We cannot presume that he will render a decision contrary to the holdings in that case.[234]

As his past expressions of bad attitude were evidence that he would, George Folta soon proved Vanech wrong.

First, in August, Folta denied the motion for a preliminary injunction that Gilmore had filed the month before. Then, although it arguably was the most important lawsuit on his docket, Folta did not calendar the case for trial until the following July.

But even if he had calendared the case expeditiously, the outcome was preordained, first by Folta's prejudice, and then when Patrick Gilmore suddenly decided to take his annual leave days before the case was tried— in order to spare himself opprobrium both in Ketchikan, where he had been born and raised, and around the Gilmore family dinner table? (His cousin, Peter Gilmore, was a cannery company lobbyist.)

On his way out the door, Gilmore handed the case file to Edward Merdes, Folta's twenty-six-year-old former law clerk, who was so new to the U.S. attorney's office that he had not yet been admitted to the bar. "Mr. Merdes was hardly more than a law clerk in experience but handled the case bravely," Elizabeth Peratrovich, a past grand president of the Alaska Native Sisterhood (the brotherhood's companion women's organization), who sat through the three-day trial, subsequently reported of the "big farce" she witnessed. "His inexperience was a great handicap and there was nothing that anyone could do to help him."[235] And indeed there wasn't, since W. C. Arnold represented Libby, McNeill & Libby.

Unlike the green-as-grass Merdes, the forty-nine-year-old Arnold, who had practiced law in Alaska for twenty-five years, was an experienced litigator who had argued *Grimes Packing Company* before the U.S. Supreme Court in 1948.

When the trial commenced and Merdes began interrogating the elderly Indian he called as his first witness, Arnold unleashed a volley of objections to the rookie prosecutor's inartfully posed questions; most of which Folta sustained. And so it went until Merdes began his closing argument, at which time, according to Robert De Armond, the *Daily Alaska Empire* reporter who witnessed the scene, "Merdes was frequently interrupted by Judge Folta for interrogation or for expression of the court's views on various aspects of the case."

> Judge Folta said that there is no doubt that most of Alaska was used by
> Indian tribes for hunting and fishing [De Armond reported], but that
> he is not satisfied that this type of use satisfies the requirements of
> actual use and occupancy.... The jurist went on to say that he does not
> believe Congress intended to give the Secretary of the Interior author-
> ity to reserve vast areas of Alaska, since it has been the policy of
> Congress to encourage settlement and development of the territory.[236]

The outcome never in doubt, in October, Folta issued his written opinion. The decision announced that "the evidence failed utterly to establish
either use or occupancy except of minute individual tracts and as to those,
not only was continuity not shown but it clearly appears that they were
abandoned."

Therefore, Folta reasoned, Secretary of the Interior Julius Krug had
exceeded his authority when he established a reservation whose boundaries encircled land and waters that the Haidas had not "actually occupied."

> [I]t is no exaggeration to say that nothing since the purchase of Alaska
> has engendered so much ill-feeling and resentment as the Department's
> reservation policy and its encouragement of aboriginal claims [the opin-
> ion gratuitously volunteered]. Whatever may be said in justification of
> reservations in the unsettled regions of Alaska, they are viewed as
> indefensible in southeastern Alaska, and generally condemned by whites
> and Indians alike as racial segregation and discrimination in their worst
> form.[237]

Years later, when he was asked how the case could have gone so wrong,
Edward Merdes answered that he had expected to lose but assumed that
the decision would be reversed on appeal.[238]

But although Oscar Chapman recommended to Attorney General James
McGranery that the Department of Justice file an appeal,[239] none was filed.

> When the case was instituted it was believed that facts could be estab-
> lished to the satisfaction of the court proving actual occupancy of the
> area by the Indians [Assistant Attorney General Perry Morton replied
> when asked to explain the dereliction]. However, the trial court found
> as a fact that such occupancy did not exist. In the federal system, the
> appellate court cannot re-examine the testimony to determine whether
> it agrees with the trial court's factual conclusion but can reverse the
> judgment only if the finding is "clearly erroneous," ... Thorough ex-
> amination in this case made it clear that such a showing could not be
> made.... The decision not to appeal was, therefore, dictated by the

different legal problems presented and not ... by a change of view of the case.[240]

Morton's post-hoc rationale is startlingly wrong: the question of whether George Folta correctly applied the evidentiary standard that Congress intended the phrase "actually occupied" (in the Alaska amendments to the IRA) to codify was one of law, rather than fact. Had that question been raised on appeal, the circuit court would have substituted its judgment for Folta's.

But the time within which to file an appeal expired, the case file was closed, and in 1954 the Department of the Interior recorded a notice in the public land records that voided the Hydaburg reservation land withdrawal.[241]

If George Folta had succeeded in abolishing the Hydaburg reservation by judicial fiat, a problem remained.

In 1935, Congress had enacted the bill that James Wickersham conceived in 1929, authorizing the Indians of southeast Alaska to file a lawsuit in the Court of Claims to obtain a money judgment as settlement of "all claims, legal or equitable for lands or other tribal property or community property rights taken from the Tlingit and Haida Indians by the United States without compensation therefor."

The Act assumed—albeit without explicitly saying so—that the proclamations that established the Tongass National Forest had extinguished Tlingit and Haida aboriginal title to the land inside the forest boundaries and that the Indians of southeast Alaska were entitled to compensation for the extinguishment. But in 1945, Richard Hanna announced in the decision he recommended to Harold Ickes that, in his judgment, "the adequacy of [the 1935] Act to meet the Alaskan situation is doubtful since no taking, or denial of aboriginal right appears, or is reflected in the evidence" presented at the Hydaburg, Kake, and Klawock hearings.

If Hanna was correct that the U.S. government's legal title to the land inside the Tongass National Forest still was clouded by an unextinguished aboriginal title, what was the situation elsewhere in Alaska?

At best the situation was legally muddled. But there was an easy solution: simply persuade Congress to enact a statute that extinguished Native aboriginal title throughout the territory. And except for the unheralded perseverance of one man, the unsung decency of two others—one of whom was the president of the United States—and the unintended intervention of William Paul, Congress would have done so.

7

James Curry and Alaska Statehood

Ernest [Gruening] holds [James Curry] in utter contempt. He would do anything he could to get him out of the Alaska scene—and so would I. I would because I think his influence is bad and that he will do the Indians far, far more harm than good.

ALASKA DELEGATE E. L. "BOB" BARTLETT, July 5, 1950[1]

FROM 1929, WHEN James Wickersham recruited him to the project, William Paul assumed that he and Wickersham would file the lawsuit that Congress in 1935 authorized the Tlingit and Haida Indians of southeast Alaska to bring in the Court of Claims to obtain compensation for the extinguishment of their aboriginal title. But by 1937, Paul's personal relationship with Wickersham was abysmal, the Bureau of Indian Affairs had not approved Wickersham and Paul's contract to represent the Indians, and a petition seeking Paul's disbarment was pending in the Juneau district court—substantial changes of circumstance to which Paul adjusted by concocting a new plan. In May of that year, Wickersham recorded in his diary:

> Henry Roden [a Juneau attorney who was a friend of both men] has talked with Wm. L. Paul and tells me that Paul told him he intended to hold up the Indian land suit, which I prepared, for the recovery of the possessory value of their lands in S.E. Alaska until his son graduates in the U[niversity] of Washington as a lawyer—in next year 1938; that he will put the son in charge of the suit, & they will manage it through a group suit of Paul and his relatives & let the rest of the Indians look out for themselves!![2]

Wickersham's hearsay description of the scheme Paul set about implementing after his disbarment (and after Wickersham informed the 1937 Alaska Native Brotherhood (ANB) Grand Camp that he would "not accept employment" as the Indians' attorney) was broadly accurate.

353

By 1939 when Bill Paul graduated from the University of Washington
Law School (a year later than Wickersham had been told he would), no
attorney had been selected, and the Tlingit and Haida Indians' lawsuit still
had not been filed. However, by that date William Paul again was in control of the ANB, so much so that when the 1939 Grand Camp convened at
Sitka in November, the delegates elected Louis Paul to a fourth term as
grand president and elected Bill Paul to succeed his father as grand secretary.

The delegates also adopted Resolution 37.

Resolution 37 designated the ANB executive committee, which one dis-
affected brotherhood member described as "Paul's machine,"[3] as the
Tlingit-Haida Central Council, the organization in whose name the Bureau of Indian Affairs wanted the Court of Claims lawsuit to be filed. To
bolster the executive committee's claim to act as the Central Council,
Resolution 37 designated each brotherhood local camp as the "tribal community" for the village in which it was located and directed the local camps
to hold elections "to ratify the governmental organization of the Alaska
Native Brotherhood ... as it is used for the purposes of these suits." Although every resident of every village would be eligible to vote, each voter
would be required to pay a $5 poll tax, which would be used to finance the
lawsuit.

William Paul wielded enough influence with enough delegates to force
Resolution 37 through the Grand Camp. But the anti-Paul delegates who
voted no were far from beaten.

That winter the local camp at Kasaan, a Haida village on the east coast
of Prince of Wales Island, mailed the other local camps a circular that
urged the repudiation of Resolution 37. Frank Johnson mailed a similar
letter. And in March, Frank Peratrovich's younger brother, Roy, sent each
camp a letter in which the Klawock camp, of which Roy Peratrovich was
president, sided with Kasaan.

> We strongly oppose the present plan of Paul attempting to pass off the
> executive committee on to us as our duly elected Central Council
> [Peratrovich announced]. Under Paul's set-up the four members of the
> executive committee at Sitka constitute a quorum and would like to
> have full control over the destiny of the rest of our people. We have no
> objections to an executive committee provided it is fairly elected and
> composed of representatives from all of the different towns in south-
> eastern Alaska, but we all know that the present Paul-influenced set-up
> is a detriment and stumbling block to the unity and well-being of our
> people.

But if there was revolt in the ranks, Paul's scheme to have an ersatz Tlingit-Haida Central Council select his son as its attorney also faced a determinative opposition inside the Department of the Interior. As Assistant Secretary Oscar Chapman informed Paul in June, the department would not allow the executive committee to act as the Central Council because the brotherhood membership was "not truly representative of all of the members of the Tlingit and Haida tribes." Not only that, but

> [t]his Department cannot countenance any levy or attempt to levy any assessment or contribution against these Indians in connection with their tribal claims where, as proposed by your organization, the payment thereof is sought to be enforced by causing the Indians to fear, without justification, that failure to pay will constitute a suspension or forfeiture of the right to participate in any benefits to be derived through the tribal claims.[4]

So, at the Department of the Interior, Resolution 37 was DOA.

To replace it, Chapman instructed Claude Hirst, the Bureau of Indian Affairs Alaska superintendent at Juneau, to order bureau schoolteachers to hold an election in each southeast Alaska village to select a Tlingit-Haida Central Council. Anticipating the influence William Paul would wield over whomever was elected, Chapman also pointedly advised Hirst that Secretary of the Interior Harold Ickes would not approve Bill Paul's selection as the Indians' principal attorney.

> This should not be construed as a reflection upon Mr. Paul [Chapman cautioned]. Our unwillingness to approve any contract with him as the principal attorney being based solely on his inexperience and his lack of knowledge of the procedure in Indian tribal claims litigation.... If the Indians desired it, consideration would be given to the matter of approving a contract of employment in which Mr. Paul was named as a party, provided some reputable experienced member of the bar, fully competent to prosecute the claims of the Indians through the Court of Claims and the United States Supreme Court, if necessary, were associated with him under the contract and was thereby made the attorney of record in the case.[5]

To make matters worse for the Pauls, when the 1940 Grand Camp convened at Klawock in November, Roy Peratrovich ran as the anti-Paul delegates' hometown candidate for grand president. When the votes were counted, Peratrovich easily defeated Louis Paul's bid for reelection.[6]

But although a setback for the Pauls, the Peratrovich-Frank Johnson faction's return to power did nothing to lessen John Collier's and Felix Cohen's anxiety that the Tlingit and Haida Indians' lawsuit would not be filed within the seven-year time limit within which the 1935 act authorized the Indians to file suit. So Collier and Cohen begrudgingly decided to bring William Paul and Roy Peratrovich to Washington, D.C., at government expense, to select an attorney. But conceding the ANB its status as the Indians' de facto spokesorganization, and conceding Paul his influence, was difficult.

> I must say to you that this invitation is extended not because of your position in the Alaska Native Brotherhood [Assistant Commissioner of Indian Affairs William Zimmerman informed Paul], and it is not to be construed as an endorsement or as a ratification of any facts by you or by the Brotherhood looking to the selection of an attorney. The invitation is extended to you because you are generally familiar with the subject matter of the suit and because you were one of those largely responsible for the passage of the jurisdictional act.[7]

When Paul and Peratrovich arrived in the capital, the city was overflowing with celebrants of Franklin Roosevelt's inauguration to a third term as president, and the two Indians were fortunate to find a room with a single bed in the basement of a hotel near the White House. Years later, Peratrovich recalled the too-much time that circumstances required the two men to spend together: "[William Paul] and I used to argue all day, and then we'd sleep together at night."[8]

Four months earlier, Paul had recommended to the ANB executive committee that it hire Grady Lewis, a Washington, D.C., attorney who had represented the Choctaw Indians in the Court of Claims and with whom he had been privately corresponding since March,[9] and who he vouched to the committee as "an able man."[10] Lewis may have been such, but there was another reason Paul wanted him retained to file the Court of Claims lawsuit. To obtain a case that might produce a million-dollar fee, Lewis had promised Paul that he would associate his sons (Fred Paul having graduated from the University of Washington Law School the year after his brother) as his co-counsel.

For that reason, while Paul and Roy Peratrovich spent six weeks interviewing attorneys, the exercise was a sham; Paul had settled on Grady Lewis prior to arriving in Washington. In February, Peratrovich finally agreed to concur in the choice; in March, Claude Hirst's teachers held their village elections; and in April, when the Tlingit-Haida Central Council convened at the bureau's expense at Wrangell,[11] the members agreed, on William Paul's motion, to retain Grady Lewis and the Paul brothers as their attorneys.[12]

But William Paul could not leave well enough alone. Congress had included a section in the 1935 act that required the commissioner of Indian affairs and the secretary of the Interior to approve the Central Council's contract with its attorneys. As a consequence, prior to the Wrangell meeting, Paul was given a standard Department of the Interior attorney contract. One of the contract's boilerplate clauses required attorneys to "be subject to the supervision and direction of the Commissioner of Indian Affairs and the Secretary of the Interior." But prior to presenting the contract to the Central Council, Paul rewrote the text to remove every vestige of Bureau of Indian Affairs control.

When he read the contract that the three council members who had been authorized to approve it had signed, George Folta, the Department of the Interior solicitor in Juneau, who in 1937 had prosecuted Paul's disbarment, was outraged.

> The contract was drafted by William Paul and his sons, and the way for it was paved in advance by the dissemination of circulars attacking the officials of the Department, their policies and motives, and espousing the doctrine of emancipation [Folta complained to Claude Hirst]. Of course the advocacy of such a doctrine is not necessarily incompatible with a genuine solicitude for the welfare of the Indians, but I do not believe in miracles and hence, I do not believe that William Paul, the would-be emancipator, occupies such an exalted position. On the contrary, there is not the slightest evidence that he has reformed. In these circumstances, his acts must be judged in the light of his past when any question arises as to the bona fides thereof, and his past is a sordid history of the exploitation of his people.[13]

So Grady Lewis and the Paul brothers' contract were not approved; and after corresponding with Bill Paul gave him a sense of the drift, Lewis withdrew from the case.[14] Later he thought better of doing so and in March 1942 tried to negotiate an acceptable arrangement between the Pauls and Assistant Commissioner of Indian Affairs William Zimmerman.[15] But Lewis was unsuccessful.

In May, with the time within which to file suit expiring in less than a month, Bill and Fred Paul filed two petitions in the Court of Claims, one on behalf of the "Tlingit Nation" and the other on behalf of the "Haida Nation," both of which the court dismissed in October 1944 on the ground that the commissioner of Indian affairs and the secretary of the interior "have refused to agree to the contracts between the Indians and the attorneys bringing these suits."[16]

By that date, however, Felix Cohen had set about finding his own attorney since the deadline for filing the lawsuit (which Anthony Dimond in 1942 had persuaded Congress to extend three years) expired the coming June.[17]

The previous summer, when he visited Alaska to interview witnesses to testify at Richard Hanna's aboriginal fishing rights hearings, Cohen had talked with several Juneau and Ketchikan attorneys about taking the case, but they declined, most likely because accepting Bill and Fred Paul as their co-counsel was one of Cohen's preconditions, the Tlingit-Haida Central Council having voted to hire them. Cohen next asked Ernest Wilkinson, one of the most prominent Washington, D.C., attorneys who represented Indian tribes before the Court of Claims. But as Cohen subsequently explained, "As I expected would be the case, he was unwilling to collaborate [with the two Paul boys]."[18] So with the deadline for filing suit again approaching, Cohen recruited James Curry.

A thirty-eight-year-old left-of-New Deal liberal son of Irish immigrants who had been born and raised in Chicago, Curry had graduated from Loyola

William Paul, Jr. (left), William Paul (middle), Fred Paul (right), circa 1960s.
ALASKA NATIVE COLLECTION PCA 33-31, ALASKA STATE LIBRARY.

University Law School and practiced law in the Windy City. In 1934 he relocated to Washington, D.C., to work as an assistant solicitor at the Department of the Interior. Assigned to assist the Bureau of Indian Affairs in implementing the Indian Reorganization Act, he made Felix Cohen's acquaintance.[19] After three years representing the bureau, Curry briefly worked as an attorney for the Puerto Rico Reconstruction Administration and then spent a stint as assistant chief attorney of the Department of the Interior Bituminous Coal Division.[20] In 1941 he moved to Puerto Rico to serve as counsel to the Puerto Rico Water Resources Authority.[21]

When he arrived in San Juan, Curry soon found himself operating as the island's de facto attorney general. As Rexford Tugwell, the governor of Puerto Rico, later noted to himself, "not having an Attorney General on whom I can rely, Curry practically serves as one—a good one too."[22]

During his several years of service as the governor's attorney, Curry wrote much of the New Deal legislation that Tugwell custom-designed for the island. And in 1943 when Curry resigned from government service to open a law office in San Juan, his client list included several of the municipal corporations he had had a hand in creating.[23]

In addition to his law office in Puerto Rico, Curry also opened an office in Washington, D.C., with C. M. Wright, a friend who recently had resigned as associate general counsel of the Reconstruction Finance Corporation.[24] Curry periodically commuted from his home in San Juan until 1949, when he closed his Puerto Rico office and moved permanently to Washington, D.C. His Washington office allowed Curry to handle his Puerto Rican clients' legal work in the national capital. But as Curry subsequently would recall, when he opened for business, he "dug up all my old friends"[25] at the Bureau of Indian Affairs. The excavation soon provided an important return.

At the principal instigation of several career bureau employees (including D'Arcy McNickle, a Flathead Indian who served as John Collier's special assistant for the bureau's relations with Indian tribes), in November 1944 seventy-five representatives of thirty-five tribes met in Denver to organize the National Congress of American Indians (known as NCAI), a new Indians-only Indian rights advocacy organization.[26] Although the Congress consisted of little more than a letterhead, the organization needed an attorney. Most likely through the good offices of Felix Cohen, D'Arcy McNickle quickly settled on James Curry because Curry agreed to work free. N. B. Johnson, the first president of NCAI, subsequently recalled how Curry was hired on:

The matter of employing an attorney was presented to the [NCAI executive] council [at the council's January 19-23, 1945 meeting in Chicago] by D'Arcy McNickle. He stated that James E. Curry was formerly an employee in the Indian Office; that he was an attorney for certain Puerto Rican interest[s] and would be stationed in Washington, D.C., part of the time and that he would be willing to represent the Indian Congress without compensation until such time as we could afford to pay him a salary. The matter was referred to the legal committee, of which Mr. McNickle was a member, with instructions to go into the matter and report to the next annual convention. In the meantime, the committee arranged with Mr. Curry to handle the legal business of NCAI without pay and so reported to the annual convention which convened in Browning, Montana, October 22-25, 1946. Under the arrangements the committee made with Mr. Curry, he was to work without pay until the end of the calendar year 1946.[27]

In 1952, Curry testified before a Senate subcommittee that he agreed to represent NCAI "not so much with the idea of profit as with the idea of public service."[28]

And the statement was true—as far as it went.

James Curry's commitment to the Native American cause was personal and heartfelt. But his pro bono representation had the intended consequence of enabling NCAI's new general counsel to hobnob with Indian leaders at the Congress's annual conventions. The hobnobbing resulted in contracts to handle legal work for more than a dozen Indian tribes that eventually annually netted Curry $16,000,[29] which during the years he earned it was a quite reasonable income.

In 1946 when Congress enacted the Indian Claims Commission Act, his access to Indian leaders through NCAI allowed Curry to obtain contracts to file lawsuits on behalf of Indian tribes that he knew when he solicited the work could earn million-dollar fees. The same year, Curry's involvement with NCAI also resulted in a contract with the Tlingit-Haida Central Council to file its lawsuit in the Court of Claims.

At the Department of the Interior, Felix Cohen occasionally became involved in legal matters that arose from the department's administration of Puerto Rico. In January 1946 when Secretary of the Interior Harold Ickes issued his second decision ratifying Richard Hanna's determination of Hydaburg, Kake, and Klawock's aboriginal fishing and land rights, Cohen was on department business in San Juan. It was from that location that he wrote Ted Haas: "I have been talking to Jim Curry about the possibility of his rendering [help to the three villages] ... now that he has a Washington office.... He is perfectly willing to do what he can, either as general counsel to the Congress of American Indians or under special arrangements with the villages concerned if more than routine services are involved."[30]

Cohen also decided that Curry should file the Indians' lawsuit (in June 1945, Congress again had extended the deadline for doing so).[31] But getting his friend the work was tricky business. In the 1940s attorneys were ethically precluded from soliciting clients, so Cohen arranged for the Robert Marshall Civil Liberties Trust to give NCAI a $2,300 grant[32] to send Ruth Muskrat Bronson to the 1946 ANB Grand Camp, which was held at Wrangell in November.

Bronson was a native of Oklahoma who, although part Cherokee, did not look Indian. In 1925, after graduating from Mount Holyoke College, which she had attended on scholarship, Bronson taught school at Haskell Institute, a boarding school the Bureau of Indian Affairs operated in Kansas. In 1928 she married and relocated to Washington, D.C., where she administered the bureau's scholarship and loan programs[33] until her retirement in 1943.[34]

The following year NCAI was organized. The founders decided "to maintain a legislative representative in Washington, D.C.," to "present testimony before Congress ... on pending legislation which affects Indian rights or welfare."[35] In the spring of 1946, when N. B. Johnson asked her to do so, Bronson (who since her retirement from the bureau had been a housewife) agreed to work out of her Georgetown home without pay as NCAI's executive secretary. The feigned purpose of Bronson's trip to southeast Alaska was to encourage the ANB to join the Congress, but her principal assignment was to persuade the Tlingit-Haida Central Council to hire James Curry.

> You will recall, from our last conversation in Mr. Cohen's office, that you were to try to get them to authorize [NCAI] to represent them on any of the following matters: the establishment of reservations, the possessory rights hearings, title extinguishment legislation, the question of limitation of fish traps, and claims [Curry wrote Bronson before she left for Alaska]. I think you understand fully that it is absolutely necessary for some such authorization to be obtained from the towns before either lawyer [i.e., Curry or Charles Wright] can spend his time effectively in Alaska.... When you have worked up sufficient demand for the services of [NCAI], it will then be opportune for either of the lawyers to come up.[36]

When she stopped at Sitka on her way to Wrangell, Bronson talked up the Court of Claims lawsuit to Alfred Widmark, who had succeeded Roy Peratrovich as grand president of the ANB. After listening to Bronson's

Ruth Muskrat Bronson. NATIONAL ANTHROPOLOGICAL
ARCHIVES, SMITHSONIAN INSTITUTION.

pitch, Widmark agreed that "something would have to be done at the convention about the land suit."[37] Bronson also lobbied Andrew Hope, the president of the Tlingit-Haida Central Council, who, as Bronson subsequently reported to Curry, related

> that at this convention of the ANB there is going to be a showdown and that if the Paul [brother]s cannot raise the money to start the land suit, or cannot make a satisfactory [attorney] contract, satisfactory to the Indian Office, they are going to be asked to withdraw. Mr. Hope asked that if they did drop the Pauls from the land suit could our organization recommend attorneys for the ANB. I told him that we could, that our own attorney for the NCAI could come up here and talk with them about the land suit, and if they liked him, they might make some arrangement with him and his firm.[38]

At Wrangell, Bronson completed her mission by persuading the brotherhood to affiliate with NCAI and persuading delegates who were members of the Tlingit-Haida Central Council to hire James Curry to file the Court of Claims lawsuit, although, as Bronson reported to Curry, the "majority want William Paul, Jr., retained in some capacity."[39]

Since it so markedly communicates both her dislike for the Pauls and William Paul's proprietary view of the lawsuit he years later would claim to have conceived, Ruth Bronson's recollection of the 1946 Grand Camp is worth quoting:

> The family (William, Sr., Louis, and William, Jr.) made every effort to and did dominate the convention [Bronson by letter informed Curry]. For three days the two Paul brothers (William, Sr., and Louis, the older men) were practically the only ones who had a chance to talk on the convention floor. They ranted at the Indian Office, they raved and they wrangled with each other until people had no chance to get their own problems before the convention. Although there was much grumbling on the side, there was nothing done about it. When I asked one woman who was complaining about the Pauls' continual "jaw fighting" as she called it why the convention did not object as there was general dissatisfaction, she said because Wrangell was the Pauls' home town and they (the home camp) were entertaining the convention, and because all the people knew William Paul, Sr., had actually done many, many things for the Native people in his younger days and they do not want to desert him now.
>
> That explains, I think, too, what feeling there may be about keeping William Paul, Jr., in the lawsuit. I doubt if Jr. is very competent as a lawyer. He has poor delivery, and he is too ready to hurl epithets at Ted Haas and other folks he thinks are against him to be very intelligent.... And there is no doubt in my mind that he is crooked. He was secretary and treasurer for the Marine Workers Union (a part of the ANB) for which he received a salary of $300 per month. But his funds were short this convention accounting and one item showed $385 for a trip to Ketchikan which turned out on investigation to be his honeymoon and not union business. Well, this was not publicized but he was quietly dropped from this job and another man, Frank Johnson, given the job. But Paul, Jr., was left in as secretary of the ANB—re-elected. When the first discussion of the land suit ended in a vote of the people to go on as they were (under the ANB) William Paul, Sr., got up on the floor and said then they had to show more confidence in his son. That it hurt a father to hear the honesty of his son questioned, etc. etc., and then he cried and ended up by saying his family had given years to the land suit and they did not intend to give it up now—that he would destroy it before he would see the family thrown out. Louis Paul got up and apologized and said he did not believe his brother realized what he was saying and to forgive him. A Wrangell woman got up and said William Paul you should be ashamed of yourself. You are our leader and the only one educated to tell us what to do in these dark times and now all you do is make us ashamed of you. None of this appears in the minutes.[40]

When Bronson returned to Washington, D.C., Curry used the last of the Robert Marshall Trust grant money to fly to Juneau. After five days of arduous meetings with William and Bill Paul and Cyril Zuboff, who had succeeded Alfred Widmark as ANB grand president, and the other executive committee and Tlingit-Haida Central Council members who were able to travel to Juneau in bad December weather, the group agreed to retain Curry as "chief attorney" of the Court of Claims lawsuit, and Curry agreed to associate Bill and Fred Paul as his co-counsel.[41]

Since Felix Cohen had brokered the arrangement, Acting Commissioner of Indian Affairs William Zimmerman approved Curry and the Paul brothers' attorney contract.[42] In October 1947 Curry filed a petition in the Court of Claims on behalf of the "Tlingit and Haida Indians of Alaska."[43] But by the time he did, the lawsuit had become something of an afterthought, since Curry had been preoccupied throughout the spring and summer with a matter of more immediate importance.

In 1940 the National Forest Service estimated that the sixteen-million-acre Tongass National Forest, whose boundaries encircled almost all of southeast Alaska, contained seventy-eight billion board feet of harvestable timber.[44] But the fact that the trees were market-grade did not mean that the timber was marketable. In 1870 when he inventoried southeast Alaska's natural resources, Maj. John Tidball predicted that "as long as the forests of British Columbia, Washington Territory, and Oregon hold equal to the demand, the lumber trade will not come so much further to obtain an inferior article at much greater expense."[45] And for three-quarters of a century Tidball's assessment of supply and demand held true.

But if the trees had no value sold as logs, whites who had an almost religious faith in the inevitability of southeast Alaska's grand economic destiny had a dream. And the dream had a name: wood pulp. As Alaska governor John Strong preached the gospel in 1914, "The cheap power and vast amount of available timber make it reasonable to assume that southeastern Alaska will in the immediate future be one of the principal pulp and paper centers of the world."[46]

In 1927 the dream almost came true when George Cameron, the publisher of the *San Francisco Chronicle,* and the Zellerbach Paper Corporation contracted to each purchase five billion board feet of timber that, as the quid pro quo for obtaining logs at deep-discount prices, Cameron and Zellerbach agreed to grind into pulp at mills constructed in southeast Alaska.[47] But the depression destroyed the economics of both projects. And then came the Second World War.

When the war ended, the National Forest Service set out anew to create a southeast Alaska mill town economy. But in January 1946, Secretary of the Interior Harold Ickes announced his final approval of Richard Hanna's determination that the Indians at Hydaburg, Kake, and Klawock held an exclusive possessory right to a quarter of a million acres of land inside the Tongass National Forest. As the trade magazine *Paper and Pulp* described the consequence, "All negotiations between the Forest Service and pulp and paper operators ceased when Mr. Ickes brought up the Indian question."[48]

In 1959 when it decided the liability portion of the Tlingit-Haida Central Council lawsuit, the Court of Claims determined that Richard Hanna was wrong (as was Felix Cohen when he assured Harold Ickes that Hanna's view of the matter was "sound") in ruling that the proclamations establishing the Tongass National Forest had not extinguished the Tlingit and Haida Indians' aboriginal title to the land inside the forest.[49] But as Secretary of the Interior Julius Krug, in 1947, described the legal uncertainty that Ickes created when he accepted Richard Hanna's conclusion that aboriginal title had not been extinguished: "[N]o attorney would be willing ... to assure [a pulp company] contractor or his underwriters that the Forest Service had a certainly good title to the timber within the boundaries of the Tongass National Forest."[50]

Given his usual attitude, Harold Ickes undoubtedly enjoyed the consternation his announcement of Hydaburg, Kake, and Klawock's possessory land rights provoked inside the Department of Agriculture (within which the National Forest Service is located). But when Julius Krug succeeded Ickes as Secretary, he had a different view. "The Indians probably have some sound theoretical basis for the claims," Krug conceded. "But I feel this is a matter which should be settled by the courts."[51]

As the twelve years that elapsed between James Curry's filing of the Tlingit-Haida Central Council's lawsuit in 1947 and the Court of Claims' first ruling in the case in 1959 would demonstrate, the judiciary—a notoriously slow-moving institution—was incapable of resolving such legally and factually complex disputes expeditiously. So in February 1947 when Frank Heintzleman, chief of the National Forest Service in Alaska, advised Julius Krug that no pulp company would purchase timber from the Tongass National Forest until the trees had been cleared of Indian claims, Krug instructed Assistant Secretary Warner Gardner to write a bill to authorize the National Forest Service to sell timber, regardless of whether the land on which the trees were located was subject to aboriginal title.

Writing the bill was simple. Enacting it was another matter. By the time the text of the bill could be cleared by the Bureau of the Budget, the 80th Congress would be so close to the adjournment of its first session that the measure could not pass the Senate except by unanimous consent. If one senator decided that it treated the Indians unfairly and objected, the bill was dead for the year. For that reason, needing a representative of the Tlingit and Haida Indians with whom he could do quick business, Warner Gardner invented one: James Curry.

When Gardner, as Curry contemporaneously explained, invited Curry as the "[representative] of the Alaska Natives to sit down with the Forest Service and the Department of the Interior and discuss this problem,"[52] Curry had no client other than the Tlingit-Haida Central Council, which he represented only for the purpose of filing the Council's lawsuit in the Court of Claims. Nor did Curry tell the client he did have that he had been asked to participate in writing a bill whose enactment would compromise Tlingit and Haida Indian claims to millions of dollars of timber.[53] Nevertheless, Curry repeatedly met with Gardner and a roomful of representatives from the National Forest Service, the Bureau of Indian Affairs, the Bureau of the Budget, the Fish and Wildlife Service, the Bureau of Land Management, the Solicitor's Office, and the pulp companies to try to work something out.[54]

In April, Curry thought he had brokered an acceptable (to Curry) arrangement: Congress would authorize the Forest Service to sell the pulp companies timber and as much land as they needed to build their mills; the National Forest Service would pay the Indians 10 percent of the sale proceeds; and if Congress or a court subsequently determined that they possessed an unextinguished aboriginal title to the land within the sale areas, the Indians could recover the other 90 percent.[55] But if there was tentative agreement, and Warner Gardner subsequently denied that there had been, it fell apart; the bill Julius Krug sent Congress in May simply provided that the proceeds from timber and land sales would "be maintained in a special account in the Treasury until the rights to the land and timber are finally determined by or under future legislation."[56]

A principal reason—if not *the* principal reason—Curry failed to broker a bill that recognized that the Indians of southeast Alaska held a legally cognizable possessory interest in the Tongass National Forest is that, at the outset of his discussions with Warner Gardner, Curry's negotiating position had been destroyed by another Paul family project gone awry.

In 1880 when Joe Juneau and Richard Harris discovered pay dirt on Gold Creek, which tumbles down a southeast Alaska mainland mountainside into Gastineau Channel, a few Tlingit Indians, known as Auks, maintained fish camps at the mouth of the stream. However, by the following summer so many Auks were living in tents on the beach in front of Juneau (as the mining camp that sprang up around the cove south of Gold Creek had been named) that Henry Glass, the captain of the U.S.S. *Jamestown,* persuaded the Indians to relocate to the mouth of Gold Creek. Rather than returning home to their villages, the Auks built plank houses along the beachfront.

Over the next thirty years the town kept growing. By 1912 when Congress moved the territorial capital to Juneau from Sitka, the Auk village on the beachfront had been surrounded by white houses and businesses. By 1913 the locale was so crowded that the town council began discussing building a road across the tideland in front of the village. But a road would have blocked the Indians who moored their canoes behind their houses from access to Gastineau Channel. When the Indians protested to Alaska delegate James Wickersham,[57] William Beattie, the superintendent of Bureau of Education schools in southeast Alaska, urged Commissioner of Education Philander Claxton to urge Secretary of Interior Franklin Lane to withdraw the tideland for the "Natives of Auk village" as a "landing place for canoes and other craft."[58] But the recommendation was ignored, the road was built (albeit on pilings high enough at several locations to allow the Indians' boats to pass beneath), and over the next quarter of a century whites began filling the tideland with rocks.

By 1940, Juneau was the largest town in the territory, and the conflict over the use of the tideland had escalated to the point that the Indians established a defense committee. Since he witnessed the document that created it, William Paul may have organized the group. If he did, he had been disbarred by that date, so the committee retained Bill Paul as its attorney.[59]

In 1942 the dispute came to a head when the U.S. attorney in Juneau petitioned the district court to condemn 10.95 acres of tideland to allow the army to construct a dock.[60] Two years later, the U.S. attorney decided that there was no third-party interest to condemn and amended his petition to allege that the army was not required to pay anyone anything.

Represented by Bill and Fred Paul, twenty-four Indians intruded into the condemnation proceeding by filing an answer to the amended petition. The answer alleged that the Indians and their ancestors had occupied the tideland since "1867, and from time immemorial prior thereto," and demanded $80,000 for the extinguishment of their aboriginal title to the 10.95 acres.[61]

When the case was heard and District Court Judge George Alexander decided that the Indians had no "compensable interest" in the disputed acreage, Bill and Fred Paul appealed Alexander's decision to the court of appeals in San Francisco, which in February 1947 issued its opinion in *Miller v United States*.[62]

For all Alaska Natives, the *Miller* decision was a disaster: the court of appeals announced in its ruling that "whatever 'Indian title' the Tlingit Indians may have had under Russian rule [to the tideland in front of the Auk village] was extinguished by the [1867] treaty [of cession]."[63]

For the cannery owners who operated fish traps in the waters surrounding Hydaburg, Kake, and Klawock and for Frank Heintzleman and other National Forest Service employees who had been horrified by Harold Ickes's announcement the previous year that large tracts of land inside the Tongass National Forest were subject to unextinguished aboriginal title, the court of appeals' pronouncement was a gift from a benevolent god. The "Daily Alaska Empire" voiced the common community sentiment:

> [T]his favorable court decision [is] ... the first ray of hope on this troublesome situation since the whole idea [of Indian aboriginal title] was cooked up back in Washington by several long-haired legal wizards under former Secretary of the Interior Harold L. Ickes.[64]

But while the decision was an important precedent, there was no way to know whether the precedent would hold until the U.S. Supreme Court decided the question.

In March 1948, Department of Interior solicitor Mastin White publicly characterized *Miller* as "unsound."[65] And in 1955 the U.S. Supreme Court would prove White correct. But throughout the spring of 1947 the *Miller* decision controlled the thinking of the attorneys who represented the National Forest Service. So it is no surprise that the Forest Service representatives who participated in Warner Gardner's discussions with James Curry objected to paying the Indians of southeastern Alaska any portion of the proceeds from the sale of Tongass timber. But the legal situation remained muddled enough for the pulp companies' attorneys to continue to advise their clients not to invest their money until Congress cleared the forest of Indian claims.

On May 21, Rep. Clifford Hope, chairman of the House Committee on Agriculture, introduced the bill that Warner Gardner had spent the spring writing as House Joint Resolution 205.

When Hope convened a hearing on May 26, Gardner began making the record for quick action by identifying "aboriginal claims" as the "major obstacle" preventing pulp companies from purchasing 40 percent of the harvestable timber in the Tongass National Forest.[66] Other witnesses presented similar testimony. Rep. James Johnson, who had replaced Hope in the chair, then asked James Curry, who was in the room, when he would be ready to present the Indians' position on Joint Resolution 205. When he rose to reply, Curry stood on razor-thin ethical ice.

After meeting with Warner Gardner for more than two months, Curry finally wrote to Bill Paul in April:

> For some weeks now we have been conducting extended negotiations with the pulp and paper industry, mostly through Warner Gardner, regarding proposals to establish an industry in Alaska. We have not previously reported to you because up to now policies have not been sufficiently definite even to report the details. I believe we are now in a position to discuss the whole problem, first with you, and then with all of our many clients.... I believe we should send to each town a summary of our negotiations to date for them to read and to prepare themselves for discussion. Thereafter, Mrs. Bronson should go to each and every town, and explain the situation generally.... At the same time, she can talk with them about signing a general representation contract.... She could also explain that the lawyers are now somewhat embarrassed by the narrowness of their authorization.[67]

To alleviate the "embarrassment" before members of Congress inquired during the House and Senate hearings on Joint Resolution 205 who it was that he represented, in May, Ruth Bronson flew to southeast Alaska to persuade the governing councils of the affected villages to retain Curry as their attorney.[68] At Felix Cohen's suggestion, Bronson cleared the trip with Acting Commissioner of Indian Affairs William Zimmerman. One of Curry's associates subsequently debriefed Curry on Bronson's meeting with the commissioner:

> Zimmerman said that the towns should have Washington counsel and that they should all employ the same attorney for the sake of efficiency. He further said that he thought that they should retain you as that attorney.... He told Ruth that she need have no conscience about recommending you to the Indians because she would be making a recommendation which was to their benefit. Cohen suggested that the contracts which you send up not carry your name but be written in blank.[69]

But if Bronson's solicitation had unofficial official sanction, Don Foster, who in 1944 had replaced Claude Hirst as the Bureau of Indian Affairs' Alaska superintendent (a position which was renamed area director), did not want Curry's runner speaking to his Indians unchaperoned. "I understand you are going specifically to discuss the proposed attempt to establish a pulp and paper industry in Alaska and the problem of obtaining adequate protection for Indian aboriginal rights in connection with said industry," Foster wrote Bronson while she still was in Washington. "I suggest that it would be desirable to have a member of my staff accompany you, and propose the name Roy Peratrovich." After moving to Juneau in 1941 to work for the territorial government, Peratrovich had gone to work for Foster in the Juneau office of the Bureau of Indian Affairs.[70]

When William Paul learned that Peratrovich would travel with Bronson, he was "mad as hops." "Do not accept any more favors from the Indian Office than you are forced to," Paul railed in a letter to Bronson, particularly from a "sycophant" like Roy Peratrovich. "We are opposed to official snoopers."[71]

Bronson, who had less use for Paul than Paul had for Peratrovich, considered Paul's disparagement of his younger rival rancorous slander and believed Bill Paul's dislike of Peratrovich to be derivative of his father's.

> I came to the conclusion that it was papa's needling that was behind Bill's objection to Roy [Bronson informed James Curry when she arrived in Juneau]. The two groups have struggled over control of the ANB and Roy and [his wife] Elizabeth have sometimes been the only ones who stood up against papa's shenanigans. Now, if Roy goes with the NCAI it will look as if the Pauls have been overshadowed, according to papa's warped way of thinking. Bill Jr. had not been in Ketchikan more than three hours until papa sent him a fifty word telegram which I did not see, but the answer he sent indicated that papa was wiring him about getting fully protected on the [attorney] contracts [that Bronson had come to southeast Alaska to persuade each village council to sign].[72]

Whatever the source of his distrust, Bill Paul shared his father's paranoia that Roy Peratrovich had arranged to travel with Bronson in order to be on hand to persuade the village councils with whom she met to cut Paul out of what he considered to be his rightful share of the legal business that Bronson was soliciting for Curry. When he voiced the suspicion, Bronson indignantly replied that she "was not interested in forwarding the career of any lawyer, either his or Curry's ... and that as I visited the towns I did not intend to urge the employment of either of them."

The profession of innocence was a look-Bill-Paul-straight-on-in-the-eye lie. Bronson subsequently confided to Curry by letter, "I did not tell Junior the strict truth ... when I told him I was not going to or [*sic*] interested in forwarding the career of any lawyer."

After clearing her conscience, Bronson then reported to Curry that when she visited Kasaan, the first village on her schedule and "where they have not met Curry but have heard much good things about him, I found myself helping vigorously to pin his halo on! ... No sales talk was necessary, but I found myself giving one just the same."[73] And three days later, Bronson would even more brazenly advise Curry that "I sincerely hope that you can come yourself. You can have all the business that develops up here for the next ten years, if you do. No one has batted an eye at the ten year [term of the] contracts [Bronson presented to the Indians who served on the governing councils of the villages she visited to sign] except Kasaan and that was a misunderstanding that you can clear up."[74]

But while Bronson allowed her dislike for Bill Paul to cloud her judgment of his intelligence, the younger Paul was no fool and knew a falsehood when he heard one. When Bronson denied that she was James Curry's agent, Paul replied that if Roy Peratrovich attended her meetings with the village councils, then Bronson had an obligation to write his name next to Curry's on the attorney contracts that Curry had prepared for the Indians to sign, regardless of whether the Indians asked her to do so.

"I accepted that incredible request in silence," Bronson subsequently reported to Curry, "and told him I could not agree to write any attorney's name in when not requested to do so.... We left it at that. If you can figure out any reason for that crazy notion except petty jealousy perhaps you are better than I am."[75] But if Bill Paul's distrust was "petty jealousy," his father's advice to Bronson to keep her distance from Don Foster was sound.

Like John Collier and most other white Bureau of Indian Affairs employees of his generation, the Alaska Area director mouthed the platitudes of self-determination but honored them in the breach. The Indians of southeast Alaska were free to decide whatever they thought best, as long as what they thought best was what his superiors at the Department of the Interior already had decided. And Warner Gardner, with whom Foster had discussed the situation during a recent trip to Washington, D.C., had decided that the Indians should support Joint Resolution 205.

In early June, Roy Peratrovich and Ruth Bronson returned to Juneau from their trip through the villages (with signed contracts that authorized

James Curry—and in most contracts Bill Paul as well—to represent each community in hand). Don Foster's interest in furthering Warner Gardner's interest in having the Indians support Resolution 205 put Roy Peratrovich in a "tight spot" when Curry began pressuring Peratrovich to inform Gardner that the Indians to whom he and Bronson had explained the situation opposed the resolution.[76]

The responsibility for telling Warner Gardner news he didn't want to hear was Don Foster's, rather than Roy Peratrovich's. But Foster, a career government bureaucrat, was trapped between the Indians for whom he was responsible and a superior to whom he was accountable, which is not to say that the Alaska area director did not struggle to find a way out. Bronson kept after him to do his job, however, and Foster finally reluctantly agreed to tell Warner Gardner that the Indians opposed Joint Resolution 205. "I tried to get Foster to say in his wire that all the towns had voted unanimously to oppose HJR 205 or similar proposals (I got to some towns before I had the actual bill in hand)," Bronson by letter informed Curry of the minor victory, but Foster refused to do so on the ground that "there is no use in throwing cold water in Gardner's face."[77]

Two weeks later the House Committee on Agriculture held a second hearing at which James Curry, the only witness, announced that the residents of the southeast Alaska Indian villages that were now his clients opposed Joint Resolution 205. He then suggested a compromise: convey Hydaburg, Kake, and Klawock legal title to the land to which (by Richard Hanna's determination) the villages' residents held unextinguished aboriginal title, and convey the other southeast Alaska Indian villages legal title to the land to which (as documented in Walter Goldschmidt's report) the residents of those villages held unextinguished aboriginal title. In exchange, the villages would relinquish their claims to the remaining 90 percent of the Tongass National Forest.

When Curry concluded, the committee members who were present to hear him float it summarily rejected his proposal.

> I certainly would not want to be a party to saying the government would have to make a settlement with your people before any disposition of the timber could be made [Republican Rep. Abe Goff of Idaho responded, pronouncing the collective judgment]. The government, as a matter of fact, does not recognize the Indians have any right to this ninety percent, and it looks to me like this committee would be going a long way to say the government had to pay off before they could go ahead with it. I do not recognize any right there at all.[78]

Alaska delegate E. L. "Bob" Bartlett, who was sitting with Goff on the dais, was similarly incredulous. But he had a considerably more generous view of Alaska Native land claims.

In 1967, John Sackett, a twenty-two-year-old Athabascan who was serving his first term in the Alaska House of Representatives, criticized Bartlett's position on the settlement of Alaska Native land claims behind his back. Bartlett, who was then Alaska's senior U.S. senator, admonished the rookie solon to "delve into history a bit" before "you start to criticize me on this score" because "I was protecting the Natives of Alaska before you were out of diapers."[79] While the scolding is uncharacteristic of a man whose gentle disposition was as ingrained a part of his nature as his unassuming physical appearance was lumpen, the senator's history lecture was accurate.

Edward Lewis Bartlett, Jr., was born in Seattle, Washington, in 1904. In 1898 his father, Edward Lewis Bartlett, Sr., had stampeded from Texas to the Klondike.[80] Rather than prospecting for gold, he began transporting supplies to the diggings. When the Klondike played out, Edward Bartlett moved his mule teams and freight wagons to Goldstream Creek, a mining district near the interior Alaska mining town of Fairbanks, where his wife and two children joined him in 1905.

Six years later, the Bartletts moved to Fairbanks, where their schoolboy son would for the remainder of his life be known as "Bob." According to his daughter, D. A. Bartlett, and his biographer, Claus-M. Naske, Bartlett's sister, Doris, who was four years old when her brother was born, decided on her own to call her new sibling "Bob" and the name stuck. However, the young Edward Lewis Bartlett, Jr.—who disliked being known as "Junior"— may have named himself "Bob" after "Captain Bob Bartlett," who became an international celebrity in 1914 when he arrived safely in Nome after the *Karluk*, the vessel he captained as part of explorer Vilhjalmar Stefansson's 1913 arctic expedition, was crushed by pack ice offshore Wrangel Island.[81]

After graduating from Fairbanks High School in 1922, Bob Bartlett moved to Seattle and enrolled at the University of Washington. Two years later he returned to Fairbanks to attend classes at the University of Alaska, in 1926 reenrolled at the University of Washington, and in 1927 quit college for good to return to Fairbanks to take a job that paid next to nothing, reporting for the *Fairbanks Daily News-Miner*.

For the next three years the twentysomething newspaperman scraped by. In 1930 persistence paid a life-altering dividend when, after a courtship that began in high school, Bartlett married Violet "Vide" Gaustad, the daughter of a local mine operator.

After a wedding in Valdez and a honeymoon spent driving the dirt road home to Fairbanks, Bartlett returned to the *News-Miner.* In the fall of 1932, twenty-eight years old and depressed about working at his dead-end $200-a-month reporting job, he decided to move to the Yukon River for the winter to cut firewood for a living.

It was at that point that Vide Bartlett decided to take her husband's life in hand. Vide's father, O. P. Gaustad, was a friend of Anthony Dimond, a prominent Valdez attorney who since 1922 had represented southcentral Alaska in the territorial senate. Gaustad and Dimond were so close that, although not well acquainted with the bridegroom, Dimond and his wife served as best man and matron of honor at Bob and Vide Bartlett's wedding.

By happenstance, at the time Bartlett began talking about moving to the Yukon to chop wood, Dimond was the Democratic candidate challenging James Wickersham in the 1932 Alaska delegate election. The U.S. House of Representatives allowed each member a staff assistant, known as a "secretary." When Dimond won the election, Vide urged her husband to write to the delegate-elect and apply for the work; he did and was hired.[82]

In April 1933 when the Bartletts arrived in Washington, D.C., the capital was awash with ambitious young men who daily were arriving from throughout the nation to staff the new president's New Deal. However, unlike most of the other congressional secretaries—a group of political wannabes that included a twenty-five-year-old Texan named Lyndon Johnson—Bob Bartlett was devoid of personal ambition. According to Vide Bartlett, "we just hated" living in Washington, D.C.[83] Years later, Bartlett would explain why: "Vide and I were appalled at the heat of the Washington summer. We had never been subject to any such thing, and in those days there wasn't general air conditioning. There were great big fans in the office making papers blow all over the room. So most of the time we suffered from the heat rather than having the fans on."[84]

The young Fairbanksians so disliked the weather that when Anthony Dimond was elected to a second term in November 1934, Bartlett arranged (undoubtedly through Dimond's good offices) to be appointed assistant director of the Alaska office of the Federal Housing Administration, another dead-end job. He worked in Juneau until 1936 when, after being terminated when the Housing Administration down-sized its Alaska office, he returned to Fairbanks. During the summers he labored at dredging the gold claim his father had been working prior to his death in 1935.

But then Fortuna spun the wheel of chance to provide Bob Bartlett a last opportunity to escape an undistinguished life of deserved obscurity.

In December 1938, Edward Griffin, the secretary of Alaska (a job whose duties were similar to those of a lieutenant governor), died of a heart attack. When he heard the news, Anthony Dimond wired Bartlett that "it would please me greatly" if his former secretary would fill the vacancy.[85] To make it happen, Dimond quickly forwarded Bartlett's name to James Farley, chairman of the Democratic National Committee, with whom patronage appointments in the Roosevelt administration were required to be cleared.[86] In January the president announced the appointment.

And then Fortuna gave the wheel a second spin.

In February 1939 when Secretary of Alaska Bartlett arrived in Juneau, John Troy, the seventy-year-old publisher of the *Daily Alaska Empire* whom Franklin Roosevelt had appointed governor of Alaska in 1933, was under threat of indictment for having signed an affidavit falsely certifying that Troy had no conflicts of interest when he knew his administration had printing contracts with his newspaper. As a consequence, Secretary of the Interior Harold Ickes ordered Troy to resign. In September, the president appointed Ernest Gruening to take Troy's place. Roosevelt did so as a face-saving way of firing Gruening from his job as director of the Department of the Interior Division of Territories and Island Possessions.

The son of a wealthy New York City ophthalmologist, after graduating from Harvard College in 1907 and Harvard Medical School in 1911, Gruening, whose avocational interest in medical school had been journalism, hired on as a reporter at the Boston *American* rather than entering the calling for which he had trained. Working his way through the ranks, by 1921 the doctor who would never practice was editor of the *Nation,* a magazine at which, over the next decade, he established a modest national reputation as an "authority on Caribbean matters."[87]

In 1933 when Franklin Roosevelt arrived at the White House, Gruening wrangled an audience with the new president, who had been a senior at Harvard College the year Gruening was a freshman, to talk about his views on Latin American policy. The self-promotion resulted in Roosevelt appointing Gruening as an advisor to the U.S. delegation to an inter-American conference at Montevideo, Uruguay. The following summer, the president's approval of Gruening's performance in Montevideo resulted in his appointment as director of the Division of Territories and Island Possessions, a new Department of the Interior agency that Roosevelt created to administer Puerto Rico, Alaska, and the Virgin Islands. A year later, Roosevelt appointed Gruening to a second job as director of the Puerto Rican Reconstruction Administration.[88]

The authority he wielded as director of both the Division of Territories and the Reconstruction Administration gave Gruening quasi-dictatorial control over the political life and economy of Puerto Rico—a power that, when his mettle was tested, he abused.

Ernest Gruening's involvement in one of the most rampageous periods in Puerto Rican history is a story beyond the scope of this narrative. However, as Governor of Puerto Rico Rexford Tugwell described the test of character Gruening flunked: his "progressivism which, until this experience [as director of the Puerto Rican Reconstruction Administration] had been largely literary, and so untested, melted quickly in the heat of tropical politics. He turned to the repressive and illiberal policies reactionaries have always employed under such circumstances."[89]

By 1936, Harold Ickes had reached a similar conclusion.

> I am very much disturbed about the situation in Puerto Rico [Ickes noted to himself in his diary]. Gruening, from being a liberal, has apparently decided that the mailed fist is the proper policy in dealing with these subject people. He has gone completely in the reverse. He is on the outs with all of his former liberal friends in Puerto Rico. Formerly he used to damn [Puerto Rican] Governor [Blanton] Winship [whose policy views on colonial administration were to the right of reactionary] up hill and down dale for his militaristic point of view. He wanted him ousted as Governor, but now apparently he and Governor Winship see eye to eye.[90]

To compound Ickes's displeasure, Gruening routinely used his access to the Oval Office to circumvent Ickes's authority to decide questions of Puerto Rican policy. By 1937, Ickes was privately railing about how much he "resent[ed] this short-cutting to the White House" of which "Gruening has been guilty of on many occasions."[91] By 1939 he was scheming to have his insubordinate subordinate replaced.[92] That May, after convincing Roosevelt of the necessity, Ickes happily reported to his diary: "The President has told me to offer Gruening the Governorship of Alaska."[93]

When Ickes did so, Gruening recognized the reassignment as the honor it was not and refused to accept it. But, undoubtedly at Ickes's instigation, in September, while Gruening was vacationing in Maine, the White House announced that the president had appointed Gruening to succeed John Troy.[94] When Gruening met with Roosevelt to decline the appointment, the president ratified his secretary of the interior's throat-slitting by commanding that "I think you ought to go."[95]

When Gruening arrived in Juneau in December 1939, it would have been difficult for him to have found anyone with whom he had less in

Ernest Gruening (left) and E. L. "Bob" Bartlett (c. 1960).
ANCHORAGE DAILY NEWS.

common than Bob Bartlett. At fifty-two, Gruening was an urbane, full-of-himself, Harvard-educated journalist of national reputation who had access to the president of the United States when he wanted it. Bartlett was a self-effacing thirty-five-year-old college dropout. But the disparate temperaments strangely meshed. As Mary Lee Council, Bartlett's longtime personal secretary subsequently would recall, "Their offices were almost adjacent and generally they would meet several times daily.... Not only did they have a close personal official relationship but they were together on a social basis. It is probably correct to say that during that entire time [1939-1944] Bob was closer to Ernest, knew him better and had more opportunity to learn his various attitudes than any other person in Alaska."[96]

By 1943, Gruening's confidence in the man who by that date was a protégé was such that when Anthony Dimond decided not to seek a seventh term in the U.S. House of Representatives, Gruening urged Bartlett to run for the office of delegate. Bartlett was tempted but hesitant; Vide Bartlett, who thought the idea "absolutely crazy,"[97] was dead set against it. But the governor refused to take "I can't decide" for an answer and set about pressuring Bartlett to enter the race.

To that end, Gruening first conned Anthony Dimond into publicly endorsing his former secretary as his successor[98] by telling Dimond that Bartlett had announced his candidacy (one of the countless mendacities Gruening, who routinely customized his means to fit his ends, committed during his thirty-four years in public life). When that ruse failed, Gruening "turned on the heat in a big way"[99] by, among other tactics, persuading Harold Ickes to promise Bartlett that he could return to his job as secretary of Alaska if he lost the Democratic primary election.

In the end, the governor got his way: Bartlett became a candidate. With Anthony Dimond's endorsement and Ernest Gruening as chief fund-raiser and unofficial campaign manager, in April, Bartlett outdistanced his two primary opponents and that fall won the general election.

At the time he did, most whites in the territory thought of Alaska Natives as step-and-fetch-it Sambos—complacent (except when drunk, which too many too often were when they visited the white towns), blubber-chewing Eskimos and subservient Indians, who willingly labored for substandard wages and, particularly in southeast Alaska, paid their betters the compliment of trying to dress and act white.

In 1944, Bob Bartlett was a forty-year-old white man who had been raised and had lived most of his life in Fairbanks (where drunken Indians in front of the downtown bars were a stereotypical commonplace). But the delegate-elect also was a man of uncommon personal decency who "never boarded an elevator, or drank from a water fountain, or got on a subway car in the Capitol, ahead of somebody else." As a member of his staff accurately eulogized Bartlett on the occasion of his death: "If you were a human being, you had enough in common with him to count in [Bob Bartlett's] book."[100] As a consequence, Bartlett's early views on the settlement of Alaska Native land claims reflected an empathy that transcended the prejudice of the society of which he now was a leader.

Three days after the September 1944 general election, Richard Hanna held his first hearing at Hydaburg, and earlier that summer the Karluk village council had tried to prevent white commercial fishermen from fishing inside the Karluk reservation. So prior to departing for Washington, D.C., in November, Bartlett released a position paper to the press that outlined his views on a politically volatile subject with which he knew he would have to deal when he assumed office.

In 1954, Bartlett wrote Patrick Paul, the grand president of the ANB: "From the outset of my service in Congress in 1945 I have stood adamantly against any scheme that would arbitrarily extinguish the rights that are asserted and then permit at the maximum only the opportunity to go before a court and obtain money."[101]

But that description of his first position on the settlement of Native land claims is inaccurate since Bartlett initially did not support allowing Natives to obtain legal title to land.

As a preliminary matter, the position paper Bartlett released to the press in 1944 promised whites that their delegate would oppose the establishment of reservations "for exclusive use or benefit of the Native race in southeastern or any other part of Alaska" with "all the vigor at my command."

But once that genuflection to the 1946 election was made, the press release continued by lecturing that "we cannot and must not overlook" that Alaska Natives had legitimate grievances because white usurpation of salmon and timber and other natural resources had "brought about the necessity for economic competition [between white and Native] the end results of which today engage our attention."

The press release then described how Bartlett thought that attention should be focused.

In 1944, Juneau was a Jim Crow town where the windows of many bars and restaurants warned "No Dogs or Indians Allowed." Windows in Anchorage and Fairbanks had similar signs. In Nome, seating in the local movie theater was segregated.[102] And after touring the territory the previous winter, a Bureau of Indian Affairs social worker described Alaska to Commissioner of Indian Affairs John Collier as a "territory where race prejudice is more shocking than in the South."[103]

At the urging of Ernest Gruening and Roy Peratrovich (who at the time was grand president of the ANB) and Peratrovich's wife, Elizabeth, in 1943 the territorial senate passed a bill to prohibit racial discrimination. But the measure failed in the territorial house of representatives on a tie vote. So the first thing Bartlett wanted was that that wrong be "righted as speedily as possible for the benefit of all Alaskans."

Of more direct relevance to the story of Alaska Natives and their land, Bartlett also wanted to prevent the Department of the Interior from using the need to protect Native aboriginal title as an excuse to establish more reservations. To accomplish that objective, his press release suggested that Congress should enact a statute that extinguished aboriginal title and then authorized all Alaska Natives—rather than just the Tlingit and Haida Indians—to file a lawsuit in the Court of Claims to obtain compensation.

> If the court makes an award and Congress passes the necessary appro-priation bill—as it surely would—we shall have gained a common objective without the objectionable features of reservations [the press release optimistically concluded]. Then there would be money avail-able for rehabilitation of Native villages—truly a desperate need; then there would be money for medical services on the scale essential if disease is to be conquered; then there would be money for economic rehabilitation. That, in my judgment, is the proper manner to settle this matter.... This would permit, and in truth encourage, a common solidarity as between whites and the Natives. It would make it possible to lift eventually the sheltering hand of the federal government from the Native people.[104]

So contrary to his recollection in 1954, the claims settlement Bartlett advocated when he arrived in the U.S. House of Representatives did not include allowing Alaska Natives to acquire legal title to land. That is why, had Bartlett asked his opinion, Felix Cohen would have objected to Bartlett's settlement terms.

As will be described, in 1945, most likely at Cohen's direction, the De-partment of the Interior would advise Bartlett that a fair settlement of their land claims required Alaska Natives to be allowed to obtain legal title to the land around their villages, after which Bartlett modified his position to conform to that view, with no public announcement or fanfare. In 1947 when James Curry informed the House Committee on Agriculture that the Indians he represented wanted legal title to the land around their vil-lages, the issue was explicitly and publicly joined for the first time.

Bartlett was under increasing pressure to clear the Tongass National Forest of Indian claims. In March the territorial legislature had memorial-ized Congress that, since "the question of Indian or aboriginal title" was a "cloud" on "pulp and paper investments," "prompt action" was needed to resolve the question.[105] And in June, Ernest Gruening brusquely reminded the man whom he, more than anyone, had been responsible for sending to Washington that "if [Joint Resolution 205] does not pass at this session Alaska pulp and paper development will be seriously retarded and perhaps lost entirely."[106]

But if conveying Indians legal title to large tracts of land was a precondi-tion for the enactment of Joint Resolution 205, for whites, the idea was anathema. As Norman Walker, who represented Ketchikan in the territo-rial senate, voiced the common community sentiment to Bartlett in July,

"The idea is immoral and ... I expect and know you will oppose this kind of legislation."[107]

The virulence that James Curry's demand for land provoked throughout southeast Alaska mooted the possibility that Bartlett could agree to such a thing. But Curry's increasingly vocal opposition to Joint Resolution 205 had the potential to derail passage of the measure in the Senate. To try to undercut Curry's credibility, Bartlett persuaded Assistant Secretary of the Interior Warner Gardner to arrange for Bureau of Indian Affairs Alaska Area Director Don Foster to fly four of Curry's clients to the capital to replace Curry as the Indians' spokesperson.[108]

Foster selected two ANB executive committee members, Frank Peratrovich and Frank Johnson, plus Andrew Hope, chairman of the Tlingit-Haida Central Council, and Fred Grant, a prominent Haida. To be fair to Foster, the selections made sense: in 1944 Peratrovich and Hope had been elected to the territorial House of Representatives (after Ernest Gruening persuaded Congress to increase the size of the legislature in order to increase the chances for Native candidates to be elected), and Johnson had been elected to the same body in 1946.

When Ruth Bronson, who still was in Juneau, caught wind of Bartlett's scheme, she urged Johnson and Hope not to allow themselves to be used. She also confronted Foster over the fact that Bartlett wanted the Indians sent east at a time when he knew that James Curry, who after testifying before the House Committee on Agriculture had returned to Puerto Rico, would not be in Washington.

Rejecting Bronson's advice, the four Indians decided to make the trip.[109] When their plane landed at National Airport, Bronson, who by then had returned from Alaska, and James Curry, who had rushed back from San Juan, were on hand to meet them.

For the next week, Curry (who, to Bartlett's undoubted consternation, retained the Indians' confidence) and Peratrovich, Johnson, Hope, and Grant met with Interior, Agriculture, and Justice Department officials, and occasionally with Bob Bartlett, to try to negotiate an arrangement. At one point an agreement seemed within reach when Mastin White, the solicitor of the Department of the Interior, drafted a new resolution that granted southeast Alaska Indian villages legal title to the million acres of land Richard Hanna and Walter Goldschmidt had determined were subject to aboriginal title, authorized the National Forest Service (rather than the Indian owners) to sell the timber, and required the proceeds to be reserved for "the benefit of the respective Native villages."[110] Curry and the Indians signed off; but before hands could be shaken, the National Forest Service representatives objected, and the deal died.

Frank Johnson, Frank Peratrovich, Andrew Hope, and Fred Grant in Washington, D.C., on July 4, 1947, after testifying before the House Committee on Agriculture opposing the enactment of House Joint Resolution 205. N. B. Johnson, president of the National Congress of American Indians (third from left); Ruth Bronson, executive secretary of the National Congress of American Indians (fifth from left); Ted Haas, chief counsel of the Bureau of Indian Affairs (third from right); Frances Lopinsky, an attorney who worked for James Curry (second from right). PHOTOGRAPH COURTESY OF FRANCES LOPINSKY HORN.

With the negotiation deadlocked, on July 1 at Bob Bartlett's urging, the House Committee on Agriculture held a hearing to provide the four Indians an opportunity to testify. Ernest Gruening sent a radiogram from Juneau to plead with them "to support the pending legislation with only such modifications as are clearly acceptable to those who have it in their power to pass the bill, [and to] trust not only in my good faith but in that of Secretary Krug and our Delegate, Bob Bartlett, for whose sympathetic and understanding attitude toward the Natives of Alaska I can vouch for no less than I can for my own."¹¹¹

But the plea was spurned, and the Indians Don Foster had handpicked to support Joint Resolution 205 publicly opposed its enactment.

Frank Johnson, the first of the four to testify and the man who in 1935 had bitterly objected to the ANB's agreement to support amending the Indian Reorganization Act (IRA) to include Alaska Natives because he objected to the idea of reservations, concluded his remarks with a warning. After having had their consciousness about their land rights raised in 1944 when Richard Hanna conducted his hearing in the village and then seeing the National Forest Service take no action to protect those rights, the Indians at Kake, Johnson's home village, had come to feel that "the only logical way they could protect their lands was possibly by the creation of reservations." "Certain people may quarrel with that," Johnson lectured, "but I am in constant touch with most of the communities and it is my honest opinion that a lot of people are coming around to that view, that there should be some sort of specific areas set aside for our people."[112]

The three other Indians gave similar testimony, which concluded with Fred Grant lecturing that in the year and a half since Secretary of the Interior Harold Ickes had identified the land on Prince of Wales Island to which the Indians at Hydaburg held aboriginal title, the National Forest Service had issued permits "to different logging operators, to permit them to take certain sections of timber out from that area," and a lime quarry had begun operating. "[A]ll this time that this has been going on," Grant drily advised, "there has been no white man that has been scalped for taking all this out of this area."[113]

Assuming so, the restraint was unrewarded. Since the Indian witnesses had been afforded an opportunity to put their opposition on the record, their opposition could be ignored. The week after Frank Johnson, Frank Peratrovich, Andrew Hope, and Fred Grant appeared before it, the Committee on Agriculture reported Joint Resolution 205 to the House of Representatives.[114] Five days later the resolution passed the House by unanimous consent,[115] a smooth sailing that reflected James Curry's inability to find a congressman who was willing to object.

Curry ultimately had no better luck in the Senate. In May, Sen. Hugh Butler of Nebraska, the right-of-Republican chairman of the Senate Committee on Public Lands, had introduced House Joint Resolution 205 in the Senate as Senate Joint Resolution 118.[116]

Butler was unsympathetic; but when Curry, Johnson, Peratrovich, Hope, and Grant testified on Joint Resolution 118 before the Committee on Public Lands, their complaints attracted the attention of Sen. Arthur Watkins of Utah. Watkins chaired the Subcommittee on Indian Affairs, which the Committee on Public Lands had organized at the beginning of the 80th Congress when the Senate abolished the Committee on Indian Affairs.

Watkins disliked James Curry. But as Bob Bartlett would pass on in a private letter to a friend, the senator was "very solicitous about the welfare of the Indians" and "most anxious that no injustice be done to them."[117] Watkins prepared a package of amendments that, among other provisions, prohibited the National Forest Service from selling land, or selling timber from land "actually possessed, used, or occupied for town sites, smokehouses, gardens, hunting and fishing cabins, or other buildings and structure, missionary stations or burial grounds, or any timber actually possessed and used by any Native tribes, Native villages, Native individuals or other persons."[118]

In the end, however, even that modest attempt to improve the situation to Indian advantage came to naught. On July 23 the president of the Senate requested unanimous consent to call up Joint Resolution 118 (with the senator from Utah's amendments attached) for debate on the Senate floor. Sen. Dennis Chavez of New Mexico objected because "the delegate from Alaska knows more about Alaska than I do" and "he states in writing [in a letter Bartlett had delivered to each senator] that the Senate joint resolution [as modified by the Watkins amendments] is very damaging to certain persons in Alaska."[119]

With consideration of Joint Resolution 118 stalled and the 80th Congress rushing toward the summer adjournment of its first session, the scapegoating began in southeast Alaska. The *Daily Alaska Empire* informed readers who wanted to take names that "opposition to the legislation on the part of Alaska Indians was responsible" for the Senate refusing to consider either House Joint Resolution 205 or Senate Joint Resolution 118, "along with the delays in consideration of the legislation brought about apparently through the efforts of Alaska Delegate E. L. Bartlett who wanted the hearings delayed until four Indian representatives from Alaska got back to Washington."[120]

But before his performance as white Alaska's champion could be further disparaged, Bartlett joined with Secretary of the Interior Julius Krug and Hugh Butler to subject Arthur Watkins to an arm-twisting. On July 26 in the early morning hours of the Senate's last all-night session prior to the summer adjournment, Watkins abandoned his amendments.

> I have great doubt as to the constitutionality of the measure but I shall not make a formal objection [the senator announced on the floor when House Joint Resolution 205 was called up]. We wanted to protect the rights of the Indians by adoption of proper amendments. Others have passed on these amendments. They think I am wrong, and for the purpose of accomplishing the building of a great pulp

industry in the Territory of Alaska, I am not going to file an objection at this time, but permit the measure to be acted upon.[121]

As enacted, Joint Resolution 205 authorized the National Forest Service to sell timber from the Tongass National Forest "notwithstanding any claim of possessory rights" and required the proceeds from timber sales to be deposited in a "special account in the Treasury until the rights to the land and timber are finally determined."[122]

Exercising that authority, in 1948 the Forest Service signed a fifty-year contract with the Ketchikan Pulp and Paper Company that authorized the company to cut 8.25 billion board feet of timber.

When the contract was signed, Secretary of the Interior Julius Krug predicted "that shortly all five of the preferred pulp mill sites in southeastern Alaska will be taken."[123] But the prediction was a fantasy. Ketchikan Pulp and Paper built a mill north of Ketchikan, which began grinding logs in 1954 and continued to operate only because the contract it signed in 1948 allowed the company to purchase timber at below-market prices. In 1956 a consortium of Japanese corporations purchased five billion board feet of timber on Baranof, Chichagof, and Kuiu Islands and built a pulp mill at Sitka that, after beginning operation in 1961, closed in 1993. In 1997 the Ketchikan mill closed as well.[124]

No other mills and no towns were built.

Rather than a legion of jobs, what Congress received in exchange for authorizing the sell-off of the nation's largest stand of old-growth timber were two pulp mills and a taxpayer subsidy to the National Forest Service to build roads and otherwise facilitate the harvest of timber that as late as 1994 averaged $34 million per year.[125]

In 1947, James Curry had no way to know that the idea of a southeast Alaska newsprint industry was a sophistry that too many years of too wishful thinking had beguiled too many people who should have known better. All he knew was that the members of the House Committee on Agriculture and the Senate Committee on Public Lands had avoided the politically unpleasant task of deciding what rights to land ownership the Tlingit and Haida Indians should be afforded as a consequence of their and their ancestors' continuous prior occupation of southeast Alaska.

But Curry's failed effort to persuade Congress not to enact Joint Resolution 205 had two important derivative consequences. The first was that it brought Native land claims to the attention of Hugh Butler, chairman of the Senate Committee on Public Lands, which at the beginning of the second session of the 80th Congress was renamed the Committee on Interior and Insular Affairs.

In 1947 when the Senate adjourned for the summer after passing Joint Resolution 205, Butler set off on a Committee junket to Alaska. He was squired around southeast Alaska by W. C. Arnold and made no effort to visit any Indian villages. When Butler and the senators with whom he was traveling arrived in Juneau, the chairman gave the ANB leaders who asked to speak with him all of twenty minutes. Cyril Zuboff, who the previous November had been elected to a second consecutive term as ANB grand president, subsequently reported to James Curry: "All the rest of the time of that committee was scheduled by the chambers of commerce."[126]

After starting out in life as a dirt poor Nebraska farmboy, in 1941 when Butler entered the Senate he had a $1 million-plus net worth that he had earned brokering grain. Being a businessman himself, three weeks of hob-nobbing with southeast Alaska businessmen convinced the senator that "the legal confusion surrounding all questions of title to real property" was impeding the economic development of Alaska and that "the controversy over what are called aboriginal rights" was a principal source of the confusion.[127]

Unintentionally validating that view, shortly after Butler returned to Washington, D.C., the Department of the Interior public affairs office erroneously announced that Secretary of the Interior Julius Krug had established a new reservation at Hydaburg. Outraged, J. S. MacKinnon, president of the Juneau Chamber of Commerce, wrote Butler that, after "stud[ying] the present deplorable situation with alarm," the members of his organization were "convinced that a major cause of the trouble is the claimed power of the Secretary of the Interior to create reservations under the [1936 Alaska amendments to the IRA]." He asked Butler to sponsor legislation to abolish existing reservations and repeal the section of the IRA that delegated to the secretary of the interior authority to establish new ones.[128] The Ketchikan Chamber of Commerce urged similar action, and in December, Butler responded by introducing Senate Joint Resolution 162.

As the Juneau and Ketchikan chambers requested, Joint Resolution 162 abolished existing reservations and repealed the section of the Alaska amendments to the IRA that delegated to the secretary of the interior the authority he had exercised to create them. For good measure, the resolution also put Congress on record as agreeing with the court of appeals in *Miller v United States* that "any aboriginal titles which may be claimed to have existed with respect to lands within the Territory of Alaska were extinguished under the terms of the treaty of June 20, 1867." It then gratuitously announced that "the United States has never recognized rights of

Natives based upon use and occupancy of lands in Alaska, except to the extent that certain individual rights have been recognized in the case of Natives in the same manner as in the case of others."[129]

The enthusiasm that Joint Resolution 162 generated among influential white businessman throughout southeast Alaska caught Bob Bartlett in a closing political vise.

Setting about trying to make good on his promise to end the Department of the Interior's preoccupation with reservations, when he arrived in Washington, D.C., in December 1944, Bartlett asked the Department of the Interior to have one of its attorneys write a bill whose enactment would accomplish that objective by extinguishing aboriginal title on fair terms.[130]

When the department delivered a draft text, Bartlett mailed a copy to the ANB executive committee. The executive committee—aka William Paul—made minor changes. On Paul's motion, the 1945 ANB Grand Camp adopted a resolution that urged Bartlett to introduce the executive committee's version of the bill.[131] In March 1946, Bartlett did so.

Denoted H.R. 5731,[132] the bill (which had been written either by Felix Cohen or Ted Haas) codified Cohen's belief that Alaska Natives should be allowed to own land. To implement that policy, H.R. 5731 authorized the secretary of the interior to negotiate with "tribes, or communities in interest" for the surrender of their "legal and equitable rights" to land and waters "not actually needed for their own use." But without explicitly saying so, the bill left open the possibility that land and waters "actually needed for [the Natives'] own use" would remain subject to aboriginal title.

Having been introduced by an obscure nonvoting freshman, H.R. 5731 died in the 79th Congress.

When the 80th Congress convened in January 1947, Bartlett reintroduced the measure as H.R. 190, but a month later the court of appeals decided *Miller v United States.* As a consequence, in June, when the House Committee on Public Lands held a hearing on H.R. 190,[133] the witnesses that the Departments of Agriculture and Justice sent to testify opposed the measure on the ground that the court of appeals had instructed that there was no unextinguished aboriginal title in Alaska whose quieting needed negotiating.[134]

Whether the court of appeals was correct that the Treaty of Cession had extinguished Native aboriginal title in 1867 was an arcane question of law that Bob Bartlett, who was not an attorney, only marginally understood. However, by 1947, Bartlett had concluded that, as a matter of economic justice, Alaska Natives should be allowed to own land around their villages. For that reason, although he did not say so publicly, he privately believed that repealing the section of the Alaska amendments to the IRA that delegated to the secretary of the interior authority to withdraw land that Alaska Natives "actually occupied" as reservations was too harsh a solution to a problem whose cause was the secretary's abuse of power rather than Congress's granting of it. As Bartlett explained by letter to Anthony Dimond when he sent Dimond a copy of Joint Resolution 162 the day after Hugh Butler introduced it,

> If the joint resolution is adopted I think despite everything I shall grieve a bit because the 1936 Act [i.e., the section of the Alaska amendments to the IRA that authorized the secretary of the interior to withdraw land] was a good one. It set up a mechanism for protection of the Indians in many cases where that mechanism might have been desirable and necessary. That there is now grave danger that the right to create reservations will be abolished altogether is due solely in my judgment to the fact that some of the "do gooders" in the Department [of the Interior] had been unable to restrain themselves. They have piled excess upon excess until people who have no devotion to the Indian cause are in a state of rebellion.[135]

But if Bob Bartlett thought that passage of Joint Resolution 162 would commit Congress to a bad policy, its introduction created a political problem for which there was no ready solution.

In southeast Alaska, Bartlett had outpolled his Republican opponent, an Anchorage attorney named John Manders, in the 1944 election, by 1284 votes to 876 votes in Juneau, Sitka, and Ketchikan and by a vote of 455 to 45 in Indian villages located inside the Tongass National Forest. In the 1946 election, Bartlett had outpolled his Republican opponent in the same precincts by similar margins.[136]

Joint Resolution 162 threatened to fracture that biracial base of support.

Prior to asking Hugh Butler to introduce Joint Resolution 162, the Juneau and Ketchikan Chambers of Commerce asked Bartlett.[137] When Bartlett, by taking no action, declined and then, when directly asked, expressed the opinion that Congress's enactment of Joint Resolution 162 would be a bad idea, his disinclination to be helpful was duly noted. R. E. Robertson, a Juneau attorney who represented the Juneau Chamber of Commerce, reported to Butler in February 1948:

> I learned that Bob Bartlett yesterday told Jim Crowdy [the president of the Alaska Miners Association] that he was not wholly for SJR 162. Bartlett said he did not think all authority to create reservations should

be taken away from the Secretary of the Interior, but simply the authority to create "large" reservations, whatever that means. I thought you would be interested in knowing Bartlett's views. Bob Jernberg [a Ketchikan attorney who represented the Ketchikan Chamber of Commerce], a Democrat, was also much disappointed when he learned Bartlett's position, although previously Jernberg had told me he didn't think Bartlett was wholeheartedly for the resolution.[138]

To compound Bartlett's problem, the month before Hugh Butler introduced Joint Resolution 162, the ANB adopted a resolution at its 1947 Grand Camp, which that year was held at Hydaburg, that urged Secretary of the Interior Julius Krug "to promulgate the order recently announced to the press initiating proceedings to establish a reservation for the village of Hydaburg."[139]

So Bartlett had next to no room to maneuver between the irreconcilable demands of two important groups of southeast Alaska voters. As he privately complained to Hugh Butler the day after the brotherhood adopted its resolution, "Almost by a miracle I got out of H. J. Res. 205 comparatively unscathed politically, but the Hydaburg reservation ... won't do me any good."[140]

The prediction proved true. When the news that Hugh Butler had introduced it reached southeastern Alaska, Josephine Peele, the president of the Alaska Native Sisterhood camp at Ketchikan, radiogramed Bartlett to demand that "you protest Joint Resolution 162." In response and to preemptively shore up his support among Indian voters, Bartlett wrote Peele a letter, which he subsequently distributed to the public by arranging for its publication in the *Congressional Record,* that carefully outlined his position on reservations and the settlement of Native land claims without announcing a position on Joint Resolution 162. "Such research as I have been able to make convinces me beyond all measure of doubt that section 2 of the Act of May 1, 1936 [i.e., the section of the Alaska amendments to the IRA that delegated the secretary of the interior authority to establish reservations] was not intended for other than establishment of comparatively small reservations, for townsites and related purposes," Bartlett explained to Peele. For that reason, "the Butler resolution ... would never have been introduced if there had always been prudent employment of the powers granted under section 2 of the 1936 Act. And especially would [it] not have been introduced if the word had not spread that those powers intended to be used in ever increasing measure."

But while he opposed the establishment of large reservations, Bartlett promised Peele that he was committed to affording Alaska Natives a fair opportunity to make their case for a settlement of land claims based on aboriginal title, "despite the findings of the circuit court of appeals at San Francisco with respect to the *Miller* case." Not only that, but "if it should be finally determined [by Congress or the courts that Alaska Natives] have possessory rights with respect to specific areas I do not think the heavens would tumble if title to these tracts was to be conveyed to them."[141]

Arthur Watkins, chairman of the Senate Committee on Interior and Insular Affairs Subcommittee on Indian Affairs, could not have cared less what James Curry and Ruth Bronson—who, when she testified before Watkins's panel, excoriated the measure as "a vicious piece of legislation"[142]—thought of Joint Resolution 162. But after listening to Assistant Secretary of the Interior William Warne explain why the Department of the Interior opposed its enactment, Watkins—who the previous year had tried to amend Joint Resolution 118 to prohibit the National Forest Service from selling timber located on land Tlingit and Haida Indians "actually possessed"—was persuaded that the resolution treated Native land rights too harshly.

As a consequence, Watkins (with its sponsor's begrudging concurrence) arranged for the Committee on Interior and Insular Affairs to amend the text of Joint Resolution 162 to eliminate the section that abolished existing reservations, as well as the section that put the Senate on record as agreeing with the court of appeals' pronouncement in *Miller v United States* that the Treaty of Cession had extinguished Native aboriginal title in 1867. Watkins also added a new section, similar to the text of the amendment he had tried to add to Joint Resolution 118. It authorized the secretary of the interior to convey to Native tribes, villages, and individuals legal title to the land they "actually possessed, used or occupied for townsites, villages, smoke houses, gardens, burial grounds, or missionary stations."[143]

Since the new version of Joint Resolution 162 still repealed the secretary of the interior's authority to establish reservations, the Department of the Interior continued to oppose its enactment. When the Senate Committee on Interior and Insular Affairs reported the new version of Joint Resolution 162 to the Senate, Sen. Joseph O'Mahoney, the committee's senior Democrat, prevented the measure from being immediately brought to the floor for a vote by announcing that he would object if the Senate tried to pass the resolution by unanimous consent.[144]

At Hugh Butler's urging, the president of the Senate on June 1 called up Joint Resolution 162 on the Senate's unanimous consent calendar. Consistent with Sen. O'Mahoney's pronouncement, Sen. Scott Lucas, the Democratic whip, objected, and the resolution was passed over. However, on June 19 in the early morning hours of the bill-trading melee of the

Senate's final all-night regular session of the 80th Congress, Butler succeeded in forcing Joint Resolution 162 through the Senate[145] and then on to the House of Representatives, whose members were in the midst of their own all-night rush to adjournment.

Because the sponsors of literally hundreds of bills were maneuvering to try to have the House act on their bills, the only way Joint Resolution 162 could be considered on the floor was by unanimous consent.

Anticipating that snafu, several days earlier George Thomas, a lobbyist for the Seattle Chamber of Commerce (which in December had voted to "join other chambers of commerce of Alaska in requesting Congress to take prompt and effective steps to stop all further promotion of aboriginal rights assertions by the Department of the Interior, and to clear the title of Alaska real estate from further assertion of such claims")[146] had begun laying the groundwork for a unanimous consent motion. As Thomas updated F. O. Hagie, vice president of the Seattle Chamber, four days before Joint Resolution 162 passed the Senate,

> I have polled the members of the Washington State delegation in the House with reference to obtaining passage of S. J. Res. 162 at the current session. All plans, of course, must be contingent on Senate approval of the bill ... [Washington] Sen. [Warren] Magnuson has been working on the Democratic objectors [in the Senate] and apparently has straightened out Senators O'Mahoney and Lucas, who were successive objectors, presumably at the request of the Interior Department.

After transmitting that progress report, Thomas confided that he also had "talked with Henry Jackson who, as a Democrat, might be disposed to support the Interior Department's objections to this measure. However, Jackson assured me he would go along and said he feels someone should clip the powers of the Interior Secretary to set up reservations and cloud title to Alaskan resources."[147]

So with the Washington state delegation wired, at 6:00 A.M., Rep. Wesley D'Ewart, chairman of the House Committee on Public Lands Subcommittee on Indian Affairs, moved that the House pass Senate Joint Resolution 162 by unanimous consent.

A conservative Republican rancher from Montana, the previous December, D'Ewart had introduced Senate Joint Resolution 162 in the House as House Joint Resolution 269. But the House Committee on Public Lands had taken no action on the resolution, according to Frances Lopinsky, a young attorney who worked for James Curry in his Washington, D.C., law office, because Norris Poulson, a Republican member of the committee's

Subcommittee on Territorial and Insular Possessions, "knew what the bill provided, [and] prevented it from passing."[148] It is difficult to believe that, if Rep. Richard Welch, chairman of the Committee on Public Lands, had wanted to report Joint Resolution 269 to the House, Poulson could have prevented the chairman from having his way.

In any event, when Wesley D'Ewart moved the House to pass Senate Joint Resolution 162 by unanimous consent, Rep. Robert Rich, a Republican from Pennsylvania, sought the floor.

An heir to the Woolrich Woolen Mill fortune, Rich had graduated from Dickinson College in Carlisle, Pennsylvania,[149] three years after William Paul had graduated from the Carlisle Indian School in the same small town, so he undoubtedly knew something about Indians.

Whether Rich truly was weary of the House passing bills that the members who still were in the chamber were too bleary-eyed to understand is not known. Since he was from Pennsylvania, Rich may have been lobbied by Isaac Sutton, a Philadelphia attorney who served as the organization's unpaid counsel, or by some other member of the Philadelphia-based Indian Rights Association. In February at the urging of Ruth Bronson, who served on the organization's board of directors, the association had passed a resolution that condemned Joint Resolution 162 "as a violation of the good faith and honor of our nation."[150] And in April, again at Bronson's instigation, each member of the association had been urged to communicate that view to his or her congressman.

Whatever his reason for doing so, when Wesley D'Ewart moved the House to pass Senate Joint Resolution 162 by unanimous consent, Rich announced: "It is now fifteen minutes after six in the morning. It is almost time to go to church. It seems to me this legislation should be deferred until some other time. I object."[151] So Hugh Butler and Wesley D'Ewart's dead-of-night attempt to repeal the secretary of the interior's authority to establish reservations had failed.

But even if it had succeeded, the passage of Joint Resolution 162 would not have settled the question of whether Alaska's 375 million acres of land (both within and without the Tongass National Forest) remained subject to unextinguished aboriginal title. For that reason and as the second consequence of James Curry's failed effort to persuade Congress not to enact Joint Resolution 205, in February 1948 the members of an Inter-Agency Committee on the Development of Alaska that Secretary of the Interior Julius Krug had organized the previous October[152] recommended that "an early and final determination of the rights of the Alaskan Natives to lands and resources used by them, now or in the past, is imperative." Until that recommendation was implemented, the committee advised, it would be "impossible to render full justice to the Natives" or for "various desirable improvements and developments" to be made that were essential to Alaska's economic development.[153]

To bring about that result, Assistant Secretary of the Interior William Warne, who chaired the committee, began negotiating with the Departments of Agriculture and Justice over the content of a bill whose enactment would extinguish Native aboriginal title on terms the three departments could jointly support.[154]

Warne, who the following year would persuade Secretary of the Interior Julius Krug to sign proclamations on his final day in office that withdrew land for reservations at Hydaburg, Barrow, and Shungnak-Kobuk, wanted each village to be allowed to own land, and he wanted the amount of land to be negotiated village by village, although, as he explained in a speech to the Seattle Chamber of Commerce, he realized that each negotiated agreement would have to "be subject to congressional approval."[155]

However, Warne's discussions with his counterparts at the Departments of Agriculture and Justice quickly gridlocked when the National Forest Service negotiators refused to allow Alaska Natives to own land beyond the curtilages of their villages and vehemently objected to the Forest Service being required to relinquish control of so much as an acre of the Tongass National Forest. As a consequence, in May 1948, Richard Neustadt, an official at the Bureau of the Budget, advised the White House that "it seems impossible at the present time to obtain agreement between the Departments of Agriculture and Interior on certain basic policy issues."[156]

But an agreement was patched together, which Richard Welch, chairman of the House Committee on Public Lands, introduced in June as H.R. 7002.[157]

After reading H.R. 7002, Frances Lopinsky advised James Curry that "all opportunity to make really big money out of the lands seems to be saved for persons of white blood."[158] The disparagement was accurate, since Warne had allowed the National Forest Service its way on every issue of consequence.

After extinguishing "all claims based upon possessory rights asserted by or on behalf of any community of Natives in Alaska to any lands or waters in such territory" over a four-year period, H.R. 7002 "immediately" extinguished claims to lands located "within the exterior boundaries of national forests." Each community of Natives and all individual Natives then were authorized to file a lawsuit in the U.S. district court for the district of Alaska to obtain monetary compensation for the extinguishments.

As further compensation, the bill authorized the secretary of the interior to convey each community of Natives legal title to the acreage its residents occupied "for towns, villages, buildings, smoke houses, cultivated fields or gardens, hunting or fishing camps, burial grounds, missionary stations, meeting places, or other improvements." As a seeming concession to Warne, the bill also authorized (but did not require) the secretary to convey a Native community title to additional lands that its residents needed to "maintain an adequate standard of living." But each conveyance of additional land was required to be approved by Congress, and if the secretary conveyed to a community of Natives additional land "within the exterior boundaries of a national forest," title to the land would be held in trust for the Indians and the National Forest Service would continue to administer the land as part of the forest. Finally, the United States retained "all oil, gas and mineral deposits within the lands granted."

Bob Bartlett had counseled the ANB, in his letter to Josephine Peele, that Hugh Butler and most of the other members of the Senate Committee on Interior and Insular Affairs believed that "no aboriginal possessory rights exist in Alaska" and that the senators' view "is indicative of what can easily be discerned in Washington by even a casual observer as an increasingly hostile attitude toward the Indian position." The failure of Joint Resolution 205 to provoke a single dissenting vote and the failure of Joint Resolution 162 to provoke more than one confirmed Bartlett's head count. As a consequence, it is not unreasonable to assume that if the House Committee on Public Lands had taken action on H.R. 7002 prior to the adjournment of the 80th Congress, both Houses would have passed the measure.

But the committee's calendar apparently was full, since the bill was not reported. For Hugh Butler and Wesley D'Ewart and other members of Congress who wanted what they considered to be the nonsense about Native land rights set straight, the committee's inattention was a consequential procedural error.

When he negotiated H.R. 7002 with the Departments of Agriculture and Justice, William Warne had not involved Bob Bartlett or Ernest Gruening. To rectify the breach of protocol, in December 1948, Warne and William Zimmerman (who still was serving as the acting commissioner of Indian affairs) met with Alaska's delegate and governor to discuss changes they wanted made to the bill.[159] Then the text was redrafted and sent to the Bureau of the Budget for the routine approval that the White House required before Secretary of the Interior Julius Krug could send the bill to Capitol Hill for introduction in the new Congress.

On the recommendation of Commissioner of Indian Affairs John Collier, in 1933, President Franklin Roosevelt had abolished the Board of Indian Commissioners, which had advised the secretary of the interior on Indian policy since 1869. Although the action was publicly justified as necessary to "increase the efficiency of the operations of the government," according to Collier's biographer, the real reason Collier had the board abolished was that "Republicans and conservatives who favored ... assimilation policies" dominated the membership.

However, now that Collier and the conservative Republican assimilationists both were gone, in April 1948 at a meeting with William Warne, Ruth Bronson and representatives of other Indian rights organizations urged Warne to urge Julius Krug to reinstitute the tradition that the secretary of the interior be advised on Indian policy by nongovernmental advisors.[160]

In January 1949, Krug did so by appointing an eleven-member National Advisory Committee on Indian Affairs,[161] whose membership, in addition to Bronson, included Oliver La Farge, the president of the Association on American Indian Affairs. In 1949 the association was the most prominent of the white "friends of the Indian" organizations; its general counsel was Felix Cohen, whom La Farge had hired when Cohen resigned from the Department of the Interior to return to private practice. The advisory committee also included Jonathan Steere, president of the Indian Rights Association, who—undoubtedly at the urging of Ruth Bronson—the previous March had excoriated Senate Joint Resolution 162 in a letter to the editor of the *New York Times*.[162]

Since writing a bill to extinguish Alaska Native aboriginal title was one of the Department of the Interior's major Indian-related projects, William Warne distributed the most recent version of H.R. 7002 for comment when the advisory committee held its first meeting in February. After reviewing the text and undoubtedly at the instigation of Ruth Bronson and Jonathan Steere, the committee demanded, by a unanimous vote, that Secretary of the Interior Julius Krug "decline to submit or support such unjust legislation."[163]

Startled by the repudiation of a bill whose content he had by that date rationalized to himself embodied a "fair and just" settlement of Native land claims,[164] Warne prevailed on the advisory committee not to publicly announce its condemnation of H.R. 7002 because to do otherwise "would embarrass him." But as Ruth Bronson subsequently explained to Oliver La Farge (who had missed the meeting at which he had been elected chairman),

> I think how he [Warne] phrased it was that he hoped we would not
> make him sorry that he had released the bill to us prematurely. His
> statement clearly implied to me that only your committee had been
> allowed to see advance copies of the proposed bill, and to discuss it
> publicly would be betraying a confidence. At the time that seemed to
> me a justifiable reason for keeping still. But after the sessions of the
> committee were over, I learned that the Department [of the Interior]
> had also released the bill to Mr. Curry, and that at the time we were
> meeting, the bill, together with Mr. Curry's analysis, was in the hands
> of the Natives of Alaska and had been for some days. I do not know
> whether Mr. Warne knew this when he asked us not to publish the
> statement [announcing the committee's objection to the new text of
> H.R. 7002]. Therefore, I do not yet know whether Mr. Warne is act-
> ing in good faith, but the situation as it has developed leaves us all
> looking rather foolish.[165]

But if Bronson thought the promise to keep their repudiation of H.R.
7002 secret risked making the committee members "open targets for criticism," the committee's announcement of its condemnation of the bill had
the potential to embarrass Harry Truman (who the previous November
had been elected to his own term as president in no small part because he
had publicly championed civil rights). So on April 27, Herbert Slaughter,
chief of the Department of Interior Legislative Division, and John Provinse,
the assistant commissioner of Indian affairs, journeyed to the White House
to discuss the situation with Stephen Spingarn and Philleo Nash, two members of the president's staff.

Spingarn, whose uncle, Arthur Spingarn, was a founder of the National
Association for the Advancement of Colored People, and Nash both had
been involved in writing the historic message on civil rights that Truman
had sent to Congress in February 1948. Nash, a University of Chicago-
trained anthropologist who had researched his doctoral dissertation on the
Klamath Indian reservation in Oregon, also had just completed a four-year
term as a member of the board of directors of the Association on American Indian Affairs.[166] It is no surprise that both men agreed with the advisory
committee that the new text of H.R. 7002 extinguished Native aboriginal
title on unfair terms. As Spingarn summarized his and Nash's meeting with
Slaughter and Provinse to Clark Clifford, Harry Truman's unofficial chief
of staff:

> Mr. Nash and I expressed the opinion that there seemed to us some
> basis for the objections about the arbitrariness of the land title extinc-
> tion features of the bill—that there was a question whether the bill in

its present form would square with the President's civil rights program. We suggested that more emphasis be placed on conciliation and negotiation with the Indians, and that a serious attempt should be made to work out a mutual agreement with them on the lands they should have, prior to the extinction of their titles. The form which a new version of the bill might take was discussed and it was agreed that Interior would prepare a new draft along these lines and submit it to me. We will then call in the Justice and Agriculture [Departments] and see if we can reach an agreement on this revised version. If not (and objection from Justice at least is likely), it will presumably be necessary to submit the matter to the President for decision.[167]

In 1949, Harry Truman operated the White House in a manner considerably different than it operates today. Each morning the day began with a meeting in the Oval Office. As Clark Clifford years later would reminisce:

These morning staff meetings had a casual air to them; today much of what took place in them would be handled by the White House Chief of Staff without the participation of the President. But President Truman did this work himself, sometimes in a haphazard manner. He began each meeting by going through the papers on his desk, handing them out to various members of the staff for action. [Charles] Ross [the White House press secretary] would raise any press or public-relations problems. After that, the rest of the staff would bring up anything they felt needed presidential attention.[168]

When he read Spingarn's report on his and Philleo Nash's meeting with Slaughter and Provinse, Clifford apparently decided not to wait for the Departments of Agriculture and Justice to object to a new Department of the Interior bill before bringing the matter to the president's attention.

As Clifford undoubtedly was aware, Truman had a personal interest in Alaska. After Ernest Gruening had urged him to give the idea a "plug" in his first State of the Union address,[169] in January 1946, Truman had been the first president to recommend Alaska statehood. In May 1948, Truman had sent Congress a special message on Alaska that urged the enactment of legislative initiatives "to assist the balanced development of Alaskan resources and to help open economic opportunities on a sound long-term basis."[170] As recently as the week prior to Spingarn's and Nash's meeting with Slaughter and Provinse, the president had privately talked up the territory to Julius Krug as "our last great frontier" which "we ought to develop ... as promptly as possible."[171]

Of equal importance and as Harry Truman subsequently explained years later, "I tried to look after Indian rights all the time I was President.

Whenever any bill came up that looked to me like a new attempt to exploit them, it got vetoed."[172]

The president also trusted his staff. When the matter was brought to his attention (most likely at the morning staff meeting), Truman accepted Stephen Spingarn's and Philleo Nash's conclusion that the bill the Department of the Interior wanted to send to Congress in his name extinguished Alaska Native aboriginal title on unfair terms. As a consequence, on May 4 the president sent Secretary of the Interior Julius Krug a private note that communicated the following order:

> I have been informed that one of the problems holding back the development of Alaska has been the matter of unresolved Native claims. Legislation has been proposed which is not satisfactory and which should not be passed. I'll appreciate it very much if the Interior Department will get up a bill which will approach a fair settlement of this unresolved situation. I think it is of vital importance.[173]

But the fact that a president of the United States has given an order does not mean that it will be obeyed. In 1951, White House aide Richard Schifter described the fate of Truman's edict as follows: "The objections to the bill were presented to President Truman, who found them justified. He consequently directed the Department of the Interior to scrap its original proposal and prepare a new bill. The interested agencies consequently resumed negotiations on this problem. Though a number of drafts were prepared, no final agreement was reached and early in 1950 the entire issue was dropped."[174]

But if the effort to negotiate a consensus inside the Departments of Interior, Agriculture, and Justice that was acceptable to the president had failed, Bob Bartlett was under continued pressure from home to persuade Congress to extinguish aboriginal title.

To relieve it, when the territorial legislature in March 1951 sent Congress a memorial that renewed its complaint that the "economic and industrial progress and development of Alaska" was being "hampered by the uncertainties of the Indian, or aboriginal title controversy,"[175] Bartlett introduced a new bill in June—H.R. 4388,[176] which Richard Schifter described as "closely resembl[ing] the drafts under consideration after the President's disapproval of H.R. 7002."[177]

Since introducing it demonstrated that he was working on the problem, for Bartlett, H.R. 4388 was better than nothing. But for Alaska Natives, H.R. 4388 was worse than H.R. 7002 since, among other onerous new sections, one required each Native village to assert its residents' land claims within two years of the date of publication of a notice in the *Federal Register,* a requirement about which William Paul subsequently correctly queried Felix Cohen: "What good is that to the thousands of our Natives who cannot read or write?"[178]

In August, Bartlett arranged for the Subcommittee on Indian Affairs (of which he was a member) of the House Committee on Interior and Insular Affairs to hold a hearing on H.R. 4388, to allow the usual suspects to voice the usual objections.[179] Speaking for his cannery company clients, W. C. Arnold objected to conveying to the Indians of southeastern Alaska title to any land located inside the Tongass National Forest.[180] C. M. Granger, assistant chief of the National Forest Service, complained that the bill recognized a "roving type" of Native use and occupancy that might be asserted "to virtually all the national forest land in southeastern Alaska."[181] And James Curry and Ruth Bronson argued that the way to settle Native land claims was for the secretary of interior to establish more reservations.

Undeterred by the discord, in November, Bartlett arranged for the subcommittee to hold hearings in Alaska.[182] The exercise accomplished nothing other than to further document the fact that Bartlett's constituency was fracturing along racial lines. In Juneau, William Paul testified on behalf of the ANB that the bill gave Alaska Natives too little. In Anchorage, Paul Robinson testified on behalf of the Anchorage Chamber of Commerce that the bill gave them too much.[183] And the Alaska Miners Association complained by letter that H.R. 4388 presumed the existence "of Native rights to huge tracts of land based upon aboriginal occupancy," when "the only rights ever possessed by the Native people of Alaska" are "to small areas for villages, individual dwellings, smoke houses, etc."[184]

Ignoring the cacophony of objection, throughout the winter and spring Bartlett met with Preston Peden, chief counsel of the House Committee on Interior and Insular Affairs; Ralph Barney, chief of the Indian claims branch of the Justice Department; Democratic Rep. Chester McMullen of Florida, who had chaired the Alaska hearings; and Wesley D'Ewart, the ranking Republican member of the Subcommittee on Indian Affairs, to rewrite the bill.[185] In May 1952 the committee released a new committee print. But no further action was taken, and when the 82d Congress adjourned in July, H.R. 4388 died.

Four months later the Republican Party slip-streamed behind Dwight Eisenhower's presidential candidacy in the 1952 congressional elections to regain the control of both houses of Congress it had lost when Harry Truman won the 1948 presidential election by running against the 80th "Do Nothing" Republican Congress.

Members of the House Committee on Interior and Insular Affairs Subcommittee
on Indian Affairs in Alaska in November 1951 to hold field hearings on H. R.
4388; Representative Wesley D'Ewart (far left), Delegate E. L. "Bob" Bartlett
(third from right). E. L. "BOB" BARTLETT COLLECTION ACC. NO. 90-176-134, ALASKA AND
POLAR REGIONS DEPARTMENT, UNIVERSITY OF ALASKA FAIRBANKS.

In January 1953, when the 83d Congress convened, Wesley D'Ewart, who
now was the second most senior majority member of the House Committee on Interior and Insular Affairs, introduced the H.R. 4388 committee
print as H.R. 1921. In March the Subcommittee on Territories and Insular
Possessions, to which H.R. 1921 had been referred inside the Committee
on Interior and Insular Affairs, reported the measure to the committee.[186]
But then the fix appeared to be derailed when a deluge of protest letters
that James Curry generated convinced Rep. Arthur Miller, the chairman of
the committee, that the bill "seems to be very controversial."[187] Contemporaneously and at Curry's instigation, Peter Nielsen, the grand secretary of
the ANB, urged Bob Bartlett by telegram to "make every effort to delay
consideration on H.R. 1921 ... until our organization can be heard from."[188]
    Rather than sending H.R. 1921 to the Rules Committee so that it could
be calendared for debate (and sure passage) on the floor, and most likely at

the behind-the-scene urging of Bob Bartlett, Miller convened a hearing in August.

As part of his duties as general counsel of the Association on American Indian Affairs, Felix Cohen had kept the ANB informed of the status of H.R. 4388. After thanking him for sending a copy of the committee print, in May 1952, William Paul, who the previous November had been elected to his first term as ANB grand secretary since 1938, had written to Cohen to ask him to "add your voice and that of your association to ours and induce the Committee to hold the bill till next Congress."[189]

Cohen did what he could to do so, but by April 1953 when the House Committee on Interior and Insular Affairs held its hearing on H.R. 1921, his involvement in the story of Alaska Natives and their land had ended. Cohen, who was only forty-five, was terminally ill with lung cancer (from which he would die in October). Arthur Lazarus, a twenty-six-year-old Yale Law School graduate who worked for Cohen at Riegelman, Strasser & Spiegelberg, the Washington, D.C., law firm Cohen had joined the previous year, picked up the staff and, testifying on behalf of the Association on American Indian Affairs in Cohen's stead, reminded the committee that "the opinions of the Indians of Alaska should be obtained before final action is taken on the pending bill."[190]

While no member of the committee (other than Bob Bartlett) had any intention of doing so, the chairman did want to know what Douglas McKay, the new secretary of the interior, thought of H.R. 1921.

A conservative former governor of Oregon, McKay was as no-nonsense an assimilationist as the last Republican secretary of the interior, Ray Lyman Wilbur. In February, McKay had lectured the Washington Press Club (in one of his first speeches as a member of the Eisenhower cabinet) that more "sensible" Indian policies were needed because "we've been 125 years getting into this mess with the Indians."[191] The package of amendments to H.R. 1921 that Assistant Secretary of the Interior Orme Lewis delivered to the committee in July reflected the new secretary's hard line. To cite but two examples, one amendment imposed the same restrictions on Native ownership of land located inside national parks and wildlife refuges as H.R. 1921 imposed on Native ownership of land located inside national forests. Another made it more difficult for Natives to obtain title to land that white trespassers occupied unlawfully.[192]

In August the committee melded the Department of the Interior's amendments into a new text of H.R. 1921, denoted Committee Print 10-A,[193] and returned the bill to the Subcommittee on Territories and Insular Possessions for further review.

If that was not calamity enough for Alaska Natives, in January 1954 the situation deteriorated further when Assistant Secretary of the Interior Orme Lewis and Deputy Attorney General William Rogers each urged the committee by letter to rewrite Print 10-A to preclude the United States from being required to compensate Alaska Natives for the extinguishment of their aboriginal title.[194]

The reason is esoteric. When it extinguished an Indian tribe's aboriginal title, Congress usually paid compensation (of some amount). But what if it did not? Was aboriginal title "private property" that the Fifth Amendment of the U.S. Constitution prohibited Congress from taking "without just compensation?" In 1945 in *Northwestern Bands v United States*,[195] the U.S. Supreme Court announced that if Congress had "recognized" aboriginal title in a treaty or statute, the "recognized" title was "private property" that the Fifth Amendment required Congress to pay compensation to extinguish. But what if aboriginal title had not been "recognized"? In 1946 in *United States v Alcea Band of Tillamooks*,[196] the Court, by a vote of 5 to 3, implied that "unrecognized" aboriginal title also was a compensable property right.

The rationale was abstruse. Four justices voted that "unrecognized" aboriginal title was "private property" within the meaning of the Fifth Amendment. Three justices voted that it was not. And Justice Hugo Black, who cast the deciding fifth vote, sided with the dissenters but thought that Congress had intended the statute that allowed the Oregon tribes that had filed *Alcea Band* to bring their lawsuit to "recognize" the tribes' aboriginal title.

After reading *Alcea Band,* Felix Cohen understood and tried to power through the problem.

> While the disagreements that split the Court three ways in its opinion-writing make it dangerous to rely on anything the Court said in this case [Cohen wrote the next year in an article published in the *Minnesota Law Review*] the fact stands out that the United States, after taking land, by congressional act, from Indians who had nothing more than an unrecognized aboriginal title to it, was required, by a five to three vote of the Supreme Court, to pay the Indians the value of the land so taken. Certainly it can make no difference to the Indians in the case whether, as Justice Black thought, they are to be paid because Congress passed a jurisdictional act allowing them to bring suit, or, as the four other justices in the majority thought ... because the action of Congress a century ago established a liability which only came before the court for adjudication in 1947.[197]

But Cohen was wrong. When the *Alcea Band* lawsuit returned to the Court of Claims, the court awarded the Oregon tribes $3.1 million as compensation for the extinguishment of their aboriginal title, and $14.2 million in interest. But interest cannot be awarded against the United States unless Congress has authorized an interest award or unless the judgment on which interest is paid is compensation for the taking of "private property" protected by the Fifth Amendment.

Since the statute that authorized the *Alcea Band* lawsuit did not authorize interest, the Department of Justice appealed the interest award back to the U.S. Supreme Court. As part of their litigation strategy, the Justice Department attorneys then cooked the books in order to argue in their brief that requiring the U.S. government to pay interest on the billion dollars of claims that were pending before the Indian Claims Commission (which Congress had created in 1946 to rid itself of having to decide case by case whether a tribe should be authorized to file a lawsuit in the Court of Claims) would cost the treasury $8 billion,[198] which in the 1950s was serious money.

The bald appeal to parsimony worked, and in April 1951 the U.S. Supreme Court issued an unsigned opinion that invalidated the *Alcea Band* interest award on the rationale that none of the Court's prior decisions—including by implication the first *Alcea Band* decision—"expressed the view that recovery [for the extinguishment of unrecognized aboriginal title] was grounded on a taking under the Fifth Amendment."[199]

For Alaska Natives, the second *Alcea Band* decision initially was of no consequence since the Truman administration did not object to H.R. 4388 requiring the U.S. government to compensate Alaska Natives for the extinguishment of claims based upon "aboriginal occupancy or title." But the summer of 1953, the new Republican Congress passed Concurrent Resolution 108, which put the House and Senate on record as agreeing with Secretary of the Interior Douglas McKay that Native Americans should not be afforded special benefits or privileges. It also ordered McKay to review all Indian-related statutes and submit recommendations by January 1, 1954, for legislation whose enactment would accomplish that objective. Since the Department of the Interior and Department of Justice letters that recommended that Committee Print 10-A be amended to deny Alaska Natives compensation for the extinguishment of aboriginal title are dated January 10, the idea of asking the committee to do so likely was an outgrowth of the Resolution 108 Indian legislation review.

In any case, on January 13 the ANB executive committee by telegram informed Bob Bartlett that the brotherhood opposed the enactment of

H.R. 1921,[200] but no member of the Subcommittee on Territories and Insular Possessions (other than Bartlett) cared. The next day the chairman of the subcommittee, Rep. John Saylor of Pennsylvania, convened a work session at which Ralph Barney, chief of the Indian claims branch of the Department of Justice, identified the provisions of Committee Print 10-A to which the Department of Justice objected. The first was the requirement that the United States pay Alaska Natives compensation for the extinguishment of their aboriginal title.[201] The following day the subcommittee held a second work session, at the conclusion of which Saylor announced his intention to have a new committee print written within a month.

So the momentum to enact H.R. 1921 was accelerating. If the new committee print denied compensation for the extinguishment of aboriginal title (as it surely would have), Alaska Natives would have been left with no money and little land other than the few acres located inside the curtilages of their villages. But thanks to William Paul, the rewriting of H.R. 1921 abruptly stopped.

The 1935 Act that allowed the Indians of southeast Alaska to file a lawsuit in the Court of Claims to obtain compensation for the extinguishment of their aboriginal title authorized the "Tlingit and Haida Indians" to litigate their claims "separately or jointly in one or more suits." The act also required the money the court awarded to be "apportioned to the different Tlingit and Haida communities" (as opposed to being paid to individual Indians) per capita, rather than on the basis of the number of acres or the monetary value of the land that was the subject of each village's claim. Consistent with both the letter and the spirit of the 1935 Act, in 1947, James Curry filed a single lawsuit on behalf of the "Tlingit and Haida Indians."

When he did, William Paul not only voiced no objection, but in 1942, Bill and Fred Paul, who would not have done so without their father's approval, had filed two lawsuits in the Court of Claims, one on behalf of the Tlingit Indians and the other on behalf of the Haida Indians. Nevertheless, in 1949, William Paul (who by that date had fallen out with Curry, who long since had aligned himself with the Frank Johnson-Frank and Roy Peratrovich faction inside the ANB) began professing outrage that Curry had malpracticed by filing one lawsuit.

In 1885 the German geographer Aurel Krause observed that "the entire Tlingit people are divided into a number of distinct tribes, called 'kon,' each of which has its permanent village and its hunting and fishing grounds."[202] In addition to Kons (today spelled Kwáans), the Indians were further divided into clans whose members, the anthropologist Kalervo Oberg would note as late as 1934, had "hunting and fishing rights [that the members of other clans recognized] to certain carefully defined areas."[203]

Reasoning from that fact post hoc, William Paul decided that, rather than one lawsuit filed on behalf of the "Tlingit and Haida Indians," Curry—whom Paul disparaged as "terribly confused both by the underlying facts that are merely historical and also by our social or tribal structure"—should have filed a lawsuit for each clan because, as he gratuitously lectured Curry, "there is no entity named 'Tlingit tribe' or 'Haida tribe' ... and your trouble is that you are trying to force the Indians to accept the Indian Bureau's concept which is not founded in fact."[204]

The rancor with which Paul turned on the man whom he had participated in hiring in 1946 is no surprise. At sixty-four, Paul was more obdurate in old age than he had been when young in his certitude that he was at all times right about everything, and anyone who disagreed with him was wrong. Nor is the sedulity that Paul brought to the task of proving his point surprising.

To make his point, Paul decided to file his own lawsuit. But to do so he needed a Washington, D.C., attorney, and in 1951 he found one.

In 1950, Paul had written to the Rev. J. Earl Jackman, secretary of the Presbyterian Board of National Missions, which supervised the church's work in Alaska, to ask for help in finding a lawyer.[205] Jackman queried Wilbur La Roe, a Washington, D.C., attorney who in 1947 had served as moderator of the Presbyterian General Assembly. La Roe recommended James Craig Peacock, a partner in a small law firm that specialized in tax law.[206]

A stolid, sixty-three-year-old pillar of the Washington, D.C., establishment (who, in addition to having graduated from Princeton and the University of Pennsylvania Law School, was a member of the board of trustees of American University), Peacock knew nothing about Indian law. But after corresponding with William Paul he became intrigued by the "nature of aboriginal title in Alaska."[207] As Paul described how it happened, "I corresponded for nearly one year with Mr. Peacock and he made extensive researches before he said he was satisfied as between the Curry theory and mine, that I was right, the essence being that we hold our land by our "nah" or tribe (some call it clan) and that is the way we would have to sue."[208]

As mentioned in the previous chapter, Paul was a Tee-Hit-Ton, one of the clans at Wrangell. In October 1951 when James Peacock filed suit in the Court of Claims, he did so on behalf of the Tee-Hit-Ton clan of Tlingit

Indians,[209] which his petition alleged had held aboriginal title to 350,000 acres of land on Prince of Wales Island.

Peacock's petition also astutely alleged that the Tee-Hit-Ton clan's aboriginal title had not been extinguished by the 1867 Treaty of Cession or the 1909 proclamation that settled the boundaries of the Tongass National Forest. Instead, the petition alleged that the clan's title had been extinguished in August 1951 when the National Forest Service—acting pursuant to the authority conferred by Joint Resolution 205—sold the Ketchikan Pulp & Paper Company timber located on the land the Tee-Hit-Tons claimed. Since the 1946 Indian Claims Commission Act granted the Court of Claims jurisdiction to adjudicate the claims of any "group of American Indians residing within the territorial limits of the United States or Alaska" that accrued after the date of the enactment of that Act, the allegations describing the timber sale provided a jurisdictional basis for the court to hear the Tee-Hit-Ton lawsuit, even though William Paul and the other Tee-Hit-Tons were Tlingit Indians for whom James Curry already had filed suit in the same court.

In April 1954 in *Tee-Hit-Ton Indians v United States,*[210] the Court of Claims issued its decision. Accepting James Peacock's contentions that the Tee-Hit-Ton clan had held aboriginal title to the land it claimed and that the title had been extinguished by the 1951 timber sale, the court reasoned that neither the 1867 Treaty of Cession, the 1884 Alaska Organic Act, nor any other federal statute had "recognized" Alaska Native aboriginal title. And since the previous year the second *Alcea Band* decision had instructed that unrecognized aboriginal title was not "private property" that the Takings Clause of the Fifth Amendment required the United States to pay compensation to extinguish, the Tee-Hit-Tons were not entitled to payment for their loss.

James Peacock asked the U.S. Supreme Court to review the Court of Claims decision, and on June 7 the Court agreed to do so.[211] Ten days later, Elmer Bennett, the Department of the Interior's legislative counsel, asked Rep. John Saylor to assemble the members of the Subcommittee on Territories and Insular Possessions to consider his request that the subcommittee take no further action on H.R. 1921 "until the Supreme Court has ruled."[212]

> H.R. 1921, by its very nature, is an attempt to blend the moral, equitable and legal considerations into one piece of legislation [Bennett explained]. We [i.e., Bennett and Ralph Barney, chief of the Indian claims branch of the Department of Justice, and the attorney who represented the United States in the Tee-Hit-Ton lawsuit] think the legal consideration might well be disposed of by the Supreme Court in

its decision ... and we, in turn, will be much better advised after the Supreme Court has spoken on this matter.[213]

After considering Bennett's request and on Wesley D'Ewart's motion, and with Bob Bartlett's wholehearted agreement, the subcommittee members voted to stop work on H.R. 1921.[214]

Aware that the second *Alcea Band* decision was a precedent that supported the Court of Claims' conclusion that the United States was not required to compensate the Tee-Hit-Tons for the extinguishment of their aboriginal title, in November, when he appeared before the U.S. Supreme Court, James Peacock argued that, unlike the Oregon tribes in *Alcea Band,* Tlingit Indians had a concept of land ownership that was tantamount to fee simple title in the white legal system. He also argued that Congress intended the 1884 Alaska Organic Act and a section of a 1900 statute to "recognize" Alaska Native aboriginal title.

Sitting in the audience, Arthur Lazarus, who had inherited the Association on American Indian Affairs as a client when Felix Cohen died, was unimpressed. Years later he reminisced that James Peacock, who "was never heard of before and very little after in terms of Indian law," was "not the man to argue that case." According to Lazarus, one of the justices asked Peacock whether he agreed that the Tee-Hit-Tons were not entitled to compensation if the Court disagreed that Tlingit aboriginal title was the Indian equivalent of fee simple ownership and Peacock answered yes. "[Justice] Felix Frankfurter slammed a book down and stormed off the bench." "It was such a wrong answer," Lazarus recalled. "I'm not saying that comment lost the case, but it damn sure didn't help it."[215]

Peacock did lose, by a vote of 5 to 3, in a decision in which Justice Stanley Reed—who in 1949 had refused to uphold the Fish and Wildlife Service regulation that prohibited whites from commercial fishing inside the Karluk reservation because he privately thought that doing so would be "too much to give the Indians"—concluded that Congress had not intended the statutes to which Peacock had referred the Court to "recognize" Native aboriginal title.

The decision was announced in February 1955, and in Alaska, most whites were exultant. As the *Ketchikan Daily News* trumpeted news of the seeming victory:

> For years the Indians have been exploited by lawyers and others who held out the bait that Indians were entitled to vast sums under aboriginal rights.... Instead of requiring the payment of huge sums on the hazy "blanket claims" for most of the lands and resources of Alaska and thereby continuing to cloud "land titles," discouraging new indus-

tries, the supreme court decision clears the way for industrial development.[216]

But the *Daily News* missed the devil's presence in the details.

Stanley Reed and the four justices for whom he spoke had decided that
Congress had not "recognized" Native aboriginal title. But in so holding,
Reed implicitly conceded that aboriginal title existed, implied that throughout most of the territory it had not been extinguished, and acknowledged
that aboriginal title protected Alaska Natives' occupancy of the land it
colored "against intrusion by third parties."[217]

So for William Paul, *Tee-Hit-Ton Indians v United States* was the drubbing
the *Ketchikan Daily News* said it was, but for Alaska Natives it was an important, if unappreciated, victory that derailed the enactment of H.R. 1921
and established the legal principles, albeit implicitly, that aboriginal title
existed and had not been extinguished.

In the U.S. House of Representatives, the U.S. Supreme Court's decision
to hear James Peacock's appeal of the Court of Claims' decision in *Tee-Hit-
Ton Indians* had the unintended consequence of ending Wesley D'Ewart's
effort to persuade Congress to enact a statute that would have extinguished
Native aboriginal title on parsimonious terms. In 1954, D'Ewart left the
House to make an unsuccessful run for the Senate. However, in the Senate
it required, first, the in-your-face objections of James Curry and then the
senator's death to prevent Hugh Butler from achieving D'Ewart's intended
end by a more indirect means.

Angered that Congress had refused to grant the territorial legislature
that it established for Alaska in 1912 the same jurisdiction to legislate that
it had granted to other territorial legislatures, in 1916, Alaska delegate James
Wickersham introduced a bill to admit Alaska into the federal union.[218]
But none of his peers in Congress took the idea of Alaska statehood seriously. Twenty-two years later, Anthony Dimond, who in 1932 had succeeded
Wickersham as delegate, kicked off the modern statehood era in a November 1943 national radio address. He argued that the territory's residents'
service to the nation during the war proved that Alaska was ready for
statehood.[219] But his peers in Congress were as unimpressed as Wickersham's
had been, and the statehood bill[220] Dimond introduced was ignored.

Two years later, Bob Bartlett succeeded Dimond as delegate and in July
1945 reintroduced Dimond's bill.[221] This time the glacier of disinterest began to melt when in January 1946 in his first State of the Union address,
President Truman urged Congress to grant Alaska statehood as soon as the
territory's residents demonstrated their support for that change of status.

In October the support materialized when a statehood referendum passed by a vote of 9,630 to 6,822.[222] In January 1947, Bob Bartlett introduced a new statehood bill. And in April the House Committee on Public Lands Subcommittee on Territorial and Insular Possessions, of which Bartlett was a member, held hearings on the measure that marked the beginning of a bitter struggle between pro-statehood whites, most of whom were recent immigrants, and anti-statehood absentee owners of the salmon canneries that dominated what little there was of a private economy in the territory. The latter correctly believed that statehood would end their influence over the regulation of the commercial salmon fishery.[223]

From the outset of that contest, W. C. Arnold, who served as the cannery owners' lobbyist and political tactician, shrewdly invoked the unsettled status of Native land claims as an excuse for delay.[224]

In 1916, James Wickersham understood the problem and had attempted to circumvent it by including a provision in his statehood bill that required the state of Alaska to disclaim all right to lands "held by any Indian, tribe or nation." But H.R. 206, the statehood bill Bob Bartlett introduced in January 1947, contained no such disclaimer. The omission did not go unnoticed, since one of the amendments Secretary of the Interior Julius Krug sent to the subcommittee (which likely had been recommended to Krug by Felix Cohen) required the state of Alaska to disclaim all right to lands "owned or held by any Indian, Aleut, or Eskimo, hereinafter called Native, or by any Native tribes the right or title to which shall have been acquired through or from the United States or any prior sovereignty."[225]

In a display of his usual combative attitude, James Curry was less discreet:

> There is a very important omission in H.R. 206 which I assume was inadvertent [Curry informed the subcommittee]. This is the lack of any provision similar to those which are universal in the western statehood bills providing for the protection of Indian property rights.... It goes without saying that unless proper provision is made for the protection of Indian property rights the Alaska Native Brotherhood and the National Congress of American Indians, and all of the various local organizations affiliated with both central groups will be opposed to the adoption of this bill.[226]

In August, Rep. Fred Crawford of Michigan, the chairman of the subcommittee, took the panel to Alaska. At the subcommittee's hearing in Fairbanks, W. C. Arnold argued that statehood should be delayed until Native land claims were settled.

> If the Indians have any claims let's have them decided [Arnold testi-
> fied with an undoubted straight face]. If they own the country I think
> that should be determined so the rest of us can leave. But it is ridicu-
> lous for the Department of the Interior to advocate the settlement
> and colonization of Alaska and urge ex-veterans and others to come
> here as they are doing on the one hand and on the other hand to assert
> the Indian title to all of the real estate and all of the fishing grounds in
> this territory.[227]

So the struggle over the extinguishment of Native aboriginal title had again been joined.

In March 1948, Bartlett introduced a new statehood bill, H.R. 5666, that included the Native land rights disclaimer section that Secretary of the Interior Julius Krug had recommended. On March 22, Rep. Richard Welch, chairman of the House Committee on Public Lands, convened the committee to report H.R. 5666. But before he could make the motion, Rep. Wesley D'Ewart unexpectedly offered an amendment to the Native land rights disclaimer section that deleted the reference to "tribal" claims. The intended legal consequence was to allow the state of Alaska to obtain title to land colored by claims of Native aboriginal title (except for the few acres under the cabins and fish camps of individual Natives). When D'Ewart offered his amendment, Richard Welch, irritated that D'Ewart wanted to rewrite a bill that the chairman wanted sent on, removed H.R. 5666 from the committee calendar.

When he did, Bob Bartlett knew trouble when he saw it. "The Indian claims matter which I had hoped would not affect the statehood bill one way or the other has now raised its troublesome head and may offer a really controversial issue," he lamented. "It could assume proportions which might endanger the statehood bill."[228]

To try to persuade D'Ewart to withdraw his amendment, Bartlett asked Felix Cohen, who now was general counsel for the Association on American Indian Affairs, for help. Cohen obliged by writing a memorandum in which he argued that the D'Ewart amendment "would encourage and spread uncertainty" and that "uncertainty concerning property rights is probably as dangerous to the future of Alaska as uncertainty concerning rights of free speech or freedom of worship."[229] But D'Ewart was unmoved because, as he curtly explained to Cohen, he had offered his amendment to bring "this matter of Alaskan Indian rights and Indian tribal rights out into the open."[230]

In the meantime, at James Curry's direction, Frances Lopinsky mailed a letter to each Indian village in southeastern Alaska that sounded the alarm and urged that telegrams objecting to the D'Ewart amendment be wired to Bob Bartlett. And Bartlett soon was besieged with protests.

The pressure on Bartlett mounting, the matter came to a head at a meeting at which Bartlett; Alaska governor Ernest Gruening; Rep. Fred Crawford, the chairman of the Subcommittee on Territorial and Insular Possessions; and Irwin Silverman, the chief counsel of the Department of the Interior Division of Territories and Island Possessions, pressed D'Ewart to withdraw his amendment. The conservative Montana rancher responded to the arm-twisting by threatening to have H.R. 5666 held in the Committee on Public Lands until the Native land claims question had been thoroughly vetted.

Irwin Silverman saved Bob Bartlett's day by concocting a face-saving compromise. If the singular references to "Indian, Eskimo, Aleut and Native" in the disclaimer section of the bill were changed to the plural, Silverman suggested, then the D'Ewart amendment's deletion of the reference to "tribes" would not comprise the validity of village land claims.[231] "[Silverman] gave it as his legal opinion that this would satisfy the Indian position," Bartlett later explained, "and D'Ewart said it would be satisfactory to him."[232]

Unfortunately for Bartlett, the arrangement began to unravel when, as Bartlett explained in a letter written the day after the Committee on Public Lands reported H.R. 5666:

> I informed Mr. Felix S. Cohen of [Silverman's interpretation of the legal effect of the modification to the D'Ewart amendment] and asked him if he believed the situation would be taken care of adequately in that manner. His answer was in the negative, in which conclusion he was later joined by Miss Frances Lopinsky, member of the law firm of Curry, Cohen & Bingham.... Before the Public Lands Committee met, Miss Lopinsky met with Congressman D'Ewart and spent more than an hour with him urging him to accept the original language. As Miss Lopinsky told me later, she was no more successful in persuading him to do so than I and the others mentioned had been at the earlier date. So, when the bill came before the committee yesterday, Mr. D'Ewart's amendment was accepted.[233]

Among his other problems (as he explained in a private note to a friend), Bartlett worried that while "I honestly don't think that the Indian position now is imperiled, I am not so sure the Indians will agree with me. More especially, I think their attorneys here won't agree."[234] And they didn't. On behalf of the Association on American Indian Affairs, Felix Cohen at that moment was busy writing a legal memorandum that trashed the Silverman modification of the D'Ewart amendment. However, by resorting to a time-tested legislative subterfuge, Bartlett succeeded in finessing the conflict.

When a congressional committee reports a bill, it files a report that explains the text. If a bill becomes law and a dispute arises over its inter-pretation, committee reports are important evidence of congressional intent. So Bartlett arranged for the report on H.R. 5666 to explain that the Com-mittee on Public Lands intended its acceptance of the D'Ewart amendment (as modified by Irwin Silverman) to produce a result opposite to the result D'Ewart intended his amendment to accomplish. According to the report, Indian groups in the continental United States were referred to as "tribes" or "bands," but Alaska Native groups were referred to as "villages" or "com-munities."

Thus, the D'Ewart amendment was simply a technical adjustment that conformed the text of the Native land rights disclaimer section of H.R. 5666 to the proper nomenclature. With respect to the committee's intent embodied in the text of the disclaimer, the report explained that "under the provisions of this paragraph, with the recommended amendments, none of the Native groups, as well as none of the Native persons would lose any legal or equitable rights which they may now have to any lands or waters within Alaska."[235]

The misdescription accomplished its purpose. After reading it, Felix Cohen wired Bartlett from New York City that "considering committee report reasonably protects Natives I have obtained release from commit-ment [to the Association on American Indian Affairs] to submit opposing brief."[236]

> It seems likely—thank goodness!—that we shall not have to worry further about Indian claims in connection with the Alaska statehood bill [Bartlett happily wrote Don Foster, the Alaska area director of the Bureau of Indian Affairs]. The D'Ewart amendment promised to provoke plenty of trouble but by some fast footwork we inserted lan-guage in the statehood report which effectively nullified any adverse effect of that amendment. Lawyers here for the Indians have told me they consider the language in the report to be entirely satisfactory and their fears have been allayed.[237]

Bartlett's euphoria, however, was premature because Joe Martin, the Republican Speaker of the House, who opposed statehood for reasons un-related to Native land claims, refused to allow the Rules Committee, which schedules bills for consideration on the House floor, to calendar H.R. 5666 for debate. The bill died in the 80th Congress.[238]

In January 1949, when the 81st Congress convened, Bartlett introduced H.R. 331, whose text was nearly identical to that of H.R. 5666; and in March the Committee on Public Lands sent the bill to the Rules Committee, where it again was mothballed by Republicans who opposed statehood because they (correctly) believed that Alaska would elect Democratic senators and by Democrats from southern states who (also correctly) believed that Alaska's Democratic senators would vote against the South on civil rights legislation.

But in January 1950, Sam Rayburn, who had replaced Joe Martin as Speaker when the Democratic Party regained control of the House of Representatives in the 1948 congressional elections, allowed the Rules Committee to be circumvented. In March, H.R. 331 passed the House.

When the bill reached the Senate, Sen. Joseph O'Mahoney of Wyoming, the Democratic chairman of the Committee on Interior and Insular Affairs, unlike Hugh Butler, the former Republican chairman, favored statehood. O'Mahoney held hearings on the measure at which W. C. Arnold urged the Senate to reject H.R. 311 because the Native land rights disclaimer section prohibited the state of Alaska from selecting land whose title was colored by Native claims and "require[d] the people of Alaska, as a condition of statehood, to acknowledge existence of unextinguished Indian title to the very homes in which they live and to accept the state lands subject to unextinguished Native rights."[239]

When the hearings concluded, O'Mahoney instructed Sen. Clinton Anderson of New Mexico, chairman of the Committee on Interior and Insular Affairs Subcommittee on Territories and Insular Affairs, to write a bill that incorporated changes on which the senators agreed.

The new bill was denoted Print A. When James Curry obtained a copy in May, he discovered that, as W. C. Arnold had recommended, the Native land rights disclaimer section had disappeared. Bob Bartlett described what happened next: "This morning Curry called me. He is agitated by the fact that one Senate amendment took out all language pertaining to Indian rights. When I visited the committee room this afternoon Nell McSherry [a staff member] showed me one wire from him protesting this and another from an official of the American Indian Rights Association. Doubtless other wires, letters and personal communications will follow."[240] And they did.

Among the protestations Curry generated, he wrote to Bill Paul to have the ANB complain to Ernest Gruening that "if the friends of statehood that agreed on this compromise clause last year are going to withdraw from their agreement" the "Natives of Alaska should withdraw their support from the cause of statehood."[241] He also had Ruth Bronson send protests to Bartlett and Joseph O'Mahoney on behalf of the National Congress of American Indians (NCAI).

Bartlett, who had had no hand in the mischief that provoked Curry's ire, tried to spin away the problem:

> [M]y present opinion also is that the omission of the [disclaimer] clause (as in Committee Draft A) would serve at least as well as the provision in the House version, and perhaps better, to effectuate this common purpose of ours [Bartlett lamely tried to rationalize to Curry]. While language similar to that contained in the House version is included in a number of State enabling acts, it is also omitted from a number of others. It may be that this language is pure surplusage. Since the language in the House version of the Alaska statehood bill is equivocal, it might be better just to omit it.[242]

But Curry was unpersuaded, and telegrams from the Association on American Indian Affairs, the Daughters of the American Revolution, the Women's Conservation League, and individual members of the 880-member Indian Rights Association, of which Ruth Bronson was a board member, continued arriving in the committee mail room.

In June the stink Curry generated accomplished its objective when the Committee on Interior and Insular Affairs released a second draft of its statehood bill into which the Native land rights disclaimer section had been reinserted. When the uproar died down, Bartlett discovered that neither W. C. Arnold nor Hugh Butler nor any other "enemy of statehood" had arranged for the disclaimer section to be removed from Print A. Rather, as Bartlett noted to himself after meeting with Secretary of the Interior Oscar Chapman, "Oscar related something else which was of great interest to me and confirmed that which I pretty well knew but of which I had no proof. Sen. Anderson was his source of information. E. G. [Ernest Gruening] was primarily responsible for deleting in Committee Print A all reference to Indian claims."[243]

But if he thought Gruening's duplicity ill-advised, since he still was angry over Julius Krug's eleventh-hour attempt to establish reservations at Hydaburg, Barrow, and Shungnak-Kobuk, Bartlett was ready to conspire with Hugh Butler to help the Senate's most notorious "enemy of statehood" stop the secretary of the interior from establishing additional reservations. In a letter to Robert Atwood, chairman of the Alaska Statehood Committee, a pro-statehood lobby group that the territorial legislature had created in 1949, written two days before Joseph O'Mahoney convened the Senate Committee on Interior and Insular Affairs for a vote to send its statehood bill to the Senate, Bartlett confided:

> I have it on high authority that either tomorrow or subsequently on the floor of the Senate an amendment will be offered, the intent of which will be to prevent the Secretary of the Interior from creating reservations during the five-year period following admission of Alaska to the Union. Whether this amendment will pertain strictly to Native reservations I have not yet been able to determine. In any event, I am willing to applaud any such move. My information is the committee is ready to accept that amendment. I have noted this as "confidential" because I suspect if word were to leak out all the Indian rights associations would be pounding on Senate doors again.[244]

Consistent with that back-channel prediction, when the committee convened, Hugh Butler offered an amendment to revoke existing reservations and repeal the secretary of the interior's authority to establish new ones. While the amendment was not agreed to, the senators agreed to add a provision to the bill that suspended the secretary's authority to establish reservations until Congress approved the Alaska constitution.

When he learned that the committee had given Hugh Butler half his loaf, James Curry was outraged.

> Curry phoned me this morning [Bartlett advised Ernest Gruening by letter]. He said he would fight statehood with any such provision. He said the Alaska Indians won't be for statehood if it is there. He may be right. He has a powerful influence on the southeastern people. I told him that he ought not to oppose statehood on any such grounds because [Secretary of the Interior] Oscar [Chapman] has said he won't sign any more reservation orders at least until he has taken a good look at the Indian problem and, of course, that would take as long as it will to get the constitution through. Curry tipped his mitt. He admitted he wants plenty of reservations in to settle the Indian land problem, and he thinks reservations are just the ticket. He added that he didn't think statehood would be such a good thing for the Indians and perhaps they aren't so strong for it now because "political leadership"— pressed, he named Gruening and Bartlett—is against reservations, and under statehood they would have more power and thus be able to fight the reservation concept more effectively. I rather feel that the do-gooders will not prevail in this.... I told Curry over the phone that it is now revealed that he is for statehood just in the same way the salmon industry is.[245]

But even if the "do-gooders" could not prevail, they could cause trouble. On July 8, Oliver La Farge, president of the Association on American Indian Affairs, in a telegram to Joseph O'Mahoney demanded that the antireservation amendment be removed from the bill.[246] On July 10, Felix Cohen informed the Congress of Industrial Organizations (CIO) that the ANB, the NCAI, and the Indian Rights Association "have pledged themselves to a fight to the finish against this rider, even to the point of urging defeat or veto of the bill."[247]

At James Curry's urging, Harold Ickes, who was living in retirement in Maine, complained to Secretary of the Interior Oscar Chapman, Commissioner of Indian Affairs Dillon Myer, and Rep. John McCormick, the House majority leader, that the Senate statehood bill treated Alaska Natives unfairly. Jonathan Steere urged members of the Indian Rights Association to write to their senators, and Curry urged the ANB to send every senator a protest letter. On July 24, Ickes published an article in the *New Republic* that, after attacking the "sneak" antireservation amendment, urged President Truman to veto the Alaska statehood bill if the amendment was not removed.[248] On August 1 the *New York Times* and the *Washington Post* published a letter in which Eduard Lindeman, vice president of the Association on American Indian Affairs, condemned the antireservation amendment as "an out-right default in our commitment to a defenseless, non-Caucasian minority."[249]

By August 4, Bob Bartlett had had enough, and in a speech delivered from the well of the House he complained that "members of the other body are receiving many letters and many personal calls" from individuals who were making a "mountain" out of a "molehill" because Secretary of the Interior Oscar Chapman had promised that no additional reservations would be established, and therefore Hugh Butler's antireservation amendment had no practical consequence.

> These men, it seems, are willing to promise [Alaska Natives] anything [Bartlett perorated]. The end result will be disillusionment and disappointment and heartache. But the suffering which surely will follow if these advisers are followed down the bitter trail will be experienced not by those who make these tinsel promises—they do not live in Alaska and never will live there—but by all of us Alaskans, white as well as Native.[250]

Not surprisingly, the animadversion left Curry and the other members of his pro-reservation lobby unfazed. On August 14, Ruth Bronson distributed a press release that accused Bartlett of misleading Congress.[251] On August 16 and 20 the *Washington Post* published letters from Oliver La Farge and Felix Cohen that railed against the antireservation amendment.[252] And on August 30, Harold Ickes followed with his own letter.

Curry and his cadre seemed to be marching in lockstep, but unbeknownst to Bartlett, there was dissension in the ranks. Despite what Felix Cohen had told the CIO, Oliver La Farge and Cohen did not feel strongly enough about the issue to want to try to kill the Senate bill, although Curry did. As Curry argued his case to La Farge, "Our only hope of deleting the clause is to convince the friends of statehood that if the anti-reservation clause is not deleted, we will be able to alienate enough voters to defeat the bill itself."[253]

Curry's strategy was analytically sound. But his belief that it could be implemented was quixotic fantasy, since Hugh Butler had an indispensable ally: indifference. On September 19, Curry mailed to eighty senators a letter about the situation. It concluded with the query, "Would you be willing to speak in behalf of these Indians when the Alaska statehood bill is debated?"[254]

The answer was no. But Curry convinced himself that his troll had snared a large fish: Sen. John Stennis, a leader of the antistatehood southern Democrats.

On November 27 when Sen. Scott Lucas, the Democratic majority leader, moved the Senate to take up the Alaska statehood bill, Stennis and Hugh Butler began filibustering the motion. Three days later, as the talking droned on, Curry boasted by letter to Peter Nielsen, the grand treasurer of the ANB, that "Sen. Stennis of Mississippi, who is leading off for the opposition to the bill, is in full possession of our material."[255] But if he was, Stennis paid the material no mind; throughout a week of bone-numbingly boring speeches, Native land claims received next to no mention.

When Lucas wearied of the talk-a-thon and withdrew his motion, the *Anchorage Daily Times* indicted James Curry as "a backstage mastermind of the bitter Senate filibuster."[256] But the *Times* got it wrong. Curry's influence had been next to none.

However, if he was anything, Curry was vigilant. And when the 81st Congress adjourned, he sent the ANB a memorandum that identified the objectives he thought the brotherhood should pursue on Capitol Hill when the 82d Congress convened. The first item on the list was removing "the anti-reservation clause from the statehood bill."[257]

But Curry needn't have bothered, since Bob Bartlett had reasoned to the same conclusion.

> I want .... to strike in its entirety that section [of the bill] prohibiting the Secretary of the Interior from creating any reservations while the final processes regarding statehood are under way [Bartlett advised Victor Rivers, a member of the Alaska Statehood Committee, two weeks after the Alaska statehood bill died in the Senate]. The section from our standpoint is not necessary. It has been most hurtful in that it has been responsible for a heavy attack on statehood itself from many groups deeming themselves friends of the Indians, and from other liberal quarters. None of them knows what it is about, but they have been incensed by this man, James Curry.[258]

Making good on Bartlett's private word, the statehood bill, denoted S. 50, that Joseph O'Mahoney introduced in the Senate when the 82d Congress convened in January 1951, contained a Native land rights disclaimer section and made no mention of suspending the secretary of the interior's authority to establish reservations.[259] But if Bartlett and O'Mahoney had decided that another fight with Curry over an issue that was more symbolic than real was not worth the political cost, Hugh Butler still had the issue in his craw. And he soon thereafter announced his intention to offer a new antireservation amendment.[260]

When he learned of Butler's plan, James Curry sent letters to each of the senators who had cosponsored S. 50 urging them "to make sure that no clause injurious to the interests of the Natives is inserted again this year."[261] While there was no senator for whom Curry's view of the situation was consequential, Bob Bartlett considered the Butler amendment another attempt to use the controversy over Native land rights to derail statehood. With Bartlett counseling that "S. 50 now does everything it ought to do in connection with Indian land claims,"[262] the Committee on Interior and Insular Affairs rejected Hugh Butler's new amendment.

But Butler was not finished. In February 1952 when S. 50 was called up for debate on the Senate floor, the Butler-Stennis coalition of Republicans and southern Democrats that had filibustered against Alaska statehood in 1950 drove their second stake through statehood's heart by rounding up enough votes to send the bill back to the Committee on Interior and Insular Affairs.[263] Statehood seemingly suffered a third debilitating blow in November, when the Republican Party regained control of the Senate in the 1952 congressional elections; and in January 1953 when the 83d Congress convened, Hugh Butler again became chairman of the Senate Committee on Interior and Insular Affairs.

While he conceded Butler his status as "*the* Republican spokesman on many matters in Washington having to do with Alaska," Bob Bartlett had no personal use for the senator from Nebraska. He considered Butler "an obstructionist" and "holder-back" who was "against statehood no matter if he every so often piously declared to the contrary."[264] But after chairing a new round of hearings in Ketchikan, Juneau, Anchorage, and Fairbanks, Butler had a change of attitude. In 1954, Butler explained his new view of the matter to the president: "After my personal visit to Alaska last summer, I am convinced the Territory is ready for statehood, under the right kind of an enabling act."[265]

But as far as Native land claims were concerned, Hugh Butler's view remained rock hard. In 1950 when, most likely at Felix Cohen's urging, Anthony Smith, a senior official of the CIO, complained to Butler that the Native land rights disclaimer section had been omitted from Print A, the new Senate Committee on Interior and Insular Affairs Alaska statehood bill,[266] Butler had retorted that "it seems to me that it is futile to talk about developing Alaska or giving Alaska statehood until the question of the Indian claims has been settled. As they stand now, they are an almost complete barrier to the development of the resources of the Territory."[267]

Now that he was in a position to settle Native claims on his own terms, in 1954, Butler drew on his authority as chairman to ensure that the Native land rights provisions of the Alaska statehood bill that the Senate Committee on Interior and Insular Affairs Subcommittee on Territories and Insular Affairs wrote on his watch were customized to his personal specifications.

Since 1947, Butler had wanted to revoke the reservations established by Harold Ickes and Oscar Chapman. So did Ernest Gruening. But having learned the lesson that the torrent of James Curry-orchestrated protests over his and Butler's previous attempts to use the statehood bill to abrogate Native land rights had to teach, in January 1954, Gruening counseled Bob Bartlett to inform Hugh Butler of the advantages of moderation. "While I think some of the Indian reservations could be abolished I think it would be strictly most unwise," Gruening advised. "It would provoke a storm and would not in any sense be worth it."[268]

When Butler and the senators who served on the Subcommittee on Territories and Insular Affairs began writing a new statehood bill, Bartlett, whom Butler allowed to participate in the subcommittee's closed work sessions,[269] made Gruening's case. Rather than abolishing existing reservations, Butler settled for including a section that repealed the secretary of the interior's authority to establish new ones.[270]

But for Alaska Natives, that forbearance was the high-water mark.

Among other provisions, the subcommittee bill authorized the state of Alaska to select and be conveyed legal title to 100 million acres of "vacant, unappropriated and unreserved" public land. In order to, as Butler subsequently explained, "make sure that the new state is not hamstrung by a cloud on titles to [its land] grants, arising from vague and unsubstantiated Indian claims to vast areas,"[271] the subcommittee rewrote the Native land rights disclaimer section of its bill to allow the state of Alaska to select any "vacant, unappropriated and unreserved" land it wanted, other than the few acres of "real property that is owned by or, for a period of at least three years immediately prior to the enactment of this act, has been in the possession and actually in the use or occupation of any Indian, Eskimo, Aleut, ... or any community of such Natives."[272]

Finally, as Butler again subsequently explained, to afford what he pronounced would be "full justice to the Native population of the territory," the subcommittee added a section to its bill that authorized the secretary of the interior

> to issue patents to the appropriate Native tribes and villages or individuals for any lands in Alaska that have been in their possession and actually in their use or occupation, for a period of not less than three years immediately prior to the effective date of this act, for towns, villages, buildings sites, cultivated fields or gardens, hunting or fishing camps, dock or landing sites, business sites, meeting places, missionary stations, burial grounds, or other like purposes.[273]

In March 1954 when the Senate Committee on Interior and Insular Affairs reported its statehood bill to the Senate, no protest of the Native land rights provisions erupted because the Native land rights lobby had disbanded. Felix Cohen was recently dead; in May 1952 when her husband had fallen ill, Ruth Bronson had resigned as NCAI's lobbyist;[274] and the previous October, James Curry had been run off Capitol Hill.

As Bill and Fred Paul learned in 1944 when the Court of Claims dismissed the two lawsuits they had filed on behalf of the Tlingit and Haida Indians because Secretary of the Interior Harold Ickes and Commissioner of Indian Affairs John Collier refused to approve their attorney contract, the statutes that delegated to the secretary and the commissioner authority to approve contracts between attorneys and Indian tribes and groups gave the commissioner of Indian affairs nearly unfettered power to prevent attorneys he disliked from representing Indians.

When he arrived at the Bureau of Indian Affairs in May 1950, of the attorneys Commissioner of Indian Affairs Dillon Myer disliked, he most disliked—indeed, loathed—James Curry. As a consequence, when he found eight of Curry's contracts and contract extensions waiting for his signature in his in-basket, Myer left them there.[275] By September this purposeful inattention provoked Curry to complain to Frank Peratrovich that he was "running out of money" because the Bureau of Indian Affairs "is rejecting my contracts wholesale, tying up my payments under the contracts that I have, and otherwise harassing me in such a way as to deprive me of income and run me out of business altogether."[276]

The ululation was not the lament of a paranoid. Myer was the ringleader of a conspiracy, whose members included Bob Bartlett and Ernest Gruening, to destroy Curry's law practice.

In 1954, Curry would complain that he had been "practically run out of the law business" because of his "aggressive defense of Indian rights."[277] It is true that Curry's uncompromising defense of the land and other rights of Indian tribe clients, such as the Pyramid Lake Paiutes of Nevada and the Mescalero Apaches of New Mexico (stories beyond the scope of this narrative), brought the wrath of senators such as Pat McCarran of Nevada and Clinton Anderson of New Mexico (not to mention the wrath of Dillon Myer) down on his head for all of the right reasons. But much of James Curry's trouble was of James Curry's making.

Curry, whom Roy Peratrovich would remember as a "gentleman" who "never once raised his voice,"[278] was always courteous to Indian clients. But his personal relations on Capitol Hill were abysmal. According to Frances Lopinsky, her boss "didn't always use good sense. He would make such statements as that if you think somebody is an SOB it's hypocritical not to tell them so. He put it in terms of being honest. He tried that one too many times on Congressmen and Senators."[279]

When asked for his recollection, William Beckerleg, who in 1948 worked as a law clerk for Curry in San Juan, recalled that Curry "was so damn smart; so assured that he was in the right, and so well prepared that he did not have a lot of patience for anyone who was not the same."[280] And even Ruth Bronson in 1952 conceded that

> Curry has managed—almost as if he worked at it—to make himself disliked even by people who ordinarily would have been disposed to help him. I confess that I myself find Jim irksome and distressing at times, and wish that by some legerdemain he might be whisked out of the picture altogether. But he has become the center of the fight [to protect Native land rights] and the symbol. I think Curry is incorruptible, and that this is part of the grim determination to destroy him.[281]

A competent lobbyist works at establishing personal relationships with congressmen and staff members with whom his clients disagree so that he can try to educate them as to why their views on a bill are misguided. But among other transgressions made in the name of "principle," Curry publicly disparaged Hugh Butler and Albert Grorud, the Senate Committee on Interior and Insular Affairs staff member who handled Indian issues, as "Public Enemy of the Indian Number One and Public Enemy of the Indian Number Two" because they opposed establishing reservations in Alaska.[282]

So it is no surprise that, as early as 1948, Curry would complain to Felix Cohen that he and Ruth Bronson "were in danger of senatorial investigation"[283] of Bronson's solicitations of business for Curry during her trip to southeast Alaska in 1947. Nor is it a surprise that in 1952 senators who served on the Committee on Interior and Insular Affairs, Republican and Democrat alike, jumped at the chance, when Dillon Myer offered it, to organize a subcommittee to investigate allegations that Curry had unethically solicited Indian tribes as clients and, after filing claims with the Indian Claims Commission to recover compensation for his client tribes' loss of their "recognized" aboriginal titles, had sold the cases to other attorneys.

During the eleven days he testified under oath at a proceeding he accurately characterized as an "inquisition,"[284] Curry attempted to deflect the senators' ire by perjuring himself, most flagrantly by swearing that "I did not send her [Ruth Bronson] up there [to southeast Alaska in 1947] to get the contracts" that authorized him to represent the affected Tlingit and Haida villages regarding what became House Joint Resolution 205, "she went of her own volition. She was not my agent, because that would have been solicitation."[285]

Since Clinton Anderson, who chaired the subcommittee, did not subpoena Curry's and Bronson's private correspondence, that falsehood was not detected. Instead, Anderson seized on Curry's statement that he hadn't "gotten a nickel for what I did in Alaska."[286]

When Curry made it, Ernest Gruening tried to prove the statement false by submitting a letter that William Paul recently had written to Joe Williams, the grand president of the ANB, in which Paul represented that since 1947 the brotherhood and his southeast Alaska village clients had paid Curry more than $4,800.[287]

When Anderson asked Curry to explain the seeming inconsistency, Curry replied: "What I referred to when I referred to not getting a plugged nickel for what I did was just that, that I had not gotten a nickel, that every nickel I got was advanced for expenses and was spent for expenses."[288]

Hoping that he had caught the target of his inquisition in a lie, Anderson tried to close the trap by subpoenaing William Paul. Paul did not have enough money for the airplane fare, even though the subcommittee would

James Curry and Frances Lopinsky.
PHOTOGRAPH COURTESY OF FRANCES LOPINSKY HORN.

reimburse the expense. So Bob Bartlett, intoxicated by the idea of seeing the man who had caused him so much grief in the criminal dock, quietly cosigned a loan for Paul at the Behrends Bank in Juneau to enable him to make the trip.[289]

Despite the high expectation, Paul's appearance before the subcommittee was uneventful. When Anderson asked whether "you have in your possession any evidence that shows whether these payments [to Curry] were for expenses or for fees," Paul answered: "No."[290] As a consequence, Bartlett regretted his impetuosity.

> It is very apparent—and I admit it—that I was a darn fool for guaranteeing the loan [Bartlett conceded in a private letter to a friend]. My certainty as to that is much greater since his appearance before the committee. Paul flubbed out entirely. He had had a talk with Sen. Anderson prior to the session but didn't produce as he told the Senator he would. Everyone is convinced that Curry got at him through Ruth Muskrat [Bronson].[291]

So James Curry escaped both the perjury indictment he deserved and the indictment he didn't.

But even so, when the Anderson subcommittee concluded its hearings in September 1952, Curry by then had had enough. Thanks to Dillon Myer,

each year since 1950 he had been losing clients and income. And thanks to
James Curry, by September 1952 he had less than no influence with members of Congress who served on the committees that exercised jurisdiction
over Indian legislation. Further, by mid-October Curry was aware that Dillon
Myer had had what Curry later sarcastically described as a "heart-to-heart
talk" with N. B. Johnson, the president of NCAI, and Ben Dwight, a founding member of the organization's executive committee. As a consequence,
Myer had persuaded Johnson and Dwight to fire Curry as NCAI's general
counsel (which they did without affording Curry the courtesy of ever being
formally notified of his termination).[292] As Dwight summarized the case
for doing so to Johnson in a November telegram:

> [I] think it unwise to postpone any longer giving [Curry] notice of
> contract termination.... I am convinced of his desire to control NCAI
> through henchmen in order that he may direct activities principally
> for his own benefit. More specifically with reference to using NCAI
> for purpose of securing contracts. Many members of NCAI have re-
> peatedly impressed me with this fact since the Oklahoma City meeting
> and predicted that sooner or later Jim Curry would either control NCAI
> or lead it to its doom. Many members still remember how at previous
> NCAI conventions Curry would have special quarters set up to carry
> on his contract negotiations with tribal representatives present.[293]

On October 29, Curry accepted his fate and issued a press release in
which—after accusing Secretary of the Interior Oscar Chapman of operating "what amounts to a dictatorship over Indian affairs" by denying Indian
tribes the right to be represented by attorneys "unless [the] lawyers agree
to being controlled by the Department [of the Interior]"—he announced
that, while he would not terminate his existing contracts, he would no
longer accept Indian tribes and groups as clients.[294] Three months later,
when the Anderson subcommittee released the report of its investigation,
the report excoriated Curry for "by methods both open and devious" having "very actively solicited contracts for Indian legal business throughout
the United States and Alaska" in violation of the Canons of Professional
Ethics, "abus[ing] his position in [NCAI] to further his own personal ends,"
and acquiring more than thirty contracts to file claims on behalf of Indian
tribes before the Indian Claims Commission which he had "assigned or
attempted to assign ... to other attorneys while retaining for himself a
substantial portion of the fees."[295]

Was James Curry as guilty as the Anderson subcommittee charged?

While the evidence on which the subcommittee based its findings was compiled by a star chamber, a close reading of the two-thousand-page transcript of the hearings Clinton Anderson chaired indicates that each of the subcommittee's condemnations of Curry's conduct had a basis in fact. Simply put, James Curry was as much in the business of representing Indian tribes and groups in order to make what he hoped would be a lot of money (and was willing to disregard his ethical obligations as an attorney to do so) as he was committed to securing his Native American clients social and economic justice. Arthur Lazarus, looking back, years later would recall:

> Curry was going around the country collecting Indian claims contracts and then brokering them. He couldn't possibly handle the cases himself so he'd get contracts and assign them over to other counsel.... [When] he set out, he was very well-intentioned. He was abrasive, but this is not a crime. I think if he had not tried to do too much his reputation would be better. It ended up with it becoming a personal thing. The issues got lost and the personality of Jim Curry became more important.[296]

In any case, with Curry gone, Felix Cohen dead, and Ruth Bronson retired, the defense of Native land rights fell to Arthur Lazarus, the young, new general counsel of the Association on American Indian Affairs. In 1954 when Hugh Butler added his anti-Native land rights provisions to the Senate Committee on Interior and Insular Affairs Alaska statehood bill, Lazarus tried to persuade two senators with whom he had connections— Herbert Lehman of New York and Hubert Humphrey of Minnesota, neither of whom was a member of the Committee on Interior and Insular Affairs—to persuade the Senate to "reject ... the changes of wording [i.e., the anti-Native land rights provisions] made by Butler's committee."[297] But when the statehood bill was debated on the Senate floor, no mention was made—either by Lehman and Humphrey or by any other senator—of the manner in which the bill treated Native land rights.

In March 1954 the Senate attached Hugh Butler's Alaska statehood bill to a bill whose enactment would grant statehood to Hawaii, and in April passed the melded measure on to the House. There Alaska and Hawaii statehood died when the Rules Committee refused to send the bill to the floor.

The failure of the U.S. House of Representatives to pass the Hawaii-Alaska statehood bill ended Hugh Butler's effort to use the enactment of an Alaska statehood bill as a procedural occasion to clear large portions of the Alaska public domain of Native claims of aboriginal title.

In January 1955 when the 84th Congress convened, the Senate roster was radically reordered. The previous July, Butler had died at the age of seventy-six after suffering a stroke in his sleep. And the previous November, Democratic candidates had won enough seats in the 1954 congressional elections to allow the Democratic Party to regain control of the Senate. As a consequence, Henry "Scoop" Jackson, who, after serving twelve years in the U.S. House of Representatives, in 1952 had been elected to the Senate, became chairman of the Subcommittee on Territories and Insular Affairs, the panel inside the Senate Committee on Interior and Insular Affairs to which the new Democratic chairman, Sen. James Murray of Montana, assigned responsibility for writing a new Alaska statehood bill.

In February, Jackson chaired three days of hearings on a Hawaii-Alaska statehood bill, denoted S. 49, that Murray had introduced, whose text, since it was identical to that of the bill that had passed the Senate the previous April, included the language in the Native land rights disclaimer section that Hugh Butler had inserted to allow the state of Alaska to obtain legal title to land to which Alaska Natives held aboriginal title. There also was a section that repealed the secretary of the interior's authority to establish reservations and a section that authorized the secretary to convey to Alaska Natives legal title to the few acres of land "actually in their use or occupation."[298]

Since 1944, Scoop Jackson had been no friend of the idea that Alaska Natives had a legally enforceable possessory interest in vast tracts of land in Alaska. And he shared Hugh Butler's dislike of reservations.

But in 1955 when Miles Brandon, a young Eskimo who was attending night school in Washington, D.C., testified on behalf of the NCAI at the hearings that Jackson chaired on S. 49 and objected to the retention of Hugh Butler's Native land rights disclaimer section, Jackson promised Brandon to give the matter "careful consideration" because "the committee has no desire to jeopardize your rights, whatever they may be."[299] William Zimmerman, who after retiring from the Department of the Interior recently had opened a Washington, D.C., office for the Association on American Indian Affairs (which was headquartered in New York City), voiced an objection similar to Brandon's.[300] Jackson responded with a similar assurance that he intended "to keep whatever rights the Indians have in status quo."[301]

The extent to which Bob Bartlett may have influenced Scoop Jackson's change of view of the matter is not known. But in 1957 when Jackson supervised the writing of the Alaska statehood bill that the Senate Committee on Interior and Insular Affairs reported to the Senate that year, he removed both the text to which Brandon and Zimmerman objected and the other anti-Native land rights sections that Hugh Butler had written into the bill.

But even if Jackson had reneged on his promises to Brandon and Zimmerman, in 1958 and with Jackson's approval the Senate discarded Jackson's bill and in the eleventh hour of the 86th Congress passed the House of Representatives' Alaska statehood bill in its stead.

So in the end, the extent to which the Alaska Statehood Act would abrogate Native aboriginal title depended on Bob Bartlett, who exercised a pervasive influence over the House bill-writing.

In 1950 when James Curry was flooding the Senate with telegrams protesting the removal of the disclaimer section from Print A of the Senate Committee on Interior and Insular Affairs statehood bill, Bartlett had promised Curry that "the question whether the Indians have aboriginal rights should not be settled or affected in any way in the statehood bill."[302] And as he later told John Sackett that he did, Bartlett kept his word. As Frances Lopinsky would remember when asked, "He [Bartlett] always insisted that he was pro-Indian and at the time of statehood I think he showed he was" since "he really did carry the ball because he was the only one up there [on Capitol Hill] who was interested in that problem."[303]

While Lopinsky was wrong that no other members of Congress cared whether he did so, she was right that in 1955, Bartlett did indeed "carry the ball" by writing a disclaimer section into the statehood bill he introduced that year. While it authorized the state of Alaska to select and obtain title to 100 million acres of "vacant, unappropriated, and unreserved [public lands of the United States in Alaska]," the Bartlett disclaimer required the state to disavow "all right and title ... to any lands or other property (including fishing rights), the right or title to which may be held by any Indians, Eskimos, or Aleuts (hereinafter called Natives)."[304]

That was the arrangement that, with Bob Bartlett's approval and next to no mention being made of the matter, Congress enacted into law in 1958.

The week prior to the beginning of the final debate on Alaska statehood on the House floor, Arthur Lazarus privately advised La Verne Madigan, the executive director of the Association on American Indian Affairs, that whoever had written the text of the disclaimer section of the House bill had been "quite conscientious in attempting to protect the Natives" but that, in his judgment, "these efforts may be ineffective."[305] As subsequent events that neither he nor Bob Bartlett could have predicted in 1958 soon would prove, Arthur Lazarus could not have been more wrong.

Epilogue

This bill proposed by the Alaska Federation of Native Associations would force our [land] selection program to a halt in any area where a claim has been filed. Under the Statehood Act we have been allowed twenty-five years to select approximately 103 million acres of federal land as state property. We have only seventeen years left and only seventeen percent of that acreage has been selected. If Native groups continue to file claims until the entire state is blanketed, our land selection program would be completely halted.... Under this proposed bill Indian title would be given lands where they were abandoned by the Natives of Alaska involuntarily or abandoned because of lack of game or other changed conditions not under their control. What this means is that if someone hunted moose around Anchorage or Fairbanks 200 years ago or chased migratory caribou over land that no longer supports caribou grazing, a Native group could claim that land today.

ALASKA GOVERNOR WALTER J. HICKEL, February 7, 1967[1]

IN JANUARY 1955 when the question was raised at hearings the House Committee on Interior and Insular Affairs held at the beginning of the 84th Congress on the various Alaska statehood bills that had been referred to the committee, Alaska delegate Bob Bartlett, was quick to assure his colleagues—after the grief James Curry and the issue had caused him in previous Congresses—that the text of the Native land rights disclaimer section in the bills that were being given principal consideration was "completely satisfactory to the Indians, Eskimos, and Aleuts in Alaska."[2]

While Bartlett (to the limited extent that he grasped the enormity of the potential conflict) was sincere in his belief that the Alaska statehood bill should preclude the state of Alaska from obtaining legal title to land colored by Native claims of aboriginal title, in 1955 in the U.S. House of Representatives the decision no longer was exclusively his to make. Unbeknownst to Alaska Natives, they had a new advocate: Oklahoma representative Ed Edmondson.

Born and raised in Muskogee, a small town in eastern Oklahoma, the thirty-five-year-old Edmondson, who, like Bartlett, was a Democrat, had been elected to the U.S. House of Representatives in 1952 from a

429

congressional election district whose residents included more Indians per capita than any other district in a state that is known for its large Native American population. As a consequence, throughout his career in the House, Edmondson steadfastly championed the idea that Congress has a special responsibility to afford Native Americans fair treatment.

Consistent with that view, after reading the text of the Native land rights disclaimer sections of the Alaska statehood bills to which Bartlett referred him, Edmondson, an attorney by trade, was not as sanguine as Bartlett that the text precluded the state of Alaska from selecting and obtaining title to land colored by Native claims of aboriginal title. As Edmundson explained to the members of the Indian Rights Association in a speech he delivered at the association's annual meeting, held the week after Bob Bartlett had assured him there was no problem: "Some of us are gravely doubtful of the legal adequacy of this language [in the Native land rights disclaimer section], and have been seeking clarification as well as assurance of immediate machinery for doing justice to these Indian and other Native groups, in the event of statehood."[3]

Making good on that pledge, two weeks later when the members of the House Committee on Interior and Insular Affairs resumed consideration of the text of an Alaska statehood bill to recommend to the U.S. House of Representatives, Edmondson offered an amendment to, as he explained to the other members,

> establish machinery whereby notice can be given and whereby the Secretary of the Interior is required to review carefully and to exercise his discretion in the matter of the lands which are claimed by the new State of Alaska under the provisions of this statehood bill. The provision under which they will take over millions of acres in the State really provides no mechanics, to my way of thinking, under which lands which are subject of existing [Native] claims could be safeguarded and prevented from passing over to the State without any remedy whatsoever to the claimants of that land....[4]
>
> [T]his will operate, if the Secretary of the Interior is diligent in carrying out the provisions of the language, to delay the passing over to the State of lands that are subject to the disclaimer provision under the language that the bill now contains.[5]

Establishing a procedure to ensure that the policy objective announced in the Native land rights disclaimer section of the bill would be achieved made excellent sense. But not to Bob Bartlett, who objected to the amendment's adoption because "a period of years might elapse before [the Secretary of the Interior made the required] determinations." He then argued that the amendment was unnecessary because "after the [U.S.] Supreme Court decision of last week [in *Tee-Hit-Ton Indians v United States*] it follows as a matter of natural sequence that this Congress must, is obligated to, morally and otherwise, enact legislation as soon as possible to set up a mechanism for adjudication of all of those [Native land] claims."[6]

Bartlett had long wanted Congress to settle Native land claims, and indeed in 1946 he had introduced the first bill whose enactment would have done so. But he knew when he made it that his argument that the Edmondson amendment was unnecessary because Congress could be counted on to enact legislation "as soon as possible" was disingenuous.

It was true, as Bartlett argued, that after rejecting the idea that their aboriginal title was "private property" that the Fifth Amendment of the U.S. Constitution required Congress to compensate Alaska Natives to extinguish, Justice Stanley Reed had concluded his opinion in *Tee-Hit-Ton Indians* by gratuitously lecturing that "our conclusion does not uphold harshness as against tenderness toward the Indians, but it leaves with Congress, where it belongs, the policy of Indian gratuities for the termination of Indian occupancy of government-owned land rather than making compensation for its value a rigid constitutional principle."[7]

But as Bartlett privately conceded to James Peacock the week after the House Committee on Interior and Insular Affairs, on his urging, rejected the Edmondson amendment: "I entertain a very lively fear, which I am sure that you and all similarly situated will share, that the Congress is not likely now or later to demonstrate overflowing generosity in view of the fact that the Supreme Court has said that there are no rights [to compensation]."[8]

To be fair to Bartlett, after orchestrating the defeat of the Edmondson amendment (whose acceptance would have been anathema to the leaders of the statehood movement back home in Alaska), he continued to do what he could to encourage Congress to enact a Native land claims settlement bill prior to enacting the Alaska Statehood Act. To that end, in June 1956, Bartlett introduced H.R. 11986,[9] a settlement bill that James Peacock pasted together from the text of the old H.R. 1921 Committee Print 10-A.[10] However, its sponsor had no expectation that the 84th Congress would take H.R. 11986 seriously. Rather, as Bartlett informed his colleagues: "It is my hope that the executive branch of government and particularly those Departments chiefly concerned—Justice and Interior and Agriculture—will examine this proposed legislation carefully during the period of congressional adjournment so the bill may be considered should it be reintroduced, as I hope will be the case, in the 85th Congress."[11]

But despite Bartlett's urging, by 1956 the three executive branch departments had lost interest in the subject. In June 1957, Bartlett reintroduced H.R. 11986 in the 85th Congress as H.R. 8190. But despite the request of Representative Clair Engle, chairman of the House Committee on Interior and Insular Affairs, that they do so, neither the secretaries of the interior and agriculture nor the attorney general sent the committee comments on the bill.[12] And since Bartlett was preoccupied with shepherding the Alaska statehood bill through Congress, H.R. 8190 languished in a committee filing cabinet; when the 85th Congress adjourned in 1958, the bill died.

For whites in Alaska who wanted Congress to extinguish Native aboriginal title on the cheap and who opposed allowing Natives to obtain legal title to large tracts of land around their villages, not encouraging Congress to enact H.R. 8190 was an Alaska history-altering mistake, because when the forty-ninth state entered the union in 1959, the state of Alaska's land selection program found itself first gridlocked and then trumped by the conflict with Native land rights that Ed Edmondson had foreseen in 1955.

In 1961 the state filed land selection applications with the Department of the Interior Bureau of Land Management that requested the bureau to convey the state title to land near the Athabascan Indian villages of Northway, Tanacross, and Minto. Alaska Area Director of the Bureau of Indian Affairs James Hawkins (at the likely suggestion of La Verne Madigan, the executive director of the Association on American Indian Affairs, who probably passed along the advice of Arthur Lazarus) filed protests on behalf of the three villages with the Bureau of Land Management office in Fairbanks. In March 1962, Madigan reported the consequence to her board: "The filing of these protests was one of Jim Hawkins' last official acts as Superintendent [i.e., area director] at Juneau [before being transferred to Minnesota]. The blocking of State selections caused an uproar in Alaska, and great political pressure was put on the Department."[13]

When the Fairbanks office rejected the protests, the Bureau of Indian Affairs appealed the rejection to the director of the Bureau of Land Management in Washington, D.C. When the paperwork reached the director's desk, Assistant Secretary of the Interior John Carver, who supervised both the Bureau of Land Management and the Bureau of Indian Affairs, ordered the Northway, Tanacross, and Minto appeals sent to his office,[14] where Newton Edwards, Carver's special assistant, cached them in a drawer in his filing cabinet.

And there the Northway, Tanacross, and Minto appeals and every other appeal of every other protest the Association on American Indian Affairs and the Bureau of Indian Affairs assisted Native villages to file to prevent the Bureau of Land Management from processing state land selection applications stayed. Years later, Arthur Lazarus would recall Edwards's unheralded contribution to the story of Alaska Natives and their land:

> I've always thought Newton Edwards was one of the unsung heroes. All those appeals [of Bureau of Land Management Alaska office rejections of village protests of state land selection applications] came to Newt and he put them in a drawer.... He was a good civil servant, but on this one thing he was sympathetic and he knew that the decision, if a decision was coming down, was going to be adverse to the Natives. So he just put all these things in a drawer.... What I got from Newt was that that was his way of handling this problem and no one upstairs was telling him that he had to get these things done.[15]

By 1965 state land selection applications that requested the conveyance of 3.25 million acres of land had been consigned by Newton Edwards to a seemingly perpetual purgatory.[16] If, for the state of Alaska, that bureaucratic calamity was not bad enough, in response to a request from Alaska Natives (who in October 1966 had assembled in Anchorage for the first statewide meeting of Alaska Native leaders in Alaska history) that he do so, in December 1966, Secretary of the Interior Stewart Udall canceled a Department of the Interior oil and gas lease sale that had been scheduled for public land near the Inupiaq village of Point Hope in the northwest Arctic "pending further consideration of protests which have been received."[17] Since the Alaska Statehood Act required the Department of the Interior to pay the state 90 percent of the proceeds that oil companies would have paid for the privilege of obtaining the leases, the cancellation was more revenue lost to the state treasury.

The die now cast, Udall, who was personally sympathetic to the need to protect Native land rights, within months expanded his decision to cancel the Point Hope lease sale into an informal statewide freeze on oil and gas leasing and all other uses of public land in Alaska. And in December 1968 on his way out of office the month after the presidential election that sent Richard Nixon to the White House, Udall made the informal freeze official by announcing that he intended to sign a public land order that in January withdrew 262 million acres of "unreserved public lands in Alaska" from selection by the state of Alaska, as well as "all forms of appropriation and disposition under the public land laws" so that the land would be available "for the determination and protection of the rights of the native Aleuts, Eskimos, and Indians of Alaska."[18]

But for the state of Alaska, there still was no end to the torment.

In March 1970, Athabascan Indians living in five interior Alaska villages filed a lawsuit in the U.S. district court for the District of Columbia that requested the court to prohibit former Alaska governor Walter J. Hickel, who had succeeded Udall as secretary of the interior, from issuing a right-of-way permit to authorize construction of the Trans-Alaska Oil Pipeline across land colored by Indian claims of aboriginal title. The pipeline was needed to move oil from Prudhoe Bay, the largest oil field in North America, which recently had been discovered on state land on the coast of the Arctic Ocean east of Barrow, to tidewater. On April Fool's Day, U.S. District Court Judge George Hart issued the injunction.

As a consequence of the lock-down, Congress in 1971 enacted the Alaska Native Claims Settlement Act (known as ANCSA) to end the Udall land freeze and open the Alaska public domain to selection by the state of Alaska and to leasing and other entries under the public land laws, including entry for construction of the Trans-Alaska Oil Pipeline. ANCSA did so by extinguishing Alaska Native aboriginal title in exchange for compensation that, had it been suggested in the 1940s and 1950s, Hugh Butler would have thought outrageous and Felix Cohen, James Curry, and William Paul would have thought beyond belief.

ANCSA authorized Alaska Natives to be paid $962.5 million.* And it authorized Natives to be conveyed legal title to forty-four million acres of land, principally around their villages, although Congress required most of the money to be managed by, and title to most of the land to be conveyed to, state of Alaska-chartered business corporations that ANCSA required Natives living in each village and within each of twelve geographic regions to organize.

---

* In 1949, James Curry brokered the lawsuit that he had filed in 1947 in the Court of Claims on behalf of the Tlingit and Haida Indians to Washington, D.C., attorneys I. S. Weissbrodt and David Cobb. Weissbrodt litigated the case to a conclusion, and in 1968 the court awarded $7.5 million as compensation for the extinguishment of aboriginal title (which the 1935 Act that authorized the lawsuit had "recognized") within the Tongass National Forest and elsewhere in southeast Alaska. Because the amount of compensation was de minimis, at the request of the Tlingit-Haida Central Council, the Alaska Federation of Natives Board of Directors soon thereafter agreed to include the Indians of southeast Alaska in the statewide land claims settlement the federation was lobbying Congress to enact. As a consequence and because Congress divided the monetary portion of the ANCSA settlement per capita, the Tlingit and Haida Indians—the most populous Native group in Alaska—received $206.5 million, 21.5 percent of the monetary portion of the settlement.

How it all happened is another very long story. But mention should be made of one important connection to this story of Alaska Natives and their land: William Paul not only lived to see it happen but had a consequential influence on the outcome.

In 1955, Fred Paul decided to try to have his seventy-year-old father reinstated to the bar. After settling accounts with the Indian fishermen at Kake (whose wages he had pocketed in 1930), in 1958, William Paul, represented by his attorney, Fred Paul, petitioned the Alaska Bar Association for reinstatement. Prior to the hearing the board of governors held on the petition, Fred asked Roy Peratrovich to testify as a character witness, but Peratrovich declined, telling Fred: "Your Dad hasn't changed."[19] Fred then recruited Walter Soboleff, a Presbyterian minister and one of the most respected Indians in southeast Alaska, and Arthur Johnson, one of the Kake fishermen his father had cheated. But as Fred later described it, the hearing was a "disaster."[20]

First, Norman Banfield, a Juneau attorney and longtime William Paul adversary, passed along to the board that several Indian clients had told him about recent "shenanigans" in which Paul had been involved "in his Native politics trying to get himself an office" (in 1955 Paul had been elected grand president of the Alaska Native Brotherhood (ANB) for the first time since 1929) and then volunteered that "the Native people that I know of, they seem to feel, the educated ones particularly, that this wouldn't be a good thing to admit him to the bar."[21] Then Arthur Johnson was nowhere to be found, and while Walter Soboleff did testify, his unenthusiastic vouching of Paul's integrity as "okay" was damning.[22] The board denied the petition for reinstatement.[23]

But Fred Paul filed a motion for reconsideration, and eight months later, on January 22, 1959, by a vote of 5 to 3, the board relented.[24] When asked years later, one of the board members who voted no recalled that the members who voted yes did so not because they thought that Paul had not been disbarred for cause. Rather, they rationalized that his reinstatement would be more symbolic than real, since Paul, who by then was seventy-three, was too old to practice law.

But they did not know their man. Throughout his long life, William Paul was an indefatigable pedagogue who, when he visited Sitka during the late 1950s and early 1960s, would lecture on Native land rights to high school students at the Sheldon Jackson School and at Mount Edgecumbe, a boarding high school the Bureau of Indian Affairs opened in 1947 in an abandoned navy installation on a small island a short distance across the water from the old Sitka Indian village.

One Edgecumbe student who fell under Paul's influence was Charles Edwardsen, Jr., a young Inupiaq from Barrow, who, when asked years later, would fondly remember Paul as "a good friend of mine."[25] Paul opened his library and archive to the inquisitive teenager, who eagerly read through the old man's voluminous files on the Tlingit-Haida Court of Claims lawsuit.

Charlie Edwardsen graduated from Mount Edgecumbe High School in 1962, after which, desultory and disorganized and too often drunk, in quick order he enrolled at the University of Alaska, dropped out, moved to Metlakatla to briefly marry a Tsimshian Indian girl, spent the summer of 1963 in southeast Alaska commercial fishing, enrolled and dropped out of a program RCA operated in New Jersey to train Natives as electronic technicians, hitchhiked to the Democratic National Convention at Atlantic City, and by 1964 was back in Barrow.

At Edgecumbe, when he read Hubert Howe Bancroft's *History of Alaska*,[26] Edwardsen had stumbled on a paragraph in which Bancroft attributed the army's problems in southeast Alaska to the Tlingit and Haida Indians' resentment that the czar had sold their land to the United States "without their consent."[27] Bancroft's spin on Alaska history caused the young Eskimo to ask himself whether the United States really "owned" the tens of millions of acres of tundra on which the Inupiat at Barrow and elsewhere on Alaska's north slope hunted and trapped and gathered.

By December 1965 the idea had so piqued the twenty-two-year-old Edwardsen's interest that he wrote a letter to each north slope village, soliciting support for creating an organization to file a land claim that would assert Inupiaq aboriginal title to every acre of land north of the Brooks Mountain Range.[28] The idea met with an immediate positive response, and on January 5, Edwardsen wrote William Paul from Barrow that "we are in the process of organizing a Native association composed of the Eskimo people of the northern slope of the Brooks range in Alaska with the express intent of securing in court our aboriginal rights and title to said land.... We wish your advice and counsel in the matter and will want you to act as attorney for the group."[29]

Paul immediately took up Edwardsen's and the Inupiaq cause and on behalf of the "North Slope Native Association" on January 18 notified the Department of Interior Bureau of Land Management that his new client—which would be renamed the Arctic Slope Native Association—asserted aboriginal title to 60 million acres of land north of the Brooks Mountain Range.[30] Paul doing so set in motion the chain of events that in December would result in Secretary of the Interior Stewart Udall's canceling the Point Hope oil and gas lease sale and imposing his informal land freeze.

In April 1967 representatives of the Arctic Slope Native Association and other Native associations that, since 1962, had begun to be organized in other regions of Alaska founded the Alaska Federation of Natives, a statewide Native organization, headquartered in Anchorage, whose principal mission was to lobby Congress to enact a statute that would extinguish Native aboriginal title on terms that the new generation of Native leaders that was coming of age thought fair.

By 1970 the terms that the federation thought fair included a forty-million acre land grant, a demand that the chairmen of the Senate and

William Paul (left), Alex Shadura, executive director of the Kenai Native Association (middle), and John Westdahl, a Yup'ik Eskimo member of the Alaska House of Representatives (right), at a February 6, 1968 meeting of the Alaska Federation of Natives in Anchorage, Alaska. The purpose of the meeting was to discuss the Native land claims settlement bill the Hickel Alaska Native Claims Task Force presented to the Senate Committee on Interior and Insular Affairs at the field hearing on that subject the Committee held in Anchorage on February 8, 1968.
TUNDRA TIMES, ANCHORAGE, ALASKA.

House Committees on Interior and Insular Affairs, which exercised legislative jurisdiction over Native claims settlement legislation, considered patent nonsense, until April 1971, when President Richard Nixon committed his administration to a forty-million-acre land settlement.

Why Richard Nixon championed the Native cause in a struggle with Congress that, without his support, the Alaska Federation of Natives had no chance of winning is a central part of the story of the enactment of ANCSA that is told in *Take My Land, Take My Life*, the companion volume. What can be said here is that the president's support for a 40-million-acre settlement would not have

William Paul in 1972 at age 87.
PHOTOGRAPH BY PETER LIDDELL,
COPYRIGHT © 1972, SEATTLE TIMES.

occurred if a majority of the rank-and-file delegates who attended the 1970 Alaska Federation of Natives convention had not cast a vote of no confidence in their leaders and their attorneys—a group of lawyers that included former U.S. Supreme Court justice Arthur Goldberg and former U.S. attorney general Ramsey Clark—by electing a forty-one-year-old Athabascan Indian named Don Wright as president of the federation.

Over the next fourteen months, Don Wright, abrasive, fractious, and socially rough around the edges, would be the right man serving in the right job at the right moment to bring the quarter-century struggle to settle Native land claims to a conclusion of historic consequence. And the man who taught Don Wright his Native land claims politics was William Paul.

Wright first met Paul in Juneau during the early 1960s. But the two men didn't get to know each other until 1967, when Wright and Paul began attending Alaska Federation of Natives board meetings—Wright as president of the Cook Inlet Native Association, which had been organized by

Natives living in Anchorage, and Paul as grand president emeritus of the ANB.

"He was basically without funds for a hotel or food in Anchorage, so I invited him into my home," Wright remembered, recounting how he, like Charlie Edwardsen, came under the influence. And once ensconced in a spare bedroom, the octogenarian occasionally stayed for months.

> He brought his lawyer's satchels full of papers [Wright recalled of his tutelage]. And every day William Paul and I sat at my kitchen table, sometimes from three o'clock in the morning, sometimes four, and discussed the issues prior to me going to meetings at eight o'clock or nine or whenever they were. He tutored me. I took what he had to offer and [in December 1967 and January 1968] I presented it to the [Alaska governor] Hickel land claims task force [of which Wright was a member]. I presented it to Ed Boyko, the [Alaska] attorney general. And I presented it when I came in contact with Ed Weinberg and Arthur Goldberg and Sen. Kuchel and Ramsey Clark. I have to give him high high credit for my education in legal and technical terms, to the point that when I went to Washington, D.C., they thought I was an attorney. And I was not. I was just a high school graduate. A lot of people, including his own sons, felt that he was eccentric and overbearing, and possibly some people thought he was senile. But he was not. He was a prince of a man.[31]

When President Richard Nixon signed the Alaska Native Claims Settlement Act into law on December 18, 1971, William Paul was eighty-six years old. And true to form, when he heard the news, he was disgruntled. "He thought the United States in the claims Act had stolen ninety percent of our land. That's a quote," Fred Paul would remember of his father's reaction. "He was entirely unhappy with it. And unhappy with his lack of influence in the settlement process."[32]

William Paul lived another six years, dying of a heart attack in Seattle, Washington, on March 4, 1977, at the age of ninety-one. When he did, Alaska Natives, busy running their corporations and their villages beset with social and economic problems that a land and monetary settlement twice the size of ANCSA would not have alleviated, paid little mind to the passing of the man who was their most important link to their historic past.

Today a new generation of Alaska Natives, for whom the name William Paul means nothing and who know nothing of the story of the settlement of Native land claims, increasingly disparage ANCSA for extinguishing Native aboriginal title on parsimonious terms. Increasingly bitterly, they rhetorically shake their fists at ANCSA village and regional corporations whose unannounced purpose, they are sure, is to hasten the destruction of traditional Native cultures by forcing Natives who sit on their boards and who own their stock to think about the world and their place in it and to make decisions regarding the commercial development of natural resources located on corporation land, in ways to which they would not otherwise be inclined. Hopefully, this story of Alaska Natives and their land may engender a reassessment of both misconceptions.

Notes

ABBREVIATIONS

AD	Anthony Dimond Papers
AL	Arthur Lazarus Papers
APA	Alaska Packers Association Records
BB	E. L. "Bob" Bartlett Papers
CC	Clark Clifford Papers
CW	Curry-Weissbrodt Papers
EEA	Edward E. Ayer Papers
EG	Ernest Gruening Papers
EWA	Edward W. Allen Papers
FSC	Felix S. Cohen Papers
HB	Hugh Butler Papers
HI	Harold Ickes Papers
HMJ	Henry M. Jackson Papers
HST	Harry Truman Official Files
IRA	Indian Rights Association Papers
JC	James Curry Papers
JK	Julius Krug Papers
PHS	Presbyterian Historical Society Records
PN	Philleo Nash Papers
RHP	Richard Henry Pratt Papers
SJ	Sheldon Jackson Papers
WG	Warner Gardner Papers
WOD	William O. Douglas Papers
WP	William Paul Papers

INTRODUCTION (PAGES 1–23)

1. This description of Bering's first and second expeditions to North America is drawn from Bancroft, *History of Alaska*, 35–74, and Fisher, *Bering's Voyages*. The accounts differ in minor detail, the most significant being the question of how the mate, Dementief, signaled to the *St. Paul* when he reached the shore of Kruzof Island. Bancroft bases his assertion that Dementief fired his musket to confirm that he had reached shore on statements in Chirikov's journal. Fisher states that after Dementief's longboat disappeared from view no prearranged signal was given and nothing more was heard from the landing party.

2. U.S. Department of the Interior, *Final Environmental Impact Statement*, 48–49.

3. According to Tlingit oral historian Mark Jacobs Jr., Dementief and the other members of Chirikov's longboat crews were not captured by hostile Tlingits. Rather, they refused to return to the *St. Paul* because the conditions on board ship on the voyage east had been intolerable and they feared that the *St. Paul* would wreck in the North Pacific on the voyage west to Kamchatka. According to Jacobs, the crewmen were accepted by the Tlingits, married local women, and eventually moved to Prince of Wales Island, where "their offspring became some of the more prominent families in the village of Klawock." Pierce, *Russia in North America*, 2–3.

4. Institute of Social, Economic and Government Research, 4, table 1.

5. Sherwood, 5, 140–41.

6. Clark.

7. Deloria.

8. Abernathy, 7–10, 38.

9. Fourteen of the fifty-five delegates who attended the Constitutional Convention of 1787 held speculative interests in western lands at the time they drafted the U.S. Constitution. In addition to George Washington and Benjamin Franklin, the group included Elbridge Gerry, Alexander Hamilton, George Mason, and Robert Morris. Beard, 95–151.

10. Fitzpatrick, 26:139.

11. *Journals of the Continental Congress*, 25:602.

12. Kappler, 5–18.

13. Prucha, *American Indian Policy in the Formative Years*, 39.

14. *Statutes at Large 1*, 137 (1790).

15. Kappler, 18–50.

16. Fitzpatrick, 33:160.

17. *Statutes at Large 1*, 443 (1795); Prucha, *Sword of the Republic*, 206.

18. *Statutes at Large 1*, 452 (1796).

19. Peake, passim.

20. Thomas Jefferson's factory policy also is worth mention. Jefferson, who was elected president in 1800, was an enthusiastic supporter of the factory system. Concerned that the Indians were growing "uneasy at the constant diminution of the territory they occupy," in 1803 he urged Congress to "multiply trading houses among them, and place within their reach those things which will contribute more to their domestic comfort than the possession of extensive but uncultivated wilds. Experience and reflection will develop to them the wisdom of exchanging what they can spare and we want for what we can spare and they want" (Richardson, 1:352). To assist Indians develop the requisite "experience and reflection," Jefferson modified factory policy in an important respect. While Washington prohibited his factory managers to extend credit, Jefferson ordered his managers to encourage Indians to take on as much debt as they were willing to assume. As he explained the plan in 1803 to William Henry Harrison, the Governor of Indiana Territory: "To promote [the Indians'] disposition to exchange lands, which they have to spare and we want, for necessaries, which we have to spare and they want, we shall push our trading uses, and be glad to see the good and influential individuals among them run in debt, because we observe that when these debts get beyond what the individuals can pay, they become willing to lop them off by a cession of lands" (Lipscomb and Bergh, 10:370).

21. Fitzpatrick, 34:391.

22. Porter, 709.

23. Ibid., 712.

24. Smith, 80.

25. Ibid., 82.

26. Porter, 725–27.

1. SOLDIERS (PAGES 25–64)

1. National Archives, "Instructions to General Jefferson Davis from General Halleck, the Commander of the Military Division of the Pacific, upon assuming Jurisdiction of Alaska," September 6, 1867, Record Group 393 (hereafter cited as RG).

2. "Isaac Dennis to *Puget Sound Argus*," October 31, 1877, in S. Exec. Doc. 59, 45th Cong. 3d Sess. 153 (1879).

3. Richard Pierce to author, October 25, 1994. According to Dr. Pierce, a distinguished historian and expert on Russian America, one of the few Russian articles that has been published about the ownership of the Russian-American Company identifies the czar as a shareholder in 1805.

4.   Tikhmenev, 244.

5.   Konstantin to Gorchakov, April 3, 1857, in D. H. Miller, 38.

6.   Pierce, *Russia in North America*, 196.

7.   D. H. Miller, 62.

8.   *Cong. Globe* 1973–76 (1852); *Statutes at Large 10,* 100, 104 (1852).

9.   Seward, 346.

10. Holbo, 36–58.

11. Utley, 173.

12. Instructions from Major General H. W. Halleck to Brevet Lieutenant Colonel R. N. Scott, September 3, 1867, in *Alaska Boundary Tribunal*, 347.

13. Colonel Scott's Report on the Indians, 1867, November 12, 1867, in *Alaska Boundary Tribunal*, 348.

14. Fry, 497.

15. Ibid.

16. National Archives, General Jefferson Davis to Adjutant General, January 4, 1866, RG 94.

17. Fry, 486–91.

18. Ibid., 492.

19. National Archives, General Jefferson Davis to Adjutant General, January 4, 1866, RG 94.

20. Fry, 493.

21. National Archives, General Jefferson Davis to Adjutant General, January 4, 1866, RG 94.

22. Sherman, 411.

23. Ibid., 724–25.

24. Howard, *Autobiography of Oliver Otis Howard*, 2:290.

25. Ludecke.

26. Mariette Davis to My Dear H, October 21, 1867, EEA.

27. U.S. Army, Alaska, 5.

28. Ibid., 6–7.

29. National Archives, General Jefferson Davis to Assistant Adjutant General, Military Division of the Pacific, October 25, 1869, RG 393.

30. Berkh, 87.

31. Gibson, 155.

32. Berkh, 89–90.

33. Gibson, 158.

34. Bancroft, *History of Alaska*, 321–22.

35. Gibson, 159.

36. Khlebnikov, *Baranof*, 29.

37. Schumacher.

38. Kuskov to Baranof, July 1, 1802, in Richard A. Pierce, *Documents on the History of the Russian-American Company*, 128–29.

39. Ibid., 144.

40. Bancroft, *History of Alaska*, 413.

41. Khlebnikov, *Baranof*, 48.

42. Lisiansky, 162.

43. Arnold, 11.

44. Ibid., 12.

45. Richard A. Pierce, *Documents*, 144.

46. Lisiansky, 166.

47. Arndt, 36.

48. Khlebnikov, *Colonial Russian America*, 4–5.

49. Tikhmenev (1978), 154.

50. Ibid., 157.

51. Ibid., 174.

52. Khlebnikov, *Colonial Russian America*, 55.

53. Chevigny, 174.

54. Khlebnikov, *Colonial Russian America*, 102.

55. Ibid., 101.

56. Ibid., 68.

57. Ibid., 70.

58. Ibid., 71.

59. Tikhmenev (1978), 353.

60. Golovin, *The End of Russian America*, 27.

61. Ibid., 28.

62. Ibid., 29.

63. Golovin, *Civil and Savage Encounters*, 84–85.

64. Tikhmenev (1978), 99.

65. Bancroft, *History of Alaska*, 572–74.

66. Michael, 96–97.

67. Ibid., 97.

68. Tikhmenev (1978), 184–85.

69. Bancroft, *History of Alaska*, 89.

70. Ibid., 88.

71. Ibid., 95.

72. Berkh, 4–5.

73. Ibid., 15.

74. Ibid., 24–25.

75. Ibid., 41–42.

76. Lamar, 561.

77. Drinnon, *Facing West*, 329.

78. National Archives, Instructions to General Jefferson Davis from General Halleck, the Commander of the Military Division of the Pacific, upon assuming Jurisdiction of Alaska, September 6, 1867, RG 393.

79. Ibid.

80. De Armond, *Lady Franklin Visits Sitka*, 44.

81. National Archives, General Jefferson Davis to General J. P. Sherburne, November 5, 1867, RG 393.

82. National Archives, General Jefferson Davis to General J. P. Sherburne, November 12, 1867, RG 393.

83. Report from F. K. Louthan on the Indian Tribes of Alaska, October 28, 1869 (hereafter Louthan), in H. Exec. Doc. 1, 41st Cong. 2d Sess. Pt. 3, 1014 (1870).

84. De Armond, *Lady Franklin Visits Sitka*, 12.

85. Report of the Board of Officers Assigned to Investigate the Homicide Committed by James Parker, April 5, 1869, in H. Exec. Doc. 1, 41st Cong. 2d Sess. Pt. 3, 1051 (1870).

86. Report of the Honorable Vincent Colyer, United States Special Indian Commissioner, on the Indian Tribes and Their Surroundings in Alaska Territory, from Personal Observation and Inspection in 1869, November 1869, in H. Exec. Doc. 1, 41st Cong. 2d Sess. Pt. 3, 982 (1870).

87. National Archives, Captain George Brady to Captain P. B. McIntire, December 16, 1869, RG 393.

88. S. Exec. Doc. 67, 41st Cong. 2d Sess. 1 (1870).

89. National Archives, Lieutenant Colonel Charles Tompkins to Lieutenant Colonel G. K. Brady, April 3, 1870, RG 393.

90. Dr. Tonner's Report on Sanitary Condition of the Sitka Indians and Their Village, October 20, 1869, in H. Exec. Doc. 1, 41st Cong. 2d Sess. Pt. 3, 1024 (1870).

91. Statement of soldier in the *St. Louis Globe*, EEA.

92. Louthan, 1014.

93. Ibid., 1051.

94. Andrews, 136.

95. National Archives, General Jefferson Davis to General James Fry, March 3, 1869, RG 393.

96. Ibid.

97. Louthan, 1015.

98. Ibid.

99. Letter from William S. Dodge, Ex-Mayor of Sitka, on Affairs in Alaska Generally, November 10, 1869, in H. Exec. Doc. 1, 41st Cong. 2d Sess. Pt. 3, 1031 (1870).

100. Bancroft, *History of Alaska*, 555–56.

101. Ibid., 558.

102. Ibid., 558–59.

103. Howard, *Famous Indian Chiefs*, 171.

104. National Archives, Report of Lieutenant D. A. Lyle on Wrangell Post, January 27, 1871, RG 393.

105. William Tamaree, "Tragedy Marred First Christmas Eve for Wrangell Indians," *Wrangell Sentinel*, May 31, 1940.

106. The following accounts of events are drawn from the reports of First Lieutenant W. Borrowe, First Lieutenant M. R. Loucks, and General Jefferson Davis, in S. Exec. Doc. 67, 41st Cong. 2d Sess. (1870).

107. Coffman, 215–20.

108. U.S. Army, Alaska, 13–14.

109. See generally National Archives, RG 94.

110. Bancroft, *History of British Columbia*, 561.

111. Report of Major John C. Tidball, December 20, 1870, in H. Exec. Doc. 5, 42d Cong. 1st Sess. 11 (1871).

112. National Archives, General Jefferson Davis to Major J. P. Sherburne, November 5, 1867, RG 393.

113. *Statutes at Large 15*, 240 (1868).

114. General Order No. 1, Headquarters Military Division of the Pacific, April 23, 1877, in *Alaska Boundary Tribunal*, 346.

115. Report of Captain J. W. White, U.S. Revenue Marine, August 12, 1877, in S. Exec. Doc. 59, 45th Cong. 3d Sess. 128 (1879).

116. Report of General O. O. Howard, June 30, 1875, in S. Exec. Doc. 12, 44th Cong. 1st Sess. 6 (1876).

117. William Gouverneur Morris to Department of the Treasury, July 23, 1877, in S. Exec. Doc. 59, 45th Cong. 3d Sess. 27 (1879).

118. William Gouverneur Morris to Department of the Treasury, July 28, 1877, in S. Exec. Doc. 59, 45th Cong. 3d Sess. 31 (1879).

119. Captain J. M. Seldon to Secretary of the Treasury John Sherman, October 18, 1877, in S. Exec. Doc. 59, 45th Cong. 3d Sess. 128 (1879).

120. Ibid., 129–30.

121. See obituary, "Noted Alaska Indian Woman Dies at Sitka," *Daily Alaska Empire*, March 16, 1931.

122. This account is drawn from Sherwood, "Ardent Spirits," 301–44.

123. Destroying of Angoon: Statement of Billy Jones, Chief of the Da-shi-ton Tribe, November 9, 1951, CW.

124. William Gouverneur Morris to Secretary of the Treasury Charles J. Folger, October 28, 1882, in H. Exec. Doc. 9, 47th Cong. 2d Sess., Pt. 2, 2 (1882).

2. MISSIONARIES (PAGES 65–110)

1. Memorandum: Education in Alaska, February 1880, SJ.

2. Young, 77.

3. The following biography of Sheldon Jackson prior to his first trip to Alaska in 1877 is drawn principally from Stewart, passim.

4. Murray, *The Skyline Synod*, 11.

5. Bailey, 77–78.

6. Richard Henry Pratt to Senator M. S. Quay, February 20, 1899, RHP.

7. Bailey, 69.

8. Ibid., 87.

9. Tikhmenev (1979), 36; Kovach, 57.

10. Veniaminov, 235.

11. Starr, 165.

12. Rezanov to the Directors of the Russian-American Company, November 6, 1805, in Tikhmenev (1979), 167.

13. Kovach, 132.

14. Golovin, *End of Russian America*, 25.

15. Golovin, *Civil and Savage Encounters*, 81.

16. Ibid., 129.

17. Ibid.

18. Golovin, *End of Russian America*, 53.

19. Ibid., 54, 56.

20. Dewey, 3.

21. Illich, 54.

22. Golovin, *End of Russian America*, 60.

23. S. Rept. 156, 39th Cong. 2d Sess. 5–6 (1867).

24. H. Exec. Doc. 1, 43rd Cong. 1st Sess. Pt. 5, i–iv (1873).

25. Ibid., vii.

26. Report of the Honorable Vincent Colyer, United States Special Indian Commissioner, on the Indian Tribes and Their Surroundings in Alaska Territory, from Personal Observation and Inspection in 1869, H. Exec. Doc. 1, 41st Cong. 2d Sess. Pt. 3, 1001 (1870).

27. Ibid., 994.

28. Ibid., 987.

29. Ibid., 1001.

30. Ibid., 1004.

31. *Statutes at Large 16*, 359 (1870).

32. F. A. Walker to Columbus Delano, March 14, 1872, in H. Exec. Doc. 197, 42d Cong. 2d Sess. 2–4 (1872).

33. Felix R. Brunot to Columbus Delano, February 14, 1872, in H. Exec. Doc. 197, 42d Cong. 2d Sess. 7 (1872).

34. F. A. Walker to Columbus Delano, March 14, 1872, in H. Exec. Doc. 197, 42d Cong. 2d Sess. 35 (1872).

35. Ibid.

36. Columbus Delano to the Speaker of the House, March 16, 1872, H. Exec. Doc. 197, 42d Cong. 2d Sess. 1–2 (1872).

37. Board of Indian Commissioners, *1872 Report*, 136.

38. *Statutes at Large 17*, 189 (1872).

39. Jackson, *Alaska*, 130.

40. Ibid., 131.

41. This account of the beginning of Clah's missionary work at Wrangell is based on Crosby, 165–71.

42. Holt.

43. E. N. Condit (n.d.), *Missions under Presbytery of Oregon*, S. Exec. Doc. 59, 45th Cong. 3d Sess. 77 (1879).

44. Stewart, 295.

45. Ibid., 299.

46. Jackson, *Alaska*, 143.

47. Hayes, 15.

48. Jackson, *Alaska*, 144.

49. Jackson, *Report on Education in Alaska*, 82.

50. McFarland to Jackson, December 10, 1877, in McFarland (June 1956), 95.

51. Ibid., February 12, 1878, in McFarland (December 1956), 228.

52.   Ibid., 228–29.

53.   Ibid., September 3, 1878, in McFarland (March 1957), 50.

54.   Ibid., 51.

55.   Ibid., October 17, 1878, in McFarland (March 1957), 53.

56.   Jackson, *Alaska*, 220.

57.   Ibid., 221.

58.   Stewart, 320–25.

59.   Board of Indian Commissioners, *1879 Report*, 91.

60.   Kendall to Schurz, December 10, 1877, in S. Exec. Doc. 30, 47th Cong. 1st Sess. 18–19 (1881).

61.   Kendall and Jackson to Schurz, October 15, 1879, in S. Exec. Doc. 30, 47th Cong. 1st Sess. 19–20 (1881).

62.   Schurz to Kendall and Jackson, December 1, 1879, in S. Exec. Doc. 30, 47th Cong. 1st Sess. 20 (1881).

63.   Hinckley, *The Americanization of Alaska*, 144.

64.   Jackson and Lanahan, *A Memorial to the Honorable Senate and House of Representatives of the United States of America in Congress Assembled*, in S. Exec. Doc. 30, 47th Cong. 1st Sess. 21 (1881).

65.   Board of Indian Commissioners, *1879 Report*, 95.

66.   Jackson to members of Congress, January 24, 1880, SJ.

67.   10 *Cong. Rec.* 596 (1880).

68.   Ibid., 644.

69.   S. Exec. Doc. 30, 47th Cong. 1st Sess. 21 (1881).

70.   Sheldon Jackson to James Bailey, March 15, 1880, in S. Exec. Doc. 30, 47th Cong. 1st Sess. 21 (1881).

71.   Memorandum: Education in Alaska, February 1880, SJ.

72.   Cohen, 28.

73.   Lamar, 561.

74.   8 *Cong. Rec.* 6 (1878).

75.   S. Exec. Doc. 30, 47th Cong. 1st Sess. 2–28 (1881).

76.   13 *Cong. Rec.* 137 (1882).

77.   Ibid., 712.

78.   John Eaton to Sheldon Jackson, January 14, 1882, SJ.

79.   13 *Cong. Rec.* 5747 (1882).

80.   H.R. 5492, 47th Cong. 1st Sess. (March 27, 1882).

81.   Hinckley, "The Alaska Labors of Sheldon Jackson," 102–13.

82.   Ibid.

83. 13 *Cong. Rec.* 5747 (1882).

84. Ibid., 5747.

85. Hinckley, *The Americanization of Alaska*, 41.

86. Ibid., 42.

87. Nichols, 41.

88. Ibid., 43.

89. *Cong. Globe*, 972–74 (1871).

90. S. Rept. 457, 47th Cong. 1st Sess. (1882).

91. S. 1426, 46th Cong. 2d Sess. (March 5, 1880).

92. W. C. Butler to Sheldon Jackson, April 1, 1880, SJ.

93. H.R. 3754, 47th Cong. 1st Sess. (April 20, 1881); S. 1153, 47th Cong. 1st Sess. (February 9, 1882).

94. Nichols, 66–67.

95. Kitchener, 34.

96. Ibid., 42.

97. National Archives, Vincent Baronovitch to General Jefferson Davis, May 26, 1869, RG 393.

98. Nichols, 69.

99. John Eaton to Sheldon Jackson, January 14, 1882, SJ.

100. Compare the text of S. 1426, 46th Cong. 2d Sess. (1880), with the text of the bill reported by the Committee on Territories, in S. Rept. 457, 47th Cong. 1st Sess. 7–10 (1882).

101. H. Rept. 1106, 47th Cong. 1st Sess. 3 (1882).

102. Mottram Ball to Sheldon Jackson, February 1, 1883, SJ.

103. 14 *Cong. Rec.* 2123–29 (1883).

104. Hinckley, "Sheldon Jackson, Presbyterian Lobbyist," 20.

105. Ibid., 21.

106. Mottram Ball to Sheldon Jackson, January 25, 1884, SJ.

107. S. 153, 48th Cong. 1st Sess. (December 4, 1883).

108. William Walter Phelps to Sheldon Jackson, December 7, 1883, SJ.

109. H.R. 994, 48th Cong. 1st Sess. (December 11, 1883).

110. Mottram Ball to Sheldon Jackson, January 25, 1883, SJ.

111. S. 72, 48th Cong. 1st Sess. (December 4, 1883).

112. 48 *Cong. Rec.* 14 (1883).

113. Ibid., 567.

114. Ibid., 565.

115. Ibid.

116.   Ibid., 565–66.

117.   Ibid., 566.

118.   Ibid., 567.

119.   Ibid., 629.

120.   Ibid., 595.

121.   Ibid.

122.   Ibid., 598.

123.   S. M. Cullom to Henry Kendall, June 27, 1884, SJ.

124.   Hinckley, "Alaska Labors," 131.

125.   Ibid., 132.

126.   Stewart, 342–43.

127.   Hinckley, "Alaska Labors," 83.

128.   Jackson, *Report on Education in Alaska*, 42–43.

129.   Ibid., 43.

130.   Lazell, 204.

131.   F. A. Johnson to Sheldon Jackson, May 1, 1885, SJ.

132.   Jackson, *Report on Education in Alaska*, 11.

133.   H. Doc. 5, 60th Cong. 1st Sess. 37 (1907).

134.   H. Doc. 39, 58th Cong. 3d Sess. Pt. 3, 604 (1905).

135.   *Roberts v City of Boston*, 59 Mass. 198 (1849).

136.   163 U.S. 537 (1896).

137.   Hinckley, "Alaska Labors," 206–7.

138.   Sarah Haynes, "Annual Report of U.S. Public School at Juneau" (1910), Bureau of Indian Affairs School Files, microfilm reel 11.

139.   H. Misc. Doc. 340, 52d Cong. 1st Sess. Pt. 7, 183 (1893).

140.   *Statutes at Large 31*, 520 (1900).

141.   *Statutes at Large 33*, 616 (1905).

142.   Jackson, *Statement of Dr. Sheldon Jackson of Alaska before the Committee on the Territories*, 5.

143.   Ibid., 6.

144.   38 *Cong. Rec.* 3081 (1904).

145.   Jackson, *Report on Education in Alaska*, 27.

146.   Stewart, 360.

147.   Board of Indian Commissioners, *1895 Report*, 25.

148.   Stewart, 364.

149.   Roberts, 79–81.

150. Stewart, 366–69; see also Henkelman and Vitt, 34.

151. Schwalbe, 16.

152. Jackson, *Report on Education in Alaska*, 28.

153. Down, 103.

154. H. Misc. Doc. 340, 52d Cong. 1st Sess., Pt. 7, 192 (1893).

155. Henderson, 220.

156. Board of Indian Commissioners, *1887 Report*, 123.

157. H. Misc. Doc. 340, 52d Cong. 1st Sess. Pt. 7, 191 (1893).

158. Hayakawa, 3.

159. *Thlinget*, December 1908.

160. Roberts, 41–42.

161. *Alaskan*, May 14, 1887.

162. U.S. Department of the Interior, *2(c) Report: Federal Programs and Alaska Natives*, task 1, Pt. A, sect. 2, table A-1.

163. H. Doc. 5, 60th Cong. 1st Sess. 37 (1907).

164. W. G. Beattie, "Annual Report of District Superintendent of Schools for Southeastern District of Alaska: 1911–1912," Bureau of Indian Affairs School Files, microfilm reel 43.

165. "Older Natives to Be Taught to Write Names," *Alaska Fishing News*, February 9, 1945.

166. Bailey, 135.

167. Jackson, *Report on Education in Alaska*, 30.

3. Capitalists (Pages 111–169)

1. *Alaska: Statement of Sheldon Dr. Jackson, of Alaska, before the House Committee on the Territories*, 58th Cong. 2d Sess. 10 (1904).

2. "Letter from William S. Dodge, Ex-Mayor of Sitka, on Affairs in Alaska Generally," November 10, 1869, in H. Exec. Doc. 1, 41st Cong. 2d Sess. 1029–30 (1870).

3. Young, 81.

4. *Alaska Appeal*, July 15, 1879.

5. Isaac Dennis to William Gouverneur Morris (n.d.), in S. Exec. Doc. 59, 45th Cong. 3d Sess. 122 (1879).

6. Notes of Conference at Fort Wrangell, September 5, 1881, SJ.

7. National Archives, General Jefferson Davis to Major General James B. Sherbourne, May 27, 1868, Record Group 393 (hereafter cited as RG).

8.   De Armond, *The Founding of Juneau*, 28.

9.   *Alaska Boundary Tribunal*, Report of Captain Beardslee, 366.

10.   Emmons, 331.

11.   *Alaska Boundary Tribunal*, Report of Captain Beardslee, 373.

12.   Willard, 128.

13.   Muir, *Travels in Alaska*, 134–35.

14.   Young, 210.

15.   Krause, 134.

16.   Willard, 169–70.

17.   Ibid., 168.

18.   Hinckley, *The Americanization of Alaska*, 122.

19.   *Alaska Boundary Tribunal*, Captain Beardslee to R. W. Thompson, Secretary of the Navy, September 1, 1880, 371.

20.   Report of Major John C. Tidball, December 20, 1870, in H. Exec. Doc. 5, 42d Cong. 1st Sess. 1–2 (1871).

21.   O. B. Carlton to Vincent Colyer, November 15, 1869, in H. Exec. Doc. 1, 41st Cong. 2d Sess. 1025 (1870).

22.   *Alaska Appeal*, November 15, 1879.

23.   S. Exec. Doc. 59, 45th Cong. 3d Sess. 114–15 (1879).

24.   Bancroft, *History of Alaska*, 663.

25.   S. Exec. Doc. 59, 45th Cong. 3d Sess. 116 (1879).

26.   Willard, 321–22.

27.   Scidmore, 116.

28.   S. Exec. Doc. 59, 45th Cong. 3d Sess. 115 (1879).

29.   Scidmore, 26.

30.   Willard, 345–46.

31.   H. Misc. Doc. 340, 52d Cong. 1st Sess. Pt. 7, 50 (1893).

32.   Muir, *Travels in Alaska*, 279.

33.   *Alaskan*, July 25, 1891.

34.   H. Misc. Doc. 340, 52d Cong. 1st Sess. Pt. 7, 22 (1893).

35.   U.S. Fish Commission, *Bulletin*, 18:50.

36.   *Thlinget*, July 1911.

37.   Ibid., September 1911.

38.   Bureau of Fisheries, *Report of Alaska Investigations in 1914*, 104.

39.   Evans, 269.

40.   Petroff, 67.

41.   *Alaskan*, July 19, 1890.

42. Ibid., November 1, 1890.

43. U.S. Fish Commission, *Bulletin*, 18:22–23.

44. Coe, 1.

45. De Armond, *Lady Franklin Visits Sitka*, 3.

46. Ibid., 24–25.

47. Coe, 13.

48. Hinckley, "The Alaska Labors of Sheldon Jackson," 179.

49. Hinckley, "The Inside Passage," 69.

50. Ibid., 71.

51. Ibid.

52. *Alaskan*, June 20, 1891.

53. Schwatka, 27.

54. *Alaskan*, September 7, 1889.

55. Ibid., April 19, 1890.

56. Scidmore, 27.

57. Ibid., 38–39.

58. Ibid., 40.

59. Ibid., 59–60.

60. Ibid., 89–90.

61. Ibid., 105–7.

62. H. Misc. Doc. 340, 52d Cong. 1st Sess. Pt. 7, 44 (1893).

63. Brooks, 299–300.

64. De Armond, *The Founding of Juneau*, 40.

65. Ibid.

66. Scidmore, 83.

67. Walter H. Pierce, 33.

68. Petroff, 32.

69. Krause, 68–69.

70. De Armond, *The Founding of Juneau*, 90–91.

71. Scidmore, 82.

72. Hunt, 110.

73. Governor of Alaska, *1886 Report*, H. Exec. Doc. 1, 49th Cong. 2d Sess. Pt. 5, 971 (1886).

74. Rickard, 43.

75. Orth, 210.

76. *Alaskan*, October 2, 1897.

77.   Brooks, 323.

78.   Walter H. Pierce, 50–51.

79.   Ibid., 50.

80.   "Ho! For the Yukon!" *Choteau Calumet*, April 2, 1886.

81.   *Alaskan*, April 24, 1886.

82.   Emmons, xxvii–xxxviii.

83.   *Alaskan*, June 19, 1886.

84.   Steckler, 230–33.

85.   Chase, 103–4.

86.   De Windt, 32–33.

87.   Hunt, 111.

88.   *Alaska Boundary Tribunal*, Statement of Claanot, June 2, 1887, 395.

89.   Adney.

90.   Haskell, 69.

91.   Ibid., 61–62.

92.   Maris, 20.

93.   De Windt, 33.

94.   Ogilvie, 109.

95.   Melody Webb, 79.

96.   *Alaskan*, June 8, 1895.

97.   Ogilvie, 153.

98.   Ibid., 127–31.

99.   Secretan, 40.

100. Ogilvie, 222.

101. Kirk, 3.

102. Sand, 32.

103. *Alaskan*, October 2, 1897.

104. Sand, 69.

105. Brooks, 361.

106. Melody Webb, 84.

107. H. Misc. Doc. 340, 52d Cong. 1st Sess. Pt. 7, 118 (1893).

108. Callahan, 128.

109. Lynch, 6.

110. Berton, 307.

111. John Sidney Webb, 672.

112. Henderson, 107.

113. Ibid., 269.

114. Cantwell, 134.

115. Henderson, 43.

116. Ibid., 132.

117. Cantwell, 133.

118. Ibid., 132.

119. Ibid., 62.

120. Ibid., 133.

121. Henderson, 82.

122. Cantwell, 80.

123. Ibid., 82.

124. Ibid., 170.

125. Henderson, 108.

126. Cantwell, 225.

127. Henderson, 104–5.

128. Cantwell, 53.

129. National Archives, C. A. Booth to the Adjutant General, January 1, 1900, RG 393.

130. Ibid., February 28, 1900.

131. Cantwell, 59–60.

132. Ibid., 184.

133. Ibid.

134. Ibid., 257.

135. National Archives, R. G. Obert to Adjutant General, July 30, 1900, RG 393.

136. Cantwell, 260.

137. Ibid., 69.

138. National Archives, Joseph R. Crimont, S.J., to General George Randall, January 1, 1901, RG 393.

139. Cantwell, 68–70.

140. National Archives, G. B. Twinehart to General George Randall, August 20, 1900, RG 393.

141. National Archives, Reverend J. Oeloff to General George Randall, December 21, 1900, RG 393.

142. Henkelman and Vitt, 153.

143. Bockstoce, *Whales, Ice and Men*, 21.

144. Bockstoce, "A Preliminary Estimate of the Reduction of the Western Arctic Bowhead Whale Population."

145. Bockstoce and Botkin.

146. H. Misc. Doc. 340, 52d Cong. 1st Sess. Pt. 7, 146 (1893).

147. Bockstoce, *Whales, Ice and Men*, 201.

148. Ibid., 241.

149. S. Exec. Doc. 132, 46th Cong. 2d Sess. 12 (1880).

150. Ibid., 13.

151. Ibid., 19–20.

152. *Nome Nugget*, July 8, 1905.

153. Bockstoce, *Whales, Ice and Men*, 137.

154. Hooper, 10–11.

155. Ibid., 11.

156. Muir, *The Cruise of the Corwin*, 24–25.

157. Bockstoce, *Whales, Ice and Men*, 138–41.

158. Ibid., 139.

159. Gambell, passim.

160. Healy, *Report of the Cruise of the ... Corwin*, 1884, 17.

161. Healy, *Report of the Cruise of the ... Corwin*, 1885, 15–16.

162. Brower, 78. In *Whales, Ice and Men*, Bockstoce quotes a version of the incident that Gilley related in 1877 that casts the trading schooner captain as a blameless victim of circumstance. Because it admits his own culpability, the version of the story Gilley told Charles Brower when the two men were aboard a ship anchored at Wales in 1886 and Gilley refused to come ashore seems more reliable.

163. Thorton, 52–53.

164. Ibid., 139.

165. Ibid., 53.

166. Ibid., xxi.

167. *Nome Nugget*, August 20, 23, 1902.

168. Allan, 118.

169. *Nome Nugget*, July 8, 1905.

170. *Seattle Post-Intelligencer*, September 24, 1905.

171. *Nome Nugget*, July 5, 1905.

172. Ibid.

173. H. Misc. Doc. 340, 52d Cong. 1st Sess. Pt. 7, 137 (1893).

174. Ibid.

175. Ibid., 143.

176. Earp, 192–93.

177. S. Doc. 357, 56th Cong. 1st Sess. 5 (1900).

178. Brooks, 382.

179. Ibid., 389.

180. National Archives, General Randall to Adjutant General, July 2, 1900, RG 393.

181. Smith, 320.

182. Brevig, 149.

183. Ibid., 151–56.

184. National Archives, Lieutenant Howard R. Hickok to Commanding Officer, Camp Nome, July 23, 1900, RG 393.

185. Ibid., Acting Assistant Surgeon to the Adjutant, Camp Nome, August 17, 1900, RG 393.

186. Renner, 14–17.

187. Ibid., 14.

188. *Nome Nugget*, August 3, 1904.

189. Ibid., August 9, 1905.

190. Ibid., December 5, 1905.

191. Ibid., August 23, 1901.

192. Ibid., August 27, 1901.

193. Ibid., September 19, 1903.

194. Ibid.

195. Ibid., September 13, 1905.

196. Ibid., August 12, 1903.

197. Ibid., January 7, 1903.

198. Ibid., August 12, 1903.

199. Ibid., November 12, 1904.

200. Ibid., October 5, 1903.

201. Ibid., November 21, 1903.

202. Ibid., December 2, 1903.

203. Ibid., December 26, 1903.

204. Ibid., January 2, 1904.

205. Ibid., January 16, 1904.

206. Ibid., March 16, 1904.

207. Ray, 28.

208. Ibid., 30–31.

209. *Nome Nugget*, April 16, 1908.

210.   Bureau of the Census, *Thirteenth Census of the United States: Population—Alaska.*

4. CONSERVATIONISTS (PAGES 171–220)

1.   E. L. "Bob" Bartlett to Bernard De Voto, January 7, 1948, BB.

2.   Nichols, 115.

3.   Hinckley and Hinckley, "Ivan Petroff's Journal"; Sherwood, "Ivan Petroff and the Far Northwest."

4.   S. Rept. 457, Appendix 24, 47th Cong. 1st Sess. (1882).

5.   S. 1426, 46th Cong. 2d Sess. (1880).

6.   H. Exec. Doc. 1, 47th Cong. 2d Sess. Pt. 5, 11 (1882).

7.   S. Rept. 3, 48th Cong. 1st Sess. 2 (1883).

8.   Connelley.

9.   Ibid., 240–41.

10.   *48 Cong. Rec.* 530–31 (1884).

11.   Ibid., 627–28.

12.   National Archives, Memoranda Relating to Black Chief Mining Company, n.d., Record Group 393 (hereafter cited as RG).

13.   Ibid., Statement of Katuganah, July 24, 1900, RG 393.

14.   Ibid., Statement of Second Lieutenant H. Erickson, July 19, 1900, RG 393.

15.   Ibid., Report to Assistant Adjutant General, Headquarters Department of Alaska, St. Michael, July 23, 1900, RG 393.

16.   John J. Healy, "Our Alaska Letter," *Choteau Calumet*, May 29, 1886.

17.   Chap. 561, *Statutes at Large 26*, 1095 (1891).

18.   U.S. Department of the Interior, *Decisions of the Department of the Interior Relating to Public Lands*, 12:583 (1891).

19.   U.S. Department of the Interior, *Decisions of the Department of the Interior Relating to Public Lands*, 23:335 (1896).

20.   R. T. Yeatman to Commissioner of the General Land Office, June 29, 1898, SJ.

21.   Ibid.

22.   National Archives, Captain Henry W. Hovey to Adjutant General, Department of Alaska, Fort St. Michael, August 28, 1900, RG 393.

23.   Hinckley, "The Canoe Rocks."

24.   Nordin, 30.

25. Gifford Pinchot claims credit for naming the new political movement "conservation" in 1907 (Pinchot, *Breaking New Ground*, 322–25). However, "conservation" had been used in the manner for which Pinchot claimed credit as early as 1873 (Clepper, 7).

26. Pinchot, "The A B C of Conservation."

27. Reiger, 118.

28. Morris, 383–84.

29. Grinnell, *Brief History*.

30. *Statutes at Large 3*, 347 (1817).

31. *Statutes at Large 4*, 505 (1832).

32. *Statutes at Large 13*, 325 (1864).

33. Carl Schurz, "The Need of a Rational Forest Policy," in McHenry and Van Doren, 289–90.

34. H. Exec. Doc. 1, 48th Cong. 2d Sess. Pt. 5, 19 (1884).

35. Clepper, 6.

36. 19 *Cong. Rec.* 688 (1888).

37. 19 *Cong. Rec.* 2195 (1888).

38. Reiger, 135.

39. Socolofsky and Spetter, 27.

40. "Care of the Forests: Meeting of the American Association in Washington," *New York Times*, December 30, 1891.

41. Proclamation No. 39, *Statutes at Large 27*, 1052 (1892).

42. Pinchot, *Breaking New Ground*, 144–45.

43. Emmons, xvii–xxxvii; Conrad; Rakestraw, 16.

44. National Archives, Reverend Harry P. Corser to Secretary of the Interior Ethan Hitchcock, September 1, 1902, RG 48.

45. Vance, 325.

46. Roosevelt, 199.

47. *Statutes at Large 35*, 2149 (1986).

48. Lieutenant Henry T. Allen, "Report of an Expedition to the Copper, Tanana, and Koyukok Rivers in the Territory of Alaska in the Year 1885," in S. Exec. Doc. 125, 49th Cong. 2d Sess. 158 (1885).

49. Janson, 7–10.

50. Mikesell, 6–7.

51. Stearns, 253.

52. See *Copper River Mining Co. v McClellan*, 138 F 2d 333 (9th Cir 1905), *cert. denied*, 200 U.S. 616 (1906).

53. Ibid., 8.

54. Ibid., 29.

55. "Mr. Guggenheim Tells Vast Plans for Alaska," *New York Times*, April 3, 1906.

56. Burch, 258.

57. Chap. 796, *Statutes at Large 31*, 658 (1900).

58. Chap. 1772, *Statutes at Large 33*, 525 (1904).

59. Harrison.

60. Birch.

61. King, 4–5.

62. 41 *Cong. Rec.* 26 (1906).

63. Glavis.

64. *1908 Report of the Secretary of the Interior*, H. Doc. 1046, 60th Cong. 2d Sess. 11 (1908).

65. "To Develop Alaska Coal," *New York Times*, May 29, 1908.

66. Nathan Miller, 504.

67. *Statutes at Large 35*, 2231 (1909).

68. Pinchot, *Breaking New Ground*, 395.

69. "Guggenheim Man Is Visiting Seattle," *Fairbanks Daily News*, July 6, 1908.

70. Glavis.

71. Gifford Pinchot to Senator Jonathan Prentiss Dolliver, January 5, 1910, in 45 *Cong. Rec.* 368 (1910).

72. Nathan Miller, 507.

73. "Alaska and Conservation," *Alaska-Yukon Magazine*, March 1911.

74. Stearns, 18.

75. Walter L. Fisher, "Alaskan Coal Problems," October 27, 1911, Bureau of Mines, *Bulletin No. 36*.

76. Ibid., 19.

77. 51 *Cong. Rec.* 76 (1913).

78. Naske and Rowinski, 42.

79. S. Rept. 1230, 71st Cong. 3d Sess. 20 (1931).

80. Franklin K. Lane to Key Pittman, Chairman, Senate Committee on Territories, May 15, 1913, in 51 *Cong. Rec.* 1584–85 (1914).

81. Prince, 528.

82. Atwood, 8–30.

83. See *Copper River Mining Co. v McClellan*, 2 Alaska Reports 134 (1903).

84. Tower, 9.

85. Ibid., 11.

86. "Wickersham Platform," *Seward Weekly Gateway*, July 25, 1908.

87. "Wickersham's Address," *Fairbanks Daily News*, June 25, 1908.

88. 51 *Cong. Rec.* 1638 (1914).

89. Wickersham diary, May 18, 1915.

90. Patty.

91. S. Rept. 1230, 71st Cong. 3d Sess. 2–3 (1931).

92. Ibid., 8.

93. "Brooks on the Coal Tie-Up," *Alaska-Yukon Magazine*, October 1910.

94. Grinnell and Sheldon, 216.

95. Morris, 382–83.

96. H.R. 11535, 57th Cong. 1st Sess. (February 18, 1902).

97. S. 2772, 56th Cong. 1st Sess. (January 30, 1900).

98. H. Rept. 951, 57th Cong. 1st Sess. 4 (1902).

99. Governor of Alaska, *1901 Report*, 16–17.

100. Grinnell, 37–38.

101. Theodore Roosevelt to Caspar Whitney, March 16, 1901, in Morison, 3:16–17.

102. *Statutes at Large 32*, 327 (1902).

103. *Conditions in Alaska: Hearings before the Subcommittee Appointed to Investigate Conditions in Alaska of the Senate Committee on Territories* (statement of Captain P. C. Rickmers), S. Rept. 282, 58th Cong. 2d Sess. Pt. 2, 149 (1904).

104. Ibid., 199 (statement of Major J. F. A. Strong).

105. Ibid., 236 (statement of William A. Kelly).

106. McLain, 282, 284.

107. S. Rept. 282, 58th Cong. 2d Sess. Pt. 1, 29 (1904).

108. Grinnell, 39.

109. G. T. Emmons, *A Report on the Condition and Needs of the Natives of Alaska*, S. Doc. 106, 58th Cong. 3d Sess. 18 (1905).

110. U. S. Department of Agriculture, *Regulations for the Protection of Game in Alaska*, 1912, Circular No. 89.

111. National Archives, A. G. Shoup to C. Hart Merriam, Chief, Bureau of Biological Survey, December 22, 1908, RG 22.

112. Ibid., Ringland, Inspector, Chugach National Forest, to Division of Forestry, U.S. Department of Agriculture, Washington, D.C., September 10, 1916, RG 22.

113. Ibid., Frank H. Foster to Charles A. Sulzer, April 30, 1917, RG 22.

114. Ibid., E. W. Nelson, Chief of the Bureau of Biological Survey, to Charles A. Sulzer, June 25, 1917, RG 22.

115. U.S. Department of Agriculture, Bureau of Biological Survey, *Regulations for the Protection of Land Fur-Bearing Animals in Alaska* (Bulletin No. 43), Regulation No. 4.

116. National Archives, Ernest P. Walker, Chief Fur Warden, to Bureau of Biological Survey, Washington, D.C., December 27, 1921, RG 22.

117. Ibid., Frank P. Williams to E. W. Nelson, Chief of the Bureau of Biological Survey, December 21, 1921, RG 22.

118. Ibid., Frank Waskey to E. W. Nelson, Chief of the Bureau of Biological Survey, January 13, 1922, RG 22.

119. Ibid., Chief Esmalka to Dan Sutherland, February 7, 1922, RG 22.

120. Ibid., Frederic W. Goodman to Dan Sutherland, November 21, 1922, RG 22.

121. Ibid., E. W. Nelson, Chief of the Bureau of Biological Survey, to Hon. Dan Sutherland, February 7, 1923, RG 22.

122. Ibid., J. W. Warwick, U.S. Fur Warden, to Ernest P. Walker, February 15, 1924, RG 22.

123. Ibid., George A. Parks, Chief of Field Division, General Land Office, Department of the Interior, to E. W. Nelson, Chief, Bureau of Biological Survey, September 29, 1923, RG 22.

124. Ibid., M. B., Official in Charge, Fur Bearers in Alaska, Bureau of Biological Survey, to E. P. Walker, Chief Fur Warden, October 20, 1923, RG 22.

125. Ibid., Report of Fur Warden's Inspection Trip Taken November 1, 1922, to November 23, 1922, Inclusive, RG 22.

126. H.R. 11535, Sec. 1, 57th Cong. 1st Sess. (February 18, 1902).

127. H. Rept. 951, 57th Cong. 1st Sess. (1902).

128. Sec. 1, chap. 162, *Statutes at Large 35*, 102 (1908).

129. National Archives, T. R. Harrison to Dr. Henshaw, Office of the Secretary, Department of Agriculture, March 11, 1916, RG 22.

130. Ibid., *1917 Annual Report of the Governor of Alaska on the Alaska Game Law*, RG 22.

131. Ibid., Solicitor, Department of Agriculture, to E. W. Nelson, Chief, Bureau of Biological Survey, February 9, 1921, RG 22.

132. Ibid., Alfred Bailey, Notes on Game Conditions in Alaska, January 1, 1921, RG 22.

133. Ibid., Circular Letter No. 4 to Alaska Game Wardens, August 18, 1924, RG 22.

134. Ibid., R. W. Williams, Solicitor, to E. W. Nelson, Chief, Bureau of Biological Survey, March 3, 1925, RG 22.

135. Nelson.

136. National Archives, E. W. Nelson, Chief, Bureau of Biological Survey, to Frank Dufresne, Deputy Game Warden, February 8, 1926, RG 22.

137. National Archives, Ernest Walker to E. W. Nelson, Chief, Bureau of Biological Survey, June 19, 1921, RG 22.

138. H.R. 12143, 67th Cong. 2d Sess. (June 23, 1922).

139. Sec. 10, chap. 75, *Statutes at Large 43*, 739 (1925).

140. U.S. Department of Agriculture, Bureau of Biological Survey, *Service and Regulatory Announcements: Alaska Game Law and Regulations and Federal Laws Relating to Game and Birds in the Territory*, Regulation No. 8 (May 1925).

141. The unlawful portions of Regulation No. 8 were repealed in 1938. Ibid., *Regulations Relating to Game Land Fur Animals, and Birds in Alaska: 1938–1939*, Regulation No. 3 (May 1938).

142. National Archives, H. E. Terhune to Bureau of Biological Survey, February 9, 1932, RG 22.

143. Ibid., H. W. Terhune to Chief, Bureau of Biological Survey, July 26, 1932, RG 22.

144. U.S. Department of Agriculture, Circular No. 9, *Amendment to Regulations Respecting Game Animals, Land Fur-Bearing Animals, Game Birds, Nongame Birds, and Nests and Eggs of Birds in Alaska*, Regulation No. 8a (August 16, 1932), RG 22.

5. WILLIAM PAUL AND THE ALASKA NATIVE BROTHERHOOD (PAGES 221–286)

1. "William L. Paul Files," *Alaska Fisherman*, February 1924.

2. Wickersham diary, October 28, 1935.

3. District Superintendent of Schools to Commissioner of Education, December 31, 1912, BIA Alaska Division, *General Correspondence: District Files, Southeastern, 1911–17*. See also Hope.

4. Littlefield and Parins, 359–60.

5. U.S. Fish Commission, *Bulletin, 43*.

6. *Verstovian*, October 1923. In August 1910, McAfee attended a conference at the Sitka Training School for Presbyterian missionaries working in the Alaska field, Beattie, 144. See also William Paul to Andrew Hope and Frank G. Johnson, February 27, 1964, WP. In his letter, Paul states that during his visit Peter Simpson and Ralph Young encountered McAfee on the street in Sitka. When they complained that because they were not citizens, they could not vote, file a mining claim, attend public school, or acquire fee simple title to land, McAfee responded by posing the rhetorical question: What would you do with citizenship if you had it?

7. William Beattie to Commissioner of Education, December 31, 1912, BIA Alaska Division, *General Correspondence: 1908–15, District Files, Southeastern, 1911–17*.

8. Kan.

9. Frances Lackey Paul. See also *Thlinget*, November 1908.

10. Frederick Paul, 43. Citations to the Paul "Then Fight for It" manuscript reference the copy of the unedited 961-page manuscript that Frederick Paul

gave to the author in 1984. A shorter version, edited in 1986 with the assistance of a grant to Mr. Paul from the Alaska Historical Commission, is on file in Anchorage, Alaska, at the Loussac Municipal Library.

11.   Davidson.

12.   Ibid.

13.   *Seward Weekly Gateway*, November 13, 1909.

14.   The year Peter Simpson was born is not known. The two suggested dates are 1864 and 1871 (Dauenhauer and Dauenhauer, 666). William Beattie, who knew both men, reported that Simpson and Edward Marsden were "about the same age" (Beattie, 23). Since Marsden was born in 1869, 1871 is the more likely of the two Simpson birth years.

15.   George Thompson Davis, 86.

16.   Peter Murray, 184–99.

17.   Beattie, 20–21.

18.   Dauenhauer and Dauenhauer, 675.

19.   Roppel; also, Dauenhauer and Dauenhauer, 667–68.

20.   Hope.

21.   Frederick Paul interview.

22.   Report of W. B. Adams on Sheldon Jackson School, 1914, PHS, Record Group 98 (hereafter cited as RG).

23.   Ibid.

24.   Peter Simpson, "As an Alaskan Sees It," *Thlinget*, December 1911.

25.   Resolution, William Beattie to Commissioner of Education, December 31, 1912, BIA Alaska Division, *General Correspondence: 1908–15; District Files, Southeastern, 1911–17*.

26.   Rev. Robert Joseph Diven, "Meeting of the Grand Lodge of Alaska Native Brotherhood at Sitka," *Verstovian*, December 1914.

27.   This biography of Matilda Kinnon is drawn primarily from Mary Lee Davis, 223–81, and Frederick Paul, 19–43. Davis based her biography on interviews she conducted with Matilda Kinnon and William Paul. William Paul correspondence from that period makes reference to the cooperation that he and his mother gave to Davis. Frederick Paul heard the same stories from his grandmother and father. See also Dauenhauer and Dauenhauer, 469–502.

28.   Mary Lee Davis, 231.

29.   "Mrs. William Tamaree Wrangell Pioneer, Taken by Death," *Wrangell Sentinel*, August 22, 1952.

30.   Crosby, 91.

31.   Frances Lackey Paul, "My Most Unforgettable Character" segment of manuscript.

32.   Young, 279.

33.   Frances Lackey Paul.

34.   Willard, 215.

35.   Ibid., 217.

36.   Ibid., 219.

37.   Young, 306.

38.   *Alaskan* (Petersburg), January 29, 1887.

39.   Ibid.

40.   Frederick Paul interview.

41.   "Old Letters from Young Writers," *Alaskan*, October 2, 1897.

42.   William Paul Autobiography, n.d., WP. William Paul wrote this autobiography for distribution at Whitworth College at the February 1972 commencement ceremonies at which he was awarded an honorary doctorate for his work for the advancement of Alaska Native rights. Although valuable (particularly as an account of Paul's adolescence and early adulthood), the document is self-serving and contains numerous misstatements and omissions.

43.   Frederick Paul, 176.

44.   This account of Richard Henry Pratt and the Carlisle Indian School is taken from Pratt and also from Gilcreast. See also Richard Henry Pratt to Adjutant General, January 13, 1903, RHP.

45.   Richard Henry Pratt, "The Way Out," in Board of Indian Commissioners, *1891 Report*, 81.

46.   Ibid., 120.

47.   Ibid., 121.

48.   Richard Henry Pratt to William Paul, November 10, 1922, RHP.

49.   Richard Henry Pratt, "Duty to Indians," *Chautauqua Assembly Herald*, August 26, 1904.

50.   Pratt, 252.

51.   U.S. Department of the Interior, *Report of the Commissioner of Indian Affairs to the Secretary of the Interior, 1880*, 180.

52.   U.S. Department of the Interior, *Report of the Commissioner of Indian Affairs to the Secretary of the Interior, 1887*, 257.

53.   U.S. Department of the Interior, *Report of the Commissioner of Indian Affairs to the Secretary of the Interior, 1881*, 185.

54.   U.S. Department of the Interior, *Report of the Commissioner of Indian Affairs to the Secretary of the Interior, 1880*, 179.

55.   Richard Henry Pratt to Sheldon Jackson, January 12, 1885, RHP.

56.   In large measure this version of the early life of William Paul is based on the William Paul autobiography (see n. 42).

57. *Red Man and Helper*, February 14, 1902.

58. *Redman and Helper*, October 3, 1902, contains a letter from Paul written from "a Phila. printery" in which Paul says hello to friends still at Carlisle and confesses, "I do get lonely sometimes." See also "The Man Behind the Land-Claims Fight," *Seattle Times*, February 6, 1972; William Paul interview in which he states that he trained at Carlisle to be a printer.

59. *Guide to Research Materials on the Carlisle Indian School in the Dickinson College Library: List and Index of Indian Students Who Attended Dickinson College*, Carlisle Historical Association.

60. Gray, 59.

61. "Old Grad Honored," *Spokane Chronicle*, February 5, 1972.

62. William Paul Autobiography, WP.

63. *Minutes of the Presbytery of Alaska 1884–1966*, April 3, 1911, PHS.

64. Frederick Paul interview.

65. *Red Man and Helper*, February 14, 1902.

66. Frances Lackey Paul, 67, 72.

67. Ibid., 46.

68. "Seventh Annual Convention Alaska Native Brotherhood," *Wrangell Sentinel*, November 25, 1920.

69. William Paul Autobiography, WP.

70. Frederick Paul interview.

71. See generally Beattie.

72. Ibid., 180–81.

73. R. A. Buchanan to Board of Home Missions, March 1920, PHS, RG 99.

74. "General R. H. Pratt: Great Educator of Indians Passes," *Alaska Fisherman*, June 1924.

75. William Paul Autobiography, WP.

76. Frederick Paul interview.

77. Frances Lackey Paul, 47.

78. William Paul to Richard Henry Pratt, January 5, 1921, RHP.

79. "The Floating Salmon Trap: Success from the Start," *Pacific Fisherman*, August 1952.

80. "Natives View of Fish Traps," *Thlinget*, January 1909.

81. Cooley, 47, fig. 9.

82. Fish and Wildlife Service, *Alaska Fishery and Fur-Seal Industries in 1920*, 47.

83. "Native Brotherhood," *Wrangell Sentinel*, December 2, 1920.

84. "Sitka Raises $500 toward Sending William Paul to Washington," *Wrangell Sentinel*, February 10, 1921.

85. Louis Paul to Richard Henry Pratt, January 4, 1921, RHP.

86. See Pub. L. 59-298, *Statutes at Large 34*, 478 (1906).

87. *Fisheries in Alaska: Hearing on H.R. 2394 before the Subcommittee on Fisheries and Fish Hatcheries of the House Committee on Merchant Marine and Fisheries*, 67th Cong. 2d Sess. Pt. 2 (1922) (statement of William L. Paul).

88. H.R. 10427, 67th Cong. 2d Sess. (February 14, 1922).

89. H. Rept. 789, 67th Cong. 2d Sess. Pt. 2, 1 (1922).

90. *Statutes at Large 43*, 464 (1924).

91. 112 U.S. 94 (1884).

92. Sec. 6, 24 *Statutes at Large 24*, 388 (1887).

93. Beattie, 151–54.

94. Ch. 24, Session Laws Alaska, 1915.

95. 57 *Cong. Rec.* 1013 (1919).

96. Ibid., 1029.

97. Ibid., 1045.

98. Ibid., 1046.

99. H. Doc. 74, 66th Cong. 1st Sess. (1919).

100. "Seventh Annual Convention Alaska Native Brotherhood," *Wrangell Sentinel*, November 25, 1920.

101. *Mason v Churchill*, District Court for the Territory of Alaska, First Division, No. 2242-A, 1922.

102. William Paul to Richard Henry Pratt, November 5, 1922, RHP.

103. "Indian Citizenship Tested," *Alaska Fisherman*, January 1924.

104. Frederick Paul, 95–96.

105. *United States v Charley Jones*, District Court for the Territory of Alaska, First Division, Nos. 792 and 793 KB, 1923.

106. *United States v Tillie Paul Tamaree*, District Court for the Territory of Alaska, Division Number One, at Juneau, No. 794 KB, 1923.

107. "Indian Citizenship Tested: Status Finally Established—Right to Vote Now Undisputed," *Alaska Fisherman*, January 1924.

108. Wickersham diary, March 30, 1923.

109. *United States v Charley Jones*, District Court for the Territory of Alaska, Division Number One, at Juneau, No. 792-KB, Motion for Special [Jury] Instructions.

110. Louis Paul to Richard Henry Pratt, April 11, 1923, RHP.

111. "Indian Citizenship Tested," *Alaska Fisherman*, January 1924.

112. "Local Man Files for Legislature," *Ketchikan Alaska Chronicle*, January 16, 1924.

113. "Wm. L. Paul Files," *Alaska Fisherman*, February 1924.

114. Ibid., 14.

115. "Arthur Frame Accuses Marshal's Office," *Alaska Fisherman*, July 1924.

116. "Attention Republicans," *Daily Alaska Empire*, March 17, 1924.

117. "Official Count: Returns of Republican Primaries by Clerk of Court," *Alaska Fisherman*, June 1924.

118. "The White Man's Way Must Prevail," *Daily Alaska Empire*, May 17, 1924.

119. Official Returns of the Election of Delegate from Alaska, Attorney General, Members of the 7th Territorial Legislature and Road Commissioner, Preferential Vote for Governor Held November 4, 1924 (Territory of Alaska—First Division), Alaska State Archives.

120. *Statutes at Large 43*, 253(1924).

121. 1923 *Alaska House Journal*, 57. See also "Bill Requiring Literacy Test Is Introduced," *Daily Alaska Empire*, March 10, 1923.

122. 1923 *Alaska House Journal*, 62.

123. National Archives, Ernest P. Walker to W. F. Bancroft, March 26, 1923, RG 22.

124. 1923 *Alaska Senate Journal*, 121.

125. HB 1, 7th Alaska Territorial Legislature,1925.

126. Ch. 27, Session Laws Alaska, 1925.

127. "First Test of Strength in Senate Indicates Literacy Bill May Fail of Passage," *Daily Alaska Empire*, April 3, 1923.

128. H.R. 9211, 69th Cong. 1st Sess. (February 11, 1926).

129. H. Rept. 728, 69th Cong. 1st Sess. (1926).

130. 67 *Cong. Rec.* 7785 (1926).

131. Personal communication from the Presbyterian Church (U.S.A.), Department of History, June 22, 1990.

132. William Paul Autobiography, WP.

133. 67 *Cong. Rec.* 12, 370–74 (1926).

134. 68 *Cong. Rec.* 3976–78 (1927).

135. Pub. L. 69-766, *Statutes at Large 44*, 1393 (1927).

136. Official Returns Compiled by Canvassing Board of the Election Held November 2, 1926, for Delegate to Congress and Senator & Representatives in the 8th Territorial Legislature, Alaska State Archives.

137. Wickersham diary, October 16, 1927.

138. "Calls the Turn on 'Committeeman,'" *Alaskan* (Petersburg), April 13, 1928.

139. 1927 *Alaska Senate Journal*, 163.

140. Wickersham diary, March 4, 1927.

141. "Primary Returns Still Coming," *Alaskan* (Petersburg), May 18, 1928.

142. "Tuesday's Primary and What It Shows," *Daily Alaska Empire*, April 26, 1928.

143. "Hunt Assigns Reasons for Opposing Paul," *Daily Alaska Empire*, October 26, 1928.

144. "Paul under Pay of Canneries, Says Hunt," *Ketchikan Alaska Chronicle*, October 27, 1928.

145. "William L. Paul Will Answer the Hunt-Frame Questions Friday Night, November 2nd," *Ketchikan Alaska Chronicle*, October 31, 1928.

146. "Democratic Club of Ketchikan," *Ketchikan Alaska Chronicle*, November 2, 1928.

147. "Paul and the Salmon Canners (Paul's Own Explanation)," transcript of speech made by William Paul at the Coliseum Theater, November 2, 1928; see Wickersham diary, October 1, 1928 (hereafter cited as Paul transcript).

148. "Paul Confesses Accepting Cannery Funds," *Ketchikan Alaska Chronicle*, November 3, 1928.

149. "Paul Betrays Indian Followers," *Daily Alaska Empire*, November 3, 1928.

150. Wickersham diary, November 4, 1928.

151. "Does One Serve Two Masters?" *Ketchikan Alaska Chronicle*, November 3, 1928.

152. "After Tonight's Meeting Turn on Your Radio," *Ketchikan Alaska Chronicle*, November 5, 1928.

153. Tally of Returns from Territorial Election, First Division—November 6, 1928, Alaska State Archives.

154. "The Voice of the People," *Alaska Fisherman*, November-December 1928.

155. Paul transcript.

156. "Platform of William L. Paul," *Alaska Fisherman*, October 1924.

157. "Previous Use of Trap Site Not Conclusive," *Daily Alaska Empire*, July 25, 1927.

158. "Death Summons David Skinner, Shipbuilder," *Seattle Times*, December 28, 1933.

159. Cooley, 130.

160. "Fish Traps or People—Which?" *Alaskan* (Petersburg), August 26, 1927.

161. Wickersham diary, November 28, 1927.

162. Ibid., December 1, 1927.

163. Ibid., November 28, 1927.

164. Ibid., December 16, 1927.

165. Frederick Paul interview.

166. "Wickersham Offers Draft New Fisheries Law," *Alaska Fisherman*, January 1928.

167. Wickersham diary, March 1, 1928.

168. "Interviews President Coolidge," *Alaskan* (Petersburg), March 30, 1928.

169. Wickersham diary, February 25, 1928.

170. Ibid., March 1, 1928.

171. Dan Sutherland to Louis Paul, December 26, 1928, WP.

172. "Politics Will Be Abandoned, Says Marsden," *Daily Alaska Empire*, November 26, 1928.

173. "Marsden in Metlakatla Flays Paul," *Ketchikan Alaska Chronicle*, November 6, 1928. Marsden's condemnation had its intended effect. In the 1926 election, Paul received 45 of the 59 votes cast at Metlakatla; in the 1928 election he received 18 of 112.

174. Frances Lackey Paul, 26–27.

175. Wickersham diary, November 16, 1928.

176. "A.N.B. Convention Largest Ever Held," *Alaskan* (Petersburg), November 23, 1928.

177. "Jottings from Convention," *Alaskan* (Petersburg), November 30, 1928.

178. "Blue Fox Industry Is Written by Joe Ulmer," *Ketchikan Alaska Chronicle*, February 16, 1923.

179. "Growth in Fur Farming Industry Shown in 1923," *Daily Alaska Empire*, January 14, 1924.

180. National Archives, U.S. Department of Agriculture, *Instructions for the Guidance of Officers of the Forest Service and the Biological Survey in Granting Permits or Leases Authorizing the Use of Government Lands in Alaska for Fur-Farming Purposes*, August 4, 1921, RG 22.

181. Ibid., William Paul to E. W. Nelson, February 18, 1924.

182. Ibid., Chief of Bureau to Colonel Greeley, March 1, 1924.

183. Ibid., Petition from the Native People of Hoonah, Alaska, to Bureau of Biological Survey, March 6, 1925.

184. "Forestry Department," *Alaska Fisherman*, December 1925.

185. William Paul Autobiography, WP.

186. "The Man behind the Land-Claims Fight," *Seattle Times*, February 6, 1972. See also Frederick Paul, 229.

187. 8 Wheat 543 (1823).

188. William Paul Autobiography, WP.

189. PL. 68-402, *Statutes at Large 43*, 886 (1925).

190. Wickersham diary, March 12, 1929.

191. Ibid., March 20, 1929.

192. Ibid., March 24, 1929.

193. Ibid., April 18, 30, 1929.

194. Ibid., November 15, 1929.

195. Ibid., November 20, 1929.

196. H.R. 8301, 71st Cong. 2d Sess. (January 8, 1930).

197. Sutherland, 33.

198. S. 1196, 72d Cong. 1st Sess. (December 9, 1931).

199. H.R. 3894, 73d Cong. 1st Sess. (March 21, 1933).

200. "Benefits from Home Rule Are Aptly Defined," *Daily Alaska Empire*, October 25, 1932.

201. "Unofficial Returns of the First Division," *Daily Alaska Empire*, November 18, 1930.

202. Frederick Paul, 208.

203. "This Actually Happened," *Alaska Fisherman*, October 1928.

204. Frederick Paul, 130–36.

205. "The Constitutional Right to Protest," *Alaska Fisherman*, November-December 1928.

206. "Court Finds William Paul in Contempt," *Ketchikan Alaska Chronicle*, March 4, 1929.

207. *Paul v United States*, 36 F 2d 639, 643 (9th Cir 1929).

208. Frederick Paul, 136.

209. Wickersham diary, November 15, 1930.

210. Ibid., February 20, 1931.

211. Ibid., November 8, 1931.

212. Ibid., November 24, 1931.

213. Ibid., February 17, 1932.

214. Ibid., May 26, 1932.

215. Ibid., February 20, 1932.

216. Ibid., June 14, 1932.

217. Ibid., June 20, 1932.

218. Ibid., June 23, 1932.

219. Ibid., July 16, 1932.

220. Ibid., July 19, 1932.

221. Ibid., July 20, 1932.

222. Ibid., July 1, 1932.

223. Ibid., July 21, 1932.

224. Ibid., July 23, 1932.

225. "Progressive Republicans" and "A Letter and an Answer," *Alaska Fisherman*, October 1924.

226. Wickersham diary, October 6, 1929.

227. "W. L. Paul Will Make Race for Att'y General," *Daily Alaska Empire*, July 30, 1932.

228. "Rustgard Flays Paul and Cole in Radio Talk," *Daily Alaska Empire*, October 31, 1932; "Roden Affirms Offer of Job to Wm. L. Paul," *Daily Alaska Empire*, November 1, 1932; "Rustgard Does Not Reply to Roden's Wire," *Daily Alaska Empire*, November 4, 1932.

229. "On Eve of Vote Drive, W. L. Paul Denies Charges," *Daily Alaska Empire*, September 27, 1932.

230. "Paul Returns from Interior Highly Elated," *Daily Alaska Empire*, October 24, 1932.

231. Wickersham diary, August 5, 1932.

232. "Paul Opens Campaign in Local Speech," *Fairbanks Daily News-Miner*, October 5, 1932; "William Paul Voices Needs of Fisheries," *Anchorage Daily Times*, October 12, 1932.

233. Wickersham diary, July 6, 1932.

234. "Unofficial Returns of the First Division," *Daily Alaska Empire*, November 18, 1930.

235. "Unofficial Returns—First Division," *Daily Alaska Empire*, November 19, 1932.

236. Resolution to the Acknowledged Democratic Party Leaders of Alaska, March 23, 1933, AD.

237. Although he finished third, Paul accomplished his objective of defeating John Rustgard; if Rustgard had received the 1,806 votes that were cast for Paul in the First Division (much less the 3,296 votes that were cast for Paul territory-wide) he easily would have defeated James Truitt, the Democratic candidate. The vote count was as follows:

DIVISION

Candidate	1st	2d	3d	4th	Total
Truitt (D)	2589	274	1595	1099	5557
Rustgard (R)	2154	442	1238	937	4771
Paul (I)	1806	178	781	531	3296

238. Simon Hellenthal to Anthony Dimond, May 18, 1933, AD.

239. William Paul to Anthony Dimond, May 25, 1934, AD.

240. William Paul to Anthony Dimond, May 22, 1933, AD.

241. H.R. 2756, 74th Cong. 1st Sess. (January 3, 1935).

242. Paul W. Gordon, Director of Education for Alaska, to John Collier, Commissioner of Indian Affairs, March 16, 1934, AD.

243. Harold Ickes to the Honorable Will Rogers, March 8, 1935, in H. Rept. 621, 74th Cong. 1st Sess. 3 (1935).

244. Ibid.

245. Judson Brown to A. J. Dimond, May 2, 1934, AD.

246. William L. Paul to Anthony Dimond, November 1, 1934, AD.

247. *Statutes at Large 49*, 388 (1935).

248. William L. Paul to Anthony Dimond, November 1, 1934, AD.

249. Wickersham diary, November 25, 29, 1935.

250. Ibid., December 10, 1935.

251. Ibid., December 12, 1935.

252. Ibid., November 10, 1937.

253. Anthony Dimond to James J. Connors, April 26, 1933, AD.

254. Anthony Dimond to William L. Paul, April 26, 1933, AD.

255. James J. Connors to Anthony J. Dimond, May 12, 1933, AD.

256. William L. Paul to Anthony Dimond, July 14, 1933, AD.

257. William Paul to Anthony Dimond, April 29, 1934, AD.

258. *William L. Paul v Justin W. Harding*, District Court for the Territory of Alaska, Division Number One, at Ketchikan, Civil Case No. 1668-KA (1933), complaint, paragraph no. 5. See also *William L. Paul v Justin W. Harding*, District Court for the Territory of Alaska, Division Number Four, at Fairbanks, Civil Case No. 3642 (1933).

259. William Paul to Anthony Dimond, June 17, 1934, AD.

260. "Ownership of Fish Trap Location Opens Dispute," *Wrangell Sentinel*, May 18, 1934.

261. *William L. Paul v Nick Bez*, District Court for the Territory of Alaska, Division Number One, No. 3802-A.

262. "Love Tangles End in Charge of Contempt," *Daily Alaska Empire*, October 26, 1935.

263. "Attorney Gets Fined $100 in Contempt Case," *Daily Alaska Empire*, October 29, 1935.

264. Wickersham diary, October 28, 1935.

265. Ibid., November 2, 1935.

266. "Paul Facing Disbarment Charges," *Daily Alaska Empire*, May 23, 1936.

267. Folta, 92.

268. Roy Peratrovich interview.

269. Ibid.

270. *United States ex rel G. W. Folta v William L. Paul*, District Court for the Territory of Alaska, Division Number One, at Juneau, No. 3918 A, Amended Information, October 16, 1936.

271. Ibid., James Wickersham to Robert Coughlin, Clerk of Court, March 1, 1937.

272. Ibid., Memorandum of Findings and Judgment, July 31, 1937.

273. William Paul to W. C. Arnold, October 31, 1936, AD.

274. National Archives, William Paul to Grand Camp, Alaska Native Brotherhood, in Convention at Kake, November 3, 1937, RG 75. See also Louis Paul to Arthur Johnson, February 1, 1939, WP, in which Louis Paul argues his brother's case as follows:

R. E. Robertson and Judge Jennings both were paid $2,500 each for trips to Washington when neither one spent more than three weeks away from Juneau representing the Chamber of Commerce. When the Dimond literacy bill was before Congress, William spent over $300 alone on transportation expense and spent several weeks in Washington to defeat that bill. His effort was successful so that our people were not barred from exercising their right of franchise. When the case of *U.S. v Charley Jones* for illegal voting was brought up Judge Wickersham asked $1,500 [actually $500] and expenses. When we asked Wickersham to represent the organization in the school case, he asked another $1,500; had any other lawyer been hired to go to Washington on the Dimond literacy bill, he would have charged from $1,500 to $2,000. When the ANB convention at Wrangell ordered William to represent them at Washington in the [effort to amend the Indian Reorganization Act], they authorized $500. He was there five months or more.... A laborer is worthy of his hire and if we hire him we should pay him. Think back to the days William published *The Alaska Fisherman* and was authorized to collect $100 per month from each [ANB] camp. I have the exact amount Wrangell camp paid and the amount they owed and the time they quit.... It will surprise you, but every camp owes on that account. And the last two years of its existence William paid $100 per month to keep it going—this from his own personal earnings.

275. National Archives, Ernest P. Walker to W. F. Bancroft, March 26, 1923, RG 22.

276. Louis Paul to Arthur Johnson, February 1, 1939, WP.

277. H. R. Trevor-Roper, "The Prophet," *New York Review of Books*, October 12, 1989.

278. James Hawkins interview.

279. Roy Peratrovich interview.

280. Ibid.

281. George Folta, "The History of the Exploitation of Indians of Alaska Is Largely the History of the Pauls," n.d., EG.

282. 1947 *Alaska House Journal*, 24.

6. Reservations (Pages 287–351)

1. Felix Cohen to Secretary Chapman, August 28, 1944, FSC.

2. Wilbur, 479–80.

3. "Wilbur Outlines New Indian Policy," *New York Times*, April 17, 1929.

4. Ray Lyman Wilbur to Louis C. Cramton, Chairman, House Subcommittee on Appropriations, November 25, 1930, in H. Rept. 2073, 71st Cong. 3d Sess. (1930).

5. 74 *Cong. Rec.* 608 (1930).

6. Secretarial Order No. 494, March 14, 1931.

7. U.S. Department of the Interior, "Status of Alaskan Natives," *Decisions of the Department of the Interior* 53:593, 605 (1932).

8. For one of Sheldon Jackson's last expressions of view on the subject prior to his retirement as superintendent of education, see Jackson, *Statement of Dr. Sheldon Jackson of Alaska before the House Committee on the Territories*, 58th Cong. 2d Sess. 7 (March 10, 1904), in which Sheldon Jackson reminds Congress that:

   The Natives of Alaska are on an entirely different footing from the Natives in any other region in the United States. There has never been an Indian agent or an Indian reservation in Alaska. The Natives of Alaska have never been under the Indian laws of the country, with the exception of the law as to the sale of liquors and breech-loading firearms. That clause, however, concerning breech-loading firearms has been repealed, so that the only restriction of the Indian laws of the United States over Alaska is as to the sale of liquor to Natives.

9. Watkins, 269–70.

10. Philp, 4–5.

11. Ibid., 16–17.

12. The biographical information on Collier is drawn from Philp, 1–117. See also Kelly, passim.

13. Harold Ickes to Francis Wilson, April 18, 1933, quoted in Watkins, 331.

14. H.R. 7902, 73d Cong. 2d Sess. (February 12, 1934); S. 2755, 73d Cong. 2d Sess. (February 13, 1934).

15. U.S. Department of the Interior, *Report of the Secretary of the Interior, 1934*, 79.

16. Moley, 257.

17. Rosenfeld, 253.

18. Rita Singer Brandeis interview.

19. Drinnon, *Keeper of Concentration Camps*, 316.

20. For a definitive history of the enactment of the Indian Reorganization Act, see Deloria and Lytle.

21. Collier, 3.

22. Ibid., 203.

23. Hearing on H.R. 7902 before the House Committee on Indian Affairs, 73d Cong. 2d Sess. 76 (1934).

24. Ibid., 498.

25. Anthony Dimond to William Paul, March 5, 1935, BB.

26. Ibid. See also Anthony Dimond to William Paul, November 19, 1935, in 83 *Cong. Rec.*, A179.

27. The following history of the founding of Metlakatla, British Columbia, and Metlakatla, Alaska, is drawn from Peter Murray, *The Devil and Mr. Duncan.*

28. Letter from William Duncan Relative to the Education of the Indians of Alaska, February 15, 1901, in S. Doc. 195, 56th Cong. 2d Sess. (1901).

29. Annual Report of the Governor of Alaska, 1900, in H. Doc. 5, 56th Cong. 2d Sess. 34 (1900). For Sheldon Jackson's view of reservations, see note 8, this chapter.

30. Jenkins, 57–89.

31. *Conditions in Alaska: Hearing before the Senate Committee on Territories*, 62d Cong. 2d Sess. (1912) (statement of Bishop Peter T. Rowe of Alaska).

32. For Beattie's involvement in establishing the first reservations in Alaska, see Louis F. Paul to the Honorable Lynn J. Frazier, December 27, 1930, author's collection: "When Prof. Beattie, now of the University of Oregon, was Divisional Superintendent of the Bureau of Education activities in southeastern Alaska some fourteen years ago, he attempted to start the reservation idea up here. His particular objective was at Hydaburg, Alaska. But he found a direct opposition to his plan as our people did not care to become direct wards of the government."

33. Executive Order 1555, June 19, 1912.

34. W. T. Lopp to Hydaburg Town Council, November 28, 1912, in Bureau of Indian Affairs, *Hydaburg, Alaska—Its History, Population and Economy* Planning Support Group Report 257, July 1978, 295–98.

35. Executive Order 4421, April 17, 1926.

36. For a list of executive order and Indian Reorganization Act reservations in Alaska, see Federal Field Committee for Development Planning, *Alaska Natives and the Land*, 444–45.

37. Bureau of Education, *Report of the Work of the Bureau of Education for the Natives of Alaska*, 1913–1914 (Bulletin No. 48), 7.

38. National Archives, P. P. Claxton, Commissioner of Education, to Secretary of the Interior, April 17, 1914, Record Group 75 (hereafter cited as RG).

39. Charles Robinson to W. T. Lopp, November 25, 1914, Bureau of Indian Affairs, *Alaska Division General Correspondence: District Files*, University of Alaska-Anchorage Microfilm.

40. National Archives, P. T. Rowe to William C. Redfield, Secretary of Commerce, March 9, 1914, RG 75.

41. Ibid., A. Evans to Commissioner of Education, December 1, 1912, RG 75.

42. Ibid., J. W. Barker, Special Agent, to A. Christensen, Chief of Field Division, General Land Office, April 8, 1914, RG 75.

43. Ibid., General Land Office, Washington, D.C., to W. T. Lopp, June 24, 1914, RG 75.

44. Ibid., Petition from Chief Kriska of Nulato and Chief Paul of Koyukuk to Arthur C. Parker, Secretary-Treasurer of the Society of American Indians, July 14, 1914, RG 75. Parker sent the petition to the Commissioner of Indian Affairs, who in turn forwarded it to the Bureau of Education.

45. Ibid., P. P. Claxton to W. T. Lopp, September 19, 1914, RG 75; George Boulter to W. T. Lopp, August 20, 1914, RG 75.

46. Patty.

47. National Archives, W. T. Lopp to George Boulter, November 9, 1915, RG 75.

48. 56 *Cong. Rec.* 7943 (1918).

49. Chap. 4, sec. 27, *Statutes at Large 41*, 3, 34 (1919).

50. Pub. L. 68-468, *Statutes at Large 43*, 978 (1925).

51. "More Reservations for Alaska," *Alaska Fisherman*, August 1930.

52. "Know Your Legislators: Frank G. Johnson," *Daily Alaska Empire*, March 19, 1947.

53. Petition from residents of Kake, Alaska, to Anthony Dimond and the Bureau of Indian Affairs, April 4, 1935, AD.

54. *Alaska Pacific Fisheries v United States*, 248 U.S. 78 (1918).

55. Fish and Wildlife Service, *Alaska Fishery and Fur Seal Industries: 1934*, 11–12; *Alaska Fishery and Fur Seal Industries: 1935*, 6.

56. William Paul to John Collier, April 1, 1935, CW.

57. "ANB Confab in Wrangell Will Close Tonight," *Daily Alaska Empire*, November 16, 1935.

58. Anthony Dimond to William Paul, December 1935, AD.

59. Kelly, 273.

60. Walter Woehlke to Commissioner Collier, April 23, 1935, CW.

61. H.R. 9866, Sec. 1, 74th Cong. 2d Sess. (January 7, 1936).

62. William L. Paul, Felix S. Cohen, and Paul W. Gordon to Commissioner of Indian Affairs, January 22, 1936, AD.

63. Pub. L. 74-538, *Statutes at Large 49,* 1250 (1936).

64. "Alonzo Hamblet Reviews Work of Brotherhood Convention," *Alaska Fishing News*, November 27, 1936; "Opposition to Paul Features ANB Sessions,"

Alaska Press, November 18, 1936; "Louis F. Paul Makes Reply to Hamblet over ANB Controversy," *Alaska Fishing News*, February 5, 1937.

65. "Louis F. Paul Makes Reply to Hamblet over ANB Controversy," *Alaska Fishing News*, February 5, 1937.

66. Drucker, 38–39.

67. "William Paul Gets Post in Indian Bureau," *Daily Alaska Empire*, August 13, 1936.

68. William Paul to Frances, Louis, and Bill Paul, February 18, 1936, WP.

69. "Paul, Peratrovich after Indian Post," *Daily Alaska Empire*, June 13, 1936.

70. Wickersham diary, February 20, 1936.

71. Mark Jacobs to Anthony Dimond, February 18, 1936, AD.

72. "Louis F. Paul Makes Reply to Hamblet over ANB Controversy," *Alaska Fishing News*, February 5, 1937.

73. Drucker, 39.

74. Judson Brown to Anthony Dimond, n.d., AD.

75. Charles W. Hawkesworth, Assistant Director of Education, to Commissioner of Indian Affairs, December 3, 1937, AD.

76. William Paul to Alaska Native Brotherhood members, October 6, 1938, WP.

77. Memorandum from John Collier to Ernest Gruening, "Indian Service Needs in Alaska, Education, Health, and General," February 28, 1938, EG.

78. National Archives, Assistant Commissioner of Indian Affairs William Zimmerman to John Fredson, Bureau of Indian Affairs teacher at Chandalar, April 7, 1938, RG 75.

79. In November 1936, Collier reported to Secretary of the Interior Harold Ickes: "Oscar H. Lipps, field representative, and William L. Paul, field agent, have been traveling in Alaska for several months making preliminary studies of organization and credit problems. It is hoped that their studies will make it possible to put the Alaska Indian Reorganization Act into effect early in the spring of 1937." Ibid., John Collier Bi-Weekly Report to Harold Ickes, November 20, 1936, RG 48.

80. "Alaskan Indian and Eskimo Villages Adopt Charters and Constitutions," *Indians at Work*, May 1940.

81. National Archives, Instructions for Organization in Alaska under the Reorganization Act of June 18, 1934, and the Alaska Act of May 1, 1936, and the Amendments Thereto, December 22, 1937, RG 75.

82. Mackenzie, 160. See also Diana Campbell, "Remembering John Fredson," *Anchorage Daily News*, May 23, 1993.

83. McKennan.

84. Mackenzie, 159.

85. National Archives, Letter, map, and petition from John Fredson to Bureau of Indian Affairs, January 1, 1938, RG 75.

86. Ibid., Notes Taken on Conference Held February 23, 1938, Reference Reservations in Alaska, RG 75.

87. Walter V. Woehlke to Commissioner Collier, June 12, 1944, FSC.

88. 43 *Fed. Reg.* 9242–45 (1943).

89. Public Land Order 128, May 22, 1943; 43 *Fed. Reg.* 9892 (1943).

90. National Archives, Dale Doty to Assistant Secretary Oscar Chapman, March 2, 1943, RG 48.

91. Diaries of Harold Ickes, 2912–13, August 18, 1938, HI.

92. Gruening, 253.

93. National Archives, Harold Ickes to John Collier, August 21, 1938, RG 48.

94. Diaries of Harold Ickes, 2922, August 21, 1938, HI.

95. National Archives, Harold Ickes to Representative James F. O'Connor, December 20, 1944, RG 48.

96. A. K. Tichenor to Marshall P. Madison, July 25, 1944, APA.

97. A. K. Tichenor to Marshall P. Madison, November 20, 1944, APA.

98. National Archives, William Zimmerman to Secretary of the Interior, August 15, 1940, RG 75.

99. W. C. Arnold to Pillsbury, Madison, and Sutro, July 5, 1944, APA.

100. *Grimes Packing Company v Hynes*, 67 F Supp 43 (D. Alaska 1946).

101. *Hynes v Grimes Packing Company*, 165 F2d 323 (9th Cir 1947).

102. *Hynes v Grimes Packing Company*, 337 U.S. 86 (1949).

103. William O. Douglas to Stanley Reed, February 1, 1949, WOD; Urofsky, 118.

104. Stanley Reed to William O. Douglas, February 1, 1949, WOD.

105. Douglas, *The Court Years*, 21.

106. 314 U.S. 339 (1941).

107. Reorganization Plan No. II, sec. 4, *Statutes at Large 53*, 1431 (1939).

108. Felix Cohen, letter to the editor, *Ketchikan Alaska Chronicle*, April 19, 1948.

109. Ibid.

110. National Archives, Felix Cohen to Commissioner of Indian Affairs, January 8, 1942, RG 75.

111. U.S. Department of the Interior, "Aboriginal Fishing Rights in Alaska," *Decisions of the Department of the Interior* 57:461 (1942).

112. 7 *Fed. Reg.* 2480 (1942).

113. Diaries of Harold Ickes, 6439–40, March 22, 1942, HI.

114. Ibid.

115. National Archives, Petition for Removal of Fish Trap at Point Colpoys on North Shore of Prince of Wales Island, April 16, 1942, RG 48.

116. *William L. Paul v Pacific American Fisheries*, District Court for the Territory of Alaska, Division Number One, at Juneau, No. 4880-A, June 23, 1942.

117. *Tee-Hit-Ton Tribe of Tlingit Indians v Pacific American Fisheries*, District Court for the Territory of Alaska, Division Number One, at Juneau, No. 4999-A, February 16, 1943. *Tee-Hit-Ton Tribe of Tlingit Indians of Alaska v Clarence Olson, as Alaska Fishery Management Supervisor of the Fish and Wildlife Service of the United States, et al.*, District Court for the Territory of Alaska, Division Number One, at Juneau, No. 5051-A, May 5, 1943.

118. National Archives, George Folta to Nathan Margold, August 3, 1942, RG 48.

119. Ibid., Warner Gardner to Secretary of the Interior, November 11, 1942, RG 48.

120. Ibid., Felix Cohen to Warner Gardner, October 15, 1942, RG 48.

121. 8 *Fed. Reg.* 2890 (1943).

122. Frederick Paul interview.

123. Association of Pacific Fisheries and Northwest Salmon Canners Association to Harold Ickes, March 27, 1942, APA.

124. Leland Groezinger to Edward Allen, April 2, 1942, APA.

125. S. 2227, 77th Cong. 2d Sess. (January 26, 1942).

126. S. 930, 78th Cong. 1st Sess. (March 30, 1943).

127. S. Rept. 733, 78th Cong. 2d Sess. 6 (1944).

128. National Archives, John Collier to Assistant Secretary Chapman, February 9, 1944, RG 48.

129. S. Rept. 733, 6, 78th Cong. 2d Sess. (1944).

130. National Archives, Harold Ickes to Louis Paul, May 28, 1943, RG 48.

131. Ibid., Harold Ickes to Lawrence Calvert, April 20, 1944, RG 48.

132. Untitled memorandum describing meeting between Claude Hirst, William Zimmerman, and unidentified BIA officials, February 6, 1937, AD.

133. Memorandum: "Economic Development Program Showing How the Funds Will Be Used," in *Repeal Act Authorizing Secretary of Interior to Create Indian Reservations in Alaska: Hearings on S. 2037 and S. J. Res. 162 before a Subcommittee of the Senate Committee on Interior and Insular Affairs*, 80th Cong. 2d Sess. 93 (1948).

134. National Archives, Application for Reserve, April 11, 1938, RG 75.

135. Ibid., Donald Hagerty to Claude Hirst, December 7, 1938; Claude Hirst to William Zimmerman, December 8, 1938, RG 75.

136. Ibid., Albert Brown to William Zimmerman, February 2, 1939, RG 75.

137. Ibid., Memorandum from Felix Cohen to Commissioner of Indian Affairs, "Work in Alaska, June 15 to July 1," July 10, 1944, RG 75.

138. Ibid.

139. H. L. Faulkner to Alaska Packers Association, July 9, 1944, APA.

140. National Archives, Felix Cohen to William Zimmerman, July 12, 1944, RG 75.

141. Ibid., Memorandum from Felix Cohen to Commissioner of Indian Affairs, "Work in Alaska, June 15 to July 1," July 10, 1944, RG 75.

142. 9 *Fed. Reg.* 9171–72 (1944).

143. National Archives, Nathan Margold to Secretary of the Interior, April 22, 1942, RG 48.

144. Ibid., Fowler Harper to George Folta, December 7, 1943, RG 48.

145. Kelly, 195.

146. National Archives, Chas. E. Jackson to Dr. I. N. Gabrielson, September 4, 1944, RG 22.

147. "Says Ickes' Plan Rob Territory of Its Taxes," *Alaska Fishing News*, September 20, 1944.

148. Transcript of Hydaburg, Kake, and Klawock hearings, EWA.

149. See notes prepared by R. E. Robertson describing the 1944 hearings, EWA.

150. "Without Benefit of Courts or Congress," *Pacific Fisherman*, December 1944.

151. Ibid.

152. National Archives, Memorandum from Felix Cohen to Commissioner of Indian Affairs, "Work in Alaska, June 15 to July 1," July 10, 1944, RG 75.

153. Edward Allen to Thomas Austern, October 7, 1944, APA.

154. National Archives, J. Steele Culbertson to Regional Director, Fish and Wildlife Service, October 11, 1944, RG 22.

155. Ibid., *Aboriginal Rights in Alaska*, Opinion of Richard H. Hanna, Examiner for the Department of Interior, n.d., RG 48.

156. Diaries of Harold Ickes, 9907, July 28, 1945, HI.

157. Ibid.

158. 10 *Fed. Reg.* 9545 (1945).

159. Edward W. Allen to A. R. Brueger, August 2, 1945, EWA.

160. H. Thomas Austern to Philip MacBride, August 7, 1945, EWA.

161. Watkins, 823.

162. *Pacific Fisherman*, March 1946.

163. Tugwell, 347.

164. Kalman, 7–26.

165. Douglas, *Go East*, 256.

166. Watkins, 661.

167. Ognibene, 32.

168. Ibid., 42–49.

169. Speech by Cassius Gates to Seattle Rotary Club, November 13, 1946, HMJ.

170. "Alaska Hearings to Open on Indians' Fishing Rights," *Seattle Times*, September 6, 1944.

171. National Archives, Memorandum from Assistant Secretary to the Secretary, July 28, 1944, RG 48.

172. Confidential Committee Print: *Investigation of Alaskan Fisheries*, 78th Cong. 2d Sess. (1944).

173. National Archives, Henry M. Jackson to Abe Fortas, December 3, 1944, RG 48.

174. Henry Jackson to Abe Fortas, [July ?] 1944, HMJ.

175. National Archives, Abe Fortas to the Secretary, December 13, 1944, RG 48.

176. Kvasnicka and Viola, 279.

177. National Archives, Alaska reservation policy statement attached to memorandum from J. C. McCaskill, Assistant Commissioner of Indian Affairs, to Commissioner of Indian Affairs William Brophy, July 21, 1945, RG 75.

178. Ibid., William Zimmerman to J. C. McCaskill, July 27, 1945, RG 75.

179. Ibid., Memorandum from Felix Cohen to Commissioner of Indian Affairs, "Work in Alaska, June 15 to July 1," July 10, 1944, RG 75.

180. Ibid., Felix Cohen to Under Secretary, July 30, 1946, RG 48.

181. Ibid., Abe Fortas to the Secretary, July 23, 1945, RG 48.

182. *Hearing on the Nomination of Julius A. Krug for Appointment as Secretary of the Interior before the Senate Committee on Public Lands and Surveys*, 79th Cong. 2d Sess. 13 (1946).

183. 11 *Fed. Reg.* 6143 (1946).

184. National Archives, Subject Index to Matters Presented during the Secretary's Trip to Alaska, August 11–22, 1946, RG 48.

185. Ibid., Dr. Walter R. Goldschmidt and Theodore H. Haas, *A Report to the Commissioner of Indian Affairs: Possessory Rights of the Natives of Southeastern Alaska*, October 3, 1946, RG 75.

186. "Secretary Krug Spends Day in Juneau," *Daily Alaska Empire*, August 19, 1946.

187. Don C. Foster to E. L. Bartlett, April 24, 1946, BB.

188. National Archives, Memorandum from William Zimmerman, Acting Commissioner of Indian Affairs, to Assistant Secretary of the Interior William Warne, "Alaska Reservations and Possessory Rights," July 21, 1947, RG 75.

189. Ibid., Memorandum from Land Division to William Zimmerman, "Proposed Alaska Reservations," July 24, 1947, RG 75.

190. Ibid., Department of the Interior Information Service, "Alaskan Native Reserve Extended," October 16, 1947, RG 48.

191. E. L. Bartlett to Julius Krug, October 27, 1947, in *Repeal Act Authorizing Secretary of Interior to Create Indian Reservations in Alaska: Hearings before the Subcommittee of the Senate Committee on Interior and Insular Affairs*, 80th Cong. 2d Sess. 155–56 (1948).

192. National Archives, Memorandum from Oscar Chapman to William Zimmerman and other Department of the Interior officials, "Indian Reservations in Alaska," November 10, 1947, RG 48.

193. 80 *Cong. Rec.* 378 (1948).

194. S. J. Res. 162, 80th Cong. 1st Sess. (December 4, 1947).

195. "Krug Is Sworn in to Succeed Ickes," *New York Times*, March 19, 1946.

196. Felix Cohen to Harold Ickes, July 26, 1948, FSC.

197. 80 *Cong. Rec.* 9348 (1948).

198. National Archives, Memoranda from Assistant Secretary Warne to Secretary Krug, "Shungnak Reserve," October 26, 1948; "Barrow Reserve," October 26, 1948; and "Hydaburg Reserve," October 27, 1948, RG 48.

199. Ibid., Under Secretary Chapman to Secretary, October 29, 1948, RG 48.

200. Ibid., Memorandum from Secretary to Assistant Secretary Warne, "Proposed Establishment of Barrow, Shungnak and Hydaburg Reservations in Alaska," November 9, 1948, RG 48.

201. Ibid., Ernest Gruening to Secretary of the Interior, December 11, 1944, RG 48.

202. Minutes of Conference No. 3, December 13, 1948, Alaska Conferences, Department of the Interior, December 9-18, 1948, JK.

203. "Warne for High Interior Post," *New York Times*, May 8, 1947.

204. "Warne Party Due Here Tomorrow," *Ketchikan Daily News*, August 29, 1947.

205. "Warne Defines Alaskan Problems," *Ketchikan Daily News*, September 2, 1947.

206. William Warne to Harold Ickes, January 30, 1950, FSC.

207. Ibid.

208. Ferrell, 192, 233.

209. Allen and Shannon, 95.

210. Ruth Bronson to Lawrence Lindley, May 12, 1949, IRA.

211. "1 1/2 Bill Plan Urged," *New York Times*, November 8, 1949.

212. Allen and Shannon, 96.

213. Clifford, 256–57.

214. William Warne to Harold Ickes, January 30, 1950, FSC.

215. *Nomination of Oscar L. Chapman to be Secretary of the Interior: Hearing before the Senate Committee on Interior and Insular Affairs*, 81st Cong. 2d Sess. 12 (1950)

216. National Archives, E. L. Bartlett and Ernest Gruening to Oscar Chapman, January 16, 1950, RG 48.

217. Drinnon, *Keeper of Concentration Camps*, 163–248.

218. Philp, 225.

219. H. Rept. 1787, 81st Cong. 2d Sess. 167 (1950). See also "Reservations Denounced as Funds Denied Indian Bureau for Pending Plans," *Daily Alaska Empire*, March 16, 1950; "Restriction Stops Indian Reservations," *Daily Alaska Empire*, March 20, 1950.

220. "Reservation Vote Split," *Anchorage Daily Times*, April 25, 1950.

221. Eben Hopson Oral History Interview, June 23, 1972, Alaska Native Interviews, State of Alaska Historical Library, Juneau.

222. "Natives Oppose Reservation Plan," *Anchorage Daily Times*, October 10, 1946.

223. Don Foster to Felix Cohen, February 27, 1950, FSC.

224. National Archives, Agreement between towns of Hydaburg and Klawock, Native Village of Kake, Hydaburg and Klawock Cooperative Associations and P. E. Harris & Company, July 1946, RG 75.

225. H. B. Friele, vice-president, Nakat Packing Corporation, to Hydaburg Cooperative Association, February 16, 1948, CW.

226. William Paul, Jr., to Alaska Area Director, Office of Indian Affairs, June 17, 1950, CW.

227. Resolution of Hydaburg Town and Reservation Councils, November 11, 1950, CW.

228. John Collier to James Curry, January 30, 1951, CW.

229. Letter to the editor, *New York Times*, February 21, 1951.

230. A. Devitt Vanech, Assistant Attorney General, to J. Charles Dennis, United States Attorney in Seattle, February 2, 1951, author's collection.

231. *United States of America v Libby, McNeill & Libby*, District Court for the Territory of Alaska, Division Number One, at Juneau, Amended Complaint, No. 6445-A.

232. *Statutes at Large 62*, 908 (1948).

233. Ibid., 898.

234. A. Devitt Vanech, Assistant Attorney General, to Patrick Gilmore, United States Attorney for the First Division, May 9, 1951, author's collection.

235. Comments by Elizabeth Peratrovich, Alaska Representative of National Congress of American Indians, on *United States v Libby McNeill & Co., No. 6445-A* "Hydaburg Case," n.d., IRA.

236. "Hydaburg Testimony Ends; No Decision Expected Soon," *Daily Alaska Empire*, July 17, 1952.

237. *United States v Libby, McNeill & Libby*, 107 F Supp 697 (D. Alaska 1952).

238. Edward Merdes, personal communication to author, May 1988.

239. Oliver La Farge, president of the Association on American Indian Affairs, to the Honorable James P. McGranery, Attorney General of the United States, December 3, 1952, PN.

240. Perry Morton, Assistant Attorney General, to La Verne Madigan, Assistant to the Director, Association on American Indian Affairs, October 29, 1953, PN.

241. "Order Designating Reservation for Indians of Hydaburg, Alaska: Notice of Invalidation," 20 *Fed. Reg.* 168 (1955).

7. JAMES CURRY AND ALASKA STATEHOOD (PAGES 353–427)

1. E. L. Bartlett to Louis C. Peters, July 5, 1950, BB.

2. Wickersham diary, May 28, 1937.

3. David Morgan to ANB local camps, March 30, 1940, WP.

4. National Archives, Oscar Chapman to William Paul, June 13, 1940, RG 75.

5. Oscar Chapman to Claude Hirst, June 13, 1940, RG 75.

6. "Frank [*sic*] Peratrovich Elected President ANB and Mrs. Laura Haller President of Sisterhood," *Alaska Fishing News*, November 18, 1940.

7. William Zimmerman to William Paul, December 28, 1940, WP.

8. Roy Peratrovich interview.

9. William Paul to Grady Lewis, March 28, 1940, WP.

10. William Paul to ANB Executive Committee, September 23, 1940, WP.

11. National Archives, Fred Geeslin, Acting General Superintendent, to Government Teachers, March 8, 1941, RG 75.

12. Ibid., Minutes of Meeting of Tlingit-Haida Claims Committee Held at Wrangell, Alaska, April 9–11, 1941, RG 75 (hereafter cited as RG).

13. Ibid., George Folta to Claude Hirst, April 23, 1941, RG 75.

14. Ibid., William Paul Jr. to John Collier, February 27, 1942, RG 75.

15. Ibid., Grady Lewis to William Zimmerman, March 25, 1942, RG 75.

16. *The Members of the Tlingit Nation v United States* and *The Members of the Haida Nation v United States*, 102 Ct Cl 209 (1944).

17. Pub. L. 77-588, *Statutes at Large 56*, 323 (1942).

18. Felix Cohen to James Curry, December 19, 1944, FSC.

19. *Repeal Act Authorizing Secretary of Interior to Create Indian Reservations in Alaska: Hearings on S. 2037 and S. J. Res. 162 before the Subcommittee of the Senate Committee on Interior and Insular Affairs*, 80th Cong. 2d Sess. 257 (1948) (hereafter cited as SJR 162 Hearings).

20. Ibid., 252.

21. *Attorney Contracts with Indians: Hearings before a Subcommittee of the Senate Committee on Interior and Insular Affairs*, 82d Cong. 2d Sess. 463 (1952) (hereafter

cited as Curry Attorney Contracts Hearings). A transcript of the hearing record is on file at the National Archives.

22. Tugwell, 394.

23. SJR 162 Hearings, 252.

24. Curry Attorney Contracts Hearings, 463.

25. Ibid., 465.

26. Harlin. See also Minutes of NCAI Convention, Denver, Colorado, November 15–18, 1944, JC.

27. N. B. Johnson to Ed Rogers, August 6, 1952, JC.

28. Curry Attorney Contracts Hearings, 465.

29. Ibid., 334.

30. Felix Cohen to Theodore Haas, January 26, 1946, CW.

31. Pub. L. 79-74, *Statutes at Large* 59, 231 (1945).

32. Felix Cohen to James Curry, September 7, 1946, CW.

33. Champagne, 1020–21.

34. "Ruth Muskrat Bronson Retires," *Indians at Work*, January–February 1944.

35. Harlin.

36. James Curry to Ruth Bronson, October 4, 1946, CW.

37. Ibid.

38. Ruth Bronson to Charles Wright and James Curry, October 30, 1946, CW.

39. Ruth Bronson to James Curry, November 19, 1946, CW.

40. Ibid.

41. "Attorneys Named for Indian Cases, Court of Claims," *Daily Alaska Empire*, January 13, 1947.

42. Rex Lee, Acting Commissioner of Indian Affairs, to James Curry, August 16, 1951, CW.

43. "Curry Claims Sixteen Million Acres Lost," *Ketchikan Alaska Chronicle*, October 1, 1947.

44. U.S. Department of Agriculture, *Tongass National Forest, Alaska*, 3.

45. H. Exec. Doc. 5, 42d Cong. 1st Sess. 5 (1871).

46. Governor of Alaska, *Report of the Governor of Alaska 1914*, 13.

47. Governor of Alaska, *Report of the Governor of Alaska 1927*, 47.

48. "Krug Wants Decision Soon on Alaska Timber Claims," *Paper and Pulp*, July 1946.

49. *Tlingit and Haida Indians of Alaska v United States*, 177 F Supp 452, 467 (Ct Cl 1959).

50. Julius Krug to Joseph Martin, Speaker of the United States House of Representatives, May 16, 1947, in H. Rept. 873, 80th Cong. 1st Sess. 2 (1947).

51.   Ibid.

52.   James Curry to Ruth Bronson, April 30, 1947, CW.

53.   James Curry to William L. Paul Jr., April 23, 1947, CW.

54.   *Tongass National Forest: Hearings on H.J. Res. 205 before the House Committee on Agriculture*, 80th Cong. 1st Sess. 16 (1947) (hereafter cited as Tongass Timber Hearings).

55.   James Curry to Ruth Bronson, April 30, 1947, CW.

56.   The House Committee on Agriculture subsequently deleted the phrase "by or under future legislation" from the text of the version of the resolution that was enacted into law. See H. Rept. 873, 80th Cong. 1st Sess. (1947).

57.   National Archives, Petition to Congress of the United States, January 22, 1914, RG 75.

58.   Ibid., William Beattie to Commissioner of Education, May 18, 1914, RG 75.

59.   Land Protective Agreement, October 24, 1940, CW.

60.   *United States v 10.95 Acres of Land*, District Court for the Territory of Alaska, Division Number One, at Juneau, No. 4940-A.

61.   *Miller v United States*, 159 F2d 997, 999 (9th Cir 1947).

62.   Ibid.

63.   Ibid., 1001.

64.   "Aboriginal Rights Memorial," *Daily Alaska Empire*, March 12, 1947.

65.   Opinion M-35028: "Administration of Native Affairs in Alaska," *Decisions of the Department of the Interior*, 60:142, 146 (1948).

66.   Tongass Timber Hearings, 4.

67.   James Curry to William L. Paul Jr., April 23, 1947, CW.

68.   Curry Attorney Contracts Hearings, 1150.

69.   Memorandum from Frances Lopinsky to James Curry, n.d, CW.

70.   Don Foster to Ruth Bronson, April 24, 1947, CW.

71.   William Paul to Ruth Bronson, May 7, 1947, CW.

72.   Ruth Bronson to James Curry, May 14, 1947, CW.

73.   Ibid.

74.   Ibid., May 17, 1947.

75.   Ibid., May 14, 1947.

76.   Ibid., June 5, 1947.

77.   Ibid., June 6, 1947.

78.   Tongass Timber Hearings, 124.

79.   E. L. Bartlett to Representative John C. Sackett, April 22, 1967, BB.

80.   "Ed Bartlett Dies at His Circle Mine," *Fairbanks Daily News-Miner*, August 29, 1935.

81. For Bob Bartlett being named by his sister, see Naske, *Bob Bartlett*, 2; also, personal communication from D. A. Bartlett to author, November 8, 2001. For Bob Bartlett naming himself, see Tom Brown, "Bob Bartlett: A Man Who Symbolized Alaska," *Anchorage Daily News*, December 12, 1968.

82. Naske, *Bob Bartlett*, 25.

83. "The Birth of Alaska as the Forty-Ninth State in the Union Told in Dramatic Story of Bob and Vide Bartlett," *Tundra Times*, February 4, 1963.

84. Council, 84.

85. Ibid., 92.

86. "Dozens Seeking Secretary's Appointment," *Daily Alaska Empire*, January 7, 1939.

87. "Gruening Takes Office," *New York Times*, August 17, 1934.

88. Bhana, 15.

89. Tugwell, 5.

90. Ickes, *The Secret Diary*, 6.

91. Ibid., 320.

92. Ibid., 636.

93. Ibid., 641.

94. "Dr. Gruening Made Alaskan Governor," *New York Times*, September 3, 1939.

95. Gruening, 283.

96. Council, 114.

97. Naske, 54.

98. "Dimond to Return to Alaska to Practice Law; Urges Hellenthal, Judge," *Daily Alaska Empire*, January 18, 1944.

99. Naske, 54.

100. Joe Josephson, "A Good and Decent Man Once Came Their Way...," *Anchorage Daily News*, December 13, 1968.

101. E. L. Bartlett to Patrick Paul, Grand President of the ANB, August 13, 1954, WP.

102. Marston, 130–40.

103. National Achives, Ruth Gruber to John Collier, January 26, 1944, RG 48.

104. E. L. Bartlett Press Release, Juneau, Alaska, November 10, 1944, BB.

105. House Joint Memorial No. 22, 18th Alaska Territorial Legislature, in 93 *Cong. Rec.* 4118 (1947).

106. Tongass Timber Hearings, 166.

107. Ibid., 183.

108. "Another Chance Lost?" *Daily Alaska Empire*, July 25, 1947.

109. Ruth Bronson to James Curry, June 16, 1947, CW.

110. Tongass Timber Hearings, 137–39.

111. Ibid., 187.

112. Ibid., 153.

113. Ibid., 164.

114. H. Rept. 873, 80th Cong. 1st Sess. (1947).

115. 93 *Cong. Rec.* 8913–14 (1947).

116. 93 *Cong. Rec.* 5635 (1947).

117. Bob Bartlett to Hugh [Wade], July 31, 1947, BB.

118. S. Rept. 433, 80th Cong. 1st Sess. (1947).

119. 93 *Cong. Rec.* 1947 (1947).

120. "Another Chance Lost?" *Daily Alaska Empire*, July 25, 1947.

121. 93 *Cong. Rec.* 10,407 (1947).

122. Pub. L. 80-385, *Statutes at Large 101*, 920 (1947).

123. "Krug Says More Pulp Mills Due Soon," *Ketchikan Alaska Chronicle*, August 3, 1948.

124. H. Rept. 600, 100th Cong. 2d Sess. Pt. 1, 5–6 (1988). See also Hal Bernton, "Sitka Pulp Mill Closes Its Doors," *Anchorage Daily News*, July 1, 1993.

125. General Accounting Office, 50.

126. SJR 162 Hearings, 278.

127. Senate Committee on Interior and Insular Affairs, Committee Print: *Official Trip to Alaska and to Reclamation Projects, Indian Reservations, and Other Interior Department Installations in the Western States*, 80th Cong. 2d Sess., 6 (1948).

128. J. S. MacKinnon to Hugh Butler, November 21, 1947, author's collection.

129. SJR 162, 80th Cong. 2d Sess. (1947).

130. The report that the Executive Committee submitted to the 1945 ANB Convention states that Grand President Roy Peratrovich was sent to Hydaburg, Kake, and Klawock to explain the Bartlett bill, which "had been written by the Department of the Interior Attorneys, who were also attorneys for Kake, Klawock and Hydaburg," Report of Executive Committee, 1945 ANB Convention, WP.

131. Resolution No. 2, 1945 Alaska Native Brotherhood Convention Minutes, WP.

132. H.R. 5731, 79th Cong. 2d Sess. (March 11, 1946).

133. The hearing (whose transcript is unpublished) is referred to and the Department of the Interior's position is described in Warner Gardner to Ernest Gruening, June 26, 1947, WG.

134. The Departments of Agriculture and Justice's opposition to H.R. 190 is discussed in "Memorandum: Conference No. 2, Alaska Working Group, Department of the Interior," December 10, 1948, JK.

135. E. L. Bartlett to Anthony J. Dimond, December 5, 1947, AD.

136. Alaska General Election Returns, September 12, 1944; Alaska General Election Returns, October 8, 1946, Alaska State Archives, Juneau.

137. E. L. Bartlett to Josephine Peele, December 13, 1947, in 93 *Cong. Rec.* A4782 (1947).

138. R. E. Robertson to Hugh Butler, February 28, 1948, HB.

139. Alaska Native Brotherhood Resolution No. 4: "Reservation for Hydaburg," November 12, 1947, WP.

140. E. L. Bartlett to Hugh Butler, November 13, 1947, BB.

141. E. L. Bartlett to Josephine Peele, December 13, 1947, reprinted in 93 *Cong. Rec.* A4782 (1947).

142. SJR 162 Hearings, 295.

143. S. Rept. 1366, 80th Cong. 2d Sess. 1 (1948).

144. Felix Cohen to Joseph O'Mahoney, May 26, 1948, IRA.

145. 94 *Cong. Rec.* 9095–97 (1948).

146. Legislative Program for Development of Alaska Approved by Board of Trustees, Seattle Chamber of Commerce, December 16, 1947, Seattle, Washington.

147. George E. Thomas to Christy Thomas, June 15, 1948, HB.

148. Frances Lopinsky Horn, Memorandum: "Resume, Alaska Situation," July 23, 1951, CW.

149. *National Cyclopedia of American Biography*, 56:429.

150. Resolution of the Indian Rights Association, February 19, 1948, IRA.

151. 94 *Cong. Rec.* 9348 (1948).

152. Julius Krug to President Truman, April 16, 1949, JK. In his memorandum to the president, Krug states that he organized the committee on October 15, 1947.

153. Alaskan Development: A Preliminary Report by the Inter-Agency Committee on the Development of Alaska, February 1948, JK.

154. A description of the negotiation over the content of H.R. 7002 is contained in Minutes of Conference No. 2 of the Alaska Conferences at Department of the Interior, December 9–18, 1948, JK. Regarding Gruening and Bartlett's lack of involvement in the negotiation, see Enclosure No. 1 attached to a letter from Ernest Gruening to Rex Lee, acting director of the Division of Territories and Island Possessions, November 13, 1948, BB, in which Gruening states: "Neither Delegate Bartlett or I saw H.R. 7002 before it was introduced in the last week of the 80th Congress."

155. 94 *Cong. Rec.* 6765 (1948).

156. Staff Report, May 11, 1948, attached to memorandum from Richard Neustadt to David Stowe, May 11, 1948, HST.

157. H.R. 7002, 80th Cong. 2d Sess. (June 19, 1948).

158. Frances Lopinsky, memorandum: "The Welch Bill to Extinguish Indian Land Titles in Alaska," January 29, 1949, WP.

159. Minutes of Alaskan Conference, Department of Interior, Conference No. 2, December 10, 1949, JK.

160. Minutes of Meeting of the Board of Directors of the Indian Rights Association, May 5, 1948, IRA.

161. *Annual Report of the Secretary of the Interior*, 363 (1949).

162. Jonathan Steere and Isaac Sutton, "The Alaska Indians: Bills before Congress Said to Deprive Them of Rights," *New York Times*, March 28, 1948.

163. Advisory Committee on Indian Affairs to Secretary J. A. Krug, March 4, 1949, memorandum: "Findings of the Advisory Committee on Indian Affairs," JK.

164. Address by William E. Warne, Assistant Secretary, Department of the Interior, before the Annual Meeting of the Indian Rights Association, Philadelphia, Pennsylvania, January 27, 1949, IRA.

165. Ruth Bronson to Oliver La Farge, July 30, 1949, JC.

166. Maria Rogers, secretary of the Association on American Indian Affairs, to Philleo Nash, May 3, 1944, PN.

167. Memorandum from S.J.S. to Clark Clifford, April 28, 1949, CC.

168. Clifford, 76.

169. Gruening, 337.

170. 94 *Cong. Rec.* 6264 (1948).

171. H.S.T. to Secretary of the Interior, April 20, 1949, HST.

172. Truman, 288.

173. H.S.T. to Secretary of Interior, May 4, 1949, JK.

174. Richard Schifter, memorandum for the President's Materials Policy Commission, Executive Office of the President: "Aboriginal Land Claims in Alaska," October 22, 1951, PN (hereafter cited as Schifter memorandum).

175. House Joint Memorial No. 11, 20th Alaska Territorial Legislature (1951).

176. H.R. 4388, 82d Cong. 1st Sess. (June 11, 1951).

177. Schifter memorandum.

178. William Paul to Felix Cohen, May 26, 1952, WP.

179. *Hearing on H.R. 4388 before the Subcommittee on Indian Affairs of the House Committee on Interior and Insular Affairs*, 82d Cong. 1st Sess. 20–21 (August 27, 1951). A transcript of the hearings held on H.R. 4388 is on file at National Archives.

180. Ibid., 19.

181. Ibid., 36.

182. *Field Hearings on H.R. 4388 before the Subcommittee on Indian Affairs of the House Committee on Interior and Insular Affairs*, 82d Cong. 1st Sess. (November 5–10, 1951).

183. Ibid., 57.

184. Charles Hebert, president of the Alaska Miners Association, to the House Committee on Interior and Insular Affairs, December 31, 1951, in transcript of hearings on H.R. 4388, National Archives.

185. *Hearing in Washington, D.C., on H.R. 1921 before the Subcommittee on Territories and Insular Possessions of the House Committee on Interior and Insular Affairs*, 83d Cong. 1st Sess. 129 (February 18, 1953). A transcript of the hearings and work sessions held on H.R. 1921 is on file at National Archives.

186. *Work Session on H.R. 1921 before the Subcommittee on Territories and Insular Possessions of the House Committee on Interior and Insular Affairs*, 83d Cong. 1st Sess. 29 (March 4, 1953).

187. *Work Session on H.R. 1921 before the House Committee on Interior and Insular Affairs*, 83d Cong. 1st Sess. 9 (March 17, 1953).

188. Ibid., 8.

189. William Paul to Felix Cohen, May 26, 1952, AL.

190. *Hearing on H.R. 1921 before the House Committee on Interior and Insular Affairs*, 83d Cong. 1st Sess. 9 (April 1, 1953).

191. "M'Kay Advocates New York Power," *New York Times*, February 26, 1953.

192. Assistant Secretary of the Interior Orme Lewis to Honorable A. L. Miller, July 30, 1953, in House Committee on Interior and Insular Affairs, Committee Print Rept. 10, 83d Cong. 1st Sess. (1953).

193. Committee Print 10-A: H.R. 1921, 83d Cong. 1st Sess. (1953).

194. Orme Lewis, Assistant Secretary of the Interior, to A. L. Miller, January 11, 1954; William P. Rogers, Deputy Attorney General, to A. L. Miller, January 11, 1954, both in Reports of the Departments of Interior, Agriculture, and Justice on H.R. 1921, a Bill to Settle Possessory Land Claims in Alaska: House Committee on Interior and Insular Affairs, Committee Print 12, 83d Cong. 2d Sess. (1954).

195. 324 U.S. 335 (1945).

196. 329 U.S. 40 (1946).

197. Cohen, "Original Indian Title," 56.

198. In an appendix to the brief it filed in *Alcea Band of Tillamooks*, the Department of Justice represented to the U.S. Supreme Court that if the Indian Claims Commission determined that all claims of Indian tribes pending before the commission were valid, the United States would be obligated to pay $1 billion as compensation for the unlawful abrogation of the tribes' aboriginal titles. But if aboriginal title was Fifth Amendment "private property," the United States would be required to pay the tribes an additional $8 billion in interest. Brief for Petitioner at 55–56, *United States v Alcea Band of*

Tillamooks, 341 U.S. 48 (1951). In fact, the U.S. liability for Indian Claims Commission judgments was slightly less than $150 million. If the United States had been required to pay interest on the judgments, the total interest payment would have been slightly more than $1 billion. Newton, 1249.

199. *United States v Alcea Band of Tillamooks*, 341 U.S. 48, 49 (1951).

200. John Hope to E. L. Bartlett, January 13, 1954, in *Work Session on H.R. 1921 before the House Committee on Interior and Insular Affairs*, 83d Cong. 1st Sess. (March 17, 1953).

201. *Work Session on H.R. 1921 before the Subcommittee on Territories and Insular Possessions of the House Committee on Interior and Insular Affairs*, 83d Cong. 1st Sess. (January 14, 1954).

202. Krause, 65.

203. Oberg, 40.

204. William Paul to James Curry, November 7, 1949, CW.

205. William Paul to Tim Casey, November 6, 1953, WP. Paul states: "I became acquainted with James Craig Peacock thru the Rev. Dr. Karl Jackman [sic], of 156 Fifth Avenue, New York City."

206. Robert Holt Myers to author, June 4, 1991.

207. James Peacock to William Paul, January 14, 1952, WP.

208. William Paul to John Hope, November 30, 1952, WP.

209. Petition, *Tee-Hit-Ton Indians v United States*, Court of Claims No. 50385, October 31, 1951, U.S. Supreme Court, Transcripts of Records and File Copies of Briefs, vol. 33.

210. 120 F Supp 202 (Ct Cl 1954).

211. 347 U.S. 1009 (1954).

212. *Transcript of Meeting re H.R. 1921 of the Subcommittee on Territories and Insular Possessions of the House Committee on Interior and Insular Affairs*, 83d Cong. 2d Sess. (June 17, 1954).

213. Ibid., 5.

214. Ibid., 8.

215. Arthur Lazarus interview.

216. "Indian Claims Decision by U.S. Supreme Court," *Ketchikan Daily News*, February 9, 1955.

217. 348 U.S. 279 (1954).

218. H.R. 13978, 64th Cong. 1st Sess. (March 30, 1916).

219. "Statehood Advocated by Dimond," *Fairbanks Daily News-Miner*, November 1, 1943.

220. H.R. 3768, 78th Cong. 1st Sess. (December 2, 1943).

221. H.R. 3898, 79th Cong. 1st Sess. (July 21, 1945).

222. Official Returns—Territorial Canvassing Board, General Election, October 8, 1946, Alaska State Archives, Juneau.

223. *Statehood for Alaska: Hearings on H.R. 206 and H.R. 1808 before the Subcommittee on Territorial and Insular Possessions of the House Committee on Public Lands*, 80th Cong. 1st Sess. (1947) (hereafter cited as 1947 Alaska Statehood Hearings).

224. The antistatehood brochure that Juneau cannery attorney H. L. Faulkner distributed to members of Congress listed "the handicaps which should be removed in advance of a consideration of statehood . . . Settlement of the matter of Indian aboriginal claims so as to eliminate completely the agitation over this subject" was first on the list. Argument on Behalf of Opponents of Statehood for Alaska, April 1947, BB.

225. 1947 Alaska Statehood Hearings, 14.

226. Ibid., 428.

227. *Alaska: Hearings on H. Res. 93 before the Subcommittee on Territorial and Insular Possessions of the House Committee on Public Lands*, 80th Cong. 1st Sess. 163 (1947).

228. Bob Bartlett to Burke Riley, April 4, 1948, BB.

229. Felix Cohen to E. L. Bartlett, March 25, 1948, BB.

230. Wesley D'Ewart to Felix Cohen, March 29, 1948, BB.

231. National Archives, James Davis, Director Division of Territories, to Assistant Secretary William Warne, April 19, 1948, RG 48.

232. Bob Bartlett to Burke Riley, April 4, 1948, BB.

233. Bob Bartlett to "Dear Friend," April 8, 1948, BB.

234. Bob Bartlett to Burke Riley, April 10, 1948, BB.

235. H. Rept. 1731, 14–15, 80th Cong. 2d Sess. (1948).

236. Felix Cohen to E. L. Bartlett, April 16, 1948, BB.

237. Bob Bartlett to Don Foster, April 19, 1948, BB.

238. Bloedel, 222–23.

239. *Alaska Statehood: Hearings on H.R. 331 and S. 2036 before the Senate Committee on Interior and Insular Affairs*, 81st Cong. 2d Sess. 307 (1950).

240. Bartlett office memorandum, May 26, 1950, BB.

241. James Curry to William Paul, Jr., May 27, 1950, CW.

242. E. L. Bartlett to James Curry, May 29, 1950, BB.

243. Bartlett Memorandum, June 23, 1950, BB.

244. Bob Bartlett to Robert Atwood, June 27, 1950, BB.

245. Bob Bartlett to Ernest Gruening, June 30, 1950, BB.

246. "Indian Group Would Alter State Bill," *Ketchikan Alaska Chronicle*, July 8, 1950.

247. Felix Cohen to Anthony Smith, Executive Secretary, CIO, July 10, 1950, CW.

248. Harold Ickes, "Alaska's Natives Need Help," *New Republic*, July 24, 1950.

249. *Washington Post* and *New York Times*, August 1, 1950.

250. 96 *Cong. Rec.* 12,066–77 (1950).

251. NCAI news release, August 14, 1950, CW.

252. "Alaska Land Rights," *Washington Post*, August 16, 1950; "Alaskan Statehood and Indian Titles," *Washington Post*, August 20, 1950.

253. James Curry to Oliver La Farge, August 22, 1950, CW.

254. James Curry to [senators], September 19, 1950, CW.

255. James Curry to Peter Neilsen, November 30, 1950, CW.

256. Robert S. Allen, "Lawyer for Alaskan Indians Worked against Statehood Bill," *Anchorage Daily Times*, December 11, 1950.

257. James Curry to Alaska Native Brotherhood, December 1, 1950, CW.

258. E. L. Bartlett to Victor Rivers, December 16, 1950, BB.

259. S. 50, 82d Cong. 1st Sess. (January 8, 1951).

260. Butler Amendment to S. 50, 82d Cong. 1st Sess. (January 25, 1951).

261. E.g., James Curry to Senator Paul Douglas, February 5, 1951, CW.

262. E. L. Bartlett to Stewart French, member of staff of Senate Committee on Interior and Insular Affairs, February 17, 1951, BB.

263. 96 *Cong. Rec.* 1537 (1952).

264. Council, 146.

265. Hugh Butler to Dwight Eisenhower, March 12, 1954, in Branyan and Larsen, 988.

266. Anthony W. Smith to Hugh Butler, May 26, 1950, HB.

267. Hugh Butler to Anthony W. Smith, June 2, 1950, HB.

268. Ernest Gruening to Bob Bartlett, January 20, 1954, BB.

269. *Statehood for Alaska: Executive Session of the Subcommittee on Territories and Insular Affairs of the Senate Committee on Interior and Insular Affairs*, 83d Cong. 2d Sess. (January 29, 1954). A transcript of the executive session is on file at National Archives.

270. Section 19(a), S. 49, in 100 *Cong. Rec.* 2905 (1954).

271. 100 *Cong. Rec.* 3167 (1954).

272. Section 3, S. 49, in 100 *Cong. Rec.* 2905 (1954).

273. Section 19(b), S. 49, in 100 *Cong. Rec.* 2908 (1954).

274. "Frank George Replaces Ruth Bronson as NCAI Director," *National Congress of American Indians News Bulletin*, May–June 1952, JC.

275. Curry Attorney Contracts Hearings, 6–7.

276. James Curry to Frank Peratrovich, September 26, 1950, CW.

277. James Curry to Wilbur Menninick, April 14, 1954, JC.

278. Roy Peratrovich interview.

279. Frances Lopinsky Horn interview.

280. W. H. Beckerleg to author, May 3, 1994.

281. Ruth Bronson to Oliver La Farge, August 24, 1952, in Drinnon, *Keeper of Concentration Camps*, 212.

282. Excerpts from the report of James E. Curry, General Counsel of the NCAI, to the Convention of the Congress at Denver, December 12, 1948, JC. See also Curry Attorney Contracts Hearings, 744.

283. James Curry to Felix Cohen, January 21, 1948, JC.

284. Curry Attorney Contracts Hearings, 1277.

285. Ibid., 387.

286. Ibid., 382.

287. Ibid., 596.

288. Ibid., 602.

289. Bob Bartlett to Hugh Wade, February 24, 1952, BB.

290. Curry Attorney Contracts Hearings, 1209–10.

291. Bob Bartlett to Hugh Wade, February 24, 1952, BB.

292. James Curry to Eva Nichols, October 19, 1952, JC.

293. Ben Dwight to N. B. Johnson, November 12, 1952, JC.

294. "Curry Says He Won't Accept Indian Clients," *Washington Post*, October 30, 1952.

295. S. Rept. 8, 83d Cong. 1st Sess. 5–15 (1953).

296. Arthur Lazarus interview.

297. Alexander Lesser, executive director, Association on American Indian Affairs, to Oliver La Farge, March 16, 1954, PN.

298. Sections 203 and 219, S. 49, 84th Cong. 1st Sess. (1955) in *Alaska-Hawaii Statehood, Elective Governor, and Commonwealth Status: Hearings on S. 49, S. 399 and S. 402 before the Senate Committee on Interior and Insular Affairs*, 84th Cong. 1st Sess. 10, 18 (1955).

299. Ibid., 98.

300. Ibid., 98–108.

301. Ibid., 104.

302. E. L. Bartlett to James Curry, May 29, 1950, BB.

303. Frances Lopinsky Horn interview.

304. Sections 3 and 5(b), H.R. 248, 84th Cong. 1st Sess. (1955) in *Hawaii-Alaska Statehood: Hearings on H.R. 2535, H.R. 2536, H.R. 49, H.R. 185, H.R. 187, H.R.*

248, H.R. 511, H.R. 555, and H.R. 2531 before the House Committee on Interior and Insular Affairs, 84th Cong. 1st Sess. 57–58 (1955).

305. Arthur Lazarus to La Verne Madigan, May 14, 1958, AL.

Epilogue (429–440)

1. Native Land Claims: An Address by Governor Walter J. Hickel to the People of Alaska, February 7, 1967, BB.

2. *Hawaii-Alaska Statehood: Hearings on H.R. 2535, H.R. 2536, H.R. 49, H.R. 185, H.R. 187, H.R. 248, H.R. 511 and H.R. 2531 before the House Committee on Interior and Insular Affairs*, 84th Cong. 1st Sess. 106 (1955) (hereafter cited as 1955 House Alaska Statehood Hearings).

3. Ed Edmondson, "The Future and the American Indian," *Indian Truth*, January–March 1955.

4. 1955 House Alaska Statehood Hearings, 381.

5. Ibid., 382.

6. Ibid., 383.

7. 348 U.S. 291.

8. E. L. Bartlett to James Peacock, February 22, 1955, WP.

9. H.R. 11986, 84th Cong. 2d Sess. (June 27, 1956).

10. James Peacock [unsigned] to E. L. Bartlett, January 3, 1956, WP.

11. 102 *Cong. Rec.* 15,426 (1956).

12. In the H.R. 8190 bill file at the National Archives the only items are a June 18, 1957 letter from E. L. Bartlett to Clair Engle, chairman of the House Interior Committee, requesting Engle to ask the secretaries of the interior and agriculture and the attorney general to submit reports on the bill; a note dated June 20, 1957, from Engle to Bartlett reporting that he had done so "and will let you know when they are received;" and confirmations from the Departments of Interior and Agriculture that the requests had been received.

13. Association on American Indian Affairs, Executive Director's Report, March 16, 1962, AL.

14. Memorandum from Director, Bureau of Land Management, to Assistant Secretary, Public Land Management, May 16, 1966, Secretary of the Interior Central Office Files.

15. Arthur Lazarus interview.

16. James Officer to Arthur Lazarus, August 10, 1965, AL.

17. 31 *Fed. Reg.* 15,494 (1966).

18. Public Land Order No. 4582, January 17, 1969, in 3 *Fed. Reg.* 1025 (1969).

19.   Roy Peratrovich interview.

20.   Frederick Paul, 203.

21.   Ibid., 205.

22.   Ibid., 201.

23.   Minutes of Meeting of Board of Governors of the Alaska Bar Association, May 28, 1958, Alaska Bar Association, Anchorge, Alaska.

24.   Ibid., January 22, 1959.

25.   Author discussion with Charles Edwardsen Jr., July 8, 1990.

26.   Gallagher, 106.

27.   Ibid., 85. See also Bancroft, *History of Alaska*, 609.

28.   Gallagher, 119.

29.   Charles Edwardsen, Jr., to William Paul, January 5, 1966, North Slope Claim File, Alaska State Historical Library, Juneau. Alaska.

30.   William Paul to Department of the Interior, Bureau of Land Management, January 18, 1966, North Slope Claim File, Alaska State Historical Library, Juneau.

31.   Don Wright interview.

32.   Frederick Paul interview.

Bibliography

References to collections, archival material, and interviews follow the main bibliography.

Abernathy, Thomas Perkins. *Western Lands and the American Revolution*. New York: Russell & Russell, 1959.

Adney, Edwin Tappan. *Tappan Adney's Biography of John J. Healy*. Hanover, N.H.: Baker Library, Dartmouth College, 1937.

"Alaska and Conservation." *Alaska-Yukon Magazine,* March 1911.

Alaska Boundary Tribunal. *Proceedings of the Alaska Boundary Tribunal, Convened at London*. Washington, D.C.: Government Printing Office, 1904.

Allan, A. A. *Gold, Men and Dogs*. New York: G. P. Putnam's Sons, 1931.

Allen, Robert S., and William V. Shannon, *The Truman Merry-Go-Round*. New York: Vanguard Press, 1950.

Andrews, C. L. *The Story of Alaska*. Caldwell, Idaho: Caxton Printers, 1943.

Arndt, Katherine L. "Russian Relations with the Stikine Tlingit." *Alaska Journal,* spring 1988.

Arnold, Robert D. *Alaska Native Land Claims*. Anchorage: Alaska Native Foundation, 1978.

Atwood, Evangeline. *Frontier Politics: Alaska's James Wickersham*. Portland, Oregon: Binford & Mort, 1979.

Bailey, Alvin Keith. "The Strategy of Sheldon Jackson in Opening the West for National Missions: 1860-1880." Ph.D. diss., Yale University, 1948.

Bancroft, Hubert Howe. *History of Alaska, 1730-1885*. Darien, Conn.: Hafner Publishing Co., 1886.

———. *History of British Columbia, 1792-1887*. San Francisco: History Co., 1887.

Beard, Charles A. *An Economic History of the Constitution of the United States*. New York: Macmillan, 1913.

Beattie, William Gilbert. *Marsden of Alaska: A Modern Indian*. New York: Vantage Press, 1955.

Berkh, Vassillii. *A Chronological History of the Discovery of the Aleutian Islands or the Exploits of Russian Merchants*. Kingston, Ont.: Limestone Press, 1974.

Berton, Pierre, *The Klondike Fever.* New York: Alfred A. Knopf, 1958.

Bhana, Surendra. *The United States and the Development of the Puerto Rican Status Question.* Lawrence, Kansas: University Press of Kansas, 1975.

Birch, Stephen. "Pioneering Capital." *Alaska-Yukon Magazine,* December 1909.

Bloedel, Richard Henry. "The Alaska Statehood Movement." Ph.D. diss., University of Washington, 1974.

Bockstoce, John. "A Preliminary Estimate of the Reduction of the Western Arctic Bowhead Whale Population by the Pelagic Whaling Industry: 1848-1915." *Marine Fisheries Review,* September-October 1980.

———. *Whales, Ice, and Men.* Seattle: University of Washington Press, 1986.

Bockstoce, John, and Daniel B. Botkin. "The Harvest of Pacific Walruses by the Pelagic Whaling Industry, 1848 to 1914." *Arctic and Alpine Research,* August 1982.

Branyan, Robert, and Lawrence Larsen. *The Eisenhower Administration 1953-1961: Documenting History.* New York: Random House, 1971.

Brevig, Tollef Larson. *Apaurak in Alaska.* Philadelphia: Dorrance & Co., 1944.

Brooks, Alfred Huse. *Blazing Alaska's Trails.* Fairbanks: University of Alaska Press, 1973.

"Brooks on the Coal Tie-Up." *Alaska-Yukon Magazine,* October 1910.

Brower, Charles D. *Fifty Years below Zero.* New York: Dodd, Mead & Co., 1942.

Burch, Franklin Ward. "Alaska's Railroad Frontier." Ph.D. diss., Catholic University, 1965.

Bureau of the Census. *Thirteenth Census of the United States: Population—Alaska.* Washington, D.C.: National Archives, Microfilm No. T624, Roll 1749.

Bureau of Education. *Report of the Work of the Bureau of Education for the Natives of Alaska, 1913-1914.* Washington, D.C.: Government Printing Office, 1915.

Bureau of Fisheries. *Alaska Fishery and Fur-Seal Industries in 1920.* Washington, D.C.: Government Printing Office, 1921.

———. *Report of Alaska Investigations in 1914.* Washington, D.C.: Government Printing Office, 1915.

Bureau of Mines. *Bulletin No. 36.* Washington, D.C.: Government Printing Office, 1911.

Callahan, Erinia Pavaloff Cherosky. "A Yukon Biography." *Alaska Journal,* spring 1975.

Cantwell, John. *Report of the Operations of the U.S. Revenue Steamer Nunivak on the Yukon River Station, Alaska, 1899-1901.* Washington, D.C.: Government Printing Office, 1902.

Champagne, Duane, ed. *The Native North American Almanac.* Detroit: Gale Research, 1994.

Chase, Will H. *Reminiscences of Captain Billy Moore.* Kansas City, Kansas: Burton Publishing Co., 1947.

Chevigny, Hector. *Russian America: The Great Alaskan Venture: 1741-1867.* London: Cresset Press, 1966.

Clark, Ramsey. Keynote Address given at Alaska Federation of Natives Annual Convention, Anchorage, 1983.

Clepper, Henry. *Crusade for Conservation: The Centennial History of the American Forestry Association.* Washington, D.C.: American Forestry Association, 1975.

Clifford, Clark. *Counsel to the President.* New York: Random House, 1991.

Coe, Douglas. *Captured Heritage: The Scramble for Northwest Coast Artifacts.* Seattle: University of Washington Press, 1985.

Coffman, Edward M. *The Old Army: A Portrait of the American Army in Peacetime, 1784-1898.* New York: Oxford University Press, 1986.

Cohen, Felix. *Felix S. Cohen's Handbook of Federal Indian Law.* Albuquerque: University of New Mexico Press, n.d.

———. "Original Indian Title." *Minnesota Law Review,* 1947.

Coleman, Michael C. *Presbyterian Missionary Attitudes toward American Indians, 1837-1893.* Jackson: University Press of Mississippi, 1985.

Collier, John. *From Every Zenith: A Memoir.* Denver: Sage Books, 1962.

Connelley, William Elsey. *The Life of Preston B. Plumb, 1837-1891.* Chicago: Browne & Howell Co., 1913.

Conrad, David E. "Creating the Nation's Largest Forest Reserve: Roosevelt, Emmons, and the Tongass National Forest." *Pacific Historical Review,* February 1977.

Cooley, Richard A. *Politics and Conservation: The Decline of the Alaska Salmon.* New York: Harper & Row, 1963.

Council, Mary Lee. "Three Steps Forward, Two Steps Back: Bob Bartlett and Alaska Statehood." University of Alaska Fairbanks, 1969.

Crosby, Thomas. *Up and Down the North Pacific Coast by Canoe and Mission Ship.* Toronto: Missionary Society of the Methodist Church, 1914.

Dauenhauer, Nora Marks, and Richard Dauenhauer, eds. *Haa Kusteeyi, Our Culture: Tlingit Life Stories.* Seattle: University of Washington Press, 1994.

Davidson, Innes N. *The Arctic Brotherhood: A Souvenir History of the Order.* Seattle: Acme Publishing Co., 1909.

Davis, George Thompson. *Metlakatla: A True Narrative of the Red Man.* Chicago: Ram's Horn Co., 1904.

Davis, Mary Lee. *We Are Alaskans.* Boston: W. A. Wilde Co., 1931.

De Armond, R. N. *The Founding of Juneau.* Juneau: Gastineau Channel Centennial Association, 1967.

————, ed. *Lady Franklin Visits Sitka, Alaska 1870. The Journal of Sophia Cracroft, Sir John Franklin's Niece*. Anchorage: Alaska Historical Society, 1981.

Deloria, Philip S. "The Era of Indian Self-Determination." Paper presented at Sun Valley, Idaho, August 1983.

Deloria, Vine, Jr., and Clifford Lytle. *The Nations Within: The Past and Future of American Indian Sovereignty*. New York: Pantheon Books, 1984.

Dewey, John. *Democracy and Education*. New York: Macmillan, 1916.

De Windt, Harry. *Through the Gold Fields of Alaska to Bering Straits*. New York: Harper and Brothers, 1898.

Douglas, William O. *The Court Years, 1939-1975*. New York: Random House, 1980.

————. *Go East, Young Man*. New York: Random House, 1974.

Down, Mary Margaret. *A Century of Service: A History of the Sisters of Saint Ann and Their Contribution to Education in British Columbia, the Yukon and Alaska*. Victoria, B.C.: The Sisters of Saint Ann, 1966.

Drinnon, Richard. *Facing West: The Metaphysics of Indian-Hating and Empire-Building*. New York: New American Library, 1980.

————. *Keeper of Concentration Camps: Dillon S. Myer and American Racism*. Berkeley: University of California Press, 1987.

Drucker, Philip. "The Native Brotherhoods: Modern Intertribal Organizations on the Pacific Coast." *Bureau of American Ethnology Bulletin*, No. 168, 1958.

Earp, Josephine. *I Married Wyatt Earp: The Recollections of Josephine Sarah Marcus Earp*. Edited by Lenn G. Boyer. Tucson: University of Arizona Press, 1976.

Emmons, George Thorton. *The Tlingit Indians*. Edited by Frederica de Laguna. Seattle: University of Washington Press, 1991.

Evans, Sheila T. "An Historical View of Selected Alaskan Natural Resources." Anchorage: Alaska Historical Commission, 1981.

Federal Field Committee for Development Planning in Alaska. *Alaska Natives and the Land*. Anchorage: Government Printing Office, 1968.

Ferrell, Robert H., ed. *Off the Record: The Private Papers of Harry S. Truman*. New York: Harper & Row, 1980.

Fisher, Raymond H. *Bering's Voyages: Whither and Why*. Seattle: University of Washington Press, 1977.

Fitzpatrick, John, ed. *The Writings of George Washington from the Original Manuscript Sources, 1745-1799*. 39 vols. Washington, D.C.: Government Printing Office, 1931-1944.

"The Floating Salmon Trap—Success From the Start." *Pacific Fisherman*, August 1952.

Folta, Richard C. *Of Bench and Bears: Alaska's Bear Hunting Judge*. Anchorage: Great Northwest Co., 1986.

Fox, Stephen. *John Muir and His Legacy*. Boston: Little, Brown, 1981.

Fry, James. *Military Miscellanies*. New York: Brentano's, 1889.

Gallagher, Hugh. *Etok: A Story of Eskimo Power.* New York: G. P. Putnam's Sons, 1974.

Gambell, Vene C. *The Schoolhouse Farthest West: St. Lawrence Island, Alaska.* New York: Woman's Board of Home Missions of the Presbyterian Church, 1910.

General Accounting Office. *Distribution of Timber Sales Receipts for Fiscal Years 1992-1994.* Washington, D.C.: Government Printing Office, 1995.

Gibson, James R. *Imperial Russia in Frontier America: The Changing Geography of Supply of Russian America, 1784-1867.* New York: Oxford University Press, 1976.

Gilcreast, Everett Arthur. "Richard Henry Pratt and American Indian Policy, 1877-1906: A Study of the Assimilation Movement." Ph.D. diss., Yale University, 1967.

Glavis, L. R. "The Whitewashing of Ballinger." *Collier's Weekly,* November 13, 1909.

Golovin, P. N. *Civil and Savage Encounters: The Worldly Travel Letters of an Imperial Russian Navy Officer, 1860-1861.* Portland: Oregon Historical Society, 1983.

———. *The End of Russian America: Captain P. N. Golovin's Last Report, 1862.* Portland: Oregon Historical Society, 1979.

Governor of Alaska. *Report of the Governor of Alaska.* Washington, D.C.: Government Printing Office, various dates.

Gray, Alfred O. *Not by Might: The Story of Whitworth College.* Spokane, Wash.: Whitworth College, 1965.

Grinnell, George Bird. *Brief History of the Bone and Crockett Club.* New York: Forest and Stream Publishing Co., 1910.

Grinnell, George Bird, and Charles Sheldon, eds. *Hunting and Conservation: The Book of the Boone and Crockett Club.* New Haven, Conn.: Yale University Press, 1925.

Gruening, Ernest. *Many Battles: The Autobiography of Ernest Gruening.* New York: Liveright, 1973.

Harlin, Lois. "The National Congress of American Indians." *Indians at Work.* Washington, D.C.: Bureau of Indian Affairs, November-December 1944.

Harrison, E. S. "What Is the Alaska Syndicate Doing?" *Alaska-Yukon Magazine,* May 1910.

Haskell, William B. *Two Years in the Klondike and Alaskan Gold Fields.* Hartford, Conn.: Hartford Publishing Co., 1898.

Hayakawa, S. I. *Language in Thought and Action.* New York: Harcourt, Brace and World, 1964.

Hayes, Florence. *A Land of Challenge: Alaska.* Philadelphia: Board of National Missions of the Presbyterian Church of the United States of America, 1941.

Healy, Michael A. *Report of the Cruise of the Revenue Marine Steamer Corwin in the Arctic Ocean in the Year 1884.* Washington, D.C.: Government Printing Office, 1889.

————. *Report of the Cruise of the Revenue Marine Steamer Corwin in the Arctic Ocean in the Year 1885.* Washington, D.C.: Government Printing Office, 1887.

Henderson, Alice Palmer. *The Rainbow's End: Alaska.* Chicago: Herbert S. Stone and Co., 1898.

Henkelman, James W., and Kurt H. Vitt. *Harmonious to Dwell: The History of the Alaska Moravian Church, 1885-1985.* Bethel: Tundra Press, 1985.

Hinckley, Ted C. "The Alaska Labors of Sheldon Jackson, 1877-1890." Ph.D. diss., Indiana University, 1961.

————. *The Americanization of Alaska, 1867-1897.* Palo Alto, Calif.: Pacific Books, 1972.

————. "The Canoe Rocks—We Do Not Know What Will Become Of Us: The Complete Transcript of a Meeting Between Governor John Green Brady of Alaska and a Group of Tlingit Chiefs, Juneau, December 14, 1898." *Western Historical Quarterly,* July 1970.

————. "The Inside Passage: A Popular Gilded Age Tour." *Pacific Northwest Quarterly,* April 1965.

————. "Sheldon Jackson, Presbyterian Lobbyist for the Great Land of Alaska." *Journal of Presbyterian History,* March 1962.

Hinckley, Ted C., and Caryl Hinckley. "Ivan Petroff's Journal of a Trip to Alaska in 1878." *Journal of the West,* January 1966.

Holbo, Paul S. *Tarnished Expansion: The Alaska Scandal, the Press and Congress, 1867-1871.* Knoxville: University of Tennessee Press, 1983.

Holt, William Sylvester. "Beginning of Mission Work in Alaska." *Washington Historical Quarterly,* April 1920.

Hooper, Calvin L. *Report of the Cruise of the U. S. Revenue Steamer Corwin in the Arctic Ocean: November 1, 1880.* Washington, D.C.: Government Printing Office, 1881.

Hope, Andrew. *Founders of the Alaska Native Brotherhood.* Sitka: New Archangel Books, 1975.

Howard, Oliver O. *Autobiography of Oliver Otis Howard.* New York: Baker and Taylor Company, 1907.

————. *Famous Indian Chiefs I Have Known.* Lincoln: University of Nebraska Press, 1989.

Hunt, William R. *Whiskey Peddler: Johnny Healy, North Frontier Trader.* Missoula, Mont.: Mountain Press Publishing Co., 1993.

Ickes, Harold. *The Secret Diary of Harold L. Ickes: The Inside Struggle, 1936-1939.* New York: Simon and Schuster, 1954.

————. "Alaska's Natives Need Help." *New Republic,* July 24, 1950.

Illich, Ivan. *Deschooling Society.* New York: Harper and Row, 1970.

Institute of Social, Economic and Government Research. *Alaska Native Population Trends and Vital Statistics, 1950-1985.* Anchorage: University of Alaska, 1971.

Ise, John. *The United States Forest Policy*. New York: Arno Press, 1972.

Jackson, Sheldon. *Alaska and Missions on the North Pacific Coast*. New York: Dodd, Mead and Co., 1880.

———. *Report on Education in Alaska*. Washington, D.C.: Government Printing Office, 1886.

———. *Statement of Dr. Sheldon Jackson of Alaska before the House Committee on Territories*. Washington, D.C.: Government Printing Office, 1904.

Janson, Lone E. *The Copper Spike*. Anchorage: Alaska Northwest Publishing Co., 1975.

Jenkins, Thomas. *The Man of Alaska: Peter Trimble Rowe*. New York: Morehouse-Gorham Co., 1943.

Kalman, Laura. *Abe Fortas: A Biography*. New Haven, Conn.: Yale University Press, 1990.

Kan, Sergi. "Russian Orthodox Brotherhoods among the Tlingit: Missionary Goals and Native Response." *Ethnohistory*, 1985.

Kappler, Charles J. *Indian Treaties, 1778-1883*. New York: Interland Publishing Co., 1904.

Kelly, Lawrence C. *The Assault on Assimilation: John Collier and the Origins of Indian Policy Reform*. Albuquerque: University of New Mexico Press, 1983.

Khlebnikov, K. T. *Baranov: Chief Manager of the Russian Colonies in America*. Kingston, Ont.: Limestone Press, 1973.

———. *Colonial Russian America: Kyrill T. Khlebnikov's Reports, 1817-1832*. Portland: Oregon Historical Society, 1976.

King, Judson. *The Conservation Fight from Theodore Roosevlt to the Tennessee Valley Authority*. Washington, D.C.: Public Affairs Press, 1959.

Kirk, Robert C. *Twelve Months in the Klondike*. London: William Heinemann, 1899.

Kitchener, L. D. *Flag over the North*. Seattle: Superior Publishing Co., 1954.

Kovach, Michael George. "The Russian Orthodox Church in Russian America." Ph.D. diss., University of Pittsburgh, 1957.

Krause, Aurel. *The Tlingit Indians*. Seattle: University of Washington Press, 1956.

Kvasnicka, Robert M., and Hernan J. Viola, eds. *The Commissioners of Indian Affairs, 1824-1977*. Lincoln: University of Nebraska Press, 1979.

Lamar, Howard R., ed. *The Reader's Encyclopedia of the American West*. New York: Thomas Y. Crowell Co., 1977.

Lazell, J. Arthur. *Alaskan Apostle*. New York: Harper and Brothers, 1960.

Lipscomb, Andrew A., and Albert E. Bergh, eds. *The Writings of Thomas Jefferson*. 12 vols. Washington, D.C.: Thomas Jefferson Memorial Association, 1904.

Lisiansky, Urey. *Voyage round the World in the Years 1803, 1804, 1805, and 1806*. New York: De Capo Press, 1968.

Littlefield, Daniel F., and James W. Parins, eds. *American Indians and Alaska Native Newspapers and Periodicals, 1826-1924.* Westport, Conn.: Greenwood Press, 1984.

Ludecke, Edward. "Our First Troops in Alaska." *Alaska-Yukon Magazine,* September 1907.

Lynch, Jeremiah. *Three Years in the Klondike.* London: Edward Arnold, 1904.

Mackenzie, Clara Childs. *Wolf Smeller (Zhoh Gwatson): A Biography of John Fredson, Native Alaskan.* Anchorage: Alaska Pacific University Press, 1985.

Maris, Omer. *Sketches from Alaska.* Chicago: Chicago Record, 1897.

Marston, Muktuk. *Men of the Tundra: Alaska Eskimos at War.* New York: October House, 1972.

McFarland, Amanda. "Letters of Amanda R. McFarland." *Journal of the Presbyterian Historical Society,* June 1956, December 1956, March 1957.

McHenry, Robert, and Charles Van Doren. *A Documentary History of Conservation in America.* New York: Praeger, 1972.

McKennan, Robert A. "The Chandalar Kutchin." *Arctic Institute of North America, Technical Paper No. 17, 1965.*

McLain, John Scudder. *Alaska and the Klondike.* New York: McClure, Phillips and Co., 1905.

Michael, Henry N., ed. *Lieutenant Zagoskin's Travels in Russian America, 1842-1844.* Toronto: University of Toronto Press, 1967.

Mikesell, Raymond F. *The World Copper Industry.* Baltimore: Johns Hopkins University Press, 1979.

Miller, David Hunter. *The Alaska Treaty.* Kingston, Ont.: Limestone Press, 1981.

Miller, Nathan. *Theodore Roosevelt: A Life.* New York: William Morrow, 1992.

Moley, Raymond. *The First New Deal.* New York: Harcourt, Brace & World, 1966.

Morison, Elting E., ed. *The Letters of Theodore Roosevelt.* 8 vols. Cambridge, Mass.: Harvard University Press, 1954.

Morris, Edmund. *The Rise of Theodore Roosevelt.* New York: Coward, McCann & Geoghegan, 1979.

Muir, John. *The Cruise of the Corwin.* Boston: Houghton Mifflin, 1917.

———. *Travels in Alaska.* Boston: Houghton Mifflin, 1915.

Murray, Andrew E. *The Skyline Synod: Presbyterianism in Colorado and Utah.* Denver: Golden Bell Press, 1971.

Murray, Peter. *The Devil and Mr. Duncan.* Victoria, B.C.: Sono Nis Press, 1985.

Naske, Claus-M. *Edward Lewis Bob Bartlett of Alaska: A Life in Politics.* Fairbanks: University of Alaska Press, 1979.

Naske, Claus-M., and L. J. Rowinski. *Anchorage: A Pictorial History.* Norfolk, Va.: Donning Co., 1981.

Nelson, Edward William. *The Eskimo about Bering Strait.* Washington, D.C.: Government Printing Office, 1899.

Newton, Nell Jessup. "At the Whim of the Sovereign: Aboriginal Title Reconsidered." *Hastings Law Journal,* July 1980.

Nichols, Jeannette Paddock. *Alaska: A History of Its Administration, Exploitation, and Industrial Development during Its First Half Century under the Rule of the United States.* Cleveland: Arthur H. Clark Co., 1923.

Nordin, D. Sven. *Rich Harvest: A History of the Grange, 1867-1900.* Jackson: University Press of Mississippi, 1974.

Oberg, Kalervo. *The Social Economy of the Tlingit Indians.* Seattle: University of Washington Press, 1973.

Ogilvie, William. *Early Days on the Yukon and the Story of Its Gold Finds.* London: John Lane, 1913.

Ognibene, Peter J. *Scoop: The Life and Politics of Henry M. Jackson.* New York: Stein and Day, 1975.

Orth, Donald J. *Dictionary of Alaska Place Names.* Washington, D.C.: Government Printing Office, 1967.

Patty, Stanton H. "A Conference with the Tanana Chiefs." *Alaska Journal,* spring 1971.

Paul, Frances Lackey. *"Mother's Memoirs."* Anchorage: University of Alaska Anchorage Archive, n.d.

Paul, Frederick. *Then Fight for It.* Seattle: Manuscript. n.d. Copy in author's possession and shorter version in Loussac Library, Anchorage, Alaska.

Peake, Ora Brooks. *A History of the United States Indian Factory System, 1795-1822.* Denver: Sage Books, 1954.

Petroff, Ivan. *Report on the Population, Industries, and Resources of Alaska.* Washington, D.C.: Government Printing Office, 1882.

Philp, Kenneth R. *John Collier's Crusade for Indian Reform.* Tucson: University of Arizona Press, 1977.

Pierce, Richard A. *Russia in North America: Proceedings of the 2nd International Conference on Russian America.* Kingston, Ont.: Limestone Press, 1990.

———. ed. *Documents on the History of the Russian-American Company.* Kingston, Ont.: Limestone Press, 1976.

Pierce, Walter H. *Thirteen Years of Travel and Exploration in Alaska, 1877-1889.* Edited and updated by R. N. De Armond. Anchorage: Alaska Northwest Publishing Co., 1977.

Pinchot, Gifford. "The A B C of Conservation." *Outlook,* December 4, 1909.

———. *Breaking New Ground.* New York: Harcourt, Brace and Co., 1947.

Porter, Kenneth Wiggins. *John Jacob Astor: Businessman.* New York: Russell & Russell, 1966.

Pratt, Richard Henry. *Battlefield and Classroom: Four Decades with the American Indian.* Edited by Robert M. Utley. New Haven, Conn.: Yale University Press, 1964.

Prince, Bernadine LeMay. *The Alaska Railroad in Pictures: 1914-1964.* Anchorage, Alaska: Ken Wray's Print Shop, 1964.

Prucha, Francis Paul. *American Indian Policy in Crisis: Christian Reformers and the Indian, 1865-1900.* Norman: University of Oklahoma Press, 1976.

————. *American Indian Policy in the Formative Years: The Indian Trade and Intercourse Acts: 1790-1843.* Lincoln: University of Nebraska Press, 1962.

————. *The Sword of the Republic.* Bloomington: Indiana University Press, 1977.

Rakestraw, Lawrence W. *A History of the United States Forest Service in Alaska.* Anchorage: Alaska Historical Commission, 1981.

Ray, Dorothy Jean. "The Sinuk Mission: Experiment in Eskimo Relocation and Acculturation." *Alaska History,* fall 1984.

Reiger, John F. *American Sportsmen and the Origins of Conservation.* New York: Winchester Press, 1975.

Renner, Louis L. *Pioneer Missionary to the Bering Strait Eskimos: Bellarmine Lafortune, S.J.* Portland, Ore.: Binford & Mort, 1979.

Richardson, James D., ed. *Messages and Papers of the Presidents, 1789-1897.* Washington, D.C.: General Printing Office, 1896.

Rickard, T. A. *Through the Yukon and Alaska.* San Francisco: Mining and Scientific Press, 1909.

Roberts, Robert O. *Tomorrow Is Growing Old.* Newberg: Barclay Press, 1978.

Roosevelt, Theodore. *The Autobiography of Theodore Roosevelt.* New York: Charles Scribner's Sons, 1958.

Roppel, Patricia. "Gravina." *Alaska Journal,* summer 1972.

Rosenfeld, Leonora Cohen. *Portrait of a Philosopher: Morris R. Cohen in Life and Letters.* New York: Harcourt, Brace & World, 1948.

Ross, Mrs. J. Thorburn. *Aaron Ladner Lindsley: Founder of Alaska Missions and Leader of Other Great Enterprises in the Northwest.* Philadelphia: Board of National Missions of the Presbyterian Church of the United States of America, n.d.

Sand, Margaret, and Ora Sand. *The Summit and Beyond.* Caldwell, Idaho: Caxton Printers, 1959.

Schmeckebier, Laurence Frederick. *The Office of Indian Affairs: Its History, Activities and Organization.* Baltimore: Johns Hopkins Press, 1927.

Schumacher, Wilfried W. "Aftermath of the Sitka Massacre of 1802." *Alaska Journal,* winter 1979.

Schwalbe, Anna Buxham. *Dayspring on the Kuskokwim.* Bethlehem, Penn.: Moravian Press, 1951.

Schwatka, Frederick. *A Summer in Alaska.* St. Louis: J. W. Henry, 1893.

Scidmore, Eliza Ruhamah. *Alaska: Its Southern Coast and the Sitkan Archipelago.* Boston: D. Lothrop and Co., 1885.

Secretan, J. H. E. *To Klondyke and Back.* London: Hurst and Blackett, 1898.

Seward, Frederick. *Seward at Washington: 1861-72.* New York: Derby and Miller, 1891.

Sherman, William Tecumseh. *Memoirs of General W. T. Sherman.* New York: Library of America, 1990.

Sherwood, Morgan. "Ardent Spirits: Hooch and the Osprey Affair at Sitka." *Journal of the West,* July 1965.

———. *Big Game in Alaska: A History of Wildlife and People.* New Haven, Conn.: Yale University Press, 1981.

———. "Ivan Petroff and the Far Northwest." *Journal of the West,* July 1963.

Smith, Elbert B. *Magnificent Missourian: The Life of Thomas Hart Benton.* Philadelphia: J. B. Lippincott, 1958.

Smith, Kathleen Lopp. "A Pioneer Family in Alaska: Ellen Lopp's Letters." Seattle: self-published, 1984. Copy in Loussac Library, Anchorage, Alaska.

Socolofsky, Homer E., and Allan B. Spetter. *The Presidency of Benjamin Harrison.* Lawrence: University Press of Kansas, 1987.

Starr, Jerome Lincoln. "The Cultural and Educational Development of Aborigines and Settlers in Russian America, 1784-1867." Ph.D. diss., New York University, 1961.

Stearns, Robert Alden. "The Morgan-Guggenheim Syndicate and the Development of Alaska, 1906-1915." Ph.D. diss., University of California at Santa Barbara, 1967.

Steckler, Gerard G. *Charles John Seghers: Priest and Bishop in the Pacific Northwest 1839-1886: A Biography.* Fairfield, Wash.: Ye Galleon Press, 1986.

Stewart, Robert Laird. *Sheldon Jackson.* New York: Fleming H. Revell Co., 1908.

Sutherland, Dan. "Dan Sutherland." Fairbanks: University of Alaska Fairbanks, n.d.

Thorton, Harrison R. *Among the Eskimos of Wales, Alaska 1890-93.* Baltimore: Johns Hopkins Press, 1931.

Tikhmenev, P. A. *A History of the Russian-American Company.* Seattle: University of Washington Press, 1978.

———. *A History of the Russian-American Company, Vol. 2.* Kingston, Ont.: Limestone Press, 1979.

Tower, Elizabeth A. "Captain David Henry Jarvis: Alaska's Tragic Hero—Wickersham's Victim." *Alaska History,* spring 1990.

Truman, Margaret, ed. *Where the Buck Stops: The Personal and Private Writings of Harry S. Truman.* New York: Warner Books, 1989.

Tugwell, Rexford Guy. *The Stricken Land: The Story of Puerto Rico.* Garden City: Doubleday & Company, 1947.

Urofsky, Melvin I., ed. *The Douglas Letters: Selections from the Private Papers of Justice William O. Douglas.* Bethesda, Md.: Adler & Adler, 1987.

U.S. Army, Alaska. Pamphlet No. 355-5: *Building Alaska with the U.S. Army, 1867-1962,* 1962.

U.S. Department of Agriculture, Bureau of Biological Survey. *Amendment to Regulations Respecting Game Animals, Land Fur-Bearing Animals, Game Birds, Nongame Birds, and Nests and Eggs of Birds in Alaska.* Washington, D.C.: Government Printing Office, 1932.

———. *Regulations for the Protection of Land Fur-Bearing Animals in Alaska.* Washington, D.C.: Government Printing Office, 1921.

———. *Regulations for the Protection of Game in Alaska, 1912.* Washington, D.C.: Government Printing Office, 1912.

———. *Regulations Relating to Game Land Fur Animals, and Birds in Alaska: 1938-1939.* Washington, D.C.: Government Printing Office, 1938.

———. *Service and Regulatory Announcements: Alaska Game Law and Regulations and Federal Laws Relating to Game and Birds in the Territory.* Washington, D.C.: Government Printing Office, 1925.

U.S. Department of Agriculture, National Forest Service. *Tongass National Forest Alaska.* Washington, D.C.: Government Printing Office, 1940.

U.S. Department of the Interior. *Decisions of the Department of the Interior Relating to Public Lands.* Washington, D.C.: Government Printing Office, various dates.

———. *2(c) Report: Federal Programs and Alaska Natives.* Washington, D.C.: Government Printing Office, n.d.

———. *Final Environmental Impact Statement: Proposed Chukchi Imuruk National Reserve.* Washington, D.C.: Government Printing Office, 1974.

U.S. Department of the Interior, Bureau of Indian Affairs. *Alaska Division General Correspondence: District Files.* Anchorage: University of Alaska Anchorage Microfilm.

———. *Hydaburg, Alaska: Its History, Population and Economy.* Planning Support Group Report No. 257. Washington, D.C.: Government Printing Office, 1978.

———. *Report of the Commissioner of Indian Affairs to the Secretary of the Interior.* Washington, D.C.: Government Printing Office, various dates.

U.S. Department of the Interior. *Report of the Secretary of the Interior.* Washington, D.C.: Government Printing Office, various dates.

U.S. Department of the Interior, Board of Indian Commissioners. *Reports of the Board of Indian Commissioners.* Washington, D.C.: Government Printing Office, various dates.

U.S. Department of the Interior, Fish and Wildlife Service. *Alaska Fishery and Fur Seal Industries.* Washington, D.C.: Government Printing Office, 1885-1958.

U. S. Fish Commission. *Bulletin of the U. S. Fish Commission.* Vol. 18. Washington, D.C.: Government Printing Office, 1899.

Utley, Robert M. *Frontier Regulars: The United States Army and the Indian: 1866-1891*. Lincoln: University of Nebraska Press, 1973.

Vance, John T. "The Congressional Mandate and the Indian Claims Commission." *North Dakota Law Review,* spring 1969.

Veniaminov, Ivan. *Notes on the Islands of the Unalaska District.* Kingston, Ont.: Limestone Press, 1984.

Watkins, T. H. *Righteous Pilgrim: The Life and Times of Harold Ickes, 1874-1952.* New York: Henry Holt and Co., 1990.

Webb, John Sidney. "The River Trip to the Klondike." *Century Magazine,* March 1898.

Webb, Melody. *The Last Frontier.* Albuquerque: University of New Mexico Press, 1985.

Wickersham, James. Diary. Juneau: Alaska State Historical Library, various dates.

Wilbur, Ray Lyman. *The Memoirs of Ray Lyman Wilbur.* Edited by Edgar Eugene Robinson and Paul Carroll. Stanford, Calif.: Stanford University Press, 1960.

Willard, Caroline. *Life in Alaska. Letters of Mrs. Eugene S. Willard.* Edited by Eva McClintock. Philadelphia: Presbyterian Board of Publication, 1884.

Young, S. Hall. *Hall Young of Alaska.* New York: Fleming H. Revell Co., 1927.

Manuscript Collections

Alaska State Historical Library, Juneau, Alaska
     Records of the Alaska Packers Association

Allen Library, University of Washington, Seattle, Washington
     Edward W. Allen Papers
     William Paul Papers
     Henry M. Jackson Papers

Beinecke Library, Yale University, New Haven, Connecticut
     Felix S. Cohen Papers
     Richard Henry Pratt Papers

Fried, Frank, Harris, Shriver & Jacobson, Washington, D.C.
     Arthur Lazarus Papers

Harry Truman Presidential Library, Independence, Missouri
     Harry Truman Official Files
     Philleo Nash Papers
     Warner Gardner Papers
     Clark Clifford Papers

Library of Congress, Manuscript Section, Washington D.C.
     Harold Ickes Papers
     William O. Douglas Papers
     Julius Krug Papers

Nebraska State Historical Society, Lincoln, Nebraska
     Hugh Butler Papers

Newberry Library, Chicago, Illinois
    Edward E. Ayer Papers

Pennsylvania Historical Society, Philadelphia, Pennsylvania
    Indian Rights Association Papers

Presbyterian Historical Society, Philadelphia, Pennsylvania
    Record Group 98-99, Alaska Mission
    Record Group 239, Sheldon Jackson Collection, Department of History of
    the Presbyterian Church, U.S.A. (University of Alaska-Anchorage Microfilm)

Rasmuson Library, University of Alaska Fairbanks, Fairbanks, Alaska
    E. L. Bartlett Papers
    Anthony Dimond Papers
    Ernest Gruening Papers

Sealaska Heritage Foundation, Juneau, Alaska
    Curry-Weissbrodt Papers

Smithsonian Institution, National Anthropological Archives, Washington, D.C.
    James Curry Papers

National Archives Materials

Record Group 22, Fish and Wildlife Service, General Administrative Files, 1890-
    1956, Alaska.

Record Group 48, Records of the Office of the Secretary of the Interior.

Record Group 75, Bureau of Indian Affairs, Alaska Division.

Record Group 94, Adjutant General's Office, Letters Received, Appointment,
    Commission and Personal Branch, General Jefferson C. Davis.

Record Group 393, Records of the United States Army Continental Commands,
    1821-1920, Department of Alaska.

Personal Interviews

Brandeis, Rita Singer. Sacramento, Calif., August 8, 1992.

Hawkins, James. Reston, Va., July 9, 1989.

Horn, Frances Lopinsky. Washington, D.C., August 4, 1988.

Lazarus, Arthur. Washington, D.C., October 5, 1989.

Paul, Frederick. Seattle, Wash., March 26, 1987, July 30, 1992.

Peratrovich, Roy. Juneau, Alaska, August 16, 1988.

Wright, Don. Fairbanks, Alaska, August 26, 1992.

Index

A

Ablikak, 161

Aboriginal title, 10, 351, 380, 394, 398, 426, 432; and monetary compensation for unlawful extinguishment of, 262–63; legal theory of, 261, 319–20; Theodore Roosevelt's view of, 186; versus "private property," 402–403, 407–408; *See also* Alaska Native aboriginal title

Adams, Rev. W. B., 225

Admiralty Island, 37–38, 63, 118, 131, 279; Angoon Tlingit Indians on, 131; Auk Tlingit Indians on, 131

Afognak Island, 243; forest reserve on, 184

Agattu Island, 47. *See also* Near Islands; Aleutian Islands

Ahtna Athabascan Indians, 299; and discovery of commercial copper deposits, 187–88; and mine copper, 186; and prohibition on market hunting, 209–210

Airplanes: used to jump Gwich'in Athabascan Indian trap lines, 314

Akutan Island, 210

Alaska (by Sheldon Jackson), 81, 91

Alaska Appeal, 113

Alaska Bar Association, 321, 435

Alaska Central Railroad, 195. *See also* Alaska Northern Railroad

Alaska civil government, 223; congressional granting of, 91–99, 172–173, 175; first municipal election of, 92; need for, 93–94; Tlingit fishing rights and, 123. *See also* Alaska Organic Act; Alaska Territorial Legislature

Alaska Commercial Company, 93–94, 97, 141–42, 216; school on Pribilof Islands, 105; on Yukon River, 142

Alaska Consolidated Canneries, 255

Alaska Copper Company, 188, 198

Alaska Democratic Party, 266

Alaska District Court, First Division (Southeast Alaska): fish trap rulings, 254, 306, 322; Hydaburg IRA reservation and, 350; Tlingit Indian citizenship verdict, 245; Tlingit Indian property ruling, 368; William Paul and, 240, 268, 278, 279, 282, 322

Alaska District Court, Second Division (interior Alaska), 278; James Wickersham and, 197–98; Karluk IRA reservation and, 317

Alaska Federation of Native Associations, 429. *See also* Alaska Federation of Natives

Alaska Federation of Natives, 11, 13, 381, 383

Alaska Fisherman, 246, 252, 256, 262, 269, 476 n.274

Alaska Fishing News, 310

Alaska Game Act (1902), 205–206; amendments to, 208; Alaska Natives and, 206–208; subsistence hunting provision of, 213

Alaska Game Act (1908), 208, 214, 217; and subsistence hunting provisions, 213–16

Alaska Game Act (1925), 213–14, 216, 218–19; author Edward W. Nelson, 217; subsistence hunting provisions of, 217–19

Alaska Game Commission, 8, 217–19

Alaska Miners Association, 328, 388, 399

Alaska Native aboriginal title, 385–86, 394, 398, 432, 434, 437, 439; and Goldschmidt report, 338, 372, 381; and Tlingit and Haida Indian lands and waters, 327–331, 338, 372, 381; and Trans-Alaska Oil Pipeline construction, 434; Athabascan Indian assertion of, 434; extinguishment by Congress of, 10, 434; Harry Truman's disapproval of extinguishment, 398;

About the Author

DONALD CRAIG MITCHELL IS A FORMER VICE-PRESIDENT AND GENERAL counsel of the Alaska Federation of Natives, organized by Alaska Natives in 1967 to fight for their historic land claims settlement. For more than two decades he has been intimately involved, both before Congress and in the courts, in the development and implementation of federal Native policy.